THE ROUTLEDGE COMPANION TO MEDIA STUDIES AND DIGITAL HUMANITIES

Edited by
Jentery Sayers

Routledge
Taylor & Francis Group
LONDON AND NEW YORK

First published 2018
by Routledge
2 Park Square, Milton Park, Abingdon, Oxon OX14 4RN

and by Routledge
52 Vanderbilt Avenue, New York, NY 10017, USA

First issued in paperback 2020

Routledge is an imprint of the Taylor & Francis Group, an informa business

Library of Congress Cataloging-in-Publication Data
Names: Sayers, Jentery, editor.
Title: The Routledge companion to media studies and digital humanities / edited by Jentery Sayers.
Description: New York : Routledge, Taylor & Francis Group, 2018.
Identifiers: LCCN 2017014964| ISBN 9781138844308 (hardback) | ISBN 9781315730479 (ebk)
Subjects: LCSH: Mass media. | Digital humanities.
Classification: LCC P90 .R673 2018 | DDC 302.23—dc23
LC record available at https://lccn.loc.gov/2017014964

ISBN 13: 978-0-367-58068-1 (pbk)
ISBN 13: 978-1-138-84430-8 (hbk)

Typeset in Bembo
by Florence Production Ltd, Stoodleigh, Devon, UK

THE ROUTLEDGE COMPANION TO MEDIA STUDIES AND DIGITAL HUMANITIES

Although media studies and digital humanities are established fields, their overlaps have not been examined in depth. This comprehensive collection fills that gap, giving readers a critical guide to understanding the array of methodologies and projects operating at the intersections of media, culture, and practice. Topics include: access, praxis, social justice, design, interaction, interfaces, mediation, materiality, remediation, data, memory, making, programming, and hacking.

Contributors: Isabel Cristina Restrepo Acevedo, Alyssa Arbuckle, Moya Bailey, Anne Balsamo, Jon Bath, Erika M. Behrmann, Nina Belojevic, Paul Benzon, Bryan Carter, Kimberly Christen, Alex Christie, Beth Coleman, Constance Crompton, Monica De La Torre, Jeanette M. Dillon, Elizabeth Ellcessor, Maureen Engel, Kathleen Fitzpatrick, Mary Flanagan, Matthew Fuller, Jacob Gaboury, Jennifer Gabrys, Radhika Gajjala, Reina Gossett, Dene Grigar, Michelle Habell-Pallán, Eric Hoyt, Kit Hughes, Patrick Jagoda, Steven E. Jones, Alexandra Juhasz, Kat Jungnickel, Lauren F. Klein, Kim Brillante Knight, Kari Kraus, Virginia Kuhn, Elizabeth LaPensée, Derek Long, Elizabeth Losh, Angelica Macklin, Shaun Macpherson, Mark C. Marino, Shannon Mattern, Peter McDonald, Tara McPherson, Shintaro Miyazaki, Aimée Morrison, Stuart Moulthrop, Anna Munster, Timothy Murray, Angel David Nieves, Amanda Phillips, Kevin Ponto, Jessica Rajko, Howard Rambsy II, Sonnet Retman, Roopika Risam, Tara Rodgers, Daniela K. Rosner, Anastasia Salter, Jeffrey Schnapp, Ray Siemens, Patrik Svensson, Victoria Szabo, Tony Tran, Annette Vee, Noah Wardrip-Fruin, Jacqueline Wernimont, Mark J. Williams, and Gregory Zinman

Jentery Sayers is Associate Professor of English and Cultural, Social, and Political Thought at the University of Victoria, Canada.

This book is dedicated to everyone at HASTAC.

CONTENTS

Notes on Contributors xii
Acknowledgments xix

Introduction: Studying Media through New Media 1
JENTERY SAYERS

PART I
Access, Praxis, Justice 7

1. **Theory/Practice: Lessons Learned from Feminist Film Studies** 9
TARA MCPHERSON

2. **#cut/paste+bleed: Entangling Feminist Affect, Action, and Production On and Offline** 18
ALEXANDRA JUHASZ

3. **Analog Girls in Digital Worlds: Dismantling Binaries for Digital Humanists Who Research Social Media** 33
MOYA BAILEY AND REINA GOSSETT

4. **(Cyber)Ethnographies of Contact, Dialogue, Friction: Connecting, Building, Placing, and Doing "Data"** 44
RADHIKA GAJJALA, ERIKA M. BEHRMANN, AND JEANETTE M. DILLON

5. **Of, By, and For the Internet: New Media Studies and Public Scholarship** 56
AIMÉE MORRISON

6. **Women Who Rock: Making Scenes, Building Communities: Convivencia and Archivista Praxis for a Digital Era** 67
MICHELLE HABELL-PALLÁN, SONNET RETMAN, ANGELICA MACKLIN, AND MONICA DE LA TORRE

7. **Decolonizing Digital Humanities in Theory and Practice** 78
ROOPIKA RISAM

8. Interactive Narratives: Addressing Social and Political Trauma through New Media 87
ISABEL CRISTINA RESTREPO ACEVEDO

9. Wear and Care: Feminisms at a Long Maker Table 97
JACQUELINE WERNIMONT AND ELIZABETH LOSH

10. A Glitch in the Tower: Academia, Disability, and Digital Humanities 108
ELIZABETH ELLCESSOR

11. Game Studies for Great Justice 117
AMANDA PHILLIPS

12. Self-Determination in Indigenous Games 128
ELIZABETH LAPENSÉE

PART II
Design, Interface, Interaction 139

13. Making Meaning, Making Culture: How to Think about Technology and Cultural Reproduction 141
ANNE BALSAMO

14. Contemporary and Future Spaces for Media Studies and Digital Humanities 152
PATRIK SVENSSON

15. Finding Fault Lines: An Approach to Speculative Design 162
KARI KRAUS

16. Game Mechanics, Experience Design, and Affective Play 174
PATRICK JAGODA AND PETER MCDONALD

17. Critical Play and Responsible Design 183
MARY FLANAGAN

18. A Call to Action: Embodied Thinking and Human-Computer Interaction Design 195
JESSICA RAJKO

19. Wearable Interfaces, Networked Bodies, and Feminist Sleeper Agents 204
KIM BRILLANTE KNIGHT

20. Deep Mapping: Space, Place, and Narrative as Urban Interface 214
MAUREEN ENGEL

21. **Smart Things, Smart Subjects: How the "Internet of Things" Enacts Pervasive Media** 222
BETH COLEMAN

PART III
Mediation, Method, Materiality 231

22. **Approaching Sound** 233
TARA RODGERS

23. **Algorhythmics: A Diffractive Approach for Understanding Computation** 243
SHINTARO MIYAZAKI

24. **Software Studies Methods** 250
MATTHEW FULLER

25. **Physical Computing, Embodied Practice** 258
NINA BELOJEVIC AND SHAUN MACPHERSON

26. **Turning Practice Inside Out: Digital Humanities and the Eversion** 267
STEVEN E. JONES

27. **Conjunctive and Disjunctive Networks: Affects, Technics, and Arts in the Experience of Relation** 274
ANNA MUNSTER

28. **From "Live" to Real Time: On Future Television Studies** 283
MARK J. WILLIAMS

29. **ICYMI: Catching Up to the Moving Image Online** 292
GREGORY ZINMAN

30. **Images on the Move: Analytics for a Mixed Methods Approach** 300
VIRGINIA KUHN

31. **Lost in the Clouds: A Media Theory of the Flight Recorder** 310
PAUL BENZON

32. **Scaffolding, Hard and Soft: Critical and Generative Infrastructures** 318
SHANNON MATTERN

PART IV
Remediation, Data, Memory 327

33. **Obsolescence and Innovation in the Age of the Digital** 329
KATHLEEN FITZPATRICK

34. Futures of the Book 336
JON BATH, ALYSSA ARBUCKLE, CONSTANCE CROMPTON, ALEX CHRISTIE, RAY SIEMENS, AND THE INKE RESEARCH GROUP

35. Becoming a Rap Genius: African American Literary Studies and Collaborative Annotation 345
HOWARD RAMBSY II

36. Traversals: A Method of Preservation for Born-Digital Texts 351
DENE GRIGAR AND STUART MOULTHROP

37. New Media Arts: Creativity on the Way to the Archive 362
TIMOTHY MURRAY

38. Apprehending the Past: Augmented Reality, Archives, and Cultural Memory 372
VICTORIA SZABO

39. Experiencing Digital Africana Studies: Bringing the Classroom to Life 384
BRYAN CARTER

40. Engagements with Race, Memory, and the Built Environment in South Africa: A Case Study in Digital Humanities 391
ANGEL DAVID NIEVES

41. Relationships, Not Records: Digital Heritage and the Ethics of Sharing Indigenous Knowledge Online 403
KIMBERLY CHRISTEN

42. Searching, Mining, and Interpreting Media History's Big Data 413
ERIC HOYT, TONY TRAN, DEREK LONG, KIT HUGHES, AND KEVIN PONTO

43. The Intimate Lives of Cultural Objects 423
JEFFREY SCHNAPP

44. *Timescape* and Memory: Visualizing Big Data at the 9/11 Memorial Museum 433
LAUREN F. KLEIN

PART V
Making, Programming, Hacking 443

45. Programming as Literacy 445
ANNETTE VEE

46. Expressive Processing: Interpretation and Creation 453
NOAH WARDRIP-FRUIN

47. Building Interactive Stories 462
ANASTASIA SALTER

48. Reading Culture through Code 472
MARK C. MARINO

49. Critical Unmaking: Toward a Queer Computation 483
JACOB GABOURY

50. Making Things to Make Sense of Things: DIY as Research and Practice 492
KAT JUNGNICKEL

51. Environmental Sensing and "Media" as Practice in the Making 503
JENNIFER GABRYS

52. Approaching Design as Inquiry: Magic, Myth, and Metaphor in Digital Fabrication 511
DANIELA K. ROSNER

Glossary of Acronyms and Initialisms 521
Glossary of Projects 526
Index 551

CONTRIBUTORS

Isabel Cristina Restrepo Acevedo is an Associate Professor and Director of the research group Hipertrópico, Arts and Technology from Universidad de Antioquia, Colombia. Her research and artistic practice explore relationships between new media art and society.

Alyssa Arbuckle is Assistant Director, Research Partnerships & Development, in the Electronics Textual Cultures Lab at the University of Victoria (UVic), where she also works with the INKE group. Alyssa holds an M.A. in English from UVic.

Moya Bailey studies marginalized groups' use of digital media to promote social justice as acts of self-affirmation and health promotion. She is interested in how race, gender, and sexuality are represented in media and medicine. She also co-curates the #transformDH initiative.

Anne Balsamo is the Dean of the School of Art, Technology, and Emerging Communication at the University of Texas at Dallas.

Jon Bath is an Assistant Professor of Art and Art History and Director of the Humanities and Fine Arts Digital Research Centre at the University of Saskatchewan. He is co-leader of the Modelling and Prototyping team of Implementing New Knowledge Environments (INKE).

Erika M. Behrmann is an activist-scholar focusing on feminist theory, postfeminism, pedagogy, postcolonialism, and their various intersections and materializations within media and gaming spaces. Her publications can be found in *Teaching Media Quarterly* (2015) and *Films for the Feminist Classroom* (2016).

Nina Belojevic completed her M.A. in English at the University of Victoria. Her work combines media studies and cultural studies with media art and physical computing practice.

Paul Benzon teaches in the Department of English and the Media and Film Studies Program at Skidmore College. His work has appeared in *PMLA*, *Narrative*, *electronic book review*, and *Media-N*, the journal of the New Media Caucus of the College Art Association.

Bryan Carter received his Ph.D. at the University of Missouri-Columbia and is currently an Associate Professor in Africana Studies at the University of Arizona, specializing in African American literature of the twentieth century with a primary focus on the Harlem Renaissance. His research also focuses on Digital Humanities/Africana Studies.

Kimberly Christen is an Associate Professor and Director of the Digital Technology and Culture Program, Director of Digital Projects for Native American Programs, and the co-Director of the Center for Digital Scholarship and Curation at Washington State University.

Alex Christie is an Assistant Professor in Digital Prototyping at Brock University's Centre for Digital Humanities. He completed his doctorate at the University of Victoria, where he worked as a research assistant with the INKE group and the Modernist Versions Project in the Electronic Textual Cultures Lab and the Maker Lab in the Humanities.

Beth Coleman directs the City as Platform Lab at the University of Waterloo, where she is an Associate Professor of Experimental Digital Media. Her research spans artistic and academic practices, addressing networked media technology and new data publics. She is the co-founder of SoundLab Cultural Alchemy, an internationally acclaimed multimedia art and sound platform. Her book *Hello Avatar* is with MIT Press.

Constance Crompton is an Assistant Professor in the Department of Communication at the University of Ottawa. She is a researcher with the INKE project and co-Director of the Lesbian and Gay Liberation in Canada project.

Monica De La Torre is an Assistant Professor in Media and Expressive Culture at the School of Transborder Studies at Arizona State University. In her research, teaching, and media production, she bridges Chicana feminist theory, Latina/o media studies, radio and sound studies, and feminist media praxis.

Jeanette M. Dillon is a 25-year media veteran pursuing her doctorate in communication at Bowling Green State University. Her research interests include health and organizational communication, particularly within nonprofit organizations and social enterprises.

Elizabeth Ellcessor is Assistant Professor in the Department of Media Studies at the University of Virginia. She is the author of *Restricted Access: Media, Disability, and the Politics of Participation* (NYU Press 2016).

Maureen Engel is Assistant Professor and Director of Humanities Computing at the University of Alberta. Formally trained as a textual scholar, her work focuses on the intricate relationships that inhere in and develop from the concepts of space, place, history, and narrative.

Kathleen Fitzpatrick is Director of Digital Humanities and Professor of English at Michigan State University. She is the author of *Planned Obsolescence: Publishing, Technology, and the Future of the Academy* and *The Anxiety of Obsolescence: The American Novel in the Age of Television*.

Mary Flanagan is an artist, designer, and media theorist. She founded and leads the game design research laboratory, Tiltfactor, at Dartmouth College, where she is the Sherman Fairchild Distinguished Professor in Digital Humanities. She also runs the game publishing company Resonym.

Matthew Fuller is a member of the editorial group of the journal *Computational Culture*. He works at the Digital Culture Unit and Centre for Cultural Studies, Goldsmiths, University of London.

Jacob Gaboury is Assistant Professor of Film & Media at the University of California, Berkeley. His work engages the history and theory of digital media with a focus on digital imaging, media archaeology, and queer theory.

Jennifer Gabrys is Reader in Sociology at Goldsmiths, University of London, and Principal Investigator on the ERC-funded project, "Citizen Sense." Her publications include

Digital Rubbish: A Natural History of Electronics and *Program Earth: Environmental Sensing Technology and the Making of a Computational Planet.*

Radhika Gajjala is Professor of Media and Communication (joint appointed faculty in American Culture Studies) at Bowling Green State University. She has published books on *Cyberculture and the Subaltern* (Lexington Press 2012) and *Cyberselves: Feminist Ethnographies of South Asian Women* (AltaMira 2004).

Reina Gossett is an activist, writer, and filmmaker. Along with Sasha Wortzel, Reina wrote, directed, and produced *Happy Birthday, Marsha!* (a short film about legendary trans activist Marsha P. Johnson, starring Independent Spirit Award winner Mya Taylor).

Dene Grigar is Professor and Director of The Creative Media & Digital Culture Program at Washington State University Vancouver.

Michelle Habell-Pallán, a Professor of Gender, Women & Sexuality Studies at the University of Washington, co-directs the UW Women Who Rock Archive. Author of *Loca Motion: The Travels of Chicana and Latina Popular Culture* (2005), she curated *American Sabor: Latinos in U.S. Popular Music* (hosted by the Smithsonian Institution Traveling Exhibition Service) and jams with Seattle Fandango Project.

Eric Hoyt is an Associate Professor of Communication Arts at the University of Wisconsin-Madison. He is the author of *Hollywood Vault: Film Libraries before Home Video*, co-Director of the Media History Digital Library, and lead developer of Lantern and Arclight.

Kit Hughes is an Assistant Professor of Media and Visual Culture at Colorado State University. Her manuscript project, *Television at Work*, details how American business developed television as a technology of industrial efficiency, ideological orientation, and corporate expansion.

Patrick Jagoda is Associate Professor of English and Cinema and Media Studies at the University of Chicago. He is also a co-editor of *Critical Inquiry* and co-founder of the Game Changer Chicago Design Lab and the Transmedia Story Lab. He is the author of *Network Aesthetics* (University of Chicago Press 2016) and co-author with Michael Maizels of *The Game Worlds of Jason Rohrer* (MIT Press 2016).

Steven E. Jones is DeBartolo Professor of Liberal Arts and Digital Humanities in the Department of English, the University of South Florida. He is author of a number of books and articles, including *Roberto Busa, S.J., and the Emergence of Humanities Computing: The Priest and the Punched Cards* (Routledge 2016).

Alexandra Juhasz is Chair of the Film Department at Brooklyn College, CUNY. She makes and studies committed media practices that contribute to political change and individual and community growth. Her current work is on and about feminist internet culture, including YouTube and feminist pedagogy and community. With Anne Balsamo, she was co-facilitator of the network, FemTechNet.

Kat Jungnickel is a Senior Lecturer in the Sociology Department at Goldsmiths College, University of London. Her research explores mobilities, digital technology cultures, DIY/DIT practices, and making methods.

Lauren F. Klein is an Assistant Professor in the School of Literature, Media, and Communication at Georgia Tech, where she also directs the Digital Humanities Lab. With

Matthew K. Gold, she edits *Debates in the Digital Humanities* (University of Minnesota Press), a hybrid print/digital publication stream that explores debates in the field as they emerge.

Kim Brillante Knight is an Associate Professor of Emerging Media and Communication at The University of Texas at Dallas, where her research and teaching focus on the interplay of power structures and identity in digital culture, with particular emphasis on the role of gender and intersectional feminism in networked environments.

Kari Kraus is an Associate Professor in the College of Information Studies and the Department of English at the University of Maryland.

Virginia Kuhn is Associate Director of the Institute for Multimedia Literacy and Associate Professor in the division of Media Arts + Practice in the School of Cinematic Arts at the University of Southern California.

Elizabeth LaPensée Ph.D. expresses herself through writing, design, and art in games. She is Anishinaabe, Métis, and Irish, living near the Great Lakes. She is an Assistant Professor of Media & Information and Writing, Rhetoric & American Cultures at Michigan State University. She designed and programmed *Invaders* (2015), a remix of the arcade classic *Space Invaders*. Her latest game, *Honour Water* (2016), shares Anishinaabe songs for healing the water.

Derek Long is an Assistant Professor of Media and Cinema Studies at the University of Illinois at Urbana–Champaign. He is currently working on a book manuscript on distribution in the early Hollywood studio system.

Elizabeth Losh is an Associate Professor of English and American Studies at the College of William and Mary. She is the author of *Virtualpolitik: An Electronic History of Govern ment Media-Making in a Time of War, Scandal, Disaster, Miscommunication, and Mistakes* (MIT Press 2009) and *The War on Learning: Gaining Ground in the Digital University* (MIT Press 2014).

Angelica Macklin is a filmmaker and doctoral candidate in Gender, Women, and Sexuality Studies at the University of Washington. She has been with the Women Who Rock Collective since 2011, organizing the unConferences and Film Festivals, building the Archive, and teaching media production. Angelica is co-Director of "Masizakhe: Building Each Other" and "De Baixo Para Cima."

Shaun Macpherson is a musician and media artist whose work combines sound design and video with analog or otherwise obsolete technology. He recently received an M.A. in English and Cultural, Social, and Political Thought at the University of Victoria.

Mark C. Marino is a writer and scholar of electronic literature living in Los Angeles. He teaches writing at the University of Southern California, where he directs the Humanities and Critical Code Studies Lab.

Shannon Mattern is an Associate Professor of Media Studies at The New School. She writes about archives, libraries, and other media spaces; media infrastructures; and mediated sensation.

Peter McDonald is a graduate student in English at the University of Chicago and a fellow at the Game Changer Chicago Design Lab. His work deals with the hermeneutics of play.

Tara McPherson teaches in the School of Cinematic Arts at USC. She is co-editor of *Vectors*, a lead P.I. on the platform Scalar, and author or editor of several books, including *Feminist in a Software Lab: Difference + Design* (Harvard University Press 2018).

Shintaro Miyazaki is currently a senior researcher at the University of Applied Sciences and Arts Northwestern Switzerland, Academy of Art and Design, Institute of Experimental Design and Media Cultures, working at the intersection of media, design, and history. He has a Ph.D. in media theory from Humboldt University, Berlin (2012).

Aimée Morrison is Associate Professor in the Department of English Language and Literature at the University of Waterloo, where she teaches new media studies. She has published on internet manifestos, mommy blogs, Facebook status updates, and videogame movies of the 1980s.

Stuart Moulthrop is Professor of English at the University of Wisconsin-Milwaukee, and coordinator of the program in Media, Cinema, and Digital Studies.

Anna Munster is a writer, artist, and educator. She is the author of *An Aesthesia of Networks* (2013) and *Materializing New Media* (2006). She is a Professor in Art and Design, University of New South Wales, Sydney, Australia.

Timothy Murray is Professor of Comparative Literature and English, Curator of the Rose Goldsen Archive of New Media Art, and Director of the Cornell Council for the Arts at Cornell University. Co-moderator of the -empyre- new media listserv, his books include *Digital Baroque: New Media Art and Cinematic Folds* (University of Minnesota Press 2008).

Angel David Nieves is Associate Professor of Africana Studies and Digital Humanities at Hamilton College, Clinton, New York. He is also co-Director of the Digital Humanities Initiative (DHi) funded by the Andrew W. Mellon Foundation (2010–16).

Amanda Phillips is Assistant Professor of English at Georgetown University. She writes about race, gender, and social justice in videogames and the digital humanities. You can find her work in *Queer Game Studies, Games and Culture, Digital Creativity, and Debates in the Digital Humanities.*

Kevin Ponto is an Assistant Professor in the Design Studies Department and the Wisconsin Institute for Discovery at the University of Wisconsin-Madison. His work focuses on the experience of visualizing data, including the development of the ScripThreads visualization application.

Jessica Rajko is an Assistant Professor at Arizona State University (ASU). Her work investigates the ethical and corporeal implications of wearable technology, big data, and the quantified self. She is a founding co-Director of the ASU Human Security Collaboratory and is an affiliated artist/researcher with the Arts, Media and Engineering Synthesis Center.

Howard Rambsy II teaches African American literature at Southern Illinois University Edwardsville.

Sonnet Retman is an Associate Professor of American Ethnic Studies at the University of Washington, where she co-directs the UW Women Who Rock Archive. She is the author of numerous essays on race, gender, genre, and performance and of *Real Folks: Race and Genre in the Great Depression* (Duke University Press 2011).

Roopika Risam is Assistant Professor of English at Salem State University. Her research focuses on digital approaches to postcolonial and African diaspora studies. Risam's work has recently appeared in *Digital Humanities Quarterly*, *South Asian Review*, and *Debates in the Digital Humanities*.

Tara Rodgers is a composer, historian, and critic of electronic music and sound. She is the author of numerous essays on music, technology, and culture, and of *Pink Noises: Women on Electronic Music and Sound* (Duke University Press 2010).

Daniela K. Rosner is an Assistant Professor of Human-Centered Design & Engineering at the University of Washington, co-directing the Tactile and Tactical Design Lab (TAT lab). Through fieldwork and design, her research examines emerging sites of creativity around digital production—from hobbyist fixer groups to feminist hacker collectives.

Anastasia Salter is an Assistant Professor of digital media at the University of Central Florida. She is the author of *What Is Your Quest? From Adventure Games to Interactive Books* (University of Iowa Press 2014) and co-author of *Flash: Building the Interactive Web* (MIT Press 2014).

Jeffrey Schnapp led the Stanford Humanities Lab between 1999 and 2009. After joining the Harvard University faculty in 2011, he founded metaLAB, where he serves as Faculty Director and co-Director of the Berkman Klein Center for Internet and Society. Among his recent books are *Digital_Humanities* (2012) and *The Library Beyond the Book* (2014).

Ray Siemens is Distinguished Professor in the Faculty of Humanities at the University of Victoria, in English with cross appointment in Computer Science. He directs the Electronic Textual Cultures Lab, the INKE group, and the Digital Humanities Summer Institute.

Patrik Svensson is a Professor of Humanities and Information Technology at Umeå University, and the former Director of HUMLab (2000–14). His current work can be loosely organized under two themes: digital humanities and conditions for knowledge production.

Victoria Szabo is an Associate Research Professor of Visual and Media Studies at Duke University. She is a member of the Wired! Lab for Digital Art History & Visual Culture and works on augmented reality and virtual worlds for critical and creative expression.

Tony Tran is an Assistant Professor in the Department of Communication at Boston College. His research interests include exploring digital diasporas and the relationships between on and offline spaces.

Annette Vee is Assistant Professor of English at the University of Pittsburgh. Her work on literacy, computer programming, intellectual property, and pedagogy has been published in journals such as *Computational Culture* and *Literacy in Composition Studies*. Her book, *Coding Literacy*, was published by MIT Press in 2017.

Noah Wardrip-Fruin is a Professor of Computational Media at UC Santa Cruz, where he co-directs the Expressive Intelligence Studio (EIS), a technical/cultural research group. His media projects have been presented by venues such as the Whitney Museum and IndieCade.

Jacqueline Wernimont is an Assistant Professor of English at Arizona State University. As founding co-Director of the Human Security Collaboratory, she works on new civil rights in digital cultures with emphases on the long histories of quantification and technologies of commemoration.

Mark J. Williams is Associate Professor of Film and Media Studies at Dartmouth College, co-editor of the *Interfaces* book series at Dartmouth College Press, founding editor of *The Journal of e-Media Studies*, and Director of The Media Ecology Project.

Gregory Zinman is an Assistant Professor in the School of Literature, Media, and Communication at the Georgia Institute of Technology. His work has appeared in *The New Yorker*, *Film History*, *MIRAJ*, and *Millennium Film Journal*. He is completing a book, *Handmade: The Moving Image without Photography*, and is co-editing, with John Hanhardt, *Nam June Paik: Selected Writings* (forthcoming from The MIT Press).

ACKNOWLEDGMENTS

As editor of this Companion, I acknowledge with respect the Lkwungen-speaking peoples on whose traditional territory I live and work, and the Songhees, Esquimalt, and WSÁNEĆ peoples, whose historical relationships with the land continue to this day.

Many thanks and much love to Brooken, Beckett, and Willem for all the hugs, support, patience, and humor along the way. I am beyond fortunate that you are in my life. Thanks as well to each of the Companion's contributors, who engaged in dialogue with me for the last four years and were (and remain) a positive force for change.

Danielle Morgan (research assistant with the MLab at UVic) produced the cover image for this Companion. Nadia Timperio (research assistant with the MLab at UVic) worked with me to prepare the Companion for publication, and Allison Murphy (research assistant with the Department of English at UVic) indexed it with me. Students in English 508 at UVic provided valuable feedback on several chapters, and Steven E. Jones, Willard McCarty, Stuart Moulthrop, and Melissa Terras offered insightful responses to the Companion during the proposal stage. Initial research for this Companion was supported by the Social Sciences and Humanities Research Council of Canada (SSHRC) and the Canada Foundation for Innovation (CFI) as well as the Departments of English and Visual Arts at UVic. Endless thanks to Cathy Davidson, Julie Klein, Tara McPherson, and Kathy Woodward for their advice and perspective early on, and to Nina Belejovic, Tiffany Chan, Katherine Goertz, Shaun Macpherson, and Danielle Morgan for their support during the MLab days. Of course, *The Routledge Companion to Media Studies and Digital Humanities* would not have been possible without the teams at Routledge and Florence Production, including Mia Moran, Erica Wetter, Emma Sudderick, and especially Jessica Bithrey, who worked with me throughout the proof-reading process.

INTRODUCTION

Studying Media through New Media

Jentery Sayers

This Companion is about *studying media through new media*: for instance, making games to better understand their mechanics and politics, writing code and developing interfaces to explore their roles in reading and literacy, stewarding texts for online annotation and public discussion, participating in social networks to locate their biases and occlusions, assembling hardware to expose norms and change default settings, or composing audio, moving images, databases, and augmented reality applications as forms of scholarship at once similar to and different from academic essays. That is quite a list. And it is not exhaustive. Yet it speaks to the Companion's principal impulse, which is to *combine media studies with digital humanities* to share with readers (especially those who are new to both fields) the various types of research that emerge.

Even though they share interests in technologies, media studies and digital humanities do not always converse. Perhaps this lack of dialogue is explained by divergent histories of theory and practice, with researchers in each field drawing from distinct canons and methodologies. In digital humanities, studies of texts from the 1800s or earlier are quite common; for numerous reasons, these texts are readily available in electronic form and thus conducive to computational analysis. In media studies, research tends to move from the 1800s forward and also focus on nontextual forms, such as sound, images, video, and games. Aside from these differences in substance and period, popular definitions of each field suggest a difference in technique, too: whereas media studies treats media and technologies as *objects of inquiry*, digital humanities *integrates* them into its methods. Or, if media studies is *about* media and technologies, then digital humanities works *with* them. Allow me to elaborate on this assumption for a moment.

Many media studies practitioners avoid the reduction of research to instrumentalism, where technologies are "neutral tools" that simply turn input into output. Against instrumentalism, practitioners should be cognizant of not only the values and histories embedded in technologies, but also how those values and histories shape interpretation. Related concerns in media studies include the risks of researchers colluding with the tech industry or adopting technologies too quickly. Early or enthusiastic adoption may be a knee-jerk endorsement of whiz-bang gadgets and alluring trends—a way to make your project appealing or relevant to the market without necessarily addressing the research questions, social issues, conceptual frameworks, matters of representation, and contexts of use at hand. Meanwhile, digital humanities practitioners experiment with and even build the infrastructures of new media, reminding us that technology is not just a metaphor or an object "over there," to be philosophized at a remove. Technologies are constructed, maintained, preserved, and consumed, and they are intricately interlaced with labor and knowledge production in and beyond the academy. In short, digital projects demand a lot of work. Where there's a technology, there's also a team, some stories, millions of files, thousands of bugs and fixes, and plenty of politics. The result is significant attention to laboratory practices and technical competencies in digital humanities.

Inspired by Tara McPherson's seminal *Cinema Journal* essay, "Media Studies and the Digital Humanities" (2009), this Companion demonstrates how such assumptions about media studies and digital humanities are in reality hyperbolic, if not mythological. Many researchers, including contributors to this Companion, move routinely across the two fields, which may mutually inform and enrich each other instead of fostering opposition. In fact, when they are combined in theory as well as practice, we could say that media studies and digital humanities work *through* new media as means and modes of inquiry. We can research media without resorting to naive enthusiasm for technologies or assuming scholarly positions from on high, somehow above or outside the very conditions we study. More specifically, we may borrow language from scholars such as Wendy Hui Kyong Chun (2005) and Karen Barad (2007) to argue that *we are entangled with the media we produce and research*, not separate from them. This position need not imply a lack of researcher awareness or a disinterest in social change. Rather, the point is to stress how all research is mediated; it is media all the way down. We influence and are influenced by our inquiries and materials, and—as exhibited by each chapter in this Companion—historicizing, assessing, and revising the roles media play in that influence renders our work more compelling and persuasive.

We might start by noting that "media" in this Companion is not synonymous with "the media," or with communication outlets and conglomerates. As an alternative, we may begin with Lev Manovich's five-part definition of new media, even if his definition privileges formal aspects over the contexts of functions and processes:

- New media are numerical representations (composed of digital code),
- They are modular (several distinct parts constitute an object),
- They are automated (their creation and maintenance involve a combination of people and machines),
- They are variable (versions eclipse originals and copies), and
- They are transcoded (a combination of computation and culture) (Manovich 2001: 27–48).

This last aspect, transcoding, is most central to this Companion, which foregrounds the *cultural dimensions* of studying media through new media: how new media are about power and control, for example. In doing so, the Companion also echoes W.J.T. Mitchell: "There are no 'pure' media" (2008: 13). Even with established categories such as sound, image, video, text, code, software, hardware, platform, interface, story, game, network, and even electricity, light, or water, it is impossible to isolate one medium from the next. Their affordances are fleeting and incredibly difficult to measure. And if no pure media exist, then it is also impossible to extract new media from the contingencies of their histories or settings, even as they transform, rot, disappear, and reappear over time, often without provenance or reference to the motivations for their composition. While anyone may unconsciously or wilfully ignore these histories and settings—these values and configurations—they are active ingredients of new media's composition; they are the stuff of making and remaking. Once they enter our frame of analysis, new media's formal or technical aspects morph from the common sense of patents, diagrams, and instruction manuals into a hairball of human and nonhuman activities or a matrix of technology and culture.

We could therefore propose that *the study of media is the study of entanglements*. How and under what assumptions is sound entwined with image? Data with design? Network with node? Old with new? Subject with object? Aesthetics with politics? This approach to combining media studies with digital humanities does not bypass specificity (as if entanglements are antithetical to granularity and difference), and it does not endorse relativism (as if entanglements either absolve us from responsibility or claim equal positioning for everyone and everything) (Haraway 1988: 584). It instead underscores how new media are simultaneously abstract and particular, inhabiting seemingly contradictory positions within systems that invite and track action. It then asks us to account for *where we are and how we participate in those systems*—in the complex mesh of apparatus with process. This is no simple task, especially when we face the litany of things media may be: both social and material, carrier and content, form and substance, portal and edge, ephemeral and permanent, you and other. Of course, practitioners usually select their preferred terms for research, and these terms unavoidably shape how people draw boundaries and assume responsibility for their demarcations.

Media. A fascinating mess. In the following pages, four palpable issues repeatedly surface from it all. These issues are not just concerns shared by some or even all the authors; they are also indicators of what makes the intersection of media studies with digital humanities unique and necessary right now.

- **Beyond Text**: With its prevalence in English departments and studies of literature and language, digital humanities frequently deems text its primary medium for both composition and analysis. Against this grain, the following chapters give us a very concrete sense of digital humanities and media studies beyond text for inquiry. By extension, they prompt practitioners to consider an array of media in tandem with a constellation of modalities, including listening, seeing, scanning, touching, skimming, hearing, watching, smelling, feeling, toggling, wearing, processing, and inhabiting. These modalities remind us how the study of media through new media is *an embodied or material activity*, which may be both situated in and distributed across space and time as well as people and machines. Embodiment (including questions of affect and labor) and materiality (including questions of inscription, plasticity, and erasure) are fundamental to research as an entanglement.
- **Labs and Collaboration**: The laboratory, broadly defined, is a core component of many chapters in this Companion. A majority, if not all, of the methods are experimental. They combine disciplines, privilege trial and error, underscore action in context, or develop custom technologies. *Rarely is this work done alone*, and even when the chapters are written by individuals they draw upon and acknowledge efforts by teams and collectives. Although they are now ubiquitous features of digital work, labs and collaboration remain understudied in the humanities. This Companion contributes additional research to address that gap.
- **Social Justice**: The content of this Companion resists formal or technical treatments of media as if technologies are outside of time, history, culture, society, and material conditions. Many of the chapters focus on the entanglements of technologies with justice, oppression, and power. Rather than asking what media *are*, they ask what media *do*.

How do new media unfold in context? How are they made, by whom, and for whom? According to what norms or standards, and with what influence on social relations? With what acknowledgments and exclusions? How do they circulate, regulate, and discipline? How are they modified or repurposed, and with what changes over time? These questions encourage a media studies and digital humanities of the *present moment*, when technologies may be modes of activism and decolonization instead of instruments or gadgets.

- **Expanding Participation**: Instead of reducing media studies or digital humanities to practices such as programming—or to the technical particulars of code and platforms—the chapters included here underscore a range of scholarly participation in new media from across disciplines and experiences. Through their methodologies, the authors may intervene in a given research area by prototyping media through new media, but they may also conduct archival research, write monographs, pursue ethnographic methods, or manage scholarly resources, for instance. One by-product of this range is a thorough account of what "making," "doing," or "building" really mean in our current moment. These forms of "active" participation need not be restricted to the creation of shiny, tangible, and measurable things. They need not rehearse the myth of lone white male inventors, either. Scholarship in this Companion involves (among other things) performing, writing, thinking, speaking, listening, resisting, revising, editing, curating, maintaining, fixing, and tinkering, the particulars of which often escape us. Through this expansive approach to participation in new media, the chapters more accurately reflect the *actualities* of research practice and move beyond the superficial hype of making and building stuff.

To give these four issues some structure, especially for readers who are new to media studies and digital humanities, I organized this Companion into five sections, followed by a Glossary of Acronyms and Initialisms as well as a Glossary of Projects mentioned in the chapters:

Part I. Access, Praxis, Justice: This section highlights social justice issues that permeate the entirety of the Companion. It also demonstrates how social justice work is enacted through new media as a form of praxis, in part by expanding the definition of "access" through an emphasis on participation, but also by sharing various modes of activism involving new media. This part features Tara McPherson on feminist film studies; Alexandra Juhasz on "ev-ent-anglement"; Moya Bailey and Reina Gossett on social media; Radhika Gajjala, Erika M. Behrmann, and Jeanette M. Dillon on cyberethnography; Aimée Morrison on public scholarship; Michelle Habell-Pallán, Sonnet Retman, Angelica Macklin, and Monica De La Torre on convivencia and archivista praxis; Roopika Risam on decolonization; Isabel Cristina Restrepo Acevedo on interactive narratives; Jacqueline Wernimont and Elizabeth Losh on a "long maker table"; Elizabeth Ellcessor on glitch and disability; Amanda Phillips on videogames and social justice; and Elizabeth LaPensée on Indigenous game design.

Part II. Design, Interface, Interaction: Design, interfaces, and interaction are too often considered additive, as if they are features layered over code just before release. Against such tendencies, this section exhibits the centrality of design to critical and creative inquiry with media. This part features Anne Balsamo on the cultural implications of design; Patrik Svensson on the design of space; Kari Kraus on speculative design; Patrick Jagoda and Peter McDonald on experience design and affective play; Mary Flanagan on critical play; Jessica Rajko on embodied thinking and wearables design; Kim Brillante Knight on wearable interfaces; Maureen Engel on deep mapping; and Beth Coleman on smart subjects in the Internet of Things.

Part III. Mediation, Method, Materiality: Instead of treating media as containers that transmit content, this section of the Companion attends to various forms of mediation, affect, and materiality important to humanities research. Many of the authors also translate mediation into a method for inquiry. Here, mediation is not something delegated to instruments or overwritten by research techniques; it is what prompts interesting questions. This part features Tara Rodgers on sound; Shintaro Miyazaki on algorhythmics; Matthew Fuller on software studies; Nina Belojevic and Shaun Macpherson on physical computing; Steven E. Jones on the eversion; Anna Munster on networks; Mark Williams on television; Gregory Zinman on moving images; Virginia Kuhn on analytics; Paul Benzon on media archaeology; and Shannon Mattern on infrastructures.

Part IV. Remediation, Data, Memory: In the humanities, how is media preserved? What role does it play in memory? When does it become "data"? And how does it change across formats over time? Moving between old and new media, the past and present, this section of the Companion addresses these questions and more. In the process, it builds on Jay David Bolter and Richard Grusin's foundational text, *Remediation* (1998). This part features Kathleen Fitzpatrick on obsolescence and innovation; Jon Bath, Alyssa Arbuckle, Constance Crompton, Alex Christie, Ray Siemens, and the INKE Research Group on futures of the book; Howard Rambsy II on collaborative annotation; Dene Grigar and Stuart Moulthrop on preserving born-digital texts; Timothy Murray on curating and preserving new media art; Victoria Szabo on apprehension through augmented reality; Bryan Carter on teaching Digital Africana Studies; Angel David Nieves on 3-D histories of South Africa; Kimberly Christen on Indigenous systems of knowledge and archival practices; Eric Hoyt, Tony Tran, Derek Long, Kit Hughes, and Kevin Ponto on applying scaled entity search to media history; Jeffrey Schnapp on the art of description; and Lauren F. Klein on data visualization and memory.

Part V. Making, Programming, Hacking: Practices such as making, programming, and hacking intertwine in many ways with writing, ethnography, and even archival work. Underscoring the critical and creative dimensions of these practices, this section surveys noninstrumentalist approaches to code, platforms, and machines that privilege inquiry over proof. This part features Annette Vee on programming and literacy; Noah Wardrip-Fruin on expressive processing; Anastasia Salter on building interactive stories; Mark C. Marino on critical code studies; Jacob Gaboury on critical unmaking and queer computation; Kat Jungnickel on learning from doing; Jennifer Gabrys on citizen sensing; and Daniela K. Rosner on design as inquiry.

Ultimately, the methods and methodologies presented here do not cohere into an exhaustive or totalizing entanglement of media studies with digital humanities. The differences between them are telling and meaningful, and—encouraged by the HASTAC community, including the affirmative work of Fiona Barnett and Cathy Davidson (see Davidson 2011)—it is in the spirit of difference that I invite readers to study media through new media. *How are the boundaries drawn, and to what effects?*

References

Barad, K. (2007) *Meeting the Universe Halfway: Quantum Physics and the Entanglement of Matter and Meaning*, Durham, NC: Duke University Press.

Bolter, J.D. and R. Grusin (1998) *Remediation: Understanding New Media*, Cambridge, MA: The MIT Press.

Chun, W.H.K. (2005) "Introduction: Did Somebody Say New Media?" in W.H.K. Chun and T. Keenan (eds.) *New Media, Old Media: A History and Theory Reader*, New York: Routledge, pp. 1–10.

Davidson, C. (2011) "'Difference Is Our Operating System'—Fiona Barnett," HASTAC, hastac.org/blogs/cathy-davidson/2011/08/03/difference-our-operating-system-fiona-barnett.

Haraway, D. (1988) "Situated Knowledges: The Science Question in Feminism and the Privilege of Partial Perspective," *Feminist Studies* 14(3), 575–99.
Manovich, L. (2001) *The Language of New Media*, Cambridge, MA: The MIT Press.
McPherson, T. (2009) "Introduction: Media Studies and the Digital Humanities," *Cinema Journal* 48(2), 119–23.
Mitchell, W.J.T. (2008) "Addressing Media," *Media Tropes* 1(1), 1–18.

Part I

ACCESS, PRAXIS, JUSTICE

1

THEORY/PRACTICE

Lessons Learned from Feminist Film Studies

Tara McPherson

> We need maps and tools, not simply to theorize with, but also to guide us to act and transform the worlds in which we live. We work, under the banner of feminism, for the improvement of women's lives.
>
> (Balsamo 2011: 49)

I

Sometime in the 1990s:

I wake to the realization that I have been dreaming in the most vivid color of my life, inhabiting deeply cinematic sequences full of interesting camera angles that shimmer with shadow and light. My dreams are highly edited, intricate nocturnal sequences of shifting narrative and points of view. Clearly my brain is processing in deeply visceral ways the lessons of film production that I am learning in a graduate seminar on feminist film, continuing to explore the visual language of film even as I sleep. Enrolled in an intense doctoral program focused on poststructuralism and feminism, I have dreamed the languages of theory as well. I have felt myself working through these languages, in and out of sleep. But this is different. These cinematic dreams are activating other senses. They inhabit other registers. They are moving me through theory toward different but related ways of knowing. They will help to inaugurate my commitment to practice, to making in the world, a making also grounded in my allegiance to feminism. They will come to guide how I engage both media studies and digital humanities, crossing the theory/practice divide.

II

"Less yack, more hack."

Despite my dedication to making, I have never really been a fan of this much-debated digital humanities (DH) slogan, which at least partially emerged from early THATCamps, those "unconferences" focused on active participation, spontaneity, and learning and building together. I do think THATCamps offer important opportunities for hands-on experimentation but am sympathetic to Natalia Cecire's observation (2011) that the early iterations of these camps tended to privilege practice over theory and also treat the "humanities" portion of digital humanities as a fixed and stable element. While Bethany Nowviskie (2014) offers a useful history of the phrase, highlighting that it in part began as a joke within a precise context and was never meant as a slogan for digital humanities writ large, I suspect that its association with certain types of DH work easily took root because a range of scholars were also beginning to critique digital humanities for undervaluing the contributions of certain types of theoretical inquiry, including theories of difference, identity, affect, and more. Around the same time, debates about whether a card-carrying digital humanist needed to code to be legitimate (Ramsay 2011), or whether digital humanities would "sunset theory" (Scheinfeldt 2012), fueled the perception that digital humanities were not sufficiently attentive to the theoretical questions that occupied the interpretative humanities for decades. What is more, Miriam Posner (2012), Adeline Koh (2012), and groups such as #TransformDH have detailed the ideological dimensions of favoring hacking while denigrating yacking, and the recent renewed emphasis on data analytics and quantitative analysis within digital humanities can also seem quite distant from the concerns of theoretically inflected humanities scholarship.

In a recent article taking up the phrase, Claire Warwick helpfully suggests that increased focus might be paid to the qualifiers "less" and "more" rather than to a binary opposition between "yacking" and "hacking." I agree. We can thus most usefully see yacking and hacking as held within a productive and dialectical relation. To take this line of thinking further, we might not even focus on "less" or "more," as if the relationship between theory and practice can be reduced to balancing a formula. Instead, we might understand the two terms to be tied together in a productive and iterative friction. Warwick looks at the tensions and debates around the establishment of English departments and notes that "neither in Cambridge nor anywhere else was it felt important that students should be taught about language by learning to write creatively" (2016: 545). Perhaps the productive relationship between yacking and hacking is harder to discern in fields such as English, where practice (in both creative writing and composition courses) and theory (typically framed as literary studies) often exist in tense relations to one another. (A multimedia journal like *Kairos* illustrates that composition programs are a site where theory and practice can more easily coexist, but literature departments often devalue composition as well.) English departments are not the only sites where "yacking" and "hacking" have been separated. Across the arts and humanities, theory and practice are often poorly integrated in our universities. Art practice is usually cleaved apart from art history. Film and media studies might integrate production in the curriculum in some cases, but few film and media scholars are also media makers. The tensions between "yack" and "hack" are not, perhaps, all that unique to digital humanities. They exist across the university in structures that make it hard to combine theory and practice in our curricula, evaluation and promotion structures, disciplinary methodologies, and privileged forms of scholarly output.

As digital humanities scholars have struggled with the right balance of yack and hack, broader debates have emerged about the relationship of theory to practice across the academy. If these tensions have simmered just below the surface of disciplines for much of the twentieth century, then the digital turn has reanimated such debates in new ways in the new millennium. Claims that critique has run of out steam (Latour 2004) have emerged at the same time that many universities have also begun to experiment with programs that integrate the applied and theoretical across numerous disciplines. My employer, the School of Cinematic Arts (SCA) at the University of Southern California (USC), has long claimed to value the integration of theory and practice. Students across SCA's divisions take courses in both "making" and theory and history. Nonetheless, this learning often happens in a rather piecemeal fashion. In an attempt to more seamlessly join critique and making within digital media studies, SCA launched the Institute for Multimedia Literacy in 1998, a research institute that eventually grew into a new SCA division, Media Arts + Practice (MAP), that includes a practice-based PhD program (in which students produce hybrid dissertations), undergraduate majors and minors, certificate programs, and more. While not a "digital humanities" program per se, the division shares with many DH initiatives a commitment to hands-on production. There are also explicit commitments to theoretical inquiry, issues of ideology and social justice, and producing multimodal scholarly research, including support for the digital journal, *Vectors*, and the authoring platform, Scalar. USC is far from alone in these endeavors within North America. A number of "theory-practice" programs have recently emerged here, joining programs in Europe, Asia, and elsewhere. Such efforts take on a wide variety of labels, from makerspaces to arts-based research to innovation labs to digital scholarship centers and more. What they typically share is a focus on multiple ways of knowing and some relationship of theory to practice—of hack to yack.

They also meet similar forms of resistance as they take shape across a variety of campuses. Some such reactions might simply be categorized as an academic resistance to change, a traditionalism within the academy that tends to favor existing structures and approaches or treats emerging paradigms with suspicion, if not outright hostility. But another vector of opposition arises from those whose worries are more specific. That is, they worry that innovation labs and makerspaces hew too closely to the neoliberal, techno-utopian logics of Silicon Valley. For instance, in a recent piece in the *Los Angeles Review of Books*, Daniel Allington, Sarah Brouilette, and David Golumbia frame digital humanities as "playing a leading role in the corporatist restructuring of the humanities" through the field's focus on "the manufacture of digital tools and archives" (2016). The limits of their position have been hotly debated across the web and social media, with many taking exception to the very broad contours of the argument that reduce all of digital humanities to a few very specific examples in English departments, and others pointing out that, of the many causes for alarm in the modern university, the increase in digital humanities programs hardly seems the most significant one (Kirschenbaum 2016; Spahr et al. 2016). Still others have underscored that the piece displaces women and scholars of color who have labored to create politically engaged DH practices (Risam 2016). Nonetheless, I think we might attend with some care to the authors' concerns that emerging programs focused on making, innovation, and creative technology might indeed be serving corporate ends to the extent that they privilege tool building or technology (or we might say, "hack") more than critique (or "yack").

More nuanced versions of this argument that DH may be complicit with corporate interests have been written by other scholars, including Gary Hall's claim (2013) that the turn toward quantitative data analysis within digital humanities is in fact incommensurable with the methods and aims of the interpretative humanities. I am sympathetic to Hall's argument. It is not hard to see that there are lines of convergence between the rise of curricular programs in digital technologies and the needs of corporate technology firms. Some of the technology programs and labs at my university as well as many others are funded by corporate benefactors, and there is no doubt that such sponsorship torques scholarship and learning in very particular ways. And yet such pressures seem to necessitate not a repudiation of the humanities intersecting with the digital, but rather a demand that humanities scholars increasingly operate within that very conjunction. If we are indeed concerned about the escalating corporatization of our campuses—from online learning platforms to new regimes of management—then an engagement with technology and the digital seems a crucial (if not the only) way to navigate these concerns. Such engagements can certainly happen (and already are happening) within the making spaces, digital scholarship centers, and digital humanities labs taking shape on many of our campuses, but they are unlikely to do so unless we move beyond the binary framed by hacking versus yacking. They will also require an explicit focus upon the ideological dimensions of technology that scholars ranging from Martha Nell Smith (2007) and Alan Liu (2012) have noted as sometimes missing from the digital humanities agenda.

III

There are precedents in the recent history of the university that suggest how such conjunctions might take shape. This volume's title actually limns one way. I find the explicit attempt to join media studies with digital humanities to be a promising gesture, one that might push each field in constructive directions and also speaks to my own intellectual trajectory. My graduate education and early scholarly career centered on film and media studies and, more particularly, on feminist film theory. While my PhD program was in an English department, the opportunity to engage in media practice did exist along the margins of the curriculum. One class in particular profoundly rejiggered how I would come to understand the relationship of making to theory, leading to the vivid dreams that opened this essay. It was team-taught by feminist theorist, Patricia Mellencamp, and video artist, Cecelia Condit. The two came together to offer the class based on a friendship that grew out of Pat writing about Cecelia's videos. The course combined students from film production and film studies at the University of Wisconsin-Milwaukee. The production department skewed toward experimental practice and was part of the art school, while the film studies program was then part of the theory-rich Modern Studies track within English. Students were encouraged to stretch outside of their comfort zones and work in a medium less familiar to them, be that print or video.

The experience deeply reconfigured how I understood feminism and collaboration, and it gave me a hands-on engagement with making that continues to influence my research—research that engages both theory and practice. The films I collaborated on years ago in that class were not very good, but they opened me up to new ways of thinking about the materiality of production practices and to different aesthetic registers, exploring what forms an explicitly feminist film language might take. They connected to my feminist activism within and beyond the academy, particularly in relation to grad student labor and reproductive politics. They eventually led me to volunteer for public access television and think more rigorously about infrastructures for production and distribution, both within and beyond the confines of commercial media. They also modeled for me the generosity and commitment that collaborations across difference require, as both Pat and Cecelia actively engaged ways of producing knowledge different than those already familiar to them. I had the opportunity to work alongside other students who were primarily artists, and this experience was incredibly invigorating, even as it was often challenging. We were investigating the possibility for making in ongoing dialogue with ideological critique. The structure of the class made it clear that the two were inextricably intertwined.

These types of interactions are incredibly important for how we might conceive of the rich possibilities of particular modes of media studies for a politically engaged digital humanities. Feminist film studies emerged from an entanglement with what is now sometimes called critical making, if the terminology of the time was different. We can trace decades of feminist media makers blurring the lines between theory and practice, from Maya Deren to Laura Mulvey to Marsha Kinder, Brenda Laurel, Sandy Stone, Anne Balsamo, Alexandra Juhasz, Sharon Daniel, and micha cárdenas, among many others. Their work powerfully illustrates how theory and making exist in rich feedback loops. It is hard to imagine Mulvey (1975) reaching the insights of her landmark essay on sexual difference and visual pleasure in film apart from her engagement with practices of production, an argument also forwarded by Miriam Posner (2015). Such exchanges between theory and practice need not only happen at the level of the individual, of course. Something quite powerful can happen when theorists and artists work together, as Pat and Cecelia illustrated.

This wedding of theory and practice was crucial to the formation of feminist film studies as a field over 40 years ago. We see this joining quite literally in the title of key essays such as Claire Johnston's "The Subject of Feminist Film Theory/Practice." The "/" signals a hybrid practice beyond the "and." Published in the journal *Screen* in 1980, the piece reports on the Feminism and Cinema Event held at the 1979 Edinburgh Film Festival. Johnston writes that, "throughout the week, emphasis was placed on the need to locate feminist politics within a conception of film as a social practice, on the dialectic of making and viewing and on film as a process rather than an object" (1980: 27). She goes on to note that the event served:

> to bring together filmmakers, film theorists and women involved in distribution and exhibition . . . to generate discussion and analysis of the conditions of existence of each of these practices, their forms and their relation to each other. The event provided a useful starting point for developing a space in which the transformation of the relationship between production, distribution, exhibition and criticism could be worked through and from which strategies could be forged.
>
> (Johnston 1980: 27)

She later argues that theory is "an endless and dialectical discursive activity, embedded in the real, and always exceeded and transformed by practice—a constant dialectic with the aim of breaking of exchange for use" (28). Thus, we see an ongoing and reciprocal, if never frictionless, exchange between making and theorizing at the very moment that feminist film studies constitutes itself as a field of inquiry. Not all feminist film scholars were wielding cameras, nor were all feminist filmmakers enamored of (or even reading) theory. The support for feminist media making, distribution, and pedagogy was also more pronounced within the UK. Nonetheless, there was a great deal of fluidity between feminist "yack" and "hack" that functioned as a dialectic force as the field came into being. There are lessons to be learned from this history for those invested in a more theoretically informed digital humanities as well as for feminist film and media theorists today.

On the one hand, the early history of feminist film theory models a vibrant relationship of making to critique. Many feminist film scholars engaged in a form of inquiry that understood theory and practice to be constitutive of one another. Forged from a commitment to change in the world along multiple vectors, these scholars and makers not only recognized that technology is never neutral; they also foregrounded the political in their various endeavors. They investigated the ways in which communication technologies worked in close concert with social systems and social inequalities, not only at the level of representation but also in their very design, implementation, and structure. They also sought to intervene in media distribution, creating new networks for the circulation of media; and, particularly in the UK, they sought to integrate making and critique through extensive pedagogical experiments within and beyond the university. These insights were often born of a deep exploration of the material forms of cinema—explorations enriched by practice. Such work is vitally important terrain for digital humanities, leading us to ask how our machines encode culture in very particular and often damaging ways while also perhaps signaling an enhanced role for artists and designers within DH endeavors.

On the other hand, feminist film and media studies today does not always exhibit such strong ties to practice as was evident at the formation of the field in the 1970s and 1980s. The conjuncture of theory and practice that was so crucial to the emerging field has been hard to maintain in many programs, with theory and practice forced apart as the discipline matured and adapted to the siloed nature of the academy, a place where "practice" and "making" are often devalued. (Hence, at my university and many others, professors of practice are not part of the tenure stream.) To the extent that Johnston and others have argued that practice refines and sharpens the work of theory, I see this split as a loss to the field. Digital media studies and digital humanities now offer the possibility of renewing the forms of dialectical inquiry so valued by feminist film scholars in the 1970s. While there is no guarantee that these programs will hold theory and practice in productive tension toward progressive ends, they can offer a space for such work to unfold.

IV

Martha Nell Smith (2007) has argued that some early computational humanities efforts were a retreat from the inroads made by theories of difference and identity, feminism included, within the academy. This certainly seems to be true, and yet Smith's own scholarly practice illustrates how powerful the routes of exchange might be between feminist theory and computational practice, as does the work of many other scholars today who are working at the intersection of digital making and theories of gender, race, sexuality, embodiment, affect, materiality, and more.

As the digital more and more infuses our everyday ways of being, writing, making, and thinking, we are also seeing a heightened call for a return to feminist modes of praxis. It is as if our daily digital immersions have reanimated a feminist longing for forms of practice that embrace yet also—in Johnston's terms—exceed theory. Such calls emerge from a wide variety of feminist scholars with diverse specialties, ranging from film and media studies to new materialisms to posthumanisms. For example, in *Vibrant Matter*, Jane Bennett writes:

> We need not only to invent or reinvoke concepts like . . . actant, assemblage . . . and the like but also to devise new procedures, technologies, and regimes of perception that enable us to consult nonhumans more closely.
>
> (Bennett 2010: 108)

Feminist philosopher Rosi Braidotti asks, "how does the posthuman affect the practice of the humanities today?" (2013: 3). She wants to "empower the pursuit of alternative schemes" (12) and calls for "combining critique with creative figurations" (163) and praxis (92). While Bennett and Braidotti push toward making again and again, their work stops short of actual practice, largely staying within the realm of theory. There is much that separates their work, but both of them strain to explicate ways of being and knowing that might push the scholar toward entanglements with making and practice beyond or in addition to language. Each understands that we are profoundly shaped by technology, caught up with it in ways that deeply impact being and acting. They, of course, understand that language is a form of making, but they are also calling for practices that exceed the discursive as we grapple with our technological imbrications. Such practices will make us dream differently.

One senses that Bennett and Braidotti also recognize that, as feminists and progressive scholars, we might produce technology and media differently, much as have feminist filmmakers. The history of feminist film studies suggests that an engagement with technological practice helps enact this dual commitment to politics and matter in ways that complement and even exceed the force of critical theory. Here, of course, we are drawn back into an interesting relation with digital humanities. Natalia Cecire (2011), Alan Liu (2012), Johanna Drucker (2012), Jamie Skye Bianco (2012), and others have urged digital humanists to get with the theoretical program, and here we have feminists calling for theory to turn (back) to practice, including making and activism. This is a promising intersection. What might emerge in this joining? While they do not operate directly under the banner of DH, we see glimpses of feminist making in the work of Sarah Kember and Joanna Zylinska (2012), who turn to both the photograph and fiction as vital forms of feminist endeavor—as creative practices that might make feminism differently. Anne Balsamo's *Designing Culture* (2011) traces over two decades of hands-on making that merges feminist insight with the technological imaginary. Her recent work with Alexandra Juhasz and many, many others on the FemTechNet coalition likewise models feminist creation, building a massive and shifting assemblage that might challenge the instrumental force of the MOOC and the corporate university. Their work recalls the work of early feminist film scholars as it engages making, theory, distribution, and pedagogy across a range of endeavors. If Claire Johnston understood the necessity of mining "the relationship between production, distribution, exhibition and criticism" in 1970s feminist film culture, then FemTechNet reanimates this insight for the digital age through its commitments to producing open access teaching materials, building noncommercial networks for the circulation of feminist ideas, and merging theory and practice.

These are vital models for digital media studies, DH, and feminism, as they operate at the pressure point between theory and practice in lively and generative ways. Other feminist scholars, including Susan Brown, micha cárdenas, Kim Christen, Beth Coleman, Anne Cong-Huyen, Sharon Daniel, T.L. Cowan, Cathy Davidson, Amy Earhart, Kathleen Fitzpatrick, Julia Flanders, Jennifer Gabrys, Radhika Gajjala, Dene Grigar, Adeline Koh, Marsha Kinder, Lauren Klein, Kim Knight, Elizabeth Losh, Alexis Lothian, Shannon Mattern, Anna Munster, Bethany Nowviskie, Veronica Paredes, Amanda Phillips, Miriam Posner, Padmini Ray Murray, Daniela Rosner, Laila Shereen Sakr, Martha Nell Smith, Margaret Rhee, Roopika Risam, Susana Ruiz, Alison Trope, Jacqueline Wernimont, and Laura Wexler, offer models of how such practice-based work might unfold. While not all of these feminists would call themselves "digital humanists," their work encompasses a commitment to theory/practice that both digital humanities and media studies should embrace. As Risam (2016) has argued, much of this work is rendered invisible in the polemics of the *Los Angeles Review of Books* publication cited earlier. What digital humanities and media studies are or will be is an open question, not a foregone conclusion. Only a subset of scholars within these fields, or within most humanities departments, is committed to politically engaged research that holds theory and practice in a productive tension.

Jane Bennett writes of the craftperson's desire to see what a material can *do* as opposed to the scientist's desire to learn what a material *is* (2010: 60). This desire to investigate the material and its potentialities is not the same as critique. It also produces different insights. The theorist might resist such a framing, arguing that she works with words as her "material," pushing them into productive new relations. She is right, but there are other materials we might engage that exist beyond the discursive realm and move us toward new alliances and new practices. Such practices can and should shape our theories, but they are not the same thing.

It is probably not an accident that the dual embrace of theory and practice in feminist film studies during the 1970s came at a time of widespread changes in communications technologies, from the advent of cheaper, more portable cameras to the broad diffusion of television. The feminists gathered in Edinburgh in 1979 understood their moment as a time in which they might intervene in systems of production, representation, distribution, and exhibition, working on many fronts and through many modalities. They valued yack as much as hack, and they held the two in lively tension. The digital technologies of our own era call us to embrace similar strategies as we confront the perils and possibilities of the widespread diffusion of the digital through our dreams, our lives, and our workplaces.

Acknowledgments

Some of the ideas for this essay were first formulated in a conversation with Henry Jenkins and published on his blog, *Confessions of an Aca-Fan*, in March 2015. They are further developed in my book, *Feminist in a Software Lab: Difference + Design* (Harvard University Press 2018). Thanks to Jentery Sayers and Amelie Hastie for thoughtful suggestions for revision.

Further Reading

Balsamo, A. (2011) *Designing Culture: The Technological Imagination at Work*, Durham, NC: Duke University Press.

Gold, M. and L. Klein (eds.) (2016) *Debates in the Digital Humanities 2016*, Minneapolis, MN: University of Minnesota Press.

McPherson, T. (ed.) (2009) "In Focus: Digital Scholarship and Pedagogy," *Cinema Journal* 48(2), 119–60.

Sayers, J. and the MLab (2015) "Kits for Cultural History," *Hyperrhiz 13*, retrieved from dx.doi.org/10.20415/hyp/013.w02.

Wernimont, J. (ed.) (2015) "Feminisms and Digital Humanities," A special issue of *Digital Humanities Quarterly* 9(2), retrieved from digitalhumanities.org/dhq/vol/9/2/index.html.

References

Allington, D., S. Brouilette, and D. Golumbia (2016) "Neoliberal Tools (and Archives): A Political History of the Digital Humanities," *Los Angeles Review of Books*, retrieved from lareviewofbooks.org/article/neoliberal-tools-archives-political-history-digital-humanities.

Balsamo, A. (2011) *Designing Culture: The Technological Imagination at Work*, Durham, NC: Duke University Press.

Bennett, J. (2010) *Vibrant Matter: A Political Ecology of Things*, Durham, NC: Duke University Press.

Bianco, J. S. (2012) "The Digital Humanities Which Is Not One," in M. Gold (ed.) *Debates in the Digital Humanities*, Minneapolis, MN: University of Minnesota Press, pp. 96–112.

Braidotti, R. (2013) *The Posthuman*, Malden, MA: Polity Press.

Cecire, N. (2011) "When Digital Humanities Was in Vogue," *Journal of Digital Humanities* 1(1), journalofdigital humanities.org/1–1/introduction-theory-and-the-virtues-of-digital-humanities-by-natalia-cecire.

Drucker, J. (2012) "Humanistic Theory and Digital Scholarship" in M. Gold (ed.) *Debates in the Digital Humanities*, Minneapolis, MN: University of Minnesota Press, pp. 85–95.

Hall, G. (2013) "Toward a Postdigital Humanities: Cultural Analytic and the Computational Turn to Data-Driven Scholarship," *American Literature* 85(4), 781–809.

Johnston, C. (1980) "The Subject of Feminist Film Theory/Practice," *Screen* 21(2), 27–34.

Kember, S. and J. Zylinska (2012) *Life after New Media: Mediation as a Vital Process*, Cambridge, MA: MIT Press.

Kirschenbaum, M. (2016) "Am I a Digital Humanist? Confessions of a Neoliberal Tool," retrieved from medium.com/@mkirschenbaum/am-i-a-digital-humanist-confessions-of-a-neoliberal-tool-1bc64caaa984#.24jhaqnbv.

Koh, A. (2012) "More Hack, Less Yack?: Modularity, Theory and Habitus in the Digital Humanities," retrieved from www.adelinekoh.org/blog/2012/05/21/more-hack-less-yack-modularity-theory-and-habitus-in-the-digital-humanities.

Latour, B. (2004) "Why Has Critique Run Out of Steam? From Matters of Fact to Matters of Concern," *Critical Inquiry* 30(2), 225–48.

Liu, A. (2012) "Where Is Cultural Criticism in the Digital Humanities?" in M. Gold (ed.) *Debates in the Digital Humanities*, Minneapolis, MN: University of Minnesota Press, pp. 490–509.

Mulvey, L. (1975) "Visual Pleasure and Narrative Cinema," *Screen* 16(3), 6–18.

Nowviskie, B. (2014) "On the Origin of 'Hack' and 'Yack,'" retrieved from nowviskie.org/2014/on-the-origin-of-hack-and-yack.

Posner, M. (2012) "Think Talk Make Do: Power and the Digital Humanities," *Journal of the Digital Humanities* 1(2), journalofdigitalhumanities.org/1–2/think-talk-make-do-power-and-the-digital-humanities-by-miriam-posner.

Ramsay, S. (2011) "Who's In and Who's Out," retrieved from stephenramsay.us/text/2011/01/08/whos-in-and-whos-out.

Risam, R. (2016) "Digital Humanities in Other Contexts," retrieved from roopikarisam.com/uncategorized/digital-humanities-in-other-contexts.

Scheinfeldt, T. (2012) "Sunset for Ideology, Sunrise for Methodology?" in M. Gold (ed.) *Debates in the Digital Humanities*, Minneapolis, MN: University of Minnesota Press, pp. 124–26.

Smith, M. N. (2007) "The Human Touch Software of the Highest Order: Revisiting Editing as Interpretation," *Textual Cultures: Texts, Contexts, Interpretation* 2(1), 1–15.

Spahr, J., R. So, and A. Piper (2016) "Beyond Resistance: Towards a Future History of Digital Humanities," *Los Angeles Review of Books*, retrieved from lareviewofbooks.org/article/beyond-resistance-towards-future-history-digital-humanities/#!.

Warwick, C. (2016) "Building Theories or Theories of Building," in S. Schreibman, R. Siemens, and J. Unsworth (eds.) *A New Companion to Digital Humanities*, 2nd edn, Malden, MA: Wiley, pp. 538–51.

2

#CUT/PASTE+BLEED

Entangling Feminist Affect, Action, and Production On and Offline

Alexandra Juhasz

The Set-Up

I have been engaged in an integrated "media praxis" that holistically links media production, theory, and criticism around social issues of value to myself and my communities for over 25 years. I have produced several large bodies of work, about a range of issues, but all share my commitment to making and theorizing media within communities and toward self- and world-changing. My media praxis—making alternative community and culture while critiquing participatory networks or hegemonic culture through an active participation within them—has moved across media forms and their related scholarly fields as technologies and their academic homes have transformed: from activist video to online spaces, from cinema to media studies to digital humanities (DH). The issues I work on have also changed over the years—AIDS, feminism, black lesbian identity and community, antiwar activism, queer families, feminist pedagogy, and digital community—but my commitment to doing this work within and about media technologies has stayed consistent. Why?

Perhaps not surprisingly, I have already answered this question online—why work *on* technologies *in* those systems?—writing there about my work on YouTube (this repeating, recycling, and returning to online expression is the particular focus [and form!] of the project I will soon be describing here: Ev-ent-anglement). "My Orientation (Toward YouTube and ThirdTube)" is one "texteo" from my born-digital, online video-book, *Learning from YouTube* (2011b: 243). There, like here, I detail my position up front because it is perhaps unusually subjective, committed, and connected, and I do not want that obscured. Self-aware, self-reflexive process is central to my media praxis:

> I am a committed media scholar and maker whose work has focused on individual and community empowerment and, by design, projects to which I am personally related. The wholistic integration of teaching, writing, media-making and politics—what I call *media praxis*—is central to my life's work, which I hope will contribute to change. I like to work within the forms I am analyzing and hoping to (use for) change. My reflexive process grounds the questions I ask of YouTube and where I

> try to push it. The project is both personal and political (i.e., feminist), as well as formal and structural in nature. Thus, a critical pedagogy aiming toward digital literacy and a civic engagement in the hopes of creative democracy are also central to my praxis. I believe that under the right conditions, citizens and students (Web 2.0's much-celebrated "users") can make expressive, critical, and beautiful media that makes relevant contributions to our culture. Thinking through (and in) these conditions is a defining orientation of my project.

In the mid-2000s, I repositioned the places and technologies undergirding my ongoing interest in user-made media for self and community empowerment, and began asking questions about the use of YouTube (and social networks, more generally) toward these potentially revolutionary ends. *Learning from YouTube* (which I "published" online with MIT Press in 2011) holds the analysis my students and I generated while attempting to theorize and produce personal, political, creative, or expressive work within one of the central, repressive corporate digital platforms that we have been given for free.

After the rather lengthy and painful process of inhabiting and critiquing this corporate platform from within, all the while learning through practice how such political and aesthetic interventions are performed, enacted, and curbed by new media networks, I wanted to be more productive and less reactive. So, in 2010, I began to teach a course called "Feminist Online Spaces" that asks my students to both find and analyze the possibilities for democratic, safe, and principled interaction online. This course inspired me to want to build more networked and generative communities, which initiated my collaboration with Anne Balsamo, with whom I co-facilitated FemTechNet (a global network of feminist scholars and artists) in 2013 as well as FemTechNet's signature course, "Feminist Dialogues on Technology," an experimental, technology-enhanced DOCC (Distributed Open Collaborative Course) in its third year-long cycle at the time of this writing. I consider all of these media-critical and -situated projects to be lab-like encounters where doing and thinking in community (often the classroom and its linked spaces) and within the sites or technologies under consideration *are* the scholarship. That is to say, the doing and the process are the product, and what is built toward those ends can also be shared and/or evaluated (Juhasz 2011a). This allocating and re-allocating of process in and as the product are what I model now, albeit within yet another technology: the paper-bound scholarly anthology. Here, I describe my most recent project, Ev-ent-anglement, one that again engages critically with social media networks from inside them; share some of my lessons learned about critical digital production and research practice; and conclude with why I think these methods (as much as my findings) matter.

Ev-ent-anglement begins with a simple enough mandate: If the internet is an unorchestrated archive of fragments of all our selves being mined to sell us more things that we never needed, then we might want to take on the empowering feminist role of editor and curate ourselves, together, into collections that matter, at least for a minute and only for us. Like any experiment, things got more complicated as theories, practitioners, places, and objects were edited in: *Our Bodies, Ourselves Redux*. Lopped. Looped. Lined. Linked. Re-aligned. Show the seams. Justice to our fragments! Like many experiments, much of the project "failed": (some) things were not built or they broke; (some) people did not participate; (some) energy waned. In what follows, I reflect on how it feels, and what I learned and can share by doing my scholarly work in this way. I explain the thinking and doing as well as the practices and theories that motivated this critical internet experiment where our object was our self and ourselves and then these objects got out of hand.

Ev-ent-anglement was a year-long, multi-sited project where participants engaged in a process of cutting/pasting+bleeding ourselves together—as we are and have been; as we have made ourselves online and off, in community, history, and action with others. The ev-ent-anglement is at once a digital platform and record that allows audience members in a room at a conference attending an event live and in person, as well as our fellow travelers on the internet and/or with a book in hand (those we can reach; those who are so inclined), to cut/paste evidence of their entangled, cooperative, and interactive role in the event so as to be part of something new. The evidence of users' presence and action takes the form of a carefully hashtagged fragment of their choice or an even more carefully penned comment. (You can entangle at will using #eventanglement or go to ev-ent-anglement.com and engage.)

The Project: Ev-ent-angelement

Ev-ent-anglement (Juhasz 2014–15) cuts and pastes an event to an entanglement, making use of hyphens for its two very visible stitches: *ev-ent-anglement*. It is currently two online entities built primarily from five events that began as scholarly talks: the first held in the Netherlands in August 2014 at the European Summer School in Women's Studies at Utrecht University; the second in Dehli at the Visible Evidence Documentary Conference in December 2014 (see Figure 2.1); the third at the Console-ing Passions Feminist Media Conference in Dublin in June 2015; the fourth in Montreal at Affective Encounters, an August 2015 gathering for feminist scholars and artists where we worked together on media and affect theory; and the fifth and final at an artist's performance space, PAM, in Highland Park, Los Angeles in November 2015, where I co-produced a culminating event with scholar and artist, VJ Um Amel (Laila Shereen Sakr) (see Figure 2.7). I call these talks "events" because their participatory and performative nature differentiates them from the more circumscribed set of routines and protocols of typical conference presentations where a professor speaks with authority and clarity

Figure 2.1 "#eventanglement on Mohamed Mahmoud St. in Cairo #mediawhore."
Source: Tweeted by Laila Shereen Sakr (@vj_um_amel) to Ev-ent-angelement 2: Dehli.

and her audience respectfully and passively listens. Here, I am indebted to Slavoj Žižek, who defines an event as: "something shocking, out of joint, that appears all of a sudden and interrupts the usual flow of things" (2014: 4). Similarly, Alain Badiou calls *an event* "a rupture in the normal order of bodies and languages as it exists for any particular situation" (2010: 242). While these theorists' interpretations of history and possible futures differ, their words, like many others to which I refer, are useful for my research praxis in that they provide mental systems, and their lovely verbal schemes, that can help to indicate the intellectual place and possibilities of my worldly (or at least digital) efforts. In this way, making theory (as do most scholars) and making art and/or practice (as do some) are linked, aligned, and differentiated: from map to territory, or territories, and back again as the work is brought into being through new boundaries for thought and production.

What I hoped would serve as event-like—shocking, or out of joint, or even something akin to a rupture—in this series of "talks" was that I asked the audience, in the room but always also online, to act with me rather than sit back and listen (or read)—to *cut* and also to *paste*—and in so doing entangle fragments of themselves into the digital record of the ever-growing and always-changing event, which itself is housed and becomes anew online as the Ev-ent-anglement. "Cuts are part of the phenomena they help to produce," writes Karen Barad (2007: 145). At the lectern, I offered intellectual, historical, and material evidence about the role of cutting and pasting in a variety of traditions and particularly for feminists (from filmmaking, to photography, self-cutting, physics, and new materialism, as evidenced in the complex Barad fragment quoted above and at all my events). The audience was invited to do the thing and verb under consideration: to cut and paste in real time by using a hashtag to deliver to me fragments of themselves and our shared event, cut from their lives and its digital record, as photos, tweets, URLs, comments, and other repurposed digital detritus.

These materials are the shared residue and building blocks of the Ev-ent-anglement: a digital place that archives, grows, and changes via the acts, interests, and values of its diverse, feminist community. Participants cut/paste into the Ev-ent-anglement, engaging in cutting one thing from and then to another, moving something from one place that was to another that will be. Cutting is a special kind of action, a "causal procedure and act of decision" that Sarah Kember and Joanna Zylinska understand as ethical (2012: 82). They explain that cutting, in the making of a photograph where something still and framed is edited from the flow of daily life, demands a choice. My project suggests that in day-to-day internet practice, this choice-making is obscured by ease and distraction. My event and its digital rendering, the Ev-ent-anglement, helps us to see obscured practices by asking my participants to do (again) something quite common, but to do so within a framework where the action becomes visible by giving it a context, a community, and a politics: a possible ethics.

While many of the fragments gifted to me during talks, or after in the asynchronous iteration of the project always online, were "about" and also made by cutting and pasting, they also pointed to and manifested the many linked and always growing sets of interests of the project and its participants. This caring and careful cutting/pasting by willing participants (and they were not all willing, by the way, one of the project's many "failures" about which I theorize later in this chapter) was initiated by a provocative invitation or script that was place-based—Utrecht, Delhi, Dublin, LA, Montreal (see Figure 2.2)—while being simultaneously online. As I moved across time and place, the digital Ev-ent-anglement grew and changed. For instance, when I was in Utrecht, new media scholar and trans theorist, KJ Surkan, entangling from afar in the US, added a poem about cutting off body parts:

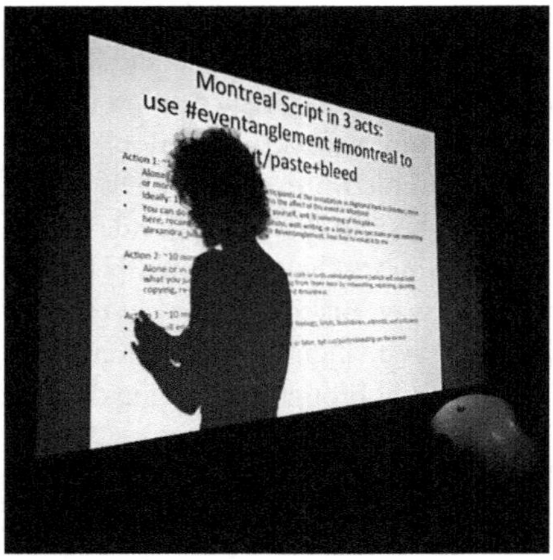

Figure 2.2 "Feminist Collectives as Shadow Archive of feminism in contemporary university. #AffectiveEncounters #eventanglement."

Source: Tweeted by T.L. Cowan (@AgingSuperModel) at Ev-ent-anglement 4: Montreal.

I have recently made a rather large cut
to myself
or rather a surgeon made it for me
out of great necessity

(It was a kind of a "do or die" situation)

This edit to my physical body invites interpretations,
many times by strangers
People whom I don't know
and who don't know me.

I don't mean to be mysterious
but
it's complicated.

Online I am a composite of many identities
gendered this way or that
and strangely
I find myself entangled in fragments of former selves
which are constantly colliding
shattering the illusion of the seamless narratives
about gender identity
about cancer
often required for the comfort of others.
#eventanglement

(Surkan 2014)

When I wrote about Alisa Lebow's keynote address at the Visible Evidence Documentary Conference as one of my own cut/pastes to the Ev-ent-anglement, other fragments from and about the Middle East, such as the Media Whore image shared above (see Figure 2.1), became part of the entanglement. It grew in this and other directions accordingly. In Dublin, Rena Bivens tweeted in a video of "Menstruation Machine" by Japanese artist, Sputniko. And so new participants (Surkan, Lebow, and Bivens), places (Middle East, Japan, and Dublin), and concepts (reconstructive and corrective bodily surgery, Arab digital activism, and menstruation) enter the complex but rooted Ev-ent-anglement. These are just three examples of the many ideas, movies, poems, pictures, links, and people that thus became objects in my archive; the Ev-ent-anglement opened out to encompass many linked lines of inquiry and activism yielding further audience attachments at later events.

Entanglements (the second fragment roughly cut with just two little dashes into the neologism, *ev-ent-anglement*) are about "joins and disjoins—cutting together/apart—not separate consecutive activities, but a single event that is not one," according to Barad (2013: 18). The word that I invented through cutting and pasting is itself about *montage*: the process of making not one from many, of "cutting together/apart." And this event (you reading me now), like any, is not one: it is my words; my stance; your thoughts; your attitudes; the words on the page; the technological infrastructure that put those words into a book and moves it to you; the behind-the-scenes labor of two programmers, Risa Goodman and Laila Shereen Sakr, who built the two WordPress sites where Ev-ent-anglement takes place; the words and viewpoints of the people I have quoted and will quote (Badiou, Žižek, Surkan, Lebow, Barad, Kember, Zylinska, and soon enough, Gregg and Seigworth); and sometimes, if participants are willing, some of our associated *feelings*, although cutting/pasting these remains the hardest part of the experiment, worthy of much more thinking, practicing, and building in its near impossibility and utter magnetism. Melissa Gregg and Gregory Seigworth have a name for this—affect—all that falls outside of things and makes events. "Affect arises in the midst of *in-between-ness*: in the capacities of a momentary or sometimes more sustained set of relations *as well as* the passage (and the duration of the passage) of forces or intensities" (2010: 1). As part of the Ev-ent-anglement, @AgingSuperModel, the queer performance artist and scholar, T.L. Cowan, shared an image (see Figure 2.3) to express some affect: an idea, feeling, and their connection to her/our experience and place.

In this event here and now, and better yet in the Ev-ent-anglement that holds it and others, you can read how I have cut/pasted editing theory and practice by way of media studies and production with fragments of what is often called "new materialism" and "affect theory" and then used this patchwork theory monster to create theoretical and practical boundaries to help enact a DH project of feminist collective, critical digital practice. Once engaged, users become objects in our archive, as do their fragments, as do the people, places, and things thereby summoned up, cut in, and linked to. This is confusing, or at least complicated, because I am often asking participants to share *affect*, which is by definition fleeting, embodied, personal, and not exactly linguistic. Obviously, in my project, and everywhere else online, people and things become objects because they are rendered as words in a database that are then ruled by algorithmic relations. If you participate, your name becomes an object, as do the things you cut/paste as digital versions of themselves; and if you describe what you think or how you felt, then that, too, once rendered as words or images or any other 0 and 1, becomes an object. In this way, the site manifests one of the central ideas of new materialism: "ideas are material in that they become rituals and then sedimented at a corporeal level" (Coole & Frost 2010: 34). Although each object becomes a thing unto itself once it is cut/pasted in, the Ev-ent-anglement also strives to keep our sights on the processes that put it and others

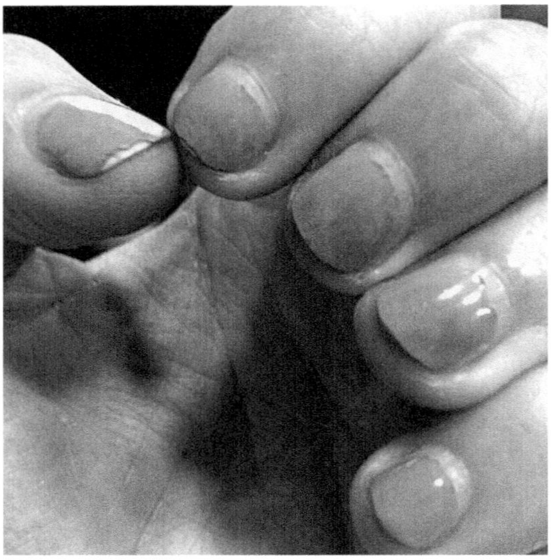

Figure 2.3 "2 Weeks. 2 feminist Workshops. 1 manicure. #What Sticks #What Chips."

Source: Tweeted by T.L. Cowan (@AgingSuperModel) during Ev-ent-anglement 4: Montreal.

into movement and connection. In this case, these connections are feminist, theoretical, anti-corporate, and collaborative, attempting to experiment with—in the doing—the changing of our conception of the digital archive from a repository of things to a process of shared feminist knowledge production: nouns and verbs; things and their processes; feminist cuts and connections that bind. With Barad in our minds, we might act knowing that matter is an actor. "[M]atter is neither fixed and given nor the mere end result of different processes. Matter is produced and productive, generated and generative. Matter is agentive, not a fixed essence or property of things" (Barad 2007: 137).

Certainly, to entangle a digital fragment of oneself, with a cut/paste via a simple hashtag, while attending what one thought was a talk, or while one is reading from a book, is neither required nor easy. Acting, doing, cutting, and making are ethical procedures that, in this case, are also public. I learned from my experiment that neither scholars nor students much like to do or make when they think they have signed up to listen or read, particularly when this doing or making will be public and lasting. (It remained a mystery to me across the project why these same people so gladly do this work for Facebook! More on this below.) The ev-ent-anglement requires audience members' "intra-action," another of Barad's terms that marks where "there is no 'between' as such[;] human and nonhuman organisms and machines emerge only through their mutual co-constitution" (2007: 151). Intra-actions are easy to render, but hard to do well. Unlike with corporate social networks, the stakes of participation in the ev-ent-anglement are made clear (in this writing for instance); the cost of action is rendered visible. For the Ev-ent-anglement, every cut/paste of a fragment of participants' digital selves, or that of others, is generously and knowingly gifted to me and the Ev-ent-anglement, rather than to the man or corporation. Yes, your fragments move through Twitter (see Figure 2.4), YouTube, WordPress, Instagram, or Pinterest to get to me: objects first to be sold before they can be gifted and hopefully lost within a more complex co-constitution. But, unlike for the corporations listed above, the Ev-ent-anglement acknowledges that there is something

Figure 2.4 Tweeted by @OtterDiscourse at Ev-ent-anglement 4: Montreal.

that exceeds the movement of the mimetic copy of some part of oneself or others so casually given away or passed on with the internet's effortless cut/pastes.

We call this the *bleed*: the actions, affects, and activities that will never be caught and saved as objects in a database. "Affect is what sticks, or what sustains or preserves the connection between ideas, values, and objects," explains Sara Ahmed (2010: 30). An ev-ent-anglement cuts and pastes participants' fragments into the digital record of an event and also takes account of the bleed: that which was not first an object but co-constituted the event, its people, its place. How do we do this? We begin by thinking about cutting and pasting in gendered terms, and in relation to power. Film/video editing, like the contemporary act of self-cutting, can be understood as a violent act of power-seeking performed in some of the many private places allocated to women in patriarchy: the editing room rather than the world itself, the bedroom and home also distinguished from the public. Yes, some kinds of cutting do not bring with them an associated paste. What *this* cut can bring with it, what it wants—its dyadic relation—is a *bleed*.

While all human bodies (and those of other animals) bleed, a particular kind of hemorrhaging will help focus the bleed's role in our feminist project of Ev-ent-anglement—one where our directives are to #cut/paste+*bleed*—because the menses are one of many in-between bodily acts that are uniquely and distinctly female. Julia Kristeva asks us to consider many bodily acts, menstruation being just one, at the border between clean and dirty, live and dead, inside and out: "Repelling, rejecting; repelling itself, rejecting itself. Ab-jecting" (1980: 13). The seeping and connecting quality of blood allows it to be a metaphoric glue, like affect, that marks the many pulls, movements, and actions of any entanglement—from in to out and on to off, from me to you to us, from digital matter to living body. Of course all people—men, those in-between or indeterminate, and females who do not menstruate—can bleed with us, too! Cyborgs all, we use technology and place to flow through distinctive binaries: let us cut/paste+bleed through these binaries! There is no in-between.

To date, there are about 100 photographs that people have cut/pasted+bled into the ev-ent-anglement, and as many tweets, often with photos in them (see Figure 2.5). There are links to websites and hours of video. People have entangled poems and their favorite authors. Many theorists have arrived after the fact, lovingly quoted by their fans, or writing new theory themselves into the project. But unlike much on the internet, our community is limited; our database is small (and yet, counter-intuitively, *enormous*) because the ideas and objects gathered

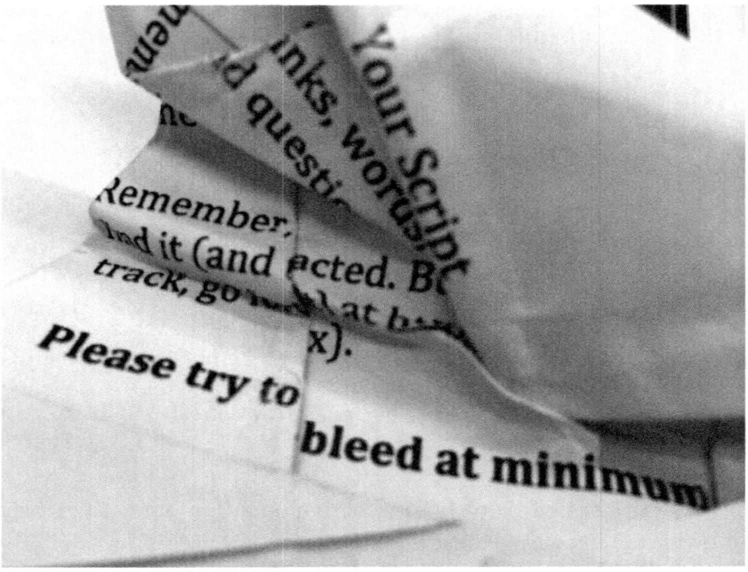

Figure 2.5 Created by Alanna Thain at Ev-ent-anglement 1: Utrecht.

are complex and deep—to know what is there demands time, and your presence is generative. In the Ev-ent-anglement, every gift is an object—whether people, places, things, or an attempt at affect—and every object can be entangled with others, initiating a bleed because it comes from a rip or a tear. When you participate, you become an object, too. And that should not be easy, or really even "fun."

In the end, the Ev-ent-anglement's form is not so different from, say, a mashup of Facebook and Pinterest, except in the highly focused set of questions it ponders (discussed above and at all the talks that initiate it); the deeply architected pathways for connection from which it is born (sure, its sits in the wilds of the internet, but you have to get there via this explanation and from committed communities that invite me to speak about it and there invite participation); the closely knit nature of the community it calls upon; our planned uses for the fragments it collects; and our willingness to honor, see, and make use of the bleeding that ensues. I discuss these differences in detail in my blog post about the Ev-ent-anglement included, below, as the third section of this chapter. I end that post, where I yet again reflect upon the successes and blindspots of this experiment, by suggesting that "the corporate Internet is the place we are, it is not the place we want or need, we can do better." This is no small thing, in that it is small! This project, one example of critical internet-based making as theorizing and activism, does not need to make popular, massive, slick, or perfect things to help us make better ideas about and practices in our lives and experiences online. Our database of objects holds only hundreds of things, not the millions that make up the great corporate bastions of Web 2.0. The interactions that inspire them are intimate, committed, and complicated (like this one between me and you). The ease of the internet and your actions in and for it are made visible through this project's complexity, technological and social rough patches, and rocky affect (in counter-distinction to the corporate *smooth*), as are the ethics of the two related, linked projects: the internet and the Ev-ent-anglement that sits within and speaks to it (see Figure 2.6).

Figure 2.6 Catching me catching and losing affect at Ev-ent-anglement 4: Montreal.

Source: From Facebook by feminist media scholar Selmin Kara.

Some Lessons Learned: "Ev-ent-anglement 3: One Current Shape for Internet Feminism and Its Many Discontents, July 3, 2015"

Here, I share with you an unedited blog post, part of the (process of) Ev-ent-anglement, written after the event, and then cut/paste+bled in. I see my blogging like my site-making, talk-giving, and chapter-writing, as another form of engaged and situated social media production and critique. I have many times experimented (as I do here) with re-purposing blog posts into more "scholarly" settings like paper-bound books (Juhasz 2012; 2013).

> No longer exactly where it started (it has had two websites and three discreet performances to date), this process- and interaction-rich project morphs yet continues as something akin to this: a living experiment that demonstrates in the doing the affordances of contemporary corporate (feminist) Internet culture and its potential alternatives. The ev-ent-anglement (perhaps poorly) enacts a feminist collective critical digital practice thereby telling us more about the corporate Internet and digital feminism.
>
> Let me explain. I built the ev-ent-anglement to consider how we might do better with the uncountable fragments of ourselves that we willingly, massively and generatively give to the man with every tweet, click, and photo. I cobbled together a theoretical armature suited to scaffold my unique intellectual and practical pursuit: how to cut/paste our fragments together making use of feminist principles toward anti-corporate ends. Collaboration; blended live and digital space; co-production of time/space/knowledge (events); the linked value of the situated and the mobile; the entangled nature of things, people, and ideas; a hunger for experiences and communities outside the corporate; an openness to complex and radical political and theoretical

critique; a commitment to learning in the doing: these are some of the many feminist and activist principles underlying the project. From them, I concocted a strange place-based practice and performance (an event) where I presented the ideas of the project—montage, new materialism, affect theory, critical Internet studies, feminist and queer theory—while simultaneously asking the audience in the room (and always also online) to entangle fragments of themselves onto the event's online record thereby marking and saving their part within the event while growing and changing its form within the ev-ent-anglement.

Because VJ Um Amel first donated some fragments online, then got more invested, and ultimately began to collaborate with me, she led the production of a new website to hold the ever-morphing collection of ev-ent-anglements fragments: cells.ev-ent-anglement.com. The new site has structuring principles related to ideas of shared-ownership, community, multiauthorship, fragmentation, bodies and their affects, collectivity, and feminism that reflect the larger project. As of now, the second website looks and even acts a lot like a hybrid (cut/paste+bleed) of two (feminist?) Internet stalwarts, Facebook and Pinterest (thanks to Natalie Bookchin for this comparison, and to the presenters on the Pinterest panel at Console-ing Passions): it automatically generates a seam-filled mosaic produced first from an author, and then from some algorithms that arrange her community's fragments that have been crowd-sourced, willfully gifted, carefully curated, and linked. And yet . . .

Here's where the differences bleed in, allowing us to see and perhaps name the current shape of Internet feminism and its many many discontents:

- Pinterest, Facebook (and other social media platforms) are corporate spaces that are free to use at great cost to users' privacy and autonomy; I pay for ev-ent-anglement with surprisingly limited personal and institutional resources.
- Corporate spaces market in and mobilize corporate goods and user-generated content (often itself about corporate goods) arranged and calibrated with some very careful measure; while there is almost no outside to the market economy, a rather significant portion of the fragments on the ev-ent-anglement are not (fully) entangled with corporate culture.
- Facebook, Pinterest (and other social media platforms) only work if things and people are bought and sold to each other; ev-ent-anglement buys and sells nothing other than platform space, the infrastructures on which it runs, and its users' time and expertise (mostly given "for free," as is so much on the Internet).
- Facebook, Pinterest (and other social media platforms) are fun and easy to use; ev-ent-anglement is intense, difficult, and convoluted in comparison. Interestingly, off-the-shelf platforms bake in more and more ease-of-use but the corporations are always simplicity-steps ahead. The role of ease cannot be overstated (see my work on slogans on YouTube; Juhasz 2011b: composite = 120).
- YouTube, Vine, Snapchat and their ilk produce a sense of community organized around the self; ev-ent-anglement organizes its community primarily through my invitation (and then that of others) to a dispersed but highly limited group of people linked by ideas, commitments, and proximity.

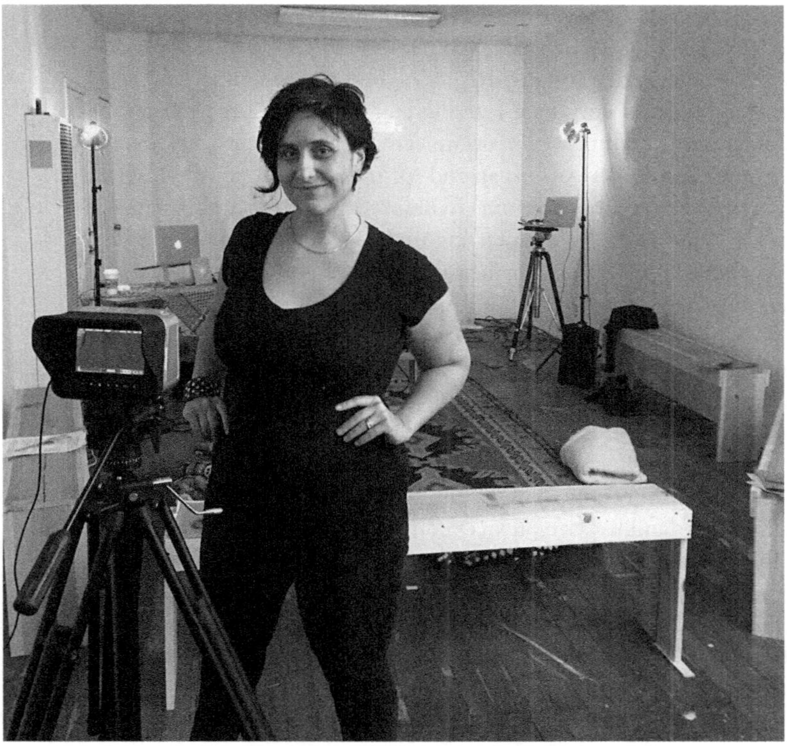

Figure 2.7 Laila Shereen Sakr (VJ Um Amel) @PAM, #eventanglement 5: Highland Park, LA.

Source: Tweeted by Alexandra Juhasz.

- Corporate spaces are built and prosper within the growth and scale logics of neo-liberalism: things are best when they get larger and hold unimaginable quantities of data; the ev-ent-anglement treasures and relies upon the close-knit, intimate, specialist interests, and commitments of its tiny community and limited data pool. There is depth and connection in the focused, but corporate spaces have other kinds of magnetism.
- Users' compulsion to engage and stay within Facebook, Instagram, Twitter and the like is high, a result of many of the features listed above: their ease of use, abundance of content, sense of community, and refined admixture of corporate and user-generated content; very few people want to engage with the ev-ent-anglement in any sustained way (or at all) mostly because it retains my signature (even as it expands), and because it is complicated and demanding of time and intellectual attention. Also, "scholars" have a hesitation to make publicly (although not on Facebook!).
- The collections of fragments that are any individual's Facebook or YouTube feed are at once satisfyingly tailored around the self, while also being fleeting, abundant, diverse, and easy; the ev-ent-anglement is co-authored and multiply-focused; it is time and space bound.

> - Twitter, Facebook, and the like are founded upon flow, speed, quantity, and brevity; much of the ev-ent-anglement sticks, taking time and space to enjoy its complexity and depth.
> - Scholars and users of corporate Internet culture perform the obligatory work of jamming "feminist" intention, activity, community, and values into spaces and practices organized primarily toward neoliberal, hegemonic and sometimes even anti-feminist aims; the ev-ent-anglement, like other "alternative," "counter-cultural," or antihegemonic spaces asks its scholars and users to name and refine the feminist values and practices that feed us and structure the space; we often disagree, which is useful when done respectfully. Of course, no space is pure, so our movement between and among and within them informs all we might know and do.
>
> The ev-ent-anglement is produced in relation to, conversation with, and defiance against corporate ownership and neoliberal aims within the Internet and every other place we go. It values feminist complexity, community, and collaboration outside the logic of capital, when possible. It tells us that the corporate Internet is expensive, commodity-driven, fun, easy, self-centered, addictive yet feeding, and malleable within these constraints. This tells me something I've known for quite awhile: the corporate Internet is the place we are, it is not the place we want or need, we can do better.
>
> (Juhasz 2015)

Why It Matters

Why do interventions like the Ev-ent-anglement matter? What kind of scholarship, art, or activism is this? As I have suggested throughout this chapter, my media praxis is most sustaining and ethical *in its process*, in its doing, in the living of it in a classroom, conference, festival, event, or chapter; a critical doing with others. In these moments of thought-out, goal-oriented critical making, I am engaged with others in kinds of living and acting that model the theoretical ideals and political aspirations that sustain me, especially when held in relief against the empty, frantic abundance of so much contemporary corporate media culture.

And here is where the principled making comes in: lived events of productive political culture can be documented, archived, or made into art or analysis. In this way, we first get the living of it, and then its sharing, and even sometimes its lasting. By making our process into matter, we mark that some people of a particular time and place lived and knew in ways other than those that dominant culture will ever represent or remember. So this kind of principled, scholarly, community-based making matters not just to our sense of purpose and connection as workers, artists, intellectuals, and citizens, but also to history—to those who follow and who are sustained by records of our efforts (see Figures 2.8 and 2.9).

For those of us trained (or training) in academia, such work and the words and images I use here to describe it do not sound or feel exactly like the "theoretical" or "analytical" traditions in which we have mostly (or entirely) been schooled. These more traditional ways of knowing and sharing our knowledge demand a distance, formality, and engagement in the realm of ideas and texts that has never been exactly or solely my project, given as I have been to actively contributing to world-, self-, and community-based change. I have

Figure 2.8 Feminist media scholars on a hike at Console-ing Passions, Dublin.

Source: Tweeted into Ev-ent-anglement 4: Dublin by Alexandra Juhasz.

Figure 2.9
"#montreal #affect #eventanglement."

Source: Shared by Ingrid Ryberg at Ev-ent-anglement 4: Montreal.

colleagues, whom I admire, whose main scholarly project is to engage with the writing of other thinkers and carefully stretch these ideas to describe the shape of other texts. What results are generative texts of their own. My work becomes part of this conversation and community when I attempt to stretch these respected colleagues' ideas (theory) onto new materials and media-objects (film, video, digital, and internet projects) that I make with others, thereby testing the worth of inspiring ideas by living by and with the actions such ideas might engender, and at the same time making anew: together producing, or at least experimenting with, the culture and community we need and value.

Further Reading

Barad, K. (2007) *Meeting the Universe Halfway*, Durham, NC: Duke University Press.
Coole, D. and S. Frost (eds.) (2010) *New Materialisms: Ontology, Agency and Politics*, Durham, NC: Duke University Press.
Gregg, M. and G. Seigworth (eds.) (2010) *The Affect Theory Reader*, Durham, NC: Duke University Press.
Kember, S. and J. Zylinska (2012) *Life after New Media*, Cambridge, MA: The MIT Press.
Žižek, S. (2014) *Event: A Philosophical Journey through a Concept*, London: Penguin Books.

References

Ahmed, S. (2010) "Happy Objects," in M. Gregg and G. Seigworth (eds.) *The Affect Theory Reader*, Durham, NC: Duke University Press.
Badiou, A. (2010) *The Communist Hypothesis*, London: Verso.
Barad, K. (2007) *Meeting the Universe Halfway*, Durham, NC: Duke University Press.
Barad, K. (2013) "Mar(k)ing Time: Material Entanglements and Re-memberings: Cutting Together-Apart," in R. Paul, P. Carlile, D. Nicolini, A. Langley, and H. Tsoukas (eds.) *How Matter Matters: Objects, Artifacts, and Materiality in Organization Studies*, Oxford: Oxford University Press, pp. 16–31.
Coole, D. and S. Frost (eds.) (2010) *New Materialisms: Ontology, Agency and Politics*, Durham, NC: Duke University Press.
FemTechNet (2013), retrieved from femtechnet.org/.
Gregg, M. and G. Seigworth (eds.) (2010) *The Affect Theory Reader*, Durham, NC: Duke University Press.
Juhasz, A. (2011a) "A Process Archive," in *Art of the Woman's Building*, Los Angeles, CA: Otis College of Art, pp. 97–123.
Juhasz, A. (2011b) *Learning from YouTube*, Cambridge, MA: MIT Press, retrieved from mitpress.mit.edu/books/learning-youtube-0.
Juhasz, A. (2011–13) "Feminist Online Spaces," retrieved from feministonlinespaces.com/.
Juhasz, A. (2012) "Video Art on YouTube," in M. Ma and E. Suderburg (eds.) *Resolutions 3*, Minneapolis, MN: University of Minnesota Press, pp. 309–24.
Juhasz, A. (2013) "YouTube Stylo: Writing and Teaching with Digital Video," in V. Mayer (ed.) *International Encyclopedia of Media Studies, Volume 2, Media Production*, Cambridge, MA: Blackwell Press, pp. 420–42.
Juhasz, A. (2014–15) *Ev-ent-anglement*, retrieved from ev-ent-anglement.com/ and cells.ev-ent-anglement.com/.
Juhasz, A. (2015) "Ev-ent-anglment 3: One Current Shape for Internet Feminism and Its Many Discontents," *Ev-ent-anglement*, retrieved from ev-ent-anglement.com/ev-ent-anglement-3-one-current-shape-for-internet-feminism-and-its-many-discontents/.
Kember, S. and J. Zylinska (2012) *Life after New Media*, Cambridge, MA: The MIT Press.
Kristeva, J. (1980) *Desire in Language: A Semiotic Approach to Literature and* Art, New York, NY: Columbia University Press.
Surkan, KJ (2014), untitled poem, retrieved from facebook.com/ksurkan/posts/10100251064401780.
Žižek, S. (2014) *Event: A Philosophical Journey through a Concept*, London: Penguin Books.

3

ANALOG GIRLS IN DIGITAL WORLDS

Dismantling Binaries for Digital Humanists Who Research Social Media

Moya Bailey and Reina Gossett

This chapter is an exercise in creating the kind of scholarship we, the writers, Moya Bailey and Reina Gossett, wish existed. As Black queer and trans women, we want more research that addresses our lives at the intersections of race, gender, class, and sexuality. We find ourselves inside and outside the digital and academic spaces that shape our engagement with the world around us. To borrow from singer Erykah Badu, we are analog girls in digital worlds, meaning we retain qualities that do not quite fit with the places we navigate (Badu 2000). We see this chapter as an opportunity to bring these tensions into the light and begin to unpack multiple dichotomies. We are aware of few academic spaces where collaborators like us are understood as collaborators. As Bailey has written elsewhere, digital scholarship necessitates a dismantling of the hierarchy between people in the academy and the people who inform their scholarship (Bailey 2015). Digital humanities is a uniquely hybrid space that prides itself on experimentation and innovation, making it a perfect platform through which to explain the shifting contexts of our lives.

The field of digital humanities (DH) combines humanist inquiry with digital tools that can aid in the research and publishing process of our scholarship. These practices can often open the traditionally siloed and inaccessible aspects of academic scholarship to the public. It is this facet of DH that we consider in this chapter, as we explore the interstitial spaces between the demarcated territories of the ivory tower and the world outside, real life and the digital world of the internet. Not only academics have the skills and means to integrate digital tools and humanistic inquiry. We argue that these distinctions are both real and imagined and as such need to be examined closely to determine the intricate and multilayered dynamics of each space.

We make two main arguments in this chapter:

1. The digital world and the ivory tower are powerful spaces for circulating ideas and creating access to our communities.
2. The power that the digital and academic worlds wield needs to be challenged, both from the inside and out.

Reina Gossett explores the radical potential of web-enabled content for people isolated by poverty and racial, gender, and sexual oppression. She argues that, while digital media makes visible communities that mainstream publics ignore, visibility can in fact incite its own violence. Gossett discusses the material human consequences of digital infrastructure that enables poor, queer, and trans people of color to have access to each other and to shape policy but also offers a word of caution that we should temper our embrace of digital visibility. This visibility can be either good or bad and even both. Gossett breaks down this binary by exposing both its merits and limits through the example of a campaign for the humane treatment of Synthia China Blast, a transgender Latina woman who has been incarcerated in New York for 21 years and held in solitary confinement for the past decade.

Moya Bailey explores the spread of her portmanteau *misogynoir*. Though Bailey created the word for her dissertation, its circulation in digital spaces was largely propelled by the work of womanist social media maven and Gradient Lair founder, Trudy. Bailey talks about the tensions between the academic origins of the word and its digital life that exceeds academic publications. Bailey uses the construction of the word's Wikipedia page to highlight misogynoir's slippery journey in and out of academia. Both narratives explain the power of situated knowledge and how different social locations are privileged over others, ultimately arguing for a more nuanced digital scholarship that can attend to these complexities.

Digitally Visible, But at What Cost

Reina Gossett

> *While clicking the "submit" button below an online comment form might look nothing like traditional images of labor—say, workers toiling on factory lines—this is the magic of capitalism once again working us over. Most of us don't even know we are working. But every Facebook post, tweet, or online article comment made on a for-profit website is a form of no-wage labor that grows the massive wealth of tech industrialists. Today, billions of us inhabit a form of volunteerism in which we work countless hours a day providing free content for social media corporations.*
>
> (Meronek & Stanley n.d.)

Some years back, having been inspired by online platforms like the Crunk Feminist Collective and the work of black feminist online laborers like Moya Bailey and Alexis Pauline Gumbs, yet feeling the intensity of transphobia filter through the experience of community isolation, I started bringing online the work and political legacy of trans women of color activists and artists living in New York City in the post-Stonewall Riots era. I wanted to know who else had felt this way and why.

Because of historical erasure and a host of other violences, many of the lives of trans people of color—specifically trans women of color, drag queens of color, and people who identified as transvestites or transsexual—were only accidentally archived. While working on this project, I frequented formal archives and came across traces and imprints—whether on film or in bequeathed papers—of the life I was searching for.

I made a Vimeo account to start video blogging and sharing interviews and archival footage. I also made a Tumblr account to write about the people whose lives touched mine, including Sylvia Rivera and Marsha P. Johnson, as well as the organization they started, Street Transvestite Action Revolutionaries. One of the videos features Sylvia Rivera fighting her way on stage in 1973 to remind a white middle class gay movement that poor people and people in prison matter. This video turned into a symbol for many people of the lingering violences of trans women of color being exiled from social movements as well as our long legacy of resisting that kind of erasure.

As the project got bigger, people began to tell me about the power they felt in the work I was doing, reflecting back the importance of our life and how meaningful that action can be for those of us who have been navigating isolation, trial, and emotional violence for a long time. That in turn has helped many of us connect with each other online and IRL in order to have an even bigger impact on social movements seeking to change structures, systems, and the way we interact with each other.

This was not my first experience navigating digital activism. In 2007 I started organizing with a Queers for Economic Justice grassroots project called the Welfare Warriors. Those of us in the Welfare Warriors had all experienced poverty, and many of us were currently living in it. We knew our experiences, if ever told, were not authored by us and certainly not meant to be shared with an audience of other queer, trans, and gender nonconforming people living in poverty. We wanted to change that and learn from each other, so we started a Participatory Action Research (PAR) group with CUNY Graduate Center. Our mission was to:

- lift up the voices of people who do not have a voice;
- document and expose injustice that exists beyond public view;
- document the creative ways that people survive, resist, have each others' backs, and foster liberation;
- share information with others about how to deal with shelters, housing, public assistance, and the courts, to make the process less hard and isolating; and
- support social change campaigns.

We did this by writing, making art and video work about living on assistance, asking each other about the experiences of being a lgbtgnc person navigating poverty, and telling our stories. We consistently discussed how isolating poverty can be, especially as it is entangled with other forms of violence, such as homophobia, racism, ableism, and transphobia. We talked about strategies and how we dealt with violence, a lot of us sharing our experiences of staying in whatever home (hotel, apartment, and shelter) we could and not going outside as a way to avoid violence.

As we started writing *A Fabulous Attitude*, our PAR report on "low-income lgbtgnc people surviving & thriving on love, shelter & knowledge," I began to learn about Twitter blogging. This followed an immersive trip with the Welfare Warriors to the 2010 Allied Media Conference, where I learned new online organizing strategies as well as the limitations, violences, and activism around the tech industry, such as where internet lines are laid down, how they displace Indigenous communities, or how Facebook and Google are gentrifying communities of color. As scholars Jian Chen and Lissette Olivares point out:

> The "virtual" network infrastructure does not only rely on conductors (cables, towers, satellites), nodes (connecting points, protocols, packet switching), and devices (computers, mobile pones, digital cameras). It also depends on a labor-intensive economy that includes creative work along with cassiterite mining, semiconductor manufacturing, [and] the production and laying of fiber-optic cables in regions of Africa, Latin America, and Asia . . . Revealing the hidden labour of the transnational bodies found on the integrated circuit is mandatory for a critical understanding of global media networks and commerce.
>
> (Chen & Olivares 2014: 247–8)

So for those of us committed to dismantling interlocking oppression, examining *how* we get the internet and *who* gets to access it is as crucial as *what* is on it.

★

In 1998 New York State passed a regulation that banned access to hormones and all surgeries commonly sought by transgender people. The impact was quick and deep, as thousands of low-income transgender people and transgender people of color were cut off from life-saving care and denied much-needed treatments. In response to the regulation, trans and gender nonconforming Medicaid recipients and allies engaged in a long term campaign to fight back, knowing that the issue was not just about policy but about who could go to a doctor, who had access to healthcare, and who could live.

In 2014, an announcement repealing the regulation came after a long campaign for healthcare that engaged a variety of strategies, including our communities combining legal advocacy in the form of a class action lawsuit against the state; IRL direct actions, such as marches and interruptions, with digital activism such as a change.org petition; online video PSAs about trans healthcare; a set of catchy infographics; and the hashtag #TransHealthcareNOW, which put pressure on the Department of Health through exposing their discrimination in public ways. One of the most thrilling efforts was in May of 2014, when a group of us involved in the campaign went to the HxRefactored Conference (which for a time advertised itself as happening in "Brooklyn, America's trendiest suburb," reflecting the very real links between tech and gentrification) for tech designers and developers, with a focus on healthcare. At the conference, New York's commissioner of health spoke.

As the commissioner was setting up his laptop, we passed out our information and then rushed the stage with a banner that read, "New York Needs #TransHealthcareNOW End Medicaid Discrimination." From the stage, we explained why we were protesting. The positive reception from the crowd—who gave us a standing ovation for the action and for engaging the commissioner of health about why New York state discriminated against trans people—completely took us by surprise, and so did the widespread media coverage of the campaign afterwards, including coverage on digital platforms such as Upworthy, Autostraddle, and Buzzfeed (Maddie 2014). Seven months later, and after 16 years of denying basic healthcare to low-income transgender New Yorkers, Governor Cuomo and the New York State Department of Health announced that New York's Medicaid programs would now cover transgender healthcare.

The repeal announcement came in response to the incredible persistence of our communities in demanding this care and grassroots campaigns led by the Sylvia Rivera Law Project (SRLP), Make the Road NY, TransJustice of the Audre Lorde Project, and the Trans Women of Color Coalition. The newly adopted regulation is not perfect—it does not cover young people under eighteen, and it does not apply to all forms of gender-affirming care. But as someone who worked on the campaign to end New York's regulation against healthcare for trans people, I consider this a momentous victory, one that reflects that trans people and our allies are powerful and capable of changing the world and each other.

While this campaign marks a certain kind of success for the digital activism tactics in our healthcare campaign, one particular moment raised significant concerns about the strategy of digital activism and visibility for the trans liberation movement, one inextricably linked to ending all forms of oppression, including the violence of the prison industrial complex.

Around the same time that the healthcare campaign received significant media attention, the SRLP launched a campaign to end solitary confinement on behalf of incarcerated community members and specifically of Synthia China Blast, an SRLP client and Prisoner Advisory Committee Member, who has been incarcerated in New York for over 21 years. Synthia, a transgender Latina woman, experienced family rejection, lack of access to safe education, homelessness, police profiling, and violence because she is transgender. The violent gender policing and various forms of trauma she experienced as a youth have only been reproduced and exacerbated while being held in various men's prisons operated by the Department of Corrections and Community Supervision (DOCCS) over the past 17 years.

Synthia has been placed in isolation for over a decade for her own "protection," but, in reality, this has negatively affected her mental health and disallowed her from accessing any programs that would incline a parole board to grant her parole. SRLP created a petition page using open source CiviCRM, featured Synthia on the SRLP Prisoner Advisory Committee blog, and partnered with actress and producer, Laverne Cox, to create a video to increase awareness of both Synthia's case and the broader use of solitary confinement, punitive or otherwise. While the video and campaign were featured on Buzzfeed, the immediate backlash was overwhelming. Anti-trans online activists used Synthia's conviction for the second-degree murder of Ebony Nicole Williams as an opportunity to pressure Laverne Cox to stop partnering with the SRLP and also put pressure on the SRLP to stop supporting Synthia (Molloy 2014). The SRLP responded with a statement in which they wrote:

> We do not research the underlying convictions of our PAC members because we do not believe a state conviction tells the entirety of a person's story. Nor do we believe that anyone should live in fear of sexual violence on a daily basis or be subjected to other forms of violence solely because of their gender identity or conviction. Not only is this a basic foundation of our work, but it is something the constitution requires.
>
> (End Solitary campaign video information 2014)

What I found powerful about the SRLP's campaign to end solitary confinement is that it does not fit a framework of respectability (the respectable nonviolent trans prisoner) in order to raise questions about who, even in incredibly marginal communities, has access to a level of visibility in the first place, without facing scrutiny and backlash. By "respectable," I mean a person whose actions and identity are most sympathetic to a white supremacist/transphobic viewer as opposed to a person whose actions and identity challenge the white supremacy and transphobia at the very roots of how "respect" or "respectable" is defined.

The decision to support someone living through such intense violence was deeply linked to a victory that took place months after the backlash from the campaign to support Synthia China Blast and end solitary confinement. New York City (NYC) decided to put new limitations on its use of solitary confinement for people in NYC jails. Having received a very different kind of online reception from #TransHealthcareNOW, and having worked to abolish the prison industrial complex and its entanglement in and enforcement of transphobia, racism, ableism, and isolation, the SRLP received backlash to its ending solitary confinement campaign. This backlash raised serious questions about using visibility through digital platforms as a means to support the liberation struggles of oppressed people. To me, the most urgent questions were: What do we open up ourselves and our communities to when we seek out visibility?

In November 2014, after the SRLP faced significant backlash around supporting Synthia, Eric A. Stanley organized a multigenerational panel of Black trans women, including myself, CeCe McDonald, Jeanetta Johnson, and Miss Major, entitled, "We Cannot Live Without Our Lives: A Conversation on Anti-blackness, Trans Resistance and Prison Abolition" at the University of California, San Diego. During the panel, we discussed and problematized the function of visibility for Black trans women, including how it could be used as a tool of criminalization and increased punishment, such as in Synthia's case, not a tenant of liberation.

So often, visibility uses the lens of respectability to determine who, even in the most vulnerable communities, should be seen and heard. I believe that, through the filter of visibility, those of us most at risk to state violence become even more vulnerable to that violence. As Eunsong Kim writes in "The Politics of Trending," when we use Twitter "trending" as a way to determine what is important, we often do not notice that we are using a framework, particularly a secret, proprietary algorithm of a company, to understand what is important:

> #Ferguson has been used over 2,000 times on March 1st alone . . . clearly surpassing the usage of the current US trends of #WeWantTheCup and contending with the usage of #ExplainAMovieByItsTitle. Basically, #Ferguson should be trending everyday. . . I bring this up to point to how the "journalistic scholarship" around visibility and trending is completely and utterly misinformed, misframed and just plain silly. The exceptional attention given to hashtag discourse by critics, news platforms and journalists—to what they perceive to be evidence of visibility—takes the focus away from the spaces created by gendered and racialized users, and rewrites it as a singular confrontation racialized/gendered users are having with white audiences within a white space. This rewriting positions trending tags to be isolated explosions. It does not labor through the possibility of communal, ongoing engagement and sustainment, for better or for worse.
>
> (Kim 2015)

Kim lays out key ways communities resisting oppression are already "hacking a commons" in the face of the violence of visibility and trending:

- the communities that congregate around tags, regardless of their trends
- the users that notice when important topic[s] (such as #Ferguson) are not trending, and use alternative tags (such as #mediablackout)
- users who pre-emptively create "when in jail" accounts (planning the heist!!!)
- anti-doxing collectives

- users on Twitter & Tumblr, that retweet/retumble posts but tag their critique (for example, this is not native looks through various "native" "indian" tags and retags the "original" with links on appropriation, genocide, and add appropriation.)

(Kim 2015)

These actions by users belie the myth of the slacktavist or armchair activist who just uses social media for consumption. There are vibrant communities using corporatized platforms in so many ways that create a new landscape for digital media. As we go forward, we must work to ensure that this work is appreciated, though perhaps some of it needs to remain invisible to propel the kind of changes we wish to see in our world.

Misogynoir and the Politics of Citation

By Moya Bailey

As a digital humanist, I often try to explain and defend the field and its potential within academia. Recent articles in both mainstream and academic presses have tried to contextualize the DH terrain for skeptical audiences (Gold 2012; Barnett 2014; Grusin 2014; Kirschenbaum 2014; Leroi 2015). Digital humanities employs digital tools in the service of humanities inquiries that would be difficult to study without these implements. I think often of Lauren Klein's coding of a script that makes James Hemmings's significance in the Thomas Jefferson archive undeniably clear (Klein 2013). What would have been a painstaking study of thousands of documents can be automated within a digital repository. DH also encompasses humanities questions posed of our digital age. For those of us already convinced of the possible breakthroughs DH can provide, internal struggles within DH often hinge on the ways in which race, gender, sexuality, and disability are frequently missing from practitioners' analysis. I am connected to a group of like-minded DH enthusiasts who strive to create social justice-oriented scholarship. Under the umbrella, #transformDH, we focus on the ways that using digital tools to help investigate concerns related to those most marginalized in society can be of great benefit to our research while simultaneously encouraging our colleagues to examine the ways race, class, gender, sexuality, and disability are present in theirs.

I have argued that there are many scholarly projects that, while not officially claimed by DH, have digital humanities components (Bailey 2015). These projects remain on the periphery of DH discussions but may find significant traction in other arenas. It is in that spirit that I wish to say a bit about my own portmanteau, *misogynoir*, and its proliferation in digital spaces, such as Tumblr, Twitter, and online journalism, despite its limited impact within scholarly communities. Although it has limited use in scholarly spaces, misogynoir's presence within academia and production by an academic give it the validity required to appear as a Wikipedia entry (Misogynoir 2015). This strange refraction, in which academic origins are privileged over the origins within the networks that use the word, offers some new theoretical terrain for DH to consider. Where can DH be done, and whose scholarship counts as DH?

As the conceiver of the word misogynoir, I appreciate its prevalence, but I know that digital feminists beyond the academy are primarily responsible for its promulgation. In particular, Trudy Hamilton, womanist scholar and creator of the site Gradient Lair, has penned several posts that expand misogynoir beyond my initial writing about the word. I highlight her work to emphasize the need for a conception of DH that makes room for people outside the academy. Digital humanities should also grapple with what humanity looks like in a digital age—a gesture that requires a focus beyond the ivory tower.

Misogynoir describes the co-constitutive, antiblack, and misogynistic racism directed at Black women, particularly in visual and digital culture (Bailey 2010). In conversations with friends and colleagues, I struggled to find a way to describe the specific types of violent imagery that seemed to target Black women in popular spaces. For example, in July 2014 the hashtag #ruinablackgirlsmonday was used to spread and celebrate images and ideas that would ostensibly ruin a Black girl's day. Many of the images and language in the hashtag perpetuate age-old stereotypes of Black women's supposed unattractiveness and hypersexual nature, while promoting white womanhood and femininity as desirable. Many of these images included white women with shapely bodies, particularly round butts, implying that there was no reason to date a Black women for her supposed curves if there are white women who look like the women in the pictures (no black girls 2014). The media malignment of Black tennis sensation, Serena Williams, particularly her depiction in digital news media, is atrocious and has been since her career started as a teenager (Cooper 2015). Similar memes often depict Black women failing at being desirable to Black men or men generally. I wanted to name this type of racialized, gendered representation as a specific constellation that targets and polices Black women's desirability, and in so doing I found that other Black women had noticed this phenomenon as well.

As a graduate student I was invited to join a people of color writing group called the Crunk Feminist Collective (CFC). In one of my earliest pieces, I used misogynoir to talk about the ways I felt Black women were being misrepresented in rap lyrics. Many in the CFC started to use the word in their own pieces for the blog, and slowly but surely it started to be adopted in other digital spaces. The crucial turning point was when womanist digital activist, Trudy, started to use it on her Tumblr, Gradient Lair.

Trudy wrote several eloquent posts in which she discussed how misogynoir operates, opening up the word to new audiences on the periphery of academic circles. Her post, "Misogyny, In General vs. Anti-Black Misogyny (Misogynoir), Specifically," provides several examples that illustrate the ways in which the anti-Black misogyny that Black women experience differs from the misogyny white women experience (Trudy 2013). This post received nearly 1,000 reblogs and likes on the Tumblr platform. Her use of misogynoir to make sense of events in her own life and in digital culture helped move the word into new spaces and prompted questions about its meaning. The word is able to move at lightning speed in this digital age. Only ten academic articles use the word despite numerous online journal articles, blog posts, and tweets, many from Trudy. Academic articles are primarily the ones cited to corroborate the word's significance to Wikipedia, despite Trudy and others' use of it in popular publications such as *Salon* and *Ebony* (Cooper 2015; Lemieux 2015).

On May 11, 2014, Michelleyc, a student at Barnard College, created a page for the word as part of a class assignment for her English class ("User" 2014). Students in the class, "The Worlds of Shange," were required to create and edit Wikipedia pages that related to themes of Ntzoke Shange's work ("Education Program" 2014). Michelleyc also edited the Wikipedia page of Michelle Wallace to include a more robust account of her work's relationship to Black feminism, and other classmates also made edits that explicitly named Black feminist contributions to existing articles.

The creation of the misogynoir Wikipedia entry was an assignment for an undergraduate class, though its introduction to that audience was through blog posts and Tumblr posts. While Wikipedia is derided by academics as an inappropriate source for students to cite in their research papers, it is becoming more acceptable for students to create Wikipedia content that draws on what would be considered more reliable sources, like academic articles and books.

However, in the rapid world of digital publishing, the articles that reference misogynoir debuted years after my initial blog post on the CFC. This lag time within academic publishing means that topics can remain contested until they are corroborated by an academic authority. Despite creating the word and being in the academy, I am not an appropriate source for the Wikipedia article unless I have published an academic article that can be cited.

Michelleyc and other Wikipedia users linked Trudy's Tumblr posts as source material for their explication of the term and its popularity. The Tumblr posts by Trudy were removed as sources for the Wikipedia article because Wikipedia has strict rules about what counts as a source. Tumblr and other blog posts are not considered reliable sources, or as reliable as print publications or academic journals. Despite the word first appearing on a blog page and growing in popularity in digital spaces that are more accessible than digital academic journals, the academic journals are what lend the word credibility. In fact, according to the talk page that documents the conversations about the entry for misogynoir, there was concern that the word should be removed from Wikipedia because it was not properly cited ("Talk" 2014). It was only in December of 2015 that Trudy was added to the entry. She is now properly credited as creating the lexical definition of the word, though she has since retreated from the web given the abuse and mistreatment she has experienced (Trudy 2015).

Wikipedia works by allowing users to generate content, which is then reviewed and edited by other Wikipedia users. There has been a lot of documentation about the ways in which cultural disparities show up in Wikipedia, particularly questions about the way that sources must be vetted via traditional media like print publications, books, TV, and movies. Blog posts are not considered valid sources. Following debate in the entry's talk page about whether my initial post on the CFC was an acceptable source, it was allowed to stay. Despite the fact that it was the digital adoption of misogynoir that drove the creation of its Wikipedia page, it is the limitedly available scholarly publications that prove that the word is important.

I think digital humanities theories and practices are of use here, where the old practices of vetting information have not been adapted to address the ever changing and quickly evolving nature of our increasingly digital world. Part of the work of DH is explaining the importance and utility of digital tools for creating new standards. When we look at DH, we see the importance of innovative and nontraditional approaches to knowledge production. If Wikipedia is an online digital encyclopedia, why would it not value the digital from which it emanates?

Though I coined misogynoir, I know I am not solely responsible for its use and successful deployment across a variety of platforms and users. Trudy and others really built the use of the word through their use and promotion. That labor should be compensated, but how do we do that? By publishing this piece in this anthology I may have validated the very thing that I wish could be validated through digital production.

Conclusion

We hope that this chapter puts into perspective the potential of DH beyond the academy and for people who are not academics. Researchers doing digital humanities work are both in and outside the academy, requiring new methodologies around publishing and promotion. Social media platforms and other digital tools are advancing social justice causes and spreading important information that needs to be heard by multiple audiences in multiple locations. This chapter is another example of the kind of work we wish to see.

Further Reading

Bailey, M. (2015) "#transform(ing)DH Writing and Research: An Autoethnography of Digital Humanities and Feminist Ethics," *Digital Humanities Quarterly* 9(2), retrieved online www.digitalhumanities.org/dhq/vol/9/2/000209/000209.html.

Bailey, M., A. Cong-Huyen, A. Lothian, and A. Phillips (2016) "Reflections on a Movement: #transformDH, Growing Up," in M. Gold and L. Klein (eds.) *Debates in the Digital Humanities 2016.*

Trudy (n.d.) *Gradient Lair*, retrieved from www.gradientlair.com.

References

Badu, E. (2000) ". . . & On."*Mama's Gun.* Universal Records.

Bailey, M. (2010) "They Aren't Talking about Me. . ." *Crunk Feminist Collective*, retrieved from www.crunkfeministcollective.com/2010/03/14/they-arent-talking-about-me.

Bailey, M. (2011) "All the Digital Humanists Are White, All the Nerds Are Men, but Some of Us Are Brave," *Journal of Digital Humanities* 1(1), retrieved from journalofdigitalhumanities.org/1-1/all-the-digital-humanists-are-white-all-the-nerds-are-men-but-some-of-us-are-brave-by-moya-z-bailey.

Bailey, M. (2015) "#transform(ing)DH Writing and Research: An Autoethnography of Digital Humanities and Feminist Ethics," *Digital Humanities Quarterly* 9(2), retrieved from www.digitalhumanities.org/dhq/vol/9/2/000209/000209.html.

Barnett, F. M. (2014) "The Brave Side of Digital Humanities," *Differences: A Journal of Feminist Cultural Studies* 25(1), 64–78.

Chen, J. and L. Olivares (2014) "Transmedia," *TSQ: Transgender Studies Quarterly* 1(1–2), 245–48.

Cooper, B. (2015) "The World Only Has Ugliness for Black Women. That's Why Serena Williams Is So Important," *Salon*, retrieved from www.salon.com/2015/07/15/why_serena_williams_is_so_important_the_world_only_has_ugliness_for_black_women%e2%80%94and_she_is_the_black_womans_champion.

"Education Program talk: Barnard College/The Worlds of Shange (Spring 2014)/Timeline" (2014) *Wikipedia: The Free Encyclopedia*, retrieved from en.wikipedia.org/wiki/Education_Program_talk:Barnard_College/The_Worlds_of_Shange_(Spring_2014)/Timeline.

End Solitary campaign video information (2014) *Sylvia Rivera Law Project (SLRP)*, retrieved from srlp.org/endsolitary/videoinformation.

Gold, M. K. (ed.) (2012) *Debates in the Digital Humanities*, Minneapolis, MN: University of Minnesota Press.

Grusin, R. (2014) "The Dark Side of Digital Humanities: Dispatches from Two Recent MLA Conventions," *differences: A Journal of Feminist Cultural Studies* 25(1), 79–92.

Kim, E. (2015) "The Politics of Trending," *Model View Culture*, retrieved from modelviewculture.com/pieces/the-politics-of-trending.

Kirschenbaum, M. (2014) "What Is 'Digital Humanities,' and Why Are They Saying Such Terrible Things about It?" *differences: A Journal of Feminist Cultural Studies* 25(1), 46–63.

Klein, L. F. (2013) "The Image of Absence: Archival Silence, Data Visualization, and James Hemings," *American Literature* 85(4), 661–88.

Lemieux, J. (2015) "This Black Feminist Classic Was a Precursor to Black Lives Matter," *New Republic*, retrieved from www.newrepublic.com/article/121925/black-feminism-named-and-celebrated.

Leroi, A. M. (2015) "One Republic of Learning: Digitizing the Humanities," *The New York Times*, retrieved from www.nytimes.com/2015/02/14/opinion/digitizing-the-humanities.html.

Maddie (2014) "Protesters Take Stage at Health Conference Because NY's Trans Healthcare Failure Is Inexcusable," *Autostraddle*, retrieved from www.autostraddle.com/protesters-take-stage-at-health-conference-because-nys-trans-healthcare-failure-is-inexcusable-237877.

Map Gallery (n.d.) *TeleGeography*, retrieved from www.telegeography.com/telecom-resources/map-gallery/index.html.

Meronek, T. and E. A. Stanley (2014) "Unintended - and Anti-Social - Consequences of Social Media Use," *Truthout*, retrieved from www.truth-out.org/news/item/22158-unintended-and-anti-social-consequences-of-social-media-use.

Misogynoir (2015) *Wikipedia: The Free Encyclopedia*, retrieved from en.wikipedia.org/wiki/Misogynoir.

Molloy, P. M. (2014) "Laverne Cox Distances Herself from Controversial Trans Inmate," *Advocate*, retrieved from www.advocate.com/politics/transgender/2014/08/26/laverne-cox-distances-herself-controversial-trans-inmate.

no black girls (@MixCouples) (2014) "Enjoying last place #ruinablackgirlsmonday," 28 July, Twitter post, retrieved from pic.twitter.com/vIDIpUHFfm. @xbreakingeven.

"Talk:Misogynoir" (2014) *Wikipedia: The Free Encyclopedia*, retrieved from en.wikipedia.org/wiki/Talk:Misogynoir.

Trudy (2013) "Misogyny, In General vs. Anti-Black Misogyny (Misogynoir), Specifically," *Gradient Lair*, retrieved from www.gradientlair.com/post/60973580823/general-misogyny-versus-misogynoir.

Trudy (2015) "Farewell," *Gradient Lair*, retrieved from www.gradientlair.com/post/130584664178/thetrudz-gradient-lair-blog-ends-2015-farewell.

"User:Michelleyc" (2014) *Wikipedia: The Free Encyclopedia*, retrieved from en.wikipedia.org/wiki/User:Michelleyc.

4

(CYBER) ETHNOGRAPHIES OF CONTACT, DIALOGUE, FRICTION

Connecting, Building, Placing, and Doing "Data"

Radhika Gajjala, Erika M. Behrmann, and Jeanette M. Dillon

> Constant revolutionizing of production, uninterrupted disturbance of all social conditions, everlasting uncertainty and agitation, distinguish the bourgeois epoch from all earlier ones.
>
> (Marx & Engels 2013 [1848])

Data is everywhere. Evidence is everywhere. The question is how do we, as researchers in the age of "big data," construct an argument that reveals the nuances of digital existence? To what end do we construct an argument? To what use do we put the evidence and data that abounds around us? What are the epistemic considerations, and how do digital ontologies shape our methods of inquiry? With today's digital pervasiveness comes the need to reexamine epistemologies and the taken-for-granted practice of research methods. Thus, constant readjustment and ambiguity mark the work of a qualitative researcher who chooses to examine digitally mediated cultures. Current modes of global being are continually mediated by virtual and actual conversations with international Others—through gadgets, screens, policy, philanthropy, gaming, organizing, Wikipedia editing, and so many other everyday things we do. As we have seen in work from the early 1990s by scholars who research cyberculture and the internet, research methods were developed as researchers encountered the internet variously as text, space, place, and screen.

This surge of experimentation and rearticulation (and anxiety) regarding methods is neither new nor unique as a response to the phenomenon of persistent communication enabled by the internet and wireless gadgets. For communication scholars engaging in computer-mediated or mobile technology, mediated communication may seem comparatively recent, but the crisis in method had already hit fields such as anthropology and history. Prior to the universal proliferation of what became the "world wide web," cultural anthropologists, such as James Clifford and George Marcus (1986), and postcolonial, feminist historians, such as Gayatri Spivak (1988) and bell hooks, were already raising concerns about voice, representation, interaction, hegemony, postcoloniality, and globalization in the 1980s and early 1990s. Thus, the encounter of critical concerns with internet-enabled networks opened up hope that there might be dialogue and collaboration among common, nonelite people across the world. Ironically, it is precisely this sort of hopefulness that foregrounds some of the interactions we currently critique for their basis in neoliberal logics that the individual is *the* motivator of change.

Markham and Baym (2009) note how media convergences have not only blurred social, geographical, and temporal boundaries, but also produced mediated identities that do not have traditionally recognizable and demographically verifiable characteristics that traditional research methods require us to name. As a result, the subject of research often fails to have stable points of reference that given categories of identity and culture offer us. Instead, we are forced to build categories based on characteristics that emerge through encounters with these convergent spaces and to chase down shifting identities as we try to understand what sorts of power structures hide within structures and hierarchies as they are rebuilt. Markham and Baym's response to this dynamic place of research is to carefully integrate and balance the use of traditional methods while being open to contemporary landscapes and epistemes. The experiences of early researchers of race, gender, and sexuality in cyberspace, including Kendall (2002), Nakamura (2002), Sunden (2003), and several others, show how traditional humanities and social sciences methods were insufficient in providing an understanding of emerging formations online. Currently, any kind of research we do on youth cultures, organizations, or globalization and nonprofit work must take into account the kinds of digital mediation that persists in the everyday of those we research. Thus, even when looking at in-person, face-to-face contexts—and not just internet-based contexts (such as games, listprocs, chat, social media, websites, or other texts)—we must be aware of challenges to older methods and epistemologies for research.

In an effort to document some struggles so as to provide direction for others engaged in similar research practices, in this chapter we write about global connections and frictions in three related contexts where millennials are engaged in philanthropy (Roy 2010). Erika draws on an examination of the *Half the Sky* movement. Jeanette draws on her study of college students engaged in social entrepreneurial projects, such as TOMS, through a physical, place-based college campus organization. And Radhika examines this intersection through a look at how do-it-yourself (DIY) prosumerism intersects with online microfinance. We describe how these research projects called for not only an engagement with epistemologies of doing (Gajjala & Altman 2006) cyberethnography but also an immersion in context through a "focus on zones of awkward engagement" (Tsing 2005: xi). These varied sites are based in "aspirations for global connection," and each in its own way "come[s] to life in 'friction'" (1).

We use these projects as points of reference as we talk about how data, evidence, and epistemic considerations play out when we examine communicative contexts shaped by contemporary neoliberal and digital ontologies. Each of these sites is deeply embedded in conversations with the "global" and the "Other" of the Western self, both implicitly and explicitly. All three of our projects aspire toward global reach, integration, and collaboration that sound hopeful but oftentimes carry contradictions within them as they examine the slippages and gaps in the micro-practices of everyday tactics and strategies. Pivotal to these integrative attempts is the ubiquity of internet and wireless connectivity. Each of these projects, therefore, relies on a web of practices, whether around philanthropy, revival of craft, or the mobilization of the western-educated millennial (regardless of race, ethnicity, or national origin) in the immaterial labor of networking the world across difference and physical boundaries.

Digital Ontology

Before we talk about data, evidence, and the epistemic considerations for researching these contexts, we need to explain our take on digital ontology. Millennials exist in time and space enveloped in a digital ethos. Like boyd (2014), Shah and Jensen (2011), and others, we feel that the term "digital natives" misrepresents this generation by implying that all young people magically know the workings of digital networks and infrastructures. Yet, the kind of millennial who engages in the philanthropic projects and networks we are researching is nonetheless mired in the context of digitality but also in offline contexts that emphasize community and generosity. Yet, as boyd notes:

> Just because teens are comfortable using social media to hang out does not mean that they're fluent in or with technology. Many teens are not nearly as digitally adept as the often-used assumption that they are "digital natives" would suggest.
>
> (boyd 2014: 22)

It is precisely this comfort in use that people may mistake as expertise. Such comfort is similar to the common assumption that, if your major is communication studies and you are able to talk or socialize in your particular social spaces, you will probably breeze through the coursework. However, the infrastructure behind technologies that shape our meaning-making is often invisible to us. Thus, in classrooms where we teach communication theory or media, students are delighted when social media is introduced as a topic of research and investigation for them in class. Several of them consider themselves to be experts; and indeed—in their limited generational, geographic, and cultural context as users—they are experts.

So, taking boyd's critique of the term "digital natives" further, we might say that the limited expertise of average, westernized millennials in their micro-social circles and as users of particular gadgets does not mean they are fluent within *global* techno-social ensembles (Latour 1987). This move is not a misreading. Notably, the term "digital natives" is often used to describe young consumers of digital gadgets. For instance, Shah and Jensen (2011) note that Marc Prensky (2001) developed the term "Digital Natives" as a way of identifying new consumer markets; however, the authors suggest that the master narratives that frame the discourse around this group of young individuals exist as two binary stories. The first is that digital natives will change the world with their expansive access to knowledge, while the second suggests that digital natives lack work ethic and empathy. Problematically, neither narrative considers the magnitude of voices within the millennial generation.

Thus remains the fact that young people are growing up and older in a world where our everyday is enveloped in communicative and interactional logics shaped through digital ontologies. This means that our challenge in both researching and teaching the millennial generation is often methodological. Therefore, Shah and Jansen note:

> Because, despite the difference in naming, the methods of understanding/analyzing these populations and the frameworks through which they are understood, remain

> unchallenged, and often contained in vocabulary and perspectives which are analogue and unable to account for the succession of changes that the rapid evolution of Information and Communication Technologies have produced across the world, in varying degrees, in the last decade.
>
> (Shah & Jansen 2011: 13)

But what is a "digital ontology?" How does it shape epistemologies of being, presence, absence, embodiment, writing, coding, crafting, conversing, and so on? What sorts of subjects are produced in this ethos of constant surveillance and digital management, where "participative management" itself becomes a "technology of power, a technology for creating and controlling the 'subjective processes'" (Lazzarato 1996: 134)? Indeed, these questions are important (and tricky) because our methods for research must function to create a "fish out of water" effect even for researchers, when oftentimes we are in the same water as our research subjects.

Coté and Pybus (2007, 2011) argue that social media sites such as MySpace and Facebook are not only considered the birth of Web 2.0, but also an emerging form of what—via Maurizio Lazzarato—they call *Immaterial Labor 2.0*, or "labour that produces the informational and cultural content of the commodity" (Lazzarato 1996: 1). According to McLeod, Rault, and Cowan, this kind of labor includes:

> affective labours that are driven by intimacy, commitment, care, love, desire, community, and community-building, but which go unrecognized, under-appreciated and un- or under-remunerated—. . . affective work that is typically ignored but absolutely expected within the queer economies of world-making, in an analogous way to "women's work" and now so uncannily familiar in "user-generated" Web 2.0 culture.
>
> (McLeod, Rault, & Cowan 2014)

Yet we cannot afford to celebrate or demonize this formation of labor as liberating or oppressive. Rather, by examining how immaterial labor both contributes to and is shaped by digital ontologies, we see how it feeds into and promotes an ethos of "continual innovation in the forms and conditions of communication (and thus in work and consumption) [and] gives form to and materializes needs, the imaginary, consumer tastes, and so forth, and [how] these products in turn become powerful producers of needs, images, and tastes" (Lazzarato 1996: 137).

Immaterial labor produces the cultural content of a commodity and serves as a modality that reinforces biopower and surveillance. Drawing from Hardt and Negri's *Empire* (2000), Coté and Pybus (2011) note that the construction of self as a digital subject becomes a constitutive practice of labor. They suggest that, by examining Web 2.0, we are able to understand how capital takes form in new cultural formats. Moreover, it is important to note that Hardt and Negri's now canonical text failed to explore computer-mediated networks due in part to its temporal location. As a result, it bypassed a multifaceted aspect of "free" labor that individuals engage on a cultural level. For example, one's tastes and preferences become advertised as they create their individual identities (Stone 1995; Beller 2013). Immaterial Labor 2.0 situates itself in the fast-paced, continuing construction of virtual identity that is often situated in a contiguous network.

As examples of biopower/biopolitical production, Coté and Pybus (2007) describe how MySpace, Facebook, and other networked spaces are composed of various, dispersed bodies. They note how power in such contexts is exercised as a discontinuous power over singular bodies, as biopower (Foucault 2001: 1009) becomes more flexible and more connected. Thus Immaterial Labor 2.0 is not a reconstruction of Marx's economic base, but rather a multifaceted *dispositif* that is linked through various networks. Immaterial labor, then, becomes a modality of biopower as it reinforces that *dispositif* through affect and capitalism (Coté & Pybus 2007: 94). In this way, a digital ontology is capitalism. This ontology "subsume[s] communication" so that there is no critical role that can be provided from the outside. Thus communication, working through "affective forms of care for producers and consumers, the mobilization of sharing and expression as instruments for 'human relations' in the workplace, or contributions to ubiquitous media circuits," serves this form of capitalism (Dean 2014; see also Brown 2015). The platform and associated network manages and regulates the subject through the use of his/her own immaterial labor as a modality. Further, the constant building of selves in these digital networks gives rise to the development of affects that rely on constant reaffirmation and negotiation of identity construction, performance, and translation. Drawing from Butler's (1990) work on performativity, Coté and Pybus argue that individuals are motivated to update their techno-identity because users "become eligible for recognition" (2011: 180). The transmission of information through relationships is central to identity formation and the creation of interlinked affective investments. This transmission in turn becomes central to the subjectivity of individuals as well as to the companies who profit from advertising in these networks. Thus, as researchers of these phenomena, the seamless and continual connecting, building, and placing of selves in online networks is what we need to simultaneously experience through immersion and research with a distance.

Connecting, Building, Placing, and Doing "Data"

In the contemporary undergraduate classroom, a typical response to feminist texts lamenting women's marginalization from technology environments, design, and even technology use suggests that students believe marginalized individuals have now "arrived" and access to technology is no longer an issue. Thus, upon reading works by technofeminist scholars such as Wajcman (1991) and many others, they seem to have a gut reaction of sorts. They note how, in the last 25 years, there has been a rapid advancement in technology and that many technological devices are now wonderfully user-friendly. They are not wrong—technological devices are indeed more *user*-friendly. However, the truth is that students have less control over the production of digital content than in the 1990s. We do not want to reject this response by constructing young women who react this way as ideological dupes. We want to take them seriously and ask, among other things, what sorts of epistemic disenfranchisement does the culture of evidence—based in a digital ontology that celebrates the *now* as new and liberating—bring forth? Young women are obviously excited to be more empowered than previous generations, perhaps because they can Google their questions, text relatives who live across oceans, or send money to the needy through PayPal transactions. As such, a response to young women is to ask if they have ever engaged in production by editing Wikipedia, designing and building layers of skins for a Second Life avatar, and so on. Notably, these are examples Radhika has regularly used in her classes, which are usually based in partial/amateur production that she herself has engaged in some form.

As educators, we might ask students to work past the creation of content via blogging and informal YouTube sharing toward more immersion in virtual environments. The suggestion of Wikipedia editing, though often considered "mere" textual content creation, is based in the knowledge that the logics of interaction (Peake 2015), monitoring, and community discussion of edits operates in conjunction with the need to learn and adhere to strict guidelines. Such a conjunction places the seeming user-friendliness of Wikipedia in question. Additionally, our suggestion of a "casual" virtual environment such as Second Life to create virtual objects is based in the knowledge that Second Life is comparatively easier for non-gamers or casual gamers to access. As a comparison to terms like "hardcore," we use "casual" in the way that most mainstream, masculinized gaming communities use them, and these terms themselves represent a binary that feminizes some gameplay while validating others (Vanderhoef 2013). We do not assume, however, that young women are not already partial users cum producers, because research tells us that, in participatory web 2.0 environments, "prosumers" (simultaneous producers and consumers) and amateur coders, designers, and builders abound. As we noted in a recent publication, two kinds of domestic space-based prosumers are made invisible in mainstream media discussions about digital labor. These prosumers are most often women working from the domestic space (at home and in feminized contexts) and making digital media products, such as how-to videos and knitting and make-up videos, that are traditionally considered to be women's work (Gajjala, Dillon & Anarbaeva, in press). Yet, in the ways evidence is presented about the "user-friendly" interfaces and "level playing fields" ascribed to digital technologies, there remains a conflation of socio-cultural literacy with technical literacy *and* a binarization of social interfaces and technical interfaces. How can this be? How do the conflation and binary exist simultaneously?

For one, many academic frameworks define "evidence" and "verification" within the confines of dominant and privileged quantitative research methods, which tend to be based in positivist paradigms. As a result, even some qualitative, interpretive research falls into this epistemology of description, with little to no attention to process and complicity of researcher location. That is, there is an unexplored assumption that we are outside of what we research. This sort of "view from nowhere" hides the ideological underpinning of contexts and elides issues of institutional and infrastructural hierarchies. Yet, the other extreme, namely claiming subjective interpretation as truth or using a sample of self and friends alone for evidence, falls into the same trap of tunnel vision. Thus, the mere acknowledgement or examination of the researcher's presence in the data space does not suffice. Self-reflexivity and accountability to multiple audiences must be continually cross-checked and verified through dialogue and interaction with subjects, co-researchers, and the multiple actors involved in the particular context being researched. Researchers need to be prepared to repeatedly revisit their findings and let go of their location as "experts" and "authorities." Even as they keep returning to the writing space to report out in academic communities and to policy makers, they also need to balance their multiple audiences and accountability links.

Davis et al. explain that the data for qualitative research consist of words: "transcripts, quotes, field notes, and texts" (2013: 320). That data, they contend, serve as evidence of information that the researcher gathered during her investigation of the site and community she studied. That said, it is understood that the most important research tool in participant observation is the researcher. Goffman (1989) saw the process of collecting data, particularly during participant observation, as one of embodiment—one that involved the researcher subjecting her whole self (e.g., body, mind, personality, etc.) to the process of collection. Further explanation about the co-dependent nature of researcher and the researched, particularly in ethnographic research, is given by Davis et al. (2013), who offer that the researcher must try to describe the life of those researched as well as the place that the researcher occupied in their lives as she studied them. This approach, they contend, is reflexive and sensitive to the privilege the researcher enjoys over the researched because of her ability to be heard. "Ethnography exceeds the capacities of quantitative—especially 'big data'—methods, providing a snap shot of those 'power plays' and conflict in action" (Peake 2015).

Integrity, therefore, is imperative when undertaking participant observation. Geertz (1973) argues that ethnographic accounts make the claim that the researcher has paid attention and accurately described the people and communications being studied. Davis et al. describe validity of qualitative research as "trustworthiness or credibility" (2013: 346). Jorgensen (1989) describes validity in similar terms and suggests that it is integrally tied to reliability. Checks of the two, according to Jorgensen, could include gathering many forms of evidence so that the researcher is not overly reliant on one. Jorgenson further advocates for researchers continually analyzing field notes, searching for patterns, identifying next questions to ask, and eventually building theory about what is uniquely communicated at the site, paying particular attention to how members are constructing meaning. Building rapport is also important in successful participant observation (Jorgensen 1989; DeWalt & DeWalt 2002; Lindlof & Taylor 2011) and allows the researcher to gather more intimate evidence than what might be collected by observation alone. Below, we give careful attention to various qualitative methods that demand the rigorous collection of evidence in online and offline spaces. We share these details to further discussion of conducting research in a digital and globalized world.

Organizing Locally, Nationally, and Internationally

Jeanette

As part of her participant observation since March 2014, Jeanette has been building rapport within a TOMS' campus club setting at a Midwest U.S. university for more than 1 year, all in an effort to understand how millennials may be connecting with TOMS, a shoe company known for its philanthropic approach to selling shoes. The TOMS volunteers use both online and offline formats for conducting their TOMS college club activities. Early observations need to be checked via informant and narrative interviews (Lindlof & Taylor 2011), but must also indicate club members's desire to be involved and immerse themselves in TOMS events and national promotions, such as One Day Without Shoes. Club members like to share stories of the events and programs that TOMS promotes in videos found on TOMS.com or YouTube. They play TOMS corporate videos at club meetings, showing the videos regularly after receiving access to a school projector in the classroom where club members meet. For instance, in February 2015, the club president played what he called a "sneak peak" of TOMS' new giving program. TOMS had yet to announce this program to the public but had secretly announced it to club leaders in advance. The video detailed the new program that funded training for birth attendants and delivery of birth kits with the goal of fewer deaths and infections, with proceeds from the sale of TOMS' tote bags. Club members expressed how they thought the program was "cool"; they also liked the design of the bag, seemingly proud that TOMS develops programs to help people around the world.

To be more involved in TOMS corporate activities, three club members competed online via the club's Facebook page to be part of a TOMS "giving trip" to Peru. Jeanette heard the winners speak about how they were looking forward to meeting staff members from TOMS headquarters and seeing TOMS philanthropy in action overseas. They also expressed that they were grateful to receive a trip out of the country, evidence that the benefits of being in a TOMS campus club are not just ideological, if they are ideological at all. TOMS club membership can be positively realized in products and services that members desire. Members do not seem like cultural dupes, either. They do not plan their activities based solely on corporate suggestions or by following other clubs' actions. For instance, TOMS' One Day Without Shoes event in 2015 was scheduled for a time when the club's university was out of school. Members therefore celebrated 1 month earlier. Members also give to causes of their choosing, not the causes TOMS has chosen, and certainly not to TOMS. The club president has said specifically that TOMS is a for-profit company, so donations raised by their club will not go to TOMS but instead to charities that club members wish to support. He also emphasized giving to *local* charities. Members appear to support that philosophy. After raising money by hosting bake sales, in December 2014 they spent more than $150 they had collected to buy toys for Toys for Tots in their university town. In what could model how TOMS talks about its philanthropy, however, members created a video of their shopping spree and posted it on YouTube.

With this participant observation in mind, we might suggest that organizing in today's world of digitization and globalization demands work online and offline by those doing the organizing. The labor is free but not necessarily exploitative, particularly when organizers feel they have been compensated in some way and in control in most ways. Today's researcher of organizing must move on and offline, too, as she participates in the organizing process. Face-to-face encounters must be seriously detailed in field notes and interviews while digital artifacts must be analyzed as visual and textual elements important to understanding face-to-face elements. The virtual is real for many organizers today, and researchers should be respectful of that perception.

Social Justice Gaming

Erika

Erika's work, on the other hand, explores the complexities and nuances throughout social gaming spaces—once again a space that orients millennials toward philanthropy. As a digital space, particularly an interactive digital space, it becomes important to examine gameplay through an inquiry that lends agency to its players. Previous scholarship has examined how basic studies on digital identity representation in videogames is not enough (Shaw 2013). In order to discern how digital spaces are used, one must be conscious of the decision-making that happens both on-screen (e.g., coding) and off-screen (e.g., gameplay decision-making). One such example is Erika's work on women's empowerment within gaming spaces that focus on social justice.

From news clips and documentaries to films and mass trade books, stories focusing on the trials and tribulations women face globally have become a popular mainstay (Mehta 2009). One such example of this phenomenon is the videogame *Half the Sky Movement: The Game*, developed by Zynga and published by Games for Change (G4C). The game is based off the *New York Times* bestseller *Half the Sky: Turning Oppression into Opportunity for Women Worldwide* (2009), written by Nicolas Kristof and Sheryl WuDunn. The book draws on liberal feminist frameworks by arguing that the best solution to female empowerment is access to capital through microfinancing. It garnered great traction in 2009, leading to a social movement campaign. The videogame has also gained great success, with over 1.3 million players worldwide (Games for Change 2014).

The *Half the Sky* videogame echoes the successful book's footsteps through its narration of issues women face globally. It follows five fictional characters around the world. Players help each character ameliorate situations of poverty by playing various mini-games and selecting narrative options. For example, the game begins in India with a character named Radhika. Radhika's child is sick, but her husband will not allow her to spend the household's money. The player must decide between speaking up to the husband or finding a way to raise money behind his back. Notably, if a player decides to "stay silent," then the game still creates a narrative in which Radhika subverts her husband's will regardless of game choice.

A cursory or critical examination might make it easy to dismiss this game as western neoliberal marketing toward millennials. Yet, such an examination would be too simplistic, as it assumes a binary in which the designers are only aiming to push a political agenda and the players are neither self-reflexive of their gameplay nor critical of the media they consume. In addition to examining how play is mediated online, one must consider the epistemologies of *how* digital media is consumed, reconfigured, and processed.

In the case of social justice games, players make certain gameplay decisions for multiple reasons. They might play for philanthropy (as many games donate money as you play along), entertainment, and/or educational purposes. Regardless of their reason, it is imperative to consider that researching interactive, digital spaces is liminal; people's lives and identities are in constant flux. Immersion in these spaces engenders a perspective that can capture this liminality.

As we continue to research digital spaces, including interactive gaming spaces, one must consider (and be okay with) liminality, specifically the liminality between self and technoself, player and character, and producer and consumer. As a method, Erika had her students play the game while journaling their decision-making process. She looked for friction and paradox between the message the game supports (that microfinancing loans and speaking up are liberatory and empowering to women) and the decisions that players made.

Her findings suggest that participants of the game do not always subscribe to its pressed narrative. For example, one black female student exclaimed that, despite the game's reinforcing narrative where women of color are saved, it was refreshing for her to play a game in which the main character was a woman of color. Her frustrations with the oversaturation of white avatars in videogames (Wohn 2011) made her more forgiving of the problematic story presented in the game's design. This example, among others, demonstrates the importance of building more nuanced methods and, more specifically, being open to liminal explanations to self, identity, and the understandings of larger socio-cultural elements that frame millennials and their experiences with games.

Prosumerism, Maketivism, and Immaterial Labor in a Web 2.0 DIY Ethos

Radhika

In her current research, Radhika (Gajjala 2015, 2016) is looking at how women engage digital technologies through domestic spaces leading into networked, public/private interpersonal spaces, specifically around DIY fiber-crafting. The over 60 women interviewed for this project have consistently indicated—implicitly and explicitly—a certain need to be working with tangible products to compensate for the ubiquity of nontangible, everyday living. They therefore work to *produce* materiality at the intersection of tangible handcrafting and digital image/text sharing. Both this process of doing and the tactile experience—the tangibility—of the offline artifact and its creation invoke a sensory experience that fosters a relational digital space. This constant harking back to tangible objects and the ritual of making keeps the practice "real." These women assert their agency through digital materiality—by intersecting tangible and digital sharing as they engage in forms of immaterial labor in various other aspects of their daily routine.

What these women do in these communities is a clear case for pedagogies of doing, both tangible and digital. Along with Alex Juhasz and Anca Birzescu, Radhika used these understandings to further develop some of her class assignments, one of which was extended for use in a FemTechNet beta class in 2013–14 (see FemTechNet Beta Class 2013). Importantly, this project is a way of being within contemporary "Maketivism" cultures and DIY communities that engage "elements of the 'hacker' ethos, but not necessarily the illegal 'cracker' ethos" (Ratto & Boler 2014: 4). This immersion, or weaving in and out, involves learning about communicative cultures and gaining real-life understanding of certain spaces. It is also a way of being for prosumers and digital laborers. "Maketivists" are engaged in what we call "epistemologies of doing." According to Ratto and Boler, they combine "the DIY (do-it-yourself) ethos of home renovation with the DIT (do-it-together) ethos of the GNU Linux and Free Software movement" (4).

Indeed, this work is a tactile, material engagement with the digital—an engagement in immaterial labor. According to Lazzarato:

> Immaterial labor finds itself at the crossroads (or rather, it is the interface) of a new relationship between production and consumption. The activation of both productive cooperation and the social relationship with the consumer is materialized within and by the process of communication. The role of immaterial labor is to promote continual innovation in the forms and conditions of communication (and thus in work and consumption). It gives form to and materializes needs, the imaginary, consumer tastes, and so forth, and these products in turn become powerful producers of needs, images, and tastes.
>
> (Lazzarato 1996: 6)

*

As these three very different projects demonstrate, (cyber)ethnography is complex. Our experiences with our research form new understandings of what might have started intuitively with past research and traditional methods. Our experiences with our students, as well as teaching through the struggle to grasp and convey a sense of being in these worlds that do not physically surround us except through screens and gadgets, challenge us as researchers and educators. This messy encounter logically leads us to adopt the very practices of the cultures we study in both teaching and research. If we are to describe practices of digital/material immersion, then we must be simultaneously *there* and *here*. But we must also narrate what happens in the process. We must show students that evidence of being there cannot be provided by merely viewing what is there from an outside gaze, just because pressing a button or clicking a mouse makes us feel present. Having said that, there are various levels of immersion or being "inside," all predicated on acquiring a variety of technical, cultural, and contextual skills. Indeed, there are degrees and layers of knowing—of evidence and verification.

Further Reading

Dean, J. (2014) "Big Data: Accumulation and Enclosure," *Academia.edu*, retrieved from www.academia.edu/7125387/Big_data_accumulation_and_enclosure.

Gold, M. K. (ed.) (2012) *Debates in the Digital Humanities*, Minneapolis, MN: University of Minnesota Press.

Levine, E. (ed.) (2015) *Cupcakes, Pinterest, and Ladyporn: Feminized Popular Culture in the Early Twenty-First Century*, Champaign, IL: University of Illinois Press.

Schwittay, A. (2014) *New Media and International Development: Representation and Affect in Microfinance (Rethinking Development)*, New York, NY: Taylor and Francis.

References

Beller, J. (2013) "Digitality and the Media of Dispossession," in T. Scholz (ed.) *Digital Labor: The Internet as Playground and Factory*, New York, NY: Routledge, pp. 165–86.

boyd, d. (2014) *It's Complicated: The Social Lives of Networked Teens*, New Haven, CT: Yale University Press.

Brown, W. (2015) *Undoing the Demos: Neoliberalism's Stealth Revolution*, Brooklyn, NY: Zone Books.

Butler, J. (1990) *Gender Trouble: Feminism and the Subversion of Identity*, New York, NY: Routledge.

Clifford, J., and G. E. Marcus (1986) *Writing Culture: The Poetics and Politics of Ethnography: A School of American Research Advanced Seminar*, Berkeley, CA: University of California Press.

Coté, M., and J. Pybus (2007) "Learning to Immaterial Labour 2.0: Myspace and Social Networks," *Ephemera* 7(1), 88–106.

Coté, M., and J. Pybus (2011) "Learning to Immaterial Labour 2.0: Facebook and Social Networks," in: M. A. Peters and E. Bulut (eds.) *Cognitive Capitalism, Education and Digital Labor*, New York, NY: Peter Lang, pp. 169–94.

Davis, C. S., H. P. Gallardo, and K. Lachlan (2013) *Straight Talk about Communication Research Methods*, 2nd edn, Dubuque, IA: Kendall-Hunt Publishing.

DeWalt, K. M., and B. R. DeWalt (2002) *Participant Observation: A Guide for Fieldworkers*, Walnut Creek, CA: AltaMira Press.

FemTechNet Beta Class (2013) retrieved from femtechnet.newschool.edu/femtechnet-site-ings-events.

Foucault, M. (2001) "Les Mailles du Pouvoir," in M. Coté and J. Pybus (eds.) *Dits et Ecrits II 1954–1988*, Paris: Gallimard, pp. 1001–20.

Gajjala, R. (2015) "When Your Seams Get Undone, Do You Learn to Sew or to Kill Monsters?" *The Communication Review* 18(1), 23–36.

Gajjala, R. (2016) "DigiNaka Located: Materializing Circuits of Affect and Care through Domestic Space," plenary presentation at *"DigiNaka" an International Seminar of the School of Media and Cultural Studies*, TISS, Mumbai, India.

Gajjala, R., and M. Altman (2006) "Producing Cyberselves through Technospatial Praxis: Studying through Doing," in P. Liamputtong (ed.) *Health Research in Cyberspace*, New York, NY: Nova Publishers, pp. 67–84.

Gajjala, R., J. M. Dillon, and S. Anarbaeva (in press) "Prosumption," in L. Van Zoonen (ed.) *International Encyclopedia of Media Effects*, Hoboken, NJ: Wiley-Blackwell.

Games for Change (2014) retrieved from www.gamesforchange.org.

Geertz, C. (1973) *The Interpretation of Cultures: Selected Essays*, New York, NY: Basic Books.

Goffman, E. (1989) "On Fieldwork," *Journal of Contemporary Ethnography* 18, 123–32.

Hardt, M. and A. Negri (2000) *Empire*, New York, NY: Penguin.

hooks, b. (1981) *Ain't I A Woman: Black Women and Feminism*, Boston, MA: South End Press.

Jorgensen, D. L. (1989) *Participant Observation: A Methodology for Human Studies*, Newbury Park, CA: SAGE Publications.

Kendall, L. (2002) *Hanging Out in the Virtual Pub: Masculinities and Relationships Online*, Berkeley, CA: University of California Press.

Kristof, N., and S. WuDunn (2009) *Half the Sky: Turning Oppression into Opportunity for Women Worldwide*, New York, NY: Alfred A. Knopf.

Latour, B. (1987) *Science in Action: How to Follow Scientists and Engineers through Society*, Cambridge, MA: Harvard University Press.

Lazzarato, M. (1996) "Immaterial Labor," in M. Hardt and P. Virno (eds.) *Radical Thought in Italy: A Potential Politics*, Minneapolis, MN and London, UK: University of Minnesota Press, pp. 133–47.

Lindlof, T. R., and B. C. Taylor (2011) *Qualitative Communication Research Methods*, 3rd edn, Thousand Oaks, CA: Sage.

Markham, A. N., and N. K. Baym (eds.) (2009) *Internet Inquiry: Conversations about Method*, Thousand Oaks, CA: Sage.

Marx, K., and F. Engels (2013 [1848]) *The Communist Manifesto*, (ed.) F. L. Bender, New York, NY: W.W. Norton & Co.

McLeod, D., J. Rault, and T. L. Cowan (2014) "Speculative Praxis towards a Queer Feminist Digital Archive: A Collaborative Research-Creation Project," *Ada: A Journal of Gender, New Media, and Technology* 5, retrieved from adanewmedia.org/2014/07/issue5-cowanetal.

Mehta, N. (2009) "Opposing Images: 'Third World Woman' and 'Welfare Queen,'" *Women's Policy Journal of Harvard* 7, 65–70.

Nakamura, L. (2002) *Cybertypes: Race, Ethnicity, and Identity on the Internet*, New York, NY: Routledge.
Peake, B. (2015) "WP: THREATNING2MEN: Misogynist Infopolitics and the Hegemony of the Asshole Consensus on English Wikipedia," *Ada: A Journal of Gender, New Media and Technology* 7, retrieved from adanewmedia.org/2015/04/issue7-peake.
Prensky, M. (2001) "Digital Natives, Digital Immigrants, Part 1," *On the Horizon* 9(5), 1–6.
Ratto, M., and M. Boler (2014) *DIY Citizenship: Critical Making and Social Media*, Cambridge, MA: The MIT Press.
Roy, A. (2010) *Poverty Capital: Microfinance and the Making of Development*, New York, NY: Routledge.
Shah, N., and F. Jansen (2011) *Book 1: To be Digital (Alter)natives with a Cause?* Delhi: Centre for Internet and Society.
Shaw, A. (2013) "Rethinking Game Studies: A Case Study Approach to Video Game Play and Identification," *Critical Studies in Media and Communication* 30(5), 347–61.
Spivak, G. C. (1988) "Can the Subaltern Speak?" in C. Nelson and L. Grossberg (eds.) *Marxism and the Interpretation of Culture*, Champaign, IL: University of Illinois Press, pp. 271–313.
Stone, A. R. (1995) *The War of Desire and Technology at the Close of the Mechanical Age*, Cambridge, MA: MIT Press.
Sunden, J. (2003) *Material Virtualities: Approaching Online Textual Embodiment*, New York, NY: Peter Lang.
Tsing, A. (2005) *Friction: An Ethnography of Global Connection*, Princeton, NJ: Princeton University Press.
Vanderhoef, J. (2013) "Casual Threats: The Feminization of Casual Video Games," *Ada: A Journal of Gender, New Media, and Technology* 2, retrieved from adanewmedia.org/2013/06/issue2-vanderhoef.
Wajcman, J. (1991) *Feminism Confronts Technology*, University Park, PA: Penn State University Press.
Wohn, D. Y. (2011) "Gender and Race Representation in Casual Games," *Sex Roles* 65(3), 198–207.

5

OF, BY, AND FOR THE INTERNET

New Media Studies and Public Scholarship

Aimée Morrison

A tweeted photo of infant sleepwear made me "internet famous" (Kane 2014). My sudden "micro-celebrity" (Marwick & boyd 2011) was enervating, and exciting, and empowering, and scary by turns. Such experiences vary widely, however, and how and why academic micro-celebrity distributes asymmetrical consequences is the subject of this chapter. I propose we must actively work to craft a new media studies of, by, and for the internet, one that seeks to *transform* rather than simply *disrupt* both scholarship and the broader social landscape. This transformation would aim to produce a new mode of what I describe as "public/scholarship," that is more democratic and expansive in its processes, and more equitable and supportive in its outcomes, for all participants. Such an outcome is by no means assured and is indeed already threatened.

It is a cliché of new media and digital humanities (DH) that digital technology is fundamentally *disruptive*—that is, that it breaks down prior social, economic, and political arrangements, and that such breakdowns have revolutionary effects. This rhetoric plays out in miniature in the academic setting. In hindsight, many of these claims seem overblown. It is hard to articulate the disruptive impact of PowerPoint, once much trumpeted: as it turns out, PowerPoint simply reproduces "the lecture" but with snazzier visual aids, and a whole lot of infrastructure spending. Similarly, there is not much revolution in new internet media used to simply further or refine status quo scholarly methods: paywalled journal articles on the web are just as inaccessible as print ones immured in academic libraries, for example.

Here, I consider viral academic speech as offering the opportunity to develop a new media studies of, by, and for the internet, or what I call "public/scholarship." Public/scholarship as a locution intends to name not a modified, adjectivized version of "scholarship" but a truly compound, see-saw form, both "public" and "scholarship" equally weighted. This mode of new media engagement can be transformative, changing both scholar and scholarship in profound and discomfiting ways.

To clarify and limit my scope for this essay, I offer this taxonomy of new media engagement, arranged from least disruptive to most transformative. I come at this from the "scholar" end of the continuum, moving toward the "public." You might reverse this instead. The boundaries between categories are fuzzy rather than sharp; overlaps will vary case by case:

1. **Publicizing and sharing finished academic work**: This includes posting your own articles on Academia.edu, placing a work in an online repository, or publishing a presentation on Slideshare.
2. **Scholarly gleaning**: Gleaning activities aggregate and organize resources for anyone to use, through, for example, curated Twitter lists, hashtags, social bookmarking, Storify, and digest blogging.
3. **Seeding**: Seeding places material online to allow others to grow it into something bigger or better or different: sharing a syllabus on GitHub for reuse and elaborations by others, or creating open documents such as the #femdh list of female coders suitable for invitations to conference keynotes.
4. **Doing research in and through the public/internet**: Collective hashtags like #dayofdh exemplify this mode: the hashtag is dispersed to participants whose use of it serves a purpose in and of itself, but the collected tweets also later become a dataset upon which further scholarship is built. #FergusonSyllabus and #CharlestonSyllabus bring academic and popular sources together, as history unfolds in real time. Public/scholarship begins to emerge as distinctions between a researching subject and a subject of research begin to break down.
5. **Affective labor and meta-discursive work**: From "Quit Lit" to the Adjunct Project at the *Chronicle of Higher Education,* to collective blogs like *Hook & Eye* and *Conditionally Accepted*, to hashtag projects like #ILookLikeAProfessor, various kinds of online scholarly writing work explicitly through new media to organize academic labor and academic communities, cutting across intersectional lines: class, institutional position, geographic location, race, and gender. The question of affect is foregrounded in these discussions about academic practices and values: the personal is political, and deliberately visible.
6. **Activist or direct intervention work**: For example, Canadian Women in the Literary Arts (CWILA) counts and counters the exclusion of female writers from formal review media. Global Outlook::Digital Humanities (GO::DH) aims to shift the direction and composition of DH using lightweight organizing and publishing tools to work around substantial infrastructure constraints as well as the disciplinary ones that are weighted against a truly global digital humanities scholarly practice.
7. **Accidentally or on-purpose going full-out public viral**: Sometimes, a bit of academic speech escapes the orbit of scholarly conversation and blazes across the sky of broader public culture. Whether the experience burns everything in its path or lights a new way often correlates to historic categories of power or exclusion. I know, because it happened to me.

It Happened to Me

My friend Christine Robinson Logel, a social psychology professor at Renison University College, snapped a photo of two pairs of infant pyjamas, juxtaposed, and posted it to Facebook. I asked her permission to share the photo on Twitter. At 12:40 on that September Monday, rushing to get to class, I tweeted the photo with the caption "Please RT this sexist set of baby jammies from Target. Boys can be heroes; girls can date heroes. #target #sexism" (see Figure 5.1).

Figure 5.1 Twitter screen capture. Tweet by Aimée Morrison (@digiwonk).

By the time my class was over, the post had already garnered more than 50 retweets, and some modified retweets from high-profile accounts were boosting the signal. Crucially, the post got re-hashtagged with further gender- and comics-related tags, which helped make the image a lot more discoverable. @EverydaySexism (220,000 followers) spliced Christine's photo to another photo, of two adult-sized t-shirts, one reading "Training to be Batman" and the other "Training to be Batman's wife," and tagged me in it (see Figure 5.2).

Twitter notifications were arriving several per minute. It took very little time for the mainstream media to notice. The first reporter, a columnist for an online news site, contacted me through Twitter, within hours (Csanady 2014). Christine and I were both recorded and interviewed for Canadian Broadcasting Corporation (CBC) talk radio and news website coverage Monday evening (van Koeverden 2014).

Overnight Monday, my notifications clogged with more than 400 messages, overwhelmingly supportive. On Tuesday, I did a TV segment for the local network affiliate, two print interviews with Canadian wire services, and a radio interview with an all-talk station locally (Perkel 2014). Retweets and modified retweets moved into the hundreds. Media requests were coming through my cell phone, the university press office, my university email, my office phone, and Twitter. Twitter users, some in my preexisting network, but most not, were alerting me every time a different media or web outlet took up the story (e.g., Dusenbery 2014; Terror 2014). Others were adding images and anecdotes to a hashtag corpus of sexist clothing (see Storified collection of these at Morrison 2014).

By Tuesday evening, the wire service stories were being posted and printed nationally. Wednesday brought more, and more diverse, media: another live talk radio interview, national broadcast TV interview, and a college radio interview. My own university's press office contacted me, a little nervous. This is the point I later describe as "peak onesie." The tweet was covered in a *Jezebel* story that appeared Tuesday overnight; later the author incorporated my submitted remarks (Rose 2014). A national all-news cable network had me in studio for a 2-minute remote, live interview: it is the first semihostile interview I have ever done, as the host opens with "people on the internet are outraged" and asks me, skeptically, "what's wrong with these pjs?" The hate mail arrived on Tuesday and built through Wednesday.

Figure 5.2 Twitter screen capture. Tweet by EverydaySexism (EverydaySexism).

On Thursday, the story received coverage in Australia, from the superhero angle, and probably related to the #WearYourSuperheroes story that originated there, and the *Mail Online* repeatedly pinged Christine and me for photo permission, as did a National Broadcasting Company (NBC) affiliate in Atlanta (Moran 2014). The story appeared on the front page of Yahoo.com. Two more student journalists from local universities contacted me. Things began to slow by Friday, a steady dribble of mentions and retweets, tapering quickly off. But even now, every couple of days, nearly 3 years later, someone retweets the image, still.

Power and Privilege in Public/Scholarship

Tressie McMillan Cottom has identified the move toward public engagement through social media as supporting a culture of academic micro-celebrity and personal branding that, instead of disrupting the neoliberal university, can instead promote it on two fronts: bringing reputational currency and prestige to the university and promoting a purported democratization of knowledge without truly changing anything (McMillan Cottom 2015b). It is undeniable that my own viral media experience operates in the ways McMillan Cottom describes, leveraging public attention to bolster my own profile as a legitimate authority at the same time as accruing reputational and attentional currency to my institution. On the ground, it looks like this: sometimes, at parties in the community where I live, or even at conferences among academics, I am introduced as "you know, she had the tweet about the pajamas!" and people are impressed, because it was kind of a big deal in socially acceptable ways, at least in my own broad employment and cultural networks. There was arguably nothing either disruptive or transformative about my viral media experience.

My experience of the public/scholarship of #sexistjammies is enframed by the intersections between my institutional position, my research area, my embodiment, and my cultural capital, mostly working to my substantial advantage. My tenured professorship and affiliation with a research institution were crucial in granting me immediate credibility as a legitimate "expert" participant in public culture. I benefit as well from the financial and professional security that tenure offers. Further, my location in the Canadian university system is marked by a political climate on and about campus issues that is generally far less polarized and antagonistic than that in the U.S. These are important advantages.

That I am a researcher of new media topics further gave me extra access to valuable social and material resources to manage this event. With around 2000 followers at the time my tweet was picked up, I was already above the 96th percentile for reach among Twitter users—the average Twitter user who logs in more than once a month has between 160 and 200 followers, depending on how this is calculated (Cir.ca 2015). I had a prior, established public persona and audience, rather than a personal or private one; self-presentation online is, after all, my core research area. Mikki Kendall has dissected how the experience of Twitter shifts based on a scale of followers: over 5,000 followers, she says, and things can get a little unpleasant and combative; over 10,000 and it is not worth reading your mentions anymore (Daniels 2015). I do not have this problem. Yet. While the scale of engagement the tweet drew was unusual, I was neither blindsided by the attention nor thrust into a position of moving suddenly from total obscurity to inadvertent internet micro-celebrity (Marwick 2013). Frankly, I had already cultivated such micro-celebrity, primed for attention and trained in getting it: I am, it seems, a good neoliberal academic subject even when I am trying to dismantle retail patriarchy.

I was also advantaged by my status as an established media commentator. For several years already, I have been very frequently called upon as an expert source on new media- and gender-related topics in print and broadcast media. Indeed, because of my media contacts, my research profile, and my faculty position, I was able to turn myself from the object of media's attention to a subject directing and framing it. I could and did reach out to journalists directly. I wanted to talk about the sexism in the pajamas, per se, but also about the arc of the feminist viral media story, generally and structurally, and I did not see this in the spontaneous coverage. I pitched the story to a digital culture radio program that airs nationally; I was allowed to suggest an angle and focus that was reflected in the questions I was ultimately asked (Young 2015). Similarly, the local newspaper, having reprinted the wire story about the controversy, decided to follow up with a story, which appeared in the feature section, on my research more broadly (Aggerholm 2014). This type of access to sympathetic and substantial media treatment is a rare privilege.

Misunderstanding Virality Produces Harm

The backlash against my viral media did ultimately arrive, both because the tweet itself was explicitly feminist and, inevitably, because I am a woman and a feminist. The Cycle of Backlash moved through my Twitter mentions, my university email account, and the comments sections of blogs and online publications, and it proceeded as it generally does in what I began to refer to as my Misogynist Insult Escalation Chart. Your chart will prob ably have similar items on it, but perhaps in a different order, depending on your membership in intersecting categories of exclusion or privilege: many scholars, were they inclined to wade through their Twitter mentions, would be well able to craft racist, ableist, or classist insult escalation charts of their own. My own experience goes like this:

1. This does not matter / I do not care / no one cares.
2. Get a sense of humor.
3. It is just Twitter / Facebook / Tumblr / The Internet, not the real world.
4. Make me a sandwich / get in the kitchen / ugly / lesbian / bitch.
5. You are wrong / this is not my experience / this is not real.

6. You have no standing / are not an expert / do not know anything.
7. I am going to get you fired / you are finished in this town.
8. I will rape you / kill you / harm your family.

Perhaps unsurprisingly, this chart recalls Joanna Russ's brilliant *How to Suppress Women's Writing* (1983), with its eleven-point plan to minimize, distract, confuse, and confound public speech by women, a problem that seems even more urgent now than in 1983. Many contemporary feminist journalists, for example, recount living in a perpetual state of fear arising from an onslaught of online rape and death threats, and many are unwilling or unable to accept those terms of employment for long (see, for example, Penny 2011; Cox 2014; Hess 2014; Dingman 2016). As Lindy West wryly puts it, "Being insulted and threatened online is part of my job" (Goldberg 2015)—and such job conditions increasingly obtain for female academics with a public presence as well. Indeed, *Model View Culture* founder Shanley Kane details how her experience of becoming "internet famous" involved her visibility being weaponized against her: becoming a "public figure" according to others' logic meant not that she gained in perceived authority, but that she lost any assumed privacy rights (2014). Having a higher platform to reach a bigger audience that does not want to hear what you have to say is a mixed blessing, at best.

From my work as a theorist in social media, I had always understood these kinds of attacks to be inevitable and substantially structural rather than strictly personal—I was expecting them. I was not expecting, frankly, to have such an easy time of it. Structural patterns have personal instantiations of course, and experiences vary widely based on intersecting categories of identity, topic, and location, a lesson I needed reminding of. I was not seriously doxxed and did not receive any really threatening Twitter mentions or emails, probably because I was mainly (but not totally) immune from racist, homophobic, and ableist attacks online: many, many people called me a humorless bitch, but only one person wanted to have me deported, for example. This was invaluable to my capacity to maintain a sort of existential equanimity that so many others have been robbed of: it is easy enough for me to joke when I suffer insults one through five, but not six, seven, or eight. Still, "going viral" even in such positive terms and with such (relatively) trivial consequences was emotionally and physically exhausting, and this truly surprised me. The constant disruption of various notifications, media calls, emails, and more, of which I was never certain which would be hostile or supportive, is enervating and unnerving, despite my comparatively easy experience. I did nothing but manage this for an entire week: no writing, no grading, no class prep, and barely attending class. I still get random hate tweets, and they still bother me.

There are real risks to taking scholarship outside the ivory tower, risks that accrue unevenly based on identity and visibility. Internet shitstorms rain down disproportionately, and with disproportionate damage, upon the more precarious: women, people with disabilities, people of color, junior scholars, and the contingently employed. McMillan Cottom writes, "Were I white or male or of a higher class, it is possible that I could leverage the adage that all press is good press" (2015b). For too many, the physical, emotional, reputational costs of "going viral" are too high to bear. Recent informal experiments, such as #raceswap, demonstrate what many of us know in our own experiences to be true: minoritized populations have their ideas challenged far more aggressively, with racist and sexist ad hominem attacks, with more threats of personal violence, and more generally trollish behavior, than white men (Carbone 2014; Nesbitt Golden 2014; Vogt & Goldman 2014; DeMarco n.d.). This is deliberate and structural. Even as academics are urged to make ourselves more public, those who would derail public/scholarship engage in organized campaigns we can liken to hostile "outing" of otherwise self-limiting and obscure internet writings by scholars, or a kind of muckraking among the AstroTurf, what the *Chronicle of Higher Education* recently described as the "Higher Ed's Internet Outrage Machine" (Schmidt 2015). While some viral academic media broadens reach and speech, other viral academic media is deliberately weaponized to suppress it. This depends largely on who is producing the speech, and about what. In the U.S., organized trolling expeditions by conservative campus organizations, some funded by national political advocacy groups, engage in missions of seek-and-destroy, looking for progressive material from precarious subjects and launching wars.

Recently, professors Saida Grundy, hired out of her doctorate directly to Boston University, and Zandria Robinson, leaving University of Memphis for Rhodes College, were both the subjects of weaponized viral media (Shahvisi 2015). Each was targeted by conservative national student organizations for public tweets addressing the intersections of race, gender, class, and power (Chasmar 2015; Hasson 2015; "University of Memphis Professor" 2015). The virality of this speech was forced upon each scholar: decontextualized tweets were surfaced, promoted, amplified, and reframed to generate maximum attention to these scholars for the purpose of having them fired or discredited and humiliated (Fadiran 2015; Jaschik 2015a, 2015c; Shavisi 2015). These incidents, and many others like them in ways that mark white supremacy as both threatened and threatening, demonstrate the skewed uses and consequences of viral academic media (see Crockett 2014; McMillan Cottom 2015a). Grundy and Robinson are black women, and both are junior faculty members, Grundy in African American Studies and Robinson in Sociology. Both were subject to organized conservative attacks their respective institutions were ill-equipped to respond to. Distressingly, neither received adequate support from their institutions. The University of Memphis merely noted that Robinson was no longer in their employ, leaving open the possibility that she had been fired rather than the actual case that she had already been recruited into a position at another school (Timpf 2015). President Robert A. Brown of Boston University, more seriously, actively denounced Grundy's tweets, characterizing them as "statements that reduce individuals to stereotypes on the basis of a broad category such as sex, race, or ethnicity" and engaging in what amounts to tone policing (Brown 2015). In both cases, the professors were targeted by conservative groups for addressing topics in critical race studies well accepted in that field, but which were violently opposed by more public audiences online; it is distressing that their institutions seemed to choose not to side with them as colleagues, but to capitulate instead to small groups of online agitators skilled at drawing and directing media attention.

Public/scholarship has never been easy, and in many ways it has become harder as internet publication and communication tools knock down the protective walls of the ivory tower. And we must remember that these walls have, in their better incarnations, sheltered vulnerable academics and created space, however imperfectly, for progressive thinking and substantial debate. (These imperfections are themselves structural and profound. The recent *Presumed Incompetent: The Intersections of Race and Class for Women in Academia* (Guttiérrez y Muhs et al. 2012), a collection of 30 personal narratives of systemic exclusion, powerfully articulates the means by which the ivory tower continues to enforce a normative academic identity that forcefully works against a more inclusive, diverse, and just academe.) The walled garden of the academy, that is, has at some times and in some ways enabled even as it restricted socially engaged scholarship. In general, the humanities academy is friendlier to marginalized and minoritized populations than the world at large can be; and in general, the world at large is more outwardly civilized than much of the internet. On the internet—the broadly construed "public" at issue here—suppressing women, people of color, people with disabilities, and otherwise marginalized subjects has become a blood sport engaged by normative subjects whose status is threatened, by simple sadists, and by groups exploiting the nature of virality to organize targeted mobs. Shiny happy talk about the imperatives of public scholarship available to any scholar with an internet connection denies the force and power of these acts of suppression and the ways they disproportionately harm some scholars in some fields more than others.

"Of the People, by the People, for the People"

It is no surprise that scholars writing on social justice issues—gender, race, class, and politics—are at the forefront of both public/scholarship and the backlash against it. Grundy ultimately favors more rather than less speech, writing: "the events we now witness with regularity in our nation tell us that we can no longer circumvent the problems of difference with strategies of silence" (quoted in Jaschik 2015b). This is the essence of a truly transformative version of public/scholarship. As Sunera Thobani, a Canadian academic who herself became the victim of a 2001 internet mob, writes: "Challenging the truth claims of dominant elites has long been a major part of the struggles of oppressed peoples for self-determination" (2003: 400). Indeed, some of the most vibrant and urgent new media public/scholarship has been produced by marginalized subjects, by those who have become public/scholars because academic and popular systems of power and reward have excluded them, or whose work has been sought out and surfaced in order to terrorize and silence. McMillan Cottom is blunt: "Put simply, all press is good press for academic microcelebrities if their social locations conform to racist and sexist norms of who should be expert" (2015b). Otherwise, not so much. Suey Park and David J. Leonard caution against the tone policing that distinguishes high-status from low-status speech online, noting that "[a]n effort to gentrify digital spaces in the name of safety and dignified discourse is sweeping the Internet," erasing marginalized voices—much of this erasure is performed by white liberal feminists (2014; see also Ross 2014). Emerging new media modes of public/scholarship must challenge rather than simply replicate how authority, authenticity, and legitimacy in intellectual work is allocated. I'Nasah Crockett flags this as well, noting the pervasiveness of antiblack racism "not only institutionally, but also at the level of the everyday . . . So of course it makes itself apparent in the supposedly brave new world (so different from any world that came before!) of social media" (2014; see also Kaba and Smith 2014). Of course it does; the sarcastic parenthetical aside speaks precisely to the disembodied dreams of utopian communication that continue to be more observed in the breach than in the occurrence.

It is easier to craft compelling rhetoric about the transformative power of public/scholarship than actually implement it. Already, as we have seen, public/scholarship is being threatened on at least two fronts. First, within universities themselves, the transformative potential in public/scholarship risks being co-opted by neoliberal logics of personal branding, good press, and "knowledge mobilization" that instead reward the powerful and maintain the status quo; in this guise, "disruptive" new media technologies simply further entrench existing powers and privilege. Second, public/scholars addressing contemporary cultural questions face substantial personal risks from internet mobs for daring to bring socially relevant research out into the world beyond the ivory tower; a secondary risk arises when their own institutions, disciplinary associations, or colleagues disavow their public/scholarship using strategies from simple tone policing to releasing blanket institutional apologies for the scholars' perceived transgressions to outright dismissal (e.g., Illinois University in the case of Steven Salaita). Some public/scholars are mobilizing to support threatened scholars, and to work out the nitty gritty details of a more equitable, more inclusive scholarship. Eric Anthony Grollman, for example, has produced a widely shared blog post detailing concrete actions that scholars, disciplinary associations, and institutions can take to support scholars under viral media attack (2015; see also McMillan Cottom 2015a for a similar take). Dorothy Kim and Eunsong Kim (2014) describe and decry a politics of academic citation that takes from but does not adequately credit or compensate the informal intellectual work of marginalized writers outside of academic systems of prestige and reward. Mia McKenzie's *Black Girl Dangerous* (2014) models transitions from blog posts to books—activist intersectional writing that moves between academic and nonacademic uses, contexts, and economies.

New media modes of public/scholarship, that is, offer us the opportunity and the imperative to transform ourselves as scholars, because our technologies and practices remain shot through with systemic biases and inequities that structure and constrain existing educational, social, political, and economic interactions and institutions. How could they not be? New media scholarship of, by, and for the internet inserts itself into, shapes, or is shaped by extant communities and emerging conversations—like #gamergate, which has terrorized scholars and game journalists alike (Cox 2014; Brown & Cuen 2015; Goodyear 2015). Whatever it is ostensibly about, it is also always already about who is entitled to speak, about what, and with what authority. It is not the abstract and utopian dreams for perfect communication envisioned in the early 1990s, suited to our more idealistic aims of seamless transmission of information. It is about whose speech is suppressed, by what means, and how this suppression can be countered; it is about whose voices are most easily amplified, by whom, and to what ultimate purpose. To neglect this work by pretending that computation "disrupts" asymmetric distributions of power and influence merely replicates these divisions we claim to wish to bridge.

Acknowledgments

This research was supported by the Social Sciences and Humanities Research Council of Canada.

References

Aggerholm, B. (2014) "Waterloo Prof's Tweet about Sexist Baby Pyjamas Woke up the World," *Waterloo Region Record*, retrieved from www.therecord.com/living-story/4919450-waterloo-prof-s-tweet-about-sexist-baby-pyjamas-woke-up-the-world/?&article_id=19286863652.

Brown, J. and L. Cuen (2015) "Gamergate's Newest Nemesis Is a Canadian PhD Student," *Vocativ*, retrieved from www.vocativ.com/tech/internet/gamergate-newest-nemesis-phd-student-natalie-zed.

Brown, R. (2015) "Letter from President Brown," *Boston University Office of the President*, retrieved from www.bu.edu/president/letters-writings/letters/2015/5–12.

Carbone, C. (2014) "What I Learned from Tweeting with a Black Woman's Avatar For #RaceSwapExp," *Thought Catalog*, retrieved from thoughtcatalog.com/christopher-carbone/2014/04/what-i-learned-from-tweeting-with-a-black-womans-avatar-for-raceswapexp.

Chasmar, J. (2015) "University of Memphis Professor: 'Whiteness Is Most Certainly and Inevitably Terror,'" *The Washingtion Times*, retrieved from www.washingtontimes.com/news/2015/jun/30/zandria-robinson-univ-of-memphis-professor-whitene.

Cir.ca (2015) "Study Shows Median Twitter Account Has Only 1 Follower," retrieved from cir.ca/news/average-followers-on-twitter.

Cox, C. (2014) "Female Game Journalists Quit Over Harassment, #GamerGate Harms Women," *The Mary Sue*, retrieved from www.themarysue.com/gamergate-harms-women.

Crockett, I. (2014) " 'Raving Amazons': Antiblackness and Misogynoir in Social Media," *Model View Culture*, retrieved from modelviewculture.com/pieces/raving-amazons-antiblackness-and-misogynoir-in-social-media.

Csanady, A. (2014) "Can Girls Be Heroes? Targets Pajamas Say No," *O.Canada.com*, retrieved from o.canada.com/news/can-girls-be-heroes-targets-pajamas-say-no.

Daniels, J. (2015) "Interview with Mikki Kendall about White Women, Feminism and Race," *Racism Review: Scholarship and Activism toward Racial Justice*, retrieved from racismreview.com/blog/2015/06/01/interview-with-mikki-kendall-about-white-women-feminism-and-race.

DeMarco, M. (n.d.) "The Race Swap Experiment—What Happens When Two Black Girls Tweet As White Guys," *Like a Boss Girls*, retrieved from www.likeabossgirls.com/race-swap-experiment-two-black-girls-experience-tweeting-white-guy.

Dingman, S. (2016) "BuzzFeed Writer's Harassment Just the Latest Example of Why Twitter Is Broken for Women," *The Globe and Mail*, retrieved from www.theglobeandmail.com/technology/harassment-of-buzzfeeds-koul-shows-how-twitter-is-broken-for-women/article28845004.

Dusenbery, M. (2014) "Photo of the Day: 'I Only Date Heroes' Pajamas for Girls," *Feministing*, retrieved from feministing.com/2014/10/01/photo-of-the-day-i-only-date-heroes-pajamas-for-girls.

Fadiran, T. (2015) "The Hollow Promise of 'Inclusivity': Saida Grundy and Boston University," *Racialicious*, retrieved from www.racialicious.com/2015/05/14/the-hollow-promise-of-inclusivity-saida-grundy-and-boston-university.

Goldberg, M. (2015) "Feminist Writers Are so Besieged by Online Abuse that Some Have Begun to Retire," *The Washington Post*, retrieved from www.washingtonpost.com/opinions/online-feminists-increasingly-ask-are-the-psychic-costs-too-much-to-bear/2015/02/19/3dc4ca6c-b7dd-11e4-a200-c008a01a6692_story.html.

Goodyear, S. (2015) "Meet The Woman Getting a PhD in Gamergate and the Death Eaters Trying To Stop Her." *The Mary Sue*, retrieved from www.themarysue.com/phd-in-gamergate.

Grollman, E. A. (2015) "How to Support a Scholar Who Has Come under Attack," *Conditionally Accepted*, retrieved from conditionallyaccepted.com /2015/07/09/attack.

Guttiérrez y Muhs, G., Y. F. Niemann, C. G. González, and A. P. Harris (eds.) (2012) *Presumed Incompetent: The Intersections of Race and Class for Women in Academia*, Boulder, CO: University Press of Colorado.

Hasson, P. (2015) "Prof. Blasted Whites on Social Media in Dissertation," *Campus Reform*, retrieved from ndm.campusreform.org/?ID=6548.

Hess, A. (2014) "Why Women Aren't Welcome on the Internet." *Pacific Standard*, retrieved from www.psmag.com/health-and-behavior/women-arent-welcome-internet-72170.

Jaschik, S. (2015a) "Regret over Tweets on Race," *Inside Higher Ed.*, retrieved from www.insidehighered.com/news/2015/05/13/professor-center-debate-over-her-tweet-white-male-students-expresses-regret.

Jaschik, S. (2015b) "Saida Grundy, Moving Forward," *Inside Higher Ed.*, retrieved from www.insidehighered.com/news/2015/08/24/saida-grundy-discusses-controversy-over-her-comments-twitter-her-career-race-and.

Jaschik, S. (2015c) "The Professor Who Wasn't Fired," *Inside Higher Ed.*, retrieved from www.insidehighered.com/news/2015/07/01/twitter-explodes-false-reports-u-memphis-fired-professor-why.

Kaba, M. and A. Smith (2014) "Interlopers on Social Media: Feminism, Women of Color and Oppression," *Truthout*, retrieved from www.truth-out.org/opinion/item/21593-interlopers-on-social-media-feminism-women-of-color-and-oppression.

Kane, S. (2014) "'Internet Famous': Visibility as Violence on Social Media." *Model View Culture*, retrieved from modelviewculture.com/pieces/internet-famous-visibility-as-violence-on-social-media.

Kim, D. and E. Kim (2014) "The #TwitterEthics Manifesto," *Model View Culture*, retrieved from modelview culture.com/pieces/the-twitterethics-manifesto.

Marwick, A. (2013) *Status Update: Celebrity, Publicity, and Branding in the Social Media Age*, New Haven, CT: Yale University Press.

Marwick, A. and d. boyd (2011) "To See and Be Seen: Celebrity Practice on Twitter," *Convergence: The International Journal of Research into New Media Technologies* 17(2), 139–58.

McKenzie, M. (2014) *Black Girl Dangerous: On Race, Queerness, Class and Gender*, Oakland, CA: BGD Press.

McMillan Cottom, T. (2015a) "Everything but the Burden: Publics, Public Scholarship, and Institutions," *tressiemc*, retrieved from tressiemc.com/2015/05/12/everything-but-the-burden-publics-public-scholarship-and-institutions.

McMillan Cottom, T. (2015b) "'Who Do You Think You Are?': When Marginality Meets Academic Microcelebrity," *Ada: A Journal of Gender, New Media, and Technology* 7, retrieved from adanewmedia.org/2015/04/issue7-mcmillancottom.

Moran, R. (2014) "DC Comics Forced to Apologise over Sexist Batman T-Shirts," *Daily Life*, retrieved from www.dailylife.com.au/dl-people/dl-entertainment/dc-comics-forced-to-apologise-over-sexist-batman-tshirts-20141001-3h379.html.

Morrison, A. (2014) "Sexist Onesies and Feminist Viral Media," *Storify*, retrieved from storify.com/digiwonk/sexist-onesies-and-feminist-viral-media.

Nesbitt Golden, J. (2014) "Why I'm Masquerading as a White Bearded Hipster Guy on Twitter (Despite Being a Black Woman)," *xoJane*, retrieved from www.xojane.com/issues/why-im-masquerading-as-a-bearded-white-hipster-guy-on-twitter.

Park, S, and D. J. Leonard (2014) "In Defense of Twitter Feminism," *Model View Culture*, retrieved from modelviewculture.com/pieces/in-defense-of-twitter-feminism.

Penny, L. (2011) "A Woman's Opinion Is the Mini-Skirt of the Internet," *The Independent*, retrieved from www.independent.co.uk/voices/commentators/laurie-penny-a-womans-opinion-is-the-mini-skirt-of-the-internet-6256946.html.

Perkel, C. (2014) "Target's 'Sexist' Baby PJs: Boys Will Be Heroes, Girls Will Date Heroes," *Global News*, retrieved from globalnews.ca/news/1592097/targets-sexist-baby-pjs-boys-will-be-heroes-girls-will-date-heroes.

Rose, R. (2014) "Target Canada Selling Sexist Superman PJ's for Girls," *Jezebel*, retrieved from jezebel.com/target-canada-selling-sexist-superman-pjs-for-girls-1641047070.

Ross, T. (2014) "Mikki Kendall and Her Online Beefs with White Feminists," *VICE*, retrieved from www.vice.com/en_ca/read/their-eyes-were-watching-twitter-0000317-v21n5.

Russ, J. (1983) *How to Suppress Women's Writing*, Austin, TX: University of Texas Press.

Schmidt, P. (2015) "Higher Education's Internet Outrage Machine," *The Chronicle of Higher Education*, retrieved from chronicle.com/article/Higher-Educations-Internet/232879/?key=HmsidgRiZSRHM3wxOGoWOGpRPC ZvYx0kN3dIangmblBUGA==.

Shahvisi, A. (2015) "Epistemic Injustice in the Academy: An Analysis of the Saida Grundy Witch-Hunt," *The Academe Blog*, retrieved from academeblog.org/2015/05/20/epistemic-injustice-in-the-academy-an-analysis-of-the-saida-grundy-witch-hunt.

"Social Media" (2014) *Model View Culture*, retrieved from modelviewculture.com/pieces/tag/social-media.

Terror, J. (2014) "Now It's Just Getting Sad: More DC Licensing Shenanigans Yield Sexist Toddler Pajamas," *The Outhouse*, retrieved from www.theouthousers.com/index.php/news/129160-now-its-just-getting-sad-more-dc-licensing-shenanigans-yield-sexist-toddler-pajamas.html.

Thobani, S. (2003) "War and the Politics of Truth-Making in Canada," *International Journal of Qualitative Studies in Education* 16(3), 399–414.

Timpf, K. (2015) "'Whiteness Is Terror' Professor Working at Rhodes College, Hailed for Her 'Sometimes Provocative' Comments," *National Review*, retrieved from www.nationalreview.com/article/420643/whiteness-terror-professor-hired-rhodes-college.

"University of Memphis Professor Zandria Robinson—'Whiteness is Terror', Whites 'Conditioned' to Commit Mass Murder" (2015) *SoCawlege*, retrieved from socawlege.com/university-of-memphis-professor-zandria-robinson-whiteness-is-terror-whites-conditioned-to-commit-mass-murder.

van Koeverden, J. (2014) "Target Baby PJs Say Boys Are Heroes, Girls Can Date Them," *CBC News*, retrieved from www.cbc.ca/news/canada/kitchener-waterloo/target-baby-pjs-say-boys-are-heroes-girls-can-date-them-1.2782450.

Vogt, P. J. and A. Goldman (2014) "#31—Race Swap," Podcast episode, *On The Media*, WNYC Studios, retrieved from www.wnyc.org/story/31-race-swap-experiment/#transcript?hc_location=ufi.

Young, N. (2015) "Anatomy of a Viral Phenomenon," Audio Recording, *Spark*, CBC Radio-Canada, retrieved from www.cbc.ca/radio/spark/anatomy-of-a-viral-phenomenon-1.2787223?autoplay=true.

6

WOMEN WHO ROCK

Making Scenes, Building Communities: Convivencia and Archivista Praxis for a Digital Era

Michelle Habell-Pallán, Sonnet Retman, Angelica Macklin, and Monica De La Torre

"If you aren't seeing women, not seeing people of color, that means it's up to us to document . . ."

— Medusa, Women Who Rock 2013 panel transcript

"Convivencia is the method. Women Who Rock is an example of the articulation of that method."

— Quetzal Flores, Women Who Rock oral history

"Convivencia has made all the difference. . . Even if it's flawed at times . . . it is the intention and process that makes all the difference."

— Martha Gonzalez, email correspondence

Figure 6.1 Women Who Rock: Making Scenes, Building Communities 2015 unConference Logo.

Introduction

Our vision of digital humanities and media production is process-driven. It is grounded in women of color feminist theorizing. Since 2011, Women Who Rock: Making Scenes, Building Communities (WWR) has brought together scholars, musicians, media-makers, performers, artists, and activists to explore the role of women and popular music in the creation of cultural scenes that anchor social justice movements in the Americas and beyond. This multifaceted endeavor reshapes conventional understandings of music and cultural production by initiating decolonial methods of research, archiving, teaching, and community and scholarly collaboration. The project encompasses several interwoven components: an annual, participant-driven community engagement conference and film festival; project-based coursework at the graduate and undergraduate levels; and an oral history archive that ties the various components together.

Though many talented and dedicated minds, hearts, and hands participate in the multiple components of WWR, this chapter is written by Michelle, Sonnet, Angelica, and Monica with a specific focus on our archival process as a transformative mode of digital humanities. Given the dynamic structure of the WWR project and its many manifestations and collaborators, we anticipate articles co-written by other sets of "we." For example, sociologist and hip hop scholar Dr. Mako Fitts Ward was a partner in the development of the first conference and co-founder of the WWR collective. Throughout the years, there is the changing "we" of the unConferences (open, informal, and collaborative gatherings where participants share interests and skills; see Figure 6.1), which have been produced in convivencia with a wide variety of community partners, including Seattle activist and youth advocate Luzviminda (Lulu) Uzuri Carpenter and the Seattle Fandango Project, along with many students, faculty, mentors, artists, and organizations, locally and internationally. The names of people who are central to the project exceed the word limit of this chapter. Moreover, the "we" of the Women Who Rock Collective is a shifting formation, dependent upon particular contexts and iterations of the project. For this essay, the four of us are a "we" who draw on our collective experiences creating the pilot Women Who Rock Oral History Archive with the University of Washington (UW) Libraries Digital Initiatives and preparing oral histories for the archive. We thought long and hard about how to design archive themes to communicate and frame its ethos and content. For this reason, the essay's structure mirrors the curatorial organization of the WWR Oral History Archive's landing page: Building Scenes (organizers and activistas), Making Communities (musicians, producers, and scene makers), Reel Rebels (film and media producers), and Write to Rock (critics, scholars, journalists, and zinesters). These four categories not only describe the particular contributions of the people included within the archive but also the aims of the project—its archivista praxis.

The four of us have spent many hours in convivencia working through questions of feminist ethics and practice in relation to digital work. It has been an intense, meaningful process. This chapter includes our experiences of "doing" digital humanities together—how we became immersed in the collection, design, development, production, and management of a networked digital archive. Our collective praxis values living process over finite product. We describe this "doing" as an archivista praxis: it is our "signature pedagogy," rooted in a method of convivencia, or the "deliberate convening, [that] builds community, creates a context for social justice work, and inspires new forms of knowledge" (Seattle Fandango Project n.d.). Our definition of signature praxis riffs on Rina Benmayor's elaboration of Lee Shulman's concept. Extending "signature pedagogies" to Latin American oral history testimonio and digital storytelling, Benmayor explains signature pedagogies as "acts that convey the personality, methods of performance, and values of a field" (2012: 509).

Over the years, some questions have shaped our perspective on collective digital praxis: How do we practice decolonial humanities in the digital age? How do we avoid turning human experience into soulless data? How do we overturn conventional modes of research that privilege individual findings over collective process? How do we work collaboratively across rank and status as faculty, graduate students, and community-based organizers, artists, and youth, being mindful of institutional power dynamics and trying to work against them? As we ask these questions, we learn through doing. The digital archive is a trace of relationships forged through collective archiving or archivista praxis. This project demonstrates the rich transformations in scholarly processes of knowledge production that women of color feminist thought inspires. We do not offer a template for digital archive building but rather an account of our own process as one of many possible methods for doing critical feminist digital humanities.

Intention: Making Scenes

Women Who Rock began with no official plan for a digital archive; it started as an idea for a class and a conference. Sonnet and Michelle wanted to co-teach a class on the politics of popular music, performance, gender, race, and power and host a conference on the same subject. We were interested in working in broad collaboration with artists and activists doing feminist work both within the university and in artist and activist spaces, locally, nationally, and internationally. We were motivated by a desire to change conventional understandings of research, pedagogy, mentoring, knowledge-production, and community at the university (see Anzaldúa 1987; Christian 1989; Todd 1996; King 2001; Taylor 2003; Hong 2008; Boyd & Roque Ramirez 2012). We wanted to find joy and camaraderie in our work, what we came to know as convivencia as we pursued the project. In 2010, we began imagining an archive that would organize our course. The course would draw together a community of students, artists, and activists engaged in the creation of a transformative archive that both reflected their own life experiences and activated a feminist network of mentors and peers. It was challenging to locate institutional support for this endeavor as we were not yet aligned with the UW Simpson Center for the Humanities or the UW Digital Libraries Initiative.

As we look back at our first conference proposal, we inadvertently named many of the core thematic inquiries necessary for a transformative digital humanities and popular music studies grounded in archivista praxis. We wanted to explore the role of music scholars, critics, performers, and archivists in crafting feminist narratives of hip hop, punk, and indie rock, and also build connections between women in hip hop, punk, and indie rock scenes that shared a similar ethos but rarely connected. We wanted to consider the politics of the archive as a site of community-making and historical praxis as well as a resource for performers, activists, media-makers, and scholars. Finally, we wanted to reflect on collaborative networks of production, performance, and distribution—to think through the uses of digital technologies for in-home production and recording as well as musical and scholarly collaboration, and to ask how an engagement with music might function as a vehicle for connecting to communities outside of the university, and vice versa. To make this woman-centered conference welcoming to local families, we included a request for child care funds (which we have never been able to procure institutionally in the life of the project).

Importantly, one of the project's largest transformations from its original proposal has been a burgeoning focus on audio/video production, an inquiry motivated by Monica and Angelica's participation in the project. Before joining UW's feminist studies doctoral program, Monica was a radio producer and host with Soul Rebel Radio (SRR), a youth-focused radio collective airing at Pacifica Network's Los Angeles affiliate. She brought her radio production skills to WWR's first annual unConference and the first WWR course. Working with a team of undergraduates to collect and archive a series of WWR oral histories, she found the course's pedagogical praxis unique: she was able to apply first-hand the decolonial and women of color feminist theories she was learning in seminars to a collaborative, digitally-based project that also seriously valued her media production skills as a research method. Digital humanities appealed to her own hybrid praxis of theorizing and creating media.

Monica's entry into digital humanities was grounded in Chicana feminist theory and praxis; she recognized the ways that concepts from women of color feminism presaged digital humanities concepts (Anzaldúa 1987; Sandoval 2000). She revisited Gloria Anzaldúa with an ear tuned to digital humanities and experienced an "aha" moment. Within Anzaldúa's 1987 theorizing of mestiza consciousness, Monica recognized key phrases also circulating within digital humanities scholarship: "rigidity means death," "remaining flexible," and "inclusion rather than exclusion" are concepts prevalent in digital humanities vocabulary (79). For instance, much of *Debates in the Digital Humanities* and the Digital Humanities Manifesto 2.0 are imbued with Anzaldúa's language, particularly in the call for a digital humanities that "affirms the value of the open, the infinite, the expansive" (Manifesto 2009: 3). In March 2013, Monica attended a digital humanities workshop where the presenter described DH's potential as a space or underscore between digital and humanities as "white space." The irony of "white space" was not lost on Monica in this predominantly white audience. Once more, she realized how crucial it is for digital humanities to critically engage with race and other modalities of difference. In her praxis, these concepts and experiences bridge Chicana feminist theorizing with digital humanities, shaping her current approach to research, teaching, and media production as an assistant professor at Arizona State University.

Angelica also came into the project early on as a community-based filmmaker and media lecturer, supporting the project by teaching oral history production classes, organizing the annual Women Who Rock Film Festival, and leading efforts to use media to document WWR activities. After 2 years volunteering with the project, it was evident that her media work was making important scholarly contributions to feminist studies. She began her PhD to continue working on the praxis of feminist digital media and digital humanities, using the WWR project as a primary site for her intellectual inquiry.

These are examples of how graduate students—some of whom have since become faculty members—have shaped the project by bringing their skills and theoretical perspectives to the project. They are in line with the "stone soup" model of convivencia (Muth 2003). The stone soup model is about using what you have to bring people together to share what they have—to create something collectively that is unique, creative, and intellectual. The mini-doc "I Saw You on the Radio" is a good example of how people came together to create a beautiful WWR radio show for one afternoon in 2011 (DeCarlo & Macklin 2011). The people who showed up made it what it was: Barbie-Danielle DeCarlo provided the space, radio air time, and her radio activista host talents; the Seattle Fandango Project brought the tarima, jaranas, and some badass bailadora activistas; members of WWR brought stories and news about the upcoming unConference; and the whole event was documented and produced by Angelica, who brought her camera and media skills. Part of the fluidity of the WWR scene is that it changes as different people (students, activists, media-makers, artists, faculty, musicians, etc.) collaborate within the project. This model is challenging for people who are accustomed to corporate organizational models, including universities, that first create roles and then find people to fill them. With WWR, we first find people, who then create their own roles within the scene. The scene becomes what people make it.

Archivista Praxis and Convivencia: Building Community

In 2010–11, with a grant from the American Music Partnership of Seattle (AMPS), Michelle and Sonnet created a course—"Making a Scene: Girls and Boys Play Indie Rock"—for undergraduate and graduate students that investigated the politics of gender and performance in music scenes. In the process, we developed a multilevel approach to mentoring graduate and undergraduate students via oral history training. This course led to the creation of a digital archive that includes oral histories produced by our students and other collaborators with WWR. After meeting with librarians who manage UW Libraries Digital Initiatives, we began a partnership to archive the interviews. The oral histories are available in English and Spanish and include artists, musicians, activists, and scholars who focus on music as a tool for social justice and decolonial practices.

In these ongoing efforts, we are trying to build an archive not in the service of the state, but rather to catalyze emancipatory dialogues, alternative histories, and feminist futures. We aim to decolonize the archive by creating it through a collective process and archivista praxis, ensuring that it is freely accessible online at no cost and providing long-term preservation for artists and activists who are documenting their own scenes and have been excluded or pushed out from "official" archives. Scholar Emma Pérez's *The Decolonial Imaginary: Writing Chicanas into History* (1999) provides a method that reframes the past in order to imagine different presents that disrupt the idea of an inevitable colonial future. The WWR archive does not simply cast back retrospectively to tell a static story of scenes and movements past; it also documents scenes and movements as they unfold in the present. In assembling the archive, we have created our own scenes, our own fluid community of inquiry. This living archive both reflects and *generates* alternative communal and creative networks and genealogies. The archive's collection will continue to expand as we continue to conduct more oral histories, generate more programing, and create new media and scholarship in coming years.

Dialoging with scholar/artivista and WWR collective member Martha Gonzalez about the concept of artivista collectivity and convivencia, we were inspired. According to Gonzalez, artivista projects work to "create a sense of *convivencia*—literally 'coexistence,'" which is "a central aesthetic principle in community building" (2015). Artivistas fuse together artistic and activist practices within larger collective endeavors in order to build relationships and create community. Gonzalez clarifies that convivencia "is the deliberate act of being with each other, and of being present to each other," with the intent of countering effects of social alienation (2014: 69). Within WWR, convivencia intentionally builds the social infrastructure needed to carry out collective digital archiving. Riffing on the concept of the artivista, "archivistas" fuse archivist and activist practices to rethink the collective possibilities of the archive, deliberately employing the networked archive as a tool to document and create the conditions of possibility for social change. Here we use the term "networked" to highlight the human relationships that connect people and communities working on related projects with similar aims. As the field tries to enact decolonial humanities in the digital age, archivista praxis provides a method for moving forward within a network of relationships.

WWR is deeply immersed in digital archive design, content collection, production, and data management. Even though the UW Libraries preserve the oral histories, the oral history participants approve a preview of their histories and retain full right of its use. Given the archive's governing vision, its conditions of emergence, and the ethical protocols around its creation, use, and expansion, digital humanities scholars Alexis Lothian and Amanda Phillips recognize it as "one of the few well-established, institutionally supported DH projects that are rooted in critical feminist media theory and praxis" (2013: 9). They view WWR as a living model of collective and collaborative feminist-of-color critique, citing it as an example of digital humanities that creates new forms of community-based, politically engaged knowledge production that might "transform the academy itself" (2013: 9–10).

Convivencia through Production: Reel Rebels

Making scenes and building community is convivencia in action, and convivencia includes documenting scenes as they are unfolding. It also includes recording the life stories of people who make up these scenes so knowledge can be shared over time and space. The WWR Oral History Archive and other WWR media projects have all emerged from the desire to connect people who are simultaneously working toward social change. They also emerged from a desire to shift the way stories are told. We are moving from a DIY (do it yourself) mode to a DIWO (do it with others) mode. This has been one of the key intellectual questions we have focused on as feminist and cultural scholars. Recognizing that convivencia has emancipatory potential, WWR media producers have asked: how do we make the process of media-making one of convivencia?

WWR infuses convivencia in our *processes* of media production. Relationships lay the ground for community and ground our technical and theoretical methods. Building a digital archive is also a very hands-on technical project that requires engaging deeply with archivista media production practice. Here, when we say "practice," we mean "doing" digital work: filming oral histories, editing video-based mini-docs, photographing events, producing radio stories, teaching and learning digital media skills, facilitating and attending skill sharing workshops, designing websites and filling them with content, being present with media equipment at community dialogues and music performances, figuring out the navigational structure and searchability functions of the WWR oral history archive, and more. What makes the archivista digital media work of WWR different from mainstream media production are its decolonizing, feminist approaches to knowledge production. Many practitioners have written books on oral history, and there are even more books on conventional filmmaking and media production practices, but most of these texts lack critical reflection on the ways media and oral history curation practices have helped reproduce colonizing and traumatic effects on the communities they aim to represent. Dominant media production methods often take a masculinist, competitive, and militaristic approach to story-making, approaching it as a "business." WWR's approach is through convivencia and community-building, guided by feminist best practices, which include, but are not limited to: production timelines based on relationships and a DIWO ethic; goals based on the politics and agendas of participatory social movements; working in multiple languages spoken within transnational relationships; moving away from a media vocabulary infused with violent symbolism, such as "shooting," "capturing," "slave," "master tape," and "shotgun mics"; and an amateur aesthetic (amateur here meaning "for the love of"), which allows different entry-points for media production and fosters mentoring relationships among media-makers at different skill levels.

The process for documenting oral histories, using media technologies to document scenes, and building the archive has many steps and layers. Since the project's inception, it has been a high quality, amateur endeavor. Various people have contributed to building the archive in different ways, including students, artists, activists, organizers, scholars, journalists, and others. WWR contributors have filmed and edited oral histories with various technologies. Students have conducted oral histories for class assignments, as independent research, and for the love of making films. Some community-based scholars have donated oral history collections, while others have volunteered their time to interview people and transcribe their stories. Beyond the oral histories, media teams have documented each WWR unConference, produced related documentaries, filmed events and shows for musicians and community organizers, and produced short films based on people and themes in the archive. The WWR Annual Film Festival derives much of its content from these efforts, offering a space to showcase movies made in the spirit of Women Who Rock. The Oral History Archive holds oral histories with a range of musicians and activists who have significantly impacted their communities but have not been placed in conversation with one another, from musicians such as Nobuko Miyamoto, Medusa, Alice Bag, and Evelyn Harris to scholars such as Daphne Brooks, Rosa-Linda Fregoso, Tiffany Lopez, and Tara McPherson; from filmmakers such as Barni Qaasim and Sheila Jackson H. to activists such as Onion Carillo and Luzviminda (Lulu) Uzuri Carpenter.

A range of technological challenges arise in such an open-source, volunteer-driven project. We have worked to create an intake system for such a large amount of media and manage our files by ensuring media consistency (for example, file types and codecs). This has involved organizing the material related to each oral history, tracking who filmed what, editing the interview, and building in a review process for interviewee sign off. There are many other questions, both technical and theoretical, that have emerged from our praxis of making WWR-related media. Through a feminist lens, WWR media-makers explore issues of composition, technical quality, interview method, control, access, criteria, purpose, and allyship in supporting community-building.

The WWR oral history archive was built in part to be a resource for students and university-based researchers; but, equally important, it was built to be accessible to community-based activists and cultural producers with social justice commitments. As a feminist archivista project, the archive and its media components must support and align with on-the-ground social justice cultural work. When its contents are used in university research, the intention is to support pedagogies of restorative justice and decolonizing scholarship that impact uneven social structures in society. The archive can also serve as an important resource for community-based activists and artists. Many activists and artists are documenting their own scenes, but do not necessarily have access to long-term preservation. Examples include the Seattle chapter of 206 Zulu's archive, which is dispersed among different people in their homes; Alice Bag's website, which features her archival collection; and Gretta Harley's archive of oral histories of women in Seattle music scenes in the 1990s, also stored on a personal hard drive. One of the benefits of having an archive housed in a public university is the ability to preserve and access knowledge over a much longer trajectory. WWR is therefore creating special collections in the archive that have been produced by activists and artists themselves, such as Gretta Harley's collection. Harley assembled these histories for her play *These Streets: A Rock 'n' Story* (2013) and requested that WWR preserve them. Media from the Chicas Rockeras of Southeast Los Angeles' Girls Rock Camp (2015) will also go in the WWR special collections. A Chica Rockera volunteered to prepare the media's metadata to gain experience before she applied to graduate programs in Information Sciences. The project has therefore become an important site for mentoring and sharing archival and media-making skills between various artist, activist, and academic communities. Our formally and informally facilitated community-based workshops, many of which take place at the WWR annual unConference, are intended to build capacity and broaden our network of people who are documenting scenes with media technologies. In turn, many people share their media with WWR, expanding the archive and using their media skills to grow communities and make even louder scenes.

Mentoring and Pedagogy: Write to Rock

Our project is unique for its integral commitment to collective doctoral mentoring and graduate and undergraduate pedagogy centered around digital humanities and the archive. Tara McPherson explains how WWR animates "an active mentorship network," where the archive is the basis for an experiment in collective mentoring (2013). For 5 years, we have run a WWR Graduate Mentor Workshop, which hosts scholars-in-residence, including established journalists, professional filmmakers and artists, and academics (from California State University, Cornell University, University of Kansas, The New School, Princeton, University of California, University of Southern California, and Yale) who are leaders in the fields of African American Studies, digital humanities, Chicano/Latino Studies, Indigenous Studies, popular music studies, feminist performance studies, and new media studies. Each scholar-in-residence provides individual feedback to at least 10 doctoral students who are housed in departments such as Communication; Comparative Literature; English; Gender, Women & Sexuality Studies; the UW Information School; the School of Music; and the School of Social Work. The workshops provide an all-too-rare space for mentoring students, many of them women of color, whose research is not always legible within their own disciplines. We support them intellectually and emotionally by working with them to present their work effectively, modeling for them how to link community engagement with research and bringing them into crucial scholarly networks. Our scholars-in-residence stay connected to their mentees in subsequent workshops and in more informal ways as well, through conferences, publications, and programs. Resonating with the way Anne Balsamo describes FemTechNet as an animated network, the WWR "animates nodes that already exist . . . bringing them into connection with each other" (2015).

Part of the urgency of WWR is the need for institutional change with regard to diversity at the University of Washington: "as of autumn 2008, the UW had the third smallest proportion of minority graduate students among our peer institutions" (Aisenberg 2013: 3). Our model successfully mentors underrepresented students, particularly women and women of color at the doctoral level. Our mentees have received highly competitive local and national awards for research, such as the McNair Scholarship, the Mary Gates Research Award, the Ford Foundation Fellowship, the Point Foundation Scholarship, and Pride Award, awards for completed dissertations such as UW's Arts & Sciences Graduate Medal, as well as appointments to postdoctoral fellowships and tenure-track faculty positions.

We use this pedagogy with our undergraduate students as well, teaching them archivista praxis as they pursue popular music studies by way of the WWR archive. In 2013, Michelle, Sonnet, and Angelica co-taught an undergraduate/graduate seminar called "Rock the Archive: Popular Music Studies and Digital Scholarship" that examined popular music studies in relation to the theory, practice, and politics of archive-building, oral history training, and digital scholarship. The class has since been transformed into a large, interactive lecture course. Propelled by a long-standing practice of emancipatory pedagogy informed by women of color feminist thought that believes "we can transform our world, by imagining it differently" (Anzaldúa 2015: 313), we have found that collaborative teaching is most effective. We each bring different strengths in terms of our training in theory, practice, and production. We have devised ways to work collaboratively but also to divide the labor of the class equitably.

After years of working together, we each lead sections of the class but often riff with each other in our class discussions. We try to model the collaborative feminist spirit that we ask our students to enact in their group projects that engage with the archive. If our teaching is a form of convivencia in the classroom and beyond, we ask our students to engage in convivencia as they work in groups with defined roles throughout the term, pursuing projects in digital humanities using archivista praxis. In a series of assignments, our students produce oral histories and other forms of media for the WWR Oral History Archive. In turn, they draw upon the archive as a credible source by which to edit existing Wikipedia entries and add new Wiki entries that help construct an alternative account of popular music focused on the women of color so often left out of the official history, a historiography mindful of social relations, power, and the politics of attribution.

Conclusion: (In)Tensions

Pushing against conventional practices within the institution is not easy, yet it is utterly necessary if epistemological innovation based in women of color feminist theorizing is to exist within its walls. It is exciting and stressful work. This project's emergence without external funding has remained a double-edged sword. We implemented it as "collaboratory," patching together small amounts of seed funding. This loose and limited funding structure allowed us the freedom to experiment without having to fulfill tightly defined outcomes. But it also created uncertainty about our roles and responsibilities: we made the path as we were walking on it. On occasion, faculty and graduate students were doing "double" work, not only fulfilling everyday university requirements with regard to teaching, research, and service, but also trying to build an institutionally supported digital archive from the ground up, develop archivista digital media production processes, teach new courses that included original digital media assignments, and undertake serious community-based feminist organizing that took up many, many hours and weekends. WWR does not replace conventional faculty responsibilities but constitutes the kind of "innovative overtime" that Lisa Disch and Jean O'Brien ascribe to "politically committed academic labor" (2007: 142). It is "a subsidy—ethical not financial—that funds programs that are necessary to the university's public mission but that do not materially enhance its profit margins" (Disch & O'Brien 2007: 142). As is surely familiar to anyone who has stumbled into a digital humanities project, grossly underestimating the time and labor that any facet of the project will require is part of its steep learning curve.

As with many digital humanities projects, it has also been unclear from the start how the institution would recognize our efforts as research. This project has been a risk for associate faculty in terms of promotion and a risk for graduate students who are entering job markets still unfamiliar with these new modes of scholarship. As faculty trying to create conditions of success for graduate students, Michelle and Sonnet consciously frame the ground-setting digital scholarship of Monica, Angelica, Christa Bell, Carrie Lanza, Martha Gonzalez, Elizabeth Ramirez, Rinna Rem, Nicole Robert, Noralis Rodriguez, Iris Viveros, and other WWR graduates and alumnae as research with profound intellectual stakes.

Other tensions stem from the institutional hierarchies of knowledge production and uneven structural power dynamics between faculty, students, and community-based cultural producers. WWR consciously works against these hierarchies by centering convivencia and collective knowledge production and understanding these efforts as a feminist women of color spatial practice. Driven by our desire to shift ways of doing academic work, WWR is about creating spaces, even if temporary, where people can wage joy and participate in social and epistemological transformation. It is about creating a praxis that includes convivencia in many spaces, not just the university. Riffing on bell hooks, Mako Fitts writes:

> [B]olstering feminist activism . . . can only be done when we are in community with grassroots activists and community organizers, with the people committed to forming transformative political coalitions and engaging projects for social change.
> (Fitts 2011: 113)

Chandra Talpade Mohanty defines solidarity as "mutuality, accountability, and the recognition of common interests as the basis for relationships among diverse communities" (2003: 7). As allies in multiple music and social justice scenes, we are committed to being part of these scenes. This means participating in organizing activities, volunteering for events, being in critical dialog with other organizers and activists, supporting individuals and groups of artists, going to shows, helping promote activities in these scenes, making room for people to showcase their work at WWR events, contributing ideas, leveraging resources, and working with communities to produce new possibilities.

Working in community, we inevitably confront familiar tensions documented by many feminists. We are committed to working through tensions as part of our convivencia archivista process. Faculty, graduate students, and community-based organizers recognize that, through this intense and imperfect collaboration, the collective brings something powerful into being that would not otherwise exist. As Tara McPherson observes, our intent is to "situate technology within social human networks rather than try to situate humans within technological networks" (2013). Making scenes and building a community is not always smooth or easy, and neither is trying to work against the grain of institutional hierarchies. WWR is a collection of committed people who are trying to figure out how to do both.

Acknowledgments

We are grateful to the University of Washington's Walter Chapin Simpson Center's Digital Humanities Summer Fellowship for support in preparing the oral histories for the UW Libraries. The authors thank the UW Simpson Center for sponsoring our training at the 2013 Digital Humanities Summer Institute at the University of Victoria, as well as supporting a retreat at The Helen Riaboff Whiteley Center to support this writing. We also thank the UW Libraries' Digital Initiative for working with us to create the pilot archive. We humbly thank all who have been involved at each stage of this collaboration.

Further Reading

Benmayor, R. (2008) "Digital Storytelling as a Signature Pedagogy for the New Humanities," *Arts and Humanities in Higher Education* 7(2), 188–204.

Everett, A. (2009) *Digital Diaspora: A Race for Cyberspace*, Albany, NY: SUNY Press.

Gonzalez, M. (2015) "Sobreviviendo: Immigration Stories and Testimonio in Song," *Diálogo* 18(2), 7–20.

Juhasz, A. and A. Balsamo (2012) "An Idea Whose Time is Here: FemTechNet—A Distributed Online Collaborative Course (DOCC)," *Ada: A Journal of Gender, New Media and Technology* 1, retrieved from adanewmedia.org/2012/11/issue1-juhasz.

Lothian, A. and A. Phillips (2013) "Can Digital Humanities Mean Transformative Critique?" *Journal of e-Media Studies* 3(1), 1–25.

McPherson, T. (2009) "Introduction: Media Studies and the Digital Humanities," *Cinema Journal* 48(2), 119–23.

Nakamura, L. (2015) "The Unwanted Labour of Social Media: Women of Color Call Out Culture as Venture Community Management," *New Formations: A Journal of Culture/Theory/Politics* 86, 106–12.

Todd, L. (1996) "Aboriginal Narratives in Cyberspace," in A. M. Moser and D. McLeod (eds.) *Immersed in Technology*, Cambridge, MA: MIT Press, pp. 179–94.

References

Aisenberg, G. (2013) "The Imperative of Diversity: Our Responsibility," in *2013 Diversity Report Follow-Up*, retrieved from grad.uw.edu/wordpress/wp-content/uploads/diversity-report-followup-2013.pdf.

Anzaldúa, G. (1987) *Borderlands/La Frontera: The New Mestiza*, San Francisco: Aunt Lute Books.

Anzaldúa, G. (2015) *Light in the Dark/Luz en lo Escuro: Rewriting Identity, Spirituality, Reality*, Durham, NC: Duke University Press.

Balsamo, A. (2015) "Women Who Rock Oral History Interview," *Women Who Rock Oral History Archive*, University of Washington, forthcoming.

Benmayor, R. (2008) "Digital Storytelling as a Signature Pedagogy for the New Humanities," *Arts and Humanities in Higher Education* 7(2), 188–204.

Benmayor, R. (2012) "Digital Testimonio as a Signature Pedagogy for Latin@ Studies," in *Equity and Excellence in Education* 45(3), 507–24.

Boyd, N. A. and H. N. Roque Ramírez (2012) *Bodies of Evidence: The Practice of Queer Oral History*, New York, NY: Oxford University Press.

Christian, B. (1989) "But What Do We Think We're Doing Anyway: The State of Black Feminist Criticism(s) or My Version of a Little Bit of History," in C. Wall (ed.) *Changing Our Own Words: Essays on Criticism, Theory, and Writing by Black Women*, New Brunswick, NJ: Rutgers University Press.

DeCarlo, B. and A. Macklin (2011) "I Saw You On The Radio," retrieved from vimeo.com/24484214.

Disch, L. and J. M. O'Brien (2007) "Innovation is Overtime: An Ethical Analysis of 'Politically Committed' Academic Labor," in K. A. Hokulani, K.A. Erickson, and J. L. Pierce (eds.) *Feminist Waves, Feminist Generations: Life Stories from the Academy*, Minneapolis, MN: University of Minnesota Press, pp. 140–68.

Fitts, M. (2011) "Theorizing Transformative Revolutionary Action: The Contribution of bell hooks to Emancipatory Knowledge Production," *The CLR James Journal* 17(1), 112–32.

Flores, Q. (2013) "Women Who Rock Oral History Interview," *Women Who Rock Oral History Archive*, University of Washington.

Gonzalez, M. (2014) "Mixing in the Kitchen: Entre Mujeres ("Among Women") Translocal Musical Dialogues," in A. E. Kinser, K. Freehling-Burton, and T. Hawkes (eds.) *Performing Motherhood: Artistic, Activist, and Everyday Enactments*, Ontario: Demeter Press, pp. 69–87.

Gonzalez, M. (2015) *Convivencia*, email.

Gonzalez, M. (2015) "Sobreviviendo: Immigration Stories and Testimonio in Song," *Diálogo* 18(2), 7–20.

Hong, G. K. (2008) "The Future of Our Worlds: Black Feminism and the Politics of Knowledge in the University under Globalization," in *Meridians: Feminism, Race, Transnationalism* 8(2), 95–115.

King, K. (2001) "Productive Agencies of Feminist Theory: The Work It Does," *Feminist Theory* 2(1), 94–98.

Lothian, A. and A. Phillips (2013) "Can Digital Humanities Mean Transformative Critique?" *Journal of e-Media Studies* 3(1), 1–25.

Manifesto 2009 (2009) "The Digital Humanities Manifesto 2.0," retrieved from www.humanitiesblast.com/manifesto/Manifesto_V2.pdf.

McPherson, T. (2013) "Women Who Rock Oral History Interview," *Women Who Rock Oral History Archive*, University of Washington.

Mohanty, C. T. (2003) *Feminism Without Borders: Decolonizing Theory, Practicing Solidarity*, Durham, NC: Duke University Press, pp. 7.

Muth, J. J. (2003) *Stone Soup*, New York: Scholastic Press.

Pérez, E. (1999) *The Decolonial Imaginary: Writing Chicanas into History*, Bloomington: Indiana University Press.

Sandoval, C. (2000) *Methodology of the Oppressed*, Minneapolis, MN: University of Minnesota.

Seattle Fandango Project (n.d.) "About Us / Quiénes Somos," retrieved from www.seattlefandangoproject.org/p/about-us-quienes-somos.html.

Taylor, D. (2003) *The Archive and the Repertoire: Performing Cultural Memory in the Americas*, Durham, NC: Duke University Press.

Todd, L. (1996) "Aboriginal Narratives in Cyberspace," in A. M. Moser and D. McLeod (eds.) *Immersed in Technology*, Cambridge, MN: MIT Press, pp. 179–94.

7

DECOLONIZING THE DIGITAL HUMANITIES IN THEORY AND PRACTICE

Roopika Risam

In recent years, the question of what it means to "decolonize" digital humanities has been broached by scholars engaged in both postcolonial digital humanities and #TransformDH, strands of the field that have pushed for greater attention to digital humanities projects and methods that foreground intersectional engagement with race, gender, class, sexuality, nation, disability, and other axes of identity that shape knowledge production. Such approaches to digital humanities have asked how to decolonize the archive (Povinelli 2011; Lothian & Phillips 2013; Cushman 2013; cárdenas et al. 2015; Risam 2015), address gaps in knowledge produced online (Lor and Britz 2005; Sheppard 2005; Koh & Risam 2013), make legible narratives and histories that have gone untold (Rawson 2014; Thorat 2015; Verhoeven 2015), understand the specificities of digital Dalit experience (Nayar 2011), locate the subaltern in cyberspace (Gajjala 2013), or use technologies to push back against existing forms of representation that may be troubling (Sanders 2014; Priego & Gil 2013; Olsen 2014). Taking a look at the theoretical basis of such work in both postcolonial and science and technology studies (STS), this chapter situates the stakes for decolonization within digital humanities, locating a historical scholarly genealogy for this work and outlining what work toward decolonization looks like in practice within digital humanities.

Situating Decolonization in Digital Humanities

Frantz Fanon, the pre-eminent Martiniquan theorist of the colonial condition, offers a comprehensive definition of decolonization in *The Wretched of the Earth*:

> Decolonization, which sets out to change the order of the world, is, obviously, a program of complete disorder. But it cannot come as a result of magical practices, nor of a natural shock, nor of a friendly understanding. Decolonization, as we know, is a historical process: that is to say it cannot be understood, it cannot become intelligible nor clear to itself except in the exact measure that we can discern the movements which give it historical form and content.
>
> (Fanon 1963: 36)

As Fanon notes, decolonization is best understood not as a temporal event but as a process. Moreover, it is a process that can only be understood through study of the intellectual, historical, and political dimensions that constitute it. It is here that digital humanities is best poised to intervene: in the affordances of digital technologies that help make decolonization legible and reveal its limits.

Fanon argues that decolonization is necessarily a violent process—violence was a tool of colonial projects, so the master's tools will dismantle the master's house. For Fanon, the violence takes physical and figurative forms—the violence engaged by the colonizer against colonial uprisings, armed struggle, the epistemic violence of colonialism, and the violent process of its undoing. In the case of digital humanities, such violence appears in discursive forms. These include reproducing colonial influences in the production of digital knowledge and centering epistemologies and ontologies of the Global North, namely the U.S. and western Europe, which in turn decenters those of Indigenous communities and the Global South. Fanon is a key figure here because his analysis is located in the dynamic between the colonizer and the colonized, between the settler and the native. This is not to say that invoking decolonization is only speaking to the political fact of colonization. On the contrary, it encompasses epistemological dimensions because the political realities of colonization are interdependent with displacement of Indigenous epistemologies and ontologies. The existence of colonization relies on not only ongoing occupation of land but also occupation of regimes of knowledge erected to maintain and legitimate such occupation.

As Kenyan writer Ngugi wa' Thiong'o (1986) argues, it is not only the colony that needs to be decolonized but also the mind of the colonized. This is a result of the way colonialism entails erasure of knowledge, belief, ways of being, and archives. It requires instantiation of structures like law, citizenship, and nationality that locate the colonizer at its center. Moreover, colonialism is not circumscribed by its temporal limits. Neo-colonialism—the control of a formerly colonized state from the outside via the operations of capitalism—demonstrates how legacies of colonialism persist after decolonization. This phenomenon manifests through globalization, cultural imperialism, foreign aid, and investment by multinational corporations.

Yet, the ways decolonization is often invoked in the context of digital humanities may do violence of their own. They risk becoming empty metaphors without specificity, equating decolonization with the need for diversity in the field. In doing so, they miss the opportunity to articulate the practices necessary for challenging the discursive violence of colonialism in digital knowledge production. This equating of diversity with decolonization is part of a trend within antiracist and other identitarian social justice movements, in which decolonization comes to signify a struggle for identity and recognition in the absence of a colonial condition. Eve Tuck and K. Wayne Yang (2012) have argued that invoking decolonization solely as a metaphor undermines the real possibility of decolonization for those whose lives are, in fact, determined by colonialism. Purely metaphorical invocations of colonization are a form of appropriation that decenters ongoing struggles for freedom of Indigenous people by recentering whiteness, even when decolonization is being invoked in favor of antiracist or other social justice-oriented movements (Tuck & Yang 2012). When we speak of social justice, it is often in favor of the liberation of oppressed people, of a drive for equity and representation in spaces where they have been disallowed. Yet, decolonization in digital humanities cannot be a simple articulation of the perceived exclusions of the field along lines of race, gender, class, ability, nation, or other axes of privilege and oppression. Such calls promote an "add and stir" approach that suggests the mere addition of "diverse" bodies will transform the practices of digital humanities (Bailey 2011). Instead, the move to decolonize digital humanities requires redress of the traces of colonialism that appear in digital scholarship, which has political and epistemological implications. While digital humanities offers tremendous potential for democratizing scholarly knowledge, such possibilities are undercut by projects that recreate colonial dynamics or reinforce the Global North as the site of knowledge production.

While many calls for the decolonization of digital humanities have articulated metaphors for dismantling the operations of power that undergird the production of knowledge in the field—the gatekeepers, reviewers, and definitions that delimit the boundaries of digital humanities—such calls efface the violence of colonialism and the violence of decolonization. Therefore, I am suggesting that—when invoking the relationship between decolonization and digital humanities—the central question is not how digital humanities itself could be decolonized but how digital humanities has contributed to the epistemic violence of colonialism and neo-colonialism. This is evident in both its implication in colonial forms of knowledge production and the ways digital humanities has contributed to historical processes of decolonization. Its further possibilities lie in resisting neo-colonialism in projects and tools.

In the context of digital humanities, we find cognates for these questions in postcolonial approaches to technology developed within STS. Sandra Harding's work, for example, has pioneered the field of postcolonial STS (Harding 1998; 2009). Among the achievements of postcolonial STS are the investigation of alternate genealogies for developments in Western science and technology as well as the drafting of counter-histories that write back to dominant narratives (Anderson 2002; Abraham 2006); recovery and development of a critical apparatus around Indigenous forms of knowledge that have historically been displaced or appropriated by Western systems of knowledge (Abraham 2005; Scott 2011); study of the postindependence legacies of colonialism on science and technology and the effects of neo-colonialism (Adas 1997; Ahmed & Stein 2004); and investigation of the conditions of global capital and politics that influence technology development within the West (Khaifan & Gough 2002; Aneesh 2006; Coe & Hess 2013; Amrute 2016).

Building on the work of Harding and others in postcolonial STS, Kavita Philip, Lily Irani, and Paul Dourish (2010) argue for postcolonial computing as a tactic for engaging with technoscience. Rooted in their critiques of the fraught universals proffered within scholarship on human-computer interactions for development, they make the case for attention to the ways that colonial technologies and ways of knowing influence design of computing technology (2010). Postcolonial computing is "a bag of tools that affords us contingent tactics for continual, careful, collective, and always partial reinscriptions of a cultural-technical situation in which we all find ourselves" (2010: 3). It engenders questions of technology and translation, mobility, labor, and infrastructure and how they manifest across cultural contexts.

Syed Mustafa Ali (2014) has proposed that "decolonial computing" is a more appropriate framework. Grounded in Charles Mills' critique of social contract theory, which argues that white supremacy subtends Mills' notion of the "racial contract," Ali draws on the decolonial theories that emerge from Latin American studies, particularly Walter Mignolo's work. The theories that emerge from postcolonial thought, Ali (2014) argues, are encumbered by the limitations of postcolonial theory, namely insufficient attention to materialist concerns and the Eurocentrism of its philosophical underpinnings. He proposes that decolonial computing reinstantiates the centrality of systemic racial equalities to these approaches to technology.

Drawing on postcolonial STS, the relationship between decolonization and digital humanities rests on the understanding that humanities-based knowledge production—whether in history, art, literature, or culture, more broadly—has historically been wielded as a technology of colonialism, as important as the technologies of the slave ship and the gun. Therefore, the question at the heart of decolonization and digital humanities is how we can use technologies to undo the technologies of colonialism. Unlike Fanon's position on the master's tools, Audre Lorde argues, "[t]he master's tools will not dismantle the master's house" (Lorde 1983). Together, the two contradictory statements support the need for the creation of new methods, tools, projects, and platforms to undo the epistemic violence of colonialism and fully realize a decolonized digital humanities. Such inquiry takes many shapes: attending to gaps within archives by interrogating existing ones and building new ones, considering how Indigenous forms of knowledge may be engaged to develop new tools, and seeking the transformative possibilities of technology without ceding to techno-utopianism.

Toward Decolonization and Digital Humanities

At stake in the possibilities for decolonization and digital humanities is the question of the relationship between theory and practice. At key points in the development of the meta-discourse that surrounds digital humanities, the two have been variously pitted against each other, seen as complementary, and described as interdependent. This conversation has taken shape through a number of themes, from the relationship between "hack" (or doing) and "yack" (or talking) (Nowviskie 2014) to the role of tacit knowledge—derived from the act of doing—as a source of theory (Scheinfeldt 2010; Turkel & Elliott 2014; Rockwell 2011; Nowviskie 2012) to the implied theory that informs the development of projects and tools (Bauer 2011). Decolonization in the context of digital humanities is not simply a matter of theory or practice but rather a combination that reiterates that any binary between the two is false. They are both essential and reminiscent of Fanon's reflection on decolonization: "If we want humanity to advance a step farther, if we want to bring it up to a different level than that which Europe has shown it, then we must invent and we must make discoveries" (1963: 255). As such, what I offer here is a look at scholarship and projects that invent and discover the theoretical and practical dimensions—or praxis—of decolonization and digital humanities.

First, the stakes of digital humanities—and therefore of decolonization in digital humanities—can only be understood in their local context. Definitions of digital humanities can only be forged by centering the local and displacing the global. Local differences in practices may be best understood through the framework of "accents"—united in a larger system but unique at the level of the local (Risam 2016). Emphasis on the local has been reiterated through the advocacy of Global Outlook::Digital Humanities, a special interest group of the Alliance of Digital Humanities Organizations, which endeavors to break down barriers to international cooperation within digital humanities writ large. Such work emphasizes the situated nature of knowledge (Haraway 1988). Embracing the process of decolonization and the contributions that digital humanities could make requires beginning with the local, the situated, which we find at the level of practice.

Among scholarly conversations that negotiate the local and the global in the contexts of decolonization, postcolonial studies has been prolific. The discursive dimensions of decolonization are readily legible to those familiar with postcolonial theory: European knowledge production has historically been complicit in colonial projects. As Albert Memmi, Edward Said, and Homi Bhabha among others have argued, these products of Europe have played a significant role in the construction of the relationship between the colonizer and the colonized, enforcing the superiority of Europe in relation to its uncivilized Other (Memmi 1965; Said 1978; Bhabha 1991). Yet, there are limits to this approach, as Ali's theory of decolonial computing suggests. One of the major critiques of postcolonial theory, which Ali echoes, is the tendency of its poststructuralist strand to privilege the power of discursive operations over materialist histories of colonialism (Ahmad 1992; Chibber 2013). Another critique, particularly from scholars in Latin American studies, is that postcolonial studies privileges the operations of British imperialism and extrapolates them for colonialism writ large (Mignolo 1993). Moreover, as Ali and others argue, postcolonial studies derives from continental European philosophy—not the local concerns of the people it purports to represent (Chibber 2013). Nevertheless, the tendency of postcolonial studies toward self-critique and its insistence on foregrounding the particular over the universal—that is to say, the local over the global—keeps alive the possibility of using it in spite of its British or Euro-centric framing; the act of contesting its possibilities for critique are themselves productive and perhaps even transformative.

Yet, a keener look reminds us of the multiplicity of the local beyond dominant national narratives and culture. The U.S., for example, continues to practice settler colonialism. Therefore, decolonization in the U.S. context requires not only the epistemological independence that wa' Thiong'o (1986) describes but also political independence for colonized Native American nations and tribes. The issue of where Indigenous communities fit within the context of decolonization is a critical one when engaging postcolonial theory in a U.S. context, which has analogues for Indigenous Australians as well as First Nations, Inuit, and Métis peoples in Canada. These national contexts require further exploration of the ways settler colonialism has shaped other nonwhite identities. In the case of the U.S., this requires clearing space for Latinx contributions, documenting African American culture, or pushing back against notions of the Asian model minority.

At stake here is how the definition of "American" has expanded and contracted, granting some the right to the putatively democratic space of the nation but foreclosing it for others. By acknowledging the relationship between settler colonialism and racial politics, we attend to the ways variously other communities have been assimilated into the definition of "whiteness" and those for whom such inclusion is impossible. Moreover, we recognize the historical and ongoing processes of racialization that have sanctioned settler colonialism, authorized Jim Crow, encouraged Islamophobia, and continue to determine immigration policies. In countries ostensibly removed from their histories of colonization, addressing decolonization means acknowledging ongoing legacies of colonialism at the local level. For example, in the United Kingdom this entails attention to postcolonial migrants and their narratives of origin and destination as well as to the effects of state-sanctioned multiculturalism as an ongoing strategy of ambiguity intended to distance the operations of colonialism from the present. These are important issues for digital humanities scholarship to consider in the context of decolonization, and they have been raised by Paul Barrett, who questions the limits of the nation as an analytical category given its implication in state institutions that provide funding (Barrett 2014). Emphasis on the local—a directive of postcolonial studies—demands acknowledgment that there is not a single world or way of being within the world but rather a proliferation of worlds, traditions, and forms of knowledge. These multiplicities only constitute a global dimension insofar as the global is itself diverse and only understood through local particularities.

Where, then, do we find evidence of the intellectual moves within digital humanities that locate decolonization at their center when produced or administered within the Global North? Emerging from Indigenous studies, a number of projects have sought to center Indigenous forms of knowledge and community need in their practice. The Mukurtu Content Management System was developed as a free, open source platform built *with* Indigenous communities to support the development of digital cultural heritage (Mukurtu n.d.).

The project began in response to needs of the Warumungu Aboriginal community in collaboration with Kim Christen and Craig Dietrich. The platform itself enables greater granular control over content than previously existing content management systems, allowing Indigenous communities to exercise cultural protocols for what should be shared and with whom. The idea that information wants to be free has been an influential one in digital humanities, privileging open access to knowledge. Yet, this approach to knowledge is grounded in epistemologies of the Global North. Presuming that freedom of information is a global phenomenon elides the cultural practices of Indigenous communities and the Global South, which often have their own cultural protocols for knowledge transmission. Unlike other content management systems for digital cultural heritage, Mukurtu enables multiple levels of access and privacy to allow communities control over the visibility of objects and artifacts. As such, it marks an important move in decolonizing digital knowledge production because it embeds Indigenous epistemology into its design.

From the perspective of Chicana studies, Chicana por mi Raza: Uncovering the Hidden History of Chicana Feminism (1965–1985), directed by María Cotera and Linda Garcia Merchant, is a digital humanities project intended to preserve the history of Chicana feminist movements in North America (Cotera & Merchant n.d.). The project was developed in collaboration with the Institute for Computing in Humanities, Arts and Social Sciences (I-CHASS) at the University of Illinois at Urbana Champaign and is financially supported by the University of Michigan. Despite its institutional moorings, the project is only possible because of the contributions of Chicana women represented in the archive who agreed to be interviewed and to share their personal artifacts from their work as feminist activists. As with many grassroots activist movements, the archives of Chicana feminists are decentralized, often held among the personal effects of the movement's participants. This decentralization poses a barrier to making the archive—and, indeed, the history of Chicana feminist activism—legible for not only historians but also the public. This project represents a community whose activism and engagement in civil rights has long gone unnoticed in historical narratives within the U.S. As a result, the project collects oral histories, posters, correspondence, and other ephemera, with the goal of providing public access to them. By making this unseen history legible, the project participates in decolonizing national narratives of activism by Chicana feminists.

Scholar, artist, and theorist micha cárdenas's work, which focuses on trans of color movements in digital media, is situated in a commitment to decolonization as well. One key example is her work on the Transborder Immigrant Tool, which she created as part of the Electronic Disturbance Theater (2007). The project repurposes obsolete cellular phone technology to create guidance tools for immigrants crossing the Mexico–U.S. border; these phones direct immigrants to water stations along their journey while also providing them with poetry. The poetry offers not only an aesthetic experience but also survival advice encoded within the poetry. cárdenas's commitments to exploring conditions of the border are also evident in her Scalar game, *Redshift & Portalmetal* (cárdenas 2014). The premise of the game, which combines principles of hypertext with performance, poetry, and film, is that humans have been forced to look beyond the earth for new places to live because of climate change (2014). Through the game, players must consider how dynamics of colonization shape such movement. As players settle on other planets, the game asks them to consider the relationship between space travel and colonization. As settlers, they must further envision new sets of practices that resist settler colonialism. cárdenas's game offers an interactive, online multimedia environment in which players experiment with creating practices of decolonization.

Finally, *Around Digital Humanities in 80 Days*, edited by Alex Gil, demonstrates a strategy of writing back to dominant narratives—in this case, dominant narratives of digital humanities—that privilege the U.S., Canada, and the U.K. in their approach to knowledge production. The project began with Gil's habit of sending emails describing digital humanities projects around the world and grew into an 80-day series of posts written by Gil and a team of editors. Open and public-facing in design, the original list from which editors selected entries was crowd-sourced, and the diversity of posts intends to foreground the range of what constitutes digital humanities praxis around the world. The resulting map depicting 80 days' worth of locations offers a challenge to center-based models and maps of digital humanities that depict the U.S. and U.K.—and, to a lesser extent, Canada—as the hotspots of digital humanities around the world. Moreover, the platform itself was built on minimal computing principles and, through its use of the Jekyll platform, is intended to provide quick load times even in low bandwidth environments, making it easily accessible around the world.

What I have offered here is a small sample of the variety of projects that, in their design *and* content, use digital cultural heritage, games, performance art, and mapping in service of decolonization for Indigenous communities, immigrant histories, and the landscape of digital humanities itself. These projects share a commitment to foregrounding that which has traditionally been relegated to the position of subaltern in dominant narratives. They resist hierarchies of knowledge that have emerged from the history and legacies of colonialism, positioning Indigenous, immigrant, and Global South knowledges at their center. Such examples avail themselves to the transformative possibilities of technology while calling attention to the ways that they resist easy answers or simple solutions to the ongoing effects of colonialism and neo-colonialism on the production of knowledge. They embrace the hybridity, plurality, contradiction, and tension that are necessary strategies of decolonization. Innovative and experimental, they are culturally located and make a contribution to our understanding of the global dimensions of digital humanities through intervention at the local level. And, at their heart, they situate the relationship between technology and the human, emphasizing how what it means to be human exists independently from neither the history and legacy of colonialism nor the technologies that made colonialism possible. As a result, the possibilities for decolonization in the scholarly contributions of digital humanities lie in continued resistance, appropriation, and theorization of the relationship between colonialism, technology, and the human.

Acknowledgments

I gratefully acknowledge Jentery Sayers for his editorial care with this chapter. This essay was also strongly influenced by the HILT 2015 course, "De/Post/Colonial Digital Humanities." Many thanks to micha cárdenas, my co-instructor; course participants, Jeremy Boggs, Ashley Bycock, Vinamarata Kaur, Joan Lubin, Emily Sessions, Danica Savonick, and Sveta Stoytcheva; and HILT directors, Jennifer Guiliano and Trevor Muñoz.

Further Reading

Fiormonte, D. (2015) "Towards Monocultural (Digital) Humanities?" *Infolet*, retrieved from infolet.it/2015/07/12/monocultural-humanities.

Galina, I. (2014) "Geographical and Linguistic Diversity in the Digital Humanities," *Literary and Linguistic Computing* 29(3), 307–16.

Gil, A. and É. Ortega (2016) "Global Outlooks in Digital Humanities: Multilingual Practices and Minimal Computing," in C. Crompton, R. J. Lane, and R. Siemens (eds.) *Doing Digital Humanities: Practice, Training, Research*, NY: Routledge, 2016.

O'Donnell, D. P., K. L. Walter, A. Gil, and N. Fraistat (2016) "Only Connect: the Globalization of the Digital Humanities," in S. Schreibman, R. Siemens, and J. Unsworth (eds). *A New Companion to Digital Humanities.* Malden, MA: Wiley, pp. 493–510.

Svensson, P. and D. T. Goldberg (eds.) (2015) *Between Humanities and the Digital*, Cambridge, MA: MIT Press.

References

Abraham, I. (2005) "The Contradictory Spaces of Postcolonial Technoscience," *Economic and Political Weekly* 41(3), 210–17.

Abraham, I. (2006) "The State of Native Americans," *Economic and Political Weekly* 40(25), 3789.

Adas, M. (1997) "Colonialism and Science," in H. Selin (ed.) *Encyclopedia of the History of Non-Western Science, Technology, and Medicine*, Dordrecht: Kluwer, pp. 214–20.

Ahmad, A. (1992) *In Theory: Nations, Classes, Literatures*, NY: Verso.

Ahmed, A. and J. A. Stein (2004) "Science, Technology and Sustainable Development: A World Review," *World Review of Science, Technology and Sustainable Development* 1(1), 5–24.

Ali, S. M. (2014) "Towards a Decolonial Computing," retrieved from www.academia.edu/6524133/Towards_a_Decolonial_Computing.

Amrute, S. (2016) *Encoding Race, Encoding Class: Indian IT Workers in Berlin*, Durham, NC: Duke University Press.

Anderson, W. (2002) "Introduction: Postcolonial Technoscience," *Social Studies of Science* 32 (5–6): 643–58.

Aneesh, A. (2006) *Virtual Migration: The Programming of Globalization*, Durham, NC: Duke University Press.

Bailey, M. (2011) "All the Digital Humanists Are White, All the Nerds Are Men, but Some of Us Are Brave," *Journal of Digital Humanities* 1(1), retrieved from journalofdigitalhumanities.org/1–1/all-the-digital-humanists-are-white-all-the-nerds-are-men-but-some-of-us-are-brave-by-moya-z-bailey.

Barrett, P. (2014) "Where Is the Nation in Digital Humanities?," *New Solitudes: Paul Barrett's Blog*, retrieved from othersolitudes.wordpress.com/2014/01/17/where-is-the-nation-in-digital-humanities.

Bauer, J. (2011) "Who You Calling Untheoretical?," *Journal of Digital Humanities* 1(1), retrieved from journalofdigitalhumanities.org/1–1/who-you-calling-untheoretical-by-jean-bauer.

Bhabha, H. (1991) *The Location of Culture*, New York, NY: Routledge.

cárdenas, m. (2014) *Redshift & Portalmetal*, retrieved from faculty.washington.edu/michamc/redshift-and-portalmetal/.

cárdenas, m., N. Beydoun, and A. Kavaloski (2015) "Decolonizing the Digital," *HASTAC*, retrieved from www.hastac.org/initiatives/hastac-scholars/scholars-forums/decolonizing-digital.

Chibber, V. (2013) *Postcolonial Theory and the Specter of Capital*, New York, NY: Verso.

Coe, N. M. and M. Hess (2013) "Global Production Networks, Labour and Development," *Geoforum* 44, 4–9.

Cotera, M. and L. G. Merchant (n.d.) *Chicana por mi Raza: Digital Memory Collective*, University of Illinois Urbana Champaign, retrieved from chicanapormiraza.org/.

Cushman, E. (2013) "Wampum, Sequoyan, and Story: Decolonizing the Digital Archive," *College English* 76(2), 115–35.

Electronic Disturbance Theater (2007) Transborder Immigrant Tool, retrieved from faculty.washington.edu/michamc/wordpress-bang/.

Fanon, F. (1963) *The Wretched of the Earth*, New York: Grove.

Gajjala, R. (ed.) (2013) *Cyberculture and the Subaltern: Weavings of the Virtual and Real*, Lanham, MD: Lexington Books.

Gil, A. (ed.) (2014) *Around DH in 80 Days*, retrieved from arounddh.org/.

Haraway, D. (1988) "Situated Knowledges: The Science Question in Feminism and the Privilege of Partial Perspective," *Feminist Studies* 14(3), 575–99.

Harding, S. (1998) *Is Science Multicultural?: Postcolonialisms, Feminisms, and Epistemologies*, Bloomington, IN: Indiana University Press.

Harding, S. (2009) "Postcolonial and Feminist Philosophies of Science and Technology: Convergences and Dissonances," *Postcolonial Studies* 12(4), 410–29.

Khaifan, A. and T. G. Gough (2002) "Comparative Analysis Between the Public and Private Sectors on the IS-IT Outsourcing Practices in a Developing Country: A Field Study," *Logistics Information Management* 15(3), 212–22.

Koh, A. and R. Risam (2013) "Open Thread: The Digital Humanities as a Historical 'Refuge' from Race/Class/Gender/Sexuality/Disability?," *Postcolonial Digital Humanities*, retrieved from dhpoco.org/blog/2013/05/10/open-thread-the-digital-humanities-as-a-historical-refuge-from-raceclassgendersexualitydisability.

Lor, P. J. and J. Britz (2005) "Knowledge Production from an African Perspective: International Information Flows and Intellectual Property," *International Information & Library Review* 37(2), 61–76.

Lorde, A. (1983) "The Master's Tools Will Never Dismantle the Master's House: Comments at 'The Personal and the Political' Panel (Second Sex Conference, October 29, 1979)," in C. Moraga and G. Anzaldúa (eds.) *This Bridge Called My Back: Writings by Radical Women of Color*, New York, NY: Kitchen Table, pp. 94–103.

Lothian, A. and A. Phillips (2013) "Can Digital Humanities Mean Transformative Critique?," *e-Media Studies* 3(1), retrieved from journals.dartmouth.edu/cgi-bin/WebObjects/Journals.woa/xmlpage/4/article/425.
Memmi, A. (1965) *The Colonizer and the Colonized*, Boston, MA: Beacon.
Mignolo, W. (1993) "Colonial and Postcolonial Discourse: Cultural Critique or Academic Colonialism?," *Latin American Research Review* 28(3), 120–34.
Mukurtu Content Management System (n.d.) Center for Digital Scholarship and Curation at Washington State University, retrieved from mukurtu.org/.
Nayar, P. K. (2011) "The Digital Dalit: Subalternity and Cyberspace," *Sri Lanka Journal of Humanities* 37(1–2), 69–74.
Nowviskie, B. (2012) "Don't Circle the Wagons," retrieved from nowviskie.org/2012/dont-circle-the-wagons.
Nowviskie, B. (2014) "On the Origins of 'Hack' and 'Yack,'" *Journal of Digital Humanities* 3(2), retrieved from journalofdigitalhumanities.org/3–2/on-the-origin-of-hack-and-yack-by-bethany-nowviskie.
Olsen, P. (2014) "Counter Modding: Towards a Theory of Postcolonial Game Studies," paper presented at *Modern Language Association Convention*, Chicago, IL, January 9–12.
Philip, K., L. Irani, and P. Dourish (2010) "Postcolonial Computing: A Tactical Survey," *Science, Technology, and Human Values* 37(1), 1–27.
Povinelli, E. (2011) "The Woman on the Other Side of the Wall: Archiving the Otherwise in Postcolonial Digital Archives," *differences* 22(1), 146–71.
Priego, E. and A. Gil (2013) "Global Perspectives: Interview with Alex Gil," retrieved from 4humanities.org/2013/01/interview-with-alex-gil.
Rawson, K. J. (2014) "Archive," *Transgender Studies Quarterly* 1(1), 24–26.
Risam, R. (2015) "Revising History and Re-authouring the Left in the Postcolonial Digital Archive," *Left History* 18(2), 35–46.
Risam, R (2016) "Other Worlds, Other DHs: Notes towards a DH Accent," *Digital Scholarship in the Humanities*, retrieved from dsh.oxfordjournals.org/content/early/2016/02/04/llc.fqv063.
Rockwell, G. (2011) "Inclusion in the Digital Humanities," *geoffryrockwell.com*, retrieved from www.philosophi.ca/pmwiki.php/Main/InclusionInTheDigitalHumanities.
Said, E. (1978) *Orientalism*, New York, NY: Pantheon.
Sanders, A. (2014) *Settler Colonialism Uncovered*, retrieved from settlercolonialism.matrix.msu.edu.
Scheinfeldt, T. (2010) "Where's the Beef? Does Digital Humanities Have to Answer Questions?" *Found History*, retrieved from foundhistory.org/digital-humanities/wheres-the-beef-does-digital-humanities-have-to-answer-questions.
Scott, C. (2011) "Science for the West, Myth for the Rest?," in S. Harding (ed.) *The Postcolonial Science and Technology Studies Reader*, Durham, NC: Duke University Press, pp. 175–97.
Sheppard, E. (2005) "Knowledge Production through Critical GIS: Genealogy and Prospects," *Cartographica* 40(4), 5–21.
Thorat, D. (2015) "Postcolonial Studies and Digital Archiving," paper presented at *HASTAC Conference*, East Lansing, MI, May 27–30.
Tuck, E. and K. W. Yang (2012) "Decolonization Is Not a Metaphor," *Decolonization: Indigeneity, Education and Society* 1(1), retrieved from decolonization.org/index.php/des/article/view/18630.
Turkel, W. and D. Elliott (2014) "Making and Playing with Models: Using Rapid Prototyping to Explore the History and Technology of Stage Magic," in K. Kee (ed.) *Pastplay: Teaching and Learning History with Technology*, Ann Arbor, MI: University of Michigan Press, pp. 175–253.
Verhoeven, D. (2015) *Be More Than Binary*, retrieved from files.figshare.com/2239209/BeMoreThanBinary.pdf.
wa' Thiong'o, N. (1986) *Decolonising the Mind: The Politics of Language in African Literature*, Portsmouth, NH: Heinemann.

8

INTERACTIVE NARRATIVES

Addressing Social and Political Trauma through New Media

Isabel Cristina Restrepo Acevedo

A simple click on the July 30, 2015 "World" section of the *New York Times* brings you to headlines describing social and political turmoil. Here are just a few examples:

> *Africa*: "'Nobody Should Be President for Life,' Obama Tells Africa"
>
> *Americas*: "Chile: 7 in Pinochet's Military Charged in Death of Protester"
>
> *Asia*: "Landslides in Western Nepal Leave at Least 33 Dead"
>
> *Europe*: "A Desperate Nightly Race as Migrants Rush the Channel Tunnel"
>
> *Middle East*: "Signs of War Crimes Seen in Israeli Hunt for Ambushed Soldier"

Common headlines like these constitute a narrative in media and journalism describing traumatic processes that have affected a great number of people over long periods of time. They provide an account of societies where dictatorial regimes, political injustices, natural disasters, economic inequalities, violence, and war mongering deeply impact people's lives, often viscerally. They describe societies in continuous turmoil, wherein traumatic events occur at individual and collective levels. Most important, the social, historical, and "official" perspective of these headlines can suppress people's psychological and sociopolitical expression of trauma, thereby reducing the opportunity for personal narration. Yet, to overcome social distress, the voices of affected people are important. Their stories—their "unofficial" perspectives—are necessary to open new dialogic spaces, where people not only reflect on the social circumstances that produce trauma but also develop critical reflections that help them mobilize toward healing and change.

According to Pilar Hernández, personal narratives are needed to understand societal trauma caused by war and political persecution (2002: 16). She writes, "the healing of trauma takes into account the development of new social identities and, in doing so, contributes to the building of social movements that question the existing social order" (17). Individual perspectives contribute to the healing process because they act as a psychology of liberation that intertwines individual and social distress. They help us examine "the concept of trauma from the standpoint of the individual within context" (24). At the same time, mobilization toward social change can be accomplished by facilitating dialogic spaces for people's actions and interactions. Dialogue is necessary because traumatic events impact people at different levels. These events impact individuals' realities and society as a whole. Along these lines, it is possible to say that the intimate and private effects of personal trauma also affect others: family, relatives, friends, neighbors, colleagues, and fellows. As Sharon Davis Massey points out, "traumatic ruptures in relationships between individuals and within and between groups occur at all levels in human systems and quickly spread from the level at which they originate, impacting others" (2009: 83). Dialogue is important because trauma is societal. It affects a group of people in a particular context (Giddo 2009: 199).

There is precedent for this sort of cultural mobilization in Paulo Freire's *Pedagogy of the Oppressed* (1972) and Augusto Boal's *Theater of the Oppressed* (Boal et al. 2008). Both Brazilian authors express the need for liberation of individuals and society through critical thinking. Specifically, Freire advocates for the liberation (or humanization) of oppressed people by allowing them to recognize the sources of oppression and then transmute that oppression by recovering self-confidence, critical thought, and creative life (Freire 1972: 31–35). Freire's theory encourages individuals to write their lives as not only passive witnesses but also active authors of their own history. He says, "Men are not built in silence, but in word, in work, in action-reflection" (76). The conceptual bases of Freire's invitation are to overcome passivity and undertake the creation and recreation of new realities (31–33). They only occur through social dialogue and interaction, in which people are equal and work toward a common goal to recover their sense of humanity.

With *Theater of the Oppressed*, Augusto Boal expands Freire's ideas of critical process by opening performative possibilities of theatrical representation to the audience. In particular, Boal advocates for the importance of physical and mental emancipation, allowing the emergence of a "Critical Conscience," which will lead to individual and social transformations:

> The audience mustn't just liberate its Critical Conscience, but its body too. It needs to invade the stage and transform the images that are shown there. To transform is to be transformed. The action of transforming is, in itself, transforming. The members of the audience must become the Character: possess him, take his place—not obey him, but guide him, show him the path they think right. In this way the Spectator becoming Spect-Actor is democratically opposed to the other members of the audience, free to invade the scene and appropriate the power of the actor.
>
> (Boal et al. 2008: xx–xxi)

In Boal's theater, audience members are openly invited to become actors, with bodies and minds intertwined in a critical process. Each participant on stage becomes a part of a group that creatively affects the scene by transforming the original premises or invitation of the artist. The power that Boal offers to spectators starts with individual self-expression, where individuals assume new identities, and moves toward collective reflection, facilitating dialogical spaces for social emancipation.

With new media—understood in our analysis as digital media, numerical representations, *and* the convergence of art and technology—the interactive and performative possibilities that spectators have in Boal's Theater are expanded to new levels of physical and mental involvement. Novel approaches to develop interactive and dialogical spaces emerge, and the possibilities for individual and social mobilization are greatly enhanced, too. Within this context, new media offers many opportunities for the development of dialogue and spaces that "give birth to new forms of text and to new forms of narrative" (Ryan 2006: 28). Specially, new media opens possibilities for audience participation as well as for unofficial narratives by individuals, collectives, and societies affected by social and political trauma. These narratives go beyond written and oral expression and, in many cases, integrate audience gestures and physical actions. At the same time, they encompass forms in which content unfolds under a creative collaboration between authors and readers. This collaboration, sometimes implicit and sometimes explicit, aligns with Michael Joyce's understanding of audience participation in what he calls "constructive hypertexts" (2003: 616–17), where the audience's active participation in content development seems to "renew an ancient promise, one which would make us know ourselves and become authors of our learning" (617). This type of audience participation is also present in Janet Murray's work:

> When the writer expands the story to include multiple possibilities, the reader assumes a more active role. Contemporary stories, in high and low culture, keep reminding us of the storyteller and inviting us to second-guess the choices he or she has made. This can be unsettling to the reader, but it can also be experienced as an invitation to join in the creative process.
>
> (Murray 1997: 38)

Additionally, new media collaboration between authors and audiences echoes the redefinition of authorship and the hegemony of the author as the privileged creator. It affords people active and creative roles in the aesthetics of reception. For instance, the French semiotician, Roland Barthes, talks about the text as a "methodological field" that requires reader activity: "the Text is experienced only in an activity of production" (1977: 157).

The aforementioned ideas help us to understand the dynamic relationships among authors, readers, and text in new media narratives. More important, they provide language for examining the potential of these narratives for dialogical spaces. Borrowing from Barthes, new media narratives constitute *methodological fields* where the content unfolds under a creative and collective collaboration between individuals, both authors and readers.

Remote Sensing and Physical and Cognitive Involvement

The creative role of the audience is enhanced by forms now at work in new media and interactive narratives: web-based applications, stand-alone devices, virtual and augmented environments, smart phone applications, teleconference systems, and interactive installations, among others. Many of these share an expanded perspective of space, intertwining screens with virtual and physical spaces, by using some sort of remote sensing technology in the collection of audience participation data. These sensing technologies capture action and interaction through sensors, web cams, and global positioning systems (GPS), among others. When used critically, they may enhance an audience's physical and cognitive engagement with a narrative. For instance, the audience may construct new relationships with themselves through representations of their own bodies and actions on screen, often in the form of avatars. In the context of new media and games, an avatar represents a vehicle for self-expression. It is "the essential unit within the network of the play community, and is the means whereby the individual player interacts with both other players and the ecosystem of the play environment" (Pearce 2009: 111). In our analysis, avatars are not merely representations of actions and bodies on a screen; they may help people build new identities and—returning for a moment to the work of Pilar Hernández—serve as strategies to heal trauma (2002: 17).

In this chapter, we will focus on the analysis of interactive narratives that use remote sensing technologies to reflect on traumatic events. These narratives create hybrid environments that intertwine digital and physical components. Such narratives also use technology as not only a tool to expand audience participation and engagement but also a symbolic medium to facilitate different levels of self-expression, creativity, and social and political reflection. By developing interactive components with computers, an interactive narrative affords collaborative wrting and authorship (Landow 1992). It also allows individuals to create and perform new identities via the relationships that emerge between actions, bodies, and representations on screens. Participants in such environments expand their self-perception and self-representation in the present moment. They live the now in a hybrid space—simultaneously here (physical space) and there (on screen).

With this focus on hybrid environments, we are departing from the premise that new media and representational environments empower people to have aesthetic and cognitive experiences via physical perception. People's bodily actions and gestures not only activate emerging narrative content but also become part of it. For example, participants may activate, alter, or even recreate sounds, images, and videos by walking, singing, dancing, and gesturing. In this environment, physical and cognitive exploration starts "within the body, as if you know by dancing" ("desde dentro del cuerpo, como si conociera danzando," Negri & Sánchez 2000: 73). In fact, the environment creates a physical and emotional connection with the emerging imagery that affords both introspective and collective reflection. The relation of people with their own representations on screen facilitates a space for action in various ways: through individual satisfaction, individual and collective physical development, experiential pedagogy, and individual, social, and political transformation, for example (Restrepo 2014). As a result, interactive narratives may serve as dialogical spaces to help people affected by trauma work toward healing and change. They may combat feelings of loneliness (Landry et al. 2010: 783), connect with other people (783), and develop actions to remodel their lives and communities (Hernández 2002: 17). In this context, the participatory characteristics of new media and hybrid spaces (simultaneously virtual and physical) may empower people's actions. Yet the environment may also produce visceral aesthetic and cognitive experiences, resulting from new or unfamiliar relations between bodies, actions, and technologies.

Interactive narratives, particularly those dealing with trauma, may benefit from a "digital ethnographic" approach, which Natalie M. Underberg and Elayne Zorn define as such:

> A method for representing real-life cultures through combining the characteristic features of digital media with the elements of story. These projects use the expressive and procedural potential of computer-based storytelling to enable audiences to go beyond absorbing facts about another culture to entering into the experience of that culture.
>
> (Underberg & Zorn 2013: 10)

In this case, audiences are invited to enter a re-created political and social situation that is filtered—both conceptually and aesthetically—with a high consideration of people's feelings. Designing interactive narratives that address trauma requires sensitive and accountable approaches, where the content of the interaction helps people overcome the negative effects of that reality without emphasizing them. Put this way, digital ethnography can improve design methodologies by bringing physiological and ethical considerations to the process while also experimenting with new forms of media and genres of narration (Ryan 2006: 28–30), including forms and genres that address social trauma.

Consider three examples, each about desapariciones (disappearances or missing people), across three different Latin American countries (Colombia, Argentina, and Mexico): my installation, *Ausentes* (*Absentees*); Leo Nuñez's *Desilusiones Ópticas* (*Optical Disillusions*); and Rafael Lozano-Hemmer's *Nivel de Confianza* (*Level of Confidence*). Although they all use remote sensing technologies to develop their semantic, poetic, and narrative components, they were selected to exemplify different levels of impact on audience participation in the configuration of narrative. In general, they playfully engage people in the traumatic situation of disappearances by tracking viewer's presence and, consequently, activating or affecting the visual imagery on the screen. They not only produce new relationships between individuals and installations, but also constitute environments where people experience transition from ludic to reflective experience. More specifically, they engage people by facilitating some emotional engagement, or what Brenda Laurel calls *dramatic pleasure*, resulting from active participation in new media spaces. According to Laurel, viewers become agents with "the power to take action" (1993: 117). She elaborates:

> When we participate as agents, the shape of the whole action becomes available to us in new ways. We experience it not only as observers or critics but also as comakers and participants. Systems that incorporate this sensibility into their basic structure open up to us a whole new dimension of dramatic pleasure. This is the stuff of dream and desire, of life going *right*. It is the vision that fuels our love affairs with art, computers, and any other means that can enhance and transform our experience.
>
> (Laurel 1993: 120)

Interactive narratives create an atmosphere that takes spectators out of their daily routines, in a manner similar to Johan Huizinga's observations in *Homo Ludens* (1955). These experiences constitute an alternate reality of sorts, with an enormous potential to capture attention and engage people in a combination of dramatic pleasure with serious reflection.

Across their conceptualization, development, and implementation, all three of the installations below also depend on some sort of interdisciplinary methodology that requires an "artistic gesture of working with algorithms" (Wilson 2002: 336) and an ethnographical approach to the psychological and social dimensions associated with the trauma of *disappearances* and their specific contexts. They facilitate space to reflect on trauma, shifting from the loneliness of personal experience to connecting individual stories and expanding the mental and physical involvement of other people. They also represent collective experiences that integrate victims and spectators on the screen through the use of remote sensing.

Ausentes

This installation departed from personal, conceptual, social, and technological considerations to reflect on disappearances in Colombia due to violence, political turmoil, and illegal drug trafficking during one of the country's most difficult times (1986–2002). Six electromechanical light-boxes with digital prints of missing people were displayed on a wall to create a dynamic database of *desaparecidos* reported in the newspapers. For the initial configuration, the machines were off, and they only turned on and moved when a spectator entered the space. This behavior was actuated using motion sensors and programmable logic controllers (PLCs). Conceptually, the piece was a dialogic space that required a spectator's disposition to participate—to act. Although the visualization of lost people individualized their stories by highlighting one person on each machine at a time, it created a collective narrative by putting them together in a series of random arrangements resulting from viewer interactions. The research process required the analysis of sources such as newspapers, reports, and videos to develop different levels of visualization, poetics, and interaction through digital media. To develop the technical components, I collaborated with Loren Schreiber in the Department of Theater at San Diego State University. Through personalized teaching and interdisciplinary dialogue, he offered technical advice for developing the electronic and interactive components of the interface (see Figure 8.1).

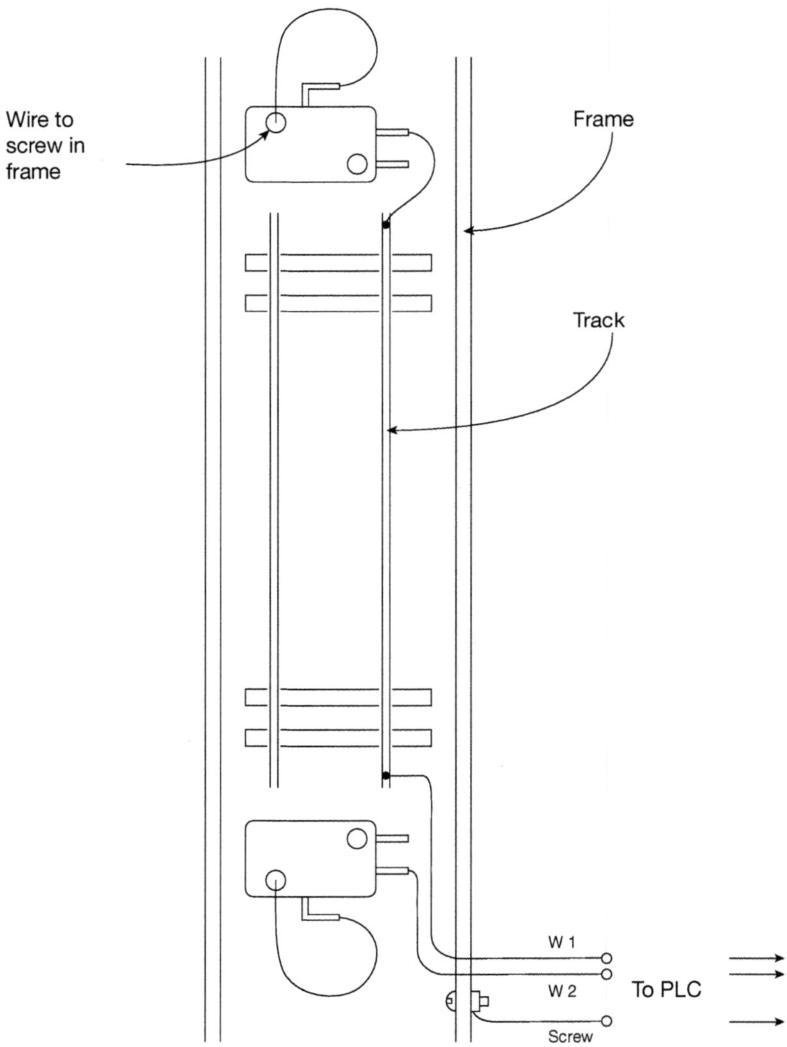

Figure 8.1 Wiring diagram for *Ausentes*.

This piece exemplified first-level audience impact in narrative configuration. Two proximity sensors detected individual presence and activated the six randomly programmed lightboxes that acted as screens displaying the preloaded images (see Figures 8.2 and 8.3). Although participants were not visually represented through avatars or photographs on the screens, they understood the correlation between their actions and the activation of imagery, even in the absence of self-representation. Without their presence or proximity to the screens, no content appeared. This relationship between spectator actions and resulting visualizations produced a

plc			INPUTS					OUTPUTS		
1	S1	Machine	Sensor	a	X0	Y0	a	Motor 1- ON	Mot-On1	1
2	MB1	1	Botton	b	X1	Y1	b	Light	L1	2
3	MT1		Top	c	X2	Y2	c	Motor 1- Reverse	Mot-Rev1	3
4	S2	Machine	Sensor	a	X3	Y3	a	Motor 2- ON	Mot-On2	4
5	MB2	2	Botton	b	X4	Y4	b	Motor 2- Reverse	L2	5
6	MT2		Top	c	X5	Y5	c	Machine2- Light	Mot-Rev2	6
7	S3	Machine	Sensor	a	X6	Y6	a	Motor 3- ON	Mot-On3	7
8	MB3	3	Botton	b	X7	Y7	b	Motor 3- Reverse	L3	8
9	MT3		Top	c	X10	Y10	c	Machine 3- Light	Mot-Rev3	9
10	S4	Machine	Sensor	a	X11	Y11	a	Motor 4 - ON	Mot-On4	10
11	MB4	4	Botton	b	X12	Y12	b	Motor 4 - Reverse	L4	11
12	MT4		Top	c	X13	Y13	c	Machine 4 - Light	Mot-Rev4	12
13	S5	Machine	Sensor	a	X14	Y14	a	Motor 5 - ON	Mot-On5	13
14	MB5	5	Botton	b	X15	Y15	b	Motor 5 - Reverse	L5	14
15	MT5		Top	c	X16	Y16	c	Machine 5 - Light	Mot-Rev5	15
16	S6	Machine	Sensor	a	X17	Y17	a	Motor 6 - ON	Mot-On6	
17	MB6	6	Botton	b	X20	Y20	b	Motor 6 - Reverse	L6	
18	MT6		Top	c	X21	Y21	c	Machine 6 - Light	Mot-Rev6	

Figure 8.2 Programming diagram for *Ausentes.*

Figure 8.3 Audience interaction in *Ausentes.*

ludic dynamic that caught people's attention and ultimately prompted more in-depth reflection about life, death, and time, especially in the context of missing people.

Desilusiones Ópticas

A second example of an interactive narrative that used a ludic—or spontaneously playful—strategy to invite critical thinking about the complex political situations of disappearances is *Desilusiones Ópticas* (*Optical Disillusions*), by Argentinian artist Leo Nuñez. The piece assumed a new level of physical and cognitive involvement by using a sensor to track actions and bodies to shape the emerging visualization on the screen. For this piece, Nuñez created an interface that conceptually and formally combined two contrasting realities: the celebration of the 1978 FIFA World Cup in Argentina and the disappearances occurring at the same time, in the same place. To engage people, Nuñez filled the floor with little pieces of paper cut from telephone directories and newspapers. Inviting interaction, the pieces represented confetti used during soccer game celebrations. Nuñez writes that, during the World Cup:

> People celebrated the success of the football team by throwing papers in the air to show their joy only a few meters from where the greatest atrocities were commited [*sic*] in the country. The time spent in the installation allows viewers to see both realities of the era.
>
> (Nuñez n.d.)

This playful action became the starting or, better yet, breaking point to initiate individual and collective reflections about the past. Active bodies and smiling faces were some of the gestures that built an emerging choreography to reveal the cruel reality behind the celebration. By physically participating, the spectator unveiled the faces of people who disappeared during the dictatorship. This visualization corresponded with a reality veiled, ignored, or not officially discussed for many years.

Disolusiones Ópticas exemplified second-level audience impact in narrative configuration by giving audience members visual presence on the screen, where their bodies were traced and their actions were emulated. In this sense, spectators became silhouettes who arranged and expressed the imagery of disappeared people by throwing confetti in the air. When compared with the first-level audience impact of *Ausentes*, where participants had no self-representation on the screen but their actions directly triggered content, the silhouette form of *Disolusiones Ópticas* combined abstract self-visualizations with preloaded images on the screen through an interface driven by remote sensing. Nuñez further experimented with this approach in *Rostros*, a piece that intertwined spectators' faces on screen with the faces of missing people. The spectators became part of the visualization, and the work thus became a space to reflect on trauma. According to the artist, being part of the system not only intertwined spectators with images of reality but also prompted their awareness of how they are involved in, or complicit with, that reality, both past and present (n.d.). To further engage spectators in reflecting on this trauma, Nuñez used a television from the time of the regime, creating a contextual environment for the piece that evoked the nuances of time and memory.

Nivel de Confianza

Nivel de Confianza, by Mexican-Canadian artist, Rafael Lozano-Hemmer, reflected on the disappearance of students from Ayotzinapa School in Iguala, Guerrero, Mexico. Like Nuñez,

Lozano-Hemmer used a sensor to connect spectator's faces on screen with a face database of *desaparecidos*. However, in *Nivel de Confianza*, audience presence shaped not only visual imagery but also the behavior of algorithms, which endlessly searched for similarities between disappeared people and spectators. This process only ended when a spectator left the space and the installation image subsequently returned to its original configuration. Lozano-Hemmer writes:

> The piece will always fail to make a positive match, as we know that the students were likely murdered and burnt in a massacre where government, police forces and drug cartels were involved, but the commemorative side of the project is the relentless search for the students and the overlap of their image with the public's own facial features.
>
> (Lozano-Hemmer 2015)

To further active participation in *Nivel de Confianza*, Lozano-Hemmer allowed spectators to download, implement, and modify its code. This approach encouraged extensive forms of participation with the piece and the reflections it invited. Perhaps the strategy to mobilize collective reflection involves not only a public exhibition but also prompting variations of the work itself.

Conclusion

These three interactive narratives facilitate creative action with a high potential to help people reflect on and mobilize from the traumatic situation of disappearances as social and political phenomena. They are the result of collective reflections that allow for self-expression and social engagement by integrating audiences both physically and cognitively. They constitute dialogical spaces to re-signify trauma. At the same time, they enable different levels of participation and creativity within methodological fields, as both the content and narrative emerge through the creative complicity of artists with audiences.

Acknowledgments

Thanks to Earl Bradbury, Juan Gomez, and Loren Schreiber.

Further Reading

Bishop, C. (2012) *Artificial Hells: Participatory Art and Politics of Spectatorship*, London: Verso Books.

Frieling, R. (ed.) (2008) *The Art of Participation: 1950 to Now*, London: Thames and Hudson.

Kwastek, K. (2013) *Aesthetics of Interaction in Digital Art*, Cambridge, MA: MIT Press.

Lozano-Hemmer, R. (2007) *Algunas Cosas Pasan Más Veces Que Todo El Tiempo / Some Things Happen More Often Than All of the Time*, México: Turner.

Murray, J. H. (2012) *Inventing the Medium: Principles of Interaction Design as a Cultural Practice*, Cambridge, MA: MIT Press.

References

Barthes, R. (1977) *Image, Music, Text: Essays*, London: Fontana.

Boal, A., M.-O. Leal-McBride, C. A. Leal McBride, and E. Fryer (2008) *Theatre of the Oppressed*, London: Pluto Press.

Freire, P. (1972) *Pedagogy of the Oppressed*, New York, NY: Herder and Herder New York.

Giddo, S. A. (2009) "Dafur: Efforts to Forgive and Reconcile in an Unresolved Conflict," in A. Kalayjian and R. Paloutzian (eds.) *Forgiveness and Reconciliation: Psychological Pathways to Conflict Transformation and Peace Building*, New York, NY: Springer, pp. 189–206.

Hernández, P. (2002) "Trauma in War and Political Persecution: Expanding the Concept," *American Journal of Orthopsychiatry* 72(1), 16–25.

Huizinga, J. (1955) *Homo Ludens: A Study of the Play Element in Culture*, Boston, MA: The Beacon Press.

Joyce, M. (2003) "Siren Shapes: Exploratory and Constructive Hypertexts," in N. Wardrip-Fruin and N. Montfort (eds.) *The New Media Reader*, Cambridge, MA: MIT Press, pp. 613–24.

Landow, G. (1992) *Hypertext: The Convergence of Contemporary Critical Theory and Technology*, Baltimore, MD: Johns Hopkins University Press.

Landry, B. M., E. Kyoung Choe, S. McCutcheon, and J. A. Kientez (2010) "Post-traumatic Stress Disorder: Opportunities and Challenges for Computing Technology," in *Proceedings of the 1st AMC International Health Informatics Symposium, IHI '10*, pp. 780–89, retrieved from dl.acm.org/citation.cfm?doid=1882992.1883110.

Laurel, B. (1993) *Computer as Theater*, Boston, MA: Addison-Wesley Longman Publishing Co.

Lozano-Hemmer, R. (2015) "Level of Confidence," retrieved from www.lozano-hemmer.com/level_of_confidence.php.

Massey, S. D. (2009) "Forgiveness and Reconciliation: Essential to Sustaining Human Development," in A. Kalayjian and R. Paloutzian (eds.) *Forgiveness and Reconciliation: Psychological Pathways to Conflict Transformation and Peace Building*, London, UK and New York, NY: Springer, pp. 83–96.

Murray, J. H. (1997) *Hamlet on the Holodeck: The Future of Narrative in Cyberspace*, New York: The Free Press.

Negri, A. and R. Sánchez (2000) *Arte y Multitudo: Ocho Cartas*, Madrid, ES: Trotta.

Nuñez L. (n.d.) retreived from www.leonunez.com.ar.

Pearce. C. (2009) *Communities of Play: Emergent Cultures in Multiplayer Games and Virtual Worlds*, Cambridge, MA: MIT Press.

Restrepo, I. (2014) Tocar con los ojos, ver con las manos. Cuerpo, acción y tecnología en los espacios de interacción digital con monitoreo remoto, unpublished PhD dissertation, Universidad de Antioquia, Medellín, Colombia.

Ryan, M.-L. (2006) *Avatars of Story*, Minneapolis, MN: University of Minnesota Press.

Underberg, N. and E. Zorn (2013). *Digital Ethnography: Anthropology, Narrative, and New Media*, Austin, TX: University of Texas Press.

Wilson, S. (2002) *Information Arts: Intersections of Art, Science and Technology*, Cambridge, MA: MIT Press.

9

WEAR AND CARE

Feminisms at a Long Maker Table

Jacqueline Wernimont and Elizabeth Losh

Although there is a deep history of feminist engagement with technology, the FemTechNet initiative (a feminist collective of which we are both a part) argues that such history is often hidden and that feminist thinkers are frequently siloed. At the same time, initiatives to promote critical making, acts of "shared construction" in which makers work to understand both the technologies and their social environments (Ratto 2011: 254), often exclude women and girls from hacker/makerspaces that require both explicit permissions and access to implicit reserves of tacit knowledge. Even attempts to provide superficial hospitality can inflict microagressions on those who feel excluded from the sites of technology. When these bastions for tinkering under the hood promote "pinkification" with hyper-feminized projects and materials emphasizing servility, consumerism, or beauty culture, the results are often counterproductive. Take, for example, Google's recent "Made with Code" effort, which emphasized accessories and selfies as projects appropriate for girls. Even the otherwise admirable "Girls Who Code" site tends to rely on the default design schemes of stereotypical gender typing, including a curling cursive script for section heads, a color palette dominated by a rose-pink, and the iconography of sisterhood and empowerment in the graphics and scrolling images.

With the rise of popularity in hacker/makerspaces has come an old reproduction of inequality at the sites of innovation and education in which women, people of color, middle-aged and elderly citizens, queer and genderqueer people, and people with disabilities are affectively and/or economically excluded. Of course, there are also ways to decolonize the female body with makerlab projects that emphasize sexual agency, reproductive rights, and resistance to gendered violence. For instance, by integrating traditional knowledges and citizen science into their work on "DiY (Do it Yourself) gynecology" (Chardronnet 2015), the GynePunk project demonstrates how the women of the Pechblenda biolab (established outside of Barcelona as part of a larger hack community called the Calafou Collective) can occupy a hackerspace in new ways to serve disadvantaged Catalan women, sex workers, and refugees. Stefanie Wuschitz, a digital artist based in Vienna, has also piloted a number of experiments in creating temporary "Rumah Hacker" spaces in Taipei, Yogyakarta, Linz, Damascus,

Offenbach, New York, and Copenhagen that borrow from the practices of women's tribal houses in Sumatra to foster projects with nonpatrilineal, multiple parentages and an ethos that is more welcoming to women. Other feminist hackerspaces are characterized by their attention to members' security and comfort, the values of domesticity, and respect for traditional craft labor (Fox et al. 2015).

In the spirit of such experiments, #FemDH, an annual course at the University of Victoria's Digital Humanities Summer Institute (DHSI), tries to bring theory and practice together around a range of coding and physical computing activities (see Chapter 25 in this volume for more) to emphasize how the material, embodied, affective, labor-intensive, and situated character of engagements with computation can operate experientially for users in shared spaces. This includes not just desktop/laptop style computing, but also the more embedded forms of wearables and networked "smart" devices like FitBit-style health devices and home climate control tools that are increasingly prevalent for some in the western world. The goal of mixing theory and practice is to facilitate new forms of participation in which the assemblages of personal and shared computing and the abstractions and lived experiences of feminist thought mutually impinge on one another. In other words, we encourage participants to meditate upon mediation and mediate conversation together, about how the range of choices may be constrained and yet how available technologies and iterative design practices may still be potentially open to appropriation. (For more on "creative mediation" see Kember and Zylinska's work on vital processes in *Life after New Media,* 2012.)

Outpost Colonialism

In 2013, Wernimont was working with Beatriz Maldonado, then a Scripps College student, on a project to take a two-dimensional poem and transform it into a three-dimensional algorithmic object. In the course of that work, Wernimont suggested that Maldonado might be interested in exploring the LA Makerspace as a way of learning more about making traditions in digital education and practice. As teacher and mentor, Wernimont also hoped it would provide Maldonado with an opportunity to develop expertise about a local resource that she might then share with other students, staff, and faculty.

We encourage you to read Maldonado's full account of her experience, but it can be summarized in her own words: "I felt distinctly out of place" (cited with permission, Maldonado). As a Latina and first generation college student, Maldonado encountered the makerspace as an all-white space of privilege that engendered feelings of sorrow, pain, and inadequacy. Her trip was fraught with concerns about costs and transportation, including the impact her visit would have on her mom and younger brother. She felt alienation, embarrassment, and even jealousy in the course of her time at a workshop there. As she watched a "mother and son [who] were sharing their exploration of technology" in the makerspace, Maldonado reflected that she did not "have the same kinds of moments over [her] research." Her work as a research assistant and student of maker culture was not accessible to her family; there would be no shared moments of discovery for her to cherish. In a particularly cruel twist, the makerspace is housed in the LA Mart, a space virtually in Maldonado's "own neighborhood" where she grew up. It was and remains an outpost of a maker culture that is colonizing spaces within Los Angeles, even as it functionally denies access to those nearby. Like the colonial outposts of imperial Britain, the LA Makerspace marks and holds a space on behalf of new regimes of political economy. Maldonado's story bears witness to the ways in which makerspaces may actually reinforce many barriers to entry by following a script of common design choices that cater to particular kinds of users, despite promulgating an ethic of openness.

If located in gritty urban settings, like many of the Dorkbot SoCal meetups, makerspaces can feel threatening for those who are reluctant to go to buildings in areas with low foot traffic or venture into uninhabited industrial or warehouse spaces. The open access, unlocked doors, and absence of boundaries to personal space can be disconcerting to those conditioned to avoid potentially risky strangers and opportunities for harassment. The hazards of alien equipment (laser cutters, power tools, soldering irons, etc.) might seem more dangerous if one has not been socialized in the practices of machismo and male expertise around tool use. Even the dread of being forced to exhibit knowledge of math or science or subjected to mansplaining can make the ubiquitous white boards of these spaces oppressive. These spaces might also not be accessible to public transportation infrastructures or adequately compensate interns and student workers employed there. In this way, the unpaid "playbor" expected by makerspaces excludes students who must contribute income to their families, only further exacerbating existing digital inequality.

If sponsored by more security- and safety-conscious institutions focusing on K-12 populations, such as libraries, schools, or community centers, as in the case of the LA Makerspace that Maldonado visited, the play may be sanitized but the interactions can still can feel intimidating, particularly if the logics of gifted programs (and the remedial instruction and tracking for which they serve as corollaries) are reproduced. In other words, merely making the resources of a hidden curriculum visible does not make people traditionally excluded from enrichment courses in STEAM (Science, Technology, Engineering, Arts, and Mathematics) areas feel welcome. Often such spaces assume particular kinds of privileged domestic arrangements, such as access to the status of the stay-at-home mother with enough leisure time to participate eagerly and to shuttle children between activities. Older students without guides may be treated as though they are past an ideal latency period and consequently might experience particularly low retention rates (see Quattrocchi 2013; Dunbar-Hester 2014).

Maldonado's story illustrates a common experience that is all but invisible to the predominantly white maker movement. Already deeply coded as a masculine conceptual and practical space, makerspaces draw on egalitarian rhetoric while often creating and sustaining spaces in which those who fall outside of white, affluent, and heteronormative culture find little to nothing that beckons to them. As Maldonado's account attests, spaces where performances of privilege, like the mother–son tableaux, are a central part of the ethos of practice can actually do harm to those who venture in. To paraphrase Miriam Posner (2012) (who writes powerfully about an analogous valorization of code culture): if you want women, people of color, and queer people in your community, if it is important to you to have a diverse discipline, you need to do something beyond just bringing people to the table.

What Kind of Table Is This?

An objection to that final statement might read something like this: but, Professor Wernimont, you were the one who sent Maldonado down to the makerspace. You and Elizabeth Losh spend a week each summer leading a seminar in which all of the stuff of makerspaces is on full display. Bringing people to the maker table is part of what you do!

Fair enough. We join in many of the efforts of the critical making and physical computing crowds. We think that making, breaking, and making again are good endeavors on a number of levels. At the same time, part of our feminist praxis is to have spaces and conversations that are theoretical; we need to connect discussions and use of technologies to our lived histories. We do not separate "yack" from "hack" any more than one might partition a stitch-n-bitch (note the connective punctuation there!). Our feminist theories and practices focus on the ways in which we live with and within systems and technologies. We privilege knowing how things work not in order to demonstrate mastery or because of a commitment to the libertarian ideology of autonomous individuals colonizing resources; we need to know how systems and technologies work because they are sites for and vectors of the exercise of power, even if the visibility of such technocultural power should not be mistaken for transparency. Understanding by whom and how those sites and vectors are shaped and how they shape us is of real import. At the same time, we see powerful possibilities in the ways in which physical computing and wearable technology do not privilege visual apperception, in so far as it enables or foregrounds engagement with the other senses and other kinds of relationships to technology (for more on physical computing see cárdenas n.d.; O'Sullivan and Igoe 2004; Garfinkel 2014). Of particular interest to us are the ways in which physical computing and wearable technologies afford larger and real-time group interactions in ways that are more limited when working with a single device, or reading from a single screen. At the intimate scale of gingerly handling an LED or connecting a circuit, the narrower scope of granular analysis can invite extremely intimate conversations around common matters of concern. Additionally, we value the ways in which both areas of research and practice foreground the always present but sometimes hidden interactions between human bodies and computational technologies, and we would hope to push those features even further to the fore. Finally, while we remain critical of the rhetoric of empowerment and agency that has been built into these fields, we look down our own versions of a long maker table and see wire bits, spools of filament, lights, paper fragments, and half-accomplished prototypes. We find that mess an exciting counterpoint to the prevailing discourse around "good" code (see Posner 2012; also Chapters 25 and 45, this volume).

By offering a feminist DH course we are not trying to reproduce a white, male, privileged perspective on technology and making, or a kind of "Henry Rollins' School" of "do-it-yourself" digital humanities (DH) (Owens 2011). Instead, if we are going to use DIY rhetoric (as opposed to do-it-together or do-it-with-others), then we want our DIY to be of the "riot grrrls School," following the models of Bikini Kill, Bratmobile, and Mecca Normal rather than working as part of a "Rollins School" paradigm of macho antiheroism. This means creating and sustaining a sophisticated DIY infrastructure that favors women—spaces, practices, and active interventions that make it possible for women to enter and promote themselves. Echoing Amy Earhart's addition of the queer zine movement in her notion of a riot grrrl DH, we note that our riotous DH takes intersectional feminisms at its starting point and therefore eschews essentializing categories in order to dismantle/subvert structural barriers for a range of people—we do not use the riot grrrl analogy in order to replicate the white privilege seen in punk cultures (Earhart 2015; Schilt 2005). We envision infrastructure that supports as many people participating as is possible. We want to develop ways of reveling in the joyful, generative, and provocative mess that can be feminist digital technology studies.

To these ends, our reading selections for #FemDH bring a variety of feminist technology critiques in media studies, human-computer interaction (HCI), science and technology studies (STS), and related fields into conversation with work in digital humanities. Each session is organized by a keyword—a term like "archive" or "play" that is central to feminist theoretical and practical engagements with technology—and begins with a discussion of that term in light of our readings. The second half of each session is spent learning about and tinkering with Processing, a programming platform that will allow participants to engage in their own critical making processes, often by appropriating found code or sharing trial-and-error experiences. We do not teach "good code" in the way that Edsger Dijkstra (1988) argues for a "cruel" discipline-and-punish approach to computer science that rejects the "familiar," but we do teach Annette Vee's (2012) critique of Dijkstra's focus on purity and danger. Pushing against instrumentalist assumptions regarding the value and efficacy of certain digital tools, we ask our participants to think hard about the affordances and constraints of digital technologies. We ask that they jump into the mess, the joy, and the creation even as we critique.

This kind of playful, collaborative making is versatile, working in the professional (both faculty and staff) and graduate level spaces of DHSI and elsewhere. It is also serious play in the sense invoked by Barbara Christian (1996) and Donna Haraway (1991) in which play is about embodied theory and practice. Borrowing from the long table methodology of feminist performance artist, Lois Weaver, we are creating participatory learning and making events that we might describe as "long maker tables." For example, Losh has joined with Karen Gregory, T. L. Taylor, and Nishant Shah to sponsor similar short-term rapid prototyping workshops for speculative feminist technologies. Using cardboard, scissors, markers, and other materials used in interface design, participants create "labor-saving devices" aimed at forms of invisible and immaterial labor and "life support systems" aimed at those in conditions of precarity. Wernimont is using similar methodologies in her introductory Prototyping Dreams course, which asks students "how do you build your dreams?" and explores prototyping across multiple media, including physical fabrication, prose writing, science fiction, and virtual worlds, while foregrounding the ethical, social, and political implications of design decisions. Our aim in these world-building activities is not merely to include women and girls in the sites of technoculture but also to help those in networked publics understand how they were excluded in the first place, in the interest of combining digital humanities with social justice goals.

Technologies of Wear and Care

We have sketched out a vision of a "long maker table" that draws on the feminist performance art tradition in order to break into and break open makerspaces that have been traditionally coded as white, affluent, and masculine spaces. This is an intervention not only in maker culture, but also in the rising academic and professional fields that engage the Internet of Things (IoT) (a network of data collecting physical objects/devices), physical computing, and wearable technologies. As Amelia Abreu observes, western fascination with wearable technology and IoT is:

> a utopian, techno-libertarian, *entrepreneurial* vision of sensor devices playing happily with machine-learning techniques, of developing perfect metrics, and application to human bodies in order to streamline the rough edges of the physical experience.
> (Abreu 2014)

Abreu is referencing a long history of wearables and so called "smart" devices that have played a part in imagining a perfected human body within an idealized techno-environment. Susan Elizabeth Ryan (2014) carefully delineates this history in longer form in *Garments of Paradise: Wearable Discourse in the Digital Age*, although Ryan also shows how feminist designers like Margaret Orth of the MIT Media Lab attempted to make practical interventions in these visions of symbiosis and transhumanism. Ryan's text is particularly helpful for thinking through the ways in which technologies create meaning, in this case by participating in what she describes as "dress acts," or hybrid acts of communication in which the embodied behavior of wearing is bound up with the materiality of garments and devices.

Ryan argues that wearable and portable technologies, many of which are the focus of maker activities, are dense acts of communication and self-fashioning. In so doing, she works with J. L. Austin's *How to Do Things with Words*, which theorizes speech acts by foregrounding the ways in which "the issuing of an utterance is the performing of the action" (1962: 6). Ryan draws on Austin's theory of performative language to create a theory of performative dressing, in which putting on or pocketing small computing and sense devices such as a cell phone, a step counter, or bio-sensitive clothing is a form of "enhanced communication" (2014: 9). Ryan's work is powerful as an articulation of the ways in which embodied "dress acts" render the techno-body as a site of *poiesis*—a making, an action that perpetually creates the worlds and the bodies that we inhabit.

What does it mean from an intersectional feminist perspective to think about wearable technologies as "dress acts" that bring certain realities, certain modes of being, into being through a symbiosis of human bodies and materials? What possible futures become present, and what is their relationship to the techno-utopian space of commerce to which they are inextricably tied? Even as we remain critical of the hegemonic spaces of much maker culture, we see work like Ryan's articulating modes of critical making that are possible through creative appropriation of both crafted and off-the-shelf technologies.

Far from representing an off-the-rack sartorial gender-neutrality, within wearable production and use we see a more complicated gendering of certain kinds of making and wearing in which "fashion" does not operate unambiguously. The conspicuous consumption and self-regulation signaled by wearable devices such as FitBits or Jawbone self-trackers is a male-gendered wearable space, in which there is a hybridization of commerce and self-actualization with the modular, minimalist aesthetics exemplified by Apple products. The gendering of the information gathered by wearables is matched by the gender typing in the design of the circuits and boards themselves. To bring a broad conceptual discussion back to our long maker table, a comparison of Arduino Lilypad and Uno circuit boards is an obvious place to ask critical questions about why wearable technologies and sewing, rather than soldering, have become the new standard for supposedly gender-neutral inclusion efforts—where girls are introduced to programming by way of clothing, jewelry, and decoration (see projects like Made with Code or blink blink). Indeed, feminized tech fashion has come to be associated with the craft-aesthetics of Etsy, where commerce is still central but the focus is on the aesthetics (rather than performance metrics) of the female body and feminized spaces with the production of accessories, clothing, and household objects. While mainstream engagement with wearables enables dress acts that perform relatively familiar gender roles, we see opportunities for technologies of wear to be leveraged as technologies of care.

Smart technologies, many of which are small and portable, can carry the liberatory promise of alternative inputs and outputs. If we can shift the emphasis of inquiry in critical making and wearable tech toward embodied activation and away from the traditional "men look"/"women appear" structures that orient participants in visual culture, new possibilities for consciousness raising seem to emerge. More practically, smart devices may also orient users in the physical world, as in the case of the Transborder Immigrant Tool launched in 2007 by the Electronic Disturbance Theater (EDT), a digital arts collective headed by Ricardo Dominguez. EDT members repurposed inexpensive cell phones to utilize the phone's GPS technologies so that immigrants could find hidden water caches in the desert. In this way the device serves a portion of the function of a human guide as it senses the risks and rewards embedded in the landscape of the environment; it also serves as a rhapsode, uttering poetic verses at appropriate moments to provide spiritual consolation to the wandering carrier of the device.

Wearables are very often understood as technologies of quantification developed for military use; repositioning them *also as technologies of poiesis*, rhapsodic devices of comfort and affective world-making, allows us to reclaim them as technologies of care. As Abreu observes, the computational apparatuses that see, monitor, and measure us—whether for ourselves or others—rarely emphasize information about human relationships, or find value in measuring affective, social, and care-based relationships. By calling attention to both care and *poiesis*, classically understood as "to make or to form," we foreground the generative social and affective affordances of wearable and portable computing. Of course, as Jill Walker Rettberg points out in her work on the quantified self, even self-care can also be a form of discipline, and the transformation of human behavior into metrics enacts a disciplinary logic (Rettberg 2014). However, wearables present possibilities for poetic fashion, dress acts that draw our attention to materiality, commerce, consumption, and labor in productive ways. In recognizing that, in addition to computing, wearable technologies bring certain modes of being into existence, we are alerted to the ways physical computing and wearable technologies are about adapting, transforming, and contorting bodies, selves, and situations to the needs of the wearer, whether that be in a positive or antagonistic relation to the marketplace and other structures of power. Thinking through this in terms of an embodied and material *poiesis* refocuses attention on a making that is inextricably bound up in care of/for others and self as it transforms the world.

EDT member micha cárdenas (n.d.) has used wearable computing to enact specific ideas developed in her transgender cyberfeminist arts practice that focus on themes of danger and safety in inhabiting a gendered, sexualized, and racialized body in extremely complex rhetorical scenes that combine elaborate digital artifacts and challenging performance art. Working with her then-partner Elle Mehrmand in *virus.circus* (2010), cárdenas played a patient to Mehrmand's doctor "testing for viral contamination." In the performance of the piece, Mehrmand wields dildos that also function as scanners as foreplay to penetration of cárdenas's body. Mehrmand's clitoris is connected to a probing glove through a LilyPad Arduino and an accelerometer. The artists' heart rates are sensed, the pressure on Mehrmand's throat is monitored, and conductive threads sewn into cárdenas's dress register still more information. The data are all fed into a processing system that emits the ambient soundscape of the piece. One critic describes the complex rhetorical situation of "this explicit and yet tender scene" as one in which "we began to understand more fully the implications surrounding the sexualized relationship between doctor and patient" as well as "between technology and the subject" (Hoetger 2012: 1).

Affective and haptic knowledge can be promoted via viewed performance, as in the case of cárdenas's work, or through encounter, as is the case with Anouk Wipprecht's *Smoke Dress* (2013). *Smoke Dress* is printed on a 3-D printer and deploys a series of small wearable sensors and smoke machines to create a defensive fashion piece:

> [It is] a wireless and wearable tangible couture "smoke screen" imbued with the ability to suddenly visually obliterate itself through the excretion of a cloud of smoke. Ambient clouds of smoke are created when the dress detects a visitor approaching, thus camouflaging itself within its own materiality.
>
> (Lamontagne 2012; Wipprecht 2013)

As a dress that "defends" personal space by reacting to infringement, Wipprecht's piece depends upon not only the visual but also the tactile and olfactory senses. Both cárdenas's and Wipprecht's work exemplify tactical deployments of wearable technology and push against the privileging of the visual that dominates much of our learning and communication. Though still deeply gendered in both of these examples, wearables offer opportunities to explore the potential of haptic feedback to engender affective understandings of data (see Fuchs & Koch 2014). By explicitly working not just in visual modalities, these kinds of computational fashions may also point to new possibilities for expressing and understanding human relationships and affective elements of knowledge as well.

Wearables also have been used as specific interventions into the colonizing and discriminatory effects of western education systems. The E2 Textiles Project works with Salt River, Pima, and Maricopa Indian communities on training and projects in ethnocomputing: "Ethnocomputing recognizes local systems of computational knowledge at multiple levels, including data structures, algorithms, tools and theory, and uses" (Brayboy et al. 2011: 241). Craft and local knowledge systems are both forms of situated knowledge, and craftwork and codework merge as students sit with parents and grandparents developing both code and textile designs. Part of their answer to the question, "what might it look like to more fully engage cultural contexts in culturally responsive computing for Native American youth and communities?," is to use wearables as small vectors for communal (and care-ful) learning and collaborative creation. As elders help to sew or design traditional figures, the students talk about the details of programming a small device like a Lilypad or the ways that conductive materials will light up a sleeve. In 2015, students created hoodies with traditional designs that lit up only when the group held hands in a conductive circle, a different but equally powerful instance of embodied *poiesis*.

Technologies of care can express human relationships (those of the healthcare scenario, face-to-face interactions, or tribal community) as well as work to facilitate care of human persons. In addition to her performative work, cárdenas is currently working developing "Local Autonomy Networks (Autonets)" as part of "an artivist project focused on creating networks of communication to increase community autonomy and reduce violence against women, LGBTQI people, people of color and other groups who continue to survive violence on a daily basis" with networks that "are both online and offline, including handmade wearable electronic fashion and face to face agreements between people" (n.d.). Based on input from a series of performances, workshops, presentations, and discussions, cárdenas is prototyping "a line of mesh networked electronic clothing with the goal of building autonomous local networks that do not rely on corporate infrastructure to function" (n.d.). As she explains, to protect against rape, street harassment, and other forms of violence in the risky built environment of human social interaction, "garments, when activated, will alert everyone in range of the local mesh network who is wearing another autonet garment that someone needs help and will indicate that person's direction and distance" (cárdenas 2014).

While mesh networks, 3-D printing, and wearables have fantastic potentials, their development is deeply wrapped up in military and industrial pursuits and, like other technologies, are not inherently feminist (for more on military development of heads up displays (HUD), e-textiles, and other wearables, see Smailagic & Siewiorek 1996; Smailagic, Siewiorek, & Starner 2007). Transforming wearables and wearable culture into technologies of care requires both poetic and political interventions that not only bring different people to the table, but also challenge the motivations and possibilities that are literally encoded into such tools.

World-Craft at the Table

We have reframed wearables in order to highlight possibilities for embodied *poiesis* and have argued for the generative potentials for wearables and portable computing tools seen in physical computing and makerspaces. In our final turn we delve into feminist engagements with larger scale world-making. The boundaries between wearables, the IoT, "in real life," and virtual worlds are constantly in flux as new technologies and new cultures of use emerge. Even virtual worlds reflect material practices of craftivism, constructivism, and peer learning that we have emphasized with respect to our long maker table. Writing on the now-defunct virtual world of There.com, Celia Pearce observes that the successes were an effect of "expressive" avatar and animation, its ability to facilitate "bonds between people" and "open up creative channels for people who often had no idea they were even creative" (2010). A craft aesthetic can help to lower the barrier to entry, but it is easy to essentialize a single "craft aesthetic" and reinforce gendered design paradigms. As Pearce notes, part of what was so powerful about the virtual world of There.com was its willingness to be a space of play and peer learning, one in which "players find themselves inadvertently learning new things about themselves through structured social play" (2010).

As Alexandra Juhasz has observed in the course of her Ev-ent-anglement series, "off-the-shelf platforms bake in more and more ease-of-use but the corporations are always simplicity-steps ahead" (2015). Ease can be a deceptive and highly privileged technological affordance. At the same time, we opened with the observation that a certain style of DiY is unsatisfactory for creating a "long table" approach that not only brings women, people of color, and queer people to the table but also enables resistance to traditional narratives of disembodied, immaterial, nonaffective, and neutral technological engagement. Like Juhasz's ev-ent-anglement, which "treasures and relies upon the close-knit, intimate, specialist interests and commitments" of its participants (2015), we have fashioned making spaces that reject corporate and militaristic logics in favor of spaces where breaking, glitching, and theorizing are integral parts of our embodied, riotous, and poetic mode of making.

We have envisioned here a long table at which a diverse range of people might break breadboards and create new circuits. Part of what we hope to facilitate are creative engagements with technologies and ways of being that we have not yet imagined. In thinking of wearable technologies and physical computing tools in terms of technologies of wear and care, we have foregrounded the relational, material, and affective engagements that structure all of our techno-interactions. We are obviously optimistic that we can support spaces that are riotous and messy, even under the conditions of western capitalism that favor minimalism and efficiency. Nevertheless, as Juhasz suggests, the degree to which we can subvert technologies and tools designed to serve consumer, corporate, and government needs remains to be seen. Further, there is significant work yet to be done on the ways in which the simplicity and ease of use designed into platforms, tools, and hardware constrains our attempts at embodied *poiesis*. Finally, we are mindful of the many guises in which colonial outposts like the makerspaces can appear and the need to remain reflective and responsive in our own practices, which cannot escape deeply embedded structures of racism and inequality.

Further Reading

Kember, S. and J. Zylinska (2012) *Life after New Media: Mediation as a Vital Process*, Cambridge, MA: MIT Press

Nakamura, L. and P. Chow-White (eds.) (2011) *Race after the Internet*, New York, NY: Routledge.

Ryan, S. E. (2014) *Garments of Paradise: Wearable Discourse in the Digital Age*, Cambridge, MA: MIT Press.

Wyer, M., M. Barbercheck, D. Cookmeyer, H. Ozturk, and M. Wayne (eds.) (2013) *Women, Science, and Technology: A Reader in Feminist Science Studies*, 3rd edn, New York, NY: Routledge.

References

Abreu, A. (2014) "Quantify Everything: A Dream of a Feminist Data Future," *Model View Culture*, retrieved from modelviewculture.com/pieces/quantify-everything-a-dream-of-a-feminist-data-future.

Austin, J. L. (1962) *How to Do Things with Words*, Cambridge, MA: Harvard University Press.

blink blink (n.d.) retrieved from www.blinkblink.cc.

Brayboy, B., J. McK, H. R. Gough, B. Leonard, R. F. Roehl, and J. A. Solyom (2011) "Reclaiming Scholarship: Critical Indigenous Research Methodologies," in S. D. Lapan, ML. T. Quartoli, and F. J. Riemer (eds.) *Qualitative Research: An Introduction to Methods and Designs*, San Frencisco, CA: Jossey-Bass.

cárdenas, m. (n.d.) Autonets, retrieved from faculty.washington.edu/michamc/autonets.

cárdenas, m. (2014) "Local Autonomy Networks / Autonets," *Zero1 Biennial*, retrieved from 2012.zero1biennial.org/micha-cárdenas.

Chardronnet, E. (2015) "GynePunk, the Cyborg Witches of DIY gynecology," *Makery*, retrieved from www.makery.info/en/2015/06/30/gynepunk-les-sorcieres-cyborg-de-la-gynecologie-diy.

Christian, B. (1996) "Does Theory Play Well in the Classroom," in G. Bowles, M. Fabi, and A. Kaiser (eds) *New Black Feminist Criticism, 1985–2000*, Urbana and Chicago: University of Illinois Press.

Dijkstra, E. W. (1988) "On the Cruelty of Really Teaching Computing Science." cs.utexas.edu/users/EWD/ewd10xx/EWD1036.PDF.

Dunbar-Hester, C. (2014) "Radical Inclusion? Locating Accountability in Technical DIY," in M. Ratto M. and M. Boler (eds.) (2014) *DIY Citizenship: Critical Making and Social Media*, Cambridge, MA: MIT Press, pp. 75–88.

Earhart, A. E. (2015) *Traces of the Old, Uses of the New: The Emergence of Digital Literary Studies*, Ann Arbor, MI: University of Michigan Press.

Fox, S., R. R. Ulgado, and D. K. Rosner. (2015) "Hacking Culture, Not Devices: Access and Recognition in Feminist Hackerspaces," in *Proceedings of the 18th ACM Conference on Computer Supported Cooperative Work & Social Computing*, 56–68. Vancouver, BC, Canada: ACM.

Fuchs, T. and S. C. Koch (2014) "Embodied Affectivity: On Moving and Being Moved," *Front Psychol* 5, 508.

Garfinkel, S. (2014) "Building Critical Contexts." American Studies Association Annual Conference, Los Angeles, CA.

Haraway, D. (1991) "A Cyborg Manifesto," retrieved from www.egs.edu/faculty/donna-haraway/articles/donna-haraway-a-cyborg-manifesto.

Hoetger, M. (2012) "Review: Virus.circus.probe. Performed by micha cárdenas and Elle Mehrmand at GUTTED. Los Angeles Contemporary Exhibition (LACE). Hollywood, CA. 19 January 2011," *Junctures: The Journal for Thematic Dialogue* 15.

Juhasz, A. (2015) "Ev-ent-anglement 3: One Current Shape for Internet Feminism and its Many Discontents," *Ev-ent-anglement*, retrieved from ev-ent-anglement.com/ev-ent-anglement-3-one-current-shape-for-internet-feminism-and-its-many-discontents.

Kember, S. and J. Zylinska (2012) *Life after New Media: Mediation as a Vital Process*, Cambridge, MA: MIT Press.

Lamontagne, V. (2012) "TECHNOSENSUAL Review + Interview with Anouk Wipprecht," *FashioningTech*, retrieved from ning.fashioningtech.com/profiles/blogs/technosensual-review-interview-with-anouk-wipprecht.

Made with Code (n.d.) retrieved from www.madewithcode.com/home.

O'Sullivan, D. and T. Igoe (2004) *Physical Computing: Sensing and Controlling the Physical World with Computers*, Farmington Hills, MI: Gale.

Owens, T. (2011) "The Digital Humanities as the DIY Humanities," Trevor Owens, retrieved from www.trevorowens.org/2011/07/the-digital-humanities-as-the-diy-humanities.

Pearce, C. (2010) "Requiem for a World." *Gamasutra*. gamasutra.com/view/news/118796/InDepth_Requiem_For_A_World.php.

Posner, M. (2012) "Some Things to Think about before You Exhort Everyone to Code," Miriam Posner's Blog, retrieved from miriamposner.com/blog/some-things-to-think-about-before-you-exhort-everyone-to-code.

Quattrocchi, C. (2013) "MAKE'ing More Diverse Makers," *EdSurge*, retrieved from www.edsurge.com/n/2013_10_29_make_ing_more_diverse_ makers.

Ratto, M. (2011) "Critical Making: Conceptual and Material Studies in Technology and Social Life," *The Information Society: An International Journal* 27(4), 252–60.

Rettberg, J. W. (2014) *Seeing Ourselves through Technology*, New York, NY : Palgrave Macmillan Press.

Ryan, S. E. (2014) *Garments of Paradise: Wearable Discourse in the Digital Age*, Cambridge, MA: MIT Press.

Schilt, K. (2005) "The Punk White Privilege Scene: Riot Grrl, White Privilege, and Zines," in J. Reger (ed.) *Different Wavelengths: Studies of the Contemporary Women's Movement*, New York, NY: Routledge.

Smailagic, A. and D. Siewiorek (1996) "The CMU Mobile Computers and Their Application for Maintenance," Mobile Computing 353 of *The Kluwer International Series in Engineering and Computer Science*, 681–98.

Smailagic, A., D. Siewiorek, and T. Starner (2007) "Wearable Computers," in A. Sears and J. Jacko (eds.) *The Human-Computer Interaction Handbook: Fundamentals, Evolving Technologies, and Emerging Applications*, New York, NY: Taylor Francis.

Smith, J. and K. MacLean (2007) "Communicating Emotion through a Haptic Link: Design Space and Methodology," *Int. J. Humam-Computer Studies* 65, 376–87.

Transborder Immigrant Tool | b.a.n.g. lab and Electronic Disturbance Theater 2.0 (n.d.)

Vee, A. (2012) "Coding Values," *Enculturation*, retrieved from enculturation.net/node/5268.

Wernimont, J. (2012) "Making It Like a Riot-Grrrrl," retrieved from jwernimont.wordpress.com/2012/03/03/making-it-like-a-riot-grrrrl.

Wipprecht, A. (2013) SMOKEDRESS [2012] // Anouk Wipprecht | Aduen Darriba // tangible couture "smoke screen" [550gram].

Wuschitz, S. (n.d.) "RUMAH HACKER," retrieved from grenzartikel.com/projects/?p=1152.

10

A GLITCH IN THE TOWER

Academia, Disability, and Digital Humanities

Elizabeth Ellcessor

In his treatise on the state of digital humanities, Alan Liu posits that the emerging field—drawn from traditions of humanities computing and new media studies—is potentially unprepared to intervene on behalf of the humanities in contemporary academia and society. He fears that digital humanities does "not yet possess an adequate critical awareness of the . . . specifically institutional—in this case, higher education—issues at stake" (2012: 11). As a scholar of new media who uses humanistic approaches to analyze digital tools and cultures, I am implicated in this critique; little effort has been made by critical media scholars to analyze or critique the increasingly digitally mediated classrooms, course management systems, presentational media, and online education services that surround us. We miss an opportunity for powerful intervention when we look past the very digital tools and cultures that make scholarship and pedagogy possible in contemporary universities.

Digital tools and services are routinely lauded for their ability to increase *access* to texts, resources, educational experiences, and new forms of pedagogy. Yet, merely making material available is insufficient to promote genuine access.

The limitations of existing rhetorics of access surrounding the digital tools of academic life are seen clearly in the case of disability. Several cases of digital media inaccessibility have risen to national attention in recent years, most notably the injunction against campus use of e-readers that did not have controls that could be navigated nonvisually. Digital media accessibility—the technologies, processes, and cultures that enable "a person with one or more disabilities to make meaningful use of a media technology, whether through assistive technologies or through modification of mainstream technologies" (Ellcessor 2016: 11)—is a technological intervention with political impact. The different technological arrangements, needs, and uses that may characterize the use of digital media by people with disabilities reveal not only alternative ways of interacting with common tools, tasks, and services but also the normative traits of "mainstream" digital media technologies and the ideologies that they rest upon and perpetuate.

Disability is a glitch in the system, revealing the system's failures and offering a leverage point from which to pry it apart and potentially rebuild it. Peter Krapp states that "faults, glitches, and bugs are too often relegated to the realm of the accidental" (2011: 53). That is, *glitches are also constitutive of digital media technologies and their operations*. To begin from the point of failure, from the inefficiencies, from the exclusions means that it is particularly fruitful to consider the use of presentational and educational media from the standpoint of disability. Communication and disability scholar, Kevin Gotkin, proposes the glitch—"a spurious technical rupture"—as a crip moment, disrupting media systems in the same way that disability has upended conceptions of normative bodies and lives (n.d.). Within disability studies, "crip" indicates a politicized concept of disability used to question the established order of things. If the glitches in digital media are interpreted in this way, then we are, in essence, stepping outside of dominant paradigms regarding digital media in academia and looking for ways to critique it, reveal its politics, intervene, and ultimately build alternatives.

In this chapter, I review scholarship related to disability and digital accessibility, as well as literature on universal design for learning, before turning to three avenues for intervention that may enable people working within digital humanities (conceived broadly) to better understand and critique the digital tools of academia and meaningfully intervene on behalf of a more inclusive academic sphere.

Disability Studies and Digital Accessibility

The foundation of much critical and media studies work on digital accessibility lies in disability studies. A growing and interdisciplinary field, disability studies proceeds from the stance that ability (in all its forms) is a social construct with material components worthy of attention and foundational to conceptions of the body, civil society, medicine, culture, and other areas of human life. Much work has proceeded from the "social model of disability," in which an individual's impairment is only disabling in the context of a society that does not accommodate it (Oliver 1983). The lack of accommodation is attributed to ableism, an ideology that positions a normative, able body as desirable and variously excludes and devalues those who do not meet standards of ability. More recently, scholars have complicated the social model, as in Alison Kafer's "political-relational model of disability," which argues that disability is established through embodied social, material, and institutional relationships, all of which are available for political critique and action (2013: 6). When a wheelchair user confronts a staircase, the inaccessibility produces disability and enables critical awareness and action.

Much work on digital media accessibility examines how technology excludes people with disabilities and reproduces ableism. Gerard Goggin and Christopher Newell's pioneering work in *Digital Disability* sought "to cast a critical gaze upon the very technologies that are supposed to provide the solution to disability—and show how new media technologies actually build in disability" (2003: xv). Their analysis demonstrates that mainstream digital media offer opportunities for people with disabilities but also reproduce unequal relations of dis/ability. Similarly, Ingunn Moser (2006) demonstrates the ways in which new technologies reproduce distinctions between normal and deviant, abled and disabled; and Alison Adam and David Kreps (2009) argue that studies of web accessibility must incorporate critical disability studies and the perspectives of disabled communities.

The early twenty-first century also saw significant scholarship focused on quantifying and critiquing policies, technologies, and implementations of accessibility. Some of this work focuses on analysis and critique of the laws and policies that govern disability access, including those that govern the federal government and the voluntary guidelines established by the World Wide Web Consortium (Brys & Vanderbauwhede 2006; Easton 2011; Jaeger 2011;

Wentz et al. 2011). Other studies quantified compliance with laws and standards, routinely finding that inaccessibility was rampant even in sectors required to provide access to people with disabilities (Lazar & Greenidge 2006; Olalere & Lazar 2011; Hanson & Richards 2013; Bose & Jürgensen 2014).

Recent years have seen growing interest in digital media and disability, strongly influenced by both trajectories. For instance, *Disability and New Media* (Ellis & Kent 2010) incorporates a chapter dedicated to explaining and critiquing accessibility policies in the U.S., U.K., and Australia, while also turning attention to the role of disability in social media cultures and the diverse experiences of users with disabilities. Meryl Alper's (2014, 2015) work draws on media, disability, and science and technology studies to contextualize the uses of computing technology by young people with disabilities. Others have turned to the industries and professionals involved in creating policies and technologies that support accessibility (Kennedy 2011; Ellcessor 2014). There is a growing body of historical work, using archival, policy, and popular documents to trace the development of digital accessibility practices (Alper 2015; Petrick 2015). The field of digital media and disability studies is growing quickly. Taken as a whole, it "illuminates the cultural, historical, political, and economic forces that for better and for worse shape the lived experience of disability" in technologically mediated, western societies (Alper et al. 2015).

Though this literature offers robust critical perspectives on the glitch of disability, it has not addressed the media that characterize academic life. There has not been sustained attention to course management systems, presentational media (projectors, slideshows, etc.), or even the lowly PDF within critical studies of digital media and disability. In fact, most of this work looks outside of academia entirely, examining the leisure practices of people with disabilities, studying learning outside the classroom, or focusing on popular media representations. Thus, I now turn to a body of literature that applies a disability studies perspective to academia.

Universal Design for Learning

Many disability studies scholars embrace the theory of "universal design for learning," a perspective which draws upon notions of universal design in architecture and design fields to argue for the development of learning environments that work (without accommodation) for the largest possible range of people. This approach often involves curriculum adjustment, via the provision of flexible content, assessments, and supports for various forms of student engagement and learning (Rose et al. 2002: 75). Universal design for learning is understood to be a matter of inclusion, as when Jay Dolmage argues that "Universal Design as praxis is still a matter of social justice" (2008). Universal design does not, however, mean that everyone partakes of content in the same way; often it is a matter of providing options, or default accommodations, or simply flexibility. Margaret Price argues that increasing access in academia requires the creation of multiple paths, or "ways to move," that enable individuals to chart a course toward access (2011). Universal design for learning is one way of creating learning experiences that may be reconfigured according to individual needs.

Often, universal design is discussed as a strategy for increasing access, itself a complicated phenomenon. Disability scholar Tanya Titchkosky, in *The Question of Access*, interrogates the concept of access by chronicling her experiences with identity, accommodation, and inclusion within university bureaucracies. Though much of her work focuses on physical forms of accessibility, she provocatively argues that "[b]etween access and inaccessibility lies a place where it is possible to theorize the cultural configurations of embodied existence and come to experience our interrelatedness differently" (2011: 70). Questions of access, or its absence, can form a basis of knowledge and reveal the normative structures of academia in all of its dimensions.

The literature summarized here advocates for universal design of the university in its physical, cultural, institutional, and digital facets. However, universal design is not unproblematic. As Titchkosky learned in attempting to build a universally designed classroom space, budgetary and management structures of the university demanded that disability be proven and accessibility necessary before providing the limited resource of accessible classroom space. Though universal design revealed the normalcy of exclusionary ideas about "who belonged" in the university space, it was not enough to change bureaucratic functions (Titchkosky 2011: 37). Universal design is provocative, but incomplete. There is no perfect design for all people, with and without disabilities, and some people will always require specific accommodations for specific tasks. Too strong a focus on universal design can obscure these needs and even render disability (and accommodations) invisible. As Bess Williamson argues, focusing on benefits for "everyone" has resulted in "images and coverage that elided or even eliminated any actual persons with disabilities" (2012: 214). It may also have the effect of marginalizing the insights of disability experiences or cultures. When universal design becomes the only answer to the "glitch" of disability in academia, much of the critical heft of disability critique may be lost, minimizing its political impact.

If not (only) universal design, then how might digital humanities scholars intervene in the digitally mediated university? In addition to learning from advocates of universal design, we might marshal the complex understandings of access and accommodation provided by disability studies scholarship with methods and modes of intervention born of new (and old) media studies, including multifaceted analysis of digital sites and services, an engaged praxis online and off, and a political and institutional advocacy within our institutions and broader scholarly fields.

Methods and Interventions

There are three trajectories via which we might study, intervene in, and learn from the "glitch" of disability in academic contexts. First, there are analytic methods, such as critical code studies and discursive interface analysis. Second, there are opportunities for critically engaged praxis, online and off, in which disability access and inclusion are considered throughout the development of new systems. And third, drawing on activist traditions in disability studies and social justice work, digital humanists and allies may engage in direct advocacy regarding policies for the adoption of new media technologies in academic contexts.

Analytic Methods

Humanistic methods for the study of digital artifacts can productively be turned to the very media that pervade contemporary academic life. For instance, critical code studies, as defined by Mark Marino, "is the application of critical theory and hermeneutics to the interpretation of computer source code" (2006). The meanings, contexts, and instantiations of cultural values in computer code are available for analysis and reveal assumptions about able bodies that are built into these systems. Even at the level of HTML (a markup language), analysis of the code needed to render pages accessible for people with disabilities reveals the history of accessibility as a retrofit, added later and intended for a secondary audience. This retrofitting is evident in websites from the late 1990s and early 2000s, when pages linked to separate "text-only" pages for visually impaired users but also used HTML and CSS to hide those links from people using visual displays. Such deliberate masking, and separate content, reified the secondary status of accessible content. Turning critical code studies onto the course management systems used in university settings could reveal similar histories and structures of technology that continue to prioritize able-bodied users over those who need accessibility features.

Another methodological approach with promise for analysis of academic media is what Mel Stanfill refers to as "discursive interface analysis." This method entails analysis of the "norms produced by 'affordances' of websites" (2015: 1062), looking at function and aesthetics to determine how an ideal user is built into the technological system. Stanfill notes Michele White (2006) and Lisa Nakamura (2008) as examples of scholars who have published this kind of work; I would add that Tarleton Gillespie's (2003) research on the politics of web design tools, work in game studies (Montfort & Bogost 2008), Megan Sapnar Ankerson's (2012) historical analysis of Flash websites, Jason Farman's (2012) *Mobile Interface Theory*, and my own analyses of a "preferred user position" that excludes disability (2016) exemplify similar methods. This work is particularly valuable in the context of higher education because, when we investigate "which ideals, assumptions, and norms underlie design and shape the 'correct' or easiest way to use" a given technology (Stanfill 2015: 1071), we also gain insight into the normative construction of academic behavior, life, time, space, and forms of embodiment.

Critically Engaged Praxis

The second pathway through which to learn from, about, and beyond the glitch of disability comes through critically engaged praxis. Anne Balsamo discusses praxis as a "methodological approach [that] blends insights from multiple design disciplines with critical techniques of cultural interpretation that are central to the humanities and interpretive sciences" (2011: 11). In digital humanities, where design and critical work are routinely commingled, "we should," in the words of Tara McPherson, "design our tools differently, in a mode that explicitly engages power and difference from the get-go" (2014: 182). Such critically engaged design also recalls George Williams's argument for universal design in digital humanities. Williams believes that digital humanities should embrace universal design principles and work with disabled people to increase access and gain perspective on "its assumptions about how digital devices could and should work with and for people" (2012). Universally designed artifacts, he believes, would be more robust over time, across devices, and for diverse audiences. Balsamo, McPherson, and Williams all emphasize the role of critical work in the design of innovative, inclusive, and politically interventionist digital media artifacts.

While addressing the design of new tools is obviously important, we must also consider the very technologies, practices, and pedagogies that constitute our "normal" work. In my own field of film and media studies, showing a screening or short clip is a foundational means of teaching as well as conducting and presenting research. By viewing the material, it becomes available for analysis and interpretation. This, of course, poses accessibility problems for people with aural or visual impairments (and possibly for others). Left to university offices that serve students with disabilities, these challenges are addressed on a case-by-case basis, often via private streaming services that the student must access from their own computer on their own time. Such individual accommodations are, in the words of one closed-captioning professional, "not the same experience" as the shared viewing of a traditional screening or clip. In other contexts, such as a conference, there is no disability office running interference; the foundational praxis of the field may be exclusionary.

A critically engaged praxis, then, would entail consideration of how these access challenges might be met using the affordances of digital media. Addressing access could entail personally captioning or audio-describing content, using a service such as Amara from the Participatory Culture Foundation, and delivering these access measures to a full class or audience. More radically, these glitches in the research and pedagogy of film and media studies might lead to considerations about how material has been studied and what kinds of analysis are possible, impossible, and made newly possible when the screening or clip is made problematic. Just as video essays may enable different modes of thinking and comprehension than traditional written essays, so might the field of film and media studies be reimagined from a perspective in which the screening, clip, or "text" is deprioritized or made multiple. There are many means of accessing media, many of which involve extremely multimodal and complex interactions of visual, audio, textual, and tactile information. The "normal" viewing position has structured much of our scholarship, but disability and the differences in experience that it brings may open up many new questions and insights. If, as McPherson writes, video essays enable multimodal humanists to produce "work that reconfigures the relationships among author, reader, and technology" (2009: 120), so, too, could scholarship that proceeds from differential media experience, varied forms of access, and multiple, equally (un)important "texts" that reconfigure core assumptions. Networked digital media are uniquely suited to producing and representing this kind of multiplicity and might be productively used to destabilize much of the normative stance that has been developed through the history of these fields.

Direct Advocacy

Finally, there are opportunities for direct advocacy regarding the adoption of new media technologies in various academic contexts. Digital humanists and allies are well-positioned to be part of discussions about the cultural impact, exclusions, and meanings created by the adoption of particular hardware or software. Our ability to critique corporate or mainstream technologies and engage in the critical development of new media tools and artifacts enables us to lend a unique perspective to these discussions. At an institutional level, this may mean seeking involvement with disability student services or accessible media offices in order to push for more inclusive forms of accommodation, or working with information technology units as they license or develop instructional software. Student activists may also organize disability-themed clubs and events through which to advocate for more accessible campus environments.

It is equally important, however, to be aware of larger policy contexts. For instance, while nearly all U.S. universities are recipients of federal funding and thus obliged to make content accessible to people with disabilities under the Rehabilitation Act, such practices were slow to be adopted and remain far from ubiquitous. In 2010, the U.S. Departments of Justice and Education issued a joint letter to universities reminding them of their obligations under this law and the Americans with Disabilities Act: "it is unacceptable for universities to use emerging technology without insisting that this technology be accessible to all students" (Perez & Ali 2010). Thus, haphazard adoption of e-readers, tablet computers, smart boards, and other technologies must be replaced by conscientious attention to the kinds of teaching and scholarship allowed and excluded by these innovations. An awareness of the "glitch" of disability, and the ways in which new media, digital technologies, and computation are social justice issues, is imperative to ensuring that the adoption of new media technologies extends students' rights and abilities to learn.

This is not to say that all of us working in digital humanities must become experts at either laws or technologies related to digital media accessibility. There have been some indications that, "with the growth of online education, it is now largely the obligation of the instructors themselves to proactively design courses that are equally accessible to all students" (Ingeno 2013). Such a stance drastically increases the scope and quantity of instructors' labor, making accessibility oversights the responsibility of those with limited knowledge or skills in this area. Instead, it is important to be aware of opportunities to address these concerns on a large scale or via collaborative practices and norms. Resources such as Amara, Web Accessibility in Mind, and the accessibility guidelines for publication recently proposed by disability studies scholars (Straumsheim 2015) can serve important roles not merely in the creation of our own media but also as educational and outreach tools through which we engage others in these issues. A similar resource was proposed in the TEACH Act, which would have tasked the U.S. federal government with creating guidelines for the adoption of accessible technologies in higher education. Though this was not passed, awareness of its existence and advocacy for similar measures would go a long way in spreading awareness of the ways in which digital media may exclude people with disabilities.

Conclusion

This chapter has considered the ways in which digital media common to the higher educational environment function as technologies of ability, affirming normative bodies and accordant perspectives while often excluding those, such as people with disabilities, who do not embody those norms. Treating disability as a glitch in the system—a feature that offers an opportunity to see differently and critique normative structures—I have attempted to demonstrate how scholars might reimagine a range of academic technologies, practices, and contexts.

The brief overviews of literature about disability and digital media as well as universal design for learning exhibit the ways in which these conversations have developed, roughly in parallel. With its critical interest in digital technologies, digital humanities are well positioned to be a fulcrum leveraging these perspectives into actionable research methods, praxis, and advocacy. The three trajectories for action laid out in this chapter are robust and practical paths, but they are certainly not the only means by which these connections can be made. Thinking through the glitch of disability exposes academic media technologies, practices, and institutions to new forms of critique and engagement; we are emboldened to think about, make, and do things differently, and in so doing may find even more radical and transformative means of intervention in the ivory tower and beyond.

Further Reading

Ellis, K. and M. Kent (2010) *Disability and New Media*, New York, NY: Routledge.

Williams, G. H. (2012) "Disability, Universal Design, and the Digital Humanities," in Gold, M. K. (ed.) *Debates in the Digital Humanities*, Minneapolis, MN: University Of Minnesota Press, pp. 202–12, retrieved from dhdebates.gc.cuny.edu/debates/text/44.

References

Adam, A. and D. Kreps (2009) "Disability and Discourses of Web Accessibility," *Information, Communication & Society* 12(7), 1041–58.

Alper, M. (2014) *Digital Youth with Disabilities*, Cambridge, MA: MIT Press.

Alper, M. (2015) "Augmentative, Alternative, and Assistive: Reimagining the History of Mobile Computing and Disability," *IEEE Annals of the History of Computing* 37(1), 96.

Alper, M., E. Ellcessor, K. Ellis, and G. M. Goggin (2015) "Reimagining the Good Life with Disability: Communication, New Technology, and Humane Connections," in H. Wang (ed.) *Communication and the Good Life, ICA Annual Conference Theme Book Series*, New York, NY: Peter Lang, pp. 197–212.

Ankerson, M. S. (2012) "Writing Web Histories with an Eye on the Analog Past," *New Media & Society* 14(3), 384–400.

Balsamo, A. (2011) *Designing Culture: The Technological Imagination at Work*, Raleigh, NC: Duke University Press.

Bose, R. and H. Jürgensen (2014) "Accessibility of E-Commerce Websites for Vision-Impaired Persons," in K. Miesenberger, D. Fels, D. Archambault, P. Peňáz, and W. Zagler (eds.) *Computers Helping People with Special Needs, 14th International Conference, ICCHP 2014, Paris, France, July 9–11, Proceedings, Part I*, Springer International Publishing, pp. 121–28.

Brys, C. M. and Vanderbauwhede, W. (2006) "Communication Challenges in the W3Cs Web Content Accessibility Guidelines," *Technical Communication* 53(1), 60–78.

Dolmage, J. (2008) "Mapping Composition—Inviting Disability in the Front Door, " in C. Lewiecki-Wilson and B. J. Brueggemann (eds.) *Disability and the Teaching of Writing: A Critical Sourcebook*, Boston, MA: Bedford/St. Martin's, pp. 14–27.

Easton, C. (2011) "The Web Content Accessibility Guidelines 2.0: An Analysis of Industry Self-Regulation," *International Journal of Law and Information Technology* 19(1), 74–93.

Ellcessor, E. (2014) "<ALT="Textbooks">: Web Accessibility Myths as Negotiated Industrial Lore," *Critical Studies in Media Communication* 31(5), 448–63.

Ellcessor, E. (2016) *Restricted Access: Media, Disability, and the Politics of Participation*, New York, NY: NYU Press.

Ellis, K. and M. Kent (2010) *Disability and New Media*, New York, NY: Routledge.

Farman, J. (2012) *Mobile Interface Theory: Embodied Space and Locative Media*, New York, NY: Routledge.

Gillespie, T. (2003) "The Stories Digital Tools Tell," in A. Everett and J. T. Caldwell (eds.) *New Media: Theories and Practices of Digitextuality*, New York, NY: Routledge, pp. 107–26.

Goggin, G. and C. Newell (2003) *Digital Disability: The Social Construction of Disability in New Media*, Lanham, MD: Rowman & Littlefield.

Gotkin, K. (n.d.) "Crip/Glitch," *Kevin Gotkin*, Personal site, retrieved from kevingotkin.com/portfolio/crip-glitch/.

Hanson, V. L. and J. T. Richards (2013) "Progress on Website Accessibility?" *ACM Trans. Web* 7(1), 2:1–2:30.

Ingeno, L. (2013) "Online Accessibility a Faculty Duty," *Inside Higher Ed*, retrieved from www.insidehighered.com/news/2013/06/24/faculty-responsible-making-online-materials-accessible-disabled-students.

Jaeger, P. T. (2011) *Disability and the Internet: Confronting a Digital Divide*, Boulder, CO: Lynne Rienner Publishers.

Kafer, A. (2013) *Feminist, Queer, Crip*, Bloomington, IN: Indiana University Press.

Kennedy, H. (2011) *Net Work: Ethics and Values in Web Design*, New York, NY: Palgrave Macmillan.

Krapp, P. (2011) *Noise Channels: Glitch and Error in Digital Culture*, Minneapolis, MN: University of Minnesota Press.

Lazar, J. and K. -D. Greenidge (2006) "One Year Older, But Not Necessarily Wiser: An Evaluation of Homepage Accessibility Problems over Time," *Universal Access in the Information Society* 4(4), 285–91.

Liu, A. (2012) "The State of the Digital Humanities: A Report and a Critique," *Arts and Humanities in Higher Education* 11(1–2), 8–41.

Marino, M. C. (2006) "Critical Code Studies," *Electronic Book Review*, retrieved from electronicbookreview.com/thread/electropoetics/codology.

McPherson, T. (2009) "Introduction: Media Studies and the Digital Humanities," *Cinema Journal* 48(2), 119–23.

McPherson, T. (2014) "Designing for Difference," *differences* 25(1), 177–88.

Montfort, N. and I. Bogost (2008) *Racing the Beam: The Atari Video Game System, Platform Studies Series*, Cambridge, MA: MIT Press.

Moser, I. (2006) "Disability and the Promises of Technology: Technology, Subjectivity and Embodiment within an Order of the Normal," *Information, Communication & Society* 9(3), 373–95.

Nakamura, L. (2008) *Digitizing Race: Visual Cultures of the Internet*, Minneapolis, MN: University of Minnesota Press.

Olalere, A. and J. Lazar (2011) "Accessibility of U.S. Federal Government Home Pages: Section 508 Compliance and Site Accessibility Statements," *Government Information Quarterly* 28(3), 303–09.

Oliver, M. (1983) *Social Work with Disabled People*, Basingstoke, UK: Macmillan Press.

Perez, T. E. and R. Ali (2010) "Dear Colleague Letter: Electronic Book Readers," retrieved from www.documentcloud.org/documents/713149-colleague-20100629.html.

Petrick, E. R. (2015) *Making Computers Accessible: Disability Rights and Digital Technology*, Baltimore, MD: Johns Hopkins University Press.

Price, M. (2011) *Mad at School: Rhetorics of Mental Disability and Academic Life*, Ann Arbor, MI: University of Michigan Press.

Rose, D., A. Meyer, and N. Strangman (2002) *Teaching Every Student in the Digital Age: Universal Design for Learning*, Alexandria, VA: Association for Supervision & Curriculum Development.

Stanfill, M. (2015) "The Interface as Discourse: The Production of Norms through Web Design," *New Media & Society* 17(7), 1059–74.

Straumsheim, C. (2015) "Disability Studies Scholars Present Accessibility Guidelines," *Inside Higher Ed*, retrieved from www.insidehighered.com/news/2015/06/16/disability-studies-scholars-present-accessibility-guidelines.

Titchkosky, T. (2011) *The Question of Access: Disability, Space, Meaning*, Toronto, ON: University of Toronto Press.

Wentz, B., P. T. Jaeger, and J. Lazar (2011) "Retrofitting Accessibility: The Legal Inequality of After-the-Fact Online Access for Persons with Disabilities in the United States," *First Monday* 16(11), retrieved from firstmonday.org/ojs/index.php/fm/article/view/3666.

White, M. (2006) *The Body and the Screen: Theories of Internet Spectatorship*, Cambridge, MA: MIT Press.

Williams, G. H. (2012) "Disability, Universal Design, and the Digital Humanities," in M. K. Gold (ed.) *Debates in the Digital Humanities*, Minneapolis, MN: University of Minnesota Press, pp. 202–12, retrieved from dhdebates.gc.cuny.edu/debates/text/44.

Williamson, B. (2012) "Getting a Grip: Disability in American Industrial Design of the Late Twentieth Century," *Winterthur Portfolio*, 46(4), 213–36.

11

GAME STUDIES FOR GREAT JUSTICE

Amanda Phillips

In the age of GamerGate, the "social justice warrior" has become a polarizing figure in gaming culture: a hero to some (who might prefer job classes like wizard or rogue instead), but an emblem of all that is wrong with political correctness to others. GamerGate, a high-profile harassment event that began with an ex-lover's vengeful tirade against an independent game developer and eventually expanded into a wide-ranging assault on political accountability in gaming under the guise of concern for "ethics in games journalism," has unfortunately hijacked conversations about social justice in game studies, marking nearly every conversation about race, gender, and sexuality in videogames. While the use of "social justice" as an aspersion is a fairly recent development (intersecting, as well, with trends in Tumblr activism), I engage it here in its classic form: the pursuit of fairness in the many political and social systems that structure our everyday lives. Robyn Wiegman expresses it best:

> I use the phrase "social justice" as a generic figure of the political destination of identity knowledges, knowing that its meaning is precisely what is at stake in the different disciplinary and critical relations that generate identity-based scholarship. For some scholars and in some disciplinary traditions, social justice will always be measured by a state-oriented outcome, with the transformation of laws and policies signifying its political resolution. In others, the juridical solution is absolutely rejected, along with the terms by which dissent is managed in a liberal social order, such that justice is always excessive of constitutional orders and governmentality of any kind, being the eternally postponed figure of what is to come.
>
> (Wiegman 2012: 3)

Wiegman's definition leaves the end of social justice somewhat open, for the disciplines engage with the concept on vastly different terms. Videogames may seem a trivial object for those concerned with something so grand as equity, but they are an increasingly important component of the media landscapes that shape the world around us. As a scholar trained in the interpretive humanities, my social justice scholarship on games aims both to recognize the links between real-world structures of power and their diffuse ideological forms in games and to open up new futures through alternative interpretive readings. A sociologist may pursue social justice in game studies by giving voice to marginalized gaming communities. A game designer may pursue social justice by inventing new game mechanics that challenge the dominance of competition and violence in the medium. There are many, many ways to do game studies for great justice.

In the spirit of modeling social justice academic practice, I would like to start by pointing out that what I have to say in this chapter does not come from my own brilliance and experience, but from listening to and receiving the wisdom of other folks, mostly women of color, who have been theorizing and designing intersectional paradigms of justice for centuries. For this piece in particular, I am grateful to the Summer 2015 workshop participants for the Center for Solutions to Online Violence, who have helped to shape my understanding of social justice practice in online scholarship, as well as Professors Barbara Tomlinson and George Lipsitz for their help in introducing me to thinking about disciplinary disloyalty. My aim is to point newcomers in the direction of particular scholars and methodologies, and to do justice to their legacies by building on their contributions in other fields.

This chapter offers five concrete suggestions to launch your game studies for great justice. Its title derives from an old internet meme centering on the mistranslation of the introduction to Toaplan's (1991) Mega Drive port of *Zero Wing*. "All your base are belong to us" might be a more familiar part of that same translation; and as such a title might suggest, this chapter assumes some familiarity with videogames and gaming culture. It will be most useful for scholars who are acquainted with the basics of videogame or media studies but are hoping to direct their research toward a cultural studies approach that prioritizes the pursuit of systemic justice over simpler solutions like diversity and representation.

Look Beyond the Fun

Having an emotional attachment is a vital part of scholarship. Researchers do not dedicate so much time and energy to questions and texts that have no personal value for them. For scholars of social justice in particular, leading with the heart is an important way to push back against the dehumanization and impossibility of "objective" research, which frequently masks the operations of hegemony. However, it is also important to be aware of how such attachments influence one's analysis and exposure to different kinds of texts.

This is particularly important in studying videogames because of the way they historically have been linked to fun and fandom. We think of games as things we do for fun, even when we are making or studying them. Much of the popular discourse around gaming connects them to the pleasure and satisfaction that comes from achievement or overcoming obstacles, even when the point is not fun itself, but more mundane achievements like training. The popularity of gamification attests to the allure of "fun" for educators, advertisers, and gamers alike.

But fun is not everything. Bonnie Ruberg (2015) argues that the hegemony of fun in game design and culture flattens the emotional complexity of the gamic experience, and that "no-fun" can be an affective position with radical potential. She points to scholars such as Jesper Juul (2013), who writes about how failure and frustration are also important characteristics of gameplay. In fact, failing is one of the most important parts of a game, since we do it over and over again. This line of inquiry matches up with social justice disciplines that recognize how competition, winning, popularity, and mass accumulation are important components of white supremacist cisheteropatriarchy.

Let us look at three different critical lenses that might be useful in thinking about unfun aspects of gaming. Ruberg (2015) engages queer failure, a concept developed by J. Jack Halberstam (2011), to think about how queerness resists capitalist imperatives to produce. While heteronormative futures depend on the constant reproduction of children in much the same way that capitalism requires continuous production of goods to drive the accumulation of money, Halberstam suggests that queer lives that "fail" to reach these goals in fact open up new space for alternative ways of being. Drawing on this celebration of failure, which refuses the value of success in an oppressive world, can be quite powerful in the context of a gaming culture that often prioritizes domination and winning as the highest form of play.

Necropolitics is a school of postcolonial theory that interrogates how power over death and dying lend oppressive regimes significant control over populations Proposed by Achille Mbembe (2003), it can be a useful analytic for game studies work that thinks through the centrality of death and dying in games. Even though they do not involve actual loss of life, videogames engage the dimensions of technology and control that are central to necropolitical power. They are exquisite objects to think about how ideology—and, in this case, the power over (virtual) death—flows through our entertainment.

Finally, the feminist killjoy is Sara Ahmed's (2010) fun-ruining figure who is always blamed for disturbing the social solidarity of a dominant group. When friction appears in the group, she is identified as its source rather than the one who points out or suffers from its existence. In the context of the social justice wars in popular culture, it is useful to have ways to talk about the figures who are blamed for pointing out inequalities and oppressive practices. Because Ahmed's feminist killjoy specifically ruins fun, this figure is all the more appropriate for discussing social justice backlash in games.

Turning these critical lenses on the unfun parts of gaming can be quite powerful. However, theory is not the only resource for social justice scholarship. Ruberg (2015) suggests that a taxonomy of "no-fun" games might include those that annoy, anger, disappoint, and hurt. Insights can also come from "bad" games, broadly conceived: easy games, boring games, ugly games, amateurish games, glitchy games, experimental games, and unfinished games. When access to the knowledge and means of production of digital games results in an industry that is 76 percent white and 75 percent male (Weststar & Legault 2015: 11), it is important to look for inspiration beyond the expectations set by these creators. Big-budget AAA games are often popular, influential, and well-crafted, and they are increasing in narrative and aesthetic sophistication every year. However, they offer a limited range of what games can be, coming from a limited range of creative perspectives, and with one major purpose: to make money for their parent corporations. Many indie game designers also strive to achieve AAA-style polish, with similar results.

Anna Anthropy, the radical trans lesbian game designer, encourages everyone to learn how to make games. She advocates for simple tools such as Twine that open up game design to those without the programming skills often thought necessary to make games (Anthropy 2012). She and other transwomen designers, including Merritt Kopas and Mattie Brice, create minimalistic, short games that subvert AAA expectations, often telling stories or using mechanics that are not marketable in the mainstream. Their games are highly personal, occasionally unpolished, but always evocative and meaningful to play. They do not make much money, often relying on crowdfunding models to support their production. In a tragedy for justice, these transwomen have endured intense harassment for offering alternatives to the AAA industry without being able to support themselves financially.

Getting beyond fun is an important first step when choosing objects and mechanics to write about. Good critique can come from unexpected places. Do not avoid certain types of titles—indie games, for example, or AAAs—because they are not your type of game. Depending on your research question, valuable facets of an issue might be spread across a wide range of media types and genres, produced by users of varying skill levels.

Practice Strategic Disloyalty to Your Discipline(s)

The formation of the academy over hundreds of years has led to what some see as a stratification and calcification of disciplines into rigid structures that stifle critique (Allen & Kitch 1998). Debates about the utility of disciplines and their complicity in the power structure of the academy are endless, but they demonstrate one thing for certain: disciplines constrain the creation of knowledge by training their initiates in particular methods of analysis. Clare Hemmings (2011) writes about how disciplinary discourse itself can shape the way knowledge is formed, such as the historical "waves" model of feminism that erases the early contributions of women of color to feminist movements. Roderick Ferguson (2012) examines how becoming part of an institution can rob a field of its radical potential even as it provides a home and resources for the work to be carried out. The structures of our disciplines, their histories, and the conversations that we have within them are tremendously impactful on the work we can do.

This particular conversation within feminist studies is very broad; Robyn Wiegman even provides an incomplete bibliography in her footnotes (2012: 72). But I come by the wording of this section via the work of Judith Stacey (1995), who wrote of the need to be disloyal to disciplines (in her case, sociology) in order to meet the political demands of feminist scholarship. A strategic disloyalty is one that acknowledges the power and privilege of disciplinary structures, but learns to break with them at appropriate moments when they hinder rigorous social justice critique.

A discipline like game studies is relatively new and still figuring out its identity, but it already has its own history of territorial disputes and anxieties. The much-ballyhooed "Narratology vs. Ludology Debates," while ultimately dismissed as unhelpful posturing, is a perfect example of the abstract boundary-making that occurs during the formation of a discipline. This debate, which occurred in the early 2000s across the *International Journal of Game Studies* (Aarseth 2001; Eskelinen 2001; Juul 2001), collections such as *First Person: New Media as Performance, Story, and Game* (Wardrip-Fruin & Harrigan 2004), and various conference presentations (Frasca 2003; Murray 2005), was an early attempt to carve out a niche for game studies as different from the study of literature and cinema, from which many early practitioners originated. The language of these debates is revealing: some scholars felt they were being "colonized" by other disciplines whose training did not adequately prepare them to talk about games as games (ludo-) rather than as narratives or visual art (Juul 2001).

Ideological posturing aside, we can read such a struggle as vying for influence and institutional recognition in the context of an academy with access to shrinking resources. Videogames are objects of study that attract high volume enrollments, and game studies criticism has the potential to reach a broad audience. The emphasis on games as games added useful critical perspectives to the game studies conversation that may not have emerged from a purely literary or filmic standpoint, but the reaction to methods from fields like literary studies led many to downplay the utility of these fields to the study of videogames entirely. For example, Aarseth (2001) described the work of cinema and literary critics as "colonising" games, while Eskelinen described the "interpretative violence" done by Janet Murray (1997) in her reading of Tetris as a metaphor for the "overtaxed lives of Americans in the 1990s" (Eskelinen 2001: 143). Perhaps as a result of these anxieties about humanistic colonization, early game studies work on cultural issues like gender and race is less prominent than the formalist perspectives of the ludologists. Some current trends in the field, such as code studies or platform studies, require specialized technical knowledge in order for a scholarly contribution to be adequate, replicating the very barriers that limit diversity in the tech industry in the first place.

Strategically breaking with the traditions of a discipline can help us to adapt scholarly approaches to new problems. Think about the training you have received in your degree program, where it places its priorities and encourages you to intervene, and what tools it gives you to make those interventions. How do these tools shape your analysis and the questions you are able to ask? What topics do they miss or obscure?

When it is clear that breaking with tradition is the best course of action, the task can still be quite complicated. One of the most important strategies for understanding and properly implementing theory and methods from other disciplines is to familiarize yourself with its context. Critical race theory, queer theory, feminist theory—all of these have their own vocabularies, historical trajectories, and foundational texts that have shaped them over time. They have more contact points with other humanities and social science disciplines than tech fields like computer science, but they are fully developed practices in their own right that require expert knowledge for persuasive implementation.

Seeking training, whether in the form of classes, apprenticeships, or co-authoring with others, is an important part of doing interdisciplinary work effectively. Many humanities disciplines neglect training in collaboration, but interdisciplinary work might be an opportunity to strategically adopt the norms of other fields and work with multiple individuals to bring a project to fruition. The most important rule here? Whether you are primarily a feminist theorist interested games or a game studies scholar hoping to bring the perspectives of disability studies to your work, you must respect the histories of the disciplines you wish to cross and understand your own adequately before stepping out.

Reach Beyond Discourses of Diversity and Inclusion

Making videogames is a multibillion-dollar industry, and it intersects in many places with the concerns of broader social justice movements: labor rights and compensation, education, the digital divide, transnational labor, and much more. However, conversations about social justice in videogames often revolve around the quantity and quality of X type of characters in games, the recognition of X group in gaming publics, or the inclusion of X group in the industry itself—where X represents any identity category that is not "straight" or "white" or "male." Reducing diversity and inclusion to numbers is tempting because it offers an easy, tangible goal to achieve. However, it also masks more serious structural problems with a comfortable veneer with which content creators are familiar. This is how tokens are created: they are solutions to mathematical problems.

Representation and inclusion are important to help us imagine and believe in new spaces of possibility, but they are small steps in a more expansive quest for justice. More often than not, lack of diversity is a symptom of larger systemic problems rather than the cause of inequality. Increasing diversity in the workplace or in media content does not necessarily mean changing the underlying structures that created the lack in the first place. For example, Sara Ahmed (2012) has written extensively about how diversity policy in the university can substitute for substantive changes in the fabric of the institution. Ferguson's study suggests that the institutionalization of diversity actually extends hegemonic power. This can apply more widely to corporations and other institutions: if a company does not provide maternity leave or benefits, it will be difficult to retain people who give birth. If crunch time is an essential part of the work environment, it will be difficult to retain people who have reasons to be home on time—family obligations, physical or emotional wellbeing, religious practices, and so on. If subtle forms of racism, homophobia, and misogyny are part of the social fabric of the work environment, individuals brought into the fold by diversity recruitment initiatives may not be able to perform at their best level or retain interest in their jobs.

Critics such as Adrienne Shaw (2015) advocate for treating diversity as a norm rather than a goal for the games industry, and to always consider gaming within a broader social and political context. She is critical of the notion of diversity as it is deployed in conversations that pose it as a problem to figure out, noting, like so many scholars before her, that such thinking places the onus on oppressed and underrepresented groups to fix their own conditions by becoming pioneers in hostile territory. Brice (2015) directly implicates wealthy organizations that ask "diverse" speakers to work for free in order to improve their corporate climate or, in the specific case of the Game Developers Conference, add value to their high-priced event. Such actions ignore the reality that improvement requires money and structural changes that will force some to give up a bit of their power, privilege, and comfort. The games industry has a reputation for hostility toward women and people of color, preventing many from choosing to enter the field in the first place. Adding members of underrepresented groups may or may not change these dynamics. If they make it through the process, then it might be easier (for all sorts of reasons) to maintain the status quo rather than challenge it. Some might even make it harder on people from their own groups to succeed in this setting—a documented phenomenon whereby individuals metaphorically kick the ladder out behind them rather than lifting others up (Carbado & Gulati 2004; Kaiser & Spalding 2015).

When it comes to onscreen representation, social justice scholarship does not need to revolve around the male gaze or the agency of gamers over their avatars. Most of the time, such approaches investigate the obvious markers of inequality without situating them within the greater context of the technological and ludic systems of a game or the decades-long conversations about agency and gazes that have occurred in feminist and queer theory. Disciplines that prioritize social justice excel at contextualizing objects of analysis within the overlapping systems of power in which they are embedded.

For example, some of my own work investigates the discourse of the "male gaze" as it applies to the game character Bayonetta, who many critics felt was gratuitously sexualized and, therefore, a harmful representation of women in gaming. However, a close examination of the game's narrative, in-game camera functions, and battle mechanics reveal that Bayonetta's relationship to visuality is not straightforward, and that we can read her as occupying a position that resists hegemonic masculinity through excessive queer femininity and button-mashing controller mechanics. The major problem with the popular understanding of the male gaze, beyond its ubiquity in fan feminist conversations, is that it simplifies what has always been a complicated set of gendered power relationships into the heteronormative formula "man looks at woman." Bayonetta is an ideal case to understand where and how this breaks down (Phillips 2017).

The veneers of avatar and narrative design conceal game mechanics and computational processes that are often confused for technological inevitability. For example, take the common refrain from designers that a lack of computing resources prevents them from including female avatars in their games (Totilo 2010; Farokhmanesh 2014). Such explanations obscure the human decisions that underwrite game design, from physics algorithms to animation details. Reading representation in gaming as a surface-level phenomenon fails to hold the entire system and its priorities accountable for the resulting problems. Platform studies and software studies are two areas of inquiry that are interested in the relationship between culture and technological design; while Bogost and Montfort's (2009) first entry into the MIT Press Platform

Studies series did not have social justice as a primary focus, it did demonstrate the varied relationships between the material of the Atari 2600 and the creative output of its game developers.

Outside of games, Wendy Chun (2006, 2012) and Tara McPherson (2012) provide some models for understanding software production through a social justice lens, making connections between design practices and real-word power structures. Such connections can easily be made in the material of videogames. Karyl Ketchum (2009) investigates the racial politics built into the avatar creator software Facegen, which serves as the basis for avatar facial customization in a variety of games as well as an aid for police sketch artists. Reed and Phillips (2013) interrogate the motion capture interfaces used to animate games and computer-generated movies like *Avatar*, showing how these technologies use the bodies and movement of people of color to guarantee its authenticity. When platform studies critique holds social justice at its core, it can provide a robust account of the meat and bones of a project, rather than simply emphasizing the skin.

Recognize Your Ethical Responsibilities to the People You Write About

Certain topics, such as the harassment of women and other groups online, have recently captured the public's attention, making them tempting topics for analysis. As academics, we frequently benefit from writing about and commenting on such events, in informal venues like professional blogs as well as more official documents like peer-reviewed publications or interviews with the news media. Having something to say about controversy grants us social and intellectual capital.

However, the raw materials of this analysis frequently come from the suffering and public shaming of others. The accessible, fixed nature of tweets and other online speech have led many to treat them as texts that are open for public consumption rather than, for example, conversations recorded by an observer or statements made in an interview. This opens up a treasure trove of data for commentators in disciplines that have no formal procedures for interacting with human subjects: in many humanities disciplines, the text is an object, like a book or a poem, that has been released by its creator and is subject to any kind of critique without needing the permission or consent of the author. Many disciplines in the social sciences, by contrast, have elaborate procedures to ensure the anonymity and dignity of their human subjects, most of whom are made to feel like contributors to a greater intellectual project even if their participation is unpleasant. Regarding social media as "text" cuts the human subjects out of the situation entirely. We treat texts and human subjects interviews quite differently.

Since so many of us writing about videogames and other contemporary media are dealing with current events rather than historical acts that have had time to settle down, there are additional consequences to consider. For example, the speed and variety of online commentary often means that important patterns are not immediately apparent.

Platforms such as Twitter are technically public, but they are also venues for conversations that can feel very personal to the individuals involved. The openness allows likeminded community members to find each other easily and engage in distributed conversation, and the vastness of the field of conversation can lead to a false sense of insignificance with respect to the whole. In 2014, a conversation about the journalistic ethics of embedding tweets sprang up after a journalist wrote a story using the tweets of rape survivors who shared their experiences in response to a question by Twitter denizen, Christina Fox. Fox and other bloggers, such as Anil Dash, challenged what many journalists used as their primary defense: Twitter is public, and anything posted to Twitter is fair game for reporting (Knibbs 2014; McBride 2014).

But Twitter users and journalists involved in the conversation also suggested that context is key here, and that some users have a lot more to lose than others when their tweets are aggregated in a news story and shared with thousands of readers. Sudden exposure and direct linking can leave underprepared members of the public vulnerable to targeted harassment and an overflow of responses in their inbox.

This is important to consider when writing in the age of GamerGate. Academics are not journalists, of course, but we do benefit professionally from writing about these events and conversations. It is courteous to contact those individuals whose social media posts you would like to discuss, and to consider the impact of your publication on their well being. By their own accounts, many individuals embroiled in social media harassment events receive a spike in unwanted attention when someone publishes about them later. Are you quoting a public figure, or a person who appears to be conversing with friends? Are you benefitting from labor that these individuals perform for free? Will linking directly to their posts facilitate further harassment? Can you anonymize their words without reducing their effectiveness for your argument?

As of this publication, no one has changed official institutional recommendations with regard to the use of social media as text (rather than interview) and its creators as authors (rather than subjects). However, organizations such as the Center for Solutions to Online Violence are currently working to develop guidelines and best practices for scholars who are dedicated to engaging in this type of research. Theorist Moya Bailey (2015) has written about Twitter ethics in her scholarship about transwomen of color activism online, offering a model of collaborative consent that differs from IRB processes in the academy by centering the expertise of "subjects" rather than treating them in a paternalistic way.

Thorough game studies research takes into account not only representation and technological platform, but also audience reception and fan practices. So many important conversations and insights into games appear online. Until official recommendations can be made, it is best to carefully consider the context of these conversations and how to minimize the harm while still accomplishing the important work that your analysis performs.

Get Your Gear and Your Party Together

Given the volatile nature of the discourse surrounding social justice in gaming, it is important to prepare yourself for the eventuality that someone, somewhere, will take issue with what you write. Whether it is a foaming internet mob or skeptical colleague, resistance to the perspectives of social justice criticism are common. Writers in academia have historically been spared much of the vitriol that journalists and other critics have received, but this is not true for every academic writing about games.

Harassment can endanger someone physically, but it more frequently causes emotional and psychological damage to individuals who become worn down by continuous conflict. Practices like doxing (the online distribution of personal information) can be used to intimidate individuals into silence, and they can happen to academics as easily as to other individuals writing about social justice in games. It is important to consider how you would like to present yourself as a professional online, and how closely linked your public life is to your private one. Keep in mind that our positions in our institutions usually mean that our basic information—name, picture, email, and place of employment—is easily traced. Consult organizations such as Crash Override or the Fembot Collective for strategies on securing your personal information and online accounts against hacking, doxing, and other forms of harassment.

In addition to the technical preparations, it is important to cultivate personal and professional networks of individuals who are passionate about social justice. It is dangerous to go alone! Social justice is a collective pursuit. In her indictment of white academic feminism, for example, Audre Lorde (1984) repeatedly encourages us to face the chaos of our differences and unite because of, not despite, them. Solidarity across oppressive categories without reproducing the hierarchies and exclusions of patriarchy is the only way to move toward justice. For Lorde, the fear that differences such as race, class, and sexuality within the category "woman" would cause the feminist movement to splinter was itself a tool of the patriarchy that prevented feminists from achieving their goals. This sentiment has been repeated over and over by important activists and thinkers. Your comrades can be fierce defenders, valuable critics, and compassionate friends. These folks can be tremendously important in surviving what is otherwise an isolating experience.

But the direct tactics of internet vigilantes are sometimes easier to confront than the more subtle strategies of academia. Nonracial ideology, sometimes known as "colorblindness," pervades the left-leaning culture of the humanities and social sciences, enabling individuals to deny the ways in which institutions are thoroughly racialized even when they believe they are on the side of justice. Work by scholars like Eduardo Bonilla-Silva (2006) and Carl Gutierrez-Jones (2000) have supplemented the calls for intersectionality by Lorde (1984), Crenshaw (1991), and others by excavating the unacknowledged ways that whiteness controls institutions. For example, Ferguson's study of the institutionalization of diversity shows how discourses of rigor can mask what is actually an assessment of an author's identity or politics. Strategic disloyalty to one's discipline can leave an opening for technical or methodological critique from scholars who are unfamiliar with or opposed to different modes of knowledge production.

Finding like-minded scholars might seem difficult when you are just entering the field, but there are many places to look. Conferences are a good place to start: smaller, local conferences with narrow themes are great places to find colleagues with your specific interests. For example, the Queerness and Games Conference started as a San Francisco Bay Area conference that attracted a small but diverse group of academics, fans, and designers who were interested in queerness and social justice in videogames. Over the years, its attendance has grown. Larger organizations also have special interest groups and graduate support networks that can help you get started. For social justice in particular, the American Studies Association, the National Association of Ethnic Studies, and the National Women's Studies Association cover a broad range of topics, many with significant digital humanities and media studies interest groups. HASTAC is a network of scholars interested in digital humanities and media production that provides extensive support for junior scholars working in social justice disciplines.

Supportive and experienced colleagues can help assess your work and refine it to address or avoid some of these pitfalls, or simply provide encouragement and direction for placing your scholarship where it will be more productively received. In addition to my institutional mentors, I have benefitted greatly from the input and collegiality of the #TransformDH Collective, a loosely affiliated group of early-career academics working to bring social justice to the forefront of digital humanities. We share resources, write together collaboratively, and invite each other to conference panels in order to increase our chances of getting on a competitive program. Each in-person meeting is an opportunity to further refine our perspectives on social justice as they apply to our specific disciplines within digital humanities. Since no one scholar can have a view on everything, it is important to share and critique ideas, to hold each other accountable to the principles of justice and boost each other's confidence in a tough system. As social justice advocates and scholars have proven for decades, solidarity is vital to doing important, difficult work.

These tips are only a start, and it is important to remember that justice is a moving target: power is agile, and it adapts and shifts in order to maintain its foothold. Your toolkit must change over time. It is crucially important, therefore, to familiarize yourself with the fundamentals of social justice practice so that you can identify appropriate courses of action when there is no clear path. Be aware of your personal biases and the biases placed on you by disciplinary practices. Look beneath the surface to understand how power flows through structures. Place the needs, priorities, and safety of oppressed groups at the center of your work. Form scholarly and social communities to offer support, accountability, and continual learning. Social justice scholarship in game studies, or in any media studies discipline, is a small fraction of the work necessary to improve our world. While it is not sufficient by itself, it can, at its best, provide inspiration, critique, and nuanced conversation for those looking for wider-reaching cultural solutions.

Further Reading

Ahmed, S. (2012) *On Being Included: Racism and Diversity in Institutional Life*, Durham, NC: Duke University Press.

Anthropy, A. (2012) *Rise of the Videogame Zinesters: How Freaks, Normals, Amateurs, Artists, Dreamers, Dropouts, Queers, Housewives, and People Like You Are Taking Back an Art Form*, New York, NY: Seven Stories Press.

Bailey, M. (2015) "#transform(ing)DH Writing and Research: An Autoethnography of Digital Humanities and Feminist Ethics," *Digital Humanities Quarterly* 9(2), retrieved from www.digitalhumanities.org/dhq/vol/9/2/000209/000209.html.

Leonard, D. (2009) "Young, Black (& Brown) and Don't Give a Fuck: Virtual Gangstas in the Era of State Violence," *Cultural Studies ↔ Critical Methodologies* 9(2), 248–72.

Shaw, A. (2015) *Gaming at the Edge: Sexuality and Gender at the Margins of Gamer Culture*, Minneapolis, MN: University of Minnesota Press.

References

Aarseth, A. (2001) "Computer Game Studies, Year One," *Game Studies* 1(1), retrieved from www.gamestudies.org/0101/editorial.html.

Ahmed, S. (2010) *The Promise of Happiness*, Durham, NC: Duke University Press.

Ahmed, S. (2012) *On Being Included: Racism and Diversity in Institutional Life*, Durham, NC: Duke University Press.

Allen, J. and S. Kitch (1998) "Disciplined by Disciplines? The Need for an Interdisciplinary Research Mission in Women's Studies," *Feminist Studies* 24(2), 275–99.

Anthropy, A. (2012) *Rise of the Videogame Zinesters: How Freaks, Normals, Amateurs, Artists, Dreamers, Dropouts, Queers, Housewives, and People Like You Are Taking Back an Art Form*, New York, NY: Seven Stories Press.

Bailey, M. (2015) "#transform(ing)DH Writing and Research: An Autoethnography of Digital Humanities and Feminist Ethics," *Digital Humanities Quarterly* 9(2): retrieved from www.digitalhumanities.org/dhq/vol/9/2/000209/000209.html.

Bogost, I. and N. Montfort (2009) *Racing the Beam: The Atari Video Computer System*. Cambridge, MA: MIT Press.

Bonilla-Silva, E. (2006) *Racism without Racists: Color-Blind Racism and the Persistence of Racial Inequality in the United States*, 2nd edn, New York, NY: Rowman & Littlefield.

Brice, M. (2015) *Diversity of Existence*, retrieved from www.mattiebrice.com/diversity-of-existence.

Carbado, D. and M. Gulati (2004) "Race to the Top of the Corporate Ladder: What Minorities Do when They Get There," *Washington and Lee Law Review* 61(4), 1645–94.

Chun, W. H. K. (2006) *Control and Freedom: Power and Paranoia in the Age of Fiber Optics*, Cambridge, MA: MIT Press.

Chun, W. H. K. (2012) *Programmed Visions: Software and Memory*, Cambridge, MA: MIT Press.

Crenshaw, K. (1991) "Mapping the Margins: Intersectionality, Identity Politics, and Violence against Women of Color," *Stanford Law Review* 43(6), 1241–99.

Eskelinen, M. (2001) "The Gaming Situation," *Game Studies* 1(1), retrieved from www.gamestudies.org/0101/eskelinen.

Farokhmanesh, M. (2014) "Ubisoft Abandoned Women Assassins in Co-op Because of the Additional Work," *Polygon*, retrieved from www.polygon.com/e3–2014/2014/6/10/5798592/assassins-creed-unity-female-assassins.

Ferguson, R. (2012) *The Reorder of Things: The University and Its Pedagogies of Minority Difference*, Minneapolis, MN: Minnesota University Press.

Frasca, G. (2003) "Ludologists Love Stories, Too: Notes from a Debate that Never Took Place," in *Level Up: Digital Games Research Conference, Proceedings of the 2003 Digital Games Research Association Conference*, University of Utrecht, pp. 92–99.

Gutierrez-Jones, C. (2000) *Critical Race Narratives: A Study of Race, Rhetoric, and Injury*, New York, NY: NYU Press.

Halberstam, J. (2011) *The Queer Art of Failure*, Durham, NC: Duke University Press.

Hemmings, C. (2011) *Why Stories Matter: The Political Grammar of Feminist Theory*, Durham, NC: Duke University Press.

Juul, J. (2001) "Games Telling Stories?" *Game Studies* 1(1), retrieved from www.gamestudies.org/0101/juul-review.

Juul, J. (2013) *The Art of Failure: An Essay on the Pain of Playing Video Games*. Cambridge: MIT Press.

Kaiser, C. and K. Spalding (2015) "Do Women Who Succeed in Male-Dominated Domains Help other Women? The Moderating Role of Gender Identification," *European Journal of Social Psychology* 45, 599–608.

Ketchum, K. (2009) "Facegen and the Technovisual Politics of Embodied Surfaces," *Women's Studies Quarterly* 27(1–2), 183–99.

Knibbs, K. (2014) "The Ethics of Embedding Tweets," *The Daily Dot*, retrieved from www.dailydot.com/news/twitter-is-public-but.

Lorde, A. (1984) "The Master's Tools Will Never Dismantle the Master's House," in *Sister Outsider: Essays and Speeches*, Berkeley, CA: Crossing Press, pp. 110–14.

Mbembe, A. (2003) "Necropolitics," L. Meintjes (trans.) *Public Culture* 15(1), 11–40.

McBride, K. (2014) "BuzzFeed Reporter's Use of Tweets Stirs Controversy," *Poynter*, retrieved from www.poynter.org/2014/buzzfeed-reporters-use-of-tweets-stirs-controversy/242413.

McPherson, T. (2012) "U.S. Operating Systems at Mid-Century: The Intertwining of Race and UNIX," in L. Nakamura and P. Chow-White (eds) *Race After the Internet*, New York, NY: Routledge, pp. 21–37.

Murray, J. (1997) *Hamlet on the Holodeck: The Future of Narrative in Cyberspace*, Cambridge, MA: MIT Press.

Murray, J. (2005) "The Last Word on Ludology v. Narratology in Game Studies," Preface to keynote presentation, *DiGRA Conference 2005 iGChanging Views: Worlds in Play*, Vancouver, BC, retrieved from inventingthe medium.com/2013/06/28/the- last-word-on-ludology-v-narratology-2005.

Phillips, A. (2017) "Welcome to MY Fantasy Zone: Bayonetta and Queer Femme Disturbance," in B. Aslinger, B. Ruberg, A. Shaw, et al. (eds) *Queer Game Studies: Gender, Sexuality, and a Queer Approach to Game Studies*, Minneapolis, MN: Minnesota University Press.

Reed, A. and A. Phillips (2013) "Additive Race: Colorblind Discourses of Realism in Performance Capture Technologies," *Digital Creativity* 24(2), 130–44.

Ruberg, B. (2015) "No Fun: The Queer Potential of Video Games that Annoy, Anger, Disappoint, Sadden, and Hurt," *QED: A Journal in GLBTQ Worldmaking* 2(2), 108–24.

Ryan, M. (2001) "Beyond Myth and Metaphor: The Case of Narrative in Digital Media," *Game Studies* 1(1): retrieved from www.gamestudies.org/0101/ryan.

Shaw, A. (2015) *Gaming at the Edge: Sexuality and Gender at the Margins of Gamer Culture*, Minneapolis, MN: University of Minnesota Press.

Stacey, J. (1995) "Disloyal to the Disciplines: A Feminist Trajectory in the Borderlands," in D. Stanton and A. Stewart (eds) *Feminisms in the Academy*, Ann Arbor, MI: University of Michigan Press, pp. 311–29.

Totilo, S. (2010) "Why Modern Video Game Armies Lack Female Troops," *Kotaku*, retrieved from kotaku.com/5488592/why-modern-video-game-armies-lack-female-troops.

Wardrip-Fruin, N. and P. Harrigan (2004) *First Person: New Media as Story, Performance, and Game*, Cambridge, MA: MIT Press.

Weststar, J. and M.-J. Legault (2015) *Developer Satisfaction Survey 2015: Summary Report*, Toronto, ON: International Game Developers Association.

Wiegman, R. (2012) *Object Lessons*, Durham, NC: Duke University Press.

12

SELF-DETERMINATION IN INDIGENOUS GAMES

Elizabeth LaPensée

> The postindian warriors hover at last over the ruins of tribal representations and surmount the scriptures of manifest manners with new stories; these warriors counter the surveillance and literature of dominance with their own simulations of survivance.
>
> (Vizenor 1994: 5)

I have let my son borrow my phone to buy myself time to get dinner finished, when I hear him say, "Booyah! New high score! Take that, invaders!" It warms my heart. He is playing *Invaders*, a mobile game I made with art by Kiowa artist Steven Paul Judd, and music by Lakota poet and musician Trevino Brings Plenty. *Invaders* is a score-oriented, arcade shooting game that plays on the classic arcade game, *Space Invaders*, by using alien invasion as a metaphor for colonization. Even with over 10 years of experience in designing, writing for, and making art for games, this is the first fully deployed game I have worked on with an entirely Indigenous team. This marks a shift in self-determined Indigenous game development alongside a rise in other Indigenous-made and -themed digital games.

Definitions

When I say, "Indigenous," I am broadening the conversation to peoples across the world, although here I speak to work from Turtle Island (also known as North America) with a nod of gratitude and recognition for the foundational work, *Digital Songlines*, based out of Australia. In the discourse of social justice, the term "Indigenous" refers to certain contemporary communities that have experienced the often-deleterious effects of western imperial expansion. Smith points out that " 'Indigenous peoples' is a relatively recent term which emerged in the 1970s out of the struggles primarily of the American Indian Movement (AIM) and the Canadian Indian Brotherhood. It is a term that internationalizes the experiences, the issues and the struggles of some of the world's colonized peoples" (1999: 7). My worldview is informed by the way I was raised and the community I am surrounded by. I am Anishinaabe and Métis through my mother and Irish through my father, brought up in the urban Native community of Portland, Oregon. The stories and teachings that transfer from me to my work in games come from personal interactions, community gatherings, ceremonies, and learning and speaking Anishinaabemowin.

While I also develop board games, card games, and other forms of games that call into question the boundaries of digital and nondigital gameplay, I will focus specifically on digital games, including videogames, computer games, mobile games, and web games. The term "game" has several definitions depending on the disciplinary context where it is used. According to Roger Caillois, whose early work forms the foundation of most discussions of play in game theory, games are voluntary, uncertain, unproductive, and make-believe acts (1961). Jane McGonigal provides a simple alternative—"all games share four defining traits: a goal, rules, a feedback system, and voluntary participation" (2011: 21)—while Eric Zimmerman (2004) offers a more open-ended framing of games as interactive narrative systems of formal play (156–64). I appreciate the flexibility in moving between these definitions, as games should always be a space for expression that can expand perspectives. When considering the potential of games as a space to express Indigenous self-determination, I emphasize gameplay informed by the needs and interests of communities.

Self-determination refers to the right of a people (nation) to exercise sovereignty or self-rule and to determine its own political, economic, and cultural arrangements. It can refer to the efforts of Indigenous peoples to regain sovereignty after years of colonization, to restore the terms of broken treaties, or to prevent continued abuses. On an individual level, it refers to a person's ability to exercise free will without interference. Subtle orthographic appropriations that assert control over Indigenous representation also constitute acts of self-determination. Consider Simon J. Ortiz's capitalization of the "I" in "Indigenous" as a way to participate in the movement to reclaim and sustain Indigenous languages: "I capitalize I when it comes to spelling and using the term Indigenous when it pertains to peoples who are indigenous or aboriginal or native to the continents of the Americas, North and South America connected by Central America" (cited in McAdams 2010). There is also the widespread adoption of the term, "peoples," in preference to "Indigenous people" as "an important linguistic symbol of our identification as self-determining peoples" (Smith 1999: 115).

Survivance, a place from which all of my work comes, can be thought of as an act of self-determination because it asserts Indigenous presence in the contemporary world rather than representing Indigenous existence as a relic of the past. Popularized by Anishinaabe writer, Gerald Vizenor, survivance is "a portfolio word combining 'survival' and 'endurance,' but it is also more than that. Survivance connotes survival with an attitude, implying activity rather than passivity, using aggressive means not only to stay alive but to flourish" (Velie 2008: 148). Survivance involves returning to traditions with the understanding that "traditional" in the Indigenous sense means looking to those who came before us while also being malleable and thinking about the many generations ahead (Fixico 2003). For example, traditional teachings are informed by stories told before us as well as collective community understandings today. Finding new ways to express Indigenous stories and knowledge is an act of self-determination because it preserves tradition and is more precisely an act of survivance because it embraces contemporary media to do so.

Historical Perspectives

The role of digital games is becoming increasingly relevant in the discussion of self-determined representations of Indigenous identity. I strongly believe that digital games are a path for self-determined Indigenous representations by passing on teachings, telling our stories, and expressing our ways of knowing through code, design, art, music, and audio. I also believe that the capacity and depth afforded by digital games is nothing new to our communities. As Loretta Todd (1996) espouses of teachings shared by Dr. Leroy Little Bear, the internet and multidimensional representations have always been present in Indigenous communities. We can reconnect with traditional perspectives on spacetime to see just how much games and virtual reality are a form of *biskaabiiyang* (returning to ourselves) rather than embarking into a "new frontier." Nonlinear paths in a choose-your-own adventure game such as *We Sing for Healing*, for example, replicate traditional storytelling structures (King 2005).

With this in mind, it is vital that we honor those who came before us as we proceed with developing digital games. In my work, I look back to traditional games that passed on teachings in ways that would be retained while feeling secure in the context of playfulness. For example, *Rock in Fist* is a traditional game played today at events held by the Native American Rehabilitation Association. In the game, one player hides one rock in their fist while the other guesses which fist it is hidden in. The players keep track of whose score is higher using sticks as markers. When the game is through, the players roll up their stick and rocks in cloth. This game teaches youth how to connect with their intuition as well as how to properly care for and roll up a pipe in ways that pass on these lessons without harm to one's self or to a pipe. In hoping to reconnect the next generations with gameplay, it is important to note that videogames have become a medium of choice for Indigenous youth, and therefore constitute a significant transmission of images and ideologies that shape their own formation of cultural identity. The National Center for Education Statistics in 2003 reported that computer ownership increased by 46 percent among Native Americans from 1997 to 2001 (DeBell & Chapman 2006). Mirroring this increase in access to technology, educational outreach efforts are beginning to leverage videogames as a way to involve minority youth by foregrounding their own cultures over western traditions. Squire studied minority students who were not interested in playing videogames

> until they realized that it was possible to win playing as Native American characters. . . . These kids took great joy in studying hypothetical history, exploring the conditions under which colonial conquests might have played out differently. What if smallpox disease hadn't wiped out millions of Native Americans? What if they had resisted the first wave of European settlers rather than embracing them?
> (Squire & Jenkins 2003: 14)

What, then, can happen when minority youth themselves are involved in making the games they play?

Self-determined Indigenous games involving youth in the development process have a strong foundation thanks to the Skins Workshops, for which I created curriculum. The Skins Workshops are based out of Concordia University in Montreal, and they are facilitated by the research network, Aboriginal Territories in Cyberspace (AbTeC), which recently transformed into the Initiative for Indigenous Futures thanks to the guidance of co-directors, Jason Edward Lewis and Skawennati. The Workshops enable next generations with storytelling, access to game development technology, and hands-on experience in design, programming, art, sound, and producing to ultimately develop their own games (LaPensée, Lewis & Skawennati 2010; LaPensée & Lewis 2011). Similar workshops—including those held by Joseph Arthur at Hoopa Valley, Darrick Baxter (who travels to reservations teaching app development) at Ogoki Learning Systems, and the Indigenous Routes artist collective (that collaborated with Dames Making Games on workshops for young Indigenous women in Toronto)—offer models for empowering youth to create in these spaces.

Critical Issues

The majority of Indigenous representation in digital games reflects cultural attitudes toward Indigenous identity (LaPensée & Lewis 2011). The relationship of the game industry to Indigenous communities has replicated the binary of subjective observer/observable subject that has provided the primary image of Indigenous identity to mainstream culture in the past and that is susceptible to the same set of fallacies today. Armchair ethnographers, cultural theorists, and salvage anthropologists have transmitted a Pan-Indian image of Indigenous identity based on the romanticized portrait of nineteenth-century Plains people, a romanticization that is propagated in many films that sum up Native existence in images of feathers, beads, and tomahawks, and that persists in representations of Indigenous peoples in games (Marcano & LaPensée 2014). This appropriation of Indigenous identity has been propagated in the service of modernist aesthetics and political agendas. Vizenor writes,

> The stoic 'savage' survived in literature and emulsion; invented, painted and photographed by postcolonial adventurers . . . The 'savages' were separated from their social experience, reinvented as racial emblems and then isolated, abstracted, revised and used in literature as ideologies to oppose bourgeois materialism.
>
> (Vizenor 1989: 193)

The problem of representing Indigenous identity within a western worldview may persist in the work of media studies despite best efforts to ameliorate the bias of past practices. Accounts of developments in anthropological methods often congratulate the practitioners while simultaneously maintaining a problematic hierarchy. For example, Sturken and Cartwright assert the following:

> Visual and cultural anthropologists have done the most toward providing accounts of how specific Third World cultures produce and use technologies and images imported from the industrialized West. Visual anthropologists long have been among the most innovative critics and scholars in the move to both study and facilitate the agency of Third World subjects in the production and circulation of images and media texts, rather than to market media to them or study them as consumers.
>
> (Sturken & Cartwright 2001: 328)

This juxtaposition of industrialized western culture with third world culture in terms that clearly privilege the former as something necessary for Indigenous peoples to have—and thus also something they lack—maintains the binary logic of dominance that historically informs anthropological study of Indigenous ways of knowing. Recent directions call this binary into question and evince a growing awareness of the problems posed by romanticizing, exoticizing, or otherwise "othering" Indigenous cultures while also clinging to the very methods and concepts that Vizenor and others find so problematic. For example, Coman and Rothenbuhler state:

> Media anthropology grows out of the anthropology of modern societies, on one hand, and the cultural turn in media studies, on the other. It turns its attention from 'exotic' to mundane and from 'Indigenous' to manufactured culture.
>
> (Rothenbuhler & Coman 2005: 1)

The prospect of re-envisioning "exotic" Indigenous cultures as "mundane and manufactured" subjects hardly aligns with the depth of symbol and ceremony in Indigenous cultures as espoused by Vizenor and other Indigenous writers, artists, and makers. Media studies would more genuinely benefit from a complete engagement with Indigenous ways of knowing by seeing Indigenous cultures as living acts of survivance.

Games that represent Indigenous cultures as a relic of the past, and that participate in the "literature of dominance" that Vizenor classes among "treacherous conditions in any discourse on tribal consciousness" (1994: 175), dominate the options available to game players. The "mystic savage" appears in several games (LaPensée 2006 and 2007), such as in the Real Time Strategy (RTS) game, *No Man's Land* (2003), which includes units of "Prairie Indian Medicine Men" who can "cast mighty magic spells." In the RTS game, *Age of Empires III: The WarChiefs* (2006), players increase their units' speed, damage, and skills by having villager units perform mystical dances in a pit. The very fact that characters dance to increase skills is a problematic stereotype that is then compounded by physical dance moves that echo stereotypes seen in films. Digital games can thus perpetuate old stereotypes both in terms of representation as well as mechanics that take the form of actions.

At the same time, digital games have the potential to ameliorate the literature of dominance in their unique ability to engage Indigenous methods of self-determination and representation. For example, *Otsì:!! Rise of the Kanien'kehá:ka Legends* (2008–09)—developed by youth in the Skins 1.0 Workshop—is a first-person shooter that adapts traditional Kahnawake Mohawk stories such as the Flying Head. In the multilevel game, the player takes the role of the hunter and sees the world from his eyes. The gameplay begins outside of a village that has been razed to the ground. The sole survivor tells him about the Flying Head and its attack on the village and warns the player that it is now heading toward the hunter's village. The hunter has to then fight his way across the land with the help and hindrance of figures from other Kahnawake Mohawk stories (LaPensée & Lewis 2011). Videogames can thus do more than simply avoid stereotypical images perpetuated in romanticized Western icons of the nineteenth-century "American frontier." They hold the potential for authentic self-representation in ways that engage the imagination in relation to Indigenous worldviews.

Current Contributions

Digital games that contribute to survivance are on the rise. In May 2015, the University of California held the Natives in Game Dev Gathering, the first academic event of its kind, with John Romero, Allen Turner, Manuel Marcano, Renee Nejo, Jason Edward Lewis, Darrick Baxter, and me as speakers. Themes discussed at this gathering as well as games highlighted at events such as the imagineNATIVE Film + Media Arts Festival demonstrate influences from traditional stories, contemporary experiences, relational teachings, and Indigenous languages. While non-Indigenous developers occasionally fill roles such as programming, animation, and technical art in games highlighted at these events, only games with Indigenous creatives in lead roles are highlighted. The resulting talks, demos, and exhibitions promote self-determination. There is a community-wide understanding at these gatherings that the direct inclusion of communities represented in a digital game is an essential aspect of any design and development process, not just to defuse stereotypes, but because Indigenous worldviews can influence game design and generate unique gameplay. While consultation and community collaboration to varying degrees during conceptualization and implementation of games with Indigenous representations are essential, there is a greater hope that more Indigenous creatives will be given the opportunity to be directly involved in the development process with the understanding that key roles shape a game.

Storytelling

Games can be a space for retelling and reimagining historical, traditional, family, and personal stories. Already mentioned earlier in this chapter, *Otsì:!! Rise of the Kanien'kehá:ka Legends* is a computer game developed in the Unreal game engine by students in Owisokon Lahache's art class at the Kahnawake Survival School during the 2008–09 school year as part of the Skins 1.0 workshop conducted by AbTeC. It is a rich representation of several stories from the Kahnawake Mohawk community that resulted in a game narrative about an Iroquois hunter on a mission to stop the Flying Head from destroying his village. The village includes longhouses modeled after traditional Iroquois structures. Figures from other Mohawk stories, including the Hoof Lady and the Monkey Dog, interrupt the journey alongside new figures, such as the Tree People, imagined by youth. Each of these figures tells its own story; some assist him, some hold him back. The journey ends at the hunter's village, which the Flying Head is attacking. The hunter must fight him off by using the information he gathered from characters along the way (LaPensée & Lewis 2011). Youth later expanded this concept into two games: *Skahiòn:hati: Legend of the Stone Giant* (2011) and *Skahiòn:hati: Rise of the Kanien' kehá:ka Legends* (2012). In these games, youth chose to uniquely fuse together traditional stories that were not previously interconnected. In doing so, they wove new interactive stories with dimensional representations of community spaces including longhouses that can be revisited much like traditional storytelling is returned to, recalled, and retold, now available in this generation in the form of games that can be replayed.

Family stories are just as meaningful as traditional stories and can carry aspects that transfer strongly to games, such as figures that can become characters or journeys that can become levels of goals and progression. *Never Alone* or *Kisima Ingitchuna* (2014) is a puzzle-platformer that was developed for computers and consoles as a collaboration between the Cook Inlet Tribal Council in Alaska and ally game company, E-Line Media. It retells a family story about a young Iñupiaq woman, Nuna, and her fox sidekick venturing together to save her village. The game shares many stories and teachings, thanks to in-game rewards made from short film clips with storyteller Ishmael Angaluuk Hope and other community members who were interviewed during the research phase of development. This involvement is especially important when developing games with Indigenous stories, since, as shown in *Never Alone*, figures such as the mischievous Little People are real and not simply "myths." As Anishinaabekwe, I recognize Little People as *memegwesiwag*, also known as water spirits. From my Auntie I have come to understand that Little People are simply hard for us to see because they move very fast, much like how hummingbird wings appear blurry to the human eye when they are flying. This realness is represented in not only *Never Alone*'s gameplay but also the way in which the developers respected feedback from the communities involved. Although *Never Alone*'s development, including art and design, was completed in-studio by non-Indigenous team members, the key designer and artist made a genuine effort to be reciprocal in the collaboration by staying with the community for extended periods and taking care to integrate carving and other traditions into the game design. *Never Alone* has since inspired many other Indigenous people to look at games more closely for their potential to express stories, teachings, and language.

Contemporary Experiences

While *Never Alone* relates traditional and family stories by having community members revisit and reimagine in a game space, other digital games deal exclusively with contemporary issues that are contextualized by the modern experiences of Indigenous communities. *Invaders* (2015), *Wanisinowin* (2015), and *Blood Quantum* (forthcoming) express unique but interrelated concerns faced by the designers. Interestingly, each of these games is developed by Indigenous women who had a direct part in the design as well as the art. This layering of roles reinforces the strengthening of Indigenous voices in digital games while suggesting that truly self-determined games are most likely to be developed independently.

Invaders (2015), which I developed in Unity 3-D with art by Steven Paul Judd and music by Trevino Brings Plenty, playfully confronts the definition of what it means to be an invader. The game is inspired by Steven Paul Judd's original artwork, which juxtaposes a historical photo of warriors shooting arrows into the sky with the 8-bit art of the classic arcade game, *Space Invaders*. The game asks, "Who are the aliens?" The player shoots arrows at waves of alien invaders and inevitably dies. The goal is to reach a new high score for how many aliens you destroy and how many waves you survive. Lives are depicted in the images of other warriors rather than a number or heart system, making the loss of a life more visceral and also challenging players to consider the genuine losses experienced by Indigenous communities during colonization, which *Invaders* portrays as an invasion. By using *Space Invaders* as a touchstone, the game manages to reach both Indigenous and non-Indigenous players with its messages, recognizing, too, that each player is responsible for their own interpretation.

Blood Quantum (forthcoming), by Diegueno game artist and designer, Renee Nejo, addresses the ongoing eradication of Indigenous identity due to the blood quantum system, which defines Indigineity based on a measurement of blood as articulated by the government of one's tribal affiliation. Due to family choices prior to the artist/designer's birth, she technically has more "quantum" than her own identification card states (Nejo 2014). Blood quantum can be impacted if, for example, a parent or grandparent chose not to register with a tribe, if they were removed, or if a tribe was disbanded. While *Blood Quantum* deals with a very intense issue, it does so cleverly through a Real Time Strategy with two sides: gray droplets and blue droplets. The player is responsible for a community of blue droplets, who are invaded by the gray droplets, who steal away the next generation of blue droplets. The player must continue creating more generations of blue droplets while also attempting to recover any stolen droplets. However, any blue droplet near a gray droplet gradually turns gray. Additionally, a new generation of blue droplets transition to gray droplets if they have been taken. Droplets are recoverable and will return to the player's community as long as they are a certain percentage of blue, which is represented visually in the game. Although *Blood Quantum*'s aesthetic is cute and friendly, the gameplay itself is dark in tone, resonating truths about contemporary Indigenous identity.

As seen in *Blood Quantum*, questions of place and belonging echo through generations influenced by relocation and urbanization. Megan Byrne is a Métis/Cree game designer who developed *Wanisinowin* in the Indigenous Routes Collective and Dames Making Games collaborative workshop, Indigicade. *Wanisinowin* is puzzle-platformer where the player is a young girl living in the spirit world who learns that, unlike anyone else there, she is actually human. She is given a chance to go with her aunt to the human world. To do this, the player must navigate their way through a dark world without literally losing their light, or their way. The developer was raised in a city away from her cultural lands and attributes this upbringing to a loss of cultural awareness that she is currently rectifying (Toronto Game Devs

2015). Through *Wanisinowin*, she is attempting to resolve the question, "Do I belong?" The game hopes to position players to either resolve their own doubt or at least experience empathy for people who are raised with disconnection and uncertainty.

Teachings

Just as there are contemporary issues, there are also ways in which Indigenous communities live and thrive through reinforcing traditional teachings and community values. In *Gathering Native Foods* (2014), which I co-designed in collaboration with the Oregon Museum of Science and Industry and the Hibulb Cultural Center, players can choose seasonal mini-games from a map, which overlays the outline of what was traditional land with land currently protected by Tulalip tribes. Of course, land has been reduced, and the locations of traditional foods have changed. With this context in mind, each mini-game hopes to challenge players to shift their perspectives about food gathering practices toward traditional cultural values. For example, in the salmon catching mini-game, the player is given a certain number of salmon that are needed for the community feast. Since the game is a touchscreen game in a museum, the usual tendency is for the player to rapidly click on salmon as quickly as they can. However, they lose the game if they overtake, thus requiring the player to slow down and consider which salmon they should take and which they should leave for a future season. Although players can certainly choose to ignore these restrictions, the game only rewards players who follow the values of the community. In this way, *Gathering Native Foods* uses design to reflect on changes to the land and invoke ongoing values to rectify losses caused by colonization. Thus, games are exciting spaces for expressing Indigenous ways of knowing because of their ability to infuse teachings with gameplay mechanics.

Language

Teachings are also infused in Indigenous languages, which can be revitalized or reinforced in digital games. It is important to note that games should never replace in-person interactions for language. Being with speakers and engaging in conversations should always be the priority. However, due to community displacement during colonization and language loss resulting from systems such as residential schools, which banned youth from speaking their languages, there is a critical need to reach today's youth and encourage them to actively engage with Indigenous languages. Overall, digital games are promising spaces for not just passing on language but also relating teachings while doing so, thanks to their ability to combine audio, art, and interaction.

Singuistics (2016), developed with ally game company, Pinnguaq, is a singing game available on iOS that aims to pass on Indigenous languages by challenging players to sing along to songs on a drum beat. Lyrics with translations scroll across the screen as artwork from community artists provides culturally relevant, visual backdrops The game opens on a map of Turtle Island depicted in a way that is true to traditional stories, since it portrays a turtle and is also geographically accurate. Players can then select a suite of songs to sing based on communities. The Anishinaabemowin suite features the Miskwaasining Nagamojig (Swamp Singers) along with Anishinabe art displayed during songs about women and wellbeing in the language. *Honour Water* (2016) builds from the same design and features the Oshkii Giizhik Singers and Sharon Day with the hope of sharing teachings about the importance and process of healing water through the vibrations created when singing water songs. This particular game also creates awareness about the Nibi Walks, which are gatherings for walking and singing to places of water with hope for healing pollution, with an emphasis on oil spills. Gameplay is equally concerned with reinforcing cultural values and engaging players with current issues as it is with teaching language.

Recommendations for the Future

The uniqueness of these games suggests that acts of survivance need not be limited to a certain set of design expectations, such as a particular platform, genre, or gameplay mechanic. This lack of standardization is not an obstacle. Instead, it opens many possibilities for expanding expression through new technologies in game development as they emerge. I hope for a future where we are coding from the game engine up, which, for example, will enable me to express teachings such as Anishinaabeg perspectives on physics. The games described in this chapter are part of an ongoing effort to adapt existing resources in the design and dissemination of survivance games while remaining aware of next generation technologies that can be used to make games that are more and more representative of Indigenous worldviews.

The more we uplift by challenging ourselves to keep this work going, and the more we push for self-determination in Indigenous games, the more we rise in parallel, standing side by side.

Further Reading

LaPensée, E. (2015) "The Artistry of Indigenous Video Games," *First American Art Magazine* 8.

Townsend, M., Claxton, D. and Loft, S. (2005) *Transference, Tradition, Technology*, Banff: Walter Phillips Gallery Editions.

Vizenor, G. (2008) *Survivance*, Lincoln, NB: University of Nebraska Press.

Wyeld, T. G., Brett, L., Joti, C., Craig, G., Brendan, L., & James, H. (2007), "The Ethics of Indigenous Storytelling: Using the Torque Game Engine to Support Australian Aboriginal Cultural Heritage," *Digital Games Research Association* 4.

References

Caillois, R. (1961) *Man, Play, and Games*, New York: Free Press of Glencoe.

DeBell, M. and C. Chapman (2006) *Computer and Internet Use by Students in 2003: Statistical Analysis Report (NCES 2006–065)*, U.S. Department of Education, Washington, DC: National Center for Education Statistics.

Fixico, D. (2003) *The American Indian Mind in a Linear World*, New York, NY: Routledge.

King, T. (2005) *The Truth About Stories*, Minneapolis, MN: University of Minnesota Press.

LaPensée, E. (B. A. Lameman) and J. E. Lewis (2011) "Skins: Designing Games with First Nations Youth," *Journal of Game Design & Development Education* 1(1), retrieved from www.rit.edu/gccis/gameeducationjournal/skins-designing-games-first-nations-youth.

LaPensée, E. (B. A. Lameman), J. E. Lewis, and S. Fragnito (2010) "Skins 1.0: A Curriculum for Designing Games with First Nations Youth," in *FuturePlay 2010 Proceedings of the International Academic Conference on the Future of Game Design and Technology*, Vancouver, BC, May 6–7, pp. 105–12, retrieved from dl.acm.org/citation.cfm?doid=1920778.1920793.

LaPensée (Dillon), B. A. (2006) "Digital Nations and Pixel Natives: American Indian Figures in Digital Games," in *27th Annual National Popular Culture/American Culture Association Conference*, Atlanta, GA, April 12–15.

LaPensée (Dillon), B. A. (2006) "North American Indigenous Imagery and Identity in the Game World," Panel held at *FuturePlay 2006*, London, ON, October 10–12.

LaPensée (Dillon), B. A. (2006) "Odaminodaa: Game Education for Indigenous Youth," presentation at *Canadian Game Studies Association Symposium*, Toronto, ON, September 21–24.

LaPensée (Dillon), B. A. (2007) "NDNWN: Designing Games with Aboriginal Stories using the Aurora Toolset," in *Proceedings of the 2007 Conference on FuturePlay*, Toronto, ON, November 14–18, pp. 233–36, retrieved from dl.acm.org/citation.cfm?id=1328247.

LaPensée (Dillon), B. A. (2014) "Survivance as an Indigenously Determined Game," *AlterNative: An International Journal of Indigenous Peoples* 10(3), 263–75.

Lewis, J. E. and S. Fragnito "Aboriginal Territories in Cyberspace," *Cultural Survival Quarterly* 29(2), retrieved from www.culturalsurvival.org/publications/cultural-survival-quarterly/canada/aboriginal-territories-cyberspace.

Marcano, M. and E. LaPensée (2014) "What Not to Do with Native Americans in Video Games," retrieved from www.youtube.com/watch?v=A59oL1isy3w.

McAdams, J. (2010) "A Conversation with Simon Ortiz," *The Kenyon Review*, retrieved from www.kenyonreview.org/wp-content/uploads/mcadams-ortiz.pdf.

McGonigal, J. (2011) *Reality is Broken*, New York, NY: Penguin Press.

Nejo, R. (2014) "Blood Quantum," *Renee Nejo*, retrieved from www.reneenejo.com/blog/2014/8/19/blood-quantum.

Rothenbuhler, E. and M. Coman (2005) *Mass Media Anthropology*, London: SAGE.

Smith, L. (1999) *Decolonizing Methodologies*, London: Zed Books.

Squire, K. and H. Jenkins (2003) "Harnessing the Power of Games in Education," *Insight* 3, 5–30, retrieved from plato.acadiau.ca/courses/engl/saklofske/download/digital%20gaming%20education.pdf.

Sturken, M. and L. Cartwright (2001) *Practices of Looking*, Oxford: Oxford University Press.

Todd, L. (1996) "Aboriginal Narratives in Cyberspace," in M. Moser and D McLeod (eds.) *Immersed in Technology: Art and Virtual Environments*, Cambridge, MA: MIT Press.

Toronto Game Devs (2015) "Interview: Wanisinowin | Lost Creator Meagan Byrne," *Toronto GameDevs*, retrieved from www.torontogamedevs.com/blog/2015/10/10/interview-wanisinowinlost-creator-meagan-byrne.

Velie, A. (2008) "The Concept of Survivance in Gerald Vizenor's Bear Island: The War at Sugar Point," in G. Vizenor (ed.) *Survivance: Narratives of Native Presence*, Lincoln, NB: University of Nebraska Press, pp. 147–62.

Vizenor, G. (1989) *Narrative Chance: Postmodern Discourse on Native American Indian Literatures*, Norman, OK: University of Oklahoma Press.

Vizenor, G. (1994) *Manifest Manners: Narratives on Postindian Survivance*, Lincoln, NB: University of Nebraska Press.

Zimmerman, E. (2004) "Narrative, Interactivity, Play, and Games," in N. Wardrip-Fruin and P. Harrington (eds.) *First Person: New Media as Story, Performance, and Game*, Cambridge, MA: MIT Press, pp. 154–64.

Games

Aboriginal Territories in Cyberspace (2012) *Skahiòn:hati: Rise of the Kanien'kehá:ka Legends*, retrieved from abtec.org/iif/index.php/outputs/output-3.

Aboriginal Territories in Cyberspace (2011) *Skahiòn:hati: Legend of the Stone Giant*, retrieved from abtec.org/iif/index.php/outputs/output-2.

Aboriginal Territories in Cyberspace (2008–09) *Otsi:!! Rise of the Kanien'kehá:ka Legends*, retrieved from abtec.org/iif/index.php/outputs/output-1.

Byrne, M. (2015) *Wanisinowin*, videogame, PC, retrieved from meaganbyrne.carbonmade.com/projects/5702517.

E-Line Media (2014) *Never Alone/Kisima Ingitchuna*, videogame, console, PC, iOS, retrieved from neveralonegame.com.

LaPensée, E. (2015) *Invaders*, videogame, iOS, web, retrieved from survivance.org/invaders.

LaPensée, E. (2015) *We Sing for Healing*, digital game, web, retrieved from survivance.org/wesing.

Nejo, R. (forthcoming) *Blood Quantum*, videogame, PC, retrieved from www.bloodquantumgame.com.

Oregon Museum of Science and Industry (2014) *Gathering Native Foods*, videogame, PC, Portland, OR.

Pinnguaq (2016) *Honour Water*, videogame, iOS, Toronto, ON, retrieved from www.honourwater.com.

Pinnguaq (2016) *Singuistics*, videogame, iOS, Toronto, ON, retrieved from pinnguaq.com/singuistics.

Part II

DESIGN, INTERFACE, INTERACTION

13
MAKING MEANING, MAKING CULTURE
How to Think about Technology and Cultural Reproduction

Anne Balsamo

Some of the most inspiring digital humanities projects that I follow focus on the development of interactive applications that reconfigure practices of authoring and reading. Probably the most ambitious and impactful has been the development of Scalar, the database-authoring platform created by Tara McPherson and her colleagues in the Alliance for Networking Visual Culture (n.d.). Innovating new tools for collaborative authoring and reading, as well as for humanities-based data management and text navigation, the Scalar project is, in fact, a platform for new ways of knowledge construction and dissemination (e.g., see Cong-Huyen et al. 2015). Other notable digital humanities projects focus on the creation of dynamic and animated databases, such as Bruce Zuckerman's *InscriptiFact* portal, which provides access to distributed collections of digital images of pieces of The Dead Sea Scrolls (Zuckerman, Lundberg, & Hunt n.d.) and the site-specific narratives Heidi Rae Cooley (2014) assembled into a geo-spatial mobile application that traces the wanderings and recordings of a traveling salesman. Other prominent genres of technology-based humanities design-research include important work in computational humanities and experiments with electronic literature, as well as more recent projects, such as explorations in cultural analytics, born-digital scholarship, and artificial reality applications. These projects not only offer examples of new genres of humanities scholarship and provide wider access to cultural heritage collections; they also demonstrate the expansive range of the technological imagination of digital humanists.

Through the digital humanities projects I have designed and developed, I explored the concept of "transmedia scholarship." As I elaborated in my book, *Designing Culture: The Technological Imagination at Work* (2011), the scholarship I authored manifested across modalities; the "designing culture" project was expressed as an interactive documentary, video primers, digital cognitive maps, and an elaborate museum exhibition. In short, it performed its cultural work using a variety of modes of expression, across institutional domains, and through engagement with diverse theoretical frameworks. For all its expressive work, realized in various digital formats, the project was also an example of applied cultural critique. This represents the horizon and challenge of most digital humanities projects. As Alan Liu persuasively argues:

> Especially by contrast with "new media studies," whose provocateur artists, net critics, tactical media theorists, hacktivists, and so on, blend post-1960s media theory, poststructuralist theory, and political critique into "net critique" and other kinds of digital cultural criticism, the digital humanities are noticeably missing in action on the cultural-critical scene. While digital humanists develop tools, data, and metadata critically, therefore (e.g., debating the "ordered hierarchy of content objects" principle; disputing whether computation is best used for truth finding or, as Lisa Samuels and Jerome McGann put it, "deformance"; and so on) rarely do they extend their critique to the full register of society, economics, politics, or culture. How the digital humanities advances, channels, or resists today's great postindustrial, neoliberal, corporate, and global flows of information-cum-capital is thus a question rarely heard in the digital humanities associations, conferences, journals, and projects with which I am familiar. Not even the clichéd forms of such issues—for example, "the digital divide," "surveillance," "privacy," "copyright," and so on—get much play.
>
> (Liu 2012)

This struggle to develop and promote nuanced critical engagement with all things digital requires digital humanists to think more complexly about such issues as the cultural work of technology, the epistemology of data, the infrastructure of knowledge production, and the deployment of critical methods of analysis. In this chapter, I provide an overview of a reproductive theory of technology to use as a framework for the critical analysis of digital cultural heritage.

A Philosophy of Technology as a Critical Foundation for Digital Humanities

We know that the conceptual core of digital humanities builds on a longstanding engagement between the humanities and technology. As a case in point, consider its deep philosophical foundation. Contemporary philosopher of technology Carl Mitcham (1994) explains that, although the designation "philosophy of technology" is a relatively recent development within the humanities, this sub-branch of philosophy has a long genealogy: work by Rousseau and Heidegger certainly contributes to its development, even if their philosophical projects were not specifically identified as such. Mitcham and his co-editor, Robert Mackey, argue: "But precisely because technology is intimately involved with practical affairs, the stimulus to develop a philosophy of technology is more than just philosophical. It also arises from economic, social, political and environmental problems" (1972: 30). Drawing on this legacy, I assert that digital humanities projects should be based on a methodical (if not methodological) investigation of (1) the relationship between humans and technology, and (2) the way in which these relationships take shape in different historical moments, in different geopolitical contexts, and at different levels of abstraction.

This assertion shifts the focus of humanistic analysis from the more traditional philosophical investigation of the metaphysical nature of technology to a consideration of how technology, and especially the creation of new applications, acquire cultural meaning. We know that the meaning of any technology is not a transhistorical given but rather a historically specific construction produced within an extended network of meaning-making practices. This approach promotes an understanding of technology as an articulated cultural formation. Here, the influence of Raymond Williams (1981) is evident; he uses the term "formation" to describe the internal organization of a cultural arrangement. Stuart Hall uses the term "articulation" as the name for a structured totality that is neither inevitable nor unending (Grossberg 1986). For Hall, cultural forms are constructed in particular ways. The unity of a form (its sensibleness, its meaning, and its manifestation) is itself a construction, constituted by connections among different elements that make up a formation. The term "articulation" is useful in part because of the double meaning of the concept: articulation is both a process (of meaning construction) and a production. As a process of meaning construction, it refers to the act whereby one unit of an ensemble or system acquires meaning in part through the relationship with or attachment to other units of the ensemble. As a production it implies the existence of an "articulating" agent. Articulations are structured in a particular way with an internal organization that is, in turn, integrated into a broader social order. The broader social order—that serves as the extra-organizational/institutional context of a given formation—is always historically constituted. Therefore articulations must be understood as historically specific formations; they are contingent on particular historical actions and forces but not necessarily determined by them. To analyze technology using this approach is to investigate the conjunctural relations among elements of the cultural formation.

Accordingly, what is called "a technology" is an articulation among different elements; these include seemingly invisible elements and immaterial objects such as codes and standards, discursive moments such as communication practices and forms of knowledge, and nondiscursive moments such as bodily habits and affective investments. This definition of technology resists the bifurcation of technology and culture. Technologies, in this sense, are not reducible to objects; they are better understood as an assemblage of elements that are articulated one-to-another in situational and historically specific ways. The elements, when articulated and assembled, are typically referred to as "digital technologies" and include technical elements such as:

- Devices and artifacts, which themselves are reified forms of knowledge;
- Practices and processes of human labor that include social relations and disciplined forms of embodiment;
- Material conditions of production, including supply chain processes of resource extraction, modification, fabrication, and commodification;
- Structures of regulation, laws, and policies;
- Circuits of economies of value and exchange; and
- Infrastructures, which enable dissemination, activation, and disposal.

And they also always include cultural elements such as:

- Semantic conventions of form,
- Modes of address and genre characteristics,
- Embodied rituals and habits, and
- Cultural narratives and mythologies.

As Donna Haraway (1991) taught us, all technologies are reproductive technologies. I elaborate her adage in the development of what—in drawing on Marilyn Strathern's work on reproductive models (1992)—I call a reproductive theory of technology (Balsamo 2011: 10). At base, this "turn to reproduction" asserts that all technologies manifest a double logic, in that they not only replicate prior knowledges (codes, materials, processes, and forms) but also bring new arrangements into existence. This is how technologies manifest multiple and often contradictory meanings, impacts, intended and unintended uses, and contradictions.

The Practical Encounter between Digital Humanities and Cultural Studies

A *critical* digital humanities rests on the commitment to create deep analyses of the ideological effects of specific cultural arrangements. This is, at least, what I learned from the cultural scholars who create and investigate particular techno-cultural conjunctions. In that cultural studies itself builds on the work of an entire tradition of critical theory, especially the work of those associated with the Frankfurt School, the engagement between cultural studies and technology also has a long history (Balsamo 2011). From Marx through Polayni (1958), as well as Marcuse (1964), scholars whose work is central to the development of critical theory had themselves been involved in the project of investigating the specifically cultural dimensions of science and technology. Key theoretical terms such as "ideology," "the public sphere," and "capitalism" were debated and clarified specifically in reference to the practices of technologists and the expropriation of a scientific worldview in the development of industrial and postindustrial societies. Following this, I argue that humanistic research on technology, and equally important, the design of digital humanities projects (applications, platforms, etc.) must be based not simply on the analysis of the cultural values manifest in technology-under-development; they must also seek ways to intervene in the technological reproduction of structures and relations of power. Having said that, it is important to remember that, while the design of these projects might draw deeply on relevant frameworks of cultural criticism (such as feminism, critical race theory, or postcolonialism), the process of doing things differently with technology must engage *practice* as well as theory. This is the productive meeting point between digital humanities and the project of cultural criticism. The creative, practical, thoroughly *critical* aim of the best work in digital humanities is to transform technology to be more democratic and empowering. How this is accomplished varies, of course, from project to project.

We might usefully understand digital humanities projects as engaged in the research-design of a category of reproductive technologies that focus specifically on the reproduction of culture. In this sense, these projects involve the *replication* of specific narrative conventions, modes of habituated technological engagement, rituals of embodied meaning making, and media specific genre conventions. Simultaneously, they manifest the *expression* of a new cultural arrangement when they provide innovative platforms for the creation of knowledge, mediated channels for the circulation of stories, and the refashioning of long-standing genre conventions. To the extent that they often incorporate new interfaces and experimental modes of interactivity, they also occasion the acquisition of transformed habits of reading and writing, or literacies (Balsamo 2011).

Designing a Complex Media System to Augment Cultural Memory

In this section, I describe an example digital humanities project that was influenced by these considerations, including understandings about the role of technologies in the reproduction of culture and the formation of questions motivated by the engagement with cultural and media studies. The effort, known as AIDS Quilt Touch, includes three digital experiences that enable the dissemination, preservation, and co-creation of an extensive digital archive of materials from the AIDS Memorial Quilt. We began this project with a cultural question: how to preserve one of the most important cultural artifacts of the twentieth century so large (and materially heterogeneous) that it strains the archival capacity of any U.S. cultural institution? Even though sections of the material Quilt continue to circulate on a regular basis, recognition of its historical significance—as an extraordinary, ongoing, collaboratively produced cultural artifact (Kurin 2013)—is limited (Literat & Balsamo 2014). In 2006, on the occasion of the 25th anniversary of the AIDS epidemic, the *Los Angeles Times* sadly announced: "The Quilt Fades into Obscurity" (Zarembo 2006). Given that the Quilt belongs to several intertwined cultural histories, including the history of arts activism in the U.S., the history of struggles for gay and lesbian rights, and the history of public health protests (Sturken 1997), we (the project team)—informed by work in digital humanities and based on what we knew of these histories and of the Quilt's precarious status as a material artifact—expanded our initial question to ask how digital technologies could augment the experience of this cultural archive.

Under the stewardship of The NAMES Project Foundation (a nonprofit organization in Atlanta), the Quilt now comprises 48,000 individual panels that commemorate more than 98,000 names (see Figure 13.1). This represents roughly 15 percent of the number of people who have died of HIV/AIDS in the U.S. The size of the Quilt is staggering. Each panel measures three feet by three feet and is stitched into a twelve-foot-by-twelve-foot block. If the Quilt were laid out for display, then it would cover more than 1.3 million square feet. If a person spent only one minute visiting each panel, then it would take 33 days to view the Quilt in its entirety. The impact of the Quilt plays out at different scales; certainly its cultural significance is tied to its massive size, the quantity of names represented, and the spatial dimensions of its array. But its impact also plays out at the scale of individual panels, where the stories of tens of thousands of people—those who died and those who lovingly created the panels—are literally stitched into a material archive.

Encountering the Quilt is always a moving experience. While Quilt blocks continue to serve as the focal point of community HIV/AIDS awareness events, the entire Quilt has been displayed only five times in its 27-year history. The first display happened in 1987, when the first 1,920 panels of the Quilt were laid out on the Mall of Washington as part of the National March on Washington for Lesbian and Gay Rights. Subsequent displays of the Quilt unfolded on the Mall in 1988, 1992, and 1996; each time the Quilt tragically grew in size. The most recent attempt to display the Quilt took place during the summer of 2012, when The Names Project Foundation sponsored a month-long event called *Quilt in the Capital*; during that time the Quilt was also featured at the Smithsonian Institute's annual Folklife Festival.

Our approach to the conceptual design of the AIDS Quilt Touch project involved the development of a multifaceted *media system* that includes diverse elements that are *simultaneously* cultural and technological: material works as well as digital representations of textile art (quilt panels), discursive descriptors (metadata tags) as well as textual accounts (stories, memories, and recollections), and unique contributions from individual human agents (quilt makers, activists, and health care providers) as well as from social collectives (audiences and families). The AIDS Quilt Touch media system also includes new practices and protocols, unique modes of interactivity, as well as those things that are typically understood as "technologies"—digital applications and hardware devices. A critical part of the system is the creation of social protocols to engage individuals who have an *interest* in the digital archive that prompts them to contribute

Figure 13.1 A view of the AIDS Memorial Quilt displayed on the National Mall in Washington, D.C. in 1996.

Source: Photo in public domain.

and *participate* in the expansion of the archive. One of the foundational objectives was to experiment with the design of processes whereby *communities of interest* are transformed into *communities of participation*. The result is the creation of a new *socio-technical-cultural arrangement* that is deeply informed by critical analyses of the relationship between culture and technology and manifests as an (historically specific) articulation among diverse elements. As such, the project incorporates scholarly insights from not only the humanities (philosophy of technology, media studies, and museum studies) but also the fields of information design, human-computer interaction, and computer science (for relevant work, see Mitcham 1994; Bennett 1995; Tufte 1990; Friedman & Winograd 1989).

Some of the crucial elements that make up this media system include:

- Institutional partnerships,
- Financial resources,
- Cultural heritage values,
- Innovative archival practices,
- New genres of cultural memory,
- Protocols of community engagement,
- Rituals of witnessing and commemoration,
- Emergent communication practices,

- Embodied modes of digital information access,
- Digital development environments,
- Visual processing algorithms,
- Novel interactive applications,
- Technological "affordances,"
- Technological devices, and
- Sustainable infrastructures for preservation and archiving.

Working in collaboration with The NAMES Project Foundation and a distributed team of research-designers from several U.S. institutions, we developed key objectives for the project:

- Use appropriate technologies that enhance and augment the personal and embodied experience of viewing the Quilt,
- Raise awareness about the stories of the Quilt panels,
- Assist people in viewing a specific panel using location-aware technologies on mobile devices,
- Assist in the annotation of the Quilt through the creation of tags and the collection of additional descriptive materials,
- Raise awareness about the archiving needs for the Quilt,
- Communicate the cultural importance of this work of international cultural heritage,
- Raise awareness about the contemporary status of AIDS in an international context, and
- Promote the Quilt as a living memorial.

Our challenge was this: how do we respect and maintain the cultures of the Quilt while developing a digital expression of its essential qualities? How could the intimacy of seeing the physical Quilt be augmented by digital applications? The design process drew insights from the history of public art as well as histories of public discourse about HIV/AIDS. As works of public art, these applications were created to evoke new perceptions through experiments with scale, mobility, and modes of human engagement in public spaces. As a mode of public engagement, these interactives were designed to prompt conversations about the impact of the AIDS epidemic, the richness of lives lost, and the contemporary status of AIDS/HIV infection in the United States. In creating these dynamic media experiences, we were especially interested in staging experiences that communicate with younger people who, having been born in the 1990s and 2000s, are growing up in a very different culture than that of the 1980s, when the AIDS epidemic began in the U.S. In this sense, experiences with AIDS Quilt Touch serve the broader cultural purpose to create a digital memorial and a contemporary context that can bridge generational interests.

At base, the digital experiences we created enable viewers to interact with information about the Quilt in different ways: the AIDS Quilt Touch Table (see Figure 13.2) allows people to view an image of the virtual Quilt and browse a list of names; the AIDS Quilt Touch mobile application (see Figure 13.3) offers viewers an opportunity to annotate individual Quilt panels with stories and commemorations.

The application incorporates digital representations of a wide range of media forms selected from the vast Names Project archive. Because the Quilt is a richly textured, cultural, and material artifact, our experience design relies on the use of tactile modes of interactivity. Applications have been optimized for display on touch-enabled devices (interactive tabletops,

Figure 13.2 Image of people interacting with the AIDS Quilt Touch Table.

Source: Photograph by Dale MacDonald; used with permission.

Figure 13.3 Image of AIDS Quilt Touch mobile web app.

Source: Photo by Sherry Moore; used with permission.

large touch screens, and mobile, handheld devices) to provide an intimate experience of viewing Quilt information. In this sense, experiences with AIDS Quilt Touch enact what Margaret Morse refers to as a "poetics of interactivity" designed to evoke an appreciation of the different scales of significance of the Quilt (Morse 2003). Like all memorials, AIDS Quilt Touch manifests a broad range of relationships among viewers and technologies.

In that we approached the design of the AIDS Quilt Touch project informed by theoretical work in the philosophy of technology and cultural studies, we consistently struggled to understand the processes whereby a socio-techno-cultural assemblage takes form. Moreover, the project was designed as a work of political activism, to embody cultural critique for the purposes of doing something different with the technologies at hand. Of course, one of the key theoretical questions that dogged this project concerned the role of specific agents in the broad process of articulation. To paraphrase Marx (as is often done): we make history, but not under the conditions of our own making.

Cultural Criticism to What End?

In the end, we might ask the nagging question: how might digital humanities projects manifest a critical analysis of cultural reproduction? And while we are at it, we should also ask the companion question: how might digital humanities projects effectively intervene in the reproduction of oppressive cultural formations?

Whereas many digital humanities projects focus on the creation of new applications and platforms, less frequently will these projects take into account the "infrastructuring" of cultural meanings. In drawing on a definition of "the digital" that emphasizes the relationship among history, community, institutions, devices, and social relations, we were primed to appreciate how these meanings are stitched in place, not simply by the nature of technology-under-development (as it too is already comprised of sedimented layers of social-technical elements), but as much by contexts of previously articulated social and institutional relations. Every assemblage, structured as it is for a moment in time, or fluidly changing over time, coheres through the connections among elements that include those more elusive qualities, such as values, affect, and agency. Every assemblage offers possibilities for creative expression and democratic practice, but these possibilities depend in large measure on the way in which agency is distributed and manifested in our messy relationships to technology and culture. In all cases, these possibilities will involve a struggle. Assemblages reproduce dominant ideological arrangements while suppressing or short-circuiting subversive possibilities because of the differential distribution of agency and power. While we know that certain agenic subject positions are "overdetermined" in many ways—for example, within capitalism, those with access to capital will continue to play a greater role in influencing the meaning of a particular technology—it is not a simple notion of determination that makes this so. As we know, subjects are not invested with capabilities as a consequence of any single line of force. The production of subject positions with differential agency is one way in which culture is reproduced (du Gay et al. 2013).

During this project, we were privileged with an abundance of technological "agency," embodied as world-class designers, industrial technologists, and institutional partners—all members of the design and development team. There were strong institutional forces empowering us with strong technological capabilities. Theoretically speaking, our collective project was an exploration of the possibility of rearticulating a socio-techno-cultural ensemble that already preceded our arrival on the scene. As cultural theorist Jennifer Slack explains:

> The success or failure of all these efforts to rearticulate the relationship between new technologies and [other elements] is dependent upon the effectiveness of real political efforts of individuals and groups. . . . [And yet,] the outcomes of real struggles to rearticulate social relations are not foreordained.
>
> (Slack 1989: 3)

What we learned is probably common sense to most: certain parts of a socio-techno-cultural assemblage are more firmly established than others. As we know, forms of culture are literally held in place by numerous organizations, institutions, and social practices, historically rooted and ideologically reproduced at every turn. And yet, having said this, we also know that technological formations are not uniformly dominant. The challenge we took on to create this project of digital cultural heritage will reveal failings and limitations; no doubt it was already constrained by numerous blind spots and unnecessary theoretical baggage. But it was, without a doubt, designed as an applied work of cultural criticism. And like all critical analyses, it will reveal its limits even as it provokes new questions and paths of inquiry.

Further Reading

Balsamo, A. (2011) *Designing Culture: The Technological Imagination at Work*, Durham, NC: Duke University Press.

du Gay, P., S. Hall, L. Janesd, A. Koed Madsen, H. MacKay, and K. Negus (2013) *Doing Cultural Studies: The Story of the Sony Walkman*, 2nd edn, London: Sage Publications.

Gold, M. K. (ed.) (2012) *Debates in the Digital Humanities*, Minneapolis, MN: University of Minnesota Press.

Ihde, D. (1979) *Technics and Praxis: A Philosophy of Technology*, Boston, MA: D. Reidel Publishing Company.

Penley, C. and A. Ross (eds.) (1991) *Technoculture*, Minneapolis, MN: University of Minnesota Press.

Polanyi, M. (1958) *Personal Knowledge: Toward a Post-Critical Philosophy*, Chicago, IL: University of Chicago Press.

Slack, J. D. and J. Macgregor Wise (2014) *Culture and Technology: A Primer*, 2nd edn, New York, NY: Peter Lang Publishing.

References

Alliance for Networking Visual Culture (n.d.), Scalar, retrieved from scalar.usc.edu/scalar/.

Balsamo, A. (2011) *Designing Culture: The Technological Imagination at Work*, Durham, NC: Duke University Press.

Bennett, T. (1995) *The Birth of the Museum: History, Theory, Politics*, London: Routledge.

Cong-Huyen, A., G. Carpio, S. Das, G. Hoagland, M. Mirer, V. Paredes, A. Phillips, and C. Rodelo (2015) *FemTechNet Critical Race and Ethnic Studies Pedagogy Workbook*, retrieved from scalar.usc.edu/works/ftn-ethnic-studies-pedagogy-workbook-/.

Cooley, H. R. (2014) *Finding Augusta: Habits of Mobility and Governance in the Digital Era*, Lebanon, NH: Dartmouth College Press.

du Gay, P., S. Hall, L. Janes, A. Koed Madsen, H. Mackay, and K. Negus (2013) *Doing Cultural Studies: The Story of the Sony Walkman*, 2nd edn, London: Sage Publications.

Friedman, B. and T. Winograd (eds.) (1989) *Computing and Social Responsibility: A Collection of Course Syllabi*, Palo Alto, CA: Computer Professionals for Social Responsibility.

Grossberg, L. (1986) "On Postmodernism and Articulation: An Interview with Stuart Hall," *Journal of Communication Inquiry* 10(2), 45–60.

Haraway, D. (1991) *Simians, Cyborgs and Women: The Reinvention of Nature*, New York, NY: Routledge.

Kurin, R. (2013) *The Smithsonian's History of America in 101 Objects*, New York, NY: Penguin Press.

Literat, I. and A. Balsamo (2014) "Stitching the Future of the AIDS Memorial Quilt: The Cultural Work of Digital Memorials," *Visual Communication Quarterly* 21(3), 138–49.

Liu, A. (2012) "Where is Cultural Criticism in the Digital Humanities?" in Gold, M. K. (ed.) *Debates in the Digital Humanities*, Minneapolis, MN: University of Minnesota Press, retrieved from dhdebates.gc.cuny.edu/debates/text/20.

Marcuse, H. (1964) *One-Dimensional Man: Studies in the Ideology of Advanced Industrial Society*, Boston, MA: Beacon Press.

Mitcham, C. (1994) *Thinking through Technology: The Path Between Engineering and Philosophy*, Chicago, IL: University of Chicago Press.

Mitcham, C. and R. Mackey (1972) *Philosophy and Technology: Readings in the Philosophical Problems of Technology*, London: The Free Press.

Morse, M. (2003) "The Poetics of Interactivity," in J. Malloy (ed.) *Women, Art, and Technology*, Cambridge, MA: MIT Press, pp. 16–33.

Slack, J. (1989) "Contextualizing Technology," in B. Dervin, L. Grossberg, B. J. O'Keefe, and E. Wartella (eds.) *Rethinking Communication: Volume 2: Paradigm Exemplars*, Newbury Park, CA: Sage Publications, pp. 324–39.

Strathern, M. (1992) *Reproducing Anthropology: Anthropology, Kinship, and the New Reproductive Technologies*, New York, NY: Routledge.

Sturken, M. (1997) *Tangled Memories: The Vietnam War, the AIDS Epidemic, and the Politics of Remembering*, Berkeley, CA: University of California Press.

Tufte, E. R. (1990) *Envisioning Information*, Cheshire, CT: Graphics Press.

Williams, R. (1981) *The Sociology of Culture*, Chicago, IL: University of Chicago Press.

Zarembo, A. (2006) "The Quilt Fades to Obscurity," *Los Angeles Times*, 4 June 4, retrieved from articles.latimes.com/2006/jun/04/science/sci-quilt4.

Zuckerman, B., M. Lundberg, and L. Hunt (n.d.) "The InscriptiFact Digital Image Library: Project Overview," retrieved from www.inscriptifact.com/aboutus/index.shtml.

14

CONTEMPORARY AND FUTURE SPACES FOR MEDIA STUDIES AND DIGITAL HUMANITIES

Patrik Svensson

I walk into the University of Toronto's Critical Making Lab, which is a large, open space with one or two offices and a meeting room at the far end, a set of cubicles occupying the remote left side of the space, and a glassed fabrication room with at least ten different 3-D printing systems and workbenches on the immediate right. The door to the fabrication room is at the far end of the room, which means that one does not walk into the fabrication workshop when entering the lab, but rather into a mixed space with couches, cubicles, tables with materials, and separate functions, including the fabrication workshop. The lab is an attractive space with not only a great deal of visible work but also people who seem very keen to engage in dialogue. In another context, the cubicles may have reminded me of a Dilbert-inspired office landscape, yet here they come across as creative workspaces with a connection to the rest of the space. I talk to one of the cubicle inhabitants. He is an experienced industrial designer who does much of his work from the lab, drawing on the separateness of the cubicle and the openness of the large space at the same time. He talks about how he benefited from exchange with scholars, bouncing around ideas and doing projects he probably would not have otherwise done. One of the postdocs points to printed prosthetics and manufacturing devices around the room while discussing the interpretations embedded in different types of medical representations. Someone walks around the space and ushers people to participate in an event in another part of the building. It is obvious to me that the space enables the institutional operations closely connected to the basic idea of the lab—exploring how critical thinking and material making come together. Could this be a joint space for media studies and digital humanities? If not, why?

Space and infrastructure condition knowledge production, manifest conceptual underpinnings, and activate certain expectations. For example, the teacher owns a third of the space of an "agrarian" or "industrial" classroom" (Scott-Webber 2004) and is not fettered to a single position. Students are normally aligned in rows and are expected to be seated rather than moving around in the space. The presentation infrastructure in such and other knowledge environments typically consists of a centrally placed, single screen and slide software used to show a single slide at a time, thus enacting a singular, central perspective with little material support for collaborative making, retention (only one slide at a time), and alternative narrative strategies, such as scale and juxtaposition (Robles-Anderson & Svensson 2016). The classroom door, normally closed when a class is in session, reinforces the sense of a closed and self-contained environment. Similarly, hospital corridors, seminar rooms, and design studios manifest and enable certain ideas about knowledge work through their architecture and infrastructure (Iedema et al. 2006; Fällman 2007; Svensson 2015). Space and infrastructure do not determine academic work, but rather suggest and enable (sometimes strongly) certain interactional modalities that are in turn embedded in an institutional, epistemic, and social context.

Nevertheless, space is often disregarded as a central factor in higher education, supporting a view of scholarship and education as independent from their spatial and geographic contexts (Livingstone 2010). Interior architecture is templated and typically not allowed or meant to be expressive and experimental, although there is an increasing interest in alternative types of knowledge spaces (Boys 2011). We are often not aware of the conditioning set by a traditional classroom or department architecture and normally unable to influence it on a structural level, even if the use of specific spaces is always negotiated by people. Space is also precious and notoriously scarce in most university and other settings. Whatever the case, academic spaces carry both implicit and explicit values. Space manifests status and power, and it conceals power relations (Soja 1989; Lefebvre 1991). It also enacts and often reifies categories of difference, including gender, race, sexuality, and ability (Risam 2015).

This chapter explores space as an enabler for the fields of media studies and digital humanities. I suggest that the material, cultural, and conceptual elements of space make it difficult to imagine and construct institutional spaces, such as labs, without attending to the infrastructural and intellectual trajectories of the fields under discussion. A somewhat provocative question posed in this chapter is—given overlapping ideas and shared visions between media studies and digital humanities—whether we might consider manifesting such visions through shared space.

Reflections on Institutional Space and Space as a Critical Category

A major challenge when analyzing and building institutional space is the considerable gap between conceptual foundations (e.g., goals and directions of an operation that are also associated with a space) and material levels of implementation (including details such as color schemes and the exact placement of outlets). Although conceptual and material foundations are deeply intertwined and co-dependent on context as well as people, it can be useful to describe them as separate layers or endpoints. What lies between the two asserted levels is a set of conditions or mechanisms for making concepts and materials meet or entangle. Such conditions or mechanisms can be understood as design principles (Svensson 2011) and "intellectual middleware" (Drucker & Svensson 2016). *Intellectual middleware describes the systemic assumptions and conditions built into digital and physical architectures*. When applied to technological platforms, it calls for precise attention to the way tools either structure arguments or express thinking, often through protocols programmed into a platform (Svensson 2016). For example, PowerPoint is constructed around the slide as a building block, meaning it is difficult to expand content over several slides in the software. This one-slide-at-a-time logic also affects physical infrastructure (Robles-Anderson & Svensson 2016). There is little reason to have two screens in a presentation room if the pervasive presentation software only requires (and can manage) one screen.

Intellectual middleware can similarly be used to understand how physical spaces, particularly institutional spaces, embody intellectual programs that organize experience and knowledge production—not deterministically, but opportunistically. A traditional classroom setup does not determine experience and the learning that can take place, but suggests and privileges certain ways of carrying out learning activities (just like online learning environments do). Alternative ways of structuring space can suggest other opportunities for learning, especially if they are part of an organized process of evaluating and reimagining both learning situations and goals where teachers as well as students are involved. Through focusing on the entanglement of the conceptual and material, intellectual middleware as a framework helps us avoid materially based installations with limited conceptual grounding (e.g., throwing in beanbags and using bright colors without anchoring such elements in operational goals) and conceptually based thinking with little material grounding (e.g., having an idea for creating a vibrant place for exchange with limited attention paid to the intellectual role of space and infrastructure).

Design principles operate in between conceptual and material infrastructure and can be seen as a means of implementing middleware. Designing and building spaces is always an iterative process and does not start out wholly from either the conceptual or the material level. Anyone who has designed an institutional space will know that such processes are dependent on operational and conceptual ideas, stakeholders and users, available resources, existing physical structures, institutional protocols, and many different types of professional expertise. Much of the work is about negotiation, but without a basic idea and concept (that is likely to develop through the process) a very crucial part is missing.

Given a basic idea centered around, for instance, "a creative meeting place for media, humanities, and technologies," there are a number of design principles that can be suggested. For example, in such an environment it will be important to facilitate meetings and connection making across disciplines as well as projects and to accommodate different work practices. It will also be vital to make the space speak to the potential users and their knowledge practices as well as suggest other practices and perspectives. Three possible design principles for this scenario would be translucence (to stimulate easy connection making; seeing what other people are working on and allowing semi-privacy), variation and flexibility (to support different working styles and knowledge traditions), and intensity (to support many simultaneous activities and a sense of energy). Translucence provides a structured way of thinking about the layout of physical and digital spaces by supporting "see-through" and striking a balance between public and private space (Dourish & Bly 1992; Erickson & Kellogg 2000; Svensson 2011). In practice, translucence as a design principle can be manifested by glass materials, nooks for individual work, half-height furniture for some parts of the space, and ways of supporting contact between ideas, people, and threads in an online platform. Here, as always, people must be part of the solution. There is no point in providing glassed doors or compartments if most of the users cover the glass in order to get more privacy and feel more comfortable. Translucence is not the same thing as transparency, and there are ways of using glass as a material that afford privacy as well as see-through.

Generally speaking, the systematic entanglement of ideas and space/infrastructure is not given enough consideration in building and reconstruction processes. Based on accumulated experience from a large number of construction projects, international collaborations, and many conversations, I suggest that there are several reasons for this predicament. First, the operation in question often does not have an articulated set of ideas about what they want to be and become (conceptual foundation). This requires articulating an operational vision (whether it is new or the same as earlier) and a willingness to discuss what could be improved and changed. To be sure, this is challenging work. Second, architectural and constructional work relies on templates to a large degree. There are longstanding specifications for different types of spaces and functions, and, while useful, these also constrain innovation. There are also often standard ways of managing ventilation, wireless networks, and other infrastructure, although there may in fact be other possible solutions that are more appropriate for the project at hand. Resistance to alternative solutions from facilities and construction teams is rarely about die-hard opposition, but rather not understanding why that alternative solution makes sense. Communication is essential at every stage of the process. There is also a cost factor here, but costs can sometimes be shifted within a budget. Third, it is very easy to get caught up in material details instead of discussions of what needs to be changed and developed in terms of the core operation. Designing institutional space can never be about asking people what furniture or colors they like and trying to distill a common denominator from such information. Fourth, design and construction projects frequently suffer from outsourcing too much of the "middleware work." Going from large-scale ideas to construction work requires the operation to be involved and work closely together with architects, interior architects, facility managers, and contractors. Often, the operation ends up having limited say and involvement in such processes. Given the lack of articulated visions, there is simply not enough there to empower architects and others to create something that is conceptual and material in a truly meaningful way, as well as grounded in the operation and operational goals.

Any academic space will be affected by many constraints, expectations, and layers of conditioning. However, as Shannon Mattern (2007) points out, reconfiguring space is an important institutional and intellectual opportunity, and it is an opportunity that needs to be taken, requiring leadership and negotiation power. Even if space is never the only factor in academic work, it plays a key role in the articulation of ideas with practices. For instance, a change in space can remind people how important space is to a given institution. Think of the pressure that MOOCs are putting on traditional campus operations, the shift from individual offices to collaborative open-plan workspaces, or the increased interest in maker-spaces and other alternative knowledge making spaces. Possible implementations can vary from small reconfigured rooms and flexible classrooms to open lab environments, display studios, and popup spaces.

For examples of innovative spaces relevant to media studies and digital humanities, consider the following: the Critical Making Lab described at the beginning of this chapter; the fairly small but materially and intellectually grounded Transcriptions Center at the University of California, Santa Barbara (Transcriptions Center 2015); or the inflatable and mobile structure, Space Buster, used for a series of artistic and scholarly events in New York City in 2012 (Raumlabor 2015). These are mostly physical examples, which necessarily embed technologies, but there are also digital platforms—such as GitHub, the CUNY Academic Commons, and the HASTAC web platform—that can be central to academic operations. Physical and digital platforms increasingly come together in different ways, including when remote participants are integrated in physical spaces and events through Skype, or when live streamed media and Twitter open up traditional events (Svensson 2016).

Such integration of physical and digital manifestations calls our attention to space and the spatial, just like mapping platforms and locational sensory technologies. Much interest will be practically oriented, but there is also a longstanding critical interest in space and infrastructure that has been renewed under rubrics such as the spatial turn (Warf & Arias

2009), spatial humanities (Bodenhamer, Corrigan, & Harris 2010), and infrastructure studies (Parks & Starosielski 2015). Edward W. Soja describes the spatial turn as a way to creatively and critically balance the temporal and historical imaginations with spatial and geographical imaginations (2009: 12). Michael Dear (2011) points to how geospatial technologies and environmentalism have been important to leverage work at the intersection of geography and the humanities. In digital humanities, geographic technologies such as ArcGIS, Neatline, and HyperCities have played a central role in emphasizing space as a way to structure and interpret digital materials. Some of this work has been critiqued because of its heavy investment in a Cartesian model of space as well as for its focus on (standard) tools rather than critical approaches to space (Hayles 2012; Drucker 2014). Meanwhile, in media studies, there is a renewed interest in infrastructure as an object of study, including work on underwater cables and networks (Starosielski 2015). This line of work is rarely connected to actively making infrastructures or envisioning new ones. However, I suggest that media studies and digital humanities are in a good position to collectively embrace space as a critical and creative category, a position that includes engaging one's own infrastructure and intellectual middleware by critiquing *and* making.

A Fictional Experiment

Imagine that a university decides to merge and co-locate a media studies department with a digital humanities initiative. First, there is a time of turmoil, discussions, and negotiations. An organized protest among media studies departments draws nationwide attention. The main argument is that media studies is being forced to succumb to digital instrumentalism and neoliberalism and that the core of the media studies discipline is being threatened. Contributors to the digital humanities initiative state they are worried they will disappear within the much larger media studies department; they fear media studies will try to turn digital humanities into digital media studies. "They have never built a thing," one leading digital humanist reportedly says.

One of the many subcommittees formed to deal with the merger has been assigned to consider work organization and space, and it soon becomes clear that space is an important matter of negotiation. The professors from media studies emphasize the importance of individual spaces for writing as well as for supervising students. One professor tells the committee that the windowless, shelf-rich office with reading chairs and hundreds of carefully arranged books is necessary to produce rigorous intellectual arguments. While the representatives of the digital humanities initiative—which are housed in an open plan office—also argue that they need individual offices, they strongly point to the need for infrastructure to support technological work and collaboration. At one point, the administrator suggests that new, distributed (and supposedly cheap) technologies make space less important. Although she does not say it, she is thinking of locating the merger in an abandoned basement below a healthcare building slightly off campus.

As it turns out, the university allocates a studio space as well as a set of adjacent offices to the merger. Two faculty members in media studies indicate that they want their primary working space inside the actual studio space, and some digital humanists prefer more closed-off offices. While the top-down administration process make things difficult, the two groups—now merged into one—eventually decide to make the best of the situation, and there are more personal connections than were apparent at first. Furthermore, in an environment more accepting of making and experimenting, some junior media studies faculty start to develop aspects of their work that were not promoted in their previous setting. One PhD student finds a place to put the wooden models he had been building at home for a research project on the architectural manifestation of the media industry. In a *Minecraft*-like universe, the digital versions of these wooden models become source material for various enactments and algorithmically driven comparisons between types of architecture.

Several digital humanists feel that their work is becoming more integrated in the school and that there is an increased interest in their knowledge domain. "We have always shaped ideas and the scholarship," one digital humanist says, "but now the whole process makes much more sense." A key result is that a new contact zone emerges (Pratt 1991), where members of both communities come together and inflect each other's work and practices. Not everyone is happy about the situation, however, and some people continue to aggressively dismiss it. "I hate the day Silicon Valley came to the department," one senior media scholar exclaims. A few of these detractors leave or retire eventually, and over the long haul a new media studies-digital humanities configuration emerges.

The above fiction is a rather optimistic caricature with limited context, but I use it as a lead-in to discuss space, infrastructure, and intellectual middleware for media studies and digital humanities. One important perspective is that space cannot be interpreted by itself, divorced from institutional politics, epistemic traditions, individual preferences, and intellectual directions. It manifests all of these perspectives at the same time, although it does not determine our work and intellectual directions. A low-performing research team or a dysfunctional teachers' group will not necessarily improve because it gets a new center. New spatial configurations cannot by themselves solve deep organizational or intellectual problems, or guarantee Nobel Prizes. However, if a large number of researchers, students, and teachers have access to a space they like, and if it matches the present and future needs of the operation, then the likelihood of high-quality work, everyday happiness, and new developments increases. There is a growing literature that supports such reasoning and that can be helpful in analyzing, designing, and constructing space (e.g., see Ellsworth 2005; Kirkbride & Mattern 2009; Boys 2011). Another perspective is that space can be used to channel change and ideas. Given a specific institutional, epistemic, and intellectual situation, changing spatial configurations can embody new sets of ideas and possibilities. Such work includes considering the current middleware and how it connects concepts with materials, as well as suggesting new middleware with adapted conceptual and material entanglements. This is a complex process, which has to be locally grounded and simultaneously sensitive to conceptual, material, institutional, and cultural elements.

Implementing Middleware for Digital Humanities and Media Studies

As suggested in the beginning of this chapter, institutional space cannot be disassociated from the fabric of the institutional operation. Imagining such spaces requires conceptual and material thinking in the same process. This is difficult work for a good reason, as the interplay between ideas and material manifestations is complex. It gets even more complex if we consider clustering several epistemic traditions in the same space, although space is likely to play an even more central role in such cases.

Digital humanities is not a stable institutional formation, and the spatial configuration depends on the type of digital humanities envisioned. A more disciplinary model of digital humanities might be housed in a department corridor (fairly rare) or be dispersed across institutions, while many center-like operations occupy a more communal, open space. There is also a model based on heavy-duty computational work with servers, workstations, and the occasional physical archive located in the space. Yet few digital humanities operations actually manifest themselves strongly through the space and infrastructure. The same is true of media studies, but here the field is more stable, and the academic template—institutional hallways with offices—applies to most media studies operations. There is a type of media studies that is more closely aligned with production and artistic practice; however, this is fairly uncommon and often involves "outsourcing" or compartmentalizing practice (see Kirkbride & Mattern 2009 for an analysis of a terminated building project at the New School).

I suggest that both fields would benefit from a stronger, combined intellectual-material engagement. Media studies has an established intellectual agenda, but arguably needs to be more engaged with the production of technological systems and the analysis of new media platforms. On the topic of media studies, Tara McPherson writes that, "[w]ith a few exceptions, we remain content to comment *about* technology and media, rather than to participate more actively in constructing knowledge in and through our objects of study" (2009: 120). Digital humanities, on the other hand, does not have a strong tradition in extensively commenting and critiquing technology and media, but it has had a much more pronounced interest in making projects and building archives. Andrew Prescott (2012) argues that digital humanities has been driven by a conservative tradition and needs to adopt an intellectual agenda. Meanwhile, digital humanities is frequently associated with lively dialogue, reaching out to communities and providing a space for seriously discussing the humanities, while media studies is often framed as a traditional discipline with limited visible engagement.

When designing space and infrastructure, questions vary from initiative to initiative; but, for the design of institutional spaces for digital humanities and media studies, the following questions are relevant: What is the goal and vision of the initiative, associated research groups, and educational programs? What academic infrastructure can be imagined? What modes of work and collaboration are envisioned? What are the spatial conditions, and how can the articulated vision be enacted given such conditions? How can this vision be described using a language that is neither too abstract nor too material, to connect concepts with materials? What are the financial constraints? What institutional bodies and protocols are relevant to the building process?

Let us assume that a given initiative—after extensive discussion about its direction and vision—concludes there is a common interest in not only challenging and expanding the assumptions built into technology-rich platforms such as 3-D printing, maker labs, THAT Camps, and TED talks, but also doing so through a combination of critical and experimental practice (e.g., redesigning and reimagining platforms). Critical concerns include the valorization of making, the lack of attention to gendered perspectives on making, investments in a realist or positivist epistemology (3-D printing), the ways in which platforms are flat ways of thinking about systems, the presumed (but not actual) lack of hierarchies at events such as THATCamps and unconferences, and the problems with TED talks as a mode of curatorship. At the same time, there is a belief in the potential of these platforms, and the initiative expresses a clear interest in engaging them, contributing to their development, and suggesting alternative modalities.

What would the middleware look like? It could be an apparatus to critique, enact, explore, and imagine platforms. Associated design principles might include the capacity to enact and simulate different types of events and processes (e.g., a TED talk), supporting multiperspective views on platforms, enacting counter platforms (alternative conceptions of what platforms could be), and reading critically the discourse surrounding platforms in relation to current, past, or imagined examples.

The actual implementation of space will always depend on a long and complex process constrained and enabled by all kinds of factors. It is important not to let constraints and standards control the conceptually grounded vision, while also being sensitive to the institutional, financial, and spatial factors at play. With these constraints, standards, and sensitivities in mind, what kinds of space and infrastructure could respond to the critical platform apparatus described above? For example, it might be useful to analyze a large number of TED talks simultaneously, using displays and tools in a space supporting the visual juxtaposition of talks, live discourse analysis, and thematic clustering algorithms. Furthermore, TED talks could be carried out in the space through a typical TED setup, manifested next to an implementation of an alternative conception (what a TED talk *could* be). At one point, a TED event could be organized around critiquing TED. Similar and different setups could be implemented around other platforms. For instance, one part of the space could be devoted to tracing inflections in different types of platforms, including power hierarchies in THAT Camps, race in maker labs, and environmental thinking in 3-D printing and maker culture. Through a given system of technologies (screens, simulation systems, and visualization engines), any platform can be seen from multiple points of view at the same time and actually tested in a space toward newly adapted or imagined platforms. Other methodologies could include interviews (e.g., structured interviews of THATCamp participants after an event) and mechanisms to foreground platforms or infrastructures that usually "run in the background" (e.g., the web). At the center of the space, a seminar table could serve as a reminder of how our own knowledge traditions and infrastructures are also platforms with their own inflections, structures, and associated practices.

There would seem to be a considerable degree of complementarity between digital humanities and media studies and, perhaps more important, a common direction. There is already overlap; however, it has had limited institutional repercussions and could be much more far-reaching intellectually, materially, and epistemologically. The current volume testifies to the potential of such work. And if representatives for the fields agree that an intellectual-material engagement is important, then there is undoubtedly a conceptual foundation that can be developed. This foundation would not have to include all the work in both fields; rather, it could be a future-oriented inflection. Intriguingly, such an inflection would also directly relate to the complexities operating across the conceptual and material levels discussed. Concepts such as intellectual middleware and related design principles can be used to think about the mapping of institutional visions and space, but they are also central to the subject matter of digital humanities and media studies. This overlap creates interesting opportunities. Could the space enact its own middleware and provide an interpretative knowledge environment? Instead of backgrounding the conditioning and choices made, such choices could be emphasized and made apparent. By including infrastructure that challenges traditional forms of digital representation, the space itself could ask questions about the standardization, history, and embedding of digital and nondigital systems and thinking.

Acknowledgments

The author's chair is supported the Wallenberg Foundation and the Baltic Group. Part of this chapter was written in 2015–16 as part of a distinguished fellowship at the Graduate Center, The City University of New York.

Further Reading

Boys, J. (2011) *Towards Creative Learning Spaces Re-Thinking the Architecture of Post-Compulsory Education*, Abingdon, UK: Routledge.

Livingstone, D. N. (2010) *Putting Science in Its Place: Geographies of Scientific Knowledge*, Chichago, IL: University of Chicago Press.

Scott-Webber, L. (2004) *In Sync: Environmental Behavior Research and the Design of Learning Spaces*, Ann Arbor, MI: Society for College and University Planning.

Svensson, P. (2016) *Big Digital Humanities: Imagining a Meeting Place for the Humanities and the Digital*, Ann Arbor, MI: University of Michigan Press.

References

Bodenhamer, D. J., J. Corrigan, and T. M. Harris (2010) *The Spatial Humanities: GIS and the Future of Humanities Scholarship*, Bloomington, IN: Indiana University Press.

Boys, J. (2011) *Towards Creative Learning Spaces Re-Thinking the Architecture of Post-Compulsory Education*, Abingdon, UK: Routledge.

Dear, M. (2011) "Historical Moments in the Rise of the Geohumanities," in M. Dear, J. Ketchum, S. Luria, and D. Richardson (eds.) *Geohumanities: Art, History, Text at the Edge of Place*, New York, NY: Routledge, pp. 309–14.

Dourish, P. and S. Bly (1992) "Portholes: Supporting Awareness in a Distributed Work Group," in *Proceedings of the SIGCHI Conference on Human Factors in Computing Systems - CHI '92*, New York, New York, USA: ACM Press, pp. 541–47, retrieved from portal.acm.org/citation.cfm?doid=142750.142982.

Drucker, J. (2014) *Graphesis: Visual Forms of Knowledge Production*, Cambridge, MA: Harvard University Press.

Drucker, J. and P. Svensson (2016) "The Why and How of Middleware," *Digital Humanities Quarterly* 10(2), retrieved from www.digitalhumanities.org/dhq/vol/10/2/000248/000248.html.

Ellsworth, E. (2005) *Places of Learning Media, Architecture, Pedagogy*, New York, NY: Routledge.

Erickson, T. and W. A. Kellogg (2000) "Social Translucence: An Approach to Designing Systems that Support Social Processes," *ACM Transactions on Computer-Human Interaction* 7(1), 59–83, retrieved from portal.acm.org/citation.cfm?doid=344949.345004.

Fällman, D. (2007) "Supporting Studio Culture in Design Research," in *Proceedings of International Association of Societies of Design Research '07*, Hong Kong Polytechnic University School of Design, pp. 1–12.

Hayles, N. K. (2012) *How We Think: Digital Media and Contemporary Technogenesis*, Chicago, IL and London, UK: University of Chicago Press.

Iedema, R., D. Long, K. Carroll, J. Stenglin, and M. Braithwaite (2006) "Corridor Work: How Liminal Space Becomes a Resource for Handling Complexities of Multi-Disciplinary Health Care," in *APROS 11: Asia-Pacific Researchers in Organization Studies: 11th International Colloquium*, Melbourne, AU, 4–7 December, 2005, pp. 238–47.

Kirkbride, R. and S. Mattern (2009) "Chainbuilding: A New Building for the New New School," *International Journal of Politics, Culture, and Society* 22(2), 201–19.

Lefebvre, H. (1991) *The Production of Space*, Oxford, UK: Basil Blackwell.

Livingstone, D. N. (2010) *Putting Science in Its Place: Geographies of Scientific Knowledge*, Chicago, IL: University of Chicago Press.

Mattern, S. (2007) *The New Downtown Library: Designing New Communities*, Minneapolis, MN: University of Minnesota Press.

McPherson, T. (2009) "Introduction: Media Studies and the Digital Humanities," *Cinema Studies* 48(2), 119–23.

Parks, L. and N. Starosielski (2015) *Signal Traffic: Critical Studies of Media Infrastructures*, Champaign, IL: University of Illinois Press.

Pratt, M. L. (1991) "Arts of the Contact Zone," *Profession* 91, 33–40.

Prescott, A. (2012) "Making the Digital Human: Anxieties, Possibilities, Challenges," *Digital Riffs*, retrieved from digitalriffs.blogspot.ca/2012/07/making-digital-human-anxieties.html.

Raumlabor (2015) "Space Buster II & Generator NY City," retrieved from raumlabor.net/space-buster-ii-generator-ny-city.

Risam, R. (2015) "Beyond the Margins: Intersectionality and the Digital Humanities," *Digital Humanities Quarterly* 9(2), retreived from www.digitalhumanities.org/dhq/vol/9/2/000208/000208.html.

Robles-Anderson, E. and P. Svensson (2016) "'One Damn Slide After Another': PowerPoint at Every Occasion for Speech," *Computational Culture* 5, retrieved from computationalculture.net/article/one-damn-slide-after-another-powerpoint-at-every-occasion-for-speech.

Scott-Webber, L. (2004) *In Sync: Environmental Behavior Research and the Design of Learning Spaces*. Ann Arbor MI: Society for College and University Planning.

Soja, E. W. (1989) *Postmodern Geographies: The Reassertion of Space in Critical Social Theory*, London, UK: Verso.
Soja, E. W. (2009) "Taking Space Personally," in B. Warf and S. Arias (eds.) *The Spatial Turn: Interdisciplinary Perspectives*, New York, NY: Routledge, pp. 11–35.
Starosielski, N. (2015) *The Undersea Network*, Durham, NC: Duke University Press.
Svensson, P. (2011) "From Optical Fibre to Conceptual Cyberinfrastructure," *Digital Humanities Quarterly* 5(1), www.digitalhumanities.org/dhq/vol/5/1/000090/000090.html.
Svensson, P. (2015) "The Humanistiscope: Exploring the Situatedness of Humanities Infrastructure," in P. Svensson and D. T. Goldberg (eds.) *Between Humanities and the Digital*, Cambridge, MA: MIT Press, pp. 337–54.
Svensson, P. (2016) *Big Digital Humanities: Imagining a Meeting Place for the Humanities and the Digital*, Ann Arbor, MI: University of Michigan Press.
Transcriptions Center (2015) "Transcriptions | A Digital Humanities Research Center in Literature, Culture & Media," UC Santa Barbara, retrieved from transcriptions.english.ucsb.edu.
Warf, B. and S. Arias (2009) *The Spatial Turn: Interdisciplinary Perspectives*, Routledge Studies in Human Geography, vol. 26, New York, NY: Routledge.

15

FINDING FAULT LINES

An Approach to Speculative Design

Kari Kraus

The belief that the past can be faithfully recovered from historical fragments that survive in the present has numerous literary champions: Rainer Maria Rilke's headless statue of Apollo is made conceptually whole again through the power of synecdoche in "Torso of Archaic Apollo"; Wilhelm Jensen's relic of a young woman in bas-relief becomes the means to reanimate the streets of ancient Pompeii in *Gradiva*; and William Blake's minuscule grain of sand is a deep-time microcosm of the universe in "Auguries of Innocence." Heritage stewardship practices likewise reflect this part-whole epistemology: a steeple might serve as the only surviving witness to a razed cathedral; a salvaged movie trailer the only testimony to an otherwise lost film; a peripheral device the only hardware component available to stand in for a retro game system. For the trained eye of the curator, these component parts are by no means mute, but rather eloquently attest to once vividly real things that no longer exist in toto. And for the expert hand of the conservationist, they may guide a conjectural reconstruction of the lost originals (a deeply controversial undertaking alternately viewed as rash or heroic depending on taste and milieu).

For over two million years, fragments have functioned as creative resources as well. It was common in the Renaissance, for example, for artists to reconstitute lost paintings of antiquity from at least partially intact descriptions of them, as when the Italian painter Botticelli reconstructed, through a sort of visual back-formation, one of Apelles's works of art from an ancient textual account of it. And it is through a kind of fractured vision—one that is capable of perceiving what cognitive scientist Ruth Byrne calls "fault lines in reality" (2007: 5 and *passim*)—that artists, designers, and engineers bring new cultural objects and inventions into the world. Charles Babbage's Analytical Engine—the first proposed general-purpose mechanical computer—repurposed the punch cards of the Jacquard loom and the stacks of rotating cams used to operate many of the eighteenth-century automata that entranced Babbage as a child. Similarly, Samuel Morse's first working prototype of the telegraph was a patchwork of parts scavenged from his artist's studio and brother's print shop, including a canvas stretcher, type slugs, and a clock pendulum. "Many of a technology's parts are shared by other technologies," notes Brian Arthur in *The Nature of Technology*, "so a great deal of development happens automatically as components improve in other uses 'outside' that technology" (2009: 134). It is as if perspicacity in design demands the ability to see the built environment not as a coherent whole, but as a scrapyard of materials that invite radical recombination. This "broken world thinking," to invoke Steven Jackson's term (2014), is profoundly inventive, allowing us to imagine rich counterfactual alternatives to reality.

Borrowing a term from evolutionary biology, I refer to the end products of such thinking as *Hopeful Monsters*: "they are things born perhaps slightly before their time," writes the novelist Nicholas Mosley, "when it's not known if the environment is quite ready for them" (2000: 71). Hopeful Monsters often source their component parts from multiple, seemingly incongruous technologies. Steampunk, for example, revels in the heterogeneity of coils, switches, cogs, and gears. Bringing a craft sensibility to industrial components, it rejects modularity in favor of joining operations that accentuate the incompatibility of parts (Tanenbaum et al. 2012: 1589). As described by steampunk artist Thomas Willeford, the basic skill involves the ability "to see [found objects] for something they are not, and then to 'upcycle' them into something entirely different—something never intended or imagined when the various components were made" (2011: 92). This outlook is all about "learn[ing] to see something else":

> I think it is virtually impossible to explain to someone how to look at objects creatively—that is, as something that they're not. If you were the type of child who turned every cardboard box into a rocket ship, tank, or fort, simply because it was a suitable enclosure, this process might be easier for you to understand.
>
> (Willeford 2011: 16)

This type of thinking enables us to see the barrel of a ray gun in the column of an old brass lamp, or eye goggles in a plumber's pipe fittings, or a cell phone case in a dusty ignition coil (Willeford 2011 *passim*). It sensitizes us to a world full of "things that want to be made into other things" (xvii). The job of the designer is to coax these other things into being.

The common thread running through all the examples I have offered thus far is an emphasis on *subjunctive knowledge*—knowledge about what might have been or could be or almost was. This subjunctive imagination underwrites both humanistic and scientific endeavors. Reflecting on its centrality to human thinking, the cognitive scientist Douglas Hofstadter entertains the idea of a world in which the subjunctive was lost to us: "Think how immeasurably poorer our mental lives would be if we didn't have [the] creative capacity for slipping out of the midst of reality into soft 'what if's' " (1979: 643). Whether it is conjecturally restoring a historic cathedral to its former glory, bringing an imaginary technology to life through 3-D fabrication, or building the next global communications system out of the odds and ends lying about one's studio, the goal in each instance is to inhabit the possibility space of the "what-if" that Hofstadter so eloquently sketches.

A central premise of this chapter is that the subjunctive act of imagining is advanced and facilitated by Byrne's notion of fault lines. A "fault line," as understood here, is a break—either conceptual or physical—that divides an event or object into two or more parts. To return to the example of the telegraph, Samuel Morse was able to mentally perceive a generic everyday clock as riddled with fault lines. This in turn allowed him to entertain how the pendulum—as distinct from the clock face, suspension spring, weight arm, or other mechanism—might be recycled to create the telegraph receiver. Without the ability to segment an everyday object into its constituent parts, each of which can be manipulated independently of the others, Morse could never have conceived of his invention, let alone built it. Fault lines yield the fragments that artists, inventors, designers, writers, and conservators use to make, unmake, and remake the world.

FAMILY OF SUBJUNCTIVE PRACTICES	
Name	**Definition**
Conjectural Criticism	Comparisons of variants between two or more related texts, languages, organisms, or artifacts are undertaken with the purpose of reconstructing their genealogy and archetype or projecting potential descendants.
Counterfactual Games & Literature	Fictional interventions in the historical record, resulting in games, novels, and other creative products that offer "what-if" alternatives to reality, where "reality" is understood to encompass empirical data, historical documentation, and fact-based events.
Divination, Magic, & Aleatory Procedures	Paranormal epistemology; supernatural inference, perception, or apprehension of the unknown.
Forensic Imagination	Causal inference or inductive reasoning that utilizes trace evidence, microscopic information, and incidental detail. There is often an aesthetic or stylistic dimension to the way the forensic imagination is wielded.
Forgery	Replicas, copies, fabrications, adaptations, and alterations produced with the intent to deceive, or else intentionally misrepresented as authentic originals.
Recreation	The physical or virtual reconstruction of an artifact based on surviving historical data, including originals, fragments, photographs, and textual documents. Recreations can show varying degrees of fidelity to the original object.
Restoration	"A means to re-establish [a cultural object] in a completed state, which may in fact never have actually existed at any given time." ~Eugène Emmanuel Viollet-le-Duc (1814–1879)
Scientific Prediction	The use of statistical models, simulations, and testable hypotheses to forecast future events.
Speculative Design	"Speculative design" consolidates the work of various practitioners with overlapping goals, values, and techniques, including prototyping objects that embody our ideas about the near future (design fiction); designing make-believe technologies (imaginary media); and fabricating weird computer architectures, composite machines, and hybrid media (speculative conglomerations, hopeful monsters, media archaeology).
Speculative Fiction	Speculative fiction embraces a wide variety of subgenres—including science fiction, fantasy, magic realism, weird fiction, supernatural fiction, and fables—whose make believe worlds are markedly estranged from or discontinuous with reality. As a genre, it is medium-agnostic, finding expression in film, theatre, books, and other cultural forms.
Speculative Wear	The simulation of material traces of use and wear in both physical and digital objects.

Figure 15.1 Table of subjunctive practices (by the author). An expanded version of this typology—including examples, subtypes, references, and additional notes—can be found at goo.gl/OEHmGh. The term "forensic imagination" comes from Matthew Kirschenbaum's *Mechanisms: New Media and the Forensic Imagination* (2008).

Figure 15.1 presents a family of subjunctive practices, classified into eleven major types, most of which have corresponding subtypes. The "speculative design" of my title carries both a general and narrow meaning: broadly speaking, the output or end products of all eleven categories in the typology are works of speculative design. Thus, for example, a conjecturally restored painting, a reconstructed text, and a scientific simulation of a flu pandemic are all works of speculative design that fall under the respective categories of Restoration, Conjectural Criticism, and Scientific Prediction. This general sense of the term is the one I have deployed in my chapter title. Narrowly speaking, "speculative design" is also a distinct category within the typology that consolidates the work of various practitioners with overlapping goals, values, and techniques. These overlapping areas include prototyping objects that embody our ideas about the near future (design fiction), designing make-believe technologies (imaginary media), and fabricating weird computer architectures, composite machines, and hybrid media (speculative conglomerations [Hertz 2009: 127], hopeful monsters, and media archaeology).

While each practice can be considered in isolation from the others, a case study of the Whereabouts Clock—one of the dozens of enchanted objects in the Harry Potter universe—serves to illustrate how a single speculative design concept may be realized (and analyzed) using multiple conjectural approaches. By examining the history of a well-known, make-believe technology and the various knock-offs, adaptations, models, versions, and functioning prototypes it has spawned, we can gain a greater appreciation for the many faces of conjecture and how they potentially interact with one another.

Case Study: Weasley Whereabouts Clock

Making its first appearance in *Harry Potter and the Goblet of Fire* (Book 4), the Whereabouts Clock occupies the corner space of the living room in the Weasley family's ramshackle home, affectionately known as the Burrow. Although physically resembling a large grandfather clock, it is actually a locative rather than temporal device, as we learn in Chapter 3:

> Harry liked this clock. It was completely useless if you wanted to know the time, but otherwise very informative. It had nine golden hands, and each of them was engraved with one of the Weasley family's names. There were no numerals around the face, but descriptions of where each family member might be. "Home," "school," and "work" were there, but there was also "traveling," "lost," "hospital," "prison," and, in the position where the number twelve would be on a normal clock, "mortal peril." Eight of the hands were currently pointing to the "home" position, but Mr. Weasley's, which was the longest, was still pointing to "work."
>
> (Rowling 2002: 151)

By the time the clock reappears two books later, in *Harry Potter and the Half-Blood Prince*, it has undergone substantial miniaturization, as evidenced by the fact that Molly Weasley transports it from room to room as she goes about her household chores (Rowling 2013: 85). (Fans have speculated that the contradiction is a continuity error rather than a deliberate effort on J. K. Rowling's part to revise her earlier conception; see Weasley Clock n.d.)

With the launch of the Harry Potter film franchise in 2001, the clock made the leap from page to screen, becoming one of the Burrow's many cross-sited media objects. Taking their cue from the earlier representation in Book 4, prop makers extensively modded a vintage grandfather clock, adding "pendulums, gears . . . and other fanciful accessories" (Harry Potter studio tour 2012), including an entirely new clock face with whimsical hands made out of scissors ("things that want to be made into other things;" see Figure 15.3): the blades point

Figure 15.2 Post-fire version of the Weasley Whereabouts Clock used on the film set of Harry Potter.

Source: Dave Catchpole, The Making of Harry Potter Flickr Collection (Warner Bros Studio Tour London) (May 29, 2012) goo.gl/21PcNq. Released under a CC BY 2.0 license (creativecommons.org/licenses/by/2.0/). Cropped image.

to the various locations listed around the perimeter (e.g., "Quidditch," "School," "Lost," "Garden," and "Home"), while the holes in the handle grips have been re-imagined as picture frames containing tiny portraits of each family member. The clock was later redesigned as part of the larger Burrow renovation after the Weasley family home is burned to the ground in the sixth film (Sibley 2010: 58–59). Although the same grandfather clock appears to have been recycled by the set decorators for the postfire interior shots (see Figure 15.2), it has been stripped of paint and given yet another new face (McCabe 2011: 80–81, 405). Thus at least two different versions of the clock were used for the films.

In the years intervening since the various cinematic releases, the Whereabouts Clock has transitioned from a fictional object on screen into a real-world object variously created by researchers, artists, and Harry Potter fans, incorporating components such as microcontrol-

Figure 15.3 Detail of the clock face, which uses scissors in lieu of hands to point to location.

Source: Marc E. Marc, "The Weasley Clock," Harry Potter Warner Bros Studio Tour Flickr Album (September 14, 2013, goo.gl/YEEmHx). Released under a CC BY-NC-SA 2.0 license (creative commons.org/licenses/by-nc-sa/2.0/).

lers, wifi modules, and cellphones (e.g., Harper 2010: 153–192; Brudy et al. 2012; Bell 2015). These prototypes exist along a spectrum, with some attempting to show as much fidelity to the original as possible, in terms of function and/or design, and others seeking merely to produce experimental mockups that successfully mimic the "magical" behavior of the Weasley device but treat the interface as an afterthought (e.g., by using foam core and other craft materials in lieu of using an actual clock as the technological backbone of the project [wooden_one n.d.]). Others, such as the MIT Media Lab's Location Doorbell, which includes a signature chime for each family member to indicate his or her general proximity to the home, are loosely inspired by the clock rather than strict imitations of it (Rose 2014: 91–95). Some of the most compelling prototypes are the hybrid physical-digital objects that preserve the idea of a situated domestic device that blends unobtrusively into the physical environment. These exemplars adhere strongly to the visual conceit of a clock that supports "ambient awareness" of the location of each family member.

From a sociotechnical perspective, the Whereabouts Clock created by the set design team is a classic example of what David Kirby calls a *diegetic prototype*: a cinematic prop representing a make-believe technology that "demonstrate[s] to large public audiences [its] need, benevolence, and viability," thereby prompting—and this is key—real-world development (2009: 41). The hallmark of a diegetic prototype is "technological sincerity." To be convincing, it must become fully naturalized within its fictional environment, making it simultaneously ordinary and extraordinary. Or as Kirby puts it, it must "achieve the sense of an extraordinary technology appearing as ordinary within the diegetic space" (50). Ticking reassuringly in the corner of the living room, the Whereabouts Clock establishes benevolence largely through setting. It is there that we encounter it, in the cozy confines of the

Burrow, rather than in an enchanted forest or a dragon's lair. We see Mrs. Weasley glance at the clock while doing laundry, fearful for the safety of her brood. The clock thus establishes its narrative exigence while at the same time securing its status as a benign source of comfort (rather than a sinister location-tracking device infringing on personal safety and privacy).

Taken together, the Whereabouts Clocks in books, films, and real life comprise an instructive dataset of subjunctive practices. Some of the most noteworthy of these include:

- **Divinatory Practices**. In the *Harry Potter* universe, the clock itself is a sentient, psychic, or enchanted object, capable of detecting location and foretelling danger. As such, it operates within the realm of the supernatural. Outside the fictional world, the proliferating number of homebrew Whereabouts Clocks coming out of basements and research labs are augmented with sensors and microprocessors to give the illusion of sorcery. The in-world versions are powered by magic; the out-of-world versions by technology sufficiently advanced to make them indistinguishable from magic, to paraphrase Arthur C. Clarke's famous dictum (Clarke's Three Laws n.d.). Indeed, inspired by the Harry Potter universe, David Rose of the MIT Media Lab refers to the whole class of things that "seamlessly couple the dual world of bits and atoms" as *enchanted objects* (Rose 2014; Tangible Media Group n.d.). Thus the paranormal magic in the story world gives way to illusionist magic in the real world.
- **Speculative Wear**. The modded clocks created by the set design team incorporate artificially distressed and worn elements, such as yellowed parchment, to match both the antique clock purchased at auction and the comfortably shabby interior of the Burrow. Such elements contribute to the perceived benevolence and authenticity of the objects. It is as if time has gently pooled in the hollows and crevices of bygone things.
- **Recreation**. The set design team speculatively transcoded the two-dimensional textual representations of the clock into three-dimensional realia for the films. The entire ecosystem of Whereabouts Clocks is chockfull of instances of the device being converted from one set of signs into another (e.g., from text to physical model to painting). At first glance, the whole enterprise can seem to veer toward translation *in extremis*: a wild careening from one semiotic system to another. A closer look, however, suggests that a tacit set of rules or conventions is in play that attempts to preserve basic homologies across different adaptations. "[S]peculation is not a license for interpretive abandon," notes Jentery Sayers (2014). There is a sweet spot that, out of necessity, tolerates substantial variation across media without entirely forfeiting some notion of fungibility, however tenuous or loosely constructed.
- **Speculative Design**. The diegetic prototypes created for the Harry Potter films are assemblages of parts harvested from old clocks, appliances, garden tools, and other artifacts, all housed in the chassis of an old grandfather clock. As such, they exemplify several of the subtypes of speculative design contained in the typology of subjunctive practices, including steampunk, hopeful monsters, and speculative conglomerations.
- **Conjectural Criticism**. A "genetic signal" can be traced in the dataset and visualized as a family tree showing the evolutionary relationships among the different manifestations of the Whereabouts Clock. These relationships often involve hybridization, with a particular clock inheriting traits from more than one source: one of the Harry Potter clocks on CafePress, for example (HP Clock 2008), includes location words ("home," "school") characteristic of the Whereabouts Clock, but also action words ("sleeping," "eating") reminiscent of the reminder clock in the Weasley family kitchen. Designed by Rebecca Hull, the CafePress clock would thus appear to be a conflation of two distinct objects, a genealogical pattern repeatedly encountered in other kinds of cultural artifacts,

too. Moreover, many of the clocks distort or mutate the traits they acquire: by adding or subtracting the number of hands or pendulums, for example, or substituting spoon-hands for scissor-hands.

The case study of the Whereabouts Clock illustrates the value of fault lines as a resource for both analysis and design. Because one of the key functions such fissures perform is the delineation of parts, any full-fledged methodology of fault lines will need to include a theory of parts and their relationship to one another. Whether it is the fragments of speculative design or the heritable and distorted traits of conjectural criticism, *parthood* figures prominently in each case. But why are some parts of the Whereabouts Clock—like the hands—active sites of experimentation, while others—like the circular shape of the dial—relatively stable? Under what circumstances might overlooked parts of the clock be made more susceptible to mutation? How do we determine the relative salience of parts? What types of creative transformations do parts undergo? And finally, how do we discover the fault lines along which objects are dissected to produce parts?

Parthood

To help answer these questions, I conducted a study in 2014 on how individuals identify the constituent parts of objects, including broken, obsolete, and semantically ambiguous objects. Thirty test subjects at the University of Maryland were asked to examine six three-dimensional artifacts and complete a written questionnaire about them. These artifacts ranged from the familiar (a book) to the unfamiliar or imaginary (a 3-D-printed steampunk variation on the mariner's astrolabe; Whystler 2012) to the broken or visually distinctive (a fork with a bent tine and a rock that appears to have a face, a phenomenon known as *pareidolia*) (see Figure 15.4).

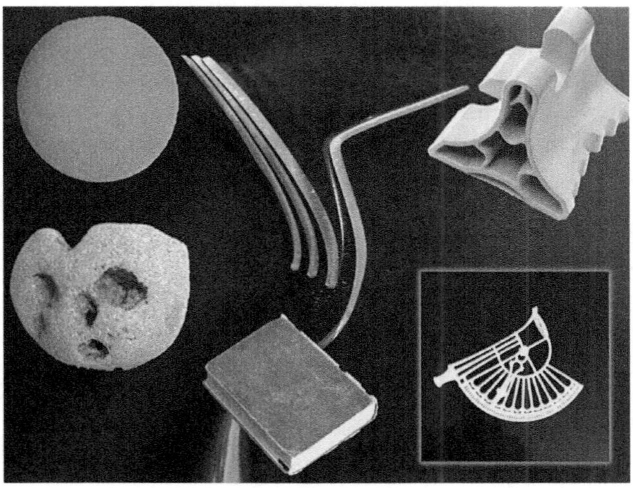

Figure 15.4 Six objects selected for the "parthood" research study (by the author). The book in this composite image is a stand-in for the one actually used.

Source: Itti at Deviant Art (itti.deviantart.com/). Book image at itti.deviantart.com/art/Stock-Old-Book-208887642. Thumbnails of the ball, geometric object, and rock are sourced from the product pages where they were purchased.

Although it is beyond the scope of this chapter to delve into the results, one finding worth highlighting is that research subjects tended to approach component analysis as a temporal as well as spatial exercise, endowing objects with inferred origin stories and biographies. Most often these took the form of speculative remarks concerning the formation, production, provenance, and/or manufacturing of the items in question. One participant theorized that the ball, for example, was "formed of a single homogenous foam (possibly cut/whittled by machine out of a more standard—possibly rectangular—shape of the material)." This line of reasoning was most pronounced with respect to the book, an object that prompted one participant to wonder if component analysis ultimately requires what we might call an *ontogenetic perspective*:

> I guess if I wanted to think more like a book scholar I'd further identify . . . the absent metal, inked letterforms that were arranged to print these words on the body pages. Interesting to think about how far you want to stretch 'included components' . . . *Is the printing press part of the book?*
>
> (Emphasis added)

Like Ireneo Funes, who (in Jorge Luis Borges's short story, "Funes the Memorious") discerns vineyards and grapes in a goblet of wine, test subjects interpreted each object as feeding them information about time through the geometry of space. Key to recovering this information is evidence of composition and wear: "I looked for any signs of wear or scratch marks," wrote a participant about an object she could not decipher, "to see [how] it had been used." Across the board, participants sought out visual traces of material change to help them individuate and enumerate the parts of an object.

The parthood study suggests the need for user experience design that, like gouges on an old wooden trunk, encodes information about the past. When visiting a web page or other online resource, we typically encounter little in the way of perceptual cues that tell us which links have been clicked most often or which images have been repeatedly viewed. Web design in general validates Brien Brothman's concern that electronic documents "may well be imperceptibly eroding our ability to experience historical pastness, for example to witness the patina of record agedness" (2010: 49). Even in cases where the user interface has been designed to communicate patterns of use or wear, the metaphors underlying those choices often feel bland and predictable. Kindle's "Popular Highlights" feature, for instance, adopts the generic convention of a dotted underline to indicate passages in books that have been highlighted by three or more readers.

Predictable displays notwithstanding, more compelling models of so-called *digital patina* do exist. Here "patina" is interpreted broadly to refer to artifacts and representations of all kinds that "carry [material] traces about time and life" (Giaccardi et al. 2014: 473). These traces are the result of chemical, environmental, and human interactions with the materials in question. Efforts to simulate such traces in the digital realm include the use of dynamic heatmaps to visualize usage statistics in Windows applications and the design of link icons that appear to rust over time the more they are clicked (Mao et al. 2000; Matejka et al. 2013). While the latter example is vulnerable to charges of skeuomorphism insofar as it transplants material properties from the real world to the virtual world, it nonetheless strives to honor the web as a time-varying environment, and to do it in a way that is immediately perceptible and comprehensible to most viewers. The design takes static webpage buttons that were visually timeless and transforms them into elements decidedly *of* time.

This act of modeling the appearance of change in software interfaces based on underlying usage data is a particularly fascinating subdomain of speculative wear. In the final section of this chapter, I propose classroom and workshop activities that draw on the typology of subjunctive practices, including the category of speculative wear.

Classroom and Workshop Activities

Speculative Wear. Using low-fidelity, paper prototyping, re-design the Kindle "Popular Highlights" feature by drawing on the principles and precepts of digital patina. Brainstorm potential real-world systems, domains, and processes that might serve as the conceptual backbone for the re-design. What would it mean, for example, to envision the most popular or frequently read words on the page as subject to extreme pressure rather than highlighting? What sort of sagging, fatigue, stress, or wobbling might result from the optical weight and compression of millions of eyes bearing down on the text? Consistent with the print metaphors underlying Kindle's hardware design, you might imagine the substrate on which the words are inscribed to be paper, but you could also mix metaphors and substitute another material in its stead. Glass shatters, ceramic breaks, and clay flattens under pressure, for instance. Or maybe chemical and environmental rather than mechanical wear serves as the basis for design: tarnishing, corroding, rusting, and oxidizing processes might all come into play.

Sensing Systems: Bibliowear. This activity involves outfitting physical books with sensors and subjecting them to processes of accelerated aging, such as dog-earing the pages, dousing them with liquid, and even lighting them on fire. What can individuals who did not witness the destruction firsthand glean about these objects as a result of their technological enhancement? If books have always been the record keepers of readers' interactions with them, how much more can we learn about a book once we have endowed it with tiny digital prosthetics that document ever so much more of its history? And what are the consequences for user privacy once we have done so?

One premise of this project is that books—like other physical objects—are already lo-fi sensors in their natural state, detecting and reacting to information about external stimuli and events. A moldy book, for example, registers the fact that there is excess moisture in the air through a multimodal output that takes the form of a musty odor and foxing stains. A book read by candlelight is likely to retain telltale traces of wax on its pages. Book historians are adept at interpreting these physical clues, often with the help of perceptual aids. Kathryn Rudy (2010), for example, has attempted to identify which pages in a small corpus of medieval manuscript books have been handled most frequently by using a densitometer, a machine that measures light reflected off a surface. The relative darkness of the edges, corners, and other white space of the page as quantified by the densitometer thus becomes a proxy for the amount of use and wear the book has undergone. Rudy adopts the densitometer as a tool to augment her *umwelt* (Eagleman 2011, 2015): the semiotic information in the environment that is available to her senses. By embedding sensors capable of detecting temperature, moisture, sound, and motion into a book, we can likewise magnify our own abilities to tell a story about its past. These sensors increase the temporal bandwidth available to us in our quest for book knowledge; they expand our umwelt by amplifying the book's capabilities as a sensing system. But that expansion comes at a cost: while it opens the doors of perception, it potentially closes the doors of conjecture. If we know the precise date, time, and place a book was opened, read aloud, or subjected to the mishaps of a careless reader who spilled coffee on it, does the world of facts begin to crowd out the world of speculation? Or does it, paradoxically, open up a new and unforeseen space for it? The purpose of this activity is to help answer these questions.

Ideally an external group of volunteers can be recruited to participate, with workshop participants serving as researchers responsible for setting up the experiment and analyzing the results. You will need two copies of the same book, one of which you will outfit with sensors designed to detect sound, motion, temperature, moisture, and open-close or bend events. You can then subject both books to identical processes of accelerated aging. A control group can analyze the sensor-free book and attempt to reconstruct its history based on material evidence, such as singed pages. A second group can analyze the companion book that has undergone the same treatment, but which has been digitally enhanced to detect various patterns of activity. How do the two groups of participants compare in terms of the level of accuracy of their reconstructions? Their modes of inference? Their propensity to embellish, surmise, conjecture, and invent? How might the precise information captured by the sensors be displayed to either heighten or limit the role of interpretation? What are the implications for privacy and surveillance?

Whereabouts Clock: Family Tree. Create a pedigree chart hypothesizing how all the various descendants of Rowling's Whereabouts Clock relate to one another. (You will want them to seek out and consider a range of models and representations for this activity, including the working prototypes created at both the MIT Media Lab and Microsoft Research, but also Instructables projects, set designs, Deviant Art paintings, Etsy crafts, etc.). You may end up with a diagram that more closely resembles a network than a tree, with converging as well as diverging edges. Try creating a visualization that depicts not only reconstructed relationships, but also descent with modification: which features of the clock are relatively stable across versions, and which ones are mutable? This exercise requires you to identify the fault lines in the Whereabouts Clock to determine traits or characteristics that are subject to transmission and distortion. As the final step in this exercise, mock up a new, speculative version of the clock that is a composite of several different traits or features inherited from its predecessors. Use your pedigree chart as a design tool to help guide your own conjectural adaptation. Consider what mutations of already existing traits you want to model and incorporate. For example, what might you use in lieu of scissors for the clock hands? Add your own customized version of the Whereabouts Clock to your diagrams, showing it as a new node that derives from and alters its predecessors. (Variation: you could also try creating an inferred ancestor to Rowling's "original" version of the clock.)

Although I have presented the foregoing list of activities as lesson plans, they should also be regarded as systematic methodological inquiries into the value of fault lines as aids to speculative design. I hope readers will test, modify, and extend these prompts to create resources that help us not only find fault lines, but also see what else they might augur for.

Acknowledgments

I would like to thank students in my 2013 Classification Theory course, who participated in an informal version of the parthood study as a class activity and made recommendations on what types of objects to present to test subjects, including the suggestion that I incorporate an object exhibiting the characteristics of pareidolia.

Further Reading

Ikemiya, M. and D. K. Rosner (2014) "Broken Probes: Toward the Design of Worn Media," *Personal and Ubiquitous Computing* 18(3), 671–83.

Kraus, K. (2009) "Conjectural Criticism: Computing Past and Future Texts," *Digital Humanities Quarterly* 3(4), retrieved from www.digitalhumanities.org/dhq/vol/3/4/000069/000069.html.

Sayers, J. (2015) "Prototyping the Past," *Visible Language* 49(3), retrieved from visiblelanguagejournal.com/issue/172/article/1232.

References

Arthur, B. W. (2009) *The Nature of Technology: What It Is and How It Evolves*, New York, NY: Free Press.

Bell, A. (2015) *The Weasley Clock Is A 'Harry Potter' DIY-er's Dream*, MTV News, retrieved from www.mtv.com/news/2273579/weasley-family-clock.

Borges, J. L. (1944) "Funes El Memorioso," ["Funes the Memorious"] in *Ficciones*, Buenos Aires, Argentina: Editorial Sur.

Brothman, B. (2010) "Perfect Present, Perfect Gift: Finding a Place for Archival Consciousness in Social Theory," *Archival Science* 10(2), 141–89.

Brudy, F., F. Steinberger, F. Praschak, and C. Böttcher (2012) *Magic Clock*, retrieved from magicclock.de.

Byrne, R. M. J. (2007) *The Rational Imagination: How People Create Alternatives to Reality*, Cambridge, MA: MIT Press.

Clarke's Three Laws (n.d.) *Wikipedia: The Free Encyclopedia*, retrieved from en.wikipedia.org/wiki/Clarke%27s_three_laws.

The Clock at the Burrow (n.d.) *Harry Potter Wiki*, retrieved from harrypotter.wikia.com/wiki/The_Clock_at_The_Burrow.

Eagleman, D. M. (2011) "The Umwelt," *2011: What Scientific Concept Would Improve Everybody's Cognitive Toolkit?, Edge.org*, retrieved from edge.org/response-detail/11498.

Eagleman, D. M. (2015) "Can We Create New Senses for Humans?" *Ted Talk*, retrieved from www.ted.com/talks/david_eagleman_can_we_create_new_senses_for_humans?language=en.

Giaccardi, E., E. Karana, H. Robbins, and P. D'Olivo (2014) "Growing Traces on Objects of Daily Use: A Product Design Perspective for HCI," in *Proceedings of the 2014 Conference on Designing Interactive Systems*, Vancouver, BC, pp. 473–82.

Harper, R. H. R. (2010) *Texture: Human Expression in the Age of Communications Overload*, Cambridge, MA: MIT Press.

Harry Potter studio tour (2012) *The Telegraph*, retrieved from www.telegraph.co.uk/travel/picturegalleries/9173352/Harry-Potter-studio-tour.html?image=8.

Hertz, G. (2009) "Methodologies of Reuse in the Media Arts: Exploring Black Boxes, Tactics and Archaeologies," Doctoral Dissertation, Visual Studies Program, University of California Irvine.

Hofstadter, D. R. (1979) *Gödel, Escher, Bach: An Eternal Golden Braid*, New York, NY: Basic Books Inc.

HP Clock Large Wall Clock (2008) *Café Press*, retrieved from cafepress.com/+hp_clock_large_wall_clock,1409806184.

Jackson, S. J. (2014) "Rethinking Repair," in T. Gillespie, P. Boczkowski, and K. Foot (eds.) *Media Technologies: Essays on Communication, Materiality, and Society*, Cambridge, MA: MIT Press, pp. 221–39.

Kirby, D. (2009) "The Future is Now: Hollywood Science Consultants, Diegetic Prototypes and the Role of Cinematic Narratives in Generating Real-World Technological Development," *Social Studies of Science* 40, 41–70.

Kirschenbaum, M. G. (2008) *Mechanisms: New Media and the Forensic Imagination*, Cambridge, MA: MIT Press.

Mao, X., Y. Hatanaka, A. Imamiya, Y. Kato, and K. Go (2000) "Visualizing Computational Wear with Physical Wear," in *Proceedings of 6th ERCIM Workshop on "User Interfaces for All,"* Florence, Italy, retrieved from ui4all.ics.forth.gr/UI4ALL-2000/files/Long_papers/Mao.pdf.

Matejka, J., T. Grossman, and G. Fitzmaurice (2013) "Patina: Dynamic Heatmaps for Visualizing Application Usage," in *Proceedings of the SIGCHI Conference on Human Factors in Computing Systems*, Paris, France, pp. 3227–36.

McCabe, B. (2011) *Harry Potter Page to Screen: The Complete Filmmaking Journey*, New York, NY: Harper Design.

Mosley, N. (2000) *Hopeful Monsters*, Champaign, IL: Dalkey Archive Press.

Rose, D. (2014) *Enchanted Objects: Design, Human Desire, and the Internet of Things*, New York, NY: Scribner.

Rowling, J. K. (2002) *Harry Potter and the Goblet of Fire*, New York: Scholastic Paperbacks.

Rowling, J. K. (2013) *Harry Potter and the Half-Blood Prince*, New York, NY: Scholastic Inc.

Rudy, K. (2010) "Dirty Books: Quantifying Patterns of Use in Medieval Manuscripts Using a Densitometer," *Journal of Historians of Netherlandish Art* 2(1–2), retrieved from www.jhna.org/index.php/past-issues/volume-2-issue-1–2/129-dirty-books.

Sayers, J. (2014) "The Relevance of Remaking," *Maker Lab in the Humanities at the University of Victoria*, retrieved from maker.uvic.ca/remaking.

Sibley, B. (2010) *Harry Potter Film Wizardry*, New York, NY: Harper Design.

Tanenbaum, J., K. Tanenbaum, and R. Wakkary (2012) "Steampunk as Design Fiction," in *Proceedings of the SIGCHI Conference on Human Factors in Computing Systems*, Austin, TX, pp. 1583–92.

Tangible Media Group (n.d.) "Vision," *MIT Media Lab*, retrieved from tangible.media.mit.edu/vision.

Weasley Clock (n.d.) *Harry Potter Wiki*, retrieved from harrypotter.wikia.com/wiki/Weasley_Clock.

Whystler (2012) *Simple Astrolabe*, Shapeways, retrieved from www.shapeways.com/product/FBS8F8973/simple-astrolabe.

Willeford, T. (2011) *Steampunk Gear, Gadgets, and Gizmos: A Maker's Guide to Creating Modern Artifacts*, New York, NY: McGraw-Hill Education TAB.

wooden_one (n.d.) "Weasley-o-Meter," *Instructables*, retrieved from www.instructables.com/id/Weasley-o-Meter/?ALLSTEPS.

16

GAME MECHANICS, EXPERIENCE DESIGN, AND AFFECTIVE PLAY

Patrick Jagoda and Peter McDonald

This chapter explores games as a major object of study in both media theory and practice. We begin by identifying two competing critical approaches to games: the proceduralist (which emphasizes rules, objectives, and systems) and the play-centric (which emphasizes modes of player response). By distinction, we advocate for a middle ground, a type of experience design that foregrounds the ways players can affect and be affected by a game: experientially, kinesthetically, and ideologically. The main site for this elaboration of affect is game mechanics. The chapter draws from close readings of existing digital and analog games, as well as techniques developed through the creative process in the Game Changer Chicago (GCC) Design Lab, to which we both belong. Ultimately, we offer a sketch of a practice-based research method for designing learning-oriented and serious games in media studies.

The Procedural and the Playful

Two primary approaches have dominated game studies since the early 2000s, one organized around procedure and the other around play. In an important study of storytelling in computational environments, Janet Murray observes that a key attribute of computers is that they "execute a series of rules" that enable dynamic interactions between the machine and human actors (1997: 71–72). Storytellers and game designers, Murray contends, can use algorithms and rules to convey interpretations. One of the most vocal theorists of proceduralism, Ian Bogost, defines it as a way of generating and making sense of processes. Processes, in turn, "define the way things work: the methods, techniques, and logics that drive the operation of systems, from mechanical systems like engines to organizational systems like high schools to conceptual systems like religious faith" (Bogost 2007: 3). Videogames are a medium that uses, and even depends on, what Bogost calls "procedural rhetoric," which "explains processes *with other processes*" in order to persuade users of a particular viewpoint (9). This procedural approach privileges a game's rules and its representation of select systems.

For example, the single-player, turn-based videogame *PeaceMaker* (Impact Games, 2007), puts the player in the perspective of either the Israeli prime minister or the Palestinian president. *PeaceMaker* produces a system in which the player's success hinges on a multifaceted political ecology. Actions reveal implicit ethical arguments: delivering peaceful speeches or establishing welfare programs are more consistently rewarded with higher scores than militaristic responses. Even more explicitly, the game posits a two-state solution as its goal. *PeaceMaker* does not produce an expository argument about responses to international gridlock (as a blog post might) nor does it craft a psychological perspective on this system (as a stream-of-consciousness novel might). Instead, the game invites players to experiment with algorithmic processes to better understand a set of political processes, as modeled by the designers.

Proceduralism has contributed to the analysis of videogames as cultural objects and influenced design practices, especially of so-called "serious games" that explicitly address social and political topics in the interest of participatory advocacy. At the same time, scholars more interested in processes of play than game structures have emphasized the limitations of procedural rhetoric as an analytic and design technique. At the forefront of the antiprocedural approach is Miguel Sicart, who contends that proceduralism is essentially a version of formalism. A consequence of proceduralism, Sicart argues, is that "it grants great power and influence to the designer," who produces the system that the player must, in turn, reverse engineer sufficiently to unpack the meaning that is inherent in it (2011). For Sicart, the limitation of proceduralism is that it marginalizes the ways in which people play by stipulating that meaning largely precedes the act of play. In other words, a game's procedural rhetoric belongs to its system of rules and objectives, rather than to the ways in which players test and transform that system. In contrast, play-centric accounts demonstrate that actions and meanings cannot prefigure play. As Alexander Galloway argues, though machine actions are key, digital games only "exist when enacted" (2006: 2). This focus on play has found proponents not only in the humanities, but also among sociology and anthropology scholars who use qualitative techniques, such as interviews, to study a plurality of player interpretations (Voorhees 2013).

In videogames, different players may indeed have distinct experiences of action, narrative, or roleplaying. For example, Kurt Squire argues that open-ended simulation or "sandbox" games, such as *Civilization III* and *Grand Theft Auto: San Andreas*, operate as "possibility spaces" in which players can "try on, inhabit, and ultimately develop new identities with trajectories for participation that extend out of the game world and into new spaces" (2008: 171–2). In other cases, a game's artificial intelligence may promote emergent gameplay by adapting dynamically to a player's skill and present situation. The "AI Director" of *Left 4 Dead* works collaboratively with players to produce dramatic encounters and spawns "Infected" enemies based on player performance, creating novel play scenarios. Even in games that are not created explicitly to promote emergent play styles, participants frequently use a system in ways that were not intended or predicted by the designers. For instance, players may find creative ways to exploit glitches, such as "rocket jumping" in *Quake* or *Halo*, that allow them to achieve greater elevation by (mis)using a weapon for mobility. In still other cases, games themselves produce variable experiences from session to session through procedurally generated characters (e.g., creatures in *Spore*) and levels (e.g., the fantasy world of *Dwarf Fortress*).

This theoretical rift is roughly parallel to the earlier split in literary criticism between, on the one hand, Russian Formalism and American New Criticism and, on the other hand, reader-response theory and deformative criticism that privileged creative interpretation. To be fair, however, procedural and play-centric theories are not mutually exclusive. Most proceduralists do, to some extent, account for the role of play in game activities. For example, Bogost notes:

> In a procedural representation like a videogame, the possibility space refers to the myriad configurations the player might construct to see the ways the processes inscribed in the system work. This is really what we do when we *play* videogames: we explore the possibility space its rules afford by manipulating the game's controls.
> (Bogost 2007: 42)

In this formulation, seemingly inexpressive processes can still enable complex forms of expression. Even so, Sicart (2014) is right that meaning is, for Bogost, *founded* in procedures whereas, for him, procedures are secondary to the possibilities of play.

Experience Design: Rules, Mechanics, and Affect

Sicart goes as far as to argue that "games don't matter" when compared to the more generalized processes of play unfolding in toys, playgrounds, technologies, and social groups (2014: 2). Though we share Sicart's investment in a broader landscape of play, as game designers we are also interested in what both procedural and play-centric theories have to teach us about game creation practices. Given the increasingly practice-based orientation of digital humanities and new media studies, especially as they are taken up in this volume, we would like to use these frameworks to think about the design of serious games. One bridge between procedures and play through design comes from Katie S. Tekinbaş and Eric Zimmerman (2003). As they show, game designers may start by creating a rule-based system and defining some of its affordances, but the success of a game ultimately depends on experience design that privileges the prospective player. As Tekinbaş puts it, a designer becomes "a socio-technical engineer, thinking about how people will interact with the game and how the game will shape both competitive and collaborative social interaction" (2007: 305). Instead of over-determining form, this orientation yields an evocative design created for ambiguous and open-ended experiences.

The concept of *experience design* suggests an internal tension insofar as it combines the control of design with the uncontrollable diversity of player experiences. Thus, design may influence experience, but only in an indirect way. Even so, rather than limiting playfulness, Tekinbaş and Zimmerman argue that rules "create multiple levels of play experience, layering strategic thinking and gradual skill acquisition on top of the physical and perceptual components of the core mechanic" (2003: 320). Game mechanics are the set of techniques for interacting with a game world that are arbitrarily mapped through an interface to player gestures and are both constrained and enabled by a game's platform, whether it is a PlayStation 4 console or an analog game board. These actions, expressed as verbs, might include "jumping" in a platformer or "targeting" in a first-person shooter. For Tekinbaş and Zimmerman, and for us, a mechanic is a key point of mediation between the player and the game that opens up the ambiguity of play. A mechanic provides a point of departure from which a variety of procedural rhetorics can proliferate. On the one hand, a mechanic is a kind of rule, an action that the game can allow or disallow; on the other, players must take up that act as their own for the game to proceed.

Mechanics arguably provide the clearest example of how constraint imposed through design can enable creativity and playfulness instead of limiting players. For example, *Super Mario World* opens up pleasurable kinesthetic sensations and bodily identifications by allowing its players to fly. However, the sense of freedom in flying only emerges against the backdrop of Mario's ordinary activities of running and jumping. Reciprocally, because flight requires a power-up and takes a significant running start, and because its duration depends on a player's skill, Mario's repertoire of jumps accumulates meanings. It might be required to traverse a level, or it might enable the enjoyment of acrobatic movements. The point we want to emphasize, contra Sicart and others, is that rules are not essentially prohibitive (as Michel Foucault already argues of rules in a broader socio-historical context). Instead, they multiply possible meanings of play by creating new contexts of action.

If the meanings of a game are negotiable, and emerge from the interplay between rules and experience, between procedure and play, then mechanics may serve to orient both game analysis and design. While game mechanics may not yield the kind of discursive argumentation of procedural rhetoric, they constitute an ideal unit of analysis for affective experiences. Though it has many connotations, the term "affect" refers essentially to a "nonconscious experience of intensity" that differs from either feelings that are personal and narrativizable or emotions that are visible and communicative (Shouse 2005). As verbs, mechanics help us think about potentials, transformations, desires, intensities, experimental engagements, and connections among players. Importantly, while the process of narrating game experiences often entails describing affects as feelings, mechanics do not merely produce unified results in which jumping elicits one kind of bodily sense whereas targeting evokes another. Jumping provokes myriad feelings, including elation, freedom, curiosity, or a sense of precarity, while targeting produces malice, satisfaction, the sense of appropriative connection to a target, or a feeling of bodily extension through a world. More than defining feelings, mechanics enable players to affect the world of the game, and in turn be affected by it opening up aleatory experiences. We are using affect here as somewhat synonymous with feeling, but also want to draw on the legacy of Spinoza for whom the possible activity and passivity of a body determines its feelings. Gilles Deleuze observes of Spinoza that "we do not even know what a body can do," and this is equally true of the gamer's or the avatar's body (1983: 36). Fundamentally, mechanics can generate proliferating affects and meanings that exceed a one-to-one signification.

As we have been discussing them, mechanics mediate between rule-bound situations and player affects. As Tekinbaş and Zimmerman put it:

> To play a game is to *experience* the game: to see, touch, hear, smell, and taste the game; to move the body during play, to feel emotions about the unfolding outcome, to communicate with other players, to alter normal patterns of thinking.
>
> (Tekinbaş & Zimmerman 2003: 314)

Though "fun" is perhaps the most frequently invoked aspect of game experience, games generate a wide range of affects. Some of these may serve persuasive purposes, but others are more ambiguous or aesthetic in nature. Procedural analyses often limit the discussion of affective experiences, restrict them to oversimplified typologies, or characterize them as ideological elements. Similarly, discussions of a game's "interactivity" often privilege agency, figured as choice that a player does or does not have. However, beyond the binary split implicit in fun or agential interactivity, players may also experience affects such as anxiety, paranoia, anticipation, and curiosity in the process of encountering hardware, interfaces, game worlds, and player cultures.

In the remaining sections, we begin to sketch out the ways that *game mechanics* might open up more nuanced forms of analysis and design strategies. To do so, we focus neither on a priori *rules, objectives, and systems* (as proceduralists might) nor *modes of play* (as play-centric theorists might). Instead, charting a middle path, we explore the meaning of mechanics in play, first in game analysis and second in game design.

The Case of "Collecting" in *Katamari Damacy*: Game Analysis

The three interpretive methods that we are comparing—practices that focus on rules (proceduralism), play (play-centrism), and mechanics (experience design)—can usefully be juxtaposed by showing how they operate in the analysis of a single game. The mechanic of "collecting" in the innovative videogame, *Katamari Damacy* (Namco 2004; see Figure 16.1), serves as a clarifying case. In this game, players use two analog sticks to control "The Prince," an alien avatar who rolls around a sticky ball that collects everything in its path. This "katamari" ball grows from an initial size of 5 cm (at which point it collects tacks and ants) to an eventual size of over 300 meters (at which point the katamari can collect cars and buildings). In each level, the katamari must reach a certain size within a time limit. In addition to the assorted mass, players collect special objects that form larger collections such as cousins of the Prince and uniquely named versions of ordinary objects. New media scholars McKenzie Wark (2007) and Steven Jones (2008) offer readings of the game that privilege procedure and play, respectively. In contrast, we offer a third reading that describes a range of affects that the game activates through collecting.

Wark's *Gamer Theory* (2007) articulates a strong version of the proceduralist thesis. For Wark, it is because a world framed by late capitalism has adopted the structure of games that this medium can help us understand the present. Particular games make aspects of capitalism easier or more difficult to see through their procedural rhetoric, or what Wark (following Alexander Galloway's neologistic combination of "allegory" and "algorithm") calls their "allegorithm." Even so, the simplest game already contains the defining qualities of capitalism. In Wark's reading, *Katamari Damacy* becomes an updated myth of Sisyphus, and an allegory for the capture of the analog by the digital. For instance, the game transforms the aleatory line of the katamari into thresholds of size and time that convert it into a binary value of

Figure 16.1 Katamari Damacy.

Source: Namco 2004.

success or failure, removing the older ambiguity of Sisphysus' task. The omnivorous tendency of the katamari to absorb even those things that appear solid, such as the walls that demarcate a level's boundaries, demonstrates the reduction of qualitative difference to numerical quantities. The katamari also operates across radically different scales, substituting a human perspective for the microscopic and the cosmic. This summary is not an exhaustive list of what Wark suggests we can see through *Katamari Damacy*, but the point is that in each case the specific procedural argument can be translated into a statement, a fact that we now know about late capitalism.

In an essay that is in part a response to Wark, Steven Jones also argues that *Katamari Damacy* tells us something essential about games. Instead of treating collecting as a symptom of capitalism, Jones characterizes this mechanic as a feature of most games in which a player picks up a weapon or a key and generates meaning through that process. In this way, collecting in a videogame is an act that is comparable to collecting on eBay or during archival research. Jones takes *Katamari Damacy* to embody a punk aesthetic in its anarchic collecting mechanic that evacuates pre-established meaning and leaves a void that demands to be filled by player actions. Because it has no content of its own, collecting in this game is "inherently an activity that points outside of itself, outside of the game itself . . . because it only truly has meaning in the context of a fanbase or other kind of community" (Jones 2008: 54). The playful path of the ball, the qualities of the objects that are rolled together, the kinesthetic pleasure of the joysticks—these are the elements from which players generate meaning.

For both Wark and Jones, *Katamari Damacy* is a privileged example because the game reflects on its material and formal conditions. In our own approach, one which privileges the way that mechanics generate affects, *Katamari Damacy* is also important because it operates as a *tour de force* of collecting, exploring the various senses of the verb that are visible in more isolated forms in games such as *Pokémon* or *Go Fish*. Unlike the real world collections that Jones explores, the objects in *Katamari Damacy* are ideal in a variety of senses that alter the feeling of collecting them. For instance, they do not degrade with time, they cannot be destroyed, and they are not removed from circulation when placed in another player's collection. Collecting is thus removed in this game from an involvement in an economy, making rare acquisitions correspond directly to virtuosic performance in the game. Desire is indexed to difficulty rather than rarity. Furthermore, because objects cannot be destroyed, the potential for growth matters more than the threat of loss, a feeling made visceral whenever players recklessly knock pieces off their katamari ball.

In *Katamari Damacy*, collecting is recontextualized by rules that idealize the world. The mechanic responds with affordances of fearlessness, virtuosic performance, and yearning. In this structure of feeling, we might recognize both the Sisyphean labor of Wark's account and the anarchic punk aesthetic of Jones. But there are other valences as well that can illuminate thematic choices within the game, such as the narrative resonance with courtly love or an alternate relation to the father that bypasses the anxiety of castration or loss. The meaning of collecting is not unitary, nor tied to the rhetorical purposes of a particular game, but neither is it vague or characteristic of all play. A mechanic constellates an array of feelings, a palette that a designer or player can reliably draw upon.

The Case of "Blocking" in *Smoke Stacks*: Game Design

Affects are key to game experience in general, but they play an especially central role in learning-oriented games. Though affect *as such* does not figure prominently in literature about educational games, related discussions about emotion inform practice-based research in digital humanities and new media studies. James Paul Gee argues that work in education has traditionally emphasized rationality and intellectual content over emotion. However, as he adds, emotion helps learners to integrate previous knowledge and organize long-term memory, focus attention and retrieve information, and evaluate possible actions (2008: 35). Games that seek to promote learning, then, must be attentive to the range of possible play experiences, including gradations of various named emotions and nonconscious intensities.

Since the 1980s, many educational games—including what Mizuko Ito calls "academic" games such as *Math Blaster* and "entertainment" games such as *Where in the World is Carmen Sandiego?* (2008: 89–116)—have offered interactive content delivery without a robust emotional experience. Similarly, serious games with social and political objectives sometimes put a greater emphasis on conveying values through game systems in a direct fashion, as Mary Flanagan and Helen Nissenbaum have described the work of the "conscientious designer" (2014: xii–xiii). While content and values are important in such games, emotions and especially obscure or illegible affects can sometimes become marginal.

The analysis of the collecting mechanic that we suggested in the previous section demonstrates the types of affects, feelings, and moods that games make available. An understanding of how core game mechanics generate such affects, and the meanings that follow from them, may be even more useful for designing games that are meant to tackle specific social issues. At the GCC Design Lab, we create both digital and board games that explore issues of social and emotional health related to topics such as unplanned pregnancy and bullying. In designing such games, we often experiment with the affective affordances of mechanics through techniques of rapid prototyping and iterative design. Because our goal is often to influence the knowledge, attitudes, or behaviors of players, an understanding of affect becomes especially important.

To briefly demonstrate how mechanics and affects are important to serious game design, we take up a case study of a board game that the authors created as part of the GCC Design Lab. This game, *Smoke Stacks*, tackles the use of tobacco products among high school youth. The game is one in a suite designed for the same *Hexacago* board, which depicts the city of Chicago broken down into hexagons. The learning objectives for *Smoke Stacks* include helping players understand marketing approaches deployed by the tobacco industry and their impact on smoking behaviors. By helping youth understand the history of tobacco legislation as well as the health effects of smoking, the game attempts to curb interest in tobacco products. In the game, four to six players take the role of tobacco companies who try to accumulate as many customers as possible. In each round, players formulate corporate strategies by bidding on cards that provide them with products (e.g., "cigarettes" or "chewing tobacco"), marketing approaches (e.g., making customers feel "independent" or "sexy"), and advertising media (e.g., "television" or "billboards"). These cards allow each player to target particular customers in certain zones on the board, while every customer increases a player's profit margin.

In creating *Smoke Stacks*, we did not privilege a uniform play experience but rather attended to the broad range of affects that mechanics might generate. The three primary mechanics in this game are collecting (picking up customers from particular urban zones), wagering (on corporate strategy cards), and blocking (keeping other players from collecting the cards they want). In our iterative design process, we were attentive, for example, to the affordances of blocking. In our research on blocking in games, we analyzed sports games, popular board games such as *Settlers of Catan*, and tower defense videogames. Across these genres, we characterized blocking as a mechanic that arises through the player's investment in a project that is under threat. In many of these games, players often go to wasteful lengths to negate a threat and regain a sense of safety, and they give up only when the situation feels utterly futile. To block, the player must understand the motives of an opponent and the details of the game system. Such understanding infuses minute actions with a sense of urgency, while sometimes generating feelings of pettiness, aggression, and desire for revenge.

In the *Smoke Stacks* design, mechanics foreground specific feelings that attend political, economic, and social systems often imagined at scales beyond individual human experience. In other words, mechanics make the abstraction of systems tangible. In the context of tobacco use, blocking gives players an opportunity to work through the affective dimensions of how certain policies may lead to a competitive race to the bottom. Players can block other players from either collecting desired cards or accumulating the maximum number of customers. The experience of blocking another player animates ways in which inequality is built into policies, even when the rationality of large-scale systems such as "the market" is meant to overshadow human motivations and feelings.

The tobacco system that *Smoke Stacks* models allows a player to experiment with elements of corporate strategy, profit motives, addictive consequences, and histories of government legislation. The game makes this affective field, which includes both systemic and historical elements, accessible and palpable through mechanics. Given the complexity of this dynamic system, the process of experience design required frequent playtesting with ongoing player feedback and designer self-reflection over several months. An iterative design method maximized the affordances of the core mechanics. Thus, rather than seeking uniform reception, the design process explored the possible experiences that each version of the game made possible.

Conclusion

This chapter offers only a sketch of a form of game analysis and experience design that privileges mechanics as a way to understand the affective dimensions of broader systems. Although we focused on a few case studies, experience design is important to a wide array of methods across games and genres. Such methods might include not only close reading but also the study of online archives of player responses to games, focus groups and interviews with players, and practice-based research that includes creating and play testing games to better understand their affordances. The field of game studies, and perhaps especially the growing area of serious game analysis and design, will benefit from a fuller understanding of the relationship between mechanics and affects.

Further Reading

Bogost, I. (2006) *Unit Operations: An Approach to Videogame Criticism*, Cambridge, MA: MIT Press.
Flanagan, M. (2009) *Critical Play: Radical Game Design*. Cambridge, MA: MIT Press
Isbister, K. (2016) *How Games Move Us: Emotion by Design*, Cambridge, MA: MIT Press.
Juul, J. (2005) *Half-Real: Video Games Between Real Rules and Fictional Worlds*, Cambridge, MA: MIT Press.
Miller, K. (2012) *Playing Along: Digital Games, YouTube, and Virtual Performance*, Oxford: Oxford University Press.
Wardrip-Fruin, N. (2009) *Expressive Processing: Digital Fictions, Computer Games, and Software Studies*, Cambridge, MA: MIT Press.

References

Bogost, I. (2007) *Persuasive Games: The Expressive Power of Videogames*, Cambridge, MA MIT Press.
Deleuze, G. (1983) *Nietzsche and Philosophy*, New York, NY: Columbia University Press.
Flanagan, M. and H. Nissenbaum (2014) *Values at Play in Digital Games*, Cambridge, MA: MIT Press.

Galloway, A. (2006) *Gaming: Essays on Algorithmic Culture*, Minneapolis, MN: Minnesota University Press.
Gee, J. P. (2008) "Learning and Games," in K. S. Tekinbaş (ed.) The Ecology of Games: Connecting Youth, Games, and Learning, Cambridge, MA: MIT Press.
Ito, M. (2008) "Education vs. Entertainment: A Cultural History of Children's Software," in K. S. Tekinbaş (ed.) *The Ecology of Games: Connecting Youth, Games, and Learning*, Cambridge, MA: MIT Press.
Jones, S. E. (2008) *The Meaning of Videogames*, New York, NY: Routledge.
Murray, J. (1997) *Hamlet on the Holodeck: The Future of Narrative in Cyberspace*, New York, NY: The Free Press.
Shouse, E. (2005) "Feeling, Emotion, Affect," *M/C Journal* 8.6.
Sicart, M. (2011) "Against Procedurality," *Game Studies* 11.3.
Sicart, M. (2014) *Play Matters*, Cambridge, MA: MIT Press.
Squire, K. (2008) "Open-Ended Video Games: A Model for Developing Learning for the Interactive Age," in K. S. Tekinbaş (ed.) *The Ecology of Games: Connecting Youth, Games, and Learning*, Cambridge, MA: MIT Press.
Tekinbaş, K. S. (2007) "Gaming Literacies: A Game Design Study in Action," *Journal of Educational Multimedia and Hypermedia* 16.3.
Tekinbaş, K. S. and E. Zimmerman (2003) *Rules of Play: Game Design Fundamentals* Cambridge, MA: MIT Press.
Voorhees, G. (2013) "Criticism and Control: Gameplay in the Space of Possibility," in M. Wysocki (ed.) *Ctrl-Alt-Play: Essays on Control in Video Gaming*, Jefferson, NC: McFarland.
Wark, M. (2007) *Gamer Theory*, Cambridge, MA: Harvard University Press.

17

CRITICAL PLAY AND RESPONSIBLE DESIGN

Mary Flanagan

In the landscape of media studies and digital humanities, games have become a popular subject of study for both their creative forms and the social practices they instigate. Because they create cognitive and epistemological environments that position the player-participant with a given collection of game elements, representations, and rules (Flanagan 2009: 10), and because they offer choices and a sense of agency that is empowering—and potentially psychologically manipulative—digital games are influential, exciting media forms worthy of critical attention. Described in this chapter, Critical Play is both a discursive method and a practical, instrumental approach toward the development of games that enrich communication, encourage in-depth reflection, and generate new conversations among game players and game designers.

Key to this discussion is an understanding of the role of media, design, and criticality in social change and overall societal improvement, as well as the notion of social responsibility. Alongside their positive elements, games have faced harsh critique; key challenges in the conversation about games arise about who makes games to begin with and for whom they are created. In pop culture, videogames are still largely described as a domain for men, even though adult women constitute half of all digital game players (ESA 2014). Hispanic players currently outnumber non-Hispanic players in the U.S. as well (Mintel 2014). Yet, while player demographics appear more inclusive than ever across the player base, equity in terms of gender in the creation of games is still slow to come. While the percentage of women working in the U.S. game industry has doubled, it remains at around 22 percent, and people of color are marginalized in the current American game industry climate (IGDA 2014). A lack of diversity in game creation spheres helps create a vicious cycle of reinforcing biased, stereotypical depictions of characters, cultures, and world rules in games and larger gaming cultures. Limited, simplistic conceptions of games proliferate from mainstream media. Unfortunately, they miss the complexity of games' messages and, moreover, their potential for personal and social benefit. Games are a part of (and some would say they are at the heart of) a massive set of societal debates about media consumption, social ills, and equity.

But things are changing. Unlike film and linear media, games sway more toward being a *systemic* art form, and such an understanding sets the stage for us to engage with the complexity games offer. For example, while studies link violent and subversive behavior to videogames

(Hull et al. 2014), they simultaneously are seen to have potential for massive, prosocial impact on culture (McGonigal 2011). These contradictory claims reveal how very little we know about the complex ways that games engage our beliefs, feelings of agency, and desires for rewards. As researchers learn more every day, games increase their influence as an artform.

There is great interest in how games promote prosocial values, due to the impact other media forms have had toward a more progressive society. For example, much has been discussed about television's role in improving gay equity in the United States; in terms of increased representation over the last 20 years, the depiction of gay couples and "out" television celebrities is associated with more positive societal attitudes (Ayoub & Garretson 2015; Craig et al. 2015). Anecdotally, the former Vice President of the U.S., Joe Biden, noted in 2012, "I think 'Will and Grace' probably did more to educate the American public than almost anything anybody's ever done so far" (Little 2012). This is not to say that the representations avoid stereotypes, or that they are always positive and multidimensional. However, media ecology provides at least some opportunity for escapism, strength, proactive action, and finding community (Craig et al. 2015). For those interested in the social impact of media, the challenge remains to push for ways toward responsible media culture that intentionally shapes culture *for good.*

Similarly, the norms depicted in digital games significantly influence culture. To give a sense of the scope of this influence, consider the fact that an estimated 33,000 people per day were downloading and playing the *Kim Kardashian: Hollywood* game a year after its release, and that it made nearly 100K USD per day (Think Gaming 2015). In 2014, there were more people playing *Candy Crush Saga* at any given moment than there were people living in Australia, Germany, or France (93 million daily active users), and the year following, it still attracted over three million active users per day (King 2014). With record sales, record numbers of players, and some games' ambitious development costs (e.g., the development of *Grand Theft Auto V* reportedly cost 266 million USD; McLaughlin 2013), games are a significant financial player in the media landscape, bringing in revenues to rival or surpass film and music industries on a global scale. Games are a key cultural force and twenty-first-century art form—their high sales figures, dominance in pop culture discourse, and sheer popularity point to their impact.

In light of the financial and cultural sway of games, designing and playing *critically* is an indispensable approach in the domain of applied media studies research and for engaging the social and cultural dimensions of digital games. Key here is the notion that media makers and game designers can *do something* about how they might alternate depictions, rewards, and so on from mere thought experiment to design studio. In an age of theory meeting practice, and a push toward experiential learning and "making," design itself operates as a mode of inquiry that can intentionally encompass a philosophical and social focus. Designing critically embodies such an intentional practice; it means being mindful of the potentially positive and negative effects of games as well as the positive and negative influences of one's own design and play processes or experiences.

Critical Play takes a historical look at how games and play can be analytical and experiential systems reflective of, but also entangled among, social and cultural norms. It incorporates past radical moves by arts and activist communities to understand games as components or counterpoints in critical theory. This is why Critical Play is an important and fundamentally unique approach: the experiential aspect of play—for all games must be playtested by actual players—moves the critique beyond a speculative conversation and creates an enactment of the imagined world. In exploring the historical foundations of games as their own form of creative expression distinct from story, image, or performance, I have argued that "critical play means to create or occupy play environments and activities that represent one or more questions about aspects of human life" (2009: 6). In past writing, I outlined approaches such as "unplaying," where players enact forbidden or secret scenes or play out unexpected scenarios (2009: 33). A Critical Play approach is one in which games are not mere thought experiments but rather actual embodied experiences that not only have the potential for social impact; they are also *likely* to change us—our perspectives, our knowledge, our biases.

Contextualizing Critical Play

Across theory and practice, what might people consider as they develop games, study them, play them, and discuss them in relationship to notions of social engagement and responsible design? Further, why is this important work for the humanities? Significant trends emerged in the late twentieth and early twenty-first centuries to advance the social responsibility of designers. In the 1990s, my longtime collaborator, Helen Nissenbaum, began publishing with Batya Friedman about values in the design of software systems (Friedman & Nissenbaum 1996). The idea here is that any software system reflects the people and culture from which it is made. As Marshall McLuhan and Barrington Nevitt famously reminded us in 1972, "New technological environments are commonly cast in the molds of the preceding technology out of the sheer unawareness of their designers" (47). Critical production therefore must rely on new methods to ensure critical making is happening. For example, it is quite easy to replicate the biases inherent in popular media forms. With other collaborators, Nissenbaum and I picked up the torch to bring values and critical introspection to digital games in 2005, while I was

Figure 17.1 Chart of possible sources of values in games, a list intended to inspire possibilities rather than be constricting in nature.

Source: From *Values at Play in Digital Games* (Flanagan and Nissenbaum 2014), used with permission.

developing the book *Critical Play* (2009). In *Values at Play in Digital Games* (2014; see Figure 17.1), we urge critics to consider how games *produce* values as often as they *reflect* values, and we demonstrate that values emerge across many game elements. Intentional interventions in games can focus on these elements, and the impact of using them can be measured empirically, if one so desires.

In effect, our approach takes a values-centric methodology to instrumentalizing the tenets of Critical Play. Verifying the impact of this approach will likely lead designers and humanists alike to social science methods for empirical validation of the lofty ideals to which they aspire. Dunne and Raby meanwhile brought the idea of responsible design to the fore from the practical discipline of architecture (2001). Sengers et al. (2005), Agre (1997), Bardzell and Bardzell (2013), Bardzell et al. (2012), and others continue the discourse on criticality and reflection in human-computer interaction to move beyond the functionality of software to its social roles and responsibilities.

The idea behind these critical-technical perspectives is that, by getting beyond the perceived "apolitical" and obvious needs of design (such as usability, reliability, and so on), we might create challenging, reflective systems instead. Designers could, for example, "force a decision onto the user, revealing how limited choices are usually hard-wired into products for us" (Dunne & Raby 2001: 45–6). Design-centric critical projects might take the form of hypothetical, high-tech innovations or even interactive fictional science laboratories that ultimately raise questions about data collection, for example. Or they might craft imaginary objects that provoke critique. These types of projects, by artists such as Natalie Jeremijenko or Critical Art Ensemble, are called "DesignArt" (Leither et al. 2013; see also Associated Press 2008). While these hybrid design-art objects are valuable, they only go so far, and as provocations often stay within the confines of the gallery. For instance, most do not make their way to the mass-produced world for which industrial design, product design, and engineering fields pave the way, and thus they may stay bound within communities where the conversations provoked already exist. They do, however, elevate the conversation about the role of design and perhaps spark systemic change at the level of industrial design. This holds less true thus far for experiments in games, especially digital games, which reach more people but have been less likely to deeply trouble the industry against which they operate, even if they raise theoretical and critical implications for the medium.

Ultimately, notions of scale relate to notions of impact, and criticality and empiricism are both essential and underutilized aspects of the creation process, with empirical verification as an ideal to which it is important to aspire. By their nature, games are ripe for criticality, but it remains up to one's strategies as a designer and player to actualize their critical potential.

Recent Examples of Critical Play

While there are many useful examples of critical games, I would like to focus here on three that showcase diverse aspects of Critical Play. Such play can utilize the mechanics in a game to convey its message or critique. The questions can be abstract, such as rethinking cooperation, winning, or losing; or they can be more concrete, involved with particular content issues (Flanagan 2009: 10). They could also focus on reshaping societal biases through game mechanics. I chose the three games for this chapter to span a range of media, which may confound traditional media studies as a discipline. The first, a card game, uses a dynamic social mechanic to counteract biases. The second game is a large collaborative event and online public art space using community participation and voice to form a relational aesthetic and prompt change through expression, representation, voice, and authorship. The final game is

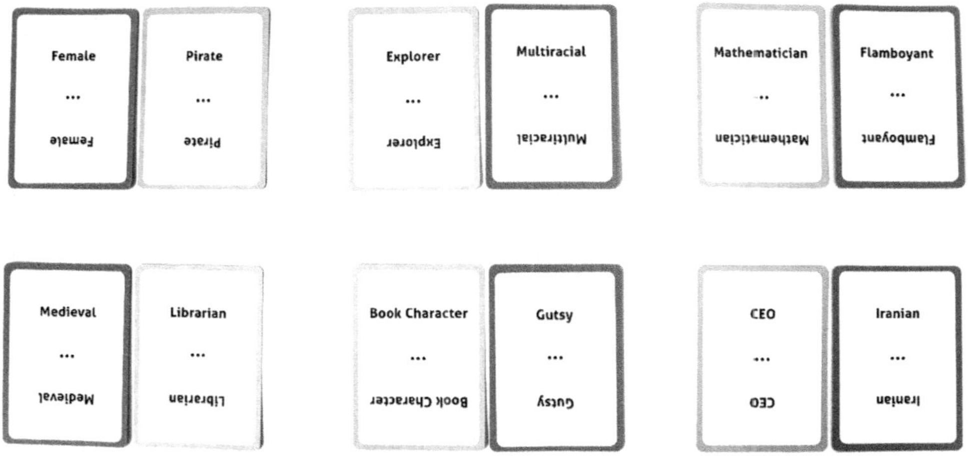

Figure 17.2 Unexpected combinations appear while playing *Buffalo: The Name Dropping Game*. These combinations disrupt the thinking that perpetuates stereotypes.

Source: Courtesy of Resonym.com.

a computer game: a single-player experience that investigates border crossing, immigration, and the various systems that govern behavior and the body. Each has its own strategy in approaching issues critically.

Buffalo: The Name Dropping Game (2012; see Figure 17.2) is a fun, party card game where players work quickly against other players to be the first to name someone who matches the cards on the table. Sometimes the game offers wildly diverse combinations of adjective and noun, such as "tattooed grandmother" or "kind bully." The first player to name an accurate match keeps the cards as points and moves on to the next fast-paced round.

Developed at the game research laboratory I lead, Tiltfactor, *Buffalo* serves as a great icebreaker or party game for groups small and large. It uses a randomizing mechanic to create unusual combinations of criteria, which, from a psychological perspective, expand a player's social categories and undermine stereotypes on conscious and unconscious levels (Kaufman & Flanagan 2015). The game positions players to overcome their own biases and prejudices as they encounter and "break up" easy mental pathways created by stereotypes. This approach corresponds with empirical work done at Harvard via Implicit Association Tests, which measure unconscious biases we might hold about race, proper jobs, language, and so on. As it turns out, countering unconscious biases is quite challenging; teaching people about the injustice of discrimination or asking them to be empathetic toward others is often ineffective. Mahzarin Banaji notes that what works, at least temporarily, is providing "counterstereotypical" images or messages (Banaji & Greenwald 2013: 151). Games are systems of rules leading to experiences that help shape the way we think and rhetorically and psychologically persuade us; games like *Buffalo: The Name Dropping Game* are in effect micro-solutions that address the psychological factors of social inequity and the microaggressions that permeate culture.

Whose criticality is the focus here? The player's? The designer's? The observer's? The scholar's? The answer is all of the above, but the designer plays a key role in framing a game and setting the stage for both conscious reflection (e.g., engaging in reflection and discussion during play) and a less conscious mindset common during design or play experiences.

Criticality in play can be fostered to bring a game's content into focus or to highlight or uncover an aspect of the content. Thus a critical attention to both playing and making provides an essential viewpoint or an analytical framework for responsible design. Through many avenues, games can represent anything from concrete incidents to abstract ideas (such as equity and cooperation), and they can do so in a wide variety of forms.

Those using Critical Play as an approach might create a platform of rules by which to examine a specific issue—rules that would somehow reflect core elements of the issue itself. As an example, *Play Your Place* (see Figure 17.3) is a series of ongoing game artworks that use drawing and play to catalyze and translate local, imaginative visions of place into games that not only exemplify community values but also contribute to real world urban planning. Crucially, every element in the game—setting, characters, and challenges—is entirely created by community members. People create their own game level by drawing a place in the town. Then they think about how their "place" could be changed for the better. They devise their own rules, drawing obstacles and rewards and building and sharing game level after level for an epic play session. The game makers also incorporate fantasy elements into their vision of everyday life. The games take the familiar format of *Little Big Planet* or *Donkey Kong*; they can be played online, on mobile phones, in schools and homes, as well as at public venues. Players take on challenges, such as obstacles, leaps, drops, prizes, and enemies, as they would in a typical 2-D platform game.

Figure 17.3 *Play Your Place* game engine and event series 2012–14, by Ruth Catlow and Mary Flanagan (LOCALLY). Here, players "Play Southend" (in Essex UK).

Source: Courtesy of the artists.

I created the platform with U.K. artist Ruth Catlow, as LOCALPLAY, to bridge the gap between urban planners and the public. The urban planners we met with at the start of the project noted that the most interesting challenge of public consultation and deliberation about a place's future is encouraging people to imagine beyond their own wants and needs toward a common good. *Play Your Place* helps people develop collective visions of place that can then be entered and played by people all over the world. Players create over time, in game instances specific to their location, and the world grows through the addition of endless drawings. Community members have created entirely fictional calamities, but often these calamities correspond with existing social and environmental challenges, such as climate change, regeneration, transit issues, and more. For example, one original game featured monsters emerging from the waters of the Thames Estuary, reflecting the dangers of rising sea levels on coastal towns. The maker used a Critical Play approach to match the social issue to the rules and various game elements they create, including available actions, points of view, player choices, and rewards. Note that, without a somewhat structured practice, making alone will not necessarily bring about criticality, at least not immediately. People have played a lot of games and have a sense of common game tropes. Criticality can be fostered by thinking through the systemic issues the maker faces with the structure of a game, and thinking about what values the rewards and choices represent for the player.

Some indie game developers have developed and distributed highly stylized fictional worlds for critical expression. *Papers, Please* (2013; see Figure 17.4) begins as a rather simple-looking, 8-bit style game. As an officer at an immigration booth, players admit people across the border of the nation of Arstotzka, a fictional former communist state that is intentionally reminiscent of former Soviet bloc nations such as Azerbaijan and Kyrgyzstan. This "former Soviet" feel is set up not only in the game FAQ but also through the game soundtrack, the national logo and art style, and the grimness of the bureaucracy in which players must work. In the game, players spend their time as immigration inspectors to control entry into Arstotzka and its recently recaptured half of the border town, Grestin. Players must sort among travelers, smugglers, spies, terrorists, and those looking for work, either admitting or denying entry to these individuals, who are waiting in a lengthy queue outside the border control booth. Sometimes documentation just does not add up, such as when a photo in a passport does not match a character representation. Players work over a month (31 in-game days) to follow the Ministry of Admission's Rules and Regulations guide in the admission of people across the border. Tension mounts as the player detects discrepancies and materials given at the border are expired or invalid. Accidentally allowing certain immigrants into the country comes at price. Players will likely make mistakes and receive citations from the Ministry. Their income may be impacted by any mistakes, and their family will suffer economically and spiritually—as the rent goes up, food prices and other costs remain high. The in-game newspaper keeps players up to date on particularly controversial characters and suspicious activities. As the game progresses, players are given notes about human traffickers and others who impact the play progression. Players may also receive large gifts from rebel parties. If players game the system without empathy and play to only benefit themselves and their family, then they might be reported by the neighbors for having too much wealth. Alternatively, their savings may be confiscated, or they may be forced to downgrade the quality of their apartments. A player's son may become sick and need medication, or a player may run out of funds entirely. Players may end the game under arrest for colluding with the rebel organization. There are several possible outcomes.

By forcing the player to conform to the rules of screening processes, and by allowing some power yet limited agency within a larger system of oppression, the game sets the stage for

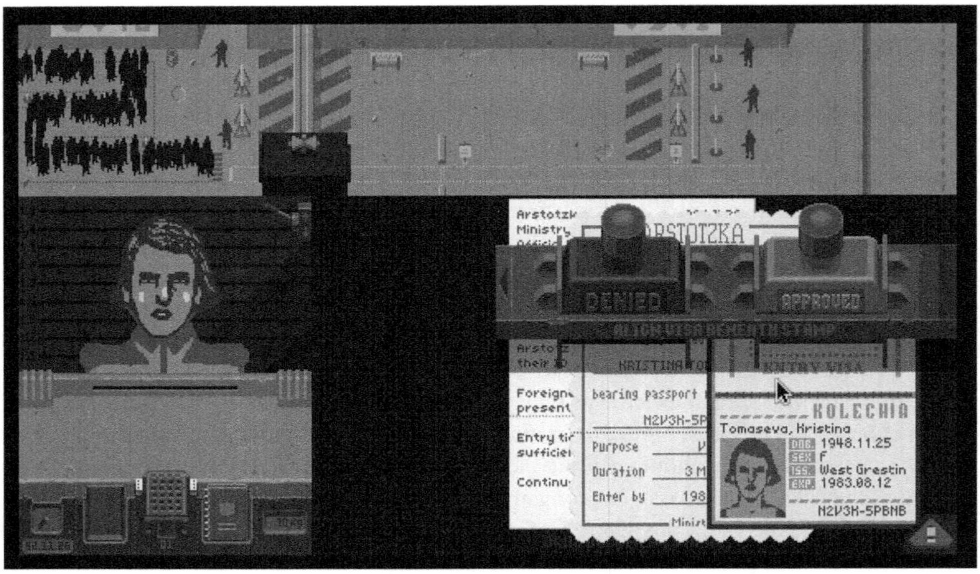

Figure 17.4 Lucas Pope's game *Papers, Please: A Dystopian Document Thriller* (2013) positions players as immigration officers who decide which immigrants can or cannot enter the fictional country of Arstotzka.

the player to be cast as an actor in moral and ethical dilemmas. For example, female characters come through, clearly as part of human trafficking campaigns, and ask for help. As the player in a position of power, do you try to help? Your supervisor tells you to detain more people as part of increased security. If you do not, will you jeopardize your family with your decisions?

Papers, Please offers an excellent example of roleplay as a character with painfully limited agency; such limitations may encourage the player to adopt a critical stance to the unfairness in which they participate. The effect is to serve as a critical witness and, perhaps on a larger level, encourage empathy toward workers as well as people in the throes of refuge-seeking and migration.

In each of these three games, different strategies for criticality emerge. In *Buffalo*, the game relies less on conscious reflection and more on unconscious psychological associations—a design mechanism that is deliberately less overt than other media intent on societal change. In *Play Your Place*, the act of creation within a grounded location and context helps engage a dialogue about community through authorship, creativity, and spectacle. While the making itself may not be critical, the reflection and practice about the rules and rewards of a real life issue do lead to deeper thought on social ills. In *Papers, Please*, a stark environment combined with a system of rules and narrative-driven tasks foster a rich sense of limited agency and inequity. The player is likely to be frustrated at their lack of agency, and their limited point of view may lead them to see the whole phenomenon of migration and border crossing in a new light. These three examples represent distinct, yet equally useful, manifestations of criticality.

Critical Play is characterized by a careful examination of social, cultural, political, or even personal themes that function as alternates to popular play spaces. The challenge, then, is to find ways to make compelling, complex play environments using the intricacies of critical thinking to offer novel possibilities in games, and for a wide range of players. As new forms of play emerge, each element of a game may foster a different sense of critical thinking, reflection, and dialogue on the part of the player. To get to this point, designers must be highly conscientious of the materials they put into play and mitigate as much as they can against the possibilities of negative associations of players with their games. (For example, some studies find associations between certain games and binge drinking, smoking, unprotected sex, and dangerous driving. For one study, see Hull et al. 2014.) Thus, the goal in theorizing a critical game design paradigm is as much about the creative person's interest in critiquing the status quo as it is about using play as a phase-changing cultural artifact.

A Practical Turn for Media Studies and Digital Humanities

Increasingly, media practice and theory are intertwined in a theory-practice dialogue that moves to praxis, and media studies and digital humanities are legitimately focusing on practice-oriented forms of critical production. If, as Latour argues, "technology is society made durable" (1991), then we must carefully examine what we craft and invent. This is a positive direction, for informed making leads to criticality outside of traditional academic texts. But the details count in the creation of new media artifacts. As noted earlier in this chapter, the impact of games and their capacity for criticality are not merely about representation. Games are a peculiar form of art that involve many other elements at play. These elements exceed those of representation and story, and games can set the stage for criticality across any media and within any story.

The fact that games are their own art form—and not mere delivery mechanisms or media—is an essential concept to grasp when understanding the role they play in criticality and social impact. Although digital games are the most popular emerging media today, games themselves can be constituted from myriad media and performance-based forms, from immersive 3-D worlds to mobile street games to 8-bit vintage arcade boxes. Games embody hybrid media forms as well, easily synthesizing elements of digital games, board games, and sports, for example. The medium itself is important but not essential to the "gameness" of a game. This makes a game a unique object for media study and one not often understood deeply by those who have researched other media.

Critical Play started in the arts, and art has helped indicate a way forward. As demonstrated in *Values at Play* (2014), we have a repeatable, scalable process involving an essential human activity—play—to create new futures. These futures, however, are real. Unlike discursive approaches to design, Critical Play actualizes and takes responsibility for the outcomes from particular games. For example, while those writing about speculative design might see a game as an avenue for discussion and possibility—a thought experiment—Critical Play assumes that games are themselves universes of actions. As experiences, they are dynamic, and their dynamics impact our thinking, minds, and lived experience. At their best, games are inspired models for social change.

Conclusion

As we move forward in playing and designing critically, the possibilities offered through other disciplines, traditions, and methods can play a key role in the practical and useful application of these ideas. At Tiltfactor, my team and I invented a new technique called "Embedded Design" to infuse some of the key ideas from social psychology into the game design process (Kaufman et al. 2015). For example, it is strategic to address psychological challenges inherent in social inequity, such as implicit biases that can limit certain groups from excelling. The psychology literature shows us that repeated exposure to stereotypes or existing prejudicial attitudes in both broader culture and media can significantly curtail even the most well-intentioned social impact design projects. A truly hybrid approach between art and science lies in the future of playing critically, as does real impact through changed psychologies and the systems such changed minds produce. The techniques of social science provide both concepts and measurement tools for validation that, if used well, can benefit this hybrid approach. "Psychology cannot tell people how they ought to live their lives. It can, however, provide them with the means for effecting personal and social change" (Bandura 1977: 213). In psychological terms, there are consequences in every game that we are only beginning to understand. The next wave of Critical Play would indicate that a deeper knowledge of social science must infuse the art of play to ameliorate, retrain, or reinvent how we approach playful engagement.

Indeed, the key challenge in any critical design space is the question of impact. The arts already serve as provocative sites for criticality, and have done so for centuries. This is valuable, and criticality needs to evolve with highly interactive art forms that are revisited on a daily basis as sites for community and lived realities. Those engaged with praxis must also confront the task to ground criticism in practical objects and systems that can be deeply experienced and are transformative in nature—phenomena that move idealistic and introspective conversations to collective, imagined realities. Games are art forms that can provide such a transitional space.

We know, too, that sheer amounts of capital sent to rectify social injustices are not the solution to societal crises: "If money could have changed the world, money would have changed the world," claims prosocial entrepreneur Sharad Vivek Sagar (2014). Media and designed objects, processes, and strategies have a much greater potential to improve society than capital alone. Yet, while there is a growing community creating "games for change," we are only beginning to understand their impact. Sherry Turkle has noted that, "[t]echnology challenges us to assert our human values, which means that first of all, we have to figure out what they are" (2010). The values of the designers and artists making games need to emerge for the next phase of Critical Play. However, many questions remain that we shall have to pursue. For instance, does Critical Play have to stay at the margins of mainstream media, or will it successfully enter a center arena? Is scale—for example, a high number of players or monumental commercial success—a logical and necessary next step for Critical Play as a practice? Will the increasing number of independently created games help create a diverse world of possibility in games and also help their positive potential flourish?

From this chapter, I hope readers get the sense that all games change us: it is just a question of understanding how and why, and taking responsibility so that change can be beneficial. Games are a rehearsal space of imagined actions and their consequences. They are themselves conversations. But they are also sites for actual decisions, actions, and feedback systems that reinforce or change biases, empathy, and more. They provide us with models for problem solving and, as I have pointed out, can limit or expand the ways we frame conflict, collaboration, resources, and competition (Flanagan 2014). Those interested in humanistic thought and the speculative nature of media do well to play critically. Games are the artwork of agency, of action, and of ritual. They are formal and relational, but mirror—and indeed may cause—progress and change. They are critical operations where transformation is triggered, new relationships are formed, and the systems of everyday life meet the randomness of the universe.

Further Reading

Boal, A. (1993) *Theatre of the Oppressed*, New York, NY: Theatre Communications Group.
Flanagan, M. (2009) *Critical Play: Radical Game Design*. Cambridge, MA: MIT Press.
Friedman, B. and H. Nissenbaum (1996) "Bias in Computer Systems," *ACM Transactions on Information Systems* 14(3), 330–47.
Latour, B. (1991) "Technology Is Society Made Durable," in J. Law (ed.) *A Sociology of Monsters: Essays on Power, Technology and Domination*, London: Routledge, pp. 103–32.
Weber, R. N. (1997) "Manufacturing Gender in Commercial and Military Cockpit Design," *Science, Technology, & Human Values* 22(2), 235–53.

References

Agre, P. E. (1997) *Computation and Human Experience*, New York, NY: Cambridge University Press.
Associated Press (2008) "Charge Dropped against Artist in Terror Case," *The New York Times*, 22 April, retrieved from www.nytimes.com/2008/04/22/nyregion/22bioart.html?_r=0.
Ayoub, P. M. and J. Garretson (2015) "Getting the Message Out: Media Context and Global Changes in Attitudes toward Homosexuality," in *Proceedings of the Western Political Science Association Annual Meeting*, Las Vegas, NV, 3 April.
Banaji, M. and A. Greenwald (2013) *Blindspot: Hidden Biases of Good People*, New York, NY: Delacourt.
Bandura, A. (1977) *Social Learning Theory*, Englewood Cliffs, NJ: Prentice-Hall.
Bardzell, J. and S. Bardzell (2013) "What Is 'Critical' about Critical Design?" in *Proceedings of CHI 2013*, New York, NY: ACM.
Bardzell, S., J. Bardzell, J. Forlizzi, J. Zimmerman, and J. Antanitis (2012) "Critical Design and Critical Theory: The Challenge of Designing for Provocation," in *DIS '12 Proceedings of the Designing Interactive Systems Conference*, New York, NY, pp. 288–97.
Catlow, R. and M. Flanagan (LOCALPLAY) (2013–15) *Play Your Place*, retrieved from www.playyourplace.co.uk.
Craig, S. L., L. McInroy, L. T. McCready, and R. Alaggia (2015) "Media: A Catalyst for Resilience in Lesbian, Gay, Bisexual, Transgender, and Queer Youth," *Journal of LGBT Youth* 12(3), 254–75.
Dunne, A. (2008) *Hertzian Tales: Electronic Products, Aesthetic Experience, and Critical Design*, Cambridge, MA: MIT Press.
Dunne, A. and F. Raby (2001) *Design Noir: The Secret Life of Electronic Objects*, Basel, CH: Birkhauser Verlag.
ESA (2014) *Essential Facts about the Computer and Video Game Industry*, retrieved from www.theesa.com/wp-content/uploads/2014/10/ESA_EF_2014.pdf.
Flanagan, M. (2009) *Critical Play: Radical Game Design*, Cambridge, MA: MIT Press.
Flanagan, M. (2014) "Creative Solutions to Crisis: Through Play," *Huffington Post*, 16 October, retrieved from www.huffingtonpost.com/mary-flanagan/crisis-solutions-found-in_b_5992492.html.
Flanagan, M. and H. Nissenbaum (2014) *Values at Play in Digital Games*, Cambridge, MA: MIT Press.
Friedman, B. and H. Nissenbaum (1996) "Bias in Computer Systems," *ACM Transactions on Information Systems* 14(3), 330–47.
Hull, J. G., T. J. Brunelle, A. T. Prescott, and J. D. Sargent (2014) "A Longitudinal Study of Risk-glorifying Video Games and Behavioral Deviance," *Journal of Personality and Social Psychology* 107(2), 300–25.
International Game Developers Association (IGDA) (2014) "Developer Satisfaction Survey 2014: Summary Report," retrieved from c.ymcdn.com/sites/www.igda.org/resource/collection/9215B88F-2AA3–4471-B44D-B5D58FF25DC7/IGDA_DSS_2014-Summary_Report.pdf.
Kaufman, G. and M. Flanagan (2015) "A Psychologically 'Embedded' Approach to Designing Games for Prosocial Causes," *Cyberpsychology: Journal of Psychosocial Research on Cyberspace*, Special Issue on Videogames, 9(3), retrieved from cyberpsychology.eu/view.php?cisloclanku=2015091601.
Kaufman, G., M. Flanagan, and M. Seidman (2015) "Creating Stealth Game Interventions for Attitude and Behavior Change: An 'Embedded Design' Model," in *Proceedings of the Digital Games Research Association (DiGRA) Conference*, Luneburg, Germany.
King Digital Entertainment (2014) F-1 form. U.S. Securities and Exchange Commission, 18 February, retrieved from www.sec.gov/Archives/edgar/data/1580732/000119312514056089/d564433df1.htm.
Latour, B. (1991) "Technology Is Society Made Durable," in J. Law (ed.) *A Sociology of Monsters: Essays on Power, Technology and Domination*, London: Routledge 38, pp. 103–32.
Leither, M., G. Innella, and F. Yauner (2013) "Different Perceptions of the Design Process in the Context of DesignArt," *Design Studies* 34(4), 494–513.

Little, L. (2012) "Joe Biden Says 'Will and Grace' Helped Change Public Opinion on Gay Rights," *Wall Street Journal*, 7 May, retrieved from blogs.wsj.com/speakeasy/2012/05/07/joe-biden-says-will-and-grace-helped-change-public-opinion-on-gay-rights/.

McGonigal, J. (2011) *Reality Is Broken: Why Games Make Us Better and How They Can Change the World*, New York: Penguin.

McLaughlin, M. (2013) "New GTA V Release Tipped to Rake in £1bn in Sales," *The Scotsman*, 8 September, retrieved from www.scotsman.com/lifestyle/technology/new-gta-v-release-tipped-to-rake-in-1bn-in-sales-1–3081943.

McLuhan, M. and B. Nevitt (1972) *Take Today: The Executive as Dropout*, New York: Harcourt Brace Jovanovich.

Mintel (2014) *Mintel Gamers and Gaming US 2014*, retrieved from mintel.com.

Nissenbaum, H. (1998) "Values in the Design of Computer Systems," *Computers in Society* 28(1), 38–39.

Pope, L. (2013) *Papers, Please*, retrieved from papersplea.se.

Sagar, S. V. (2014) Sagar quoted on Vine.com and in a tweet by @TheIncitement, 15 November, retrieved from twitter.com/theincitement/status/533808681562152960.

Sengers, P., K. Boehner, S. David, and J. Kaye (2005) "Reflective Design," in *Proceedings of the 4th Decennial Conference on Critical Computing: Between Sense and Sensibility*, New York: ACM, pp. 49–58.

Think Gaming (2015) "Kim Kardashian: Hollywood," *Think Gaming*, retrieved from thinkgaming.com/app-sales-data/8141/kim-kardashian-hollywood/.

Turkle, S. (2010) "Interview: Sherry Turkle," *Frontline digital_nation*, 2 February, retrieved from www.pbs.org/wgbh/pages/frontline/digitalnation/interviews/turkle.html.

18

A CALL TO ACTION

Embodied Thinking and Human-Computer Interaction Design

Jessica Rajko

Before beginning, I want to explain that this chapter is not a guide to embodied thinking, but rather a critical call to action. It highlights the deep history of embodied practice within the fields of dance and somatics and outlines the value of embodied thinking within human-computer interaction (HCI) design and, more specifically, wearable technology (WT) design. What this chapter does not do is provide a guide or framework for embodied practice. As a practitioner and scholar grounded in the fields of dance and somatics, I argue that a guide to embodiment cannot be written in a book. To fully understand embodied thinking, one must act, move, and do. Terms such as embodiment and embodied thinking are often discussed and analyzed in writing; but if the purpose is to learn *how* to engage in embodied thinking, then the answers will not come from a text. The answers come from movement-based exploration, active trial-and-error, and improvisation practices crafted to cultivate physical attunement to one's own body. To this end, my "call to action" is for the reader to move beyond a text-based understanding of embodiment to active engagement in embodied methodologies. Only then, I argue, can one understand how to apply embodied thinking to a design process.

The use of the term "embodiment" in HCI has dramatically increased since the turn of the new century. Following branches of embodied theory that use third-person, empirical methods of observation, design practices typically place bodies in the role of the active subject, and the researcher in the role of the passive observer (Schiphorst 2008: 67). Somatic techniques and various forms of contemporary dance offer a different perspective on embodiment, placing the observer and the subject in one body. As defined by Thecla Schiphorst, "Somatics techniques are intended to be used 'by the self on the self' in order to refine knowledge and precision through the use of the human body in action" (2008: 52). Somatics techniques such as Laban Movement Analysis, Alexander Technique, Feldenkrais Method, Body-Mind Centering, and Bartenieff Fundamentals provide methods for engaging in self-inquiry through movement and action. This first-person approach to embodied thinking cultivates knowledge from the *every-day* body. By focusing on self-study, it allows practitioners to build upon their own capacity to move, rather than expecting people to meet a particular level of expertise to engage in the practice.

Contemporary dance applies these techniques in the training of highly technical or *virtuosic* bodies; however, somatics is often used to help dancers unlearn physically harmful, habituated movement patterns and relearn movement that is both healthy and virtuosic. Dance has also made its own contributions to embodied thinking by creating practices to engage in collective rather than individual exploration. Improvisational forms such as contact improvisation (postmodern dance), cyphering (urban dance), and various social dance forms place embodied thinking within a social context. In this, they provide methods for expanding self-knowledge into a social framework, giving space for practitioners to understand how their own actions affect the actions of others. These improvisational forms primarily exist within their respective fields of dance; however, improvisational techniques have been cultivated for and are often practiced by individuals without prior dance training.

The Ephemeral, Allusive, and In-Between Nature of Embodied Thinking

> It is often difficult to put into words, and even harder to justify to politicians, the ways in which dance works its magic—the basis of its transformative powers. We tend as a culture to value only what is tangible and measurable whereas dance is all about the ephemeral, the allusive, and the in-between.
>
> (Clarke 2007: 35)

The idea of "embodied thinking" is one that is well understood in the fields of contemporary dance and somatics, but one often difficult to capture in words on a page. Scholars and practitioners have explored many methods of sharing and reflecting upon embodied practices in writing; however, these writings become more of a reflective practice than a holistic account of an embodied experience (Kozel 2007; Bacon 2010; de Lima 2013). Familiar, yet constantly changing, embodied thinking is a method of processing our world through our moving bodies. Simple enough to define, a written description of "embodied thinking" lacks the ability to articulate how embodied thinking is understood in and through a body in motion. For example, reading step-by-step instructions on how to juggle does not mean one will immediately master the skill. The written instructions provide an initial framework for knowing. Action-based exploration teaches one how to juggle. A novice must feel the weight of the balls as they are held and learn to coordinate the visual cues of a ball falling with the physical sensation of the body aligning for a catch. The muscular exertion of the body must be calibrated to toss the ball "just so." All of these skills must be coordinated into a finely tuned set of actions that overlap and build upon each other like waves. Each of the senses must work in harmony and dynamically adapt to the shifting landscape of the balls in motion.

Now, given that I bring perspective to this term from the field of dance, it is easy to assume that, by "moving body," I refer to a highly active or highly trained, *virtuosic* body (as in the example of a juggler). Here, then, is where I wish to trouble perceptions of embodiment by referring back to my earlier descriptions of somatics as being for the *every-day* body and contemporary dance's use of somatics as a means to *unlearn* harmful movement patterns. Beyond unlearning, dance also explores embodied thinking as a means to cultivate dancers who are highly attuned to a multisensory awareness of their surroundings. In "Trans-meaning: Dance as an Embodied Technology of Perception," Cecília de Lima explores the ways in which dance "works its magic" not through physical spectacle but by processing and understanding our world through all of the senses:

> In the case of dance, it becomes clear that its particular "technological expertise" is not so much to do with virtuosity or the capacity of the body to move, but is more about having an improved awareness of movement related to the proprioceptive sense.
>
> (de Lima 2013: 20)

She goes on to define the *proprioceptive sense* through the work of J. J. Gibson (1966, 1979), stressing that: (1) perceptive systems are active mechanisms for receiving different sorts of stimulus information from the environment, (2) these diverse perceptive systems function in interrelation, and (3) perception is based on the skill to move.

The ability to dynamically perceive the world is one that is afforded simply by the fact that bodies move. The idea of movement is often associated with highly visible, voluntary movements, such as reaching for an object, sitting, standing, or walking. However, as we begin to turn our awareness to the body, it becomes clear that the body is always moving. Our heart beats; our chest rises and falls with each breath; our eardrums vibrate; our eyes move in their sockets to shift perspective. These micro-movements are highlighted in dance artist Steve Paxton's signature piece, "small dance." In this work, the solo dancer stands in one place, experiencing the micro-shifts of the body as it adjusts in relationship to gravity, breath, and other bodily processes (BodyCartography Project 2011). This piece attunes the dancer to the ways in which our body experiences the world through motion, reminding us that, even as we perceive ourselves as being still, we are moving. It also highlights the ease with which we adapt to ongoing stimuli and repetitive actions, removing them from the foreground of our conscious. For example, take the fairly common act of walking. Walking is a complicated process we learn as children through rigorous trial-and-error. Embodied thinking is crucial to this developmental process. Now, as adults, the act of walking is an action upon which we rarely consciously reflect. We walk frequently, but are highly desensitized to the act of walking itself. In dance, we often use walking to engage in embodied thinking practices and prompt simple questions such as:

- How do my feet feel upon the floor as I walk?
- What body part(s) are initiating or driving my walk?
- What am I seeing, hearing, feeling around me right now?
- How am I walking in relationship to the other people in the room?
- How am I breathing?
- How am I dynamically organizing my body, and am I comfortable?
- How does my perception of the world change if I change the way I walk by moving faster? Slower? Backwards? Sideways?

The purpose is not to answer these questions, but to open our awareness to our constant and ever-changing state of transformation. These questions foreground our habituated ways of moving and help us recognize the many sensations we experience without our conscious awareness.

Tuning into our proprioceptive sense not only heightens our self-awareness but also helps us understand how we come into contact with our world. Drawing on Maurice Merleau-Ponty's idea of "flesh," Susan Kozel writes:

> The body is a weave of different materialities, the body is a dynamic process, the body navigates the world at the intersection of a cluster of languages (verbal, physical, archetypal, mnemonic, and unconscious). It is electric, biological, and cultural. The body is a pattern of information and the body is both a site and a mapping onto sites. Above all, for Merleau-Ponty, bodies are flesh, and flesh is more than just bodies.
>
> (Kozel 2007: 33)

We experience ourselves as anatomical beings, kinesthetic beings, multisensory beings, sociocultural beings, and emotional beings; beings in conversation with space, objects, and others—beings who act and are acted upon in the world. The ability to move from a first-person embodied perspective to an understanding of how this perspective acts upon the world is how we learn empathy. In this, somatic practitioners argue that somatic and improvisational techniques are a form of "empathetic training." Furthermore, the dynamic flow from individual to collective or communal perspectives is how we build ethical relationships with ourselves and others both directly through interaction and indirectly through the objects and technologies we create (Schiphorst 2008: 65).

Embodiment and Interaction Design: Moving Beyond Rhetoric to Methodology

The term embodiment, or embodied thinking, is one that has been adopted into the language of many different practices, including interaction design. This is in no small part due to Paul Dourish's seminal work, *Where the Action Is: The Foundations of Embodied Interactions* (2001). Here, he builds an argument for embodied design by drawing from the fields of tangible computing, social computing, and phenomenology. In his sixth chapter, "Moving Toward Design," Dourish articulates a framework for embodied design in six principles. While listing these principles by no means fully captures their meaning, it does provide a glimpse into the nature and value of his work. These principles are: computation is a medium; meaning arises on multiple levels; users, not designers, create and communicate meaning; users, not designers, manage coupling; embodied technologies participate in the world they represent; and embodied interaction turns action into meaning (2001: 155–188). Similar to the means by which I situate my own argument for action, Dourish clearly states that his book (and any design theory text, for that matter) cannot guarantee design success. In this, he recognizes the value of learning from design practice as much as from design theory. While Dourish's principles have been built upon by other researchers in the field (Buchenau & Suri 2000; Klemmer, Hartmann, & Takayama 2006; Djajadiningrat, Matthews, & Stienstra 2007), this work misses one pertinent point: embodiment is not something one achieves merely through observation and design. Embodiment is a *way of being*. Dourish repeatedly refers to embodiment as a way of being in, actively engaging with, and coming to understand our world; however, when addressing the application of these ideas, the conversation repeatedly turns back to instances in which a community of users or designers is engaging with the technology. While this context-specific articulation of embodiment makes sense for both his research and the book's audience, it isolates embodiment into a specific setting, such as the design task at hand, ultimately detaching it from the broader world in which it exists. In this way, the designers are encouraged to "call upon" an embodied way of thinking within the design process; however, clear methods for somatic awareness are rarely suggested. Such a focus brings me to the following critical statements: (1) embodied thinking is not practiced solely through interaction design, and (2) a designer's understanding of embodiment must move beyond the designed interaction. This second point is particularly pertinent as we move forward to a discussion of wearable technology (WT).

A Breakdown in Embodiment: Google Glass

As a designer, it is feasible to imagine that one can develop a comprehensive understanding of how technology meets the world when it is permanently fixed in a given environment (i.e., a point of sale terminal in a grocery store). In the case of WT, however, the convenience of a fixed environment does not exist. Consider Google Glass, which came to the market with great hype and enthusiasm in early 2015, but failed to fully take off. In his 2015 keynote at South by Southwest (SXSW), Google X's "Captain of Moonshots," Astro Teller, blames too much media attention for Google Glass's failure: "The thing that we did not do well, that was closer to a failure, is that we allowed and sometimes encouraged too much attention to the program" (Teller 2015). Later, in the question and answer session, he describes his surprise at the backlash of privacy concerns that arose from having a camera on the device: "I'm amazed by how sensitively people responded to some of the privacy issues. . . When someone walks into a bar wearing Glass . . . there are video cameras all over that bar recording everything." He goes on to describe how this is not "really" a conversation about privacy because Google Glass is only one of many cameras in the bar. Teller's statements both reveal how he devalues an honest concern (i.e., personal privacy) and demonstrate how a single component (i.e., the camera on a pair of Google Glasses) cannot be decoupled from the broader world in which it exists. The voyeuristic nature of the camera comes not only from the fact that it is an instrument meant for recording moving images but also from the way in which it is worn. Permanently facing outward on a moving body, the camera is always at eye level, always reminding others that it is there. It roves and seeks out new vantage points as its wearer moves, settling to stare directly into the eyes of another during a conversation. When people look at someone wearing Google Glass, they do not see two eyes staring back at them; they see three. The third eye could be recording everything. It is unblinking, always seeking new information; it also feels alive because it is connected to a living being. It cannot be put away. It just watches, while some "Glasshole" controls it.

Google Glass clearly demonstrates the many ways in which an interactive technology can fail to recede into the background given the myriad of environments in which it might be situated. This is particularly relevant in highly public, social contexts. In the case of privacy, Google Glass rubbed up against the world in a way that was most felt by those who were proximate to Google Glass wearers, hence the emergence of the derogatory name, Glasshole. The discomfort felt by people near technology users and wearers is a newer phenomenon not wholly accounted for in contemporary HCI design practices. Despite the increased production and consumption of portable and wearable devices, design practices still focus solely on the user or community of users, taking little account for those merely within proximity. Given HCI design does not prioritize or even account for the broader social implications of portability and wearability, it is highly unlikely that the social backlash encountered by Google Glass wearers would have been discovered within a design studio. Herein lies my argument for the embodied practices of somatics and movement improvisation.

Embodied practices teach us how to experience the world differently, how to open up our thinking to a phenomenological awareness—to a way of knowing that is situated in not only experiencing new ideas but also re-experiencing familiar spaces, actions, and interactions over and over again as if they were new. Had a Google Glass project member with experience in a somatic practice visited a public space such as a bar or café and applied embodied thinking (even without wearing the device), it is possible they would have foreseen some of the ways in which Google Glass was a failure, particularly how it would affect those *not* wearing the device. This way of meeting the world decenters users (and their relationship with the technology) from being the only valuable subjects of observation. Furthermore, it questions the relationship between objects, people, and spaces by asking, "What is happening here? How is this space being influenced right now?" rather than, "What *should* be happening here? How *should* people adapt to me and what I make?" This distinction of "is" versus "should" is conveyed in many of Dourish's principles, but perhaps most clearly when he states that "the manipulation of meaning and *coupling* (or connection that arises during the course of an interaction) are primarily the responsibility of users, not of designers" (2001: 172). In this, we imagine *users* as anyone directly affected by the technology, both those using the technology and those proximate to the user. This reimagining of the term "users" expands Dourish's principle beyond its original intention and suggests designers are responsible to everyone affected by the technology within the design process. Had Teller and his team broadened their perspective of user beyond those wearing Google Glass, maybe they would have understood that the public's privacy concerns really are about privacy because the user made it this way. Different perceptions of privacy are not better or worse, only different. Just because people did not respond the way Teller thought they *should* have, does not make their concerns any less important, real, or meaningful to them.

Aesthetics and Embodied Agency in the Ever-Evolving Wearable Technology Landscape

As learned from Google Glass, knowing how technology affects our everyday experience is particularly important as we move into the field of WT. Beyond considering the broader social implications, I now turn back to our personal experience with WT as it relates to our bodies. Once interfaces are worn on bodies, an understanding of how they flow in and out of our dynamically shifting embodied experience becomes critical. We come into a different relationship with objects once they are worn rather than held. Portable objects (like mobile phones) blend more easily into the din of our everyday experience. They can be put away, hidden, and set aside. However, WT comes into a different relationship with us. Making contact with the flesh and tracking bodily functions in places (e.g., face, chest, and hips) often not touched by others, WT's physical relationship with the body is more intimate than that of portable objects, which are primarily operated by hand. Engaging in a multisensory relationship with intimate, often highly personal spaces of the body, WT thus has a deeper impact upon our embodied agency.

The idea of agency has often been considered apart from a corporal understanding of the self, where mental states are rendered superior to and somehow distinct from embodied states (Campbell et al. 2010: 1–2). However, embodied or corporal experience is central to how we understand both self and agency, and WT reveals the trouble with separating agency from bodies: wearers cannot easily distinguish their self-identity from the technology itself. The visual aesthetics, multisensory feedback, and physical materials of devices continuously interweave with a wearer's embodied experience. In this, WT is successful when it gives the user control to shape and define relationships. WT is far less successful, and in fact reduces embodied agency, when it acts upon people in ways that demand attention or recognition without consent. This reduction or loss of embodied agency can come in many forms, including unwelcomed and uncontrollable haptic, sonic, or visual cuing; distractingly "loud" visual design; wearer discomfort; and reductive representations of embodied experiences that do not give agency to the user to contextualize the data. Again, if we broaden the concept of *user* to be all those affected by WT, then it is easy to imagine how these unwelcomed intrusions can apply to both the wearer and those proximate.

Issues of embodied agency are heightened when WT is adopted and imposed upon people by a company or organization. In 2002, Ana Viseu conducted a case study in which she studied Bell Canada field technicians wearing small computers fashioned to fit in shoulder bags. Similar to many of today's wearable technologies, the computers handled much of the "busywork," such as dispatch, communications, and fieldwork logs, that technicians were accustomed to doing. The computers did all of this work, collecting considerably more information than workers could themselves and freeing up time for them to do other things. This freedom was seen as a means to give workers increased agency within their everyday processes, but the actual sentiment among them was that of agency loss (Viseu 2005: 176). For instance, the highly organized software system required entry into prescribed fields and removed workers' ability to contextualize their notes. The software also removed their ability to correct mistakes in their work and decreased the amount of contact they had with their managers. These changes fundamentally altered the workers' self-identity, and the wearable computers became a recurring reminder of agency loss. In this scenario, WT allowed workers to physically move more naturally and freely within their work environment. In theory, this freedom should have improved their embodied experience. However, interaction design choices removed almost all embodied agency from the system at hand and left workers with devices onto which they could no longer inscribe themselves.

Since Viseu's experiment in 2002, data tracking through personal wearable devices has become nothing less than pervasive. Individual users are now choosing to self-track with WT, a behavior revered by the Quantified Self (QS) movement (Quantified Self 2015). Fitbit, for example, has become the most popular health- and fitness-tracking device on the market, making over 745 million USD in 2014 alone (Park 2014). While it has clearly been embraced by some sectors of western culture, its framework looks very similar to that of Bell Canada's wearable computers: a wearable/portable device that automatically tracks and logs user behavior. The unsettling implications of such devices have become more publicly transparent now that businesses and insurance companies are partnering with Fitbit to provide "perks" to users. Fitbit's corporate wellness program partners with businesses interested in tracking the health of their employees and lowering health insurance rates. Health insurance companies, such as United Health, Kaiser Foundation Group, Humana Group, and Aetna, are now developing perks programs that reward members for tracking and sharing their health data (Olson 2014). For instance, Discovery Health's "Vitality" health program offers "Vitality Points" to members who wear fitness tracking devices (Bernard 2015). Both Humana Group and John Hancock now partner with Vitality to offer similar rewards programs to their customers (John Hancock Vitality Program 2015; Humana 2016).

While aiming to shed light on the human experience, the QS movement compresses experience down to a lossy dataset large in size but devoid of critical contextual information. This type of tracking may be convenient and relatively easy to analyze, but it is based on a large set of assumptions about what types of behaviors are producing the data and how devices are being used. This concern is satirically highlighted in the work of artists, Tega Brain and Surya Mattu. Pushing back on the influx of health promotion programs such as Vitality, Brain and Mattu developed *Unfit Bits*: motion-generating devices that "set your data free" by connecting Fitbits to metronomes, bicycle tires, and other repetitive motion objects (Brain & Mattu 2015). *Unfit Bits* critically push back against the QS movement, demonstrating the futility and arbitrariness in attempting to harness embodiment with massive quantities of data—a vital, much needed critique as the QS movement continues to grow.

While theories in embodied interaction design take us far, they cannot account for the value of engaging in embodied practices. In this, I challenge designers to become agents in their own embodied discovery by engaging in a somatic practice. This work is not easy, neat, or quick. Embodied thinking takes time to cultivate. It is difficult to articulate in words, and the ways in which it affects our work is not always easy to explicitly understand. The urgency to address this challenge has been felt by many in the WT design community for some time now. My biggest question as a somatic practitioner and dancer is when and why WT is necessary. Furthermore, who has the right to make WT? The inherently pervasive and invasive nature of WT means that we need designers who deeply care about these questions and want to take responsibility for ways WT affects not only potential users but also broader society. The potentially profound sociocultural impact that WT can and is having means that designers need to cultivate a deep, embodied ethos of care, one that recognizes the power of influencing people's embodied agency.

Cultivating responsible technologies will require a transdisciplinary approach, one in which somatics, movement improvisation, experience prototyping, and HCI design practices are integrated without predetermined prioritization. Some progress can be made through the work of interdisciplinary teams that include somatic practitioners, but I argue that real progress will come when all members of a design team learn to value and engage in embodied thinking. In this, I reiterate my call to action: I encourage readers to enrich the theoretical understanding of embodiment to one that is experienced through not only words on a page but also the bodies with which we are so intimately interconnected.

Further Reading

Cohen, B. B. (1986) "The Action in Perceiving," *Contact Quarterly* 12(3), 22–26.

Hackney, P. (2003) *Making Connections: Total Body Integration through Bartenieff Fundamentals*, New York, NY: Routledge.

Ryan, S. E. (2014) *Garments of Paradise: Wearable Discourse in the Digital Age*, Cambridge, MA: MIT Press.

Rywerant, Y. and M. Feldenkrais (2003) *The Feldenkrais Method: Teaching by Handling*, Laguna Beach, CA: Basic Health Publications.

Schiphorst, T. (2009) "Body Matters: The Palpability of Invisible Computing," *Leonardo* 42(3), 225–30.

References

Bacon, J. (2010) "The Voice of Her Body: Somatic Practices as a Basis for Creative Research Methodology," *Journal of Dance & Somatic Practices* 2(1), 63–74.

Bernard, T. (2015) "Giving Out Private Data for Discount in Insurance," *New York Times*, retrieved from nyti.ms/1FepJeK.

BodyCartography Project (2011) "small dance," *Vimeo*, retrieved from vimeo.com/19001115.

Brain, T. and S. Mattu (2015) Unfit Bits, retrieved from www.unfitbits.com.

Buchenau, M. and J. F. Suri (2000) "Experience Prototyping," in *Proceedings of the 3rd Conference on Designing Interactive Systems: Processes, Practices, Methods, and Techniques*, ACM, p. 424.

Campbell, S., L. Maynell, and S. Sherwin (2010) *Embodiment and Agency*, Pennsylvania, PA: Penn State University Press.

Clarke, G. (2007) "Mind Is as in Motion," *Animated: Foundation for Community Dance*, retrieved from www.independentdance.co.uk/rsc/MindIsAsInMotion.pdf.

de Lima, C. (2013) "Trans-Meaning: Dance as an Embodied Technology of Perception," *Journal of Dance & Somatic Practices* 5(1), 17–30.

Djajadiningrat, T., B. Matthews, and M. Stienstra (2007) "Easy Doesn't Do It: Skill and Expression in Tangible Aesthetics," *Personal and Ubiquitous Computing* 11(8), 657.

Dourish, P. (2001) *Where the Action Is: The Foundations of Embodied Interaction*, Cambridge, MA: MIT Press.
Gibson, J. J. (1966) *The Senses Considered as Perceptual Systems*, Boston, MA: Houghton Mifflin.
Gibson, J. J. (1979) *The Ecological Approach to Visual Perception*, New York, NY: Psychology Press.
Humana (2016) retrieved from www.humana.com/vitality.
John Hancock Vitality Program (2015) retrieved from www.jhrewardslife.com.
Klemmer, S. R., B. Hartmann, and L. Takayama (2006) "How Bodies Matter: Five Themes for Interaction Design," in *Proceedings of the 6th conference on Designing Interactive systems* ACM, p. 140.
Kozel, S. (2007) *Closer: Performance, Technologies, Phenomenology*, Cambridge, MA: MIT Press.
Olson, P. (2014) "Wearable Tech Is Plugging into Health Insurance," *Forbes Magazine*, retrieved from www.forbes.com/sites/parmyolson/2014/06/19/wearable-tech-health-insurance.
Park, J. (2014) Form S-1 Registration Statement, Fitbit Inc., retrieved from www.sec.gov/Archives/edgar/data/1447599/000119312515176980/d875679ds1.htm.
Quantified Self: Self Knowledge through Numbers (2015) retrieved from quantifiedself.com.
Schiphorst, T. (2008) *The Varieties of User Experience: Bridging Embodied Methodologies from Somatics and Performance to Human Computer Interaction*, PhD dissertation, University of Plymouth, ProQuest Dissertations Publishing.
Teller, A. (2015) "Moonshots and Reality" [Keynote video file], *South by Southwest*, retrieved from live.sxsw.com/detail/videos/sxsw-live/video/4147825546001.
Viseu, A. A. B. (2005) *Augmented Bodies: The Visions and Realities of Wearable Computers*, PhD dissertation, University of Toronto, ProQuest Dissertations Publishing.

19

WEARABLE INTERFACES, NETWORKED BODIES, AND FEMINIST SLEEPER AGENTS

Kim Brillante Knight

Bodies have a history of troubled relation to machines. From metaphors of Cartesian dualism that align the body/mind split with machine/code (see Moravec 1988; Kurzweil 1991, 1999), to popular and scholarly rhetoric that celebrated the networked computer as a means of social interactions that transcend the body (see Stone 1991; Rheingold 1993; MCI 1997), to the project of recovering histories of the bodies who labored on early machines, such as the women who programmed early computers (see Stanley 1995; Abbate 2012), bodies have never been in a stable, locatable position in relation to machines.

Wearable technology does little to clarify this relationship. Steve Mann is often cited as the forefather of wearable computing and has earned a reputation as the world's first cyborg. Much of Mann's early work grows out of asymmetrical systems of surveillance (Mann 1998). His experiments in wearing recording or computing equipment in public spaces were in response to him frequently being subjected to surveillance without the option to look back. In the decades that Mann has been wearing his devices, he has been assaulted, had them forcibly removed, and reported experiences of extreme disorientation from wearing them (Buchanan 2013). Mann's evolving relationship to his equipment and the resulting anxieties and physical effects indicate that the relationship between bodies and machines remains in flux.

Oft-cited examples of earlier wearable technology derive from the worlds of computation and art: Edward Thorp and Claude Shannon's wearable counting device (developed for cheating at roulette) and Atsuko Tanaka's 1956 "Electric Dress." There are likely many examples that could be added to these two. One that I find particularly noteworthy is VALIE EXPORT's 1968 performance art, *Tapp und Tastkino* (*Tap and Touch Cinema*). In the performance, EXPORT wears a television-shaped shell over her upper torso. Viewers are invited to experience what EXPORT calls the "first immediate women's film" (Medien Kunst Netz n.d.). The viewer parts curtains, reminiscent of those that hide a stage or movie screen, and places their arms inside the box, which sits over EXPORT's breasts. This example is notable for the prominence given to the body as mediated rather than as a carrier or platform for the technology.

Much current research is devoted to the development of wearable devices in engineering, computing, and medical fields. In the fields of fashion or design, wearable computing is largely treated as a means to achieve aesthetic ends, or as part of a wider context of technological developments in areas such as textile innovation. There is less research that addresses the cultural or ethical dimensions of wearable computing. In media studies or digital humanities, there is a fair amount on technologies that are sometimes worn on the body, such as portable cassette players, virtual reality hardware, MP3 players, and mobile computing. However, research on wearable computing proper—computing technologies designed primarily to be worn on the body as a garment or accessory—is still in the nascent stages. Pedersen's *Ready to Wear* (2013) addresses the rhetoric around wearable technology as augmented reality, and Rettberg's *Seeing Ourselves through Technology* (2014) addresses multiple modes of technological self-representation. One of these modes is the Quantified Self movement, a community that uses data tracking, often from fitness trackers, as a means to know the self. Ryan's *Garments of Paradise: Wearable Discourse in the Digital Age* (2014) is probably the most in-depth treatment to date of wearable technology from a humanist perspective. Ryan, an art historian, emphasizes the need to treat wearable technology through the lens of dress and takes the reader through a richly detailed history of wearable computing as evolving out of the "Borg Lab" group at MIT, with Steve Mann and Thad Starner among its notable alumni.

The interface is central to Ryan's reading of wearable technology. The interfaces of wearable tech are either invisible or, if visible, material and critical. Her emphasis on visibility of the interface seems to largely break down into applied research for commercial development, which strives for invisibility, and art, in which the technology is foregrounded either as an aesthetic strategy of dress (material) or for the purposes of social critique that she calls "dress acts" (critical). Dress acts are material analogues of "speech acts." They are performative in that clothing creates a text from which some meaning can be decoded, though this meaning is variable since it is embedded in historical and cultural signifying structures (Ryan 2014: 10).

Material, lived bodies are absent from Ryan's formulation of the "dress act." Her engagement with the body is most often as a generalized construction of embodiment (subjectivity as experienced through the culturally produced body and, in this particular case, its relation to technology), with an occasional focus on gendered systems of meaning. She acknowledges this oversight, writing, "I leave specific feminist theoretical analysis to future scholarship" (2014: 4). We share an interest in developing a critical framework for wearable computing and an interest in the role of the interface. Indeed, a feminist theoretical analysis of interfaces would re-introduce the materiality of the body, conceptualizing the interface as part of a dress-body-technology assemblage.

The body is never a neutral site of the interface. For instance, *Tap and Touch Cinema* explicitly refuses the ruse of neutrality, a refusal it shares with other feminist, touch-based performance art. Vasseleu writes, "Broadly speaking, feminist artists latched onto the fact that touching pertains to a bodily act and affect, not a bodiless presence devoid of social and historical context or cultural standing" (2015: 296). Touch has a bodily presence, even when it is not between two bodies, but instead the zone of contact in a dress-body-technology assemblage. Though the garment and/or device may remain materially stable, the ways they shape and are shaped are influenced by bodily presence. The body is framed by touching them as well.

In short, as an interface, the dress-body-technology assemblage is not a stable entity. It is a process. The importance of the interface as a process can be traced in multiple recent theories. For example, in *Window | Interface,* Eckmann and Koepnick theorize the interface not as a neutral window, but as always having been a zone of contact, which HCI allows us to understand with new awareness. Koepnick writes, "Instead, interfaces are sites of virtual transport and dislocation that have the power to carry us to other temporal and spatial orders while also inserting different orders into our own physical surroundings" (2007: 19). Much of Koepnick and Eckmann's theorizing is related to the increasing ubiquity of screen-based interfaces in the mid-2000s. As Eckmann notes, the window/screen as an interface not only has a material function, but also acts as a conceptual paradigm (2007: 61). Thus, even though the screen is absent in most wearable media, it still functions as a conceptual device that frames the processual operations of the dress-body-technology assemblage.

Galloway elaborates on the concept of interface as process, suggesting that the interface only exists in the process of contact. Like Kopenick and Eckmann, his theory begins with an articulation of the interface as a zone of contact. This is not a seamless union or bridge. Rather, the interface is the "generative friction" in this contact (Galloway 2012: 31). He suggests that the differences between layers, and between layers and interface, are never easily discernible. For example, in a web page, there is little to distinguish between the ASCII characters displayed on the page and those that are used in the markup language to produce that display (2012: 33). The interface as process is:

> [T]hat moment where one significant material is understood as distinct from another significant material. In other words, an interface is not a thing, an interface is always an effect. It is always a process or a translation . . . a fertile nexus.
>
> (Galloway 2012: 33)

This reframing of the interface from a thing, with a stable identity, to an effect, always in process, allows us to account for the material conditions in which different bodies result in different body-dress-technology assemblages.

Consider various performances of *Tap and Touch Cinema.* In images of a 1968 performance, EXPORT is not wearing a shirt; her bare arms extend out from the television box and her abdomen is visible. Her long blonde hair is teased in a style reminiscent of Brigitte Bardot (Museum of Modern Art n.d. a). In images from a 1969 performance, EXPORT is wearing a long-sleeved sweater, and her hair is styled in a more conservative manner (Museum of Modern Art n.d. b). This second performance, in which EXPORT is less exposed and dressed more conservatively, invites the viewer to experience a slightly different mediated body. These images from two separate performances provide us with a representation of different iterations of a dress-body-technology assemblage that is never stabilized. In the wearable technology interface, that fertile nexus of distinction has implications for issues of embodiment and subjectivity.

These implications arise out of both dress and technology. After first establishing that the body is "always and everywhere culturally interpreted" (Entwistle 2000: 13), Entwistle describes dress as "situated bodily practice" for a body that is the "active and perceptive vehicle of being" (29). In other words, dress is a situated practice that impacts embodiment. In *Technologies of the Gendered Body*, Balsamo argues for the role of technology in materially redesigning the body. She describes the techno-body as a "boundary concept" in an ideological tug-of-war between the organic/natural and the technological/cultural (1996: 5). The body can no longer be understood as having any originary, natural state. Instead, the organic can only ever be known in relation to the culturally produced body that is increasingly framed through technology in the second half of the twentieth century. Neither wholly technological nor wholly organic, the techno-body is both at once. Though Balsamo's work refers mostly to analog forms of technology, her concept of the techno-body articulates a perspective that, if anything, becomes more urgent in an era of emerging wearable technologies and ubiquitous mobile computing. This is particularly true of her assertion that "[n]ew body technologies are often promoted and rationalized as life-enhancing and even lifesaving. Often obscured are the disciplining and surveillant consequences of these technologies—in short, the biopolitics of technological formations" (Balsamo 1996: 5). I will return to this critique later, but for now it suffices to establish the concerns of wearable media as growing out of the wider milieu of the techno-body.

None of these theories can be reduced to suggesting that dress or technology simply translates the perceptions of the body into a projection of self. The process is more complex than that. Grosz suggests that the "body must be psychically constituted in order for the subject to acquire a sense of its place in the world and in connection with others," while at the same time, "social inscriptions of bodies produce the effects of depth" (1994: xii–xiii). In other words, the body is in a mutually constitutive relationship with a socially situated self. Grosz uses the metaphor of a Möbius strip to describe the relationship between inside and out in terms of embodied subjectivity. The relationship between body, dress, and self involves both performance and inscription. For instance, in Ryan's concept of "dress acts," to wear a garment is to perform signification, to situate a body within a historically specific system of signification in a particular cultural location. At the same time, a body is never a blank canvas onto which signification is draped. Bodies are never outside of culture. They are always inscribed by the social. Thus, a body that is dressed is already marked by gender, race, class, and other manifestations of subjectivity. Further, these bodies are also inscribed by the norms that arise out of legislation, medicine, and other institutions (Grosz 1994: 142). Our sense of the body arises from the material and social inscriptions upon it, and our sense of the self is simultaneously imbricated with this social body.

The dress-body-technology assemblage of wearable technology functions as a fertile nexus not just between user and computing device, but between the fashioned, technological, and embodied subject. This subject is often theorized as a cyborg being. It is important to consider the connection between the fertile nexus of the wearable tech interface and theorizations of the radical potential of the cyborg subject. In "A Cyborg Manifesto," Donna Haraway suggests that the figure of the cyborg presents an opportunity: "a cyborg world might be about lived social and bodily realities in which people are not afraid of their joint kinship with animals and machines, not afraid of permanently partial identities and contradictory standpoints" (1991: 154). The cyborg for Haraway is a potential means of resisting the "informatics of domination," the material and ideological shift to hierarchies and power structures grounded in networks, technological virtuosity, and biopolitics, enacted through global capitalist culture (1991: 162). As a fertile nexus of bodies, machines, and inscriptive practices of dress, wearable technology presents one means through which a material enactment of a cyborg assemblage has radical possibility.

Kathleen McDermott's Urban Armor collection is a series of wearable garments in which we glimpse the cyborg's radical possibility. Of particular note is the "Personal Space Dress"; its skirt expands when activated by a proximity sensor in order to protect the wearer from unwanted contact (Taylor 2014). The choice of a feminine garment—a dress—calls attention to the way women in particular are subject to harassment in public spaces. McDermott's use of pink and white lace signifies a high degree of girlishness, akin to "sweet lolita," a Japanese street fashion subculture. Interpretations of lolita vary. For Winge (2008) and others, lolita style challenges Japanese gender norms by demanding the gaze through the spectacle of dress, while remaining untouchable behind the facade of doll-like subjectivity (2008: 60). McDermott's garment employs the same tension: it demands the gaze by invoking lolita style as it also refutes touch through sensors and motors. It emphasizes bodily presence and foregrounds the importance of touch by denying it through surrogate technological agency. It is no accident that McDermott's demo video occurs on a train. Though it was filmed in Hong Kong, the invocation of Japanese street fashion filmed on public transit undoubtedly makes reference to issues of harassment on public transport in Japan that have received significant recent news coverage. Here we have an assemblage of dress (lolita style), body (the body of model Annick Lung), and technology (proximity-activated motors) that signals kinship and affinity among women who experience public harassment across cultures, while drawing particular attention to the issues faced by young women on public transport in Japan. While not unproblematic, the Personal Space Dress does operate through the zone of contact in a body-dress-technology assemblage that evokes cyborg subjectivity as a challenge to oppressive gender regimes.

Most wearable technology, however, does little to realize its cyborg potential. The most ubiquitous wearable technology today is the fitness tracker. It generally comes in the form of an arm or wristband that explicitly marks the wearer as a techno-body. The sleek gadget features dark colors and silver metallic touches, though an increasing number of devices and accessories are being developed for an audience who would prefer more fashion-oriented aesthetics. The wearer is no longer limited to only a geek-chic or fitness aesthetic and may align the device with a wider range of dress choices. Though the device itself may be screenless, it is functionally inseparable from the interface of a mobile or web application that offers a more complete perspective on the wearer's data. The devices often include a vibration motor or speaker to offer status notifications through tactile or auditory signals, thus augmenting its integration with the body's kinesthetic and sensory capabilities.

No description of the fitness tracker would be complete without attention to the body that forms part of the wearable technology assemblage. The device marks the techno-body as one that is interested in health and/or understanding the self. But the interface between dress-body-technology is also shaped by the gender, race, class status, and relative fitness of the wearer. Consider, for instance, how interpretations of fitness trackers may morph in relation to norms regarding which bodies are constructed as already "fit" versus those that are othered in some way, via age, gender, race, or ability. The device interfaces with the body on which it is worn and inscribes a relationship to "fitness," but the body also inscribes the device itself in terms of its status as an effective management tool, laudable aspiration, or useless accessory. In other words, the device is affected by the bodily presence of the specific body on which it is worn. The interface can never be actualized before the device is worn. Once the device is donned, the assemblage of dress-body-technology begins to enact the ongoing process of interface effect. The interface is activated as a process in the zone of contact between dress, body, and technology.

As I mentioned earlier, Grosz suggests that, in the process of inscription, "[the body is] made amenable to the prevailing exigencies of power" (1994: 142). The fitness tracker hearkens back to Balsamo's warning about technologies that contribute to the "biopolitics of technological formations" and to Haraway's "informatics of domination." Intended to manage the behavior of a population, the device produces data that has clear personal privacy implications and is a latent tool of legislative inscription—data from trackers has been used in various legal proceedings, for instance (Crawford 2014). In addition, the fitness tracker inscribes a techno-body as narrowly self-focused. The logic underlying this device is that more data is needed for a better self. The narrative of this feedback loop between data and self (i.e., the Quantified Self) creates a myopic focus on self-determination and supports fantasies of meritocracy. If one can just understand one's data and act upon that understanding, one can improve oneself. If one cannot, then it is a failure of inadequate data, poor understanding, or a lack of will, but never a failure of neoliberal self-determination.

Balsamo notes, "whatever label they attract, the cyborg serves not only as the social figure of the mass-mediated popular culture of American techno-science, but also as the figuration of posthuman identity in postmodernity" (1996: 18). The posthuman is a term with various meanings, though in this case Balsamo is referring to technological embodiment. In this model of the cyborg as posthuman identity, Haraway's potential kinship and affinity is suppressed in favor of the neoliberal subject who values personal responsibility above collectivity (see Barnard Center for Women 2013). As the most ubiquitous current form of wearable technology, the fitness tracker presents a rather bleak landscape.

In imagining alternative landscapes, one wonders what the Quantified Other or the Quantified Self-in-Kinship might look like. In other words, how does the dress-body-technology assemblage shift when it is widened to account for the self as an already-social self? How can the dress-body-technology interface refuse the neoliberal biopolitics of technological formations? These questions might be the impetus for subaltern counterpublics that emerge in response to the neoliberal norms of current wearable technology. Nancy Fraser defines subaltern counterpublics as "parallel discursive arenas where members of subordinated social groups invent and circulate counter discourses, which in turn permit them to formulate oppositional interpretations of their identities, interests, and needs" (1990: 67). For instance, Mothership HackerMoms is a makerspace whose membership is open only to women with children. The organization provides a physical and discursive space in which the particular needs and priorities of maker moms can be formulated into discourses counter to those of dominant maker culture.

Dunne and Raby argue that critical design can be one means of articulating counter-discourses. They assert that everyday objects can be designed to articulate social and ethical issues in ways that are more accessible to the public than government research, which is often linguistically and philosophically opaque; art, which often remains in sterile gallery settings; and, film and literature, which may be relegated to the realm of fantasy (2005). These "products" (i.e., objects that are embedded in our everyday material culture) can be designed in such a way that they resist or challenge oppressive norms. Dunne and Raby cite Tobie Kerridge, Nikki Stott, and Ian Thompson's "Biojewellery" project, which uses bits of human bone to grow the material to make engagement rings, which are already potent cultural symbols. By incorporating organic matter into the engagement ring, Biojewellery challenges norms of what can be commodified and the transactional nature of courtship and marriage rituals.

Material end-products are not the only way in which design can contribute to counterpublic formation. DiSalvo emphasizes the processes of public formation, which may be prompted by the design of objects using the tactics of projection and tracing. In projection, objects are designed to project possible outcomes of current scientific or technological scenarios (2009: 55). In tracing, design objects guide users to uncover the histories and/or current infrastructures of existing scenarios (57). In both cases, the impact of design tactics are found less in the finished product and more in the processes of discovery that they prompt, and these processes may lead to the articulation of a public (59). There are many artists and designers who are engaging with discovery, articulation, and critical design in their material practices (see Quinn 2002; Ryan 2014).

For the remainder of this chapter, I focus on how the university classroom might also be a space in which such questions are addressed and counterpublics are articulated. I approach Fashioning Circuits (see Figure 19.1), a public humanities project that coordinates research, university coursework, and community workshops, from this perspective. The university courses for Fashioning Circuits are taught from within a humanities framework, and they are intended to be inviting and supportive to populations, namely women and underrepresented people of color, who are marginalized in typical computer science spaces. From the very outset of the courses, the goal has been to articulate a counterpublic to dominant computing publics by creating a space in which women and underrepresented people of color feel comfortable learning and have the freedom to pursue projects that reflect their priorities and needs. Depending on whether Fashioning Circuits is taught via independent study or formal coursework, the gender ratio varies from 50 percent to 100 percent of students identifying as women. The ratio of students of color is anywhere from 30 percent to 50 percent people of color, which is much higher than dominant computing publics, such as those of computer science degree programs or Silicon Valley tech companies.

In addition to engaging this audience, there are two foundational approaches that help challenge norms and articulate counterpublics. The first is the reading list. The dress-body-technology assemblage is a given in Fashioning Circuits and serves as the organizing logic for theoretical readings. The students are mostly upper division students in Critical Media Studies. I can reasonably assume that they are already versed in the social considerations of technology and that they will bring that experience to the classroom. So I assign course readings that address issues such as the role of clothing in the performance of gendered, raced, classed, and sexual identities; cultural appropriation; respectability politics and the policing of bodies; and the ethics of consumption and global labor practices. These form a foundation before we move on to readings that more explicitly address wearable technology. The students also establish a grounding in intersectional feminist epistemologies and learn to consider how networked bodies are not just connected in technical networks, but also in networks of global flows of capital, production, and consumption. By emphasizing social construction, systemic power, and intersectional identities, the reading list is constructed to highlight the fault lines in the notion of the neoliberal subject.

Ratto describes the "review of relevant literature and compilation of useful concepts and theories" as one of the stages of critical making (2011: 253). In this case, the relevant literature and useful concepts are connected to wearable technology as a dress-body-technology assemblage. This connection influences the second foundational tactic of Fashioning Circuits: critical making. Critical making is a multivalent means of incorporating the body of the student into Fashioning Circuits. As a collective, the classroom tends to be a much more diverse space than dominant computing publics. Students are more likely to be engaged in creating alongside others like themselves than they would otherwise. The makings of a counterpublic are initiated in the embodiment of the students, who bring with them situated knowledge. Drawing on Papert and other theorists of constructionism, Ratto suggests that critical making has value in "connecting the sensorimotor 'body knowledge' of a learner to more abstract understandings" (2011: 254). Students bring or develop new embodied epistemologies in the acts of sewing, coding, and electronics work. Challenging gender binaries, every student engages in work that has been traditionally viewed as hypermasculine and that which is coded as hyperfeminine, often at the same time. Circuit boards and microcontrollers are paired with fabric and conductive thread, resisting the dichotomies of gendered labor.

Figure 19.1 A Fashioning Circuits community workshop participant handsews a Lilypad Arduino and LEDs.

The assignment structure and classroom practices are intended to reinforce thinking beyond dominant paradigms of wearable technology. For the final project, students are required to conceptualize and produce something that makes a statement or solves a social problem. Shared classroom practices are an important factor in these projects. Significant amounts of class time are devoted to workshops where students can engage in "doing it with others" (DIWO). Workshops address various topics, such as an introduction to the sewing machine and fabric tools or collecting analog data from environmental sensors. The DIWO model is supportive of affinity-building, but also of the individual needs of students for troubleshooting and problem-solving. In addition, many of the hardware, software, and tutorials we use are open source materials. Kinship and affinity are created as part of a collective where we consistently enact Pierre Lévy's knowledge space, in which "nobody knows everything, everyone knows something" (1997: 14). This destabilizes self-reliant and self-determining notions of neoliberal subjectivity and instead emphasizes the strength and value in our interdependence. The classroom becomes the grounds for counterpublic formation (i.e., a space for the enactment of the shared values of reciprocity and inclusivity in opposition to the informatics of domination that privilege masculinized communication and individual virtuosity).

The classroom is undoubtedly a space of social inscription. In Fashioning Circuits, students are enacting their own inscriptions of dress and adornment in creating their own wearable objects. In addition, the theoretical readings and emphasis on embodied knowledge are often an early, or even a first, exposure to learning in a feminist framework. On occasion, students whom I describe as "feminist sleeper agents" have their curiosity ignited by the course and are awakened to a more active engagement with issues of intersectional feminism. The course itself is an interface effect, where feminist epistemologies and critical making meet in a zone of contact that projects alternate realities in which kinship and affinity are privileged and the needs and viewpoints of marginalized or underrepresented groups are prioritized.

Further Reading

Abbate, J. (2012) *Recoding Gender: Women's Changing Participation in Computing*, Cambridge, MA: MIT Press.

Barnard Center for Research on Women (2013) "What Is Neoliberalism?" retrieved from vimeo.com/71978595.

Entwistle, J. (2000) *The Fashioned Body: Fashion, Dress, and Modern Social Theory*, Cambridge, U.K.: Polity Press.

Quinn, B. (2002) *Techno Fashion*, Oxford: Berg.

Rettberg, J. W. (2014) *Seeing Ourselves through Technology: How We Use Selfies, Blogs, and Wearable Devices to See and Shape Ourselves*, New York, NY: Palgrave.

References

Abbate, J. (2012) *Recoding Gender: Women's Changing Participation in Computing*, Cambridge, MA: MIT Press.

Balsamo, A. (1996) *Technologies of the Gendered Body: Reading Cyborg Women*, Durham, NC: Duke University Press.

Barnard Center for Research on Women (2013) "What Is Neoliberalism?" retrieved from vimeo.com/71978595.

Buchanan, M. (2013) "Glass Before Google," retrieved from www.newyorker.com/tech/elements/glass-before-google.

Crawford, K. (2014) "When Fitbit Is the Expert Witness," *The Atlantic*, retrieved from www.theatlantic.com/technology/archive/2014/11/when-fitbit-is-the-expert-witness/382936.

DiSalvo, C. (2009) "Design and the Construction of Publics," *Design Issues* 25(1), 48–63.

Dunne, A. and F. Raby (2005) "Towards a Critical Design," Catalogue essay, *Le Design Aujourd'hui*, Centre Pompidou, France, retrieved from www.dunneandraby.co.uk/content/bydandr/42/0.

Eckmann, S. (2007) "Seeing and Performing," in S. Eckmann and L. Koenick (eds.) *Window | Interface*, Chicago, IL: University of Chicago Press, pp. 61–86.

Entwistle, J. (2000) *The Fashioned Body: Fashion, Dress, and Modern Social Theory*, Cambridge U.K.: Polity Press.

Fashioning Circuits (2012) retrieved from fashioningcircuits.com.

Fraser, N. (1990) "Rethinking the Public Sphere: A Contribution to the Critique of Actually Existing Democracy," *Social Text* 25/26, 56–80.

Galloway, A. (2012) *The Interface Effect*, Kindle edition, Cambridge, U.K.: Polity Press.

Grosz, E. (1994) *Volatile Bodies: Towards a Corporeal Feminism*. Bloomington, IN: Indiana University Press.

Haraway, D. (1991) "A Cyborg Manifesto: Science, Technology, and Socialist-Feminism in the Late Twentieth Century," in *Simians, Cyborgs and Women: The Reinvention of Nature*, New York, NY: Routledge, pp. 149–81.

Koepnick, L. (2007) "The Aesthetics of the Interface," in S. Eckmann and L. Koepnick (eds.) *Window | Interface*, Chicago, IL: University of Chicago Press, pp. 15–49.

Kurzweil, R. (1991) *The Age of Intelligent Machines*, Cambridge, MA: MIT Press.

Kurzweil, R. (1999) *The Age of Spiritual Machines*, New York, NY: Penguin.

Lévy, P. (1997) *Collective Intelligence: Mankind's Emerging World in Cyberspace*, trans R. Bononno, Cambridge, MA: Perseus Books.

Mann, S. (1998) "Reflectionism and Diffusionism: New Tactics for Deconstructing the Video Surveillance Superhighway," *Leonardo* 31(2), 93–102.

McDermott, K. (n.d.) "Urban Armor," retrieved from urbanarmor.org.

MCI (1997) *MCI TV Ad 1997*, retrieved from www.youtube.com/watch?v=ioVMoeCbrig.

Medien Kunst Netz (n.d.) "Tapp und Tastkino," retrieved from www.medienkunstnetz.de/works/tapp-und-tastkino/images/1.

Moravec, H. (1988) *Mind Children: The Future of Robot and Human Intelligence*, Cambridge, MA: Harvard University Press.

Mothership HackerMoms (2012–15) retrieved from mothership.hackermoms.org.

Museum of Modern Art (n.d. a) "VALIE EXPORT. TAP and TOUCH Cinema 1968," retrieved from www.moma.org/collection/works/109931?locale=en.

Museum of Modern Art (n.d. b) "VALIE EXPORT. TAPP und TASTKINO (TAP and TOUCH CINEMA) 1969 (1989)," retrieved from www.moma.org/collection/works/159727?locale=en.

Pedersen, I. (2013) *Ready to Wear: A Rhetoric of Wearable Computers and Reality-Shifting Media*, Anderson, SC: Parlor Press.

Quinn, B. (2002) *Techno Fashion*, Oxford: Berg.

Ratto, M. (2011) "Critical Making: Conceptual and Material Studies in Technology and Social Life," *The Information Society* 27, 252–60.

Rettberg, J. (2014) *Seeing Ourselves through Technology: How We Use Selfies, Blogs, and Wearable Devices to See and Shape Ourselves,* Kindle edition, New York, NY: Palgrave.

Rheingold, H. (1993) *The Virtual Community: Homesteading on the Electronic Frontier*, New York, NY: Addison-Wesley.

Ryan, S. E. (2014) *Garments of Paradise: Wearable Discourse in the Digital Age*, Cambridge, MA: MIT Press.

Stanley, A. (1995) *Mothers and Daughters of Invention: Notes for a Revised History of Technology*, Cambridge, MA: Rutgers University Press.

Stone, A, R. (1991) "Will the Real Body Please Stand Up?" in M. Benedikt (ed.) *Cyberspace: First Steps*, Cambridge, MA: MIT Press, pp. 81–118.

Taylor, K. (2014) "The Personal Space Dress: Preserving the Wearers' Right to Personal Space," *Fashioning Circuits*, retrieved from fashioningcircuits.com/?p=2488.

Vasseleu, C. (2015) "Resistances of Touch," *Signs* 40(2), 295–300.

Winge, T. (2008) "Undressing and Dressing Loli: A Search for the Identity of the Japanese Lolita," *Mechademia* 3, 47–63.

20

DEEP MAPPING

Space, Place, and Narrative as Urban Interface

Maureen Engel

Maps are everywhere. They are the most significant contemporary mediator between people and the spaces we inhabit. Importantly though, they no longer get folded up and placed in glove boxes, waiting for the next road trip, nor are they consigned to those quaint old volumes called "atlases." Now, the map is always with us—in our pocket, on our phone, on our dashboards; it checks us in on FourSquare, shows us the nearest Starbucks, and gives us turn-by-turn directions to our destination. Indeed, the map has become so ubiquitous as to become invisible. It is not solely a representational object but rather an embedded technology—a true medium and extension of ourselves into space. This embeddedness marks the map's final transition to indexicality—that is, the map makes a truth claim about what is "there," and it tells us "you are here." Like a technological begging of the question, it transparently reflects that which it also represents.

Yet we also know that maps are complex graphical, representational, and narrative objects. They have historically been used for everything from navigation to empire building. Rather than relying on the power of the map to *reveal* what is already there, "deep mapping" foregrounds the fact that the affordances of the map can be used to *construct* the complex stories of human thought, culture, history, and production—in short, that the objects of humanities study can be analyzed, critiqued, understood, and articulated through a spatial interface as much as through a linguistic one. In deep mapping, the map is the principal tool of communication, analysis, and argument, similar to the way language performs that function in writing. Of course, maps have always been symbolic and representational, even as they have sometimes, or popularly, made claims to empirical truth and correctness. The difference of the deep map is that it acknowledges its complexity, conflict, politics, and history in its very foundation. As the Polis Center's definition of deep mapping contends, "Where traditional maps serve as statements, deep maps serve as conversations" (n.d.). Deep mapping is a way to open up questions rather than resolving them, to communicate *knowledge* rather than simply *information*.

This chapter provides an overview of the complex confluence of technologies, knowledge frameworks, and social forces that undergird and make possible the emergent field of deep mapping. It also provides examples of deep mapping practices. Philosophical developments in the way we analyze and understand space, technological advances in how we represent and interface with that space, and material developments in how space is physically structured and navigated have all contributed to new methodologies and new representational strategies. The result is deep mapping: a practice that challenges the empirical and representational assumptions of maps. It contests the cartographic bias of what might "count" as a map while simultaneously building palimpsests, narratives, cartographies, and critical interfaces to space and place. This chapter begins by placing mapping and cartography (for it is important to remember that they are not necessarily the same thing) in their own historical context to situate them as *productions* rather than simply *reflections*. It then examines how these domains shift with the advent of computerized cartography and geographic information systems (GIS), two technological developments that happen contemporaneously with the chapter's next theme: new philosophical understandings of space and place. The chapter then looks at how those parallel developments become intertwined through such practices and domains as spatial humanities, the geoweb, neogeography, critical cartography, and deep mapping. Finally, it presents a few examples of deep mapping as an urban interface and suggests some avenues for further exploration, pointing readers as much toward its future promise and unfinished platforms as to its existing methods and experiments.

Mapping in Context

For much of modernity, the map has been the purview of geographers and cartographers. Historians of science may have read and analyzed maps, but the creation and circulation of maps was principally solidified in the discipline of geography and the profession of cartography over the last few centuries. From early modernity through the eighteenth century, advances in mathematics, geometry, and astronomy, among other fields, simultaneously allowed for and made desirable an increase in map accuracy and indexicality, giving rise to what we now think of as "the map." It is important, however, to begin with the understanding that this articulation is a historically located and constructed concept of the "map" and its purpose. Ancient mapping technologies, such as the Babylonian map of the world, or medieval technologies, such as the mapa mundi, concerned themselves as much with symbolic relationships among peoples, places, and the unknown (including the spiritual) as they did with strict geography. Modern mapping, in contrast, has sought ever-increasing accuracy in representing the physical and mathematical relations contained in space. Maps in modernity developed and mastered a specific purpose: to accurately describe physical spaces such that they could be navigated or administered. Indeed, radical cartographers contend that, throughout modernity, the map has been inextricably linked to the project of exploration and, by extension, empire and colonialism. As European empires expanded, becoming larger and more complex, the need to symbolize them via physical features, transportation routes, boundaries, and resources became a more and more vital enterprise (see, for example, Harley 1989; Harvey 2001). Denis Wood (2010) argues that the map is a performative technology. He provides an excellent history of the concomitant rise of the map and the nation, and contends that the map is the unique technology that *calls into being* the nation state, giving "the elusive idea of the state concrete form" (31). The very origin and development of what we call "the map" is as much about creating what is "there" as it is about empirically reflecting or representing it.

Fast-forward to the contemporary, where computer-generated maps and mapping systems, including the advent of GIS in the mid-twentieth century, further extend this prioritization of empiricism. GIS is an entire computational system for collecting, storing, and analyzing data about space. Taking data about space and making it available for computation opens up huge possibilities for what we can know, learn, and represent about that space. A simple example will suffice: where, on an analogue paper map, we would measure the distance between point A and point B with a ruler (or a string, or a span of our fingers) and then compare that distance with the map's scale to determine the distance between two points, we now need only identify those two points and the power of computation does the rest. Just as that particular instance of *measuring* is faster and more accurate via computation, so, too, are other operations that geographers carry out with maps. GIS allows faster and more accurate measurement, comparison, quantification, and interpolation. Further, all of these data points in a GIS—whether they represent relief lines specifying elevation, flow rates of a river, or even neighborhood coffee shops—can be reused on different maps for different purposes. Such systems are used for everything from mapping weather patterns to planning the placement of emergency response services. In fact, in many of its applications, GIS relies on computational power to answer questions and solve problems. It allows scientists to predict the path of a hurricane by calculating all known data about a storm and its environment, or it can calculate where a fire station would be within acceptable time distances from the greatest number of structures or citizens. The mathematical and predictive possibilities of GIS are key reasons for its expanding influence and industry integration. Yet the advent and deployment of terms like "data" and "computation" solidify and extend the truth claim of a map. Its geometric and mathematical basis found a logical extension in computation.

Reconceptualizing "Space"

At root, GIS subscribes to and perpetuates the story that mapping tells about its own indexicality, and computational advances in mapping technologies and GIS reinforce empiricism and quantification. We know, however, that the development of disciplines, practices, and domains of knowledge are not singular, uniform, linear, or consolidated. Contemporaneous philosophical and theoretical advances in how we think about and conceive of space have challenged geography's quantitative foundations. Within the discipline of geography, such subfields as human geography and critical geography have long histories of revising the emphasis on quantification and accuracy and have instead approached space as a meaningful, historical, and/or political site of human activity.

In *The Image of the City* (1960), Kevin Lynch was among the first in the field of geography (though technically he was an urban planner) to think about the relationship between people and the spaces they inhabit instead of analyzing spaces as a priori objects. Lynch's work examined the mental maps that people have of their urban environments, and he proposed that they imagine spaces in relation to key geographic features: paths, edges, districts, nodes, and landmarks. Lynch's work initiated a significant change, as it accounted not just for the empirical *fact* of space but also the *meanings* people inscribe in it.

Over 30 years later, Lynch's initial impulse to think of space *relationally* is extended and enhanced in the work of Doreen Massey (1994), who integrated the political philosophies of Marxism and feminism into geography. Massey compellingly articulated the concept of "place" as a construction and constellation of social relations weaving together at a particular locus. If one zooms in from the satellite toward the globe, holding all those networks of social relations in one's head, then each "place" can be seen as a particular, unique site of intersection. Place is, indeed, a meeting point. This marks an important departure from conventional geographic thinking for two reasons: first, it challenges the idea that geography can adequately describe (in both senses of that term) that which it might "contain." Second, instead of a single focus on the relation between humans and the spaces they occupy, as embodied in human geography, Massey's work also put spaces into dialogue with other spaces, allowing us to think of space as articulated moments in networks of relations and understandings (1994: 7). Massey's call for a new way to imagine space from within geography drew on a significant body of theory interrogating the concept of "space" from sociological and philosophical perspectives.

Michel Foucault offers one such philosophical perspective in "Of Other Spaces: Utopias and Heterotopias" (1986 [1967]). Foucault argues that, while the nineteenth century was concerned above all with themes of time and history—development, accumulation, and the slow, inevitable course of so-called progress—we are now in an era defined by the characteristics of space. Massey fundamentally echoes Foucault's assertion that

> [T]he space in which we live, which draws us out of ourselves, in which the erosion of our lives, our time and our history occurs, the space that claws and gnaws at us, is also, in itself, a heterogeneous space. In other words, we do not live in a kind of void, inside of which we could place individuals and things. We do not live inside a void that could be colored with diverse shades of light, we live inside *a set of relations* that delineates sites which are irreducible to one another and absolutely not superimposable on one another.
>
> (Foucault 1986: 3, my emphasis)

Space is thus not an empty container for human actions, a kind of void to be geometrically demarcated and filled, but rather a set of relations. Human action and meaning do not straightforwardly occur within space; space is co-constitutive of those very actions. Space is multiple and complex, already inscribed with meaning, and generates relations as much as it "houses" them.

Henri Lefebvre in *The Production of Space* (1992 [1974]) is likewise interested in freeing the concept of space from its perception as not only geometric and mathematical (i.e., *physical space*) but also a metaphorical mise-en-scène for knowledge and ideas (i.e., *mental space*). Lefebvre instead theorizes a third term, *social space*, which proposes that space is produced by social actions and actors. This gesture provides social space with far more nuance than a concept like physical space, while simultaneously providing structure and substance in a way that the concept of mental space lacks.

These theorizations of space clearly distance it from a purely indexical or empirical thing by demonstrating the ways that it becomes meaningful through human interaction—the historical and the contemporary, the creative and the everyday. These new understandings of space occur contemporaneously with the technological developments we looked at earlier: computer-based mapping technologies and GIS. The result of their union is an interest in producing maps that account for more nuanced analyses of space and also represent spaces differently than strict empirical or indexical approaches. If, as Michel de Certeau contends, "space is a practiced place" (2011: 117), then our task is to analyze and express the *practice* itself as the interrelation between space and place. The four main practices that have arisen from this nexus are counter mapping, neogeography, the spatial humanities, and deep mapping. While the topic of this chapter is deep mapping, it is important to understand how the same basic concepts and technological advances find slightly different expressions through these practices. It is also important to understand that the boundaries between where one of these practices might end and another begin are highly subjective and ever shifting. Each practice readily and frequently borrows from the others.

New Mapping Practices

Counter-mapping and neogeography both use the map itself as the primary mode of expression and argument—they make things that can be readily identified and read as "maps." Counter-mapping is premised on the argument that maps are expressions of power, and that they most frequently serve dominant power structures. As its name suggests, counter-mapping aims instead to map places and territories *counter* to dominant power structures, and to use the map as a tool of politically engaged discourse. William Bunge's maps of Detroit are pioneering examples of counter-mapping and still stand as emblematic examples of the power of maps as political agents (see Wisniewski 2013 for an expanded commentary on Bunge's work, including reproductions of many of his maps of Detroit). "Where Commuters Run Over Black Children," arguably his most famous map, plots the locations of children struck and killed by cars in an inner city neighborhood. That the neighborhood is predominantly African American, and that the collisions occur on major commuter routes to the white suburbs, give the map its title, politics, and power.

Still in the realm of mapmaking, neogeography "consists of a set of techniques and tools that fall outside the realm of traditional GIS . . . Essentially, Neogeography is about people using and creating their own maps, on their own terms" (Turner 2006: 2–3). Neogeography principally employs free online mapping tools, the so-called "geoweb," like Google Maps or Open Street Map, eschewing expensive applications like ArcGIS; it also relies heavily free and open-access data sets to produce maps. Alan McConchie (2015) persuasively traces the genealogy of neogeography through a computational history of hacking, crowdsourcing, and making instead of a history of geography or cartography. As such, neogeography blurs the boundaries between mapmaking and application building on the one hand, and producers and consumers on the other. It is the map-based province of the *prosumer*—a term coined by Alvin Toffler to name a person who blurs the boundary between producing goods and consuming them.

The spatial humanities and deep mapping, on the other hand, are less strictly focused on the creation of actual maps and instead conduct research that takes the spatial as a starting point for knowledge production. They concern themselves with a broad range of texts, including narrative, visual, and cartographic texts, to engage in humanistic inquiry in a new way. As with all of the new spatial practices outlined here, it is difficult to draw clear or simple distinctions. Still, it is possible to broadly describe the spatial humanities as a more formal practice, where geotools, be they professional-level GIS or consumer-level Google maps, are used to address the conventional questions and problems of the humanities. One example is the work of Anne Kelley Knowles (2013), who asked the question, "What could Robert E. Lee actually see at the battle of Gettysburg, and how does that change how we understand that historical event?" By reconstructing the physical landscape of the battle in a GIS, and literally putting Lee on the battlefield, Knowles proved that Lee could not have known the extent of the reinforcements arriving on the federal side because he literally could not see them. Here, the technologies of the map are used to investigate an historical question, with groundbreaking results.

Deep Mapping

Deep mapping is an amalgam of each of these approaches. It combines the spatial humanities' scholarly treatment of "space" as an analytic with neogeography's interest in an open and participatory geoweb and counter-mapping's self-conscious remaking of maps to challenge dominant power structures and discourses. In so doing, it interrogates not just the scholarly concepts of space and place, but also the very practice of mapping itself.

One approach to achieving the goals of deep mapping is application development—that is, building applications that allow users to make maps differently. The *HyperCities* platform is an excellent example of just such a project. Developed by Todd Presner, David Shepard, and Yoh Kawano at UCLA, its method is "thick mapping" rather than deep mapping. "Built on the idea that every past is a place" (Presner 2009), *HyperCities* allows users to place a wide variety of media objects, including images, historical maps, texts, and tweets, into a map interface to explore the layered histories of city space. The platform arises from a need for researchers in the spatial humanities to access affordances different than those of standard GIS platforms. One such affordance is allowing users to specify not just the geographic co-ordinates of their objects but also the temporal ones. In *HyperCities*, users can navigate by time as well as by space. Using the timeline feature in the interface, objects on the map appear and disappear according to the temporal range the project creator assigned to them. The result is the ability to construct a multilayered history of a small geographic area and show changes over time and space.

The multiple layers of history also play a central role in The Museum of London's "Streetmuseum" app, which exemplifies what is possible when digital content, maps, locative technology, and the dense histories of urban spaces are brought together. The app maps a number of locations where significant historical events took place in greater London. Once they are at the sites of these events, users can hold up their tablet, "see through" their screen (the app activates the rear camera on the tablet), and view historical photographs superimposed on the contemporary reality of the location. Imagine standing at the gates of Buckingham palace and seeing the superimposed image of suffragette Emmeline Pankhurst being arrested, or imagine seeing a building falling to the ground on Queen Victoria Street during a bombing raid in 1941. These are the sorts of deep mapping experiences that capture precisely what Lucy Lippard means when she says:

> Place is latitudinal and longitudinal within the map of a person's life. It is temporal and spatial, personal and political. A layered location replete with human histories and memories, place has width as well as depth. It is about connections, what surrounds it, what formed it, what happened there, what will happen there.
>
> (Lippard 1997: 7)

Pipelines

Lippard's metaphors of width and depth, and her enunciation of place, have been particularly enabling in my own work on Edmonton, Alberta, Canada, a city whose layered history I have been learning about and excavating for some years. Here, I belong to a research cell called the *Edmonton Pipelines Project*. *Pipelines*, as we call it, is a collection of distinct yet reciprocal projects (under the direction of different scholars, including undergraduate and graduate students) that share common spatial, theoretical, and/or methodological ground. Each project approaches the deep map as both a method and metaphor, using depth both as *concept* and *instantiation* to engage with issues of history, suburbia, gentrification, and urban planning. In a geographical location too frequently assumed to be without geographical depth (e.g., the flatness of the prairies) and historical depth (e.g., the erasure of precolonial and ecological history), Edmonton in many ways serves as a model of the North American city of the twentieth century. If cities such as Montréal and New York stand as idealized forms for the urban, it is the Edmontons, the Tulsas, the Phoenixes, and the Salt Lakes that serve as the model for what most cities *are* (not what they aspire to be). Reintroducing depth to that urban conversation disrupts the very flattening of discourse that renders these types of cities under-narrated, uninteresting, and somehow always already known.

While we initially imagined *Pipelines* to be a singular effort that could somehow synthesize the disparate ideas and visions of its collaborators, we soon realized that we would require different methods and strategies to accomplish the varied thematic and localized aims of our interests. Indeed, we realized that one strength of deep mapping is the capacity to collect different scholarly pursuits together—to juxtapose them under a single umbrella, without any necessary adherence to methodological purity. Thus, each of the projects that make up *Pipelines* can at once stand alone while also contributing to the collective expression of a shared ambition. For example, the Rossdale project is building a layered historical map of the area with the same name, an area inhabited for some 6000 years with a deep Indigenous, colonial, civic, and industrial history, to name but a few of its intersections. As project director, Heather Zwicker, urges:

> Stand in one spot in the Rossdale Flats to apprehend the complexity of place. If you look closely at the boreal bush along the bike trails, you can discern raspberry canes and apple trees on the riverbanks, domestic remnants of the backyards from houses expropriated in the 1970s to build the "Ribbon of Green." Where you stand and marvel, trying to imagine that disappeared cityscape, will be on a riverbank hollowed by coal extraction: a formative city phenomenon beneath the plane of the visible. Beneath that vision, another made forcibly invisible by the false celebration of this city as a hundred-year-old entity: aboriginal Rossdale, routinely inhabited for six thousand years.
>
> (Zwicker n.d.)

In this description, we can see the depth that the Rossdale project evinces. By juxtaposing the long history of human habitation in the form of Indigenous history and settler domesticity (historical depth), the industrial legacy of coal extraction (geographic depth), the civic impulse to park development (political depth), and the ecological footprint of the boreal bush (environmental depth), the Rossdale *Pipelines* project stands as an exemplary instance of how to think and represent the complexity of depth.

Daniel Laforest's Vertical Suburbia *Pipelines* project encourages a different kind of depth. It argues that suburbia is perceived almost exclusively on the horizontal plane. The crowd-sourced project challenges its contributors to look differently, to produce images that highlight the verticality of suburban landscapes. Other *Pipelines* document and narrate "desire lines," or "unsanctioned paths worn by frequent footsteps" (Luckert n.d.). Still others take the block-by-block makeup of the city and rearrange it chronologically rather than spatially, or they ask what aspirational urban planning projects have never actually come into being. Taken together, the *Pipelines* projects represent a sustained and varied engagement with what constitutes space and place, what might count as a "map," and how we might insert "depth" into our theories and methods alike. While we take our name, *Pipelines*, from the oil and gas industry on which the city's economy is largely based, we use the term metaphorically, to denote the ways that each of our deep mapping endeavors is a way of channeling meaning, rather than oil, through dense city spaces.

The field of deep mapping is changing rapidly, like technologically influenced fields always do. New internet-based mapping tools and plugins emerge at a pace that makes mastering them almost impossible; new open source GIS applications, such as QGIS, allow developers to build out the kind of functionality that they want to see in their GIS; new platforms, like *HyperCities*, encourage humanists to experiment with spatial arguments in an environment that demands subject matter expertise rather than technical expertise; and all of this is happening in an environment where users of all types are generating geographic data that scholars cannot even begin to capture and have only just begun to study. The deep map has emerged, for humanists, as a new method of argument and a new form of scholarly production. It is exciting to anticipate what it might offer once it is an established, rather than an emergent, praxis.

Acknowledgments

The Edmonton Pipelines Project was supported by a Social Science and Humanities Research Council of Canada grant and a Kule Institute for Advanced Study grant.

Further Reading

Bodenhamer, D. J., J. Corrigan, and T. M. Harris (eds.) (2010) *The Spatial Humanities: GIS and the Future of Humanities Scholarship*, Bloomington, IN: Indiana University Press.

Lippard, L. (1997) *Lure of the Local: Senses of Place in a Multicentered Society*, New York NY: The New Press.

Lynch, K. (1960) *The Image of the City*, Cambridge, MA: MIT Press.

Wood, D. (2010) *Rethinking the Power of Maps*, New York, NY: Guilford Press.

References

de Certeau, M. (2011) *The Practice of Everyday Life*, trans. S. F. Rendall, Oakland, CA: University of California Press.

Foucault, M. (1986 [1967]) "Of Other Spaces," *Diacritics* 16 (Spring), 22–27.

Harley, J. (1989) "Deconstructing the Map," *Cartographica*, 26(2) (Spring), 1–20.

Harvey, D. (2001) *Spaces of Capital: Towards a Critical Geography*, New York: Routledge.

Knowles, A. (2013) "A Cutting-Edge Second Look at the Battle of Gettysburg," *Smithsonian Magazine*, retrieved from www.smithsonianmag.com/history-archaeology/A-Cutting-Edge-Second-Look-at-the-Battle-of-Gettysburg.html.

Lefebvre, H. (1992 [1974]) *The Production of Space*, trans. D. Nicholson-Smith, Hoboken, NJ: Wiley.

Luckert, E. (n.d.) *Lure of the Local: Senses of Place in a Multicentered Society*, New York NY: The New Press.

Luckert, E. (n.d.) *Theories of Space: Mapping Desire Lines in Edmonton*, retrieved from desirelines.edmontonpipelines.org/.

Lynch, K. (1960) *The Image of the City*, Cambridge, MA: MIT Press.

Massey, D. (1994) *Space, Place, and Gender*, Minneapolis, MN: University of Minnesota Press.

McConchie, A. (2015) "Hacker Cartography: Crowdsourced Geography, OpenStreetMap, and the Hacker Political Imaginary," *ACME: An International E-Journal for Critical Geographies* 14(3), 874–98.

Pipelines (n.d.) retrieved from edmontonpipelines.org/.

Polis Center (n.d.) "Deep Maps and Spatial Narratives," Indianapolis, IN: Indiana University-Purdue University Indianapolis, retrieved from polis.iupui.edu/index.php/spatial-humanities/deep-maps-and-spatial-narratives/.

Presner, T. (2009) "HyperCities 2.0 Launches with Mobile Media Tours," retrieved from www.toddpresner.com/?p=115.

Turner, A. (2006) *Introduction to Neogeography*, Sebastopol, CA: O'Reilly Media, retrieved from highearthorbit.com/neogeography/book.pdf.

Wisniewski, K. (2013) "An Atlas of Love and Hate: Detroit in the 1970s," retrieved from architizer.com/blog/radical-cartography.

Wood, D. (2010) *Rethinking the Power of Maps*, New York, NY: Guilford Press.

Zwicker, H. (n.d.) "Project Description," *Rossdale: An Edmonton Pipeline*, retrieved from rossdale.edmontonpipelines.org/project-description.

21

SMART THINGS, SMART SUBJECTS

How the "Internet of Things" Enacts Pervasive Media

Beth Coleman

Always Crashing in the Same Car

When Charlie Miller and Chris Valasek hacked a Jeep Cherokee in 2015, it was the first known remote-control takeover of an automobile (Greenberg 2015). The coders wrote a patch that got them into the Jeep's control system via a vulnerability in the car's networked entertainment components. During a test drive, the driver gradually lost control. First, the air conditioning system started to blast, and then the radio began blaring. Even though he consented to the test drive, the driver was quickly startled—and then panicked—when Miller and Valasek cut the acceleration while the car was moving down the highway, bringing it to a sickeningly slow pace with cars and trucks amassed behind it. To gain control of the acceleration again, the driver had to pull off the highway and *restart* the vehicle.
The stunt demonstrated several traits of the Internet of Things (IoT):

- networked automation can trump local, autonomous control
- networked technologies have direct impact on our sense of privacy and control
- networked media allows for a hyper-extension of reach and vulnerability.

Known variously as "smart" technologies, ambient intelligence, and social machines, an IoT further extends our reach across networked information (internet and mobile computing) into the material world. There are objects such as "smart" cars that drive themselves and "smart" tiles that tell us where our dumb objects, such as keys and bikes, are hiding. They sense the environment, removing the need for our attention to complete certain tasks (e.g., opening a door or noticing when a traffic light turns green). Among other things, an IoT further automates our physical habitat and daily habits of memory and action. We find ourselves extended, again, with a new level of reach—a remote control that looks a bit like magic—*even as we are rendered more exposed.* Remote control means we can reach and be reached. As demonstrated by the Jeep hack, the extension goes in both directions: more power to act and more vulnerability to be acted upon.

This is a world in which interaction takes pride of place. In fact, such interaction increasingly establishes what "place" means and how we come to inhabit it—what we might call modes of *X-reality*, the merging of informational and physical world (Coleman 2011). Each mode, with its corresponding information and communications technology (ICT), moves the point of transmission increasingly away from a stationary computer and toward mobility, location, and the phenomenal world. But, as the technology gets "smarter," is the human subject getting dumber? Put differently, what does a "smart subject" look like in this configuration?

As illustrated by the car hack, an IoT interaction is fairly *invisible*. It is an interaction based on the conditions of pervasive media in which devices talk to each other, automatically updating agendas, programs, scripts, and so on—creating a network of machine-to-machine (M2M) communication. This M2M communication is so important that the European Technology Platform on Smart Systems defines an IoT as "a world-wide network of uniquely addressable interconnected objects, based on standard communication protocols" (EPoSS 2008). They describe a merger of the informational and material world in which common objects—beyond one's cellphone and tablet—are imbued with computational power that allows them to be identified, activated, or controlled across a network. This is the radio frequency identification (RFID) tag that makes physical packages easy to scan and locate for speedy delivery. These are the data chips in mass transportation cards that say how many people boarded at which station and when they exited. These are "smart" technologies different than other, older computational technologies along two primary lines: they sense information about the physical environment, and they broadcast that information. Industrial age machines, such as thermostats, gauge the temperature and other aspects of their environment. Items such as smart phones and tablets receive and broadcast information. An IoT object such as the Nest "smart" thermostat heats up your house via remote control and transmits temperature data over the course of time (through the month, year, and so on). The device offers a pleasing, streamlined design from physical object to interaction. It also creates a real-time "data portrait" of the heat signature of a household. The question about such pleasing IoT devices is not whether they work (they do), but to whom the information is broadcast.

Oh! You Pretty Things

One finds important differences between early automation, such as the autopilot program, and pervasive automation, as described by the IoT. These differences are articulated along the lines of technological design, public policy, and the people who use them—"end-users" or citizens, depending on how one describes the relationship. This "depending" gives a false sense of chance operation, a roll of the dice, when in actuality the description of designed objects is also the description of an ontology—the perspective of its framework and properties, as defined by the domain in which it exists—where the affordances (technological aspects) and the social aspects (behaviors around connectivity, privacy, and searchability) are programmed along the lines of specific expectations regarding transparency, service, and ownership.

In this light, what is the difference between the self-driving car of the near future and a plane's autopilot program, a real-time feedback system first introduced in the 1920s? Both automate a procedure that had previously commanded human attention; both "sense" the environment for critical feedback that determines course of action. The "smart" technology, though, is new in its increasing scale of application . . . in its emerging ubiquity. We have ever more tiny computational devices that can be activated toward interaction with humans and automation with other machines. But the difference does not rest singularly with ubiquitous computing as a technological platform. It also reflects a cultural assumption of *pervasive mediation*—a radical increase in the power of automation. The system design of the autopilot was conceived as prosthesis: when the pilot tired, the autopilot could be engaged for nonemergency conditions. The shift with the driverless car is semantic (how we program its purpose) and procedural (how it enacts its designed functions). The car's smart system becomes the de facto driver—all the time, for all conditions.

"Smart" does not necessitate sentience. But it does involve programming qualities of the sensitive and sensible. Literally, a self-driving car needs to understand the sensory factors of road conditions as well as the sensibility (mood, orientation, etc.) of other drivers on the road. The sensory and affective spectrum must be translated into machine-readable language with a bouquet of real-time, real-world variables. Thus, sensing the environment and acting upon that input is increasingly in the "hands" of machines we have designed. And out of ours.

This is not necessarily bad news for activities such as driving, flying planes, or running the HVAC and lights system. Human judgment is demonstrably not as good at these activities as well-programmed machines (with the exception of some circumstances, such as emergencies). In the narrow view of highway safety, the automation technology keeps getting better, and we are not very good drivers en masse. In the larger scope of a pervasive automation, the outlook is not as sanguine.

In a comprehensive analysis, Anzelmo et al. discuss the formulation of an IoT and the technological, commercial, legal, and social aspects of its development (2011: 6–7). In defining the scope of an IoT, they write, "it is a network of connected objects. *Vehicles, machine components, domestic consumable durables, the clothes on your back*, all are being hooked up to a network with a speed most of us have yet to comprehend" (2, emphasis added). And in fact, what they describe is more or less a technologization of everything. In the history of interaction design and computation, Mark Weiser (chief scientist at Xerox Palo Alto Research Center), first articulated this vision of ubiquitous computing in 1991 when he looked at desktop computing and predicted that the future would be tiny computers and giant touchscreens scattered throughout the environment (Weiser 1991); there would be clouds of computing—ethereal and communitarian—as opposed to static hunks of plastic with awkward interfaces. That is the path we are on with IT companies, such as Apple and Google, leading the way on minimal, pervasive, customized, and closed design.

Although it looks like technology is the issue, in fact it is the social that is at stake. As Anzelmo et al. point out, the implications for this emergent technology reach across domains of technical standards, privacy protection, and politics: "[t]herefore, while many technical challenges remain to be overcome, the main themes and discourse around the Internet of Things are primarily social in scope and intent" (2011: 3). It was only in 2012 that Apple officially released an unlocked iPhone, its series of smart phones, allowing the user to put in a SIM card of her choosing (AT&T). Until that point, the design default had been to lock-up user access to the network information of the device. Despite the fact the one pays a tidy sum to buy the phone, one has to know to ask (and pay) for an unlocked phone or know how to hack it.

The iPhone design delivers sleek form and services with increasing obfuscation of the system of selection, reporting, and delivery. (Is the open OS Android significantly better? Yes and no.) It is certainly a pretty thing that we want, as demonstrated by Apple sales (Williams-Grut 2015). In contrast, one must bring intelligence to the device to know how to handle its privacy settings that lockout the user. And this is the scenario played out with increasing frequency: *"smart" outlines a particular model of service delivery and data acquisition.* The necessary intelligence to interpret how the device does what it does remains fairly esoteric.

A key aspect of the hard-to-know smart systems of algorithmic recommendations and cloud computing (where "our" bits are and how they are being served up) is that *they are not for us.* The data are not part of the user experience of "smart." The data are for the machines to learn faster in a M2M capacity. Such a machinic dialogue can be found in the quotidian act of your cellphone talking to wifi networks it "knows" (or has accessed in the past) without having to ask you. In the right hands, your bicycle and your washing machine reveal forensic evidence. We have programmed our cellphones and thermostats and cars to remember for us, to find our way, to make us feel at home. In this role of helpmate, the machines tell on us, describing our everyday in a newly intimate manner. Our acts are legible as data, if someone cares to read this affective broadcast.

We Pack and Deliver Like UPS Trucks

The Tile IoT technology is a small, white plastic disk no bigger than a quarter, if a quarter were square. The Tile works as a tracking device, signaling its location to one's phone using a micro Bluetooth tracker—for home (short range) and outside (distance) use. In either case, it is a device-to-device communication with the human as the end-user in the exchange of information. In the case of short-range wireless connection, within 100 feet the Tile can transmit its location and that of the item to which it is attached—keys, wallet, dog collar, and so on—to the phone running the Tile app. The Tile signals its location with a loud tone until it is located. At greater distances, the Tile will use *other* people's phones to signal location, a kind of M2M relay, until the location is broadcast to the Tile owner. Notably, for distance broadcast, the cellphones that form the informational chain run the app *outside the supervision of their humans,* who must enable background "community" support, after which the tracking is anonymous.

Short-range Tile use is fairly quotidian (which does not make it *secure*). We have long been able to program our IT machines with tracking devices so we can find them in local range (e.g., "Find My iPhone" became a standard application when the iPhone 1 entered the 2007 market at $500). The question of what information telecom and internet providers possess about users remains primarily a background one because these companies have had access to this information since the beginning of mobile telephony. The fact that noncomputational objects, such as keys, can now signal location is the reason Tile exists as a commercial endeavor. Yet the most significant change relates to a shift in register in M2M engagement. The civic, or perhaps one must say "public," use of the app presents a new form of IoT interaction that invokes the idea of a "community" of users who enable their devices to help crowd-solve the problem of a stolen bike or missing purse. This next level of machinic communication allows devices from an ad hoc Bluetooth network to ambiently track an object across a territory. Thus, a secondary effect of the Tile device finding your things for you is a *mapping* of things: where things go and how they can be found becomes an aggregated heap of data of how Tile *users* (you) move around the city. (And this is a distinctly urban app; it requires locative density of users to function as a "community.")

As with the transit smart cards introduced in Hong Kong, London, and Amsterdam, the issue of efficiency (getting on the train without stopping to buy a ticket) provides a great deal of data on how people use public transportation. This data can help with issues of traffic flow, congestion, and so on. It makes sense to have civic data on how the trains run.

But to have civic data on how *people move* requires a degree of transparency and protection of privacy that does not yet exist. The Tile tracking device, without stating it, invites one to opt into a level of precision tracking at an unprecedented scale. The closest corollary to this locative technology is an ankle monitor, the mandatory IoT bauble of those under house arrest so authorities can remotely monitor their location. (The ankle monitor uses radio frequency and global positioning systems for local and distance broadcast.) Or, we could imagine ourselves as packages en route for delivery with an available status update at any point along the way, much like delivery services such as UPS and FedEx keep track of their shipments once the objects leave the dispatch point. Historically, governments and businesses had to go through a lot of trouble to track the movements and activities of their citizens. Because our environment reaches increasingly toward a full broadcast of all actions that can be translated into digital information (e.g., purchases, "likes," steps, heartbeats, and location), the only way not to participate in a Big Data surveillance society is to take great pains to opt out.

The curtailing of civil rights is neither abstract nor far off. The Tile promotional video describes a scene where a young woman's bike is stolen. The network of connected devices (smart phones running the Tile app in the background) send an alert, tracking the object through the streets of the city, then anonymously relaying its position to the owner. If one plays out the implied Tile scenario, then one sees the community of good users—the good looking, global creative class made up of people who live in renovated industrial spaces and exercise a lot. We do not see the perpetrator of the crime: the bike thief. One can only imagine that the perp is *someone else*—someone not imagined in the neoliberal system of things and services.

As a tracking device, the Tile accelerates locating the purloined object and, one must assume, the person who took it . . . or the person in whose hand it is found. It further automates a ruthless social logic of have and have not where we can track people who take our stuff *without* ostentatious surveillance equipment or law enforcement. The Tile does not make someone steal a bike, but it does accelerate an automation of crime and punishment that further truncates presumption of innocence and contextual nuance. It closes down on a logic of inclusion and exclusion that only reinforces societal expectations of who makes up a criminal underclass of petty crime. And yet, this is only the cover story of services delivered. In its promise of efficiency, the Tile also tracks "us."

The orientation of IoT design is not a democratic process; the development is accelerated by the global network economies manifested with the second wave—the world wide web and e-commerce—of the internet. The biggest media companies in the world dominate it: Apple, General Electric, Google, Microsoft, Amazon, Siemens, and Facebook, with huge activity around Smart City builds from IBM, Intel, AT&T, and Cisco, among others. The IT industry loves Smart Things, and that love is the primary reason a new robot uprising (small AI, not big AI) is taking place. Smart objects signal a massive expansion of computational objects. Peter Semmelhack, founder of the open-source hardware company Buglabs, explains that the business future of "social machines" cannot be underestimated: "Right now there is an enormous pool of untapped information residing in all of the machines we've designed, built, and launched into the world" (2013: 28). However, Semmelhack makes clear in his IoT business model that this future does not *preclude* design that makes data both transparent and open. In other words, there are possibilities for design protocols that grant us control over when we want to be located and when we do not.

People have found their own workarounds for the always-on, always-identifiable dimensions of ubiquitous computing. Turning off networked devices, purchasing "burner" phones, encrypting information, redirecting IP addresses, anonymous darknets . . . these are all strategies from the hacker underworld that have emerged in everyday practices of regular people. Certainly, the IoT is not a design culture without its distributed disruptions—its pockets of citizen makers and hackers who innovate toward degrees of freedom. "Faraday pockets" that sheath cellphones from remote snooping emerged as the cool accoutrement of the digerati in 2015 (Lomas 2014). This IoT pocket protector is a charming object within a high-tech consumer culture where "we" are in control ("we" being educated and privileged ICT users, who are often the same class as ICT makers). Needless to say, the Faraday pocket does not address the systemic issues of ubiquitous data collection.

Such affordances to protect or alert are not common practice in IoT design because there is interest neither in the tech community nor among users to make available the valuable data gleaned from IoT devices. Transparency is far outside of our cultural habits around ICTs. Activists and outlaws have plenty of practice with these issues, but normal citizens do not. Bruce Sterling makes this point when he states:

> The real problem . . . is that the reader thinks he's the hero of the story. To the vacuum company, he was the "customer" or "consumer." In the legacy internet days, he was the "user." In the Internet of Things, he lacks those privileged positions, "user" and "customer." An Internet of Things is not a consumer society. It's a materialised network society. It's like a Google or Facebook writ large on the landscape.
>
> (Sterling 2014: 26–29)

He identifies a shift in subject position outside the inherited consumer model that has arisen quickly as a societal norm (i.e., "free" services for user information). Additionally, in materializing the informational network, the IoT forecasts a world of ubiquitous computing where everything is animated around us (Coleman 2012).

One effect of augmenting everyday objects and the built environment is a new norm of seemingly unfettered access, which is mostly a smokescreen If we look at the situation in relation to interaction and ubiquitous computing, this model breaks down very quickly across several dangerous avenues. The two most egregious are privilege (for whom are these services designed) and exclusion from system knowledge (who has access to this information). What Guy Debord theorized as the seductive "spectacle" of the twentieth century and Baudrillard as the procession of "simulacra," the IoT takes a turn of the screw *beyond*, toward a material interaction that inhabits the landscape. And we find ourselves "participating" in that system of information collection: surrounded by sensor networks and surveillance cameras while carrying tracking devices.

Around the cultural edges of this massive technological build, we are beginning to hear voices calling for the Smart Subject to become a Smart Citizen—activated and engaged in a battle for (degrees) of autonomy—who is the civic face of ubiquitous technology systems. Against the IoT endgame, author and open internet advocate, Cory Doctorow, analyzes the progression of a surveillance society through a historical lens: first, it is the criminals who are stripped of rights, then the infirmed and children on whom tactics of control and surveillance are auditioned. After, these techniques are applied to society as a whole (Doctorow 2015). By waiving our rights for services ("free"), we participate in this development whether we know it or not.

What the IoT design ontology still lacks are the civic aspects of free and open—and not simply as developer tools. Increasingly, civic media design is a growing demand. Groups such as Future Everything have corralled advocacy for this position across diverse sectors of academic, technological, and activist work. This ad hoc group takes the position that a Smart Citizen paradigm must include Smart Things with trackable, transparent activity. It is in fact citizens who need to take the lead in programming our "smart" future:

> On the one hand there is the view that Smart City design should allow for the disruptive ways in which people use technology. But there is also a stronger claim here, namely that citizens can, and should, play a leading role in conceiving, designing, building, maintaining our cities of the future.
>
> (Hemment & Townsend 2015: 2)

In how Future Everything names the problem and points toward a solution, one can only be struck by the incredible difficulty of "seizing" the means of the production. This really would be a revolution.

Call Me Maybe

So who is the driver in the world of the driverless car? The steersman of cybernetics is not the human driver but the system (Weiner 1965). However, important aspects of that system are *programmed* toward particular outcomes. We can data mine to optimize website use and make recommendations (common uses of Big Data). Or we can data mine to solve traffic problems (another common use of Big Data). We might also data mine phenomena such as the distribution of wealth and educational resources (e.g., Occupy Wall Street), environmental monitoring (Amsterdam Smart Citizen Lab), and so on. These are issues that civic activist groups rally around, and they call for more open access to databases as well as a transparent formulation of what data has been acquired and under what conditions. As critics of the coming IoT have noted, there is more complexity in the *social adoption and ethical standards* than in the technical development of this next turn in networked media design.

The terror (and the glory) of the IoT is not the singularity—the robotic "last days" that movies such as the *Terminator* series and a long line of sentient AI speculative fiction describe. Rather, the terror is losing all standards of decorum—of a right to self and unfettered relation to others. Decorum is a Latinate word meaning, "right and proper," which in modern parlance essentially means, "good manners." In calling for the rights and property of the Smart Subject, I suggest the root meaning. And in advance of "smart" systems, advocates of the Smart Citizen ask for a mandate of decorousness—a kind of decency in the design and use of IoT technologies.

This is a change away from the raging consumer service model; such an economy simply fulfills the user pleasure principle and only accelerates the role of humans as one Smart Thing among others. Change would thus entail new design ontologies based more closely on open-source and open-civic platform models, and it would prescribe a societal awareness of how (and why) these technologies work. Which is to say, the massive adoption of a Smart Citizen view is highly unlikely. It cannot simply be legislated, even if there were the political will. To ask people to *desire* decorum around privacy, ownership of one's data, and knowledge of public data systems is a tall order.

What, then, is the territory between abandoning control and developing better systems for sustainability? Can we have our benign IoT and eat it too? Probably not. But maybe. It depends on how collective awareness of these technologies develops and what fuels it. Based on the mass adoption of social media in the early 2000s, prospects are not great. Yet, as noted, one finds growing communities of discontent and refusal that take diverse manifestations. As the avatar Citizen Four, Edward Snowden's self-immolation in the world of national security certainly served as a catalyst for awareness.

There is no IoT outside of a surveillance network. The hacks, the points of resistance, the increased awareness of how such information systems behave are the best options if one is to imagine a *free agent* within the context of pervasive mediation and ubiquitous computing. If machines are now part of a sensing system, increasingly interpreting sense and sensibility, then the differential rests with an ability to be a good actor—that is, decorous *and* contentious, working toward comprehension. "Smart" is shorthand for outsourcing information and responsibility. If intelligence implies *an act of interpretation*, then we have an opportunity at this turning point to discern between convenience (what looks like more free services) and engagement (what looks like more hard work). Otherwise, we will indeed always be crashing in the same car.

References

Anzelmo, E., A. Bassi, D. Caprio, S. Dodson, R. van Kranenburg, and M. Ratto. (2011) "Discussion Paper on the Internet of Things," Berlin, Germany: Alexander von Humboldt Institute for Internet and Society.

AT&T (n.d.) "Unlock Phone or Tablet," retrieved from www.att.com/esupport/article.html#!/wireless/KM1008728.

Coleman, B. (2011) *Hello Avatar: Rise of the Networked Generation*, Cambridge, MA: MIT Press.

Coleman, B. (2012) "Everything Is Animated," Special Issue on "Animation and Automation," *Body & Society* 18(1), 79–98.

Doctorow, C. (2015) "Art, Design, and the Future of Privacy," Panel held at *Pioneer Works*, September 17, retrieved from boingboing.net/2015/09/09/nyc-to-do-art-design-and.html.

EPoSS (2008) "Beyond RFID—The Internet of Things," retrieved from www.smart-systems-integration.org/public.

Greenberg, A. (2015) "Hackers Remotely Kill a Jeep on the Highway—with Me in It," *Wired*, retrieved from www.wired.com/2015/07/hackers-remotely-kill-jeep-highway.

Haraway, D. (1988) "Situated Knowledges: The Science Question in Feminism and the Privilege of Partial Perspective," *Feminist Studies* 14(3), 575–99.

Hemment, D. and A. Townsend (2015) "Here Come the Smart Citizens," in D. Hemment and A. Townsend (eds.) *Smart Citizens*. Manchester, UK: Future Everything Publications, pp. 1–3.

Lomas, N. (2014) "UK Menswear Brand, The Affair, Wants to Make Privacy Tech a Fashion Statement," *TechCrunch*, retrieved from techcrunch.com/2014/09/04/unpocket.

Semmelhack, P. (2013) *Social Machines: How to Develop Connected Products that Change Customers' Lives*, New York, NY: Wiley.

Sterling, B. (2014) *The Epic Struggle of the Internet of Things*, Kindle Edition, Moscow, Russia: Strelka Press.

Weiner, N. (1965) *Cybernetics: Or Control and Communication in the Animal and the Machine*, 2nd edn, Cambridge, MA: MIT Press.

Weiser, M. (1991) "The Computer for the 21st Century," *Scientific American* September, 94–104.

Williams-Grut, O. (2015) "Apple's iPhone: The Most Profitable Product in History," *Independent*, retrieved from www.independent.co.uk/news/business.

Wolfe, C. (2009) *What Is Posthumanism?* Minneapolis, MN: University of Minnesota Press.

Part III

MEDIATION, METHOD, MATERIALITY

22
APPROACHING SOUND

Tara Rodgers

> I am sitting in a room different from the one you are in now. I am recording the sound of my speaking voice and I am going to play it back into the room again and again until the resonant frequencies of the room reinforce themselves so that any semblance of my speech, with perhaps the exception of rhythm, is destroyed . . .
>
> (Chadabe 1997: 75)

So begins the voice of Alvin Lucier in a 1980 recording of his composition, *I Am Sitting in a Room* (1969), a prominent work in electronic and experimental music history. As heralded by these opening words, Lucier's recording unfolds over 40 or so minutes, with 32 iterations of the spoken text played back into a particular room—the living room of his house in Middletown, Connecticut (Lovely Music n.d.; Lucier 1980: 37). Lucier played each iteration of the recording into the room, re-recorded it with a microphone onto tape, and then spliced these together in sequence. The "resonant frequencies of the room"—the pitches reproduced most prominently because of a room's dimensions and materials—gradually transform, and eventually take over, the distinct contours of Lucier's voice and words If a listener does not know the premise of this composition and starts the recording 30 or more minutes in, the sounds seem more akin to haunting oscillations of a pipe organ or accordion than to the deliberate intonations of a male speaking voice that set the piece in motion (Lucier 1990). The material qualities of the room and tape medium are central to how this project is conceived; the rhythms and irregularities of Lucier's speaking voice also contribute unique dimensions to the composition, even as the sounds grow more abstract.

The score for *I Am Sitting in a Room* includes the text to be read as well as instructions for performing the piece with two tape recorders, a microphone, and a loudspeaker (Lucier 1980: 30–31). Over the years, many artists have performed and re-interpreted it. Recent variations demonstrate how digital audio coding formats, such as MP3 compression, transform sound quality in ways analogous to the effects of room ambience and tape recording that Lucier explored in his original composition (Sterne n.d.). A key artistic contribution of Lucier's piece—the captivating thing that keeps it relevant—is that the repetition of the exercise exposes auditory processes and effects that are barely discernable in everyday encounters with sound and shows how these physical phenomena can inspire creativity. I reference *I Am Sitting in a Room* at the outset of this chapter precisely because it encapsulates key issues confronted by soundmakers and theorists: relationships and boundaries between sounds and other sounds, bodies and audio technologies, sounds and spaces, self and others.

I am writing this essay on a laptop that serves not only as a tool for writing but also as a hub of my own soundmaking practice (Rodgers 2015b). (I use "soundmaking" and "soundmaker" to refer to diverse ways of working creatively with sound, such as music performance and production, DJing, circuit bending, sound art, and design.) You are sitting in a room or inhabiting an environment different from the one I am in now, undoubtedly with new or different ways of working with sound at your disposal. Creative practices and available tools vary over time with complex cultural forces that result in technological change, and always with each soundmaker's cultural location and identity. The intersections of such factors as race, gender, geographic location, ability, and socioeconomic status inform access to resources, the amount of time available for creative pursuits, and the aesthetic contours of sonic expressions. For this volume on media studies and digital humanities, then, I write from a particular time and cultural location in the spirit of Lucier's *I Am Sitting in a Room*, attempting to elucidate creative approaches to sound that address enduring questions and concepts even as particular soundmaking tools and practices vary widely, and eventually become obsolete or inaccessible.

The Materiality of Sound

The title and implicit theme of this essay, "Approaching Sound," carries a dual meaning. First, it refers to ways of thinking about sound that provide a foundation for creative projects and practices. Read with a different inflection, the phrase *approaching sound* also acknowledges the physical reality that sound is always approaching us. This is well encapsulated by a common illustration in audio textbooks that shows a human figure on the receiving end of sound waves bouncing around a room, with their directions indicated by arrows (Huber & Runstein 1997: 48; White 2006). Scenes of approaching sound are not always so tidy or implicitly pleasurable; for example, music has been used by the U.S. military as a means of torture, and the impact of sound in contexts of war or policing—such as a bomb exploding in close proximity—can have immediate and devastating effects on the body even before this sensory experience is interpreted as sound (Cusick 2008; Daughtry 2012; Goodman 2012).

Sound consists of audible vibrations that are "a dynamic patterning propagated through a medium . . . a transitory event in time" (Henriques 2011: xvii). In part because of its perceived ephemerality, sound in Western philosophy and cultures is "constantly subjugated to the primacy of the visual, associated with emotion and subjectivity as against the objectivity and rationality of vision . . . in essence, fundamentally secondary to our relationship to the world and to dominant ways of understanding it" (Hilmes 2005: 249; see also Sterne 2003: 1–5). This cultural primacy of the visual infiltrates many aspects of daily life, often in subtle ways. Note that *seeing* stands in for *understanding* in the phrase, "I can see why." Feminist theorists have shown how visual technologies and techniques have bolstered claims to scientific objectivity and fortified uneven distributions of power (Haraway 1988). In one contemporary example of this, biometric technologies used by government agencies to identify and classify citizens—like body scanners at airports—often have an effect of further marginalizing and criminalizing vulnerable populations (Magnet 2011). Such visual technologies and techniques are predicated on the distancing of a knowing subject (in this case, the state and its agents) from bodies under surveillance, which consolidates and sustains power by concealing its modes of operation.

Vibrations—including that specific class of audible vibrations experienced as sound—present alternative ways of apprehending reality that can point toward political sensibilities that emphasize complexity, interconnection, and interdependence rather than modes of distancing and control. Indeed, philosophers have taken up the concept of vibration to reimagine boundaries between things, and between subjects and objects, because vibration "moves material, and moves through material," and it "can move simultaneously through subjects as well as objects, bridging internal and external worlds" (Trower 2012: 6, 8–9). To flesh out these concepts, we can turn to musicians and composers who have elaborated theories of listening that promote a politics of reflexivity and interconnection. Evelyn Glennie, a virtuosic percussionist and composer who is profoundly deaf, has developed a creative practice and philosophy of hearing based on sensing vibrations throughout the whole body. Glennie claims, "Hearing is basically a specialized form of touch," and her accounts of hearing emphasize the interconnectedness of sight, sound, and touch, as well as the intimate interplay of bodies and musical instruments (1993, 2003). She implies that those who are able to hear well through the ears actually limit significantly their experience of sound (and of the world) by not attending to the myriad ways that vibrations register throughout the body. While Glennie emphasizes whole-body dynamics of sensing sound, the composer Pauline Oliveros's practice of Deep Listening centers on expanding attentiveness to sounds as they are perceived "both acoustically and psychologically" (2005: xxii). Deep Listening can inform improvisation, composition, and being in the world; it aims to expand "attentional dynamics" to sound so that "one is connected to the whole of the environment and beyond" (xxiii). Oliveros has long cultivated expanded consciousness of sound; in *Sonic Images*, a series of prompts first presented in 1972, she asks, "Who is very familiar to you? Could you recognize this person only by the sound of her or his footsteps?" (1984: 52). By challenging her audience to consider how well they know someone by subtle auditory cues alone, Oliveros calls into question cultural tendencies to privilege visual ways of knowing.

Sound Relations: Embodiment, Identity, and Community

To the extent that we are able to isolate "sound itself" as a distinct phenomenon, we can say that it embodies and catalyzes a diffuse set of relations. An artist and critic, Brandon LaBelle, offers a cogent summary:

> Sound is intrinsically and unignorably relational: it emanates, propagates, communicates, vibrates, and agitates; it leaves a body and enters others; it binds and unhinges, harmonizes and traumatizes; it sends the body moving, the mind dreaming, the air oscillating.
>
> (LaBelle 2008: ix)

What happens when sounds are "made?" Textbook accounts are a good place to start; core ideas are remarkably consistent over the last century and document stories of sound that are common in audio-technical cultures. A 1965 *Life Science Library* text explains:

> Sound originates when a body moves back and forth rapidly enough to send a wave coursing through the medium in which it is vibrating. But sound as a sensation must be received by the ear and passed on to the brain, where it can be registered as an event taking place in the world about the listener.
>
> (Stevens et al. 1965: 10)

Over the course of a day, the ear, brain, and/or other parts of the body register proximate and distant vibrations of such elements as another's vocal cords, the wings or legs of insects, strings on a guitar, mechanical vibrations of passing vehicles, or various digital sounds made audible from the realm of zeros and ones by a digital-to-analog converter on a computer or mobile device. Most of us are routinely exposed to such sounds and sounding bodies as a transitory assemblage. The sound and performance artist, Laetitia Sonami (2004), has said that when she began to work with sound creatively, one of the first things she did was to develop an active-listening exercise: writing down each sound she heard to learn to recognize sounds in isolation from and in relation to one another (see also rsitoy 2015). Sound enrolls the listening body in a web of material connections that transect boundaries of subjects, species, organic and inorganic matter, and bodily interiors and exteriors. Sonami's exercise suggests a way to document one's location within a complex environment connected and transected by sound.

While sound is a formidable material force, it is also "a potent and necessary means for accessing and understanding the world . . . it leads away from itself" (Kahn, cited in Sterne 2012b: 6). Sound's relational aspects and propensities are what make it resoundingly political. Sounds that are organized into music compositions and performances present audible relations of individual elements to complex wholes that provide powerful metaphors through which we can make sense of our selves and relationships to others. Sonic and musical patterns are "an abstraction of the social" (Shank 2014: 244) and also "participate in social formation" (McClary 1991: 7): we learn who we are as socially differentiated bodies and subjects in part through our engagements with sound and music. Because sound is felt by the body in complex ways, it holds particular power to move us physically, emotionally, intellectually, and politically:

> We confront our own bodies through the experience of patterned sounds, and we confront the bodies of others through our interpretations of those patterned sounds . . . [O]ur sense of the social is necessarily affected.
>
> (Shank 2014: 246)

Anyone who has joined with others in voicing a collective chant or cheer at a sporting event or political rally, or who has felt empowered by the sonic rush of a high-volume concert, has sensed this process by which sound and music elicit embodied experiences of identity and community.

Being in the presence of others is, of course, not a requirement for sensing sound and music's meaningful depths and political possibilities. Listening privately to recorded music is a common way that many listeners encounter social differences, such as differences of race and culture, for the first time. Music and songs activate the imagination as "almost-places of cultural encounter that may not be physical places but nevertheless exist in their own auditory somewhere" (Kun 2005: 2–3). Some listeners may use such auditory encounters as prompts for examining their own cultural location, but such reflexivity is certainly not a given. Imani Perry, an interdisciplinary scholar of race and culture, has analyzed how the consumption of hip hop by some white suburban men is an extension of longstanding, problematic patterns in the U.S. of white appropriation of African American music and culture. While suburban white teens may identify their own feelings of social isolation or frustration with elements of hip hop sounds, lyrics, and styles, Perry notes that their circumstances are "an individualized and modest parallel" to the structural racism, economic discrimination, and ever-present threat of violence faced by Black men:

> The question is whether the use of hip hop will remain purely selfish or will translate to a generation of whites who as adults will have a politics that addresses the frustration of broader social marginalization of African Americans.
>
> (Perry 2004: 126)

In some contexts, listening to recorded music alone or with others can foster productive senses of connection and belonging. For example, Susan Driver's research on queer girls and popular culture proposes that music's unique combination of sonic, kinetic, verbal, and non-verbal modes of signification make it "a vital tool in shaping queer youth self-perceptions, imaginative longings, and political commitments" (2007: 196). Jenna, one of her informants, explains:

> Walking around listening to [Le Tigre's] queer music on my headphones sometimes feels like I'm wearing armor . . . it kind of protects me from the straight world I live and work in, especially if I'm having a bad day.
>
> (Driver 2007: 226)

With these examples in mind, we might think of listening bodies as sonic-political transducers. *Transduction* refers to the conversion of one form of acoustic energy into another by microphones, loudspeakers, and even parts of the ear—such as when an electrical signal becomes an audible sound wave as it passes through the technology of a loudspeaker (Huber & Runstein 1997: 20–22). Transduction serves as a useful metaphor for what both Imani Perry and Jenna describe (see also Keeling 2013 and Helmreich 2015). Sound and music are absorbed by individuals—with varying modes of consciousness and interpretation—and then converted into kinetic and social modes of engaging with others, with the potential to mobilize various kinds of political work in the world.

Sound Limits and Parameters

What are sound's limits? We can approach this question in a few different ways. First, perceptions of sounds are contingent upon the bodies of beholders and relations among them. As the sound artist Bill Fontana notes, "a sound is all the possible ways there are to hear it" (n.d.; see also LaBelle 2008: 235). Sound studies scholar Jonathan Sterne elaborates:

> [T]he boundary between sound and not-sound is based on the understood possibilities of the faculty of hearing—whether we are talking about a person or a squirrel. Therefore, as people and squirrels change, so too will sound.
>
> (Sterne 2003: 11–12)

The range of frequencies associated with "normal" human hearing (20 to 20,000 Hz) varies widely among human subjects according to environmental context as well as physical ability, which changes for everyone over time due to such factors as illness, exposure to sound, and age. And, while we likely have a mental image of an ear that is particular to the ears we see on ourselves and companion species, the ear as a sound-sensing organ takes myriad shapes and locations on the bodies of other species—such as on the abdomens and legs of common insects ("Vibrational Communication" 2011; "Listen Up" 2012).

Capacious definitions of sound might accommodate a multispecies vibrational ecology that is felt across this diversity of ears; more bounded approaches to sound seek to understand one species' (or one culture's or community's) auditory norms and communication practices. David Dunn (1992, 1996, 2001; Dunn & van Peer 1999) has explored interspecies communication in many of his sound works: for example, by staging a duet outdoors between an analog electronic oscillator and a mockingbird, and by using underwater recordings to amplify for human listeners the complexity of sonic communication in "the emergent mind of the pond."

Maryanne Amacher (1999) took a different approach in her compositions and performances, mining the limits and idiosyncrasies of human auditory perception. Amacher researched and produced what she called "third ear music," in which an avalanche of frequencies played at an extremely high volume triggers the perceptual phenomenon of oto-acoustic emissions—meaning that listeners' ears seem to emit sounds while also receiving them (see also Amacher 2008 and Ouzounian 2006).

A soundmaker's palette encompasses various parameters of sound, such as frequency, loudness, duration, and timbre, and it is not surprising to find sonic experimentalists working at the edges and extremes of these parameters. Like Amacher, who pushed at the limits of sound frequency and loudness, others have creatively explored parameters such as duration and timbre. Many of Eliane Radigue's (2003) compositions embody extremes of duration, using sustained tones of the ARP 2500 synthesizer that evolve slowly with barely discernable modulations of harmonics over time (see also Guitton 2009). Radigue works on what she calls the "inside of a sound"—making subtle and precise changes to timbre while the overall composition coalesces around what seems to be one long sound, fueled by its relative constancy of pitch (Rodgers 2010: 54–60). Antye Greie (aka AGF) recounts a story that Radigue once gave her an assignment to work on a single sound in the studio for four days—cultivating a level of craft that challenges the typically fast-moving pace of digital audio editing (Rodgers 2010: 214). On the other end of the duration spectrum, *microsound* aesthetics and practices "treat sound as collections of infinitesimally small particles" (Demers 2010: 71). Iannis Xenakis's *Concret PH* (1958), an early work in this area, was assembled from very short fragments on tape of the sounds of burning charcoal. Contemporary explorations of microsound employ granular synthesis software to amass evolving soundscapes from detailed variations to the pitch, speed, and timbre of extremely small sound fragments in succession (Chadabe 1997: 34–35; Demers 2010: 71–74; see also Price 2005; Carlson 2015). John Cage's *4′33″* (1952) is a well-known composition that innovated in areas of loudness and duration, by embracing silence as a central element (calling attention to the many incidental sounds in a concert hall) and using structured segments of sound and silence (calling attention to the function of duration in music composition) (Chadabe 1997: 25). For examples of explorations at the outer edges of timbre—the harmonic or textural quality of sound that makes the same note played on two different instruments sound distinct from each other—we can look to some contemporary hip hop producers who "work in the red," pushing bass frequencies until they distort in particular ways (Rose 1994: 74–78), and to noise musicians' creative uses of feedback and circuit-bent devices so that "'unimagined sounds happen'" in each performance (Novak 2013: 153–61).

Sound is also delimited by its media of transmission, the acoustic spaces in which it resonates, and the constraints of sound reproduction technologies that play it back. Lucier's *I Am Sitting in a Room* exemplifies how media (such as tape) and acoustic spaces transform the experience of sound. There are many other common examples of these phenomena, such as the reverberant effects of singing in the shower or the eerie sense of quiet brought about by a fresh snowfall to an otherwise bustling neighborhood (Exploratorium n.d.; Fallik 2005). As for how audio technologies frame what we hear, the recording engineer Jamie Tate (2013) playfully depicts this dynamic in his cartoon, "Modern Recording," which illustrates how tens and even hundreds of thousands of dollars' worth of high-end audio equipment are routinely used in professional studios to record music that eventually gets played back through a 99-cent MP3 file and $12 earbuds that reproduce only a fraction of the range of frequencies captured by the recording (see also Sterne 2012a). If we listen through those earbuds in an environment with considerable ambient noise, such as on a subway ride, the range of audible frequencies is limited even further. In arguably every instance, to attend to sound by listening or feeling its vibrations is to discover how it is ever interdependent with its material and social contexts.

Conclusion: Sound Knowledges in the Making

Every time we cut and paste a piece of an audio file in a digital audio workstation, or reach for a knob on a synthesizer, what we know about sound in that moment is informed by a range of historical and cultural factors. Knowledge of sound circulates in audio-technical discourse and also resides within musical instruments and sounds themselves: "Every field of sonic practice is partially shaped by a set of knowledges of sound that it motivates, utilizes and operationalizes" (Sterne 2012b: 9). Consider the simple wave shapes on a synthesizer interface that mark the kinds of sounds that emerge. Wave metaphors, integral to audio-technical language, are ancient concepts that were sustained by a Euro-American cultural milieu at the turn of the twentieth century in which fascinations with the sea abounded. Writers of acoustics textbooks aligned the physical properties of sound waves with the connotations of fluidity and excess associated with female bodies throughout Western history and philosophy. Late-nineteenth- and early-twentieth-century narratives in acoustics texts also employed themes of maritime voyage, in which the experiential navigation and technological control of sound waves reflected a masculinist and colonialist imagination. Adorned with simple wave shapes and marketed with names like "Odyssey" and "Voyager," modern synthesizers bear traces of this history, while the subjects at the center of electronic music histories—white and male composer/technologists—inherit a certain legacy of the archetypal, intrepid explorer who is tossed by, and must tame, the unruly seas (Rodgers 2016). Along similar lines, Andra McCartney (1995) has documented pervasive metaphors of domination and control in electroacoustic music and shown how some women composers have adopted alternative ways of characterizing their work. The ways that audio technologies are shaped by gender and other modalities of identity "is, at least in part, a discursive process; . . . it unfolds as part of the verbal and textual interactions that accompany music production," whether in the studio or in print or online forums (Porcello 2005: 276; see also Porcello 2004; Tamarisa 2014).

And yet, the fact that linguistic modes of description do not fully capture sonic communications has sparked many novel methods of music notation and creation. Anthony Braxton (1985) has innovated a diagrammatic scheme of music notation, using letters, numbers, shapes, drawings, and colors, with philosophies and meanings elaborated in his *Tri-Axium Writings* (Tri-Centric Foundation 2014). Fred Frith (1999) provided instructions to groups of improvisers for interpreting photographs of inanimate objects; the resulting music is presented on his album *Stone Brick Glass Wood Wire* (see also Sauer 2009 for an extensive collection of graphic scores). These examples illustrate the capacious symbolic imaginary of sonic expression (and the complexity of audio-visual relations) that extends beyond the constraints of descriptive terms.

As soundmakers and sound students, then, we should be attuned to how historically and culturally specific metaphors and descriptive language frame our knowledge of sound, as well as to sound's potential for complex communications of its own kind. Instruments and interfaces are often where these two trajectories join forces: technological designs crystallize sound knowledge into material forms that, in turn, generate more sounds. Knowing an instrument's history and interrogating the logic of its design can be a productive starting point for creative interruption and innovation. The form of late-twentieth-century analog synthesizers—with oscillator, amplifier, and filter components respectively devoted to the modulation of loudness, pitch, and timbre—is indebted to Hermann von Helmholtz's nineteenth-century theories of perception that analogized this tripartite structure of sound to the properties of color: brightness, hue, and saturation (Rodgers 2015a: 216–17). Many digital audio tools continue to remediate analog styles, such as the graphical user interfaces that resemble analog mixers and software effects processors that are decorated with virtual wood paneling; these older interfaces often persist because they are familiar and remain marketable. But for every software interface that resembles a traditional multi-track mixer with separate channels and faders for each sound, a soundmaker might develop a wholly different visual and tactile method for combining and controlling sounds, based on alternate histories or theories of sound and instrument design, or on other sources of inspiration (see Rodgers 2010: 139–55).

Sound is both a carrier of cultural knowledge and an expressive medium modulated by individual and collaborative creativity. Annea Lockwood's (1989) "sound map" compositions, which combine the sounds of rivers and recorded interviews with people whose lives are shaped by rivers, exemplify this. Listening to a river and how it moves can reveal ecological complexity as well as the cultural and economic histories of a particular location (Rodgers 2010: 114–27). Lockwood's choices of microphones, interview subjects, and recording locations in and around the rivers frame these sonic narratives in specific ways.

The soundmakers' ideas and work I highlight throughout this chapter provide a sampling of creative methods for approaching sound. These methods include attentive listening, modulating sonic parameters and pushing at their limits, experimenting with notation, and interrogating conventions of instrument design. Along the way, cultural theories and analyses teach us about the various ways that sounds, audio technologies, and listening practices have histories and politics.

In my own work, soundmaking generates questions that I try to answer with historical research and cultural analysis; that research and writing, in turn, lends a deeper understanding of the issues and stakes in my creative practice. I also appreciate the argument by the musician and educator, Michael Bierylo, that soundmaking and critical writing can be two separate and analogous projects. In an interview on designing the music production curriculum at Berklee, Bierylo describes how a "track" of music produced for a course in that program functions like a "term paper" elsewhere: "Being able to produce your musical idea is essential to sharing and communicating that idea. The production is part of the process of creation . . . in both subtle and sophisticated ways" (Ableton 2015). Soundmaking and writing may share a common purpose of communicating a concept or argument, yet each emerges from a distinct set of practices—a craft that can be learned and innovated. Approaching sound through both of these critical and creative ways of working can uncover its complex expressive and political power.

Further Reading

Born, G. (1995) *Rationalizing Culture: IRCAM, Boulez, and the Institutionalization of the Musical Avant-Garde*, Berkeley: University of California Press.

Davies, H. (2002) "Electronic Instruments: Classifications and Mechanisms," in H. -J. Braun (ed.) *Music and Technology in the Twentieth Century*, Baltimore, MD: Johns Hopkins University Press, pp. 43–58.

Oram, D. (1972) *An Individual Note of Music, Sound, and Electronics*, London: Galliard.

References

Ableton: Artists (2015) "Berklee's Michael Bierylo on Designing a Modern Music Curriculum," retrieved from ableton.com/en/blog/michael-bierylo-designing-music-curriculum.

Amacher, M. (2008) "Psychoacoustic Phenomena in Musical Composition: Some Features of a 'Perceptual Geography,'" in J. Zorn (ed.) *Arcana III: Musicians on Music*, New York, NY: Hips Road/Tzadik, pp. 9–24.

Braxton, A. (1985) *Tri-Axium Writings, vol. 1–3,* Lebanon, NH: Frog Peak Music.

Carlson, C. (2015) *Borderlands Granular*, retrieved from www.borderlands-granular.com/app.

Chadabe, J. (1997) *Electric Sound: The Past and Promise of Electronic Music*, Upper Saddle River, NJ: Prentice Hall.

Cusick, S. G. (2008) "'You are in a place that is out of the world . . .': Music in the Detention Camps of the 'Global War on Terror,'" *Journal of the Society for American Music* 2(1), 1–26.

Daughtry, J. M. (2012) "Belliphonic Sounds and Indoctrinated Ears: The Dynamics of Military Listening in Wartime Iraq," in E. Weisbard (ed.) *Pop When the World Falls Apart: Music in the Shadow of Doubt*, Durham, NC and London: Duke University Press, pp. 111–44.

Demers, J. (2010) *Listening through the Noise: The Aesthetics of Experimental Electronic Music*, New York, NY: Oxford University Press.

Driver, S. (2007) "'Your Music Changed My Life. I Needed Something Queer': Musical Passion, Politics, and Communities," in *Queer Girls and Popular Culture: Reading, Resisting, and Creating Media*, New York, NY: Peter Lang, pp. 195–232.

Dunn, D. (2001) "Nature, Sound Art, and the Sacred," in D. Rothenberg and M. Ulvaeus (eds.) *The Book of Music and Nature: An Anthology of Sounds, Words, Thoughts*, Middletown, CT: Wesleyan University Press, pp. 95–107.

Dunn, D., with R. van Peer. (1999) "Music, Language and Environment," *Leonardo Music Journal* 9, 63–67.

Exploratorium. (n.d.) "Why Does My Singing Sound So Great in the Shower?" retrieved from www.exploratorium.edu/music/questions/shower.html.

Fallik, D. (2005) "Researchers Keep Ear to the Snow," *Philadelphia Inquirer*, retrieved from articles.philly.com/2005–02–22/news/25444409_1_new-fallen-acoustics-snow.

Fontana, B. (n.d.) "Listen to Sound Sculpture Excerpts," *Bill Fontana website*, resoundings.org/Pages/possible%20ways%20copy.html.

Glennie, E. (1993) "Hearing Essay," retrieved from www.evelyn.co.uk/hearing-essay.

Goodman, S. (2012) *Sonic Warfare: Sound, Affect, and the Ecology of Fear*, Cambridge, MA: MIT Press.

Haraway, D. J. (1988) "Situated Knowledges: The Science Question in Feminism and the Privilege of Partial Perspective," *Feminist Studies* 14(3), 575–99.

Helmreich, S. (2015) "Transduction," in D. Novak and M. Sakakeeny (eds.) *Keywords in Sound*, Durham, NC and London: Duke University Press, pp. 222–31.

Henriques, J. (2011) *Sonic Bodies: Reggae Sound Systems, Performance Techniques and Ways of Knowing*, London: Continuum.

Hilmes, M. (2005) "Is There a Field Called Sound Culture Studies? And Does It Matter?" *American Quarterly* 57(1), 249–59.

Huber, D. M. and Runstein, R. E. (1997) *Modern Recording Techniques*, 5th edn, Boston, MA: Focal Press.

Keeling, K. (2013) "Electric Feel," *Cultural Studies* 28(1), 49–83.

Kun, J. (2005) "Introduction: Strangers among Sounds," *Audiotopia: Music, Race, and America*, Berkeley, CA: University of California Press, pp. 1–28.

LaBelle, B. (2008) *Background Noise: Perspectives on Sound Art*, London: Continuum.

"Listen Up: Crickets Have Had Ears on Their Legs for More Than 50 Million Years" (2012) *University of Colorado Boulder News Center*, retrieved from www.colorado.edu/news/features/listen-crickets-have-had-ears-their-legs-more-50-million-years.

Lovely Music, Ltd. (n.d.) "Titles: Alvin Lucier; I Am Sitting in a Room," retrieved from www.lovely.com/titles/cd1013.html.

Lucier, A. (1980) *Chambers: Scores by Alvin Lucier; Interviews with the Composer by Douglas Simon*, Middletown, CT: Wesleyan University Press.

Magnet, S. (2011) *When Biometrics Fail: Gender, Race, and the Technology of Identity*, Durham, NC and London: Duke University Press.

McCartney, A. (1995) "Inventing Images: Constructing and Contesting Gender in Thinking about Electroacoustic Music," *Leonardo Music Journal* 5, 57–66.

McClary, S. (1991) *Feminine Endings: Music, Gender, and Sexuality*, Minnesota, MN: University of Minnesota Press.

Novak, D. (2013) *Japanoise: Music at the Edge of Circulation*, Durham, NC and London: Duke University Press.

Oliveros, P. (1984) "Sonic Images," in *Software for People: Collected Writings, 1963–1980*, Baltimore, MD: Smith Publications, pp. 52–54.

Oliveros, P. (2005) *Deep Listening: A Composer's Sound Practice*, New York, NY: iUniverse.

Ouzounian, G. (2006) "Embodied Sound: Aural Architectures and the Body," *Contemporary Music Review* 25(1/2, February/April), 69–79.
Perry, I. (2004) *Prophets of the Hood: Politics and Poetics in Hip Hop*, Durham and London: Duke University Press.
Porcello, T. (2004) "Speaking of Sound: Language and the Professionalization of Sound-Recording Engineers." *Social Studies of Science* 34(5), 733–58.
Porcello, T. (2005) "Afterword," in P. D. Greene and T. Porcello (eds.) *Wired for Sound: Engineering and Technologies in Sonic Cultures*, Middletown: Wesleyan University Press, pp. 269–79.
Price, S. (2005) "Granular Synthesis: How It Works and Ways to Use It," *Sound on Sound*, retrieved from www.soundonsound.com/sos/dec05/articles/granularworkshop.htm.
Rodgers, T. (2010) *Pink Noises: Women on Electronic Music and Sound*, Durham and London: Duke University Press.
Rodgers, T. (2015a) "Synthesis," in D. Novak and M. Sakakeeny (eds.) *Keywords in Sound*, Durham and London: Duke University Press.
Rodgers, T. (2015b) *Analog Tara / Pink Noises*, retrieved from www.analogtara.net.
Rodgers, T. (2016) "Toward a Feminist Epistemology of Sound: Refiguring Waves in Audio-Technical Discourse," in M. Rawlinson (ed.) *Engaging the World: Thinking after Irigaray*, SUNY Press.
Rose, T. (1994) *Black Noise: Rap Music and Black Culture in Contemporary America*, Hanover and London: Wesleyan University Press.
Sauer, T. (2009) *Notations 21*, New York, NY: Mark Batty.
Shank, B. (2014) *The Political Force of Musical Beauty*, Durham and London: Duke University Press.
Sonami, L. (2004) Interview with the author, 8 May.
Sterne, J. (2003) *The Audible Past: Cultural Origins of Sound Reproduction*, Durham and London: Duke University Press.
Sterne, J. (2012a). *MP3: The Meaning of a Format*, Durham and London: Duke University Press.
Sterne, J. (2012b) "Introduction to Sonic Imaginations," in J. Sterne (ed.) *The Sound Studies Reader*, New York: Routledge, pp. 1–17.
Stevens, S. S., F. Warshofsky, and the editors of *Life*. (1965) *Sound and Hearing*, New York: Time Incorporated, Life Science Library.
Tamarisa, A. (2014) "Muff Wiggler: Sexism in Audio Cultures," *Bluestockings Magazine*, retrieved from bluestockings-mag.com/2014/04/17/muff-wiggler-sexism-in-audio-cultures.
Tate, J. (2013) "Just for Fun," *Rukkus Room Studios*, retrieved from www.rukkusroom.com/Fun.html.
Tri-Centric Foundation. (2014) "Braxton Musical Systems," *The Tri-Centric Foundation*, retrieved from tricentric foundation.org/musical-systems.
Trower, S. (2012) *Senses of Vibration: A History of the Pleasure and Pain of Sound*, London: Continuum.
"Vibrational Communication in Insects and Spiders" (2011) *Map of Life*, University of Cambridge, retrieved from www.mapoflife.org/topics/topic_584_Vibrational-communication-in-insects-and-spiders.
White, Paul. (2006) "The Studio SOS Guide to Monitoring and Acoustic Treatment," *Sound on Sound*, retrieved from www.soundonsound.com/sos/feb06/articles/studiosos.htm.

Audio and Video Examples

Amacher, M. (1999) *Sound Characters (Making the Third Ear)*, Tzadik, CD 7043.
Dunn, D. (1992) *Angels and Insects*, What Next? Recordings, CD WN0009.
Dunn, D. (1996) *Music, Language and Environment*, Innova, CD 508.
Frith, F. (1999) *Stone Brick Glass Wood Wire*, I Dischi di Angelica, CD.
Glennie, E. (2003) "How to Truly Listen," *TED Talk*, February, retrieved from www.ted.com/talks/evelyn_glennie_shows_how_to_listen.
Guitton, M. (2009) *A Portrait of Eliane Radigue* (documentary), retrieved from vimeo.com/8983993.
Lockwood, A. (1989) *A Sound Map of the Hudson River*, Lovely Music, CD 2081.
Lucier, A. (1990) *I Am Sitting in a Room*, Lovely Music, CD 1013.
Radigue, E. (2003) *Geelriandre/Arthesis*, Fringes Recordings, CD Fringes Archive 01.
rsitoy (2015) *the ear goes to the sound: the work of Laetitia Sonami* (documentary), retrieved from earsoundfilm.com.
Sterne, J. (n.d.) "Alvin Lucier Cover," retrieved from sounds.sterneworks.org/projects/alvin-lucier-cover.

23

ALGORHYTHMICS

A Diffractive Approach for Understanding Computation

Shintaro Miyazaki

Knowing how to use, program, and deploy software is a key skill in today's society. It comprises the core of curricula in so-called STEM (science, technology, engineering, and mathematics) disciplines. This chapter offers a critical, humanities-based approach to software that engages the growing importance of algorithms without resorting to wholly affirmative or wholly negative interpretations. I consider this approach "diffractive," instead of reflective, a distinction which I explain further below.

The entry into a critical understanding of digital media, algorithms, and their growing cultural impact often takes place by studying the visible aspects of media aesthetics (Manovich 2013; Bruno 2014; Cubitt 2014). Other approaches examine social networks and their properties through data visualization (Rogers 2013), or they concentrate on alphanumeric code (Cox 2012; Montfort et al. 2012). Similarly, approaches in digital humanities are often focused on textual methods (Berry 2012; Jones 2013; Gardiner & Musto 2015), which are based in visual perception. However, this chapter argues that, for a comprehensive understanding of algorithms and computational culture, it is important to train a nonvisual sensitivity toward information technology. To cultivate this sensitivity, I developed a method called, "algorhythmics," which arose after a playful, heuristic synthesis of *algorithm* with *rhythm* (Miyazaki 2012, 2013a).

Focusing on algorhythmics, this chapter is divided into four sections: the first offers brief definitions and explanations of algorhythmics as a diffractive approach to computational culture; the second presents methods and discusses some benefits of algorhythmics via case studies; the third describes another case study and further addresses the framework required for doing algorhythmics; and the final section offers some recommendations for future directions and extensions.

Algorhythm = Algorithm + Rhythm

"Algorithm" is a term used in computer science that means a finite sequence of step-by-step instructions active in computers as core modules of software. They are procedures mostly for solving a problem or task. Prior to the existence of either computer science or algorithms, Plato defined "rhythm" as a time-based order of movement (1967–1968: 664e–665a), where movement is a material process that can be measured by a technical instrument. Rhythm, then, is an effect of ordering and measurement (Miyazaki 2013a: 136–141). By extension, "algorhythmics" are time-based, technological processes, which occur when matter is modulated by symbolic and logical structures, such as instructions written as code. Algorhythms are the timing effects of computation. Such processes are micro-events, which operate on scales and levels that are usually below or beyond our perceptual threshold. Still, they are ubiquitous and operate across all aspects of our life. They are—as I show below—highly influential, especially in cases where they become dysfunctional.

The synthesis of algorithm with rhythm does not merely merge materialism with immaterialism, signals in circuits with text-based code, the real world with the symbolic world, or physics with mathematics. Rather, it is to be understood as a kind of diffraction or interference pattern (Barad 2007: 71). One easy way to generate such patterns or wave phenomena is by dropping two stones in a pond and observing the resulting ripples on the water surface. They interfere and mix into each other in interesting ways. Similarly, the research fields of algorithmics and rhythmics could positively interfere with each other, still maintaining their specificity and characteristics.

According to Karen Barad and Donna Haraway, diffraction is an alternative to reflection, which is the common term used in conjunction with critical inquiry or critical thinking (Barad 2014: 172). Diffraction happens when moving waves encounter an obstacle or slit that is a size close to their wavelength. The disturbed waves then create new patterns. While a reflective inquiry is based on a change of direction—a returning and mirroring of the thing under study—a diffractive inquiry transforms and bends its subject to create a range of alternative approaches for studying a subject, object, or process (Barad 2007: 89). As a diffractive approach for understanding computational culture, algorhythmics not only looks for interesting patterns across computer science (algorithms) and real-world phenomena (rhythms), but also includes thinking about how to render these often unperceivable processes into sensible phenomena. In this way, it involves bridging research fields where technical measurements are essential with those where human perception and cultures are examined. Algorhythmics is thus more than a recommendation to cultivate a time-based sensitivity toward processes where computation and data are involved; it demands skills and methods to quite literally *make sense* of these processes.

Algorhythmic Sensitivity

Methods of media transformation between the senses are important for practicing algorhythmics. Turning a selection of alphanumeric values (data) into an audible stream of sound (sonification), or transforming these into visible structures on a flat plane (visualization), demonstrates simple procedures of media transformation, which equips and augments human sensitivity with machines and media. In a project called *Algorhythmic Sorting* (2010–11), I collaborated with programmer, Michael T. Chinen, to make a piece of software that let us aurally and visually compare the efficiency and performance of different algorithms while ordering and sorting randomly generated numbers. We could see and listen to "bubble," "merge," "quick," "insertion," "shell," and "heap sort" algorithms. Each generated distinct audible rhythms and visible patterns (see Figure 23.1). This experiment acted as a proof of concept for algorhythmics, since it allows even nonprofessionals to quickly understand how algorithms perform differently, or how algorithms are bound to time and embody different types of timing. Understanding the efficiency and performance of algorithms is crucial to also understanding the sociopolitical and economical aspects of digital cultures, because algorithms are now common components of most infrastructures.

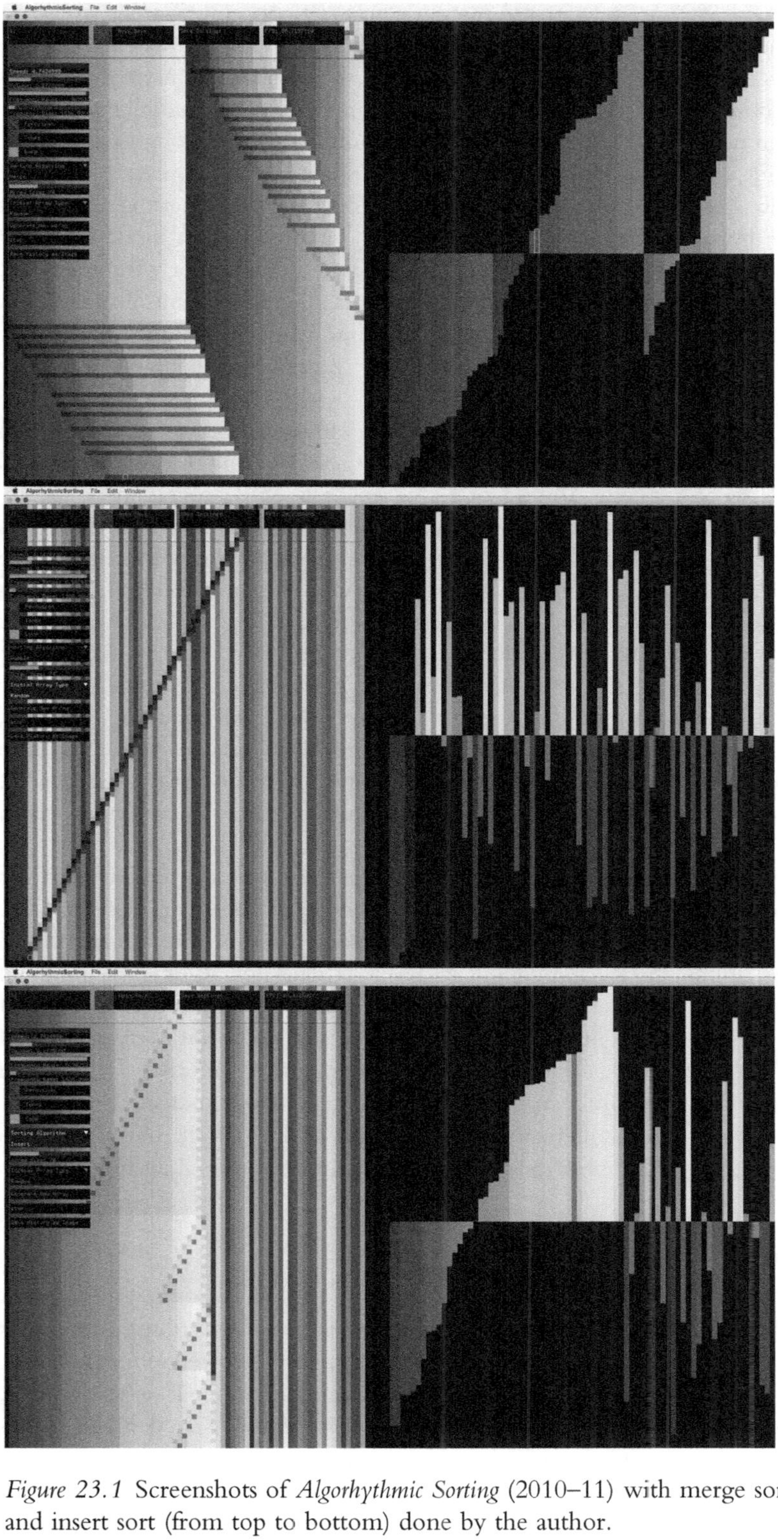

Figure 23.1 Screenshots of *Algorhythmic Sorting* (2010–11) with merge sort, bubble sort, and insert sort (from top to bottom) done by the author.

For another proof of concept, I transformed electromagnetic emissions of operating computing machinery into audible sounds (audification) by amplifying signals coming from long cables and electromagnetic coils. This simple trick lets you hear the material processes of computers and other digital gadgets. Placing a coil connected to an amplifier and loudspeaker near the central processing unit (CPU) of a MacBook Pro reveals a lot of interesting sounds. After loading the desktop, you are able to hear noisy buzzes connected to mouse movements as well as sounds connected to window loading, program starting, and other processes. All these processes correspond with the CPU. The micro-units inside the CPU chip emit small electromagnetic waves, which get transmitted to the coil or wire. These get amplified, and then drive the membrane of the loudspeaker. The movement of the speaker creates pressure differences in the air that we hear as sounds. Most of these fluctuations are too fast to be heard, but some are slow enough that they generate distinguishable rhythms of noise and melody.

In fact, this simple trick was practiced from the late 1940s until the early 1960s during the era of electronic mainframe computing, when the speed of computation was still in the realm of hundreds of kilohertz. Instead of a coil, engineers and programmers directly connected some part of the computer—mostly data busses or parts of storage—to amplifiers and loudspeakers. It was a quick-and-dirty way to get perceivable feedback from otherwise silent machinery (Miyazaki 2012, 2015). Other examples where audible feedback was produced from otherwise silent media include audiocassettes for data storage (1970s), acoustic coupled modems in the early age of preinternet networks (1960s and 1970s), and dial-up internet and telefaxing (1990s). Even the transmission of presumably silent ethernet communication protocols can be turned into streams of algorhythms (Miyazaki 2013a). Also, wireless communications (via Wi-Fi, Bluetooth, GSM, and UMTS) have specific rhythms and fluctuations, which we can listen to with some minor technical effort (Miyazaki 2013b). This is quite useful to understand the coverage of digital wireless networks in urban environments.

In short, algorhythmic sensitivity allows people to experience and understand the structures of a wide variety of key media operations, their fundamental principles, and their timings. This implies a sensorial, nonlinguistic approach to the inner workings of computational gadgetry. Since algorithms operate throughout all levels of data storage, transmission, and processing, algorhythmics builds aesthetic, cultural, and technical competences in areas of computational culture and digital humanities. This is especially important because most of the processes in this realm are usually imperceivable. Algorhythmic sensitivity as a mental state of inquiry might afford new links and reconfigure the understanding of an object under examination, since it provides an alternative to its text-based description. Including these nonlinguistic aspects of digital humanities is highly important for a critical analysis of algorithmic cultures.

Understanding Media with Other Media

Algorithms usually act on hidden micro-levels. Bulks and networks of algorithmic procedures build our technological unconscious (Thrift 2004). Algorithms are involved in management, business, finance, supply chains, logistics, postal systems, air traffic, war, media entertainment, telecommunication, and knowledge production, but they are typically hidden and unimportant—mere tools, services, and means of human control.

The significance of the algorithmic micro-world is often only learned through technological breakdowns with massively hazardous consequences. Crashes of financial markets, e-commerce, communication networks, or power-grids show us that a small mistake in calculation, timing, scheduling, or routing can lead to unforeseen malfunctions. For instance, on January 15, 1990, AT&T's long-distance telephone network in North America crashed and was disabled for 9 hours. The reason for the crash was a small programming mistake implemented via a software update for line-switching computers across the country (Miyazaki 2016). The mistake was written in the programming language C. The update did not act in the intended way, and the timing of the network's operations were thus slightly out of order. The resulting algorhythmics were a sort of stuttering. Rhythms not usually detected by self-monitoring operating systems became effective during the updating process, when the routing maps of a station were actualized. When this happened, the automated shutdown procedure was initialized, and a station would go offline. The first station went offline for unknown reasons. It sent a "go offline now" message to all its neighboring computers. Receiving this message, neighboring stations crashed as well, because they needed to update their routing maps. After a short break of four to six seconds, they would be online again and communicate with neighboring computers. This again caused crashes, as even more computers would update their routing maps. In this way, the crashing and shutdown of the line-switching computers repeated rhythmically, cascading over the entire long-distance telephone network for nearly 9 hours.

This crash is just one example of thousands of algorithmically caused breakdowns one can find in common information sources. Whenever scholars equipped with an algorhythmic sensitivity learn that algorithms were involved in such malfunctions, they might determine which algorithms were responsible and ask themselves how the overall orchestration of these events would sound. Would it have a rhythm? Would it be repetitive? An open and sensitive mindset, which regards things as constantly in flux and also emphasizes the importance of making the unperceivable sensible, might be productive, since it pushes humanities scholars beyond common methodologies framed by reading and writing. Doing algorhythmics involves an interest in understanding media phenomena with different media. Listening to electronic signals via a loudspeaker or making them visible with either an oscilloscope or LEDs are examples of such very basic operations. How would a digital image sound? What does a sound recording look like? What does browsing the net sound like? Even though being sensitive to some aspects of a process—here, timing and rhythms—inevitably reduces or eclipses other modes of perception, such a reduction does not imply that some forms of perception or inquiry are superior to others.

Again, algorhythmics is a diffractive practice, which is open for interferences between low-level re-engineering, technical measurement, and hardware tinkering on one side and critical theory, musicology, theater or film studies, and art history on the other. It is a scholarly gesture of bridging and thus includes both tentative and speculative elements, but also some kind of engagement with the materiality, technicality, and performativity of the matter under study.

Beyond Algorhythmics

The theoretical framework for algorhythmics was strongly influenced by the work of Wolfgang Ernst and his method of media archaeology (Ernst 2011, 2013), but is as well informed by different approaches within media studies, including media ecology, political ecology, and ecological history (Fuller 2005; Bennett 2010; Parikka 2013). As my example of the AT&T crash demonstrates, it is not only crucial to grasp the workings, effects, and rhythms of one algorithm. It is also important to get an idea of the relations and feedback loops involved, such as when algorithms start to interact with each other in unintended ways.

An aesthetics of technological ecosystems—a techno-aesthetics of the twenty-first century—is required, one that does not forget that today's systems consist of millions of interconnected, algorhythmic micro-worlds. The growing ecosystem of intelligent machines and small invisible devices, which are connected to our smart phones, tablets, and laptops, generate a never-ending stream of algorhythmic effects that may influence processes on a planetary level. How do agents affect each other in such ecosystems? How does a trend spread across them? How can we hear and see such trends? How do complex timings and behaviors evolve and emerge in ecosystems? What are the habits of our data-driven society? How do we study their trajectories?

Using algorhythmics to understand computing and grasp how deeply these micro-operations are built into almost all aspects of society might be an important milestone during general education of the future. Equally essential to learn are the ecological consequences of "bad" algorhythmics. A future scenario for education might include a cabinet of curiosities with various algorhythmic models, which explain different layers, levels, and spheres of computation, including their benefits and dangers. Students could use these media to understand other media as well as the relationships between media. We have created a continuously expanding and evolving, heterogeneous new world based on algorithmic structures. To understand its wonders, dangers, futures, and histories is a never-ending, but surely rewarding, task.

Further Reading

Barad, K. M. (2007) *Meeting the Universe Halfway: Quantum Physics and the Entanglement of Matter and Meaning*, Durham, NC: Duke University Press.

Berry, D. M. and M. Dieter (eds.) (2015) *Postdigital Aesthetics: Art, Computation and Design*, New York, NY: Palgrave Macmillan.

Huhtamo, E. and J. Parikka (eds.) (2011) *Media Archaeology: Approaches, Applications, and Implications*, Berkeley, CA: University of California Press.

Mitchell, W. J. T. and M. B. N. Hansen (eds.) (2010) *Critical Terms for Media Studies*, Chicago, IL: University of Chicago Press.

References

Barad, K. M. (2007) *Meeting the Universe Halfway: Quantum Physics and the Entanglement of Matter and Meaning*, Durham, NC: Duke University Press.

Barad, K. M. (2014) "Diffracting Diffraction: Cutting Together-Apart," *Parallax* 20(3), 168–87.

Bennett, J. (2010) *Vibrant Matter: A Political Ecology of Things*, Durham, NC: Duke University Press.

Berry, D. M. (2012) *Understanding Digital Humanities*, New York, NY: Palgrave Macmillan.

Berry, D. M. and M. Dieter (eds.) (2015) *Postdigital Aesthetics: Art, Computation and Design*, New York, NY: Palgrave Macmillan.

Bruno, G. (2014) *Surface: Matters of Aesthetics, Materiality, and Media*, Chicago, IL: University of Chicago Press.

Cox, G. (2012) *Speaking Code: Coding as Aesthetic and Political Expression*, Cambridge, MA: MIT Press.

Cubitt, S. (2014) *The Practice of Light: A Genealogy of Visual Technologies from Prints to Pixels*, Cambridge, MA: MIT Press.

Ernst, W. (2011) "Media Archaeography: Method and Machine versus History and Narrative of Media," in E. Huhtamo and J. Parikka *Media Archaeology: Approaches, Applications, and Implications*, Berkeley, CA: University of California Press, pp. 239–55.

Ernst, W. (2013) *Digital Memory and the Archive*, Minneapolis, MN: University of Minnesota Press.

Fuller, M. (2005) *Media Ecologies: Materialist Energies in Art and Technoculture*, Cambridge, MA: MIT Press.

Gardiner, E. and R. G. Musto (2015) *The Digital Humanities: A Primer for Students and Scholars*, New York, NY: Cambridge University Press.

Jones, S. E. (2013) *The Emergence of the Digital Humanities*, Abingdon, UK: Routledge.

Manovich, L. (2013) *Software Takes Command*, New York/London: Bloomsbury Academic Press.

Mitchell, W. J. T. and M. B. N. Hansen (eds.) (2010) *Critical Terms for Media Studies*, Chicago, IL: University of Chicago Press.

Miyazaki, S. (2012) "Algorhythmics: Understanding Micro-Temporality in Computational Cultures," *Computational Cultures: A Journal of Software Studies* 2, retrieved from computationalculture.net/article/algorhythmics-understanding-micro-temporality-in-computational-cultures.

Miyazaki, S. (2013a) "AlgoRHYTHMS Everywhere—a Heuristic Approach to Everyday Technologies," *Thamyris/Intersecting* 26, 135–48.

Miyazaki, S. (2013b) "Urban Sounds Unheard-of: A Media Archaeology of Ubiquitous Infospheres," *Continuum* 27(4), 514–22.

Miyazaki, S. (2015) "Going Beyond the Visible: New Aesthetic as an Aesthetic of Blindness?" in D. M. Berry and M. Dieter (eds.) *Postdigital Aesthetics: Art, Computation and Design*, New York: Palgrave Macmillan, pp. 219–31.

Miyazaki, S. (2016) "Algorhythmic Ecosystems: Neoliberal Couplings and Their Pathogenesis 1960–Present," in R. Seyfert and J. Roberge (eds.) *Algorithmic Cultures*, Abingdon, Oxfordshire: Routledge, pp. 128–39.

Montfort, N., P. Baudoin, J. Bell, I. Bogost, J. Douglass, M. C. Marino, M. Mateas, C. Reas, M. Sample, and N. Vawter (2012) *10 PRINT CHR$(205.5+RND(1));_: GOTO 10*, Cambridge, MA: MIT Press.

Parikka, J. (2013) "Green Media Times: Friedrich Kittler and Ecological Media History," *Archiv Für Mediengeschichte* 13, 69–78.

Plato (1967–68) *Plato in Twelve Volumes*, Vols. 10, 11, trans. R. G. Bury, Cambridge, MA: Harvard University Press, retrieved from perseus.tufts.edu/hopper/text?doc=urn:cts:greekLit:tlg0059.tlg034.perseus-eng1:2.665.

Rogers, R. (2013) *Digital Methods*, Cambridge, MA: MIT Press.

Thrift, N. (2004) "Remembering the Technological Unconscious by Foregrounding Knowledges of Position," *Environment and Planning D: Society and Space* 22, 175–90.

24

SOFTWARE STUDIES METHODS

Matthew Fuller

What is the consistency of computational culture? What are the ways in which the objects of computer science and its more informal offspring operate in the world? Looking into such issues, it can be readily seen that a cunningly diffuse and multilayered aspect of the question of method is understanding what constitutes the problem. Luckily, for the development of a field such as software studies, computational media cultures are abundantly generative of such things. Problems flourish. From questions about the foundations of computing to the articulation of cultural tendencies and political systems across commodity platforms, via the questions of power, aesthetics, and processes of subjectivity, problems abound, and that is only to mention a few that are properly named as such. Any short survey of methods in the field can therefore only be partial and indicative, picking out a few general trends. The kinds of problems addressed arise, too, at the emergence of software studies at the beginning of this century. However, from such a starting point, software studies has become the grounds for a diversity of methods, concerns, and conceptual and practical resources. This chapter maps a few of these and give some sense of their consistency and trajectories. In this, as a survey, it will necessarily be limited due to the vitality and range of activity in the field. Read it, then, as an aperitif, before investigating further.

To frame the question of the problem, a little genealogy is in order. From a certain set of angles, software studies arises from a background of bemused frustration at the ways in which "high level" media theory would tend toward subsumptive generalization about the "virtual," or about "cyberspace," without attending to the howl and screech of a dial-up modem or the particular dance of pixelated entities among the Graphical User Interface (GUI) that constituted everyday activity in the "knowledge economy." A parallel here can be drawn with software art, which articulated itself in part against the media art and net art that often ignored the specific materials from which it was made, a condition that—as those materials became both increasingly interesting and increasingly overcoded—became untenable. Equally, as social theory drew upon the active constitution of society by systems, media, and tools, alongside those entities that had hitherto been understood to be social, the capacity to recognize what Scott Lash (2002) called "Technological Forms of Life" became pressing. Amid this, too, the imperatives underlying the development of the field are driven by an emphasis on the complexly materialist, fortified by the empiricism of the abstract found in both the more generous reaches of poststructuralist legacies and those aspects of meta-mathematics and computer science that had always recognized the cultural dimensions of their activity.

More recently, software studies finds itself in the curious position of being a scholarly stick-in-the-mud as certain aspects of computational culture become sprinkled like glittery mica on trays of theoretical cupcakes: decorative, indigestible, and garnishing the semiotically retrospective and materially stale. For instance, algorithms are increasingly emphasized as an explanatory actor, although in a surprisingly large quantity of scholarship this explanatory power is asserted without their contextualization within other systems in which they are embedded, and even without ascertaining what an algorithm might be. A scan of the literature shows that it is entirely possible to have a social or literary theorist discourse on "algorithms" without any references other than to others of their ilk. This kind of elective solipsism of disciplines is familiar to those navigating interdisciplinary terrains and is also articulated through the kinds of citation politics that other such fields, such as feminist research, have become all too familiar with (Fábos & Haddad 2013). We are in the amusing position where the emphasis on materiality is elevating technical content to the same kind of generalizations that, say, the more banal pronouncements of postmodernity suffered from in their heyday. Social theory, too, often brings along its upstairs–downstairs split between high theory and empiricism.

There is an art to the interplay between the rigors imposed by attention to material qualities and conditions with all their constraints, limits, and capacities; their specificities and individuations; and those entailed also by the particular epistemic and ontogenetic capacities of abstractions. To address such topics, software studies approaches might characteristically tend to identify specific algorithms, articulate their genealogy, recognize and work with their characteristics, and see them as part of a larger assemblage—one that is not in turn immune to the adventures of conceptual rigor (see Mackenzie 2010). All this requires something of an avidity for research. Such a condition also drives it toward noncanonical texts and sites as sources of interest. This drive in turn is a methodological choice that sets it at a tangent toward theoretical work aiming to array itself solely among well-cited or paternalistically approved books. Showing that one is in dialogue only with those of the correct lineage is a rhetorical technique that has the democratic advantage that the canon is seemingly available to us all, whether we like it or not; but it also may be affected as a technique of foreclosure. Part of this condition is due to the febrile pleasures of academic politics, in which it is assumed that the study of new media has yet to fully establish itself as a legitimate field and, to do so, must exaggeratedly exhibit the habits of conformism and deference special to the various overlapping pyramid schemes that are, among other things, operative in the university.

Another way to frame the question of methods is to partially arrive at it via two fields that contribute to software studies. In different ways, cultural studies and computing both emerged in the aftermath of the Second World War, forged by the necessity for an interdisciplinary bringing together of multiple methods, materials, and problematics. In different times, software studies emerges as a minor mutational fold within these discourses, at the cusp of the inventive enthusiasm of the world wide web and the internet, and the transition to the version of the same which we now inhabit. The various crises and possibilities in knowledge, technology, institutions, and epistemic potential that each of these represents feed into the specific traits of software studies as a field.

With cultural studies, software studies shares a taste for vulgar objects that pass below the threshold of critical perception due to their mundane or tedious nature. Ostensibly boring entities, manuals, slide presentations, and technical specifications are all probed for interesting traces as admixtures of high technology and low theory. Just as crystals grow differently in variable electromagnetic fields, which can in turn be examined through the variations in growth patterns to which they contribute, the relatively "pure" formalisms that software articulates in such materials can also retain interesting patterns of resonance with wider formations.

Relatedly, one may sense into software by the ways it comes into composition with users. And here, ignorance of software's conventions has been highly revealing. It must be possible to read software in a way that is partially naïve, stupid, heading in the wrong direction, mysterious, uninformed by a disciplinary history. To watch a person encounter a machine for the first time is exciting; one might learn from their dissonant interpretation what experienced preconceptions have become. Unfortunately, even with the confusions of users moving between operating systems, today the state of inexperience with computational entities is a rare resource. But there are ways in which it is mobilized, bearing indeed some relation to Jacques Rancière's formulation of the "ignorant," where people learn by moving along in a manner in which "one shouldn't move along—the way children move, blindly, figuring out riddles" (1991: 10). Indeed, given its value, ethnographical techniques have been utilized to capture this moment, or to set up a pretext in which it can be removed from the stories of products (Wilkie 2010). There is a kind of sense in which this naivety, as a prerequisite for the genesis of thought, may seek new objects of encounter.

One way such naivety may fruitfully manifest is by asking scrupulously simple questions. Indeed, the cunning and intelligence required for the deployment of a simple question is a key concern for programmers attempting to instruct machines, and for anyone working to elicit material from what is now characterized as big data (Kitchin 2014a; Elmer, Langlois & Redden 2015). The artful projects of the working groups convened by Lev Manovich, such as *Selfie City* (Software Studies Initiative 2014), work in this mode, and one can say that they operate at a number of levels. Ostensibly, they are navigations of certain sets of data. A question is asked of a flow of images that conform to a certain categorical norm, that of date, kind, genre, keyword, location, and so on. These categorical terms are those that arise out of the specific nature of the system, which is partly that of a database whose genealogical roots are in set theory. Corralled as it often is within categorical architectures and tucked behind Application Programming Interfaces (APIs), it is difficult to get significant traction on the material, except in reconfirming its preconditions.

To work around this, data are captured and *withdrawn* from such systems and then subject to other kinds of query: for instance, using color saturation to navigate variations in images tagged with the names of certain cities, or image-recognition software is used to analyze the tilt of the head characteristic of selfies in a certain location. The findings of such work are partly in this activation of the parodically positivist formalisms that undergird computational culture and subtend big data. Genuinely trivial details in aggregate become something else; they constitute part of cultural form. To navigate these and aggregate them in turn becomes part of a dual capacity of critical exploration and seamless involvement that is both troubled and fascinating.

Working through the ways in which computational forms change established modes of culture, politics, and society and establish new ones has—like the traces of forces acting on a crystal—been very palpable in certain cultural-economic forms, such as publishing, music, and film, where they have had massive systemic effects. In other disciplines, such as philosophy, the articulation of these predispositions and capacities has been less immediately discernable but also intriguing, with the development of platforms and the mobilization of previously more marginal actants, but also cognitive speed-ups and conceptual hazing becoming more visible. Here, computational forms become one of the fields in which the crystal grows.

Related in certain ways to the question of operative stupidity and the principle of the pyramid scheme in academic citation patterns is the entrenchment of Pareto-principle-type citation patterns due to the material specificity of contemporary publication (Becker & Stalder 2009). When the search engine becomes the primary basis of scholarly research, the keyword becomes a crucial pivot for the articulation of fields. Thus, in speeded-up research cultures, ever-ready to pronounce what passes for a novelty, it is possible for communities working in related domains to entirely bypass each other's work due to over-dutiful following of links.

Earlier I noted that software studies methods include something of the fastidious, painstaking work of the archive following a specific object. Here, there is a useful correlation with work suggested by Kopytoff (1986) and in the figure of the boundary object formulated by Susan Leigh Star and James Griesemer (1989). A key factor to note is that many objects in software studies are multiscalar. To fix only on the immediately empirical—say, on the position of a specific procedure within a wider assemblage—would also be to risk missing, via simply descriptive means, some of the more abstract dimensions of such an assemblage. The mathematical and logical conditions of such an entity are also inherently formed among non-uniform fields of metaphysical "radiation" set in motion by mathematical conditions (Fazi & Fuller 2016). Equally, their articulation can be probed in relation to the epistemic conditions of certain kinds of data cultures and economies. To recognize the multidimensionality of the problem is by no means to deny the pleasures or necessity of micro-scalar analyses, but rather to emphasize the ways in which positing an analysis of a part triggers in turn the positing of a putative whole.

To return, then, to the relation of the method to the problem, part of the work of software studies has been to burrow into and articulate the relations between different scales in which software becomes manifest without proposing any pre-existing, hierarchically ordered set of conditions to which such things must correspond, without at the same time failing to notice that such orderings are multiple and highly operative. To this end, there is a discussion of software in terms of the data-structures known as "stacks" in the work of Ben Bratton (2016) and Rob Kitchin (2014b), among others, examining the ways in which the mutual ordering and dependencies of separate scales of abstraction and operation produce functional wholes. When, via an overly normalized and normative empiricism, work in this domain risks a simple recapitulation of systemic technical description, it is also challenged by a materialism operating "below the stack" by, for instance, focusing on the social and even alchemical histories of the minerals that end up in dialogue with software in the work of artists such as Jonathan Kemp, Martin Howse, and the group YoHa. Both of these tendencies afford further dialogue with wider questions of infrastructure and the scholars, from Sergio Bologna (1991) to Keller Easterling (2014), who have traced these inter-relations via political economy and spatial approaches.

Questions of infrastructure appear, too, in much of the work on understanding the fundamental components of large-scale web platforms. There is a sense that a key movement in much contemporary work is an investigation of the operations, significance, and underlying forces and consequences of social media and the apparatuses of production, storage, dissemination, and analysis that they constitute. Numerous articles have seen scholars address the functioning of Google's PageRank or Adwords; Facebook's OpenGraph; the shifting nature of database systems, from relational to NoSQL; and other mechanisms that deftly bring together theoretical resources drawn from different strands of cultural and social theory as well as histories of organization and mathematics (Dourish 2014; Kaldrack & Röhle 2014).

Treating the entities of such "abstract infrastructure" as inherently cultural, social, and political and also interrogating how computational media install and format modes of being and becoming in the present are fundamental to the genesis of software studies methods.

One of the conditions here is the changing status of media. Friedrich Kittler neatly boiled down the condition of media as being those mechanisms to do with the production, storage, and dissemination of information. The systems in the last paragraph added *analysis* to this triad. Here, analysis is the breaking down of complex entities into what, at a certain scale, can be read as nominally fundamental units, and working out their immanent, potential, or emergent relationships. Media have in many cases become a subset of computational systems. As a condition of their constitution as digital systems and, thanks to Alan Turing, as procedural systems that are inherently composed of discrete entities and steps, computers are constitutionally predicated upon analysis. Analysis and control combined are part of what make the move to computational generality such a significant, if not unprecedented, shift. It is in how this power of computational analyses is coupled with other forms native to the arts and humanities that we should now turn.

The collectively authored book, *10 PRINT CHR$(205.5+RND(1)); : GOTO 10* (Montfort et al. 2014), proposes that the single line of code set out in its title can be read, rewritten, divagated from, and used as the basis for memory and reverie in a compelling way. Here, close reading is the pivot around which a world can be spun out from a crystal of code. In related terms, a number of similarly minuscule objects have been examined for how their minor variations can become highly revealing entry points into a wider set of phenomena. Anne Helmond's (2013) discussion of the historical changes to the hyperlink or URL—from something hard-coded into an HTML document to an artifact generated on the fly by a database system—exemplifies this approach. By looking at such changes, insights into how websites are used and embody different modes of social and cultural activity can be readily elicited—for instance, in the trajectory from something hand-coded and available to all users to being an ostensibly secure, one-time only transaction. Related articulations of such telling detail are evident in Ben Grosser's (2014) account of his plug-in, the "Facebook Demetricator," which removes numerical and temporal data from the interface of the social media site. Another recent approach is to combine analytical methods from police data forensics with a survey of software manuals to articulate a history of metadata for author information (Fuller, Mazurov & McQuillan, forthcoming). In these and many other projects, there are numerous contributions to debates about what constitutes an object of study, entangled with the methodical means of staging such an encounter. Work by Wendy Chun (2011), Alex Galloway (2012), Annette Vee (2012), Taina Bucher (2013), Shintaro Miyazaki (2012), and numerous others propose methods integrated with particular lines of inquiry around certain scales at which software exists.

An additional mode of analysis, drawn from technical practices, is that of reverse engineering. Here, Adrian Mackenzie suggests:

> One strategy is to begin by describing the most distinctive algorithmic processes present, and then ask to what constraints or problems these processes respond. From there we can start to explore how software transforms relations.
>
> (Mackenzie 2008: 50)

Such a methodical frame corresponds with the process of observation and decomposition adopted in Robert W. Gehl's (2014) research on social media. It also provides an impetus for working directly on software systems via programmatic comparisons between input and output (Feuz, Fuller & Stalder 2011; Skeggs & Yuill 2015). Such research involves setting up one system to interrogate another. Applied to a target such as predominant web-based services, this interrogation may involve establishing user accounts, scripts, and servers that feed data into a system to generate results and then make comparative analyses of them. Sometimes described as an "algorithm audit" (Sandvig et al. 2014) and strongly developed by researchers such as Latanya Sweeney (2013), these techniques are especially notable in formulating a progressive program of research on the empirical operations of computational systems that constitute privatized forms of public resources.

One of the difficulties here is negotiating the privileged position that quantification is allocated in different kinds of discourse, where the numerically describable stands in for the empirical. Such quantitative research is often that most embraced and, if not actually discussed, replicated in the press. Nevertheless, as a means of reflexively working through how computational forms operate, it is an intensely valuable set of approaches. In a context where massive amounts of economic, social, and cultural actions are processed in computational environments, quantitative research is a mode of action conducted on a tactical basis by multitudes of actors, including algorithms employed by competing companies to understand the operations of others. We can say, too, that as reverse engineering becomes a mode of sociability—for instance, one prods a person to see if they elicit the signs taken for friendship—it is also a mode that becomes increasingly omnipresent.

Methods result in many cases from the conjunction of an intensive question with a problem. A case that is interesting to the point of fascination demands subtle attention to cracking it. Here, the mode of study adequate to a digital entity or process achieves the tender revelations of a hack. Exemplary in this regard are the edited volume and exhibitions of artworks put together by Olga Goriunova (2010, 2011, 2014) on the theme of *Fun and Software*. One of the guiding concerns in this strand of Goriunova's work is to draw out the ways in which software is attached to obsessive pleasures of multiple kinds. This series of projects draws rich attention to the articulation of logics, processes, systems, and other modes of computational artifact as they are not only manifest in—and given grounds and shaped by—the nature of software but also provide a condition of life that is both sensual and abstract. Crucial to note in the *Fun and Software* series is that scholarly modes of research are challenged by those that are anterior to the question of academic form. The condition of software is understood to be fundamentally existential. Aesthetics provides routes into such a condition, but so also do the reflexive accounts of cultural and technical practitioners. There is a close involvement here, too, with the immanent mode of criticism established in software art and the properly speculative dimension required when thinking about the various scales of abstraction and concretion found in software cultures. (Related approaches such as design fictions and speculative design are important to map here.) Here, software studies develops close affinities to the philosophical approaches of writers such as Luciana Parisi (2013) that mobilize reflections on the ontological conditions of mathematical technologies.

Following from this, the question of method is one coeval with multiple modes of being as much as with the problems into which those modes are crystallized. Appropriate methods involve grinding up such crystals to see what they do when ingested, describing what they mix with and the forms they take, or gazing deeply into them to divine the nature of the present.

Further Reading

Computational Culture: A Journal of Software Studies, retrieved from www.computationalculture.net.
Ekman, E. (ed.) (2013) *Throughout: Art and Culture Emerging with Ubiquitous Computing*, Cambridge, MA: MIT Press.
Manovich, L. (2013) *Software Takes Command*, London: Bloomsbury.
Ulrik Andersen, C. and S. Bro Pold (eds.) (2011) *Interface Criticism: Aesthetics Beyond the Buttons*, Aarhus, Denmark: University of Aarhus Press.

References

Becker K. and F. Stalder (eds.) (2009) *Deep Search: The Politics of Search beyond Google*, Vienna: StudienVerlag.
Bologna, S. (1991) "The Factory-Society Relationship as an Historical Category," trans. E. Emery, retrieved from libcom.org.
Bratton, B. (2016) *The Stack: On Software and Sovereignty*, Cambridge, MA: MIT Press.
Bucher, T. (2013) "Objects of Intense Feeling: The Case of the Twitter API," *Computational Culture* 3, retrieved from computationalculture.net/article/objects-of-intense-feeling-the-case-of-the-twitter-api.
Chun, W. H. K. (2011) *Programmed Visions: Software and Memory*, Cambridge, MA: MIT Press.
Dourish, P. (2014) "*NoSQL: The Shifting Materialities of Database Technology,*" *Computational Culture* 4, retrieved from computationalculture.net/article/no-sql-the-shifting-materialities-of-database-technology.
Easterling, K. (2014) *Extrastatecraft: The Power of Infrastructure Space*, London, UK: Verso.
Elmer, G., G. Langlois and J. Redden (eds.) (2015) *Compromised Data: From Social Media to Big Data*, London: Bloomsbury.
Fábos, A. and E. Haddad (2013) "Toward a Feminist Analysis of 'Impact': Sondra Hale's Scholarship and Activism in and Beyond the University," *Journal of Middle East Women's Studies* 10(1), 53–81.
Fazi M. B. and Fuller, M. (2016) "Computational Aesthetics," in P. Christiane (ed.) *A Companion to Digital Art*, Oxford: Blackwell.
Feuz, M., M. Fuller, and F. Stalder (2011) "Personal Web Searching in the Age of Semantic Capitalism: Diagnosing the Mechanisms of Personalization," *First Monday* 16(2).
Fuller, M., N. Mazurov, and D. McQuillan (forthcoming) "The Author Field," in G. Bachmann, Y. Hui, and S. Lash (eds.) *Technics and Data*, London: Sage.
Galloway, A. (2012) *The Interface Effect*, Cambridge, MA: Polity.
Gehl, R. W. (2014) *Reverse Engineering Social Media: Software, Culture, and Political Economy in New Media Capitalism*, Philadelphia, PA: Temple University Press.
Goriunova, O. (2010) *Funware* (Exhibition), Arnolfini, Bristol, September–November 2010
Goriunova, O. (2011) *Fun with Software* (Exhibition), MU and Baltan, Eindhoven, November 2010–January 2011.
Goriunova, O. (ed.) (2014) *Fun and Software: Exploring Pleasure, Paradox and Pain in Computing*, London: Bloomsbury.
Grosser, B. (2014) Facebook Demetricator, retrieved from bengrosser.com/projects/facebook-demetricator.
Helmond, A. (2013) "The Algorithmization of the Hyperlink," *Computational Culture* 3, retrieved from computational culture.net/aerticle/the-algorithimization-of-the-hyperlink.
Howse, M. (2015) "-micro research—Martin Howse [London/Berlin]," retrieved from 1010.co.uk/org.
Kaldrack, I. and T. Röhle (2014) "Divide and Share: Taxonomies, Orders and Masses in Facebook's Open Graph," *Computational Culture* 4, retrieved from computationalculture.net/issue-four-2.
Kemp, J. (2016) retrieved from xxn.org.uk.
Kitchin, R. (2014a) *The Data Revolution: Big Data, Open Data, Data Infrastructures and Their Consequences*, London: Sage.
Kitchin, R. (2014b) "Thinking Critically About and Researching Algorithms," *The Programmable City Working Paper* 5.
Kopytoff, I. (1986) "The Cultural Biography of Things: Commoditization as Process," in A. Appadurai (ed.) *The Social Life of Things: Commodities in Cultural Perspective*, New York, NY: Cambridge University Press.
Lash, S. (2002) "Technological Forms of Life," in *Critique of Information*, London: Sage.
Mackenzie, A. (2008) "Codecs" in M. Fuller (ed.) *Software Studies*, Cambridge, MA: MIT Press.
Mackenzie, A. (2010) *Wirelessness: Radical Empiricism in Network Cultures*, Cambridge, MA: MIT Press.
Miyazaki, S. (2012) "Algorhythmics: Understanding Micro-Temporality in Computational Cultures," *Computational Culture* 2, retrieved from computationalculture.net/article/algorhythmics-understanding-micro-temporality-in-computational-cultures.
Montfort, N., P. Baudoin, J. Bell, I. Bogost, J. Douglass, M. C. Marino, M. Mateas, C. Reas, M. Sample, and N. Vawter (2014) *10 PRINT CHR$(205.5+RND(1)); : GOTO 10*, Cambridge, MA: MIT Press.
Parisi, L. (2013) *Contagious Architecture: Computation, Aesthetics and Space*, Cambridge, MA: MIT Press.

Rancière, J. (1991) *The Ignorant Schoolmaster: Five Lessons in Intellectual Emancipation*, K. Ross (trans.) Stanford, CA: Stanford University Press.

Sandvig, C., K. Hamilton, K. Karahalios, and C. Langbort (2014) "Auditing Algorithms: Research Methods for Detecting Discrimination on Internet Platforms," presented at *Data and Discrimination: Converting Critical Concerns into Productive Inquiry*, a pre-conference at 64th Annual Meeting of the International Communication Association, May 22, Seattle, WA.

Skeggs, B. and S. Yuill (2015) *Values and Value*, retrieved from values.doc.gold.ac.uk/.

Software Studies Initiative (2014) *Selfie City*, retrieved from www.selfiecity.net.

Star, S. and J. Griesemer (1989) "Institutional Ecology, 'Translations' and Boundary Objects: Amateurs and Professionals in Berkeley's Museum of Vertebrate Zoology, 1907–1939," *Social Studies of Science* 19(3), 387.

Sweeney, L. (2013) "Discrimination in Online Ad Delivery," *Communications of the AMC* 56(5), 44–54.

Vee, A. (2012) "Text, Speech, Machine: Metaphors for Computer Code in the Law," *Computational Culture* 2, retrieved from computationalculture.net/article/text-speech-machine-metaphors-for-computer-code-in-the-law.

Wilkie, A. (2010) "User Assemblages in Design: An Ethnographic Study," PhD thesis, University of London.

Yokokoji M. and G. Harwood (n.d.) "YoHa (English translation 'aftermath')," retrieved from yoha.co.uk.

25

PHYSICAL COMPUTING, EMBODIED PRACTICE

Nina Belojevic and Shaun Macpherson

In recent years, the increasing public availability of inexpensive, powerful electronics—such as microcontrollers and radio-frequency identification (RFID) tags—and the proliferation of do-it-yourself-themed websites and online communities have fostered the emergence of physical computing, a set of tools, technologies, and practices used by artists, technologists, academics, and hobbyists. Physical computing pushes human–computer interaction (HCI) beyond the logics of the screen by facilitating computer interaction with bodies and objects off-screen, in the physical world. While HCI can be broadly historicized—even insofar as considering cultural anxieties over the replacement of human workers by automated machines or the development of the computer mouse by Douglas Engelbart in 1967 as early examples—physical computing is typically defined as the practice of combining hardware design with computer programming to create networked, interactive devices and environments.

A core effect of physical computing is the creation of new devices and networks that challenge conventional ideas about interfaces and interactions between bodies, technology, and the environment. In *Physical Computing*, Dan O'Sullivan and Tom Igoe describe the practice as making a "computer for the rest of you" (2004: xvii). Such interactions expand not only the computer's range of actuation (or expression) beyond modes of HCI, but also the ways that computers "sense" physical matter and environmental behaviors. What results are novel modes of expression and interaction, achieved by programming sensors to translate input (e.g., temperature, touch, sound, or wireless data transmissions such as Twitter feeds) into machine-readable data. Algorithms then transform that data into output, both on- and off-screen (e.g., light, sound, rotating a servomotor, or triggering some digital behavior).

Such expanded capabilities offer nearly limitless potential for the development of technologies across a range of social, cultural, and political applications, from social justice to surveillance to data collection. For example, the Autonets project (2015), started by a group of artists led by micha cárdenas, uses small, wearable microcontrollers, which are programmed and sewn into pieces of clothing, to create autonomous, local networks that enable women, LGBTQI people, people of color, and others to stay connected and locate each other. With Autonets, physical computing enables its network of wearers to anticipate and thereby avoid potentially violent situations, while also increasing safety among communities susceptible to violence or discrimination. cárdenas describes the project as "fashion hacking for social re-organization, recoding the meaning of fashion symbols such as hoodies that have associations ranging from Trayvon Martin to the Black Bloc, or femme fashion elements like dresses and bracelets, into symbols of connectivity and autonomy" (cárdenas 2015).

On the other hand, the novel modes of HCI afforded by physical computing are also used to develop corporate interests. Google's Advanced Technology and Projects Group (ATAP) recently released Project Tango, a smartphone and tablet designed to "give mobile devices human-scale understanding of space and motion" (Google 2014). Project Tango combines computer vision with geolocation sensors inside the device to track its motion in three dimensions while geometrically mapping the space around it. Such behavior opens a range of interactive possibilities: from rapid three-dimensional mapping of an indoor environment to augmented reality apps that integrate their physical surroundings to assist people with disabilities. Of course, since Google is funding the project, it is also reasonable to speculate how the information gathered by these devices will serve the company's grander project of data collection—that Project Tango's slogan is, "The future is awesome. We can build it faster together," hints that the company's next era of world-mapping will be crowd-sourced. Though developed at a much different scale than Autonets, Project Tango similarly works to simulate a mode of perception, process sensory information algorithmically, and convey that information to larger networks. In so doing, both projects draw attention to different social issues that frame the interfaces between bodies and technology.

Since it networks digital and nondigital environments, physical computing requires a mix of programming, electronics, and mechanical knowledge on the part of the operator. This knowledge is gained through hands-on experience—code must be written and de-bugged, schematics must be translated into circuit-building, and parts must be hammered, cut, drilled, soldered, glued, sewn, and otherwise manipulated. As such, physical computing's investment in handicraft often corresponds closely with "maker culture," a term that broadly encompasses the practices of people interested in building their own tools, devices, and interactive technologies. Maker culture shares with physical computing practitioners an interest in making the practices of software programming, electronics prototyping, and manufacturing more accessible to nonspecialists.

Spurred by ever-increasing access to materials and online communities of practice, maker culture represents itself as a shift in the way individuals and small groups explore the materiality of HCI, with the independence and entrepreneurial energy of the Whole Earth Catalogue subscribers of the 1960s, the Silicon Valley garage-programmers of the 1970s, and the open-source enthusiasts of the 1990s and 2000s. As was largely common with these communities, the culture's ethos is bound up in a technocultural narrative of open access and instrumentalist responses to social and economic issues. To this end, the virtues of individual empowerment and egalitarianism are often foregrounded in maker culture, with the belief that DIY practices constitute forms of radical dissent in the face of black-box, corporate technologies. While some of these practices gesture toward the centrality of human bodies in computing, their rhetoric is more invested in outlining a socioeconomic subject that is at once communitarian (sharing with and borrowing from the open-source community) and libertarian (practicing resistance against the cultural hegemony of proprietary goods and regulated services). Yet, as is the case with other grassroots technology movements, making and physical computing remain heavily implicated in discourses of late capitalism and commercialism, as evidenced by the heavy branding campaign of the O'Reilly-operated *Make* magazine and its how-to imprint as well as the rising ubiquity of "maker faires," which were started by *Make* and involve heavy trademark licensing fees and requirements. Hence, what is first framed as a liberatory practice by its champions is susceptible to naïveté and complicity with neoliberal ideologies.

What typically get overlooked by such criticism—absent of attention to process as it often is—are the ways in which the practices and outcomes of physical computing do not simply naturalize technology, but rather emphasize a material understanding of the digital and physical processes taking place all around us. Eschewing the black-box opacity of screen-based, proprietary technologies, physical computing emphasizes an experimental approach to better understanding and creating new technologies: it both provides an alternate framework vis-à-vis the proprietary nature of consumer tech culture and facilitates a broader understanding of how and where networked technologies influence our bodies, as well as the things and events near us.

By foregrounding the materiality of electrical operations and computational processes, physical computing also pushes against the increasing naturalization of digital interfaces—that is, the seeming "disappearance" of digital devices due to their ubiquity across many elements of contemporary life. For example, a line of code that causes electricity to pulse through a light-emitting diode (LED) to turn it on and off at regular intervals demonstrates the relationship between a digital process (the binary digital command that determines when the electrical signal will fire through the LED) and the physical object (the LED) itself. The conversion of signal data into observable behavior foregrounds the transductive processes that underlie any interface between digital and physical things.

Transduction, broadly defined, is the conversion of one form of energy into another. While this term originates in the sciences, it has been taken up in the context of computation as a way to understand, as Matthew Fuller puts it, the process of "how this becomes that" (2007: 85). Many technologies easily demonstrate the cause-and-effect principles of transduction: for example, a light bulb transduces electricity into light and heat, while a microphone transduces sound waves into fluctuating currents of electricity. Even the transductive processes of early analog computers could be partially observed and thus more easily grasped—latch relay switches were large enough that their switching mechanism could be seen or heard (the click of the switch was audible), and thus the operator was able to understand the material way a computer could perform, say, sequential logic operations.

With the continuing miniaturization of digital technologies, physical transduction has become increasingly complex and harder to observe without specialized equipment. Thus the ways that contemporary electronics and data processing actually work is relegated to what is graphically expressed on screens, an effect of computing Nick Montfort calls "screen essentialism" (2004). Innumerable critical discourses have taken shape that indicate the profound effect screen essentialism has on contemporary technoculture, from the ecstatic communication theorized by Jean Baudrillard (2012) in the 1980s to the vibrant discussions surrounding digital labor and cognitive capitalism among scholars such as Jonathan Beller (2006), Nick Dyer-Witheford (1999), Maurizio Lazzarato (1997), Tiziana Terranova (2004), McKenzie Wark (2004), and many others. Physical computing's emphasis on the material aspect of digital technology offers both a contribution to these critical discourses and a potential for new approaches to critical analyses and computational practices.

A Brief History of Physical Computing

Physical computing first emerged through academic channels as a means to explore how HCI could facilitate studies of computation by pushing beyond the screen and in part reviving the concept of the feedback loop. In 2001, Casey Reas and Benjamin Fry—then graduate students in the Aesthetics and Computation Group at MIT's Media Lab—wrote an open-source, integrated development environment (IDE) called Processing, a simplified coding environment for generating interactive digital visual graphics and designs. Visual artists themselves, Reas and Fry set out to create a programming language that could be easily learned by designers and artists, with an emphasis on writing "sketches" (or programs) for interactive graphics (Reas & Fry 2010: vii). They articulate this idea in *Getting Started with Processing* (2010): "Processing offers a way to learn programming through creating interactive graphics. There are many possible ways to teach coding, but students often find encouragement and motivation in immediate visual feedback" (1).

Reas and Fry's approach to computation—that engagement with a user-friendly, programmable system is reinforced through "immediate visual feedback"—is echoed by Tom Igoe in *Making Things Talk* (2007). Igoe cautions his readers to remember the operator end of the interaction: when creating interactive design projects, it is vital to "give some indication as to the invisible activities of your objects" and build indicators such as "an LED that gently pulses while the network transfer's happening, or a tune that plays" (2007: 47). According to Igoe, people using a device or interacting with a system do not need to know what is being communicated—or how this becomes that—at all points. But they do need to be aware that communication is taking place.

At the core of what Reas, Fry, and Igoe suggest is that operators remain invested in the *process* of computing—that, when a given function's invisibility is reified as a physical mechanism, people become aware of (and presumably invested in) the network's communications. Such mechanisms are rendered both knowable (in that we are aware that they are taking place) and unknowable (in that we do not actually know how the process is taking place). This making visible the invisible perpetuates a sort of fetish: the physical indication of an otherwise invisible software process constitutes in operators a sense that the unknowable functions of software have tacitly exposed themselves in a way that surpasses the mode of representation (be it light, text, sound, or something else).

Reas and Fry later adapted Processing to work as the IDE for Arduino, an open-source microcontroller platform that has become one of the primary tools in physical computing communities. Arduino was developed by a team at the Interaction Design Institute Ivrea in Italy as a means to provide students with an inexpensive microcontroller platform. Led by Tom Igoe, Massimo Banzi, David Cuartielles, Gianluca Martino, and David Mellis, the development team made Arduino an open-source hardware platform: designs and parts lists for the board were shared freely, meaning people could assemble their own boards for the price of parts rather than buy a manufactured one. This low-cost, open-source approach to hardware was intended to make hardware as accessible to new users as Processing was for software. This accessibility was important, as Arduino provides interoperability with Processing, extending the program's interactive elements beyond the realm of on-screen graphics by providing input and output pins that enable an operator to connect sensors and actuators to the board and program behaviors using the modified IDE.

While, through microcontroller platforms such as Arduino as well as the Raspberry Pi, process indicators can ostensibly free operators from the visual domain (e.g., a "tune that plays" makes processes knowable via auditory conveyance), the insistence of screen-centric HCI persists: such expanded sensory diversity is tied to the visual insofar as what is knowable is expressed in visual terms (e.g., Igoe's "invisible activities of your objects"). When programming a microcontroller, this continued adherence to the visual persists because the construction of a schema for translation and communication is written in the IDE, which, as most interfaces do, functions according to a metaphorical relationship—anchored in visual paradigms—between operator and machine. Although such paradigms are conducive to rendering technologies friendly to operators without expertise in computing or manufacturing, they also reduce the complexity of technological processes, mask or reify them, and curb the range of critical or creative approaches.

Physical Computing and the Graphical User Interface

The proliferation of such interfaces resulted in what Wendy Chun calls the empowerment of operators, whose ability to directly manipulate and engage with computational processes afforded by the graphical user interface (GUI) "offers [them] a way to act and navigate an increasingly complex world" (2011: 176). Interestingly, empowerment remains tied to the ability to manipulate and engage with process, though the process has grown increasingly mediated by automation or digitization over time, from manipulating analog computation (e.g., flipping relays in the 1950s) to attending to screens (e.g., writing a sketch in Processing). In other words, the emphasis has gradually shifted from a hands-on interface with electronics to a visual and arguably abstract mode of HCI. Such screen essentialism results in a mode of production that privileges the visual display of information while obscuring the balance of a platform's processes, hardware and electronic circuitry included.

However, programmable microcontrollers—emblematic of physical computing's primary "purpose"—also represent a departure from GUI-based HCI. O'Sullivan and Igoe write that "we need computers that respond to the rest of your body and the rest of the world. GUI technology allows you to drag and drop, but it won't notice if you twist and shout" (2004: xvii). Though they adhere to the parlance of conventional HCI—falling back on the metaphor of visuality that the computer "sees" our physical, embodied expression—they nevertheless shed light on the inherent constraints and limitations of the desktop computer's interaction with nondigital environments (interactions that are typically limited to the computer screen, mouse, and keyboard, and tools that allow operators to manipulate symbolic representations of data on a screen). Their point is that screens are for people, and physical computing is an exploration of HCI for the computer.

In other words, the cybernetic function of microcontrollers in physical computing interfaces—specifically the feedback loop of sensors, software, operators, and actuation—facilitates a broader discussion about access between humans and objects, objects and objects, and so on. Such interfaces resist the screen essentialism at work in the GUI. Jef Raskin, who created the interface for Apple's Macintosh project (arguably the first consumer-level GUI), echoes O'Sullivan and Igoe's critique. Acknowledging his own culpability, he claims that GUIs are not conducive to the cognitive processes at play in the way people work: "Human adaptability has its limits and . . . GUIs have many features that lie outside those limits, so we never fully adapt but just muddle along at one or another level of expertise" (Raskin 1993). Physical computing functions as a response to GUI reliance by expanding the range of interaction. For instance, an operator can communicate with a digital environment via a motion sensor, an electret microphone, or a photoresistor, thereby exposing the screen-based paradigm and ableist norms of embodiment that inform most interface designs while also increasing the scope and capacities of computer perception.

Physical Computing and Critical Practice: Highlighting Embodiment

Just as physical computing expands the range of possible interactions between digital and analog environments—and, in so doing, offers a renewed attention to materiality in the context of technocultural critique—so, too, does it open a range of potentially interesting and valuable methodologies for research across media studies and critical practices, particularly in the context of the humanities, arts, and social sciences. Scholars and artists, such as Leah Buechley, Critical Art Ensemble, Electronic Disturbance Theater, Jennifer Gabrys, Garnet Hertz, Tom Igoe, Natalie Jeremijenko, Kim Knight, Kari Kraus, Matt Ratto, Jentery Sayers, and William J. Turkel, among many others, apply a critical lens to physical computing projects and techniques toward an awareness of the cultural, social, and political factors at work in technologies. For critical practitioners, physical computing can be applied as a form of close study that complicates scholarly objectivity and employs a more experimental approach to theoretical analysis. This approach results in highlighting embodiment (of both humans and nonhumans) as a fundamental part of HCI. Because physical computing requires elements to be taken apart and assembled, circuits to be designed and built, and code to be programmed and debugged, it is an intrinsically embodied practice—one that relies on the practitioner's combined physical and mental attention in more tactile ways than forms of observation through other senses commonly used for humanities analysis, such as reading, looking, or listening. In this way, physical computing offers a form of practiced media study that not only observes but also moves inside the black boxes ubiquitous across contemporary life.

Such an approach also provides a purposeful way to trouble (or augment) a kind of top-down, theory-first approach to studies of technology. While transductive processes in the production and perception of, say, sound waves (for example) can be theoretically mapped, an embodied perspective—akin to Donna Haraway's "situated knowledge" paradigm (1988)—allows the researcher to explore the cognitive or social impacts of such information in ways not necessarily afforded by a theory-first approach. A consciously embodied approach provides a purposeful way to raise important questions for cultural critique: where do these materials come from? How are they produced? How does transduction occur? What cultural, social, economic, or political factors are obfuscated under the screen of user friendliness? Why is this technology built in this way? What gets foregrounded is not only the materiality of transduction (for instance, when we feel a small electric shock while touching a circuit board attached to a battery), but also the practitioner's place in a multitude of ecologies, ranging from operational processes to histories of technologies to the labor, modes of production, resources, and socioeconomic relations that are always circulating under the veneer of digital technologies. Importantly, recognizing this embodiment draws the user's attention to their own partial perspective and lack of access to certain knowledge, a point that is particularly important for media studies.

Example Projects: *BodyPlay* and *Ghost Tree*

The possibility for critical insights that may not be as apparent via a top-down, conceptual approach can be practically demonstrated through creative projects. For instance, consider several physical computing art pieces by Nina Belojevic, a co-author of this chapter. First, her interactive wall installations for the *BodyPlay* series (see Figure 25.1) depict body parts using a combination of mixed media visuals and microcontroller-based interactivity to encourage critical inquiry into the audience's relationships with technologies, interfaces, art, and bodies. The process of creating these pieces required not only the conceptualization and development of visual elements, but also the exploration of sensors and electronic triggers that enact and foreground these relationships. One piece, *Connect the Wires*, triggers different colored light cycles when two wires that emerge from a silicone nipple are connected.

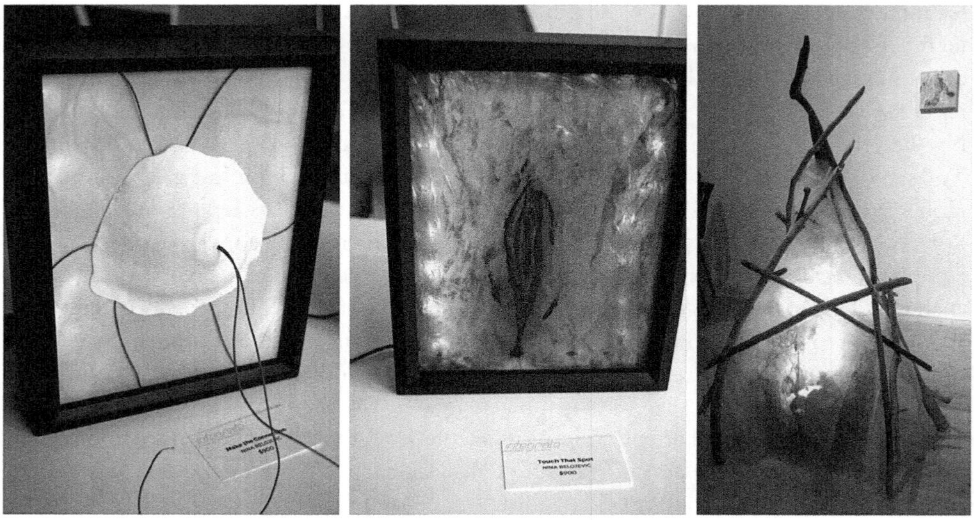

Figure 25.1 Left and center: *BodyPlay* wall pieces. Right: *Ghost Tree*.

Source: Images courtesy of Nina Belojevic.

Another, *Touch that Spot*, brightens up and displays various color patterns when conductive parts of the image are touched.

Both pieces use LED strips to create their responsive effects—colorful light patterns, movements, and cycles. While the capabilities of these LED strips are vast and allow for endless applications, they are relatively easy to program, even for someone new to physical computing. That said, even simple circuit construction such as this one necessitates specific material considerations for proper and reliable execution. For example, to regulate the power between the strips and the microcontroller, a capacitor, soldered in a specific configuration, is essential. Without it, the initial onrush of electrical current can damage the delicate LEDs inside the strip. If the wrong terminals are connected and a short circuit occurs, then any part of the circuit may be damaged. While recalling such a process might seem banal to media studies scholars, it highlights the cognitive, aesthetic, and material connections—or the interfaces and transductions—that must be made to create a computational art piece that conveys some meaning, be it social, political, or aesthetic.

When approached through critical media studies, physical computing projects can also highlight how digital technologies are not disembodied concepts or metaphors, but rather situated in different ecologies of place and context. Belojevic's sound-responsive piece, *Ghost Tree* (see Figure 25.1), was originally commissioned as a set piece for a local musician. Constructed from a combination of found materials and Arduino-based circuitry, *Ghost Tree* translates different sonic frequencies into preassigned color patterns; what results is an object that glows with particular colors based on the notes and chord arrangements performed by the musician. Belojevic was later invited to display *Ghost Tree* at a noise music event, where the decibel level was substantially higher than that of the initial performance. She was forced to make on-the-fly adjustments to the piece for its input (a small electret microphone) to function effectively in this different sonic environment. In the absence of the time and means to rebuild the circuit or reprogram the Arduino, she created an effective sound dampener over the input using tissue paper and electrical tape. Not ideal, but it worked, and *Ghost Tree* successfully interacted with the much louder music. The effectiveness of the device was mitigated by a complex ecology, which included different sonic environments, affordances of the materials, and the integration of further materials that altered the behavior of the device in a given context.

Embodied interactions and explorations such as the examples given above encourage unique ways of seeing and studying technologies—techniques that do not rely on a removed study of an object, but rather encourage the development of situated knowledge that experiences what is at hand and then follows a path of inquiry. It makes possible a reciprocal methodology whereby complex and inaccessible elements of technologies can be studied and communicated through experimental practice, which may make it possible to communicate new insights in words, create a discourse around them, and share perspectives that can then feed back into hands-on computing. This approach relies on much more than the interfaces we are provided with: images we see on screens, user-friendly interactions with metaphors, sounds we hear through speakers, or code we can read. It follows the flow of electricity through wires, resistors, and capacitors, out of sensors and into chips, from computer to actuator, and from air to the sensory receptors in our skin, eyes, and ears. The landscape of the circuit can be felt with our hands and seen with our eyes; and while the transduction of energy may not be fully visible to us, its operations are more easily felt and discerned when we become physically invested in them.

Further Reading

Banzi, M. (2009) *Getting Started with Arduino*. Sebastopol, CA: O'Reilly.

Belojevic, N. (2014) "Circuit Bending Videogame Consoles as a Form of Applied Media Studies," *New American Notes Online* 5, retrieved from nanocrit.com/issues/5/circuit-bending-videogame-consoles-form-applied-media-studies.

Fuller, M. (2007) *Media Ecologies: Materialist Energies in Art and Technoculture*, Cambridge, MA: MIT Press.

Macpherson, S. (2014) "A Computer for the Rest of You: Human-Computer Interaction in the Eversion," Master's Thesis, University of Victoria.

Nakamura, L. (2014) "Indigenous Circuits: Navajo Women and the Racialization of Early Electronic Manufacture," *American Quarterly* 66(4), 919–41.

O'Sullivan, D. and T. Igoe (2004) *Physical Computing: Sensing and Controlling the Physical World with Computers*, Mason, OH: Cengage Course Technology.

Scholz, T. (ed.) (2013) *Digital Labor: The Internet as Playground and Factory*, London: Routledge.

References

Autonets (2015) *Local Autonomy Networks*, retrieved from autonets.org.

Baudrillard, J. (2012) *The Ecstasy of Communication*, Cambridge, MA: MIT Press.

Beller, J. (2006) *The Cinematic Mode of Production: Attention Economy and the Society of the Spectacle*, Hanover, NH: Dartmouth College Press.

cárdenas, m. (2015) "Local Autonomy Networks: Post-Digital Networks, Post-Corporate Communications," *Media-N* (2013), retrieved from median.newmediacaucus.org/caa-conference-edition-2013/local-autonomy-networks-post-digital-networks-post-corporate-communications/.

Chun, W. H. K. (2011) *Programmed Visions: Software and Memory*, Cambridge, MA: MIT Press.

Dyer-Witheford, N. (1999) *Cyber Marx: Cycles and Circuits of Struggle in High Technology Capitalism*, Chicago: University of Illinois Press.

Fuller, M. (2007) *Media Ecologies: Materialist Energies in Art and Technoculture*. Cambridge, MA: MIT Press.

Google (2014) Project Tango, retrieved from www.google.com/atap/project-tango/.

Haraway, D. (1988) "Situated Knowledges: The Science Question in Feminism and the Privilege of Partial Perspective," *Feminist Studies* 14(3), 575–99.

Igoe, T. (2007) *Making Things Talk: Practical Methods for Connecting Physical Objects*, Sebastopol, CA: O'Reilly.

Lazzarato, M. (1997) "Immaterial Labor," in P. Virno and M. Hardt (eds.), *Radical Thought in Italy: A Potential Politics*, Minneapolis, MN: University of Minnesota Press, 133–50.

Montfort, N. (2004) "Continuous Paper: The Early Materiality and Workings of Electronic Literature," *MLA Convention*, 28 December. Philadelphia, PA.

O'Sullivan, D. and T. Igoe (2004) *Physical Computing: Sensing and Controlling the Physical World with Computers*, Mason, OH: Cengage Course Technology.

Raskin, J. (2013) "Down with GUIs!" *Wired* 1(06) (Dec. 1993), retrieved from wired.com.

Reas, C. and B. Fry (2010) *Getting Started with Processing*, Sebastopol, CA: O'Reilly.

Terranova, T. (2004) *Network Culture: Politics for the Information Age*, Ann Arbor, MI: Pluto Press.

Wark, M. (2004) *A Hacker Manifesto*, Cambridge, MA: Harvard University Press.

26

TURNING PRACTICE INSIDE OUT

Digital Humanities and the Eversion

Steven E. Jones

I have argued elsewhere (Jones 2014) that a new digital humanities emerged around 2004–2008 in response to changes in technology and how digital networks were perceived—what author William Gibson has called the *eversion* of cyberspace. Gibson coined the term cyberspace in a 1982 short story, but it became famous in his 1984 cyberpunk novel, *Neuromancer*, where it was the name for an online realm that was an abstract, disembodied nonspace, above and beyond the physical world, a kind of wireframe landscape familiar in movies such as *Tron*, for example. Through the 1980s and 1990s, popular notions of the internet—widespread access to which was only just emerging—were dominated by the metaphor of cyberspace. It was where people went when they went online.

But starting about 2007, Gibson overwrote his own earlier metaphor: "Cyberspace, not so long ago, was a specific elsewhere, one we visited periodically, peering into it from the familiar physical world. Now cyberspace has everted. Turned itself inside out. Colonized the physical" (Gibson 2010). To "evert" is to turn inside out—as when an umbrella flips upward in a rainstorm, exposing its carrier to the weather. That image of exposure, the sense of being inside the network, of soaking in it, is what the eversion feels like. The digital network, with its connected data, is now recognized as being down here, in the world all around us.

This new perspective on the network, the eversion, was made possible by a series of changes between 2004 and 2008—for example, simple geographic information systems (GIS) based on the Google Maps application programming interface (API) (which was in turn made possible by the availability of U.S. satellite data after May 2000), the widespread introduction of mobile cellphones (and the integration of the cellular network with the internet), RFID and NFC chips for radio-frequency tagging of physical objects, increasingly pervasive data (thanks to embedded processors and sensors), as well as data-driven social network platforms, such as Facebook and Twitter, that promoted and exploited all of these changes.

Cyberspace was just a metaphor, a way to represent the experience of being connected to the internet. Gibson famously called it a "consensual hallucination." The eversion represents a new consensus about our experience of digital technology, a shift in the collective imagination of the network. What Gibson calls the eversion, N. Katherine Hayles characterizes as a shift from virtual reality to mixed reality:

> Instead of constructing virtual reality as a sphere separate from the real world, today's media have tended to move out of the box and overlay virtual information and functionalities onto physical locations and actual objects. Mobile phones, GPS technology, and RFID (radio frequency identification) tags, along with embedded sensors and actuators, have created environments in which physical and virtual realms merge in fluid and seamless ways.
>
> (Hayles 2010: 148)

A raft of new or newly configured technologies were introduced in the first decade of the 2000s, but the shift from virtual to mixed reality was ultimately a cultural phenomenon, a response to technologies but not fully determined by them. Like the everted umbrella, the metaphorical membrane of cyberspace no longer divided the human world from the ambient weather of the digital realm. At least in the developed world—though not only there—for better or worse, people began to take it for granted that the everyday world is a data-saturated, mixed reality. Cyberspace had turned inside out.

In *Spook Country*, William Gibson has a character remark that cyberspace was just "a way we had of looking where we were headed, a direction. With the grid, we're here. This is the other side of the screen. Right here" (Gibson 2007: 64). But "here" in this case is less a destination and more a point along a trajectory. Eversion is a useful metaphor precisely because it names a *process* of turning out toward the world. At roughly the historical moment of the eversion, between about 2004 and 2008, a new digital humanities emerged. This was not an entirely new field but—growing out of the long traditions of humanities computing, media studies, and library and information science, in particular—a new direction for practice: from merely *digitizing* humanities materials (mostly paper-based archives) to exploring the implications of the eversion, the new mixed reality.

The new digital humanities has often been associated with programming, tinkering, and making, sometimes with making tools for practical applications, such as building digital archives or scholarly websites. But these experiments were produced in many cases by practitioners who were keenly aware of the eversion as it happened—the rise of social networks, casual and mobile gaming, the geospatial turn and data mapping, distributed cognition, augmented reality, 3-D printing, wearables, and methods inspired by the maker movement—and digital humanities practitioners responded by bringing these new developments into their classrooms, libraries, labs, and centers, where the developments became the objects of critical attention. Much of the hands-on, practical digital humanities work that emerged around 2004–08 was undertaken as an experimental engagement with the materialities of mixed reality. In this way, the new digital humanities of the 2000s tested theoretical questions, in the workshop or lab, but also out in the world, where the network was already having important social, geospatial, and object-based effects on people, places, and things.

People

In the 1980s and 1990s, cyberspace was often visualized as a lonely landscape (despite the fact that actually going online was usually an intensely social experience). With the eversion, the social nature of networks moved into the spotlight. Beginning with talk of "Web 2.0" applications around 2004, there was an increasing focus on the fact that networks are people.

Now, of course, "social media" has become a cliché with supporting ideologies of its own. The institutional sexism revealed and organized in #gamergate, as well as the unsavory subreddits and comment sections across the internet, continue to demonstrate the violent underside of the social network (and of human social relations in general). At the bottom line, the technology companies that control most of the popular social network platforms see their billions of users as a potential data resource to be mined or harvested for profit, often with privacy sacrificed in the process. They are often joined (and sometimes subpoenaed) by government agencies engaging in networked surveillance.

All of this is to recognize that networks exist as a result of social interactions and that their most important effects are social. The social possibilities of networks also include opportunities for a wide range of people to contribute to making knowledge that has been the purview of the humanities, especially in the areas of public heritage or shared cultural resources. The social constitution of networks raises important questions for digital humanities and media studies. One way to address such questions is in practice, by building platforms or using existing ones to engage people in crowdsourced scholarship, for example, to create digital archives and artifacts, while at the same time self-consciously testing the limits of crowdsourcing methods.

Crowdsourcing is not by any means unique to the humanities. One well-known example of "citizen science," The Zooniverse, calls itself "the largest online platform for collaborative volunteer research," which "provides opportunities for people around the world to contribute to real discoveries in fields ranging from astronomy to zoology" (n.d.). Its motto is "people-powered research." The networked platform allows for interested online volunteers (there are reportedly over 1 million) to contribute in small ways to a variety of research projects, from identifying individual humpback whales (actually, helping to train computer algorithms to identify them) to classifying data on everything from animals trapped in the Serengeti to stars and planets to subatomic particles. Micro-contributions to Zooniverse projects often amount to sorting or "scrubbing" large datasets of whatever kind. At present, only one of the projects listed by the site is classified as humanities research: Ancient Lives. Based at Oxford University, it enlists online volunteers to transcribe and help identify ancient papyrus fragments containing bits of Greek literature and other kinds of texts. While many contributors may be self-selected readers of Greek with an interest in papyrology, the project is open to anyone. Brief introductory essays are available, aimed at participants of varying skills. The project includes hundreds of thousands of images, and transcribers can browse databases of Ancient Greek texts to search for strings of letters or words that match their transcriptions. Human labor (across a broad swath of the population, potentially anyone with an interest and the ability to transcribe texts from the images) is combined with automated processes to analyze large sets of data.

This is "digitization" in the broad sense: transcribing from physical sources, producing metadata, and preparing archival materials for digital analysis. The first step, transcribing print materials to produce machine-readable texts, has been particularly amenable to crowdsourcing. Computers are getting better at reading images and printed texts, and optical character recognition (OCR) software has improved in recent decades. But, especially when it comes to older books, accuracy is still a problem, and the whole process of digitization requires significant contributions from humans as well as machines. A basic form of this combination can be seen in reCAPTCHAs, the bits of scrambled text at many website logins, in which humans collaborate with machines to edit scanned texts, one piece at a time.

Archives or databases of born-digital materials can also be seen as crowdsourced, in the sense that they are collectively produced in the first place by massively social networks, such as Twitter streams linked by hashtags and devoted to particular topics or historical events. A project at the Maryland Institute for Technology in the Humanities (MITH), directed by Ed Summers and Neil Fraistat, began with a collection of 13.5 million tweets posted in the first 2 weeks after the shooting of Michael Brown in Ferguson, Missouri on August 9, 2014. In the immediate wake of the shooting, Summers was inspired by Zeynep Tufekci's "What Happens to #Ferguson Affects What Happens to Ferguson" (Tufekci 2014). The Twitter stream marked by the hashtag #Ferguson (as well as #BlackLivesMatter) represented data out in the world, with obvious social and political implications. How data were distributed online (Tufekci was particularly interested in the issue of net neutrality), filtered, archived, and analyzed also mattered. Summers decided to use Twitter's open search API and a command-line program that he had previously scripted in Python (named twarc, for "Twitter Archive") to collect and archive Ferguson-related tweets for analysis (Summers 2014). The 13.5 million tweets represented data (both local and global) produced in the aftermath of the shooting, and patterns based on geolocation are potentially significant. It was not just a question of graphing trending subtopics. As Neil Fraistat pointed out in an interview about the project, a tweet is more than its 140 characters: besides carrying links and media files (images or audio), it comes with metadata, including in some cases geolocation (Kast & McKone 2015). And a collection of tweets is more than the sum of its parts. Mining, analyzing, and then visualizing or mapping the collection's data can be revealing, often in unexpected ways.

Despite clichés about the lone scholar scribbling in his (*sic*) cubicle, forms of distributed research are traditional in some areas of the humanities, especially the production of large reference works or scholarly and critical editions. It is no accident, therefore, that some of the earliest humanities computing projects (led by Roberto Busa, S.J., starting in 1950), which aimed to create lexical research tools through "literary data processing," required large teams of punched-card operators and other collaborators. This work included building a massive lemmatized concordance to the works of St. Thomas Aquinas, but also the analysis of some of the then-recently discovered Dead Sea Scrolls. At one point, Busa attempted to divide and distribute some of the tasks of digitizing and analyzing the Scrolls. Rather than a "crowd," he enlisted a relatively small, international, and interdisciplinary community of experts in ancient philology. Aside from that limited scale, he asked for a familiar kind of micro-curation of small pieces comprising a larger work—in this case, the lemmatization of a Hebrew, Aramaic, or Greek text to be punched onto cards and processed as linguistic data.

Computing in the humanities often works by "atomizing" source materials, for example, breaking texts down into individual words or letters, which can then be analyzed across a range of different dimensions. The micro-contributions of crowdsourcing fit perfectly into this process, and the division of labor into many small, discrete tasks opens the work to amateurs and volunteers. This is one way in which digital humanities research has turned outward to the social world. At the same time, the advent of social-networking platforms, which I have characterized as part of the eversion, has allowed for the massively collaborative production of new data, most of it potentially open to analysis, while raising ethical questions about the labor, privacy, and consent of the people whose contributions or whose data are being aggregated, mined, and analyzed.

Places

If the eversion means that cyberspace leaked out into the world, then the precondition was turning off "selective availability" to U.S. satellite data in May 2000. Global Positioning System (GPS) directions improved immediately. Within a few years, Google Maps was released as a platform for connecting maps to location data and—crucially—many other kinds of data. In other words, this offered a form of GIS readily available online and relatively simple to build, thanks to the Google Maps API (2005). These changes led to what became known as the geospatial web, and to countless map-based applications, including many digital humanities projects. Location has always been studied by historians, literary scholars, and other humanities researchers. But new digital humanities projects often build layered combination of maps and data—representations of geographical places linked to analyzable, digital information. In literary studies, for example, fictional locations in nineteenth-century novels can be treated not just as settings but as manipulable data to be plotted, mapped, and analyzed. Or patterns in the long-term history of publishing—collected by mining and analyzing millions of digitized books—can be examined statistically, keyed to historical maps, and correlated with other data, such as economic data representing national gross domestic products.

That last example is taken from a project by Matthew Wilkens of the University of Notre Dame, "Mapping and Modeling Centuries of Literary Geography across Millions of Books" (Wilkens 2015). Wilkens combines natural language processing with GIS (via the Google Maps Geocoding API) to first extract and then analyze geographic references to place in the HathiTrust corpus, which contains the digitized texts of 12 million published books. The project investigates relationships between "patterns of literary attention"—which places get mentioned the most in texts—and "demographic and economic factors in the United States between 1800 and 2010." Wilkens first extracts references to place from the texts, then statistically associates those references with geographic data using Google's API, and, finally, maps the results. This approach allows him to see patterns across time, connecting references to place in American literature with data about economic influence during the time of publication, for example. Like other digital humanities projects of this sort, this project connects data with representations of place. It is not just that digital tools are applied to maps; projects like this make it clear that there is no clean line separating the physical from the digital. Work of this kind begins with the eversion's spatially tagged mixed reality, in which digital data are already everywhere in the world.

Things

The eversion was made possible by satellite data as well as the increased use of sensors, transponders, cameras, and small processors in the physical environment—by the distribution of computing out in the world. The internet itself now depends not only on copper and fiber-optic cable spanning the globe but also on radio waves permeating the atmosphere, experienced as WiFi and cellular connections (along with additional short-range protocols, such as Bluetooth). Cards of various kinds, toys, game tokens, key fobs, appliances, pets, things we wear and things we carry, even our bodily interactions with the physical environment of buildings and streets—all are potentially connected, networked, whether we are always aware of the connections or not. The Internet of Things (IoT) is an old idea, but, in the past decade or two, what was once called (with some exaggeration) "ubiquitous computing" has become a mundane reality, sometimes in the most banal ways. Consider, for instance, the spread of QR codes as machine-readable optical quick-response tags. It is now assumed that almost any object can be made to collect, use, and transmit data of various kinds through everted networks, and that networks consist of many possible connections among things of all kinds.

In a kind of thought experiment or design fiction, author Bruce Sterling imagines the advent of what he calls "spimes" (a portmanteau of "space" and "time"), each an object consisting of a physical thing plus data about the thing, resulting in a cloud or halo of data about the thing's interactions with humans and the environment as it moves through the world (Sterling 2005). A spime would be data-rich, and each interaction with it would become part of the potentially available data. Today's tagged or "chipped" things are mere harbingers of spimes, nowhere near as sophisticated as what Sterling imagines, but his concept is an important reminder that the effect of the eversion is to make us think about the physical objects around us in a new way, as potentially linked to ambient data. This view of mixed reality raises important social, political, philosophical, and ethical questions for the humanities. And digital humanities can address some of these questions in practice, in part by making and exploring the possibilities of data-saturated things—prototyping and theorizing design fictions, as Kari Kraus has argued (2012; see also this volume)—and in part by engaging in critical analysis of developments out in the world.

This is the remit of the Maker Lab in the Humanities at the University of Victoria, which opened in 2012, inspired in part by extra-academic makerspaces that emerged in the era of the eversion. The Maker Lab is a hands-on research lab focused on the intersection of humanities research with "tacit learning through physical computing, fabrication, material culture studies, and comparative media studies" (Sayers 2012). Work in the Lab often takes the form of tinkering or experimenting with everything from small Arduino and Raspberry Pi circuit boards to 3-D printers and scanners, videogames, maps, chips, and wires as well as code—and it includes self-conscious research on its own status as well as on the implications of the laboratory as a model for humanities research, by asking: "How can experimental methods inform materialist research and cultural criticism?"

Similarly, Harvard's metaLAB is "dedicated to exploring and expanding the frontiers of networked culture in the arts and humanities" (metaLAB n.d.). Its research focuses on what it calls the "artifactual knowledge" and the design of exhibitions that "conjoin media and physical objects," on "digital extensions of physical exhibitions," and on the "animation" of archives and built environments. Like the Maker Lab in the Humanities, the metaLAB resists the idea that digital humanities tinkering and making is a refuge from theory: it sees its hands-on research with mixed-reality objects and environments as addressing "fundamental questions regarding experience in a connected world, democracy and social justice, the boundaries between nature and culture." Founding co-director of the metaLAB, Jeffrey T. Schnapp, has said that the "defining design challenge of our epoch" is "to weave together information and space in a meaningful fashion" (Schnapp 2015; see also this volume). And the premise behind this challenge is one aspect of what I have been calling the eversion: the fact that "every cultural object is a network; every collection is a set of collections." He asks rhetorically whether there are "any 'analog only' cultural objects left in museums today" and argues instead that "nearly all cultural objects, whether belonging to the remote past or the immediate present, circulate surrounded by a halo of data and capta."

> [D]ata is the defining cultural material of the twenty-first century: it is our marble and clay, our coal and petroleum; but raw data alone don't do anything; they have to be collected, processed, curated, and shaped.
>
> (Schnapp 2015)

Although Schnapp is speaking directly to the design of museums here, what he says applies to the digital humanities as a whole, both the mixture of digital and physical materialities and the role of data—not only in museums but in everyday lived experience—as points of focus for engaged humanities research.

Schnapp's aphorism about the "halo of data *and capta*" (my emphasis) reminds us that, as Drucker (2011) suggests, the etymology of the term, "data," is itself problematic from a humanities perspective. Data assume what is "given" as its starting point, rather than what is taken or construed by humans. But, as should be clear by now, the eversion—the shift in perspective occasioned by the turning inside out of the network in relation to the physical world—has come with a heightened awareness of the collaborative roles played by objects and observers, computers and humans, in collecting, curating, and analyzing the data that saturate the everyday experience of people, places, and things—and of the profound questions raised by these processes.

The statistical analysis of large corpora of texts as linguistic data is perhaps the best-known example of digital humanities practice today. In the larger context of the eversion, it is revealed as only one way to experiment with the relationship between physical objects (such as printed books) and digital data, one among many ways that humanities researchers can explore the implications of the mixed-reality world.

Further Reading

Gibson, W. (2007) *Spook Country*, New York, NY: Putnam's.

Hayles, N. K. (1999) *How We Became Posthuman: Virtual Bodies in Cybernetics, Literature, and Informatics*, Chicago, IL: University of Chicago Press.

Jones, S. (2014) *The Emergence of the Digital Humanities*, New York, NY: Routledge.

Sayers, J. (2015) "Why Fabricate?" *Scholarly and Research Communication* 6(3), retrieved from src-online.ca/index.php/src/article/view/209/428.

References

Drucker, J. (2011) "Humanities Approaches to Graphical Display," *Digital Humanities Quarterly* 5(1), retrieved from digitalhumanities.org/dhq/vol/5/1/000091/000091.html.

Gibson, W. (2007) *Spook Country*, New York, NY: Putnam's.

Gibson, W. (2010) "Google's Earth," *New York Times*, 31 August, retrieved from nytimes.com/2010/09/01/opinion/01gibson.html.

Hayles, N. K. (2010) "Cybernetics," in W. J. T. Mitchell and M. B. N. Hansen (eds.) *Critical Terms for Media Studies*, Chicago, IL: University of Chicago Press, pp. 144–56.

Jones, S. (2014) *The Emergence of the Digital Humanities*, New York, NY: Routledge.

Kast, S. and J. McKone (2015) "The Politics of Archiving #BlackLivesMatter," *Maryland Morning* (radio broadcast), WYPR Radio, May 15, retrieved from wypr.org/post/politics-archiving-blacklivesmatter.

Kraus, K. (2012) "Rough Cuts: Media and Design in Process," *The New Everyday*, New York: New York University and *MediaCommons*, retrieved from mediacommons.futureofthebook.org/tne/pieces/introduction.

metaLAB (n.d.), *metaLAB at Harvard*, retrieved from metalab.harvard.edu/.

Sayers, J. (2012) "The Humanities Lab as a Makerspace," *The Maker Lab*, September 5, retrieved from maker.uvic.ca/makerspace.

Schnapp, J. T. (2015) "Aphorisms on the 21st Century Museum," *Jeffrey Schnapp*, January 26, retrieved from jeffreyschnapp.com/aphorisms-on-the-21st-century-museum/.

Sterling, B. (2005) *Shaping Things*, Cambridge, MA: MIT Press.

Summers, E. (2014) "A Ferguson Twitter Archive" 30 August, Retrieved from inkdroid.org/journal/2014/08/30/a-ferguson-twitter-archive/.

Tufekci, Z. (2014) "What Happens to #Ferguson Affects Ferguson: Net Neutrality, Algorithmic Filtering and Ferguson," *The Message*, August 14, retrieved from medium.com/message/ferguson-is-also-a-net-neutrality-issue-6d2f3db51eb0.

Wilkens, M. (2015) "Mapping and Modeling Centuries of Literary Geography across Millions of Books," at Digital Humanities 2015, Global Digital Humanities conference, Sydney, Australia, July 3.

27

CONJUNCTIVE AND DISJUNCTIVE NETWORKS

Affects, Technics, and Arts in the Experience of Relation

Anna Munster

"The Internet is over," Prince famously proclaimed in an interview with British newspaper *The Daily Mirror* in 2010. Comparing the entire way in which music distribution and marketing had fallen into the "middling" hands of both networked corporations and downloaders to the grip and branding filter that MTV held over pop music during the 1980s and 1990s, Prince's declaration was naïve and savvy at the same time. The sheer statistics, the growth, and now diversification of platforms and apps such as Reddit, Instagram, and Snapchat, which circulate memes, stories, images, and commentary on popular music, would suggest that online networking *is* the main environment for music distribution and consumption. And yet Prince's characterization of the internet as a control space for audiovisual content, similar to MTV's tight grip over the marketing of popular music's image, is interesting. According to Prince, by 2010 the internet was no longer a space for directly networking one's music with one's audience, because it had become an environment in which direct connectivity was no longer possible.

Prince is not the only one to have declared the demise of a certain kind of "direct" online connectivity. Fifteen years earlier, in an opinion piece published for *Newsweek*, Clifford Stoll (1995)—systems administrator and author of *The Cuckoo's Egg* (1989), a myopic into his stalking of a KGB hacker—had already bemoaned the chaotic and unedited realm of voices that online interactions had become. Although Stoll saw chaos and chatter where Prince decried the presence of opaque middleware, a similar sentiment pervades their views on the culture and enterprise of going online—the lack of authentic personal contact and connectivity. More recently, Andrew Keen steadfastly criticized the internet for its celebration of narcissism and self-expression and its lack of authentic connection with other minds (2007, 2015). Prince, Stoll, and Keen all represent quite different positions on the massification of networked cultures and economies. But they also indicate that, for at least 20 years, online culture has felt as if it were already an environment in which corporatism, middleware, and other forms of "RL" organization were facets of its terrain. The internet had fast become an environment consistently failing to live up to the utopian ideals of its early advocates, such as Stuart Brand and Larry Brilliant, who founded the WELL (Whole Earth 'Lectronic Link), one of the earliest online communities, in 1985.

There are a myriad of other tales about network experience that fall somewhere else, on neither side of the utopian/dystopian divide. During the 1990s, artists and writers were eager to crawl on, slip into, and fall down any cyber-hole that would lead them into shared networked spaces, projects, and discussions. Such falls were often quite literal. For example, in connecting to LambdaMOO (a text-based multiuser online environment and community set up in the early 1990s by Pavel Curtis at Xerox PARC), one entered its topography through a text-based description of a space called "the Closet." A dark and confined "rabbit hole," players experienced the feeling of bumping up against hanging coats, boots, and sometimes other online sleeping denizens, before using the @ command to fumble into other "rooms" in the environment (see Quittner 1994). "The Closet" opened out into a "Living Room," where other players in the community also hung out. Another potential encounter in the "Living Room" was with a "magical" couch that frequently caused players' objects to fall through it. All such falls, encounters, and spaces occurred via typed text descriptions, @ commands, and dialogue generated by members. I was first shown how to log on to LambdaMOO by the artist, Francesca da Rimini, who, at that time and across much of the 1990s and into the 2000s, fell in and out of various online environments, avatars, and communities and had been part of VNS Matrix. These four women, seriously and with a dash of humor, described their online and digital mission to be "terminators of the moral code, mercenaries of slime" (VNS Matrix 1991).

I never made it out of "the Closet" into LambdaMOO proper—the text commands dictating the modes of interaction and navigation with the MOO space remained obscure to me. And so, in tune with this rambling topology of associations, I fell out of this environment into other online projects, such as the Australian *recode* list for new media arts and culture, active for a few years in the late 1990s and moderated by Julianne Pearce, likewise a member of VNS Matrix. There are few traces of the *recode* list online after it perished at the hands of intense debate and disagreements over funding for new media arts in the Australian context as well as the posting styles of net art contributors such as Mez Breeze (Lovink 2002: 204). I later bumped into the *fibreculture* list after an email correspondence with Mitchell Whitelaw, a theorist, sound designer, and data artist and designer who informed me that, to find the list site, I needed to search for "fibre" not *cyber*culture. I settled with the *fibreculture* network, which morphed into an online open access journal, *The Fibreculture Journal*, still readable and accessible today.

This kind of meandering and ambulatory movement of falling and flailing around and across networked sites, conversations, and projects produced an itinerant feel to networked experience. Online experience felt to me like a kind of stumbling upon, falling into, and groping toward. Entry into and knowledge of lists, networks, and environments were both contingent and somewhat secretive—you had to know someone or else discovery was more or less serendipitous. Networked projects and sites were both mysteriously obscure and yet surprisingly open and welcoming. Online engagement was infused with an affective atmosphere that can still be detected when scanning over list archives—a collective sense of exhilaration joined with frustration. Projects emerged out of and attempted to generate a respect for difference in their sensibility, yet equally collapsed easily under the weight of trolling and unrealistic political ideals. Critique and creation co-existed. VNS Matrix, for example, were both infiltrators *and* critics of spaces they perceived to be already over-determined by sexism, "mainframeism," and a palpable sense of alignment between the life worlds of geeks, hacker masculinity, and computation. List networks on network culture were at once generative *and* damning of network forces, online governance structures, and emergent corporate forms of computational and technical capitalism. A generation of "net" artists such as Heath Bunting, Olia Lialina, and jodi.org made work online that already engaged with the heterogeneity of networks as simultaneously "open" and proprietary, available technically to the amateur and hobbyist *and* imbued with a technical episteme indebted to a cold war legacy.

A lived doubling of both engagement and critique, then, colored my entry into online culture and has come to shape my ongoing concern with (an) aesthesia of networks. This is not to make a claim for these earlier online events and engagements as *authentic* forms of network experience. In approaching network experience, I want to instead suggest that networks—as sociotechnical assemblages, as singular and nonlocalized, as standardized communicative protocols operating across open architectures—must also be thought in close proximity to the affectivity of technically inflected experience. The proposition for "an" aesthesia of networks, then, is to think network technicity in relation to the perceptual and affective components of network experience as well.

Many of these earlier experiments with platforms for distributed communications generated a particular kind of aesthesia that is at once nonlocal and intensely embodied. In discussing the experimental network of artists who gathered and performed using the first online, real-time multimedia collaborative performance software, *KeyWorx*, in the late 1990s and early 2000s, Sher Doruff makes a similar observation:

> . . . translocal experience, as an embodied experience, is amplified because your body is . . . you have the sensation of . . . how can I say this? The effect of intensities of translocal performance when it's indeterminate and you're collectively negotiating and making choices together and you're playing off those choices as a jazz band would or as a dancers might . . . the translocal becomes incredibly, intensely physicalised, but your feeling of space is nonlocally oriented.
>
> (Doruff 2012)

What online networking experiments initially made palpable was a kind of stumbling into relation with the differentials of technical speeds, geographical spatial dispersion, and the life rhythms of differing time zones. Things, projects, and online experiences both flowed rapidly into one another and moved on just as quickly, building dense intensities and rapid perishings. In spite of all proclamations about the demise of the internet—whether these have to do with a loss of immediacy or melancholia about the ceding of political ideals to communicational capitalism—the potential to generate novel technosocial and techno-aesthetic events continues for contemporary networked experience.

All this is quite different from an *aesthetics* of the network, which, it could be argued, has definitively taken command of culture, politics, and life. Such aesthetics instills a global cultural imaginary of interconnectivity, dominated by a link-node topology, and technically supported by the algorithmic crunching of the innumerably vast hoarding, querying, and patterning of data. Such an aesthetics functions less as a formal mode for analyzing contemporary networked culture than as a silent, operative system that supports and perpetuates Western military operations, information architecture and infrastructure, the reliance on data visualization as an unquestioned empirical reality, and the sensibility of sociality as reducible to sets of likes and dislikes. Arjun Appadurai's concept, developed in the face of a newly minted global sociality of the 1980s and 1990s, puts it well:

> [T]he imagination has become an organized field of social practices, a form of work (both in the sense of labor and of culturally organized practice) and a form of negotiation between sites of agency ("individuals") and globally defined fields of possibility.
>
> (Appadurai 1990: 5)

This global social imagination has become a "networked" one, seeping through granular and macro dimensions via social practices and military, political, and economic operations and exchanges.

Why name this aesthetics? When glancing at a few key publications, marketing forms, and information domains, it is very clear that a recurring and formalized model of *imaging* life as a network has taken hold. Throughout the end of the twentieth-century and into the first decade of the twenty-first, the U.S. military has reimagined warfare as "network-centric" (Verton 2003). The Command and Control Research Program of the U.S. Department of Defense published a series of books during this period, culminating in a graphic principle called "power to the edge," embedding an image of the network as flexible, opening out on to an enemy's networks, and diffusing control throughout its organizational structure (Alberts & Hayes 2003). In a similar vein, the new image of the contemporary business enterprise is of "agility" (see Hugos 2009). Here, the "hierarchy" of the "boss" at the top of the pyramid controlling the flow of information and decision-making is replaced by an image of a network of autonomously functioning units, coordinated by a chief officer. The units are immediately responsive to the interactions that they have with their customers, an emerging market situation, or (shifting) client base. These interactions between company and customers are viewed as "edges," the concept taken from mathematical graph theory used to describe the links that join the nodes in network analysis. Customers, then, have become "nodes" in the network of the company itself; the company that is able to be agile and flexible in terms of its edges (here, literally the "edge" that both separates *and* links company and client) will best adapt to the changing directions in which its market or clients are moving. The image of the network that permeates these new business models imagines only soft differences between corporation and client because the client is as much a part of the networked corporation as is its internal organizational structure.

And at the very heart and/or edge of all this social imagining, we also find the network *as* aesthetic in the emergence of the eponymous "New Aesthetic." Infamously pronounced in the vaguest of terms on the social media and blogging platform Tumblr, the New Aesthetic pointed to the commonplace of networked infrastructure such as satellite imaging and drones as a generator of contemporary visual culture and also spoke online from the design(ed) space of blogs and Tumblrs run mainly by people working within the creative industries (Bridle 2011a, 2011b). The New Aesthetic partakes in the social imagining of life as networked inasmuch as it situates itself as the immediate and immediately responsive interface to the media, technologies, and techniques of informatically connected and generated life.

What ties these three dimensions—the military/logistical, the business/organizational, and the creative/medial—of the contemporary network together is the extent to which networking has become less a system or infrastructure and more a sensibility. Of course, the shift to network-centric warfare that has become the U.S. military's *modus operandus* involves a carefully calculated set of maneuvers being put into place for personnel. Similarly, the reorganization of enterprise according to "agile" principles and responsivity is a considered one. Nonetheless, there is a sense in which a particular *affectivity* conditions all three modes of instilling the network as a sociotechnical assemblage. This affectivity is precisely a *diffuse vagueness*, the state of being permanently everywhere but in no one fixed location—of ongoing readiness to act, interact, or respond. Such affect is both a condition for and an ongoing effect of the network itself. Brian Massumi suggests that this kind of "readiness potential," this priming for action and being primed to act wherever and whenever it may occur, is the hallmark of contemporary *infra-connected* neoliberalism (2014: 13–14). What is "connecting" individuals at a more than one-to-one level (*infra* in the sense of both below and further on) is not an infrastructure of cables, routers, packets, and switches but a *diagram* of diffuse readiness in which being prompted, responsive, and participatory is glued together with informatic flows. If the internet is over, then it is because the online world has ceased to exist as a place or medium for analysis and critique. It has given way, instead, to an entire *dispositif*, to deploy Foucault's concept (1980) of the heterogeneous ensemble of discursive, institutional, administrative, and technical elements that power exercises in the social field. This *dispositif* is the agile readiness of *networking*. In the end, though, we will need to find a different way to speak about how—through this diffuse, *infraconnected*, logistical neoliberal sociotechnicality—a system gives way to diagrams *and* aesthetic objects give way to affective sensibilities, processes, and techniques of information. In response to this modulation, I have proposed the concept of (an) aesthesia of networks (Munster 2013).

An *aesthesia*, I think, might tentatively hold in the same moment an oscillating tension between, on the one hand, numbness, boredom, and the predictability of a template or connectivity and, on the other, the intensive joy of networking as a shared event of translocal relation. It speaks to the diffuse creep of the connective edge that is constantly "liking," "predicting," and "capturing" across social media, network architectures, and logistical chains—an advance of nodes and edges that is anaesthetizing. But it also speaks to edging as a process of inventing, often via aesthetic techniques, new modalities of relation that bring us into as yet unknown assemblages with the nonhuman, the more-than-human, and the infrahuman. A network *aesthesia*, rather than "anaesthesia," might allow us to not count the already similar, already nodal but encounter what we do not know, sense, or own—the imperceptible. Such an aesthesia also requires us to rethink the movements of networks: a shift away from connectivity toward conjunction and its companion, disjunction.

Indeed, these movements and relations of conjoining and disjoining resonate with the sensibility and affectivity discovered and generated by earlier artistic and medial experiments with distributed networked communications. Now, in what is sometimes circumscribed as a "post internet" context (see, for example, Steyerl 2013), it is important to rethink these affective and intense events of memes, media, projects, and collectivities by carefully attending to how networks involve processes and flows of both continuity (conjunction) and cuts (disjunction) rather than the reified image of expansionist connectivity. In order to get at what networked life is like for *us* as individuated humans, we should proceed from the processual aspects of the experiences of networks, many of which involve technical, nonhuman operations such as recursion, redundancy, and nonlinear dynamics. Yet, far from sinking into a sea of complex technical jargon and protocol—although, even so, holding on to some technical precision—I propose that we can approach these operations via the decidedly nontechnical theories of experience found in the late-nineteenth- and early-twentieth-century writings of William James.

James's vocabulary for theorizing experience is scattered with images and processes that are well suited to thinking through network relations as diffuse generators and shapers of contemporary experience. For him, experience is loosely wrought; hanging together through relations of proximity between things and beings as these bump up together, pass into one another, settle, and transition (James 1912: 43–56; 1977: 256–269). James's emphasis on relations as the most immediately felt or sensed aspect of experience lead him to comment on how conjunctions and disjunctions operate as events that qualitatively contour relations: "If I ask you where some object of yours is, our old Memorial Hall, for example, you point to my Memorial Hall with your hand which I see" (James 1912: 79). Here, "with," "my," "your,"—but also the concepts of proximity and distance with which James is dealing when he discusses both seeing and remembering Memorial Hall—are not subjects, objects, or points to be measured and connected. They are all relations that fundamentally impinge on, modulate, and organize even the seemingly simplest of experiences. In such an everyday experience, we can see the germs of a process-oriented mode of engaging with the world functioning on a different plane than connecting the nodes. In more recent aesthetic, philosophical, and political theory (for example, Lapoujade 2000; Massumi 2011), this emphasis on conjunctions and disjunctions as the critical operators that bring together the political, social, and cultural spheres with the mico-dimensions of perceptual and affective experience is known as "relationality."

The link-node image is one in which "nodes" are given substantive status—they are treated as objects or subjects, such as "friends" on social media, that have already formed and just need to be added to the network. A process-oriented approach that takes relations as the real generators of experience instead suggests that "nodes" are only produced by and through their relations. A "friend" in a social network is therefore something much more fleeting, in a state of ongoing composition across a range of both technocultural forces and microsocial comings and goings. A process-oriented approach to networking offers us a way out of the hold the link-node network image has on contemporary social imagining. Attending carefully to the materialities of such relationality—rather than to the scale-free (see Barabasi & Bonabeau 2003: 52) and somewhat anchorless link-node model—is key to contemporary networked cultures.

An aesthesia of networks—or, more plainly, networking as experience—joins the heterogeneity of humans and nonhumans into arrays that are constantly deforming and reorganizing through dynamic recursions, tending toward both repetition and difference. We find ourselves loosely "concatenated," to borrow a Jamesian term (1977: 221), with both other humans and informatic machines, enmeshed in an architecture that is dependent on forces internal and external to specific networks and results in the generation of massively redundant, criss-crossing routes between and across networks as well as older formations, such as the sovereign state and the assembly line. An aesthesia of networks is a proposition for thinking and feeling through networked cultures, art practices, new publics/socialities, and emerging formations of networked capitalism that are made possible via the operations of complex, relational life today.

How, for example, can we understand the deformations that the moving image and moving image culture undergo in networked culture, without ignoring the complexity of the conjunctions or relations the moving image now has? Such conjunctions include, but are not limited to, cinema's relations with different media delivery and distribution platforms; the engagement of amateurs and fans with images, merchandise, and the cultivation of audiences; the global uptake of the moving image in local contexts; and the differentials of labor for the film industry that such globalization has generated. Cinema has not only materially transformed but become a wholly different kind of movement—literally from moving image to streaming data. And this shift—material, formal, and operational all at the same time—opens a complex reassembly of the political economy of images, of new publics and modes of producing the moving image—indeed, of new kinds of labor that provide the condition and engine for making streams of images. To account for such relationality, a conception of the network as an online or even offline set of links and nodes simply will not wash.

Instead, we should look to artists in tandem with sociotechnical and process-based thinkers, all of whom are particularly good at touching upon the complexity of such experience and rendering the conjunctions and disjunctions of networking as dilatory and contracted openings. Take, for example, Kevin Lee's *Transformers: The Premake (a desktop documentary)*, an online video originally posted to Vimeo in 2014 (Lee 2014). Here, Lee creates a whole new possibility for a networked genre—the desktop documentary—that emerges as a conjunction of disjunctive online visual culture sources, environments, platforms, and techniques. Trawling through 355 YouTube videos shot by fans and amateurs (including himself) of the shooting and production of *Transformers: Age of Extinction* (dir. Michael Bay 2014), Lee unleashes and contours a set of problems around media, labor, and affective capitalism in funny and poignant ways. Not only do these YouTube clips reappear in Lee's documentary, but they are also composed into his process of actually searching for and watching online videos. They are composited against and with other online platforms, such as Google Maps, to provide a kind of postnarrative "plot"—made possible by the ubiquity of tracking provided by network metadata—of where, when, and how fans captured material about the making of a Hollywood blockbuster.

Lee recomposes all this content and its various networked platforms and processes via screencasting software. This approach captures and remakes all his searching, querying, and downloading into a relentlessly smooth stream, and it brings this labor *together with* the aggregates of creative fan labor (Deuze 2007: 57) manifest in the YouTube clips themselves. All these amateur clips of the making of the *Transformers* movie, as well as Lee's "premake," appeared online before the release of the Hollywood film in cinemas. This timing is crucial. Lee's desktop documentary foregrounds this "pre-production" not as simply medial background to contemporary cinema but rather as the affective surplus labor *produced in advance and retrospectively parasited* in the generation of audiences for the Hollywood release.

And yet, of course, this pool of audience, marketing, and advance excitement is unpaid, uncredited, and under-valued in the political economy of the studio film system. Such affective labor is nonetheless increasingly necessary for the circulation of any media in a mixed economy of online/offline production, circulation, and distribution. While a number of social and cultural media theorists have drawn attention to questions of free and material labor (for example, Terranova 2004; Scholz 2013: 1–10), Lee's film takes us into the intensive/affective and extensive/spatial experience of networks that *is* the materiality through which affective/creative/cognitive capitalism functions.

Transformers: The Premake is not simply a critique of how the fan labor of capturing and uploading snippets of upcoming film releases feeds global media franchises such as Hollywood cinema. The compositional techniques deployed by Lee both trace standard online geotagging/mapping visualization practices *and* provide a sense of the rhythms and intensities that translocally straddle and propel networked aesthesia. At 5′22″ into his video, Lee scrubs across a map of the U.S. populated by clusters of fan videos assembled according to sites where the actual *Transformers* movie was being shot. We move from Monument Valley in Utah, with only one fan video, to Texas, with eight fan videos, then to Detroit, with a thriving cluster of 115 fan videos. Skipping quickly from Washington state (with only one fan video), we are suddenly propelled halfway across the globe to Hong Kong, where production on the movie gathered 52 fan videos in its wake.

On the one hand, we get the sense that the art of Hollywood filmmaking travels smoothly across global spaces with little care for the specificities of the places in which it lands—these are all just cities that offer the producers tax breaks and concessions. On the other hand, the spatial montage of fan videos laid out as a grid within each city gives a sense of the city itself being filmed through the pulsing, polyrhythmic activities of its citizens and fans on their mobile phones. We scrub across to Detroit's mosaicked grid of fan videos, and the cityscape feels momentarily animated, alive across the flickering of moving images. This is quickly juxtaposed against its ruined urban infrastructure, as Lee selects two fan videos among the grid and zooms in to reveal *Transformers* being shot in a landscape of burnt-out, vacant blocks. That urban setting is the reality of a city that has been ravaged by the shift from an industrial economy to a networked service industry. Even the movie industry will not save it. While not for a moment idealizing the vitality of all the creative labor undertaken by fans, *Transformers: The Premake* nonetheless refuses to cede its affectivity to the appetite of the Hollywood franchise. Something remains: a kind of glimpse into the ways in which imploded cities might nonetheless hold intensities and vitalities—still generate other modes of living through the rhythms and everyday media practices of their inhabitants. Lee both pools the videos together and assigns them to city sites; he draws us into the rhythms that pulse across and between each city grid, across a global network. He plunges us into the quirkiness of a single fan's capture of the production of *Transformers*.

In my analysis of online videos that go viral, I suggest that:

> Something elusive moves and moves us; something not quite quantifiable is generated when these videos are uploaded and then circulate through networks. Something that is felt, shared, and spread through online audiences and networks. Something that does not yet have substance, even so, has force. As these viral videos *go viral*, they become an element at work in the individuation of networked affectivity. They enable a collective (heterogeneous) capacity to affect and be affected in online networks.
>
> (Munster 2013: 103)

A similar, infectious affectivity inhabits Lee's *Premake*. Although the affectivity of fan labor generates a pool of marketing potential for the Hollywood system, it also creates a perspective on cities, habitation, and everydayness in networked cultures that reveals an eye for quirkiness among audiences/citizens. This quirkiness, together with the polyrhymicity of YouTube media and practices of social imagining, ensure the networked imagination cannot simply settle for an image of connectivity. The "join"—the passing of one experience into or across to another—is the process that shifts us from a "network" to qualitative network*ing*. There is still an open proposition at work for inflecting the qualities of relations, for contouring the rhythms, refrains, and passages toward aesthesias of networks.

Further Reading

Doruff, S. (2012) "Multimedia Mixing and Real-time Collaboration: Interview with Sher Doruff about the Development and Use of *KeyWorx*, the Translocal and Polyrhythmic Diagrams," *The Fibreculture Journal* 21.

James, W. (1977 [1912]) "The Thing and Its Relations," in *Essays in Radical Empiricism*, New York: Longmans, Green, pp. 92–122.

Massumi, B. (2011) "Conjunction, Disjunction, Gift," *Transversal*, retrieved from eipcp.net/transversal/0811/massumi/en.

Munster, A. (2013) *An Aesthesia of Networks: Conjunctive Experience in Art and Technology*, Cambridge, MA: MIT Press.

Steyerl, H. (2013) "Too Much World: Is the Internet Dead?" *E-flux Journal* 49, retrieved from www.e-flux.com/journal/too-much-world-is-the-internet-dead.

References

Alberts, D. and R. Hayes (2003) *Power to the Edge*, Washington: CCRP Publications.

Appadurai, A. (1990) "Disjuncture and Difference in the Global Cultural Economy," *Public Culture* 2(2), 1–24.

Barabasi, A.-L. and E. Bonabeau (2003) "Scale-Free Networks," *Scientific American* 288(5), 50–59.

Bridle, J. (2011a) "The New Aesthetic," *Really Interesting Group* weblog, retrieved from www.riglondon.com/blog/2011/05/06/the-new-aesthetic.

Bridle, J. (2011b) "The New Aesthetic," retrieved from new-aesthetic.tumblr.com.

Deuze, M. (2007) *Media Work*, London: Polity.

Doruff, S. (2012) "Multimedia Mixing and Real-time Collaboration: Interview with Sher Doruff about the development and use of *KeyWorx*, the Translocal and Polyrhythmic Diagrams," *The Fibreculture Journal* 21.

Foucault, M. (1980) "The Confession of the Flesh," in C. Gordon (ed.) *Power/Knowledge: Selected Interviews and Other Writings*, New York, NY: Pantheon Books, pp. 194–228.

Hugos, M. (2009) *Business Agility: Sustainable Prosperity in a Relentlessly Competitive World*, Hoboken, NJ: Wiley.

James, W. (1912) *Essays in Radical Empiricism*, New York, NY: Longmans, Green.

James, W. (1977) *The Writings of William James: A Comprehensive Edition*, Chicago, IL: University of Chicago Press.

Keen, A. (2007) *The Cult of the Amateur*, Boston, MA: Nicholas Brealey.

Keen, A. (2015) *The Internet Is Not the Answer*, New York, NY: Atlantic Monthly Press.

Lapoujade, D. (2000) "From Transcendental Empiricism to Worker Nomadism: William James," *Pli: The Warwick Journal of Philosophy* 9, 190–99.

Lee, K. (2014) *Transformers: The Premake*, Online video, retrieved from vimeo.com/94101046.

Lovink, G. (2002) *Dynamics of Critical Internet Culture: 1994–2001*, Amsterdam: Institute for Network Cultures.

Massumi, B. (2011) "Conjunction, Disjunction, Gift," *Transversal*, retrieved from eipcp.net/transversal/0811/massumi/en.

Massumi, B. (2014) *The Power at the End of the Economy*, Durham and London: Duke University Press.

Munster, A. (2013) *An Aesthesia of Networks: Conjunctive Experience in Art and Technology*, Cambridge, MA: MIT Press

Prince (2010) Interview with P. Willis, "Inside Prince's Bizarre Life at Paisley Park," *Daily Mirror*, retrieved from mirror.co.uk/3am/celebrity-news/inside-princes-bizarre-life-paisley.

Quittner, J. (1994) "Johnny Manhattan Meets the Furry Muckers," *Wired 2.0*, retrieved from archive.wired.com/wired/archive/2.03/muds.html.

Scholz, T. (2013) "Introduction," in T. Scholz (ed.) *Digital Labor: The Internet as Playground and Factory*, London and New York: Routledge, pp. 1–10.

Steyerl, H. (2013) "Too Much World: Is the Internet Dead?" *E-flux Journal* 49, retrieved from www.e-flux.com/journal/too-much-world-is-the-internet-dead.

Stoll, C. (1989) *The Cuckoo's Egg: Tracking a Spy through the Maze of Computer Espionage*, New York: Doubleday.

Stoll, C. (1995) "Why the Web Won't Be Nirvana," *Newsweek*, retrieved from newsweek.com/clifford-stoll-why-web-wont-be-nirvana-185306.

Terranova, T. (2004) *Network Culture: Politics for the Information Age*, London: Pluto Press.

Verton, D. (2003) "IT at the Heart of Shock and Awe," *Computerworld*, retrieved from www.computerworld.com/article/2581364/business-intelligence/it-at-heart-of—shock-and-awe-.html.

VNS Matrix (1991) "A Cyberfeminist Manifesto for the 21st Century," Screenshot from *All New Gen* computer game, retrieved from *Media, Art, Net* online database, www.medienkunstnetz.de/works/all-new-gen.

28

FROM "LIVE" TO REAL TIME

On Future Television Studies

Mark J. Williams

As is true across media studies, the growing field of television studies is experiencing a series of methodological crossroads with the rise of digital culture and technology. A survey of both historical and emergent critical issues in the field will suggest new prerogatives for study and analysis in the twenty-first century.

Some of the crossroads in TV studies are related to shifting definitions of "television," always a polysemantic, overdetermined object. Even though the term "television" is ubiquitous, and most everyone uses the term with confidence, what "TV" describes varies considerably over time and has multiple valences even among its contemporary audiences and critics. Is television a growing collection of moving image texts? An electronic device, a combination of devices, or perhaps a piece of furniture? Is it a range of modes of production, from prohibitively expensive, multicamera shoots to images captured and shared on the fly? Is it available to everyone or via limited distribution, accessed according to a schedule or consumed in binge reception, watched alone or together, in physical proximity or linked by social media, on one screen or many? Does it emanate from vast multinational corporations, neighborhood community centers, state governments, or "viewers like you?" How large is the image, with what resolution, and how rich is the sound? Is it broken up by ads, funded by sponsors, or cravenly selling something? Is it local, networked, in the air, under the ground, paid for on-demand, free of charge, or tied to a monthly billing cycle? Television is all of these things, situationally and historically—and the list of characteristics presented here is far from comprehensive. Such complexity offers many opportunities for nuanced and sophisticated analysis, which drives the field of television studies as well as interest in television more broadly. This chapter will introduce many hallmark and emergent directions of study while also suggesting new methods and emphases moving forward. But first, we should briefly recognize a vintage, blindered view of television: TV as "bad object."

Despite several generations of claims about the "golden ages" of television (including TV today) and the rise of complex approaches to TV within media history, cultural studies, and theory and philosophy, television is still available as a ready straw man at the apex of multiple broadside attacks against "the media." Critiques of TV can certainly be warranted and valuable, and they often contribute to public and professional deliberations that affect change and growth in media practice, reception, consumption, and impact. Skepticism is a virtue when watching

TV, part of our due diligence as viewers. And bad television exists just as bad art exists in any format or medium. (Indeed, depending upon one's tastes, "bad" television tends to be readily available as a camp delight when in need of distraction: #craptacular.) But hyperbolic binaries too often structure both popular and critical discourse about television, including dubious claims about the passivity of the TV audience and correlative assumptions about the dearth of insight and creativity on television. The scale of this available mythology (e.g., the boob tube, the idiot box, and the wasteland) has been at times pervasive and unreflective—rudimentary and banal in its defense against the rudimentary and banal. The casual adoption of such attitudes was distilled in a February 2000 *Onion* satire: "Area Man Constantly Mentioning He Doesn't Own a Television." The refutation of television as bad object is a battle mostly won and serves here as a fundamental example of the opportunity to revise and restructure the sometimes simplistic, but more often sophisticated, systems of difference that shape the field.

A historicized perspective about television and a considered analysis of television studies are important to the entertainment value and pleasures sought by consumers of television. They are also important to understanding the social values that reside in television's broad appeal, regulatory framework, responsibilities toward the public interest, and complex modes of address (see Newcomb 1974; R. Williams 1974; Ellis 1985; Streeter 1996). This critical discourse often engages in language and concepts that are unfamiliar to many everyday television audiences. Complex ideas that enrich many areas of cultural and media studies are often crucial to the progress of television studies as well. With that in mind, this chapter mobilizes critical constructs and methodological differences within television studies as they relate to the rise of digital technologies and media. A key arc of consideration is the seemingly linear and arguably triumphalist progression from "live" to "real time," provisionally an arc from analog media to digital media. More than just a matter of how television is perceived over time, this arc deeply influences methods for interpretation.

A Brief History of Now: Modernity, Postmodernism, and Television

In "The Painter of Modern Life," the iconoclastic French poet, Charles Baudelaire, famously wrote:

> Modernity is the transient, the fleeting, the contingent; it is one half of art, the other being the eternal and the immovable . . . You have no right to despise this transitory fleeting element, the metamorphoses of which are so frequent, nor to dispense with it.
>
> (Baudelaire 1972 [1863]: 403)

Media invented since the early nineteenth century, including photography, but perhaps especially electronic media, are deeply imbued with this fugitive genealogy—with this transience. In fact, if the ur-definition of television is an electronic means of vision at a distance, then its technological forebears resonate with the dynamism and fleeting presence of Baudelaire's modernity.

James Carey's study of the telegraph (1989) is a meaningful starting point. Although the telegraph is now defunct, its invention in the 1840s initiated a transformation of mediated communication. If, classically, space and time mutually define one another, then telegraphy introduced a fundamental schism of modernity: for the first time, information traveled faster than physical motility. This is a profound disjuncture, one to which we have grown accustomed but continue to grapple with. It had an enormous impact on the concept and material practices of reporting and receiving the news (and therefore an impact on history and even our notion of history), raising still pertinent questions about who controls the dissemination of information, at what speed and rate, to whom, and under what conditions. Ultimately, the socio-cultural impact of the telegraph led to fundamental changes in language, transportation, commerce, the law, and subjectivity itself. The subsequent invention of electronic communication devices, such as telephony and radio (1870s–1890s), both amplified and complicated the temporal and spatial characteristics of telegraphy, especially as they gradually situated and threaded these characteristics into the everyday practices of public, domestic, and private/individualized environments. Radio was even called wireless telegraphy, at least initially, before its eventual ubiquity as a broadcast medium in the 1920s. Of course, it is not difficult to imagine the relevance of this history today, considering the weave of complex immediacy we experience via television's multiplatform modes of address and reception. Who controls the dominant flow of programming, what is at stake in the variable selectivity of information across television and social media, what tiered and uneven access may exist, what potential exists for online participation, and how do distractions dilute or obscure pertinent information? All of these issues are flavored by the promised spontaneity of electronic interfaces, with their history in technologies such as telegraphy.

In fact, the historical disjuncture of electronic communication defines today's notion of *liveness*, or "live" (with scare quotes), a term which suggests that quotidian experience is electronically mediated by default. After all, electronic media can now represent an event almost simultaneous to the moment it occurs. Liveness, once posited as an essential technological and textual capacity for television, has been staunchly resisted as such (Feuer 1983). In place of liveness, the immediacy of electronic representation—rife with ephemeral references and capable of collapsing distance in a flash—describes a technological capacity as well as performance, reception, and affect, which carry an elusive or fugitive charge reminiscent of Baudelaire's modernity. Some of this charge can be recognized in commonplace disavowal, expressed through statements such as, "I know this is mediated, but I experience it live."

How, then, to consider this new sense of the world and one's place in it, via considerable changes in the use and exchange values of information at high speeds? We might begin by identifying an electronic culture *dispositif* to describe the ethereal yet sustained complex of electronic communication and mediated "liveness" (M. Williams 2003). A *dispositif* refers to details of historically specific configurations of a given medium, paying attention to its technological characteristics, limits, and affordances, its representational capacities and tendencies, and attendant dynamics of subjectivity. Such identification demands an enhanced questioning of how electronic culture is constructed, but also a critical mindfulness about modern epistemologies and their effects. For instance, the proliferation of electronic culture was only possible after decades of intensive infrastructure development, such as the expansion of transportation and power grids that were tied to forceful socio-economic manipulation and exploitation. The resultant capacity for liveness thus complicated the rich history of discontinuous, nineteenth-century media, which are now ripe for rediscovery in the context of today's global communications (Starosielski 2015). Amid this infrastructural shift toward the grid, the capacity for inscribing or recording "live" phenomena was critical and even axiomatic to several key media of the 1800s—for example, photography (1840s), phonography (1870s), and motion pictures (1890s) (Uricchio 2010).

The histories of these media are prioritized in public memory, based primarily on their iconic repeatability. Recording technologies for electronic media were technically complex and expensive to adopt or utilize, developed only after variable periods of contingency and experimentation (Sterne 2003). Despite the incredible impact of these media during their emphatically "live" periods, this history is often disregarded by studies of electronic culture, due in part to difficulties in accessing early media and technologies. However, print and paper materials from this era are increasingly available at archives and online. For example, consider the vintage trade and fan periodicals collected at sites such as the Media History Digital Library. Further development of these resources will prove them transformative as catalysts for research about neglected histories, including additional research on communications and media infrastructures that are routinely disavowed in experiences of immediacy today.

Combining studies of electronic culture with renewed attention to such periods of early media and ephemerality can afford surprising critical insight. Robert Vianello (1985) detailed the critical role that broadcast networks played in developing a strategic mutability of liveness as a means to consolidate power and control over U.S. airwaves, first in radio and then in television. In the U.S., local broadcast stations were the technological and financial backbone for both of these media, radio developing in the 1920s and television after World War II. The FCC mandated local station licenses to regulate and develop broadcasting. Licensing helped ensure that powerful technologies would serve the public interest and not follow top-down development, solely at the behest of special interests and sizable corporate entities in the largest cities. (The FCC also determined, after decades of debate, that advertising would be the economic fulcrum of broadcasting in the U.S., as opposed to alternative funding models around most of the world.) Once local stations grew sufficiently numerous, broadcasting networks emerged by sitting atop them, via network affiliations and by gleaning national advertising rates that could pay for elaborate "live" programs broadcast across the country. This national identity for networks was deployed at various points of advantage during "The American Century," promoting the implicit unity of a national audience—what Benedict Anderson (1983) would call an imagined community—during eras of challenge and strife in the 1930s and 1940s.

"Live" programs, especially those aired by networks during prime time, often featured elaborate production values (e.g., stars and other creative talent) that local stations could not match. That is, they were highly constructed and very performative. As a result, such practices established a qualitative distinction between network and local "live" and then mobilized that distinction in the political economy of the broadcast industry. Crucially, the long-term value of these politics involved inscription and recording technologies: once networks secured control across the "live" broadcast terrain, they could again reconfigure the value of "live" by shifting modes of production to recorded programming, which would realize still more lucrative economies of scale (e.g., address to multiple time zones or reruns and syndication of successful programs).

The early television era featured all of the technologies discussed above as "current" media formats to be utilized and deployed as necessary. There was not a simple transposition of network power to the new medium, based in part on the fraught economics of postwar America and the slow development of technology that could carry the bulkier television signal (Sterne 1999). Networks may have been expected to dominate someday, but once again local stations were the backbone and fulcrum for future development. 1952 was a pivotal year, as a temporary freeze on television stations licenses was lifted and a "live" signal could, for the first time, be regularly telecast across the United States. The experimentation and innovation of early television was gradually over-written by "live" network television and the emergence of filmed or "canned" programs from west coast studios and production centers—a practice that enhanced homogenization of class difference and whitening of televisual content (Lipsitz 1990). The capacity for recorded programs grew with the invention of videotape in the 1950s, leading to a similar shift in business models from the radio era, privileging network power and production companies that specialized in recording (Vianello 1985; Lafferty 1999; Kompare 2005).

The rise of local and network television news provided a different valence of recording and storage media, since most every station would send out professional 16 mm camera and sound personnel to capture some variant on the news of the day. In surprising quantities, the original in-camera footage or edited footage from this era (1950s–1970s) still exist in local cultural heritage institutions and national archives. As virtually untapped resources of public memory and social history, these materials are enormously valuable to contemporary researchers.

The infamous era of three- or four-network U.S. television has received a lion's share of attention in television history and criticism, including classic studies of network television decision-making, programming, and social impact (Boddy 1990; Spigel 1992) and legions of textual analysis about specific programs, events, and episodes—far too numerous to reference here. As this era of influence began to wane with the rise of cable and satellite transmissions, television criticism challenged constitutive practices of the industry as a cultural institution and new capacities for engagement with, if not control over, the medium. Television had become available 24/7, its schedule reinforcing ideological assumptions about the gendered workday and workweek, yet featuring complex textual configurations with pan-textual implications (Browne 1984). TV was also recognized as a site of seemingly endless availability and consumption, reflecting subjective crisis management regarding political economies of address and reception (Houston 1984), a medium available for fertile theoretical consideration yet potentially guilty of tautological self-recognition: a mirror serving pleasure in search of legitimacy (Elsaesser 1992). Scheduled events of cultural, national, and international importance could be planned and ritually configured according to the participation of a vast televisual audience (Dayan & Katz 1992). Domestic technologies of remote control and selective inscription (e.g., VCRs) led to enhanced options of when and how to consume TV—to time-shift or "zip" through programs and commercials and also save them for later in a personalized archive (Friedberg 2006).

This was the era when the rise of digital channels of access (via cable and satellite), but also advances in digital graphics, demonstrably changed television into an almost literalized object of postmodernism, driven by multiple industry logics that produced what Caldwell (1994) calls "televisuality": an exhibitionist performance of both style and content that underscores how television is constructed. It was a response to not only a perceived crisis in the changing economics of television, but also audience demands for aesthetic and conceptual innovations, such as high culture appropriations and pronounced strains of irony and pastiche. This transformation of the medium contributed heavily to a signal transfiguration of liveness into the act of articulation. "Live" once implied a technological *relation* to a referent that a medium, such as television, was in the process of representing. However, its definition changed alongside TV's emergence as both a virtual mirror of continuous time and experience and a spectacle of commercial networked address. In short, liveness became a *description* of what TV is showing at the moment, in the flow of the mediated now, regardless of the referent.

What is live now matters less than the status of liveness. After all, what could be less "live" than C-SPAN?

But these vertiginous dynamics of representation periodically, if not methodically, return to an ontological baseline when disaster and catastrophe occur (Doane 2006), with 9–11 serving as a predominant example in contemporary U.S. history. Suddenly, the performative exhibitionism of media is mitigated (at least temporarily), the coverage becomes protracted and strains for phantom legibility, and, perhaps most tellingly, the commercial imperatives of the medium come to a near halt. Repetition of footage and scant pieces of information stand in for a progressive understanding of traumatic events and explanations of them. These mediated exercises serve to conditionally re-boot televisual liveness, a process which today is conjoined by the additional channels of discourse that mobile and social media enable—participatory roles of response and inquiry with the potential to both enhance and mollify the effects of catastrophe to the presumption of quotidian experience.

This example affords consideration of the far more moderate modalities of anxiety and disruption that are commonplace to valuations of interactive and participatory digital media today, especially the sea change growth of networked mobile devices such as smart phones—media that are more often discussed in terms of "real time" rather than liveness. Real time represents a curious border zone of the electronic *dispositif*, situationally deployed across analog and digital media to describe the duration of a mediated present. Like liveness, real time is a flexible and mutable term that refers to mediation of the present; like liveness, real time also refers to a situational valuation of mediation. It proffers a virtual transposition of values as its limit point: the act of mediation itself may render something exceptionally inflected (more live, more real, or more present) than it would be if encountered otherwise, outside mediated networks. In the context of digital media, real time often competes with liveness as a modality, associated with desire (and anxiety) about the near future rather than a present tense wired to the mediated past. The contemporary charge of real time seems indelibly connected to the modern logic of acceleration (Virilio 1997), a logic invested in realizing the near future. But real time regularly suggests individuated control while within the media network(s), a capacity to navigate autonomously but also have one's autonomy confirmed (Samuels 2008). This capacity does not describe a false autonomy, though it often relies upon an active disavowal of the distinction between self and networked device.

A correlative technology is the DVR, which amplifies and exacerbates the personalized control introduced by the VCR. DVR temporality is keenly imbricated in the real time *dispositif*. The device allows the user to selectively freeze and control "live" content and then flash or fast-forward through real time to re-synchronize with the present. This represents a new wrinkle of time within television culture and suggests an attendant desire within DVR temporality: to continue to fast-forward and "record" into the future, to accelerate into the near future. This desire can be described as a real time subjunctive (M. Williams 2003), situated within related yet contradictory temporal mediations of subjectivity. For example, the consumerist public sphere of mobile phones and social networks is premised upon our movement through a persistent "now," where we are recognized or hailed (as consumer participants). This sphere is not equivalent to our identities and rights as citizens. Yet, corporate and state forces assume a sphere of dataveillance and subjection, which condition the real time media environments of consumerism, often through our unwitting reliance on complex metadata feedback loops to confirm an experience that the networks in which we engage believe in us (Stiegler 2011). Is the desire to participate in these environments by virtue of invitation, opportunity, interdiction, or a fugitive lure charged with promise and anxiety about a future we do not wish to be absent from?

Television Studies: Next Steps

A great deal of contemporary research in television studies has circled around evident concern and enthusiasm about the crises facing the television industries as well as television as an object of study, including whether "television" will endure widely anticipated changes wrought by disruptive technologies and complexities of commercial competition. Lotz (2014) provides a formative overview of contentious, "post-network" dynamics of television. Multiple conferences and anthologies have been devoted to different variants on television and the digital (television after TV, television and the internet, digital television, television as digital, post-TV, must-click TV, etc.), alongside the landmark unconference, journal, and collection of *Flow TV* (Kackman et al. 2010). Other scholarship credits television as the key precursor to the internet (Murphy 2011), celebrates TV narrative complexity (Mittel 2015), actively legitimizes TV in the new media context (Newman & Levine 2011), and even declares TV's victory over digital culture (Wolff 2015). As a barometer of cultural acceptance, The Peabody Awards have taken the lead in recognizing web series and other alternative formats of television in their annual awards of excellence.

Churn in the television media environment has been especially productive for the emerging field of media industries studies, featuring initiatives to map and understand the innovations of decentered matrixes of production and new eco-systems of multiplatform distribution and reception. Amid concerns of collusion between scholarship and industry practice, forceful yet nuanced studies have been produced on topics such as labor issues in global media production (Curtin & Sanson 2016) and the mixed potential for participatory politics in social media (Jenkins, Ford, & Green 2013). Other groundbreaking research resources have been produced from outside academia. For example, consider the Internet Archive's "Political TV Ad Archive," which is developing a tracking system to reveal the funding background of ads, together with capabilities to fact-check and track memes found within ads.

What was once reported as warlike hostilities between online media, streaming services, and the legacy broadcast television industry is now being framed through deeply complementary services, which pointedly underscore TV as an enduring framework that provides endless consumption, with slogans such as "Come TV with Us" (Hulu) and "You've Fallen Into the #Showhole" (Amazon Fire TV)—the promise of plentiful programming for postbinge despair. Notable for a blank irony that borders on clueless is Comcast's "Everything is Awesome" ad (2016). It features elegant editing and a faux rap break to signify the transmedia options of cable and broadband. The ad figuratively channels the brand as a seamless array of guaranteed family harmony and connectedness; whether together or alone, all of it is "real"—which is to say, apparently without any buffering delays. It also adapts *The Lego Movie* (2014) theme, featuring rhymes such as, "Everything is awesome, everything is cool when you're watching a screen, everything is awesome when you're sharing a meme." Apps, selfies, interactive DVRs, shows-to-go: these are delights to be shared across platforms, devices, and audiences to produce a familial sense of immediacy, belonging, and domestic security, even if you happen to be riding a public bus. The Comcast song even describes "an awesome internet that's super-'Whoa!'" The subjunctive "now" of figurative plenitude is literally articulated as the slogan in the concluding tag line, "Xfinity: the future of awesome."

Beyond the hype and chic coziness of such an appeal, significant questions persist about the mediated public sphere, the future of public memory, and how our "real time" engagement with television might best inform awareness and diligence about these topics. Digital anxiety is often related to shifts in economies of avowal. For example, as a result of digital culture's crisis of indexicality, how can we trust what we see? But changes in economies of avowal necessarily entail changes in economies of disavowal (and, more broadly, attendant economies of occlusion, repression, and foreclosure). These may be among the principal spaces where radical difference and socio-political intervention germinate and reside in digital culture. It should be our prerogative, then, to inform our research with critical thinking aware of the past and outside what dominant media industries would have us believe.

Further Reading

Barker, T. (2012) *Time and the Digital: Connecting Technology, Aesthetics, and a Process Philosophy of Time*, Hanover, NH: Dartmouth College Press.

Bennett, J. and N. Strange (eds.) (2011) *Television as Digital Media*, Durham, NC: Duke University Press.

Chun, W. H. K., A. Fisher, and T. Keenan (eds.) (2016) *New Media, Old Media: A History and Theory Reader*, 2nd edn, New York, NY: Routledge.

Ernst, W. (2002) "Between Real Time and Memory on Demand: Reflections on/of Television," *South Atlantic Quarterly* 101(3), 625–37.

Galili, D. (ed.) (2016) "Early Television Historiographies," *Journal of e-Media Studies* 5(1), retrieved from journals.dartmouth.edu/cgi-bin/WebObjects/Journals.woa/1/xmlpage/4/issue/.

Hu, T-H. (2012) "Real Time/Zero Time," *Discourse* 34(2–3), 163–84.

Jenkins, H. (2008) *Convergence Culture: Where Old and New Media Collide*, New York, NY: NYU Press.

The Media Ecology Project, retrieved from sites.dartmouth.edu/mediaecology/.

Noble, S. U. and B. Tynes (2016) *The Intersectional Internet: Race, Sex, Class, and Culture Online*, New York, NY: Peter Lang Publishing, Inc.

Parks, L. (2005) *Cultures in Orbit: Satellites and the Televisual*, Durham, NC: Duke University Press.

Scannell, P. (2014) *Television and the Meaning of "Live": An Enquiry into the Human Situation*, Cambridge, UK: Polity.

Sewell, P. (2014) *Television in the Age of Radio*, New Brunswick: Rutgers University Press.

Smith-Shomade, B. (2012) *Watching while Black: Centering the Television of Black Audiences*, New Brunswick: Rutgers University Press.

Spigel, L. and J. Olsson (eds.) (2004) *Television after TV: Essays on a Medium in Transition*, Durham, NC: Duke University Press.

Thompson, E. and J. Mittell (eds.) (2013) *How to Watch Television*, New York, NY: New York University.

Williams, M. (2016) "Networking Moving Image History: Archives, Scholars, and the Media Ecology Project," in C. Acland and E. Hoyt (eds.) *The Arclight Guidebook to Media History and The Digital Humanities*, Falmer: REFRAME/Project Arclight, retrieved from projectarclight.org/book.

References

Anderson, B. (1983) *Imagined Communities: Reflections on the Origins and Spread of Nationalism*, New York, NY: Verso.

Baudelaire, C. (1972 [1863]) "The Painter of Modern Life," in P.E. Charvet (trans.) *Baudelaire: Selected Writings on Art and Artists*, London: Cambridge University Press, 390–436.

Boddy, W. (1990) *Fifties Television: The Industry and Its Critics*, Urbana, IL: University of Illinois Press.

Browne, N. (1984) "The Political Economy of the Television (Super) Text," Special Issue, "Television/Film: Cultural Perspectives on History and Theory," Nick Browne (ed.) *Quarterly Review of Film Studies* 9(3), 174–82.

Caldwell, J. (1994) *Televisuality: Style, Crisis, and Authority in American Television*, New Brunswick, NJ: Rutgers University Press.

Carey, J. (1989) *Communication as Culture: Essays on Media and Society*, Boston, MA: Unwin Hyman.

Curtin, M. and K. Sanson (eds.) (2016) *Precarious Creativity: Global Media, Local Labor*, Oakland, CA: University of California Press.

Dayan, D. and Katz, E. (1992) *Media Events: The Live Broadcasting of History*, Cambridge: Harvard University Press.

Doane, M. A. (2006) "Information, Crisis, Catastrophe," in W.H. K. Chun and T. Keenan (eds.) *New Media, Old Media: A History and Theory Reader*, New York: Routledge, 251–64.

Ellis, J. (1985) *Visible Fictions: Cinema, Television, Video*, London, UK: Routledge & Kegan Paul.

Elsaesser, T. (1992) "TV through the Looking Glass," *Quarterly Review of Film & Video* 14(1–2), 5–27.

Feuer, J. (1983) "The Concept of Live Television: Ontology as Ideology" in E. Ann Kaplan (ed.) *Regarding Television: Critical Approaches—An Anthology*, Los Angeles: The American Film Institute, 12–22.

Friedberg, A. (2006) *The Virtual Window: From Alberti to Microsoft*, Cambridge, MA: MIT Press.

Houston, B. (1984) "Viewing Television: The Metapsychology of Endless Consumption," Special Issue, "Television/Film: Cultural Perspectives on History and Theory," Nick Browne (ed.) *Quarterly Review of Film Studies* 9(3), 183–95.

Internet Archive (n.d.), Political TV Ad Archive, retrieved from politicaladarchive.org/.

Jenkins, H., S. Ford, and J. Green (2013) *Spreadable Media: Creating Value and Meaning in a Networked Culture*, New York, NY: NYU Press.

Kackman, M., M. Binfield, M. Payne, A. Perlman, and B. Sebok (2010) *Flow TV: Television in the Age of Media Convergence*, New York, NY: Routledge.

Kompare, D. (2005) *Rerun Nation: How Repeats Invented American Television*, New York, NY: Routledge.

Lafferty, W. (1999) " 'A New Era in TV Programming' Becomes 'Business as Usual': Videotape Technology, Local Stations, and Network Power, 1957–1961," in Special Issue, "U.S. Regional and Non-Network Television" Mark Williams (ed.) *Quarterly Review of Film and Video* 16(3–4), 405–19.

Lipsitz, G. (1990) *Time Passages: Collective Memory and American Popular Culture*, Minneapolis, MN: University of Minnesota Press.

Lotz, A. (2014) *The Television Will Be Revolutionized*, 2nd edn, New York, NY: NYU Press.

Media History Digital Library (n.d.), retrieved from mediahistoryproject.org/.

Mittell, J. (2015) *Complex TV: The Poetics of Contemporary Television Storytelling*, New York, NY: New York, NY University.

Murphy, S. (2011) *How Television Invented New Media*, New Brunswick, NJ: Rutgers University Press.

Newcomb, H. (1974) *TV: The Most Popular Art*, New York, NY: Anchor Books.

Newman, M. Z. and E. Levine (2011), *Legitimating Television: Media Convergence and Cultural Studies*, New York, NY: Routledge.

The Onion (2000) "Area Man Constantly Mentioning He Doesn't Own A Television," *The Onion* 36(4), retrieved from theonion.com/article/area-man-constantly-mentioning-he-doesnt-own-a-tel-429.

Samuels, R. (2008) "Auto-Modernity after Post-Modernism: Autonomy and Automation in Culture, Technology, and Education," in T. McPherson (ed.) *Digital Youth, Innovation, and the Unexpected*, Cambridge, MA: MIT Press.

Sconce, J. (2000) *Haunted Media: Electronic Presence from Telegraphy to Television*, Durham, NC: Duke University Press.

Sewell, P. (2014) *Television in the Age of Radio*, New Brunswick, Canada: Rutgers University Press.

Spigel, L. (1992) *Make Room for TV: Television and the Family Ideal in Postwar America*, Chicago, IL: University of Chicago Press, 1992).

Starosielski, N. (2015) *The Undersea Network*, Durham, NC: Duke University Press.

Sterne, J. (1999) "Television under Construction: American Television and the Problem of Distribution, 1926–1962," *Media, Culture & Society* 21, 503–30.

Sterne, J. (2003) *The Audible Past: Cultural Origins of Sound Reproduction*, Durham, NC: Duke University Press.

Stiegler, B. (1998–2011) *Technics and Time* (3 volumes), Redwood City, CA: Stanford University Press.

Streeter, T. (1996) *Selling the Air: A Critique of the Policy of Commercial Broadcasting in the United States*, Chicago, IL: University of Chicago Press.

Uricchio, W. (2010) "TV as Time Machine: Television's Changing Heterochronic Regimes and the Production of History," in Jostein Gripsrud (ed.) *Relocating Television: Television in the Digital Context*, London, UK: Routledge, pp. 27–40.

Vianello, R. (1985) "The Power Politics of 'Live' Television," *Journal of Film and Video* 37(3) (Summer, 1985), 26–40.

Virilio, P. (1997) *Open Sky*, New York, NY: Verso.

Williams, M. (2003) "Real-Time Fairy Tales: Cinema Pre-Figuring Digital Anxiety" in A. Everett and J. T. Caldwell (eds.) *New Media: Theories and Practices of Digitextuality*, New York, NY: Routledge, pp. 159–78.

Williams, R. (1974) *Television: Technology and Cultural Form*, New York, NY: Schocken Books.

Wolff, M. (2015) *Television Is the New Television: The Unexpected Triumph of Old Media in the Digital Age*, New York, NY: Portfolio.

29

ICYMI

Catching Up to the Moving Image Online

Gregory Zinman

Online video has reached escape velocity: at present, video traffic accounts for over three-quarters of U.S. internet bandwidth; YouTube counts over one billion people as users; and three hundred hours of new video are uploaded to YouTube every minute—only three years ago, it was only 60 hours per minute (Boris 2014). The figure will be higher by the time you read this. Now, more than ever, there is quite literally too much to see.

Digital humanities have long been concerned with issues of scale, but, save for some important exceptions (Burgess & Green 2009; Snickars & Vonderau 2009), scholars have yet to fully contend with a medium—online video—that commands an attention to scale as one of its fundamental characteristics. Nevertheless, the *experience* of online video is nearly always one of overabundance and, concomitantly, loss. ICYMI, the acronym for the internet/txt slang "in case you missed it," may thus be the defining *impression* of online video. Relentlessly hashtagged and reposted, ICYMI points out noteworthy videos you may not have seen. The shorthand's putatively helpful tone papers over an individual's proliferating anxiety as she attempts to stay *au courant* with all of the "essential" memes, GIFs, trailers, soundbites, vines, and vids marked as such. Save for live-streaming video of press conferences or webcam shows, catching up to the past—whether from the last century or only a few minutes ago—is online video's fundamental mode of viewership. In a content-heavy mediascape in which web pages are constantly updated and browsers are incessantly refreshed, media gets buried. One of the only chances for a video's survival within the attention economy is if it is taken up in the ecology of social media: reblogged, re-tweeted, posted, and shared. A close cousin to that other internet-inspired self-diagnosis, FOMO ("fear of missing out"), ICYMI speaks to the impossibility of keeping up. The resulting discomfort is produced by the notion that *not* seeing the video takes one out of the circulation of information—to have not seen means to not participate, to not comment, to not register within a designated community.

Regardless of what one thinks is "worth watching," the staggering scope and potential of online video—what Richard Grusin has dubbed "the YouTube sublime" (2009: 60)—has forestalled a significant academic bibliography on the subject, even as those concerning social networks and computational media have swelled in recent years. Considering the subject's quickly changing terrain, which pulses at a speed well beyond that of conventional academic publishing, the dearth of scholarship is understandable. Online video's expanding reach presents a further challenge. Just think: the moving image online encompasses not only streaming cinema and television content from services such as Netflix, Amazon, and Hulu, but also video platforms such as YouTube, Vimeo, and DailyMotion; micro moving image platforms such as Vine; social media platforms, such as Twitter, Facebook, Snapchat, and Instagram; as well as live streaming, interactive platforms such as Skype, Google Hangout, FaceTime, and Periscope—not to mention the host of ever-proliferating sites and platforms for watching pornographic video. Video online therefore encompasses nearly every imaginable instantiation of the moving image, and the tendency toward the production of more content, increased viewership, and bigger business seems both inevitable and irrevocable. Online video is a locus of culture and capital, and it is therefore incumbent upon us, as media scholars and students of same, to think hard about its technologies, methods, and meanings.

How, then, do we approach the study of the moving image online? How do we catch up to our video present? How much of online video deserves scrutiny beyond its obvious ephemeral pleasures? When we think of the moving image, we tend to think first of film and television. Perhaps not surprisingly, a number of conceptual rubrics associated with cinema and media studies can be applied to an analysis of the moving image online. When our focus shifts from traditional film and television to the moving image online, we have an opportunity to expand the parameters of screen studies by revealing continuities and ruptures between newer and older forms of media.

One key difference between online video and earlier varieties of the moving image is the position and role of the viewer, particularly with regard to the idea of labor. In a visual field where videos come to us and we reach out to find others with a search bar or simple click, the ease of access and manipulation of the visual image has resulted in an effacement of labor. YouTube, Google, and Facebook employ thousands of workers whose responsibilities include screening and removing new uploads that depict beheadings, torture, child pornography, bestiality, and animal abuse. Many of these workers do not make it past a few months on the job, and there is now more content than can be effectively screened by humans (Chen 2014). Online video gives us a chance to think about digital labor through the material and affective economics that are put into play with every keystroke and followed link.

There are numerous conceivable approaches to the subject of online video, so this chapter sets out a small series of conceptual lenses—Content, Viewing, and Genre—through which we can begin to see the online moving image as a technology, artistic medium, economy, and social structure. My focus largely centers on YouTube, not only because it is the largest repository of online video, but also because it stands as the third most trafficked website on the internet (Alexa 2015), behind Facebook and Google—the latter owns YouTube, and the former makes extensive use of its resources. YouTube is hardly the only place where people are watching video, but it is a major hub of video culture—the site where the moving image is being liked, shared, aggregated, quantified, and reshaped.

Content

ICYMI: The most watched online video of 2014 was a piece of grassroots filmmaking by Polish YouTuber, Sylwester Wardega, aka SA Wardega. Wardega dressed up his small dog, Chica, in a tarantula costume and filmed people's terrified reactions when confronted by the comically uncanny animal in a subway station, in a dimly lit park, or while stepping into a parking garage elevator (Luckerson 2014). More than 125 million people watched "Mutant Giant Spider Dog," and its success encapsulates many features of contemporary online video. For one, animals, particularly cats and dogs, enjoy a place of privilege in online video—a digital mainstreaming of the myriad appearances by pets in avant-garde films by Chris Marker, Maya Deren, Andy Warhol, Kenneth Anger, and Carolee Schneemann, among others. Wardega's video is also short, running roughly three and a half minutes, making it perfect for a bit of procrastination from whatever task is at hand, for waiting out a long coffee line on a mobile phone, or for breaking up a scroll through one's social media feed. It carries the documentary impulse that defines a swath of online amateur filmmaking while conflating the real and imaginary. It is user-generated in terms of content, viral in its success and spread, and global in its reach, supported by Wardega's dedicated Facebook and YouTube profiles, not to mention a number of fansites and ancillary pages (Chica, it should be noted, has her own Facebook profile). As slight as it may be, the success of "Mutant Giant Spider Dog," at first glance, seemingly encapsulates the promise of online video as a participatory and democratic medium, as expressed by scholars such as Henry Jenkins (2006), Clay Shirky (2008), and Sam Ford and Josh Green (2013), in which barriers to production, distribution, and fame have been lowered to the point that ostensibly anyone can make a video that can compete on the media playing field with content by any professional filmmaker or company. At the same time, however, more sustained economic critiques of digital culture have begun to emerge. Most notably, Christian Fuchs (2012) argues that internet platforms such as YouTube cannot be considered participatory if the ownership structure is not in fact participatory, and Alexandra Juhasz's video-book, *Learning From YouTube* (2011), points to the many ways YouTube's design primarily functions as means of digression and distraction from deep critical engagement of any kind. By corporate intention and through user experience, individuals are left out of the negotiations, decisions, and strategy of video sharing sites, all while signing away personal data that can be used by industrial authorities to shape exactly those business decisions. Jonathan Beller (2006) suggests that in the economy of the internet, attention is the most significant indicator of value, with the result being that "to look is to labor" (115). Online viewers thus find themselves simultaneously assuming the roles of consumer, laborer, and commodity.

Tellingly, the second most watched online video of 2014 was an ad—the very thing viewers hope to avoid (or at least claim to) by watching content online, and a potent example of how capital has staked a significant claim on the moving image online. In "Winner Stays," a 4-minute advertisement for Nike's "Risk Everything" campaign, shot by the agency Wieden + Kennedy, school-aged participants in a pickup game of soccer miraculously transform themselves into some of the world's greatest professional players. As the scene shifts from the schoolyard to a flashbulb-popping, 50,000-seat arena, the camera cuts from the fevered pitch to fans cheering on the action as they watch the game broadcast on televisions in bars and cafes around the world. The players sport signature Nike cleats, while in the stands, NBA star Kobe Bryant and *Sports Illustrated* swimsuit model Irina Shayk lend credence to the machismo-laden one-upmanship on display below. Meanwhile, one of the children metamorphoses into the Incredible Hulk before further transforming, strangely, into Team USA's goalkeeper, Tim Howard. The short ends with a call for participation via social media, replete with a hashtag: #riskanything.

What was implicit in the production of "Mutant Giant Spider Dog"—that fame and fortune can be achieved by anyone, anywhere—is made explicit in the Nike video. Amateurs become professionals with transmedial potential, watched and adored by millions. At the same time, the ad is a riot of cross-promotional branding, which ranges between the subtextual (e.g., Victoria's Secret by the association with Shayk and the NBA by association with Bryant); the literal (e.g., the "Fly Emirates" logo adorning the Paris Saint-Germain F.C. jersey of Zlatan Ibrahimović), and the absurd (e.g., the CGI apparition of Disney-owned Marvel's jade giant). This surreal bricolage of human and intellectual properties is emblematic of Francisco Casetti's formulation of the experience of online video: "We no longer find ourselves faced with an exchange, but a circulation; no longer in front of a merely factual reality, but a reality born of a recombination of information packets" (2015: 173). Nike offers a GIF-ready, pre-emptive remix, smashing together bodies and brands to pleasure and entice an eager, twinned audience: one that is staged in the commercial, and one ready to click through the same. Having so thoroughly mixed the real with computer-generated fantasy, "Winner Stays" concludes with a gesture toward the public, but serves ultimately as further promotion for the brands and celebrities at hand.

Made at opposite ends of the video production scale, with radically different levels of financial and technical support, these two videos nevertheless capture the still-developing and uneasy relationship between professional and amateur makers online. YouTube's slogan used to be "Broadcast Yourself," a populist motto celebrating grassroots self-expression. That initial euphoria has given way to a sober tagline that reflects the site's increased reliance on ad revenue and material that can hold viewers' attention in a crowded virtual marketplace: "Hosts user-generated videos. Includes network and professional content." The divide between amateur and professional is simultaneously blurring distinctions even as it generates insurmountable gaps. Of the 30 most watched YouTube videos since the site arrived online in 2005, only one of them—"Charlie Bit My Finger Again," a home-video of an infant chomping his older brother—was made by an individual rather than a corporation. 27 of the remaining 29 slots are filled by professionally budgeted and executed music videos (YouTube 2015).

This is the shifting nature of capital at work in online video. Jean Burgess states:

> As YouTube, Inc. moves to more profitably arrange and stabilize the historically contentious relations among rights-holders, uploaders, advertisers and audiences, some forms of amateur video production have become institutionalized and professionalized, while others have been further marginalized and driven underground or to other, more forgiving, platforms.
>
> (Burgess 2012: 53–54)

Of course, the majority of videos on YouTube receive fewer than 500 views, and amass even fewer subscribers (Frommer & Angelova 2009). Online video is not simply supported by the millions of hours of unpaid labor that go into creating and maintaining user-generated content, but, most important to the shareholders and businesspeople running the sites, it is increasingly supported by a hierarchical star-system—a firmament which now includes Wardega—responsible for generating ad revenue.

For all there is to see online, there is an equal or greater amount of moving image material that remains *offline*. What gets digitized and uploaded (and not subsequently taken down) depends on a complex negotiation of legal rights, costly preservation efforts, and business strategies, as well as the initiative of enterprising individuals willing to fly in the face of intellectual property claims. The resultant gaps in the online video record produce a surfeit of parallel, ghostly content—a forgotten history of the moving image comprised of marginalized, amateur, forgotten, and restricted work that will never make it to our screens.

Viewing

How we watch online video not only presents a problem of scale, it also presents a problem of diversity. Videos are consumed on desktop computers at work, on laptops, on tablets, on phones, on watches, and across façades and billboards of urban centers. This does not mean that all of these surfaces, screens, and displays hold viewers' attention equally. Each carries associations and conventions of use and is highly contextualized by the time and place in which it is engaged. Viewing conditions are situational and in perpetual flux: the single viewer of Facebook and Instagram engages online video differently from the couple settling down to stream a few episodes of *Game of Thrones*, or a preteen slumber party where individuals watch *The Lego Movie* on separate devices so that they can IM one another in real time as it plays. What is being watched where, how, and by whom is something that has not yet been extensively studied, and remains far from understood. Yet online video's now-familiar condition of one viewer, one screen, harkens back to some of the earliest moving image technology, such as Edison's Kinetoscope, which also had a small screen that could only be accessed by one viewer. More than a marker of mere convenience, this personalization of media consumption is less a recursion to past media conventions than a symptom of how both media experiences and communities have been made immaterial, the "weak ties" described by Nicole Ellison and danah boyd that "would fade away were it not for the ease with which people can communicate, share, and maintain simple connections" (2013: 159). Viewing online video thus produces a divided consciousness in which the user continuously toggles between personal interest and a global connection with myriad like-minded groups. To address these new viewing contexts, Tara McPherson has coined the term "volitional mobility" to describe the "scan-and-search" experience of viewing content online (2006: 205). The term implies agency and ability, a means of surveying an ever-expanding media horizon before drilling into a particular facet of the landscape. However, in addition to users seeking out and curating collections of videos online, more and more we find that online video comes to viewers.

Video comes to viewers in a number of different but interrelated ways. People see videos embedded in their social media streams on Facebook, Twitter, Instagram, and Tumblr. Videos viewed on these platforms may even start automatically, momentarily pausing the user's infinite scrolling of updated content. Videos displayed within and transmitted by social media tend to be extremely short and are meant to register briefly. Still others are linked within posts or comments. One's "volitional mobility," her behaviors and choices online—or, what gets clicked and how long one lingers—comes back to her algorithmically. Your social media reacts to your choices. You are "fed" more of the kinds of things you have previously clicked on, and the same is true of sites such as YouTube, where your global searches serve, first and foremost, to hone the specificity and variety of the online video that comes to you. Your searches beget searches undertaken not by you, but by algorithms developed to keep you watching more, to sprinkle a trail of video breadcrumbs that are followed to various destinations. During an interview in 2014, YouTube spokesman Cristos Goodrow described the millions of lines of code comprising the platform's proprietary algorithm:

> I don't think of it as one thing, I think of it as lots of little pieces that are trying to accomplish the overall goal of connecting you with what you're looking for or what we think you might want to watch.
>
> (Kreft 2014)

A reason cited by many viewers who now claim to prefer watching content online to offline is that they feel free of programming, liberated from scheduled times and places of viewership (Battaglio 2015). Our behaviors and click-throughs imbricate us in what I call *algorithmic viewing*, a kind of subtle and individually tailored programming that users may not be fully aware of ("what we think you might want to watch") or even care about. Echoing Wendy Chun's theorization of how computational environments pose the problem of not only what is not known but also what cannot be perceived phenomenologically, the processing rate of algorithms exceeds people's knowledge capacity *and* perception (2011: 1–18).

Algorithmic viewing also applies to the increasing numbers of nonhuman watchers of online video. YouTube employs automated copyright violation detection, so that rights holders can be alerted to others using their content without permission, and geofiltering software to restrict access to content depending on viewers' locations. Bots designed to watch and ratchet up YouTube views became so widespread that, in 2012, YouTube changed its proprietary algorithm to reflect not the number of times a video was watched, but the amount of time spent watching specific videos. Advances in computer vision have trained robots to watch cooking tutorials on YouTube and recognize objects (e.g., apples and wire whisks) as well as cooking techniques in videos. It is not impossible to imagine online viewing as both a template for machine learning and a site for combinatory expressions of computer and human vision resulting in new modes of the moving image.

Computer vision may allow for comprehensive viewing of online video by nonhuman agents, but there are also heaps of material that go unseen by human viewers. Roughly 30 percent of videos on YouTube account for 99 percent of what is actually watched on the platform (Whitelaw 2011). The vast majority of the online video repository simply gets swept away in the wake of online video's big whales. Regardless of who is or is not watching, it is worth asking what is ultimately more valuable to Google: the content uploaded to YouTube by people, or the computer vision harvesting, processing, and analyzing its metadata. Indeed, accounting for who or what is viewing online video is just one way that media scholars can begin to conceptualize the changing nature of viewing in the digital age.

Genre

As heterogeneous as online video content and viewing may be, certain generic tendencies have emerged. While related to conventions associated with film and television, these tendencies nevertheless establish new vistas for the moving image.

For instance, online video has given rise to certain new classifications of moving image practice. Compiled tropes are the visual lingua franca of today's viral videos. Meme-based "supercuts" are now staples of online video production and consumption. Like a web-based instantiation of Lev Manovich's (2000) database cinema, they collect a repeated action, bit of dialogue, or composition from a single film, television show, or genre (think of every instance of Chewbacca roaring in the *Star Wars* films, sequences of tough guys walking away from explosions in slow motion, or scenes of Tom Cruise running). Found-footage practices that were once the province of the filmic avant-garde (e.g., Bruce Connor's *A Movie* (1958)) have become the way video is made, disseminated, and understood online.

When online video is relegated to the realm of pleasant diversion, how it hails viewers or deploys questionable choices often goes unacknowledged or unchallenged. In exploring the intersections of laughter with the ethics and practices of remix culture, Jaimie Baron (2014) identifies a tendency that she calls "(in)appropriation," or the foregrounding of disparity between source material and its repurposing. Baron's research points to the necessity of interrogating remix culture and its negotiations with not only public and private domains, but also issues of race, class, gender, and power.

Remix is hardly the only wellspring for new genres, however. *Machinima*, in which users employ real-time 3-D graphic engines to create new computer animations, is wildly popular and demonstrates the shrinking gaps between animation, videogame cut scenes, and traditional cinema. It also serves as a promotional tool for existing games or even visual archives of obsolete ones. Relatedly, but even more widespread, is *Let's Play*: video that demonstrates videogame playthrough, usually accompanied by a gamer's running commentary. Swedish gamer PewDiePie (né Felix Kjellberg) is the reigning champion of the genre; the 56 million people who have signed up to follow his virtual exploits makes his the most subscribed channel in all of YouTube (Guinness World Records 2015). *Tutorials*, in which on-camera personalities offer tips on the mechanics of hairstyling, makeup, plumbing, circuit-bending, sweep-picking guitar techniques, and so on, also indicate a shift from a text-based culture to a moving-image one. The widespread popularity of particular tutors, such as makeup demonstrator Michelle Phan, indicates how what was once the province of the how-to book or dreary instructional film has become a launching point for transmedial branding. *Unboxing*, or videos in which recent purchasers of commercial goods both film and narrate their experiences of taking things they bought out of the original packaging, speaks to the simultaneous commodity fetishism and documentary impulse that inform a great deal of online video. In these object-oriented strip teases for eager consumers, viewers can see if the purchase comes as advertised while marveling at the sight of a device emerging from its glossy packaging. At the same time, unboxing videos and examples of its related genre, "haul" videos—the visual cataloging of multiple purchases—act as unpaid advertising, and thus labor, for the brands and products on display. For instance, five days after the release of the iPhone 6S, nearly 300,000 unboxing videos featuring the device appeared on YouTube.

Online video is changing and repositioning the use and understanding of the moving image within the digital mediascape. To the suggested directions for further investigation laid out above, we might add others: how online video has influenced the notion of celebrity, the varieties of collective and individual affect engendered by online video, the question of digital video preservation, how online video complicates notions of temporality in the moving image, the study of marginalized networks and alternative viewing platforms, and the efficacy and reach of social justice movements in online video. Several recent projects highlight the possibilities of using online video as a method of conducting innovative scholarship in the humanities, from Matthias Stork's (2011) video essays on "chaos cinema" to my own website dedicated to handmade cinema (2012) to Virginia Kuhn's use of computer vision for large-scale analysis of images (see Chapter 30, this volume). In other words, online video affords us the opportunity to formulate new histories and theories of the moving image and, in doing so, expand the boundaries of humanistic inquiry. ICYMI: the field of online video is ready—if not necessarily waiting.

Further Reading

Strangelove, M. (2010) *Watching YouTube: Extraordinary Videos by Ordinary People*, Toronto, ON: University of Toronto Press.

References

Alexa (2015) "How Popular Is YouTube.com?," retrieved from www.alexa.com/siteinfo/youtube.com.
Altman, R. (2007) *Silent Film Sound*, New York, NY: Columbia University Press.

Baron, J. (2014) "(In)appropriation: Productions of Laughter in Contemporary Experimental Found Footage Films," in L. Westrup and D. Laderman (eds.) *Sampling Media*, Oxford: Oxford University Press, pp. 168–82.

Battaglio, S. (2015) "TV Networks 'on the Defensive' as Online Video Outlets Take Market Share," *Los Angeles Times*, retrieved from www.latimes.com/entertainment/envelope/cotown/la-et-ct-upfront-preview-ads-cable-tv-20150509-story.html.

Beller, J. (2006) *The Cinematic Mode of Production: Attention Economy and the Society of the Spectacle*, Hanover, NH: Dartmouth College Press.

Boris, C. (2014) "In the Next 60 Seconds, 300 Hours of Video Will Be Uploaded to YouTube," *Marketing Pilgrim*, retrieved from www.marketingpilgrim.com/2014/12/in-the-next-60-seconds-300-hours-of-video-will-be-uploaded-to-youtube.html.

Burgess, J. (2012) "YouTube and the Formalization of Amateur Media" in D. Hunter, R. Lobato, M. Richardson, and J. Thomas (eds.) *Amateur Media: Social, Cultural and Legal Perspectives*, London: Routledge, pp. 53–58.

Burgess, J. and J. Green (2009) *YouTube: Online Video and Participatory Culture*, Cambridge, UK: Polity.

Casetti, F. (2015) *The Lumière Galaxy: Seven Key Words for the Cinema to Come*, New York, NY: Columbia University Press.

Chen, A. (2014) "The Laborers Who Keep Dick Pics and Beheadings out of Your Facebook Feed," *Wired*, retrieved from www.wired.com/2014/10/content-moderation/.

Chun, W. H. K. (2011) *Programmed Visions: Software and Memory*, Cambridge, MA: MIT Press.

Ellison, N. and d. boyd (2013) "Sociality through Social Network Sites," in W. H. Dutton (ed.) *The Oxford Handbook of Internet Studies*, London: Oxford University Press, pp. 151–72.

Frommer, D. and K. Angelova (2009) "Chart of the Day: Half of YouTube Videos Get Fewer than 500 Views," *Business Insider*, retrieved from www.businessinsider.com/chart-of-the-day-youtube-videos-by-views-2009-5.

Fuchs, C. (2012) "Class and Exploitation on the Internet," in T. Scholz (ed.) *Digital Labor: The Internet as Playground and Factory*, New York, NY: Routledge, pp. 211–24.

Grusin, R. (2009) "YouTube at the End of New Media" in P. Snickars and P. Vonderau (eds.) *The YouTube Reader*, Stockholm: National Library of Sweden, pp. 60–67.

Guinness World Records (2015) "Most Subscribers on YouTube," *Guinness World Records*, retrieved from www.guinnessworldrecords.com/world-records/most-subscribers-on-youtube.

Jenkins, H. (2006) *Convergence Culture: Where Old and New Media Collide*, New York, NY: NYU Press.

Jenkins, H., S. Ford, and J. Green (2013) *Spreadable Media: Creating Value and Meaning in a Networked Culture*, New York, NY: NYU Press.

Juhasz, A. (2011) *Learning from YouTube*, Cambridge, MA: MIT Press.

Kreft, E. (2014) "You Just Got 'Tubed: How the Secret Algorithm Perfected by YouTube Gets You Clicking on the Next Video (and the Next and the Next . . .)," *The Blaze*, retrieved from www.theblaze.com/stories/2014/04/25/you-just-got-tubed-how-the-secret-alogrithm-perfected-by-youtube-gets-you-clicking-on-the-next-video-and-the-next-and-the-next/.

Luckerson, V. (2014) "These Were the Most Popular Videos on YouTube in 2014," *Time.com*, retrieved from time.com/3625337/youtube-most-popular-videos-2014.

Manovich, L. (2000) *The Language of New Media*, Cambridge, MA: MIT Press.

McLagan, M. (2006) "Introduction: Making Human Rights Claims Public" *American Anthropologist* 108, 191–95.

McPherson, T. (2006) "Reload: Liveness, Mobility, and the Web," in W. Chun and T. Keenan (eds.) *New Media, Old Media: A History and Theory Reader*, New York: Routledge, pp. 199–209.

MyTop100Videos (2012, automatically updated) "Most Viewed Videos of All Time," *YouTube*, retrieved from www.youtube.com/playlist?list=PLirAqAtl_h2r5g8xGajEwdXd3x1s Zh8hC.

Shirky, C. (2008) *Here Comes Everybody: The Power of Organizing without Organizations*, New York, NY: Penguin Books.

Stork, M. (2011) "Chaos Cinema: The Decline and Fall of Action Filmmaking," *Indiewire*, retrieved from www.indiewire.com/2011/08/video-essay-chaos-cinema-the-decline-and-fall-of-action-filmmaking-132832/.

Whitelaw, B. (2011) "Almost All YouTube Views Come from Just 30% of Films," *Telegraph*, retrieved from www.telegraph.co.uk/technology/news/8464418/Almost-all-YouTube-views-come-from-just-30-of-films.html.

Zinman, G. (2012) *Handmade Cinema*, retrieved from www.handmadecinema.com

30

IMAGES ON THE MOVE

Analytics for a Mixed Methods Approach

Virginia Kuhn

> Whether we like it or not, it is the movies that mold, more than any other single force, the opinions, the taste, the language, the dress, the behavior, and even the physical appearance of a public comprising more than 60 percent of the population of the earth.
>
> (Panofsky 2002 [1934]: 70)

Everything I want to say about the need for video analytics (broadly defined as the use of computational methods to analyze filmic archives), as a component of humanities research is encoded in the above epigraph. The essay from which it is taken, "Style and Medium in the Motion Pictures" (2002 [1934]), was written over 80 years ago. A highly respected art historian, Panofsky argued that cinema should be considered art, his somewhat qualified claim and resignation notwithstanding. His reference to the public influence of media, as well as his use of statistical evidence (regardless of the precision of his "60 percent"), are emblematic of current debates in the humanities—those framed as "public humanities" and "digital humanities," respectively. Quantification is a somewhat odd move for someone so famous for close-reading the iconography of visual art, and yet I argue that it provides essential context for qualitative methods. Panofsky's essay and his attendant lectures were sensationalized simply because of the subject matter. Cinema had not been considered art by most critics prior to the 1930s. However, for my current purposes, the richness of Panofsky's essay lies in his discussion of cinema's potential, specifically the "dynamization of space" and "spatialization of time" (2002 [1934]: 71). Considering the medium's complexity as well as its increasing ubiquity, a mixed methods approach to cinema studies is vital because no single method is adequate on its own. And research is sorely needed. Moving images bombard us, impacting our lives in ways we have yet to adequately understand.

The abundance of consumer grade recording devices and online networks that can house and stream video combine to render filmic media (also called moving images) a common form of communication and expression, whose sources are varied and numerous. They include analogue media, such as digitized films and television shows; massive databases of instant video (e.g., Netflix, Hulu, and Amazon); hosting sites (e.g., YouTube, Vimeo, and the Internet Archive); TED talks; academic video, including recordings of conferences, lectures, and tutorials; and, finally, incidental footage from surveillance cameras, drones, and body cameras (e.g., GoPro). Further, as depth cameras—for example, RGB-D, Kinect, and Leap Motion—with motion sensors proliferate, they create big, fat files that contribute to the vastness of these databases.

This proliferation of filmic media does not mean these databases are particularly useful for research. Even as the recording of images is now commonplace, their organization, arrangement, and modes of access are far less straightforward. That is to say, while the processes of production have been automated, those for accessing media have not, leaving a vital aspect of culture essentially unavailable to researchers. As Lev Manovich pointed out more than a decade ago, "by the end of the 20th century, the problem was no longer how to create a new media object such as an image; the new problem was how to find an object that already exists somewhere" (2005: 35). Indeed, filmic archives are characterized by incomplete metadata and wildly divergent content tagging schemas. Since there is more media produced daily than can be viewed in a lifetime, the situation will only amplify as time passes (ReelSEO 2015).

This is the climate in which computational approaches to studying media have emerged. Cultural analytics, data analytics, big data, information visualization, distant reading, network analysis—all are founded on the notion that today's media landscape is too vast for a single human to study with any sort of breadth or, indeed, depth. Yet one of the most troubling aspects of computational approaches to research is the way they are often misunderstood by humanities scholars and, as such, simply dismissed. The issue is not strictly a matter of quantitative versus qualitative methods, or even formal analysis versus critical theory. Such divides are exacerbated when it comes to computational analysis, which seems to somehow exceed human perception or cognition, orienting toward the hard sciences and away from an emphasis on the individual. To make matters worse, some of the most prominent proponents of computational methods, such as Lev Manovich and Franco Moretti, criticize manual approaches like close reading and instead rely almost entirely on computation. Manovich (2011) argues that, to date, the study of culture has relied on either *shallow data*, such as statistics, or *deep data*, such as close reading and thick description, and these methods should be replaced by the use of pattern recognition to analyze massive cultural data sets that are generated and disseminated via social media and web technologies. Moretti argues that the very act of close reading is premised upon an extremely small number of canonical texts, since scholars only invest such effort in the artifacts that are deemed valuable (2013: 48). Though clearly this is not a zero sum game—close reading can exist with distant reading and pattern recognition—criticisms of close reading have alienated many humanists, and this alienation risks limiting the knowledge that might be gained from computational approaches, which could benefit from the input of researchers who see themselves as more analogue than digital. From this angle, a mixed methods approach is strategic since it implies choosing appropriate methods for a particular project rather than simply denouncing any particular one.

Before proceeding, it is important to expose the exigency for studying filmic media as well as the specific challenges inherent in this type of computational research. Only then will my argument for video analytics as part of a mixed methods approach fully resonate with other methods, such as close reading, hermeneutics, and ethnography, in media studies and digital humanities. If, however, the choice of methods is viewed in binary terms, then the work produced will necessarily lack the nuance expected by scholarly communities. It is worth remembering, too, that current methodologies, like the academic disciplines from which they proceed, were reified during an analogue era and may need rethinking for a digital or computational context. This rethinking should also make explicit the processes by which knowledge is produced, opening them up to analysis and re-evaluation should they no longer prove viable. Moreover, the complexity of a globally networked world demands a collaborative approach to research across disciplines and institutions, and this collaboration means methods will come under scrutiny (Balsamo 2011: 9; see also Lear Center 2010; Kuhn 2010).

Filmic media both reflects and shapes society, but the precise processes by which this occurs remain unclear, as do their cumulative effects. Study after study reveals the often subliminal impact of visual media on human beings, from stereotype threat to psychic numbing, from the relationship between edit lengths and attention span to the physical effects of vision via mirror neurons (Slovic 2007; Steele 2011). And since the medium operates at the affective level (much of which occurs below the threshold of consciousness or at least outside the range of verbal language), it is vital to study not only the narrative content but also the formal properties, both among and across genres. However, none of this research is tenable without the curating, indexing, tagging, and cataloguing necessary to make filmic archives searchable and discoverable. These databases need metadata, or "data about data" (e.g., titles, dates, creators, and descriptions). Metadata comes from the audio and visual features of filmic media and should include information about format, content, context, and provenance. The generation of this metadata may require some degree of automation, in addition to some form of collaborative editing, the most common example of which is Wikipedia.

Human Vision, Computer Vision

Automating image analysis is no trivial matter, in part because human vision is quite different from computer vision. In fact, popular programs such as CAPTCHA were created to discern between the two. An acronym for Completely Automated Public Turing test to tell Computers and Humans Apart, CAPTCHA distinguishes "bots" from humans by asking people to type distorted letters on a screen into a website's text box. This procedure helps to reduce the likelihood of website hacks. In the process, people also help computers to interpret images as plain text. When compared with computers, human visual perception allows people to sharpen the blurriness of distorted letters and read them as distinct from their backgrounds, literally separating the text from the context. Computers often have difficulty making such distinctions.

Even if a strength of human vision is its ability to contextualize images, this capacity may also result in flawed apprehension, where people either filter out too much information or fill gaps too thoroughly. In *Now You See It* (2011), Cathy Davidson offers a great example of such filtering. She notes that the impetus for the book came after a colloquium during which participants were shown a video that tracks "attention blindness," a phenomenon that effectively cloaks an object in one's visual field when the body or the brain is otherwise engaged. The now-viral video features six people—three wearing white shirts and three wearing black shirts—passing two basketballs. Viewers are told to count the passes by the white-shirted players as the players bob in and out of the other players. In the course of gameplay, a person in a gorilla suit enters the frame, gestures, and then leaves. Most people do not see the gorilla since they are focused on isolating the three players and counting how many times the ball is passed. The opposite effect can happen, too, as people fill gaps in a visual narrative to give it meaning. This attention blindness is why audiences typically do not notice continuity errors in films. Of course, such lapses in vision are revealed upon repeated viewings and the sustained analysis made possible by those technologies that allow video to be stopped, started, slowed, and replayed.

By contrast, computer vision attends to all aspects of the visual field and does not privilege one pixel over another. It scans every detail of an image without filling in narrative gaps. While advances are being made in machine learning or "neural networking," training an algorithm *what* to identity is quite tricky (Hern 2015). The bottom line is that, at present, computerized image detection cannot replace human vision; however, it significantly narrows the conditions for human interpretation of visual materials. In this way, computer vision algorithms function much like search engines, endowing the indexing process with an element of discovery. This automation, however, still requires human intervention, whether to verify results or to train the algorithm in the first place, a process that is labor intensive (Li 2015; Pangburn 2016).

Manual Tagging and Crowdsourcing

Clearly, more is better when it comes to annotating the content of moving image media, since annotation allows for the search and discovery of content. But some types of metadata are easier to generate than others. For instance, the voice and sound tracks of filmic media are less daunting to automate than image tracks. Also, advances in audio signal processing have paved the way for music detection applications such as Shazam. These applications are fairly accurate, but voice recognition programs are less precise. Still, transcripts are often available, particularly with studio films, which begin development in script form. There are also several ventures, such as The Closed Captioning Project, which asks users to transcribe video, often as a classroom project, providing searchable captions for researchers. Although this method is still manual, it contributes to the larger repository and the labor is spread out across users. And even as people tend to add nonlinguistic utterances and inflections when speaking, automating the process of speech recognition is less daunting than image recognition.

Manual tagging is a very different story. The creation of content tags for image-based media is not only labor intensive but also inexact. This is true when labeling objects as well as their contextual elements, or what Sara Shatford Layne (1986) calls "ofness" and "aboutness," based on Panofsky's three levels of pictorial meaning (1955). First, there are many human languages and dialects, and within each language different words may have similar meanings. Second, word choices and tagging schemas for image labeling are not straightforward, nor are they ideologically neutral. This bias impacts any application they undergird. For instance, Anne Balsamo interprets semantic mapping tools such as the *Visual Thesaurus* and convincingly shows how the deep structures on which such tools are built subtly reinforce the gender stereotypes of a culture (2011: 186–89). Finally, there is an inevitable gap in meaning when words stand in for images. For all of these reasons, then, content tagging is vital to research with filmic media, but it is insufficient on its own.

In addition to tagging ofness and aboutness, or objects and their contextual materials, or "things and stuff" (Heitz & Koller 2008: 2), metadata is also needed to identify formal properties of filmic media, such as shot type, camera angle, color palette, and the like. These elements shape meaning. For example, low camera angles bestow power to the image in relation to the viewer, while people and objects in the foreground are given more weight than those in the middle and backgrounds (Kress & van Leeuwen 2006: 140–42). Color likewise functions to make meaning, particularly with regard to the representation of human beings and their skin tones, which are impacted by cool or warm color timing (Kuhn 2012).

Between the interprestive slipperiness and the vastness of filmic media, crowdsourcing becomes a viable mode for content tagging. Crowdsourcing describes the combined efforts of thousands or millions of people, each completing a relatively trivial task, the cumulative effect of which contributes to a far larger endeavor, one that would be otherwise untenable. Further, when there are varying interpretations, crowdsourcing can offer a system of checks and balances (Frick 2015). Just as Wikipedia became a leading database of information, crowdsourcing proves attractive in this case, given its ability to use content tags created by many people.

All things considered, then, the optimal approach to research with filmic media would pair the strength of human analysis with the computational power and speed of machines. It would also allow for the study of media's conceptual and formal qualities. Though utterly necessary, formal analysis is not adequate on its own, since its interpretation hinges on the cultural, political, and technological affordances that shape creation. However, in solving some of the technological issues, it is easy to become preoccupied with tools and lose sight of critical engagement with this media. This risk is one reason why Alan Liu contends that digital humanities needs cultural criticism and must take a more active role in the issues that confront contemporary culture. He suggests that "digital humanists will need to show that thinking critically about metadata, for instance, scales into thinking critically about the power, finance, and other governance protocols of the world" (2012: 495). Indeed, identifying the ways in which seemingly neutral systems like metadata standards are not ideologically neutral and, in fact, impact what can be found and what remains invisible is the hallmark of critical theory.

Cultural critique is also a necessary component of media literacy, but while critique provides an analysis of things as they are—identifying and interpreting problems—it seldom offers alternatives to those problems. A productive approach would generate the folowing questions: Which metadata schema might be more inclusive? How might we mitigate the negative impacts of sexist representations of women that are rampant in mass media? Further, when screens disappear, giving way to images that are embedded in objects and the environment, and so less obviously staged, the need for critical evaluation, media literacy, and guidelines for the ethical use of media increases dramatically.

Exemplars

Since the combination of computational techniques with critical analysis is such a compelling approach to filmic media, it is rapidly gaining ground among digital humanists and computer scientists. This growth is evidenced by the recent blossoming of projects that deploy computational methods to aid in reading the formal and conceptual features of filmic media (Tsivian 2005; Manovich & Douglass 2008; Casey et al. 2012; Hoyt & Acland 2013). Some of these methods involve annotation tools, while others measure and visualize media in new ways. Annotation tools include ANVIL (anvil-software.org), created by Michael Kipp, and ELAN, developed at the Max Planck Institute for Psycholinguistics. Both are useful for a single scholar's analysis, but they are desktop programs lacking networked functionality such as online collaboration and integration with existing film databases, thereby limiting their potential for broad analysis and interoperability. The Semantic Annotation Tool, a project recently launched by Mark Williams and John Bell, promises to help remedy this limitation via a web-based tool with a server that will allow researchers to share their notes with their colleagues. Shared annotations will be hugely helpful in making film archives discoverable and searchable. Still, image-processing applications are needed. Not only do they hold the potential to automate approaches to time-based media, they also provide a way to compare the formal elements of film across genres and linguistic orientations.

One of the best-known proponents of image processing via computer vision is Lev Manovich, who founded the Software Studies Initiative in 2005. Manovich has embarked upon several projects that visualize large quantities of images (including photographs, page images, digitized paintings, and film frames) that create a mosaic of sorts, using thumbnails of the images themselves to form the larger visualization. For this purpose, the research team at the Software Studies Initiative developed ImagePlot, an application that can be used in combination with ImageJ, which helps medical researchers compare magnetic resonance imaging (MRI) scans and other biological scans, and is thus useful for manipulating images and visualizing them in "stacks" that afford a three-dimensional component. This approach is interestingly deployed in the service of film analysis by Kevin Ferguson, who argues for a renewed interest in cinema as a volume even as it is instantiated in a two-dimensional form (2015).

Elsewhere, Barry Salt and Yuri Tsivian are well known for measuring the shots of a film—the length of each section between edits—and, along with computer scientist Gunars Civjans, have developed a tool called Cinemetrics, which measures the average shot length (ASL) of a particular film. While shot length can be (and has been) measured manually, the ability to compare the ASL of films across time and space has proven transformative for Tsivian, who reports having "felt [his] heart beat faster, for it turned out that between 1917 and 1918 the cutting tempo of Russian films had jumped from the slowest to the fastest in the world" (2005). Frederic Brodbeck, by contrast, combines shot measurement and visualization, creating "movie fingerprints" that are aesthetically pleasing yet short on analytic potential (n.d.). While these types of projects are proliferating, their findings are either purely artistic (and thus not immediately useful) or somewhat obvious (e.g., action films are more frenzied). More conceptual and practical work will be needed before the field can hone this method, possibly combining it with textual annotations and other image processing applications to make it a more meaningful research tool.

Combining textual and visual tools was the impetus for the Video Analysis Tableau (the VAT), a system that builds on several of these tools to establish a software workbench for video analysis, annotation, and visualization (Kuhn et al. 2015). The VAT—a project I lead and whose team includes supercomputing scientists, media scholars, and digital humanists—employs a host of algorithms for machine reading in addition to user-generated tagging and annotation, using both current and experimental discovery methods. This work is supported by the National Science Foundation's XSEDE program (Extreme Science and Engineering Discovery Environment), uses open source code, and is built on the Clowder framework as its database and interface.

Upon ingestion into the VAT, footage is processed with extractors that segment the video, convert it to a common codec to facilitate previewing, and create a novel visualization that serves as a barcode of sorts (see Figure 30.1). This preprocessing allows users to quickly preview a video by looking at its major segments and then selecting a particular frame to be queried across a specified collection of videos. Searching based on that query frame, the system returns the 10 most similar frames for each of the computer vision algorithms (also known as descriptors), which create histograms of the frame to identify features (such as image boundaries or distributions of color), detect edges, or look for transformations in texture. Each result returned includes a calculation of relative distance from the query frame to the frame returned, providing a pedagogical component as users get a glimpse of the deeper structures upon which the VAT is built.

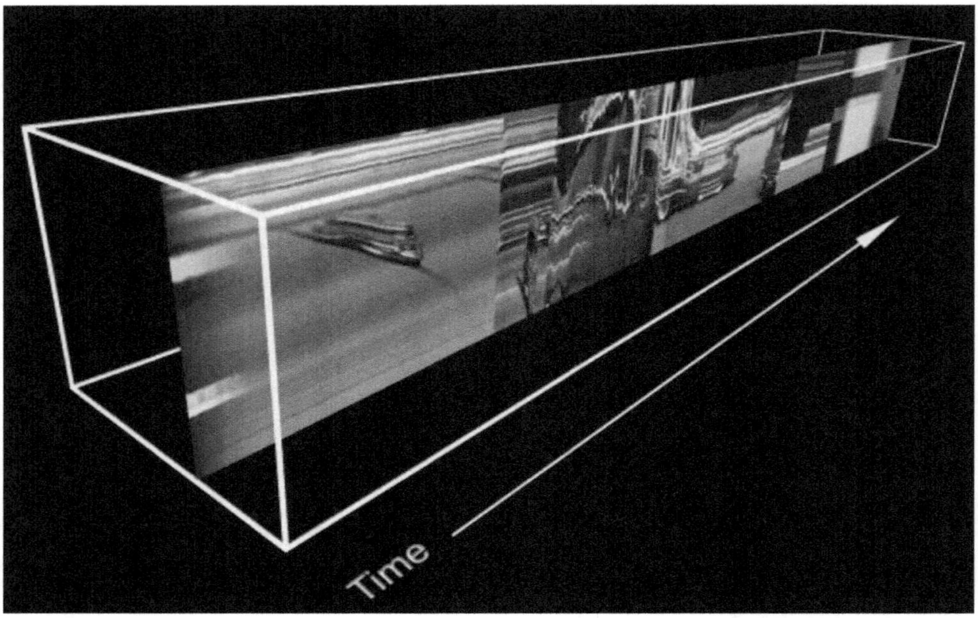

Figure 30.1 Screen shot of the VAT's "Movie Slice" barcode visualization, which affords a spatial view of films. Visualization by Dave Bock.

Source: Image care of the author.

By assessing the various results returned, users begin to understand the logic of the particular descriptor, encouraging a type of algorithmic literacy. They can then hone their query frame based on this understanding, even as they construct new research questions and pursue further inquiry. For instance, in an early test case, we were looking for depictions of cigarettes and people smoking. The query frame used was the best representation of a person holding a cigarette close to her mouth. The frames returned included copious images from television news, which featured reporters speaking into microphones or holding them out to others whom they were interviewing. This makes sense as the system searches for small objects held at an angle. In order to further enhance the search, then, we focused on color distribution, looking for instances of white near those of flesh colors. We also had luck finding smoke in a frame by focusing more on the DCT (discrete cosine transform) descriptor, which works at the boundaries of an object, allowing us to find "fuzzy" borders that indicate smoke over an image.

While the VAT is nascent, its development team is focused on establishing a community of users such that the project's evolution is directed by and responsive to the scholarly community, rather than an individual or corporation. Indeed, I suspect that—via a mixed methods approach—the VAT and projects like it will enrich cinema and media studies by making visible those artifacts that may have been overlooked by scholars so far.

New Directions: Cinema Studies and Neuroscience

While the projects discussed in the previous section will become more compelling the more they are adopted, there is ample room for continued experimentation with computational approaches to filmic media. Perhaps the most exciting and intriguing emergent work lies at the crossroads of cinema studies and visual neuroscience. Neuroscientists have long used MRIs and fMRIs (functional MRIs, which measure blood flow) to track brain activity in order to study how the brain reacts to various stimuli in real time. While MRIs can be quite uncomfortable and loud, there is some promise among research with sounds and images as researchers use headphones and other padding to dampen the machine's noise and amplify the sound of the stimulus. For instance, Pia Tikka (2008) uses fMRI scans to track brain activity while people view filmic media. This work builds on Tikka's ambitious doctoral dissertation that includes a monograph, short film, and video documentation of a gallery installation. The written portion charts the practical and theoretical work of film pioneer, Sergei Eisenstein, as Tikka argues for a research-based practice (as Eisenstein did in 1935) instead of the practice-based research that has dominated university-level arts education. She notes that, rather than "proposing a readymade theory in conclusion, perhaps the extended reach of the mind's conceptual grasp (read 'research') may provide the practical domain of cinema with new insights" (2008: 18). The media elements of the dissertation do just this, documenting her Helsinki gallery installation, which consisted of four chairs that were wired to track viewers' skin response and heart rates as they viewed a short film, whose subject ranged from the quotidian (a laundromat) to the violent (a rape). This work provides evidence of media's physical impact on viewers—a notion that is vaguely accepted as true, though seldom given much credence. A systematic study of this impact will go a long way toward understanding the relationship between media inundation and human health.

Filmmaker and critic, Peter Wyeth, offers a conceptual framework for such efforts, contending that we have shortchanged the extraordinary power of cinema by ignoring the sciences. In *The Matter of Vision: Affective Neurobiology and Cinema*, he uses recent work in brain science and evolutionary biology to arrive at his three main premises: vision is a primary source of human intelligence, the visual detection of movement is a key function of human perception, and emotion is the mind's default state, with reason being but a filter of affect (2015: 12). Obviously, if these premises are correct, then they suggest the importance of and a natural affinity for cinema—a visually rich medium, full of movement with an affective dimension. Being familiar with much of the underlying research, I find Wyeth's arguments plausible. However, without a mixed methods and interdisciplinary research agenda, it will be difficult to assess and enhance this research.

Perhaps it was Panofsky's early call to treat cinema as art that pushed it away from its early engagement with science, or maybe cinema studies' roots in literary criticism confined filmic media to the arts and humanities. Regardless of the cause, one thing is clear: that moment has passed.

Further Reading

Dinsman, M. (2016) "The Digital in the Humanities: A Special Interview Series," *Los Angeles Review of Books*, retrieved from lareviewofbooks.org/feature/the-digital-in-the-humanities.

Drucker, J. (2015) "Database Narratives in Book and Online," *Journal of Electronic Publishing* 18(1), retrieved from quod.lib.umich.edu/j/jep/3336451.0018.113?view= text;rgn=main.

Manovich, L. (2013) "Visualizing Vertov," *Software Studies Initiative*, retrieved from softwarestudies.com/cultural_analytics/Manovich.Visualizing_Vertov.2013.pdf.

Ross, S. (2014) "In Praise of Overstating the Case: A Review of Franco Moretti, *Distant Reading* (London: Verso, 2013)," *Digital Humanities Quarterly* 8(1), retrieved from www.digitalhumanities.org/dhq/vol/8/1/000171/000171.html.

References

ANVIL annotation software (n.d.) retrieved from anvil-software.org.

Balsamo, A. (2011) *Designing Culture: The Technological Imagination at Work*, Durham, NC: Duke University Press.

Brodbeck, F. (n.d.) Cinemetrics project website, retrieved from cinemetrics. fredericbrodbeck.de.

Casey, M., M. Williams, and T. Stoll (2012) *ACTION: Tools for Cinematic Information Retrieval*, retrieved from aum.dartmouth.edu/~action/index.html.

Cinemetrics software (n.d.) retrieved from cinemetrics.lv.

Cutting, J. E., J. E. DeLong, and C. E. Nothelfer (2010) "Attention and the Evolution of Hollywood Film," *Psychological Science* 21(3), 432–39.

Davidson, C. (2012) *Now You See It: How Technology and Brain Science Will Transform Schools and Business for the 21st Century*, New York, NY: Viking.

ELAN annotation software (n.d.) retrieved from tla.mpi.nl/tools/tla-tools/elan.

Ferguson, K. L. (2015) "Volumetric Cinema," in *[in]Transitions*, 17 March.

Frick, W. (2015) "What to Do When People Draw Different Conclusions from the Same Data," *Harvard Business Review blog*, retrieved from hbr.org/2015/03/what-to-do-when-people-draw-different-conclusions-from-the-same-data.

Heitz, G. and D. Koller (2008) "Learning Spatial Context: Using Stuff to Find Things," *ECCV 2008 Proceedings of the 10th European Conference on Computer Vision*, October 12–18, Marseille, FR.

Henn, S. (2014) "When Women Stopped Coding," in *Planet Money*, episode 576, National Public Radio, retrieved from www.npr.org/blogs/money/2014/10/21/357629765/when-women-stopped-coding.

Hern, A. (2015) "Yes, Androids Do Dream of Electric Sheep," *The Guardian*, 18 June, retrieved from www.theguardian.com/technology/2015/jun/18/google-image-recognition-neural-network-androids-dream-electric-sheep.

Hoyt, E. and C. Acland (2013) "Project Arclight: Analytics for the Study of 20th Century Media," Digging into Data Challenge, retrieved from diggingintodata.org/awards/2013/project/project-arclight-analytics-study-20th-century-media.

Image Plot (n.d.) Software Studies Initiative, retrieved from lab.softwarestudies.com/p/imageplot.html.

ImageJ software (n.d.) National Institutes of Health, retrieved from imagej.nih.gov/ij.

Kress, G. and T. van Leeuwen (2006) *Reading Images: The Grammar of Visual Design*, 2nd edn, New York, NY: Routledge.

Kuhn, V. (2010) "The Techno-Humanist Interaction," *EDUCAUSE Review* 45(6), 58–60, retrieved from er.educause.edu/~/media/files/article-downloads/erm1067.pdf.

Kuhn, V. (2012) "The Rhetoric of Remix," in F. Coppa and J. Levin Russo (eds.) "Fan/Remix Video" special issue, *Transformative Works and Cultures* 9, retrieved from dx.doi.org/10.3983/twc.2012.0358.

Kuhn, V., A. Craig, M. Simeone, S. Puthanveetil Satheesan, and L. Marini (2015) "The VAT: Enhanced Video Analysis," in *Proceedings from the 2015 Extreme Science and Engineering Discovery Environment XSEDE conference*, Atlanta, July, article 29.

Lear Center (2010) "Creativity and Collaboration in the Academy: Technology and the future of research," Annenberg School of Communication, University of Southern California, retrieved from learcenter.org/-project/collab.

Li, F. (2015) "How We're Teaching Computers to Understand Pictures," *TED talks*, retrieved from ted.com/playlists/310/talks_on_artificial_intelligence.

Liu, A. (2012) "Where Is Cultural Criticism in the Digital Humanities?" in M. Gold (ed.) *Debates in the Digital Humanities*, Minneapolis, MN: University of Minnesota Press, pp. 490–501.

Manovich, L. (2005) *The Language of New Media*, Cambridge, MA: MIT Press.

Manovich, L. (2011) "Guest Column: Lev Manovich Takes Us From Reading to Pattern Recognition," *The Creators Project*, January 20, retrieved from thecreatorsproject.vice.com/blog/guest-column-lev-manovich-takes-us-from-reading-to-pattern-recognition.

Manovich, L. and J. Douglass (2008) "Cultural Analytics," Software Studies Initiative, retrieved from lab.software studies.com/p/cultural-analytics.html.

Marini, L., et al. (2015) Clowder interface and database, retrieved from isda.ncsa.illinois. edu/clowder.

Moretti, F. (2013) *Distant Reading*, London, UK: Verso.

Pangburn, D. (2016) "Here's What Actually Goes into Creating Artificial Intelligence," *The Creators Project*, retrieved from thecreatorsproject.vice.com/blog/artificial-neural-network-visualization.

Panofsky, E. (1955) *Meaning in the Visual Arts: Papers in and on Art History*, Garden City, NY: Doubleday.

Panofsky, E. (2002 [1934]) "Style and Medium in Motion Pictures" in A. Vacche (ed.) *The Visual Turn*, New Brunswick: Rutgers University Press, pp. 69–94.

ReelSEO (2015) "500 Hours of Video Uploaded to YouTube Every Minute [Forecast]," retrieved from www.reelseo.com/youtube-300-hours.

Shatford Layne, S. (1986) "Analyzing the Subject of a Picture: A Theoretical Approach," *Cataloging & Classification Quarterly* 6(3), 639–62.

Simons, S. (2012) "But Did You See the Gorilla? The Problem with Inattentional Blindness," in *Smithsonian Magazine*, retrieved from www.smithsonianmag.com/science-nature/but-did-you-see-the-gorilla-the-problem-with-inattentional-blindness-17339778/?no-ist.

Slovic, P. (2007) "'If I Look at the Mass I Will Never Act': Psychic Numbing and Genocide," *Judgment and Decision Making* 2(2), 79–95, retrieved from journal.sjdm.org/7303a/jdm7303a.htm.

Steele, C. (2011) *Whistling Vivaldi: How Stereotypes Affect Us and What We Can Do*, New York, NY: Norton.

Tikka, P. (2008) *Enactive Cinema—Simulatorium Eisensteinense*, Helsinki: University of Art and Design.

Tsivian, Y. (2005) Cinemetrics: Movie Measurement and Study Tool Database, retrieved from cinemetrics.lv/index.php.

Wyeth, P. (2015) *The Matter of Vision: Affective Neurobiology and Cinema*, New Barnet, UK: John Libbey Publishing.

31

LOST IN THE CLOUDS

A Media Theory of the Flight Recorder

Paul Benzon

CNN's coverage of the March 24, 2015 crash of Germanwings flight 9525 offered an uncanny crystallization of both the specific archival issues involved in flight data recording and the larger question of the digital archive. An early headline on the story announced, "Plane obliterated in crash; data recorder found." This strange parataxis—itself fittingly no longer available online—encapsulates a peculiarly contemporary condition of information in which storage and loss, memory and forgetting, and recovery and oblivion exist in constant tension and reverberation. Situated at the uncanny overlaps of these forces, the flight recorder provides a unique vantage point on the dark heart of data storage in the modern era. The flight recorder is a globally circulating data object designed to protect the information that it holds from extreme material stress; indeed, its singular purpose is to record and retain information when all else around it is damaged or destroyed. Yet it is also, paradoxically, a tool of erasure in all but the most extreme and singular cases: in the case of an uneventful flight—no crash, no hijacking, no crisis—a great deal of the information captured by a flight recorder can be and almost always is erased. Moreover, in the event of a crash, the status of flight data is often highly sensitive in both material and governmental senses of the term. Data recovery is highly delicate due to potential damage from pressure, heat, and immersion, while the data itself is not subject to Freedom of Information Act requests and is usually accessible to a small set of National Transportation Safety Board employees (National Transportation Safety Board 2002: 1).

Whereas data forensics in digital humanities is often the province of scholars and archivists working across changing hardware, platforms, and standards to preserve and share digital history, the forensics of the flight recorder is largely a matter of singularity and secrecy, in which the information recovered is rarely if ever circulated in any public fashion. Indeed, the device's inscriptive endurance is deeply bound up with its inscriptive ephemerality—in a sense, it records and stores in order to be able to erase. Yet it is precisely in this tension that the device becomes most illuminating, shedding light on why and how we record, store, and delete as well as on which institutions have the power to conduct these processes and define their parameters.

Paul Virilio understands the existence of the modern accident as the "fortuitous" product of "archaeotechnological invention . . . To get what is heavier than air to take off in the form of an aeroplane or dirigible is *to invent the crash*, the air disaster" (2007: 10). If we accept Virilio's proposition, then we should also acknowledge a third component in this contemporaneity: just as the invention of mechanized flight is inextricable from the invention of the plane crash, this duality is itself inextricable from the invention of flight recording. This is true in simple historical terms: the Wright brothers' first flight in 1903 was recorded by the first flight recorder, measuring duration, distance, and propeller rotation (Grossi 2006: 35). Yet it is also true in epistemological terms: we might say, following Virilio, that modernity's capacity for the air disaster would not exist in the same way without the parallel technological capacity for recording the physical parameters of that disaster. However, the flight recorder is a marked exception to the saturating media coverage that has characterized aviation disasters from the Hindenburg crash, captured and replayed on multiple newsreels, to the contemporary media spectacles of September 11, 2011 and the disappearance of Malaysia Airlines Flight 370. Whereas the mass media records of these disasters constitute them as always-accessible events, circulating publicly in real time, flight recorders situate the data of a disaster as private or only selectively accessible.

Thinking Inside the Box: Toward an Archaeology of Inscriptive Extremity

In this chapter, I read the flight recorder as an object whose history and technology offer a unique perspective on the material particulars of data storage and on how those particulars frame questions of inscription, memory, and erasure that are central to media studies. These questions have been a recurring concern among scholars of digital media in recent years, offering a valuable line of inquiry into how various technologies shape practices of knowledge production, remembering, and forgetting at a range of individual, institutional, and cultural levels. Writing of "the complex nature of transmission and inscription in digital settings," Matthew Kirschenbaum describes hard drives as "mechanisms of *extreme* inscription—that is, they offer a limit case for how the inscriptive act can be imagined and executed" (2008: xii, 74). The flight recorder—a specialized kind of hard drive, at least in its most common current incarnation—constitutes a particularly powerful instance of the extremity Kirschenbaum describes, a device in which the shifting capacities of data storage are leveraged against both the irreducible possibility of disaster and the possible destruction of the very storage technologies in question. It is also a test case for examining these issues through two qualities: its status as a historically and materially contingent data object, and its place within current conversations about mobile wireless connectivity and cloud-based network culture. Ultimately, it reveals the importance for media studies and digital humanities of critical methods that foreground both the profound contingency of data capture across historical time and technology and the status of the digital archive as grounded in partiality. Attending to contingency and partiality as central to the materiality of data—both analog and digital—by way of the flight recorder allows scholars and students of media studies to see the devices, infrastructures, and institutions that surround and contain that data as also contingent through their relationship to data. These contingencies, then, reveal one powerful way in which media history itself is contingent, open to critical rethinking along variant social and historiographic lines.

My approach to the history of the flight recorder follows the methods of a subset of media studies known as media archaeology. According to Jussi Parikka, media archaeology is:

> [A] way to investigate the new media cultures through insights from past new media, often with an emphasis on the forgotten, the quirky, the nonobvious apparatuses, practices and inventions. In addition . . . it is also a way to analyse the regimes of memory and creative practices in media culture—both theoretical and artistic. Media archaeology sees media cultures as sedimented and layered, a fold of time and materiality where the past might be suddenly discovered anew, and the new technologies grow obsolete increasingly fast.
>
> (Parikka 2012: 2–3)

As Parikka's language suggests, the concept of archaeology has multiple valences in this context. Media technologies are themselves archaeological, storing information to be recovered, inscribing record upon record to be unearthed by scholars engaging with devices. Yet media archaeology also invites scholars to perform similar excavations at a more abstract level upon media history itself: to recover forgotten technologies and protocols, dead ends, and lost technologies, and to consider these histories alongside their contemporary counterparts. This second valence is particularly relevant in the case of the flight recorder: while excavation of specific data is a largely restricted practice, in excavating the device's history we might begin to see new formulations of the relation between memory and storage across time. In working along the lines described by Parikka, we might also in turn seize upon some of the historiographic payoff of media archaeology as a critical method, revealing alternate historical possibilities and alternate understandings of the flight recorder that run counter to mainstream conceptions of technological change as characterized by a "glossy, high-tech 'Californian ideology'" of constant social betterment through innovation (Parikka & Hertz 2012: 427).

If unauthorized civilian scholars cannot in most cases examine the records produced by specific flight recorders—if we cannot easily go "under the hood" of this technology, to use another term from Parikka, to trace how it stores and deletes specific records—perhaps it makes sense to begin with the device's own history as a source of disappearance and contingency (2012: 83). In doing so, we have to confront the deceptively simple question of etymology: if the contemporary flight recorder is almost universally colored bright safety orange, so as to be found more easily amid wreckage or underwater, why is it commonly and colloquially referred to as a black box? The simplest answer is that, prior to international standardization of the device in the latter part of the twentieth century, early models were quite literally black, either painted black or encased in an actual black container. However, this explanation is only part of a more complex technological history. One possible origin of the term derives from slang usage by the British Royal Air Force (RAF) circa World War II to refer to a navigational or bomb-aiming device on a plane ("black box"). This usage was in circulation before the widespread use of flight recorders and provides a strange kind of mirror image to the material conditions of the flight recorder: while the RAF black box is a technology of vision without any lasting recorder, allowing the pilot or bombardier to see down to the ground while in flight, the flight recorder, which did not acquire the nickname "black box" until some 20 years later, exists to produce an after-the-fact record of flight following a crash. The former is transparent in the literal sense of the word—it is meant to be seen through—while the latter is intended to be sealed shut.

Yet both are instances of the larger overall category of the black box as a closed technological system, another meaning of the term that signifies a device with opaque inner workings, seemingly universally reliable, but only capable of being parsed in terms of its input and output. This sense of the black box within scientific discourse has a long history beyond the scope of this discussion, but Bruno Latour's explanation of the term sheds light on how this broader category might inform the specific conditions of the flight recorder as a data object. Latour argues:

> [S]cientific and technical work is made invisible by its own success. When a machine runs efficiently . . . one need focus only on its inputs and outputs and not on its internal complexity. Thus, paradoxically, the more science and technology succeed, the more opaque and obscure they become.
>
> (Latour 1999: 304)

Latour's explanation here has technical and sociological resonances, but also, in the case of the flight recorder, material ones as well. Since the introduction of the modern flight recorder in the 1950s, major airlines have followed the policy of erasing and overwriting flight records except in the case of a crash or other emergency, largely in response to pressure by pilot's unions for continued privacy. In this sense, as long as a flight is uneventful, it has no permanent record via the flight recorder; the black box and its informational content only "appear" in the case of dysfunction and destruction.

This ephemerality took shape through various different technological constraints across the early history of the device. The HB recorder, or Hussenograph, first developed as a prototype in 1939 and in a limited run in 1941, stands as an early example. Named after its inventors, François Hussenot and Paul Beaudouin, the Hussenograph essentially functioned through photographic capture. It contained an oscillograph that measured changes in several flight parameters and projected them as light beams across a series of mirrors onto photosensitive paper inside an otherwise lightproof box. This process created an intricate pinhole camera that recorded numerical data through light rather than conventional optical photographic images (Beaudouin 2005: 207). Captured over time by the slow movement of the paper across the focal plane in front of the light beam, the resulting record had to be read as well as seen. It was photographic in the literal, schematic sense of the term—a figure made in light that was writing as much as it was image. Yet of course the uniqueness of this mechanism—an uncanny electrocardiograph for the vital functions of the plane—was precisely its greatest vulnerability. Flight data recorded as photographic information were, in Greg Siegel's words, "all but defenseless. Whether stored in cockpit or cabin, film lay unguarded, unprotected, its photochemical materiality vulnerable to aviation catastrophe, its corpus subject to 'mutilation,'" to say nothing of simple accidental exposure to light (2014: 101).

The cockpit voice recorder (CVR) introduced a similar uneasy tension between recording and erasure with regard to sonic material. Australian chemist David Warren, developed the first proposal for what would become the CVR in 1954 (Witham 2005). Based on existing wire recording technologies, Warren's proposed device could record the last 2 minutes of flight, a duration that was eventually expanded to 30 minutes in his first prototype in 1958. In both cases—and indeed throughout the history of the CVR, from Warren's initial designs to later versions employing magnetic tape and eventually the solid state digital storage currently used in most commercial planes—duration, permanence, and ephemerality existed in a complex relationship with both the medium in question and the issue of pilot privacy. As Siegel notes, early flight recording of the sort made possible by the Hussenograph was "fundamentally impersonal," a wholly numerical and data-centric operation (2014: 121). Warren's introduction of the capacity to reproduce the human voice, however, concurrently introduced an accompanying array of "disconcertingly personal" questions about the social, ethical, legal, and practical stakes of that reproduction (122). To address these concerns, Warren foregrounded the centrality of erasure to his mechanism. Since the widespread accept ance of the CVR, each flight recorder has included this voice component as well as a flight data recorder (FDR). Yet even the magnetic tape CVRs used until the late 1980s only stored records of the last 2 hours of a flight, in comparison with up to 25 hours of numerical data that could be captured on the accompanying FDR. Thus, the CVR's relatively short recording times created an "endless-loop recording pattern" that resulted in a kind of crystalline short-term-only memory, a perpetual newness of the sonic archive by way of the machine's perpetual overwriting (Grossi 2006: 38). While this feature was largely due to the limitations of the mechanisms and recording media in question, Warren also incorporated the capacity for deliberate erasure by design. He created the CVR to be self-erasing, noting that: "If no accident occurs, anything said during flight is obliterated during the time taken to taxi in," lost to what Warren (1954) described as the "short memory" of the CVR. In this sense, then, flight recorders hold no standing record of anything but accidents and other emergencies. Their short memories are inseparable from disaster, trauma, and testimony; their material record of flight as uneventful, by contrast, is forgotten, lost to the archive.

From Clouds to Contrails

Perhaps unsurprisingly, interest in a networked, wireless flight recording system has intensified considerably in recent years, stimulated by increasingly ubiquitous access to wireless internet connectivity on the ground as well as by a number of widely publicized airplane crashes in which the object of the flight recorder played a crucial and visible role, often by way of its absence or unrecoverability: the incineration of the recorders on the planes that crashed into the World Trade Center in 2001, the extended delay between the June 2009 crash of Air France Flight 447 in the Atlantic Ocean and the May 2011 recovery of the plane's recorders, and the wholesale disappearance in 2014 of Malaysia Airlines Flight 370, with little to no recorded evidence, to name a few of the most infamous instances. Writing in *Wired* magazine, Jerry Adler articulates the commonsensical argument for wireless flight recording in our current technological moment:

> If real-time stock quotes can be transmitted to anyone with a smartphone, why does the vital work of investigating an airplane crash still depend on reading physical memory chips that must be rescued from the wreckage?
>
> (Adler 2011)

In keeping with the desire for unbroken global accessibility encapsulated by Adler, advocates of wireless flight recording often imagine it in stark contrast to the opacity of the black box. For example, Krishna Kavi calls such a proposed system "a glass box, that is, a system that would be transparent because it would be in the cloud—not a cottony puff in the sky but rather the network of servers and databases that covers ever more of the world every day," providing "ubiquity, invulnerability, unlimited storage, and unparalleled powers of search" (2010). Given the concurrence of these imagined qualities with the aerial environment in question, Kavi seems to protest too much the association with "cottony," ephemeral clouds. In recent years, a wide range of major technology corporations have employed the rhetoric of *the* cloud in marketing their services to consumers, promising a stability of storage that seems predicated on sidestepping questions of materiality: Apple's iCloud, Microsoft Cloud, and Amazon Cloud Player and Kindle Cloud Reader, for instance. At the same time that he dismisses association with this rhetoric, Kavi's invocation of the cloud seems to imagine the same sort of transcendent permanence by way of dispersion: data as atmospheric, everywhere and nowhere at once.

Yet a number of technical, legal, and geopolitical obstructions have as yet kept these archival fantasies from realization. Perhaps the largest is, as Kavi notes, "the lack of a uniform communication medium. The world, after all, is covered by many different wireless systems—some designed for cities, some for rural areas, others for use over the ocean" (2010). Here we find the often suppressed materiality of the cloud manifesting as a powerful, palpable obstruction. Yet, even if a workaround to this multiplicity is possible, as Kavi suggests it is, any technical solutions would leave larger issues, such as intellectual property, infrastructure ownership, and cost responsibility, to be resolved over the complex terrain of airspace between and across nations. Questions of storage and transmission also pose obstacles to the widespread acceptance of wireless flight recording. In the current case of an un-networked flight recorder, all voice data remain onboard, thus facilitating regular erasure. By contrast, however, streaming data directly to the ground would produce a record of flight activity that (while certainly not permanent) would be more stably stored and widely accessible, and that would surely meet with considerable resistance from pilots' unions with regard to privacy—a return to the initial concerns raised by Warren's innovations. As Adler notes, bandwidth limitations and costs would also complicate the viability of streaming technology.

In response to these issues, advocates of wireless flight recording have suggested effectively splitting the difference between streaming and onboard recording by splitting numerical and voice data. Kavi proposes

> economizing on the bandwidth by streaming only flight data, not the cockpit voice recording. The voice recording would go into an onboard recorder, as it does today. In fact, to ensure against the loss of communication to the ground station, we suggested that the current black box technology might continue, as a backup.
>
> (Kavi 2010)

In another quintessentially media-archaeological moment, we find here a strange holdover of earlier inscriptive modalities within this new configuration. The old, seemingly obsolete object of the recorder persists alongside precisely the technology that would render it obsolete, mirroring and redoubling it in uncanny, unsettled ways, not as vestige but as "backup"—hardly a secondary role when questions of recording, storage, permanence, and ephemerality are at stake as they are here. Yet the very need for a backup within a system that purports to be always accessible—a backup that is itself still irreducibly vulnerable, no less—belies the stabilizing rhetoric of the cloud trumpeted by major technology corporations. The overall configuration Kavi suggests here is ultimately a more complicated and unstable archival constellation of old and new, wired and wireless, that reveals the overdetermined materiality and historicity of information within the totalizing archival condition that characterizes our contemporary moment.

Thus given the inadequacy—perhaps even the danger—of using the cloud as a metaphor to understand the workings of digital storage, particularly in the case of flight recorder information, I want to offer another pertinent metaphor that captures the problematics of black box storage more richly and rigorously: the concept of the data contrail posed by Kathi

Inman Berens. Berens uses the idea of the contrail to describe the unstable archive produced by netprov, a genre of "networked improvised narrative" performed live and in interaction with readers on the social media website, Twitter. She says of netprov that this "[e]phemeral networked text art leaves confusing inscribed conversations in the 'cloud' that are erratically visible after the echo of live speech has quieted" (2015). In contrast to the transcendent permanence of the cloud, these confusing inscriptions take shape as data contrails, "digital traces of real-time reader participation that slowly decay and become less coherent over time" (2015). The conditions of ephemerality are of course different for flight recorders than they are for the alphabetic, networked archive Berens discusses, and thus my use of the metaphor is different from, although resonant with, hers. Yet this is precisely the point; indeed, no metaphor can perfectly capture the workings of digital technology, perhaps particularly not the complex workings of digital storage, so often invisible to the naked eye. As Shannon Mattern argues, there is "a material dimension, a 'heavy architecture,' to even our most seemingly ephemeral and placeless . . . media technologies," an infrastructure that implicates forces of labor, capital, ecology, and geopolitics, among others, and the flight recorder, whether wired or wireless, is no exception (Mattern, this volume: 321). Neither the cloud nor the contrail can transcend this weight. Yet the metaphor of the contrail allows for a richer rendition of the archival workings of the flight recorder than that of the cloud in both its emphasis on material vulnerability and its origination within the discourse of air travel: condensation trails, as they are more formally known, are the long, cloudlike streams that are produced by the condensation of water vapor from airplane engines and disappear shortly after their creation. Machine-made clouds, they are—like flight recorders—an ephemeral record of air travel.

The metaphor of the contrail moves the status of data away from the abstracted and the natural (as in the case of the cloud) and toward the contingent and the constructed. It allows us to frame the data of the flight recorder not as diaphanous and immaterial, but rather as a slippery, elusive kind of skywriting. In doing so, it allows us to foreground important trajectories of process, manufacture, apparatus, and, perhaps most important, ephemerality within our understanding of data storage, thus prompting us to see the importance of absence as well as persistence for media-archaeological thought and research. Indeed, partially literalizing the metaphor of the contrail, bending it from Berens's original usage partway back to its aerial origins, also turns us back to what we might see as the most important element of the flight recorder archive, namely the vast majority of material that is erased, excised from this archive for reasons of error, privacy, efficiency, and banality. Perhaps this dominant gap in the archive of the flight recorder suggests that the most urgent archaeology of modern and contemporary storage media attends to moments of obsolescence and instability to highlight the often irreversible production of absence, whether by design or by contingency, as a crucial site of inquiry for media studies—a sheet of overexposed photographic paper in the Hussenograph, a wire or foil recording distorted by unimaginable heat and pressure, a solid state drive erased after landing in all but a miniscule percentage of flights, an obliterated aircraft for which the surviving black box is at once sign, record, vestige, and surrogate.

Even in the instances when they do survive, these records and devices are often off-limits, particularly to the humanistic scholar outside the inner circles of aviation. Yet their absence from the public historical record casts a long shadow on how we might frame the question of storage and inscription from a media-archaeological approach. The detours and anachronies across the history of the flight recorder are not its only crucial products; there are also these irretrievable shadow documents: the evanescence—of the record, the device, the planes themselves—that shows us technological materiality most starkly and profoundly. Perhaps what is most important about flights is their contrails.

Acknowledgments

I am grateful to Lauren F. Klein and Jentery Sayers for their thoughtful comments on earlier drafts of this essay.

Further Reading

Derrida, J. (1998) *Archive Fever: A Freudian Impression*, Chicago, IL: University of Chicago Press.
Dworkin, C. (2013) *No Medium*, Cambridge, MA: MIT Press.
Ernst, W. (2012) *Digital Memory and the Archive*, Minneapolis, MN: University of Minnesota Press.
Huhtamo, E. and J. Parikka (eds.) (2011) *Media Archaeology: Approaches, Applications, and Implications*, Berkeley, CA: University of California Press.

References

Adler, J. (2011) "Banish the Black Box: There's a Better Way to Capture Plane Crash Data," *Wired*, retrieved from www.wired.com/2011/06/ff_blackboxes/.
Beaudouin, D. (2005) *Charles Beaudouin: une histoire d'instruments scientifiques*, Paris: EDP Sciences.
Berens, K. (2015) "Live/Archive: *Occupy MLA*," *Hyperrhiz* 11, retrieved from hyperrhiz.io/hyperrhiz11/essays/live-archive-occupy-mla.html.
"black box, n." (2015) *OED Online*, Oxford University Press.
Grossi, D. (2006) "Aviation Recorder Overview," *Journal of Accident Investigation*, 2(1), 31–42.
Kavi, K. (2010) "Beyond the Black Box," *IEEE Spectrum*, retrieved from spectrum.ieee.org/aerospace/aviation/beyond-the-black-box/0.
Kirschenbaum, M. (2008) *Mechanisms: New Media and the Forensic Imagination*, Cambridge, MA: MIT Press.
Latour, B. (1999) *Pandora's Hope: Essays on the Reality of Science Studies*, Cambridge, MA: Harvard University Press.
National Transportation Safety Board (2002) "Flight Data Recorder Handbook for Aviation Accident Investigations," Washington, retrieved from www.ntsb.gov/investigations/process/Documents/FDR_Handbook.pdf.
Parikka, J. (2012) *What Is Media Archaeology?* Cambridge, U.K.: Polity.
Parikka, J. and G. Hertz (2012) "Zombie Media: Circuit Bending Media Archaeology into an Art Method," *Leonardo* 45(5), 424–30.
Siegel, G. (2014) *Forensic Media: Reconstructing Accidents in Accelerated Modernity*, Durham, NC: Duke University Press.
Virilio, P. (2007) *The Original Accident*, Cambridge, U.K.: Polity.
Warren, D. (1954) "A Device for Assisting Investigation into Aircraft Accidents," *Aeronautical Research Laboratories/Mechanical Engineering Technical Memo* 142.
Witham, J. (2005) *Black Box: David Warren and the Creation of the Cockpit Voice Recorder*, South Melbourne: Lothian.

32

SCAFFOLDING, HARD AND SOFT

Critical and Generative Infrastructures

Shannon Mattern

Everyone from tech manufacturers and app developers, to sci-fi authors and filmmakers, to real-estate developers and engineers, are conjuring up utopic visions of "sentient cities" and "quantified selves"—data-driven entities that uphold the primary virtues of efficiency and economy. Our bodies, regulated by sensors and algorithms, will become lean, high-performance machines; and our cities—ever clean and green—will respond, in real time, to our individual and collective social needs. If we dig past the enticing renderings and techno-fetishist rhetoric that characterize these plans, then we come to recognize the number of intertwined and layered networks, protocols, and practices—the interlocking *infrastructures*: smartphones, sensors, data sets, regulations, and various public and proprietary service providers—that would have to sync up perfectly for these "seamlessly" efficient digital futures to become realities. And we have to wonder about the critical issues that those connections, and potential disconnections, might raise regarding the roles that technology plays in our lives. These future data-driven scenarios—whether they are purely speculative designs or real plans for implementation—can serve us as critical tools to think with: "critical scaffolding" for analysis that, ideally, informs the way we build our future infrastructural worlds.

Infrastructure, Hard and Soft

The term "infrastructure" typically conjures up images of roads, railways, bridges, military structures, and other public works—heavily material stuff. And this is what "infrastructure" referred to when the term was first used in the mid-1920s. According to a U.S. Presidential Commission, by the late 1990s the term came to encompass "man-made systems and processes that function collaboratively and synergistically to produce and distribute a continuous flow of essential goods and services": systems like transportation, oil, gas distribution and storage, water supply, emergency management, government services, banking and finance, electrical power, and information and communications (President's Commission 1997). Yet the heavily material stuff persists even in the information age. Seemingly immaterial, ubiquitous, and placeless digital networks rely upon data centers, power plants, fiber-optic cables, satellites, mines yielding coltan and copper, and assembly-line workers and e-waste handlers regularly exposing themselves to toxic materials (Gabrys 2011). These are among digital culture's myriad material infrastructures.

As sociologists Susan Leigh Star and Geoffrey Bowker (2006) remind us, though, intellectual and institutional structures and operations—measurement standards, technical protocols, naming conventions, bureaucratic forms, etc.—are *also* infrastructures. The scenario I painted earlier demonstrated that agreeing on, or being forced to comply with, technical protocols, measurement standards, and classification systems (all intellectual and administrative infrastructures) is necessary in order for the software and hardware to do their jobs (see Galloway 2004 for more on protocol). Star and Bowker suggest, too, that infrastructure is inevitably a flexible term, often defined with regard to context and situation. They describe infrastructure as "that which runs 'underneath' actual structures[,] . . . that upon which something else rides, or works, a platform of sorts"; but then acknowledge that "this common-sense definition begins to unravel when we . . . look at multiple, overlapping and perhaps contradictory infrastructural arrangements. For the railroad engineer, the rails are only infrastructure when she or he is a passenger" (230; see also Bowker & Star 1999: 35). In other words, infrastructure can easily flip between figure and ground.

It becomes "figure" especially when snafus occur: when that otherwise invisible platform malfunctions and calls attention to itself—as is the case when we encounter dead zones, or suffer natural disasters, or carry our locked smartphones into foreign lands, or when our devices fail to sync or operate on different frequencies, or when various stakeholders do not adhere to the same protocols, or when the legal machinery and bureaucracy codifying these standards collapses under its own weight, or when government firewalls block access or corporations deem a market insufficiently lucrative to deserve a "hookup." And of course there are parts of the world where breakage and disconnection are the *norm*. And there are technicians who routinely monitor and repair cables and transformers and satellite dishes; for these people, infrastructure is commonly "figure" by default.

Infrastructure as Critical Structure: What Critical Tools and Frameworks Does a Focus on Infrastructure Offer Us?

A Deeper, Networked Media History

Even the infrastructural "ground" has its own substrate, its own platform, too. While the term infrastructure was not put into common use until the 1960s, and is thus commonly associated with modern telecommunications, the *idea* of infrastructure has existed since the dawn of civilization (see Mattern 2015). People have always needed physical, intellectual, political, and economic substrates on which to build their settlements, and those ancient structures have had residual effects across history. Digital infrastructures follow many of the same paths—the same, or very similar, conduits; similar network structure—as did early telecommunications infrastructure. "Because of the costs of developing new telecommunications networks," geographers Stephen Graham and Simon Marvin note, "all efforts are made to string optic fibers through water, gas, and sewage ducts; [and] between cities, existing railway, road, and waterway routes are often used" (1996: 329). And many early telecommunications hubs are urban centers built up over centuries in part through strength in publishing and a flourishing print culture. Cities thus become magnets for new technological development thanks to capital accumulated under old media regimes. Digital infrastructures are often predicated on their analog predecessors; old media infrastructures begat new media infrastructures.

I have written elsewhere on the deep history and temporal entanglements of urban media infrastructures—on the ways in which the rise of trade and the need for record-keeping necessarily made early human settlements into infrastructures for writing, with even the buildings' and cities' clay walls serving as substrates for written texts; and the ways in which, in the early days of democracy, cities were designed, or emerged through trial and error, to be conducive to public address and interpersonal communication (Mattern 2013a, 2015). Thinking about media infrastructure through this deep historical perspective—which requires that we borrow insights and methods from other fields, such as archaeology and urban history—helps us to recognize that media histories are entwined with the histories of our cities and civilizations, and that cities have long constituted infrastructural environments that support their essential role as communicative spaces.

The principle of "path dependency" explains how previous choices and patterns in designing and constructing systems, regardless of the circumstances or conditions under which those choices were originally made, limit our options in future developments: where the cable was lain in the past determines to some degree where we position our new conduits, which file formats have become the industry standard inform our design and production decisions, and how users have come to expect to interact with media—the habitual gestures of flipping pages and swiping screens, for instance—influences how we build familiarity and novelty into interaction design. Yet those previous "paths" are not rigidly deterministic. As Edwards et al. note, "The eventual growth of complex infrastructure and the forms it takes are the result of converging histories, path dependencies, serendipity, innovation, and 'bricolage' (tinkering)" (2007: 6–7). As we will see later, chance and human agency also have roles to play in the evolution of infrastructures and the unfolding of media and technological history.

Media Networked across Scale

Thinking about media infrastructure as networked and layered helps us to recognize that media can be embodied on a large scale—that media's modes of operation, and their aesthetics and ideologies, can be spatialized and materialized in the landscape. Today's media infrastructures encompass handheld devices and the microchips that make them work, as well as global networks and even extraterrestrial objects, like satellites, which are in turn affected by cosmic forces such as sun flares and space dust. When we think about infrastructures, then, we must also think about the granularity of our observations. Graham and Marvin list various scales of infrastructural analysis, including the corporeal, the local, the urban, the regional, the national, the international, and the global (2001: 411). Infrastructures cut across these scales and, in their role as "critical structures" or scaffolds, can even help to model "scalar thinking." Thinking at the scale of the media object (e.g., the book, the smartphone, or the modem), for instance, or the individual human-media interaction, compels us to "telescope out" and consider how those objects have been shaped across time, and how they are networked across space. Paul Edwards argues that scale need not be conceived as merely a geographic quality; it is also possible to consider scales of force (from the human body to the geophysical), scales of time (from human time to geophysical time), and scales of social organization (from individuals to governments) (2003: 186).

Expanding our unit of analysis—"scaling out" from the page, screen, or device—helps us appreciate the intermingling of various systems. For their production, distribution, and consumption, media rely on the power grid, transportation networks, waste removal systems, and even, in the case of paper production and data storage, the availability of water to power the mills and cool the server rooms. Thus, media infrastructures are inevitably part of infrastructural "constellations" involving myriad other nonmedia-related networks. And those networks are often layered and entangled into historically "deep" systems—systems with different paths of evolution or paces of operation. Scaling *out* in scope or space thus often enables us to dig *deeply* into our networks' histories.

Virtuality's Material Scaffolding

As we have already discussed, thinking about infrastructures—particularly the fact that these networks are always *inter*-networked and mutually evolving, reinforcing, and limiting one another—also reminds us that there is a material dimension, a "heavy architecture," to even our most seemingly ephemeral and placeless (i.e., mobile or ubiquitous) media technologies. As sociologist Adrian Mackenzie argues in *Wirelessness: Radical Empiricism in Network Cultures*:

> While the notion of wireless networks implies that there are fewer wires, it could easily be argued that actually there are more wires. Rather than wireless cities or wireless networks, it might be more accurate to speak of the rewiring of cities through the highly reconfigurable paths of chipsets. Billions of chipsets means trillions of wires or conductors on a microscopic scale.
>
> (Mackenzie 2010: 64–5)

That material scaffolding scales both up and down, in and out: down to the elements mined for those chipsets and conductors; up to the systems of labor that support that mining as well as the global manufacture, distribution, and sale of gadgets; out to the networks of satellites and undersea cables as well as the governmental and corporate policies that manage and monetize them (see Parks 2005; Blum 2012; Mayer 2011; Starosielski 2015). We will inevitably find hardware and, as we will discuss below, "wetware" or biopower behind our ostensibly immaterial networks; we simply have to expand our searches—across scales, depths, and altitudes—to find it.

Human Infrastructure

Perhaps paradoxically, while we are considering the potent forces of "deep history" and path dependency, and the heavy engineering that powers our technologies, an infrastructural framework also leads us to acknowledge the role of humble human agency. People have not been mere *beneficiaries* of infrastructure; they have actually served as integral links within those infrastructural networks, providing labor for material extraction or service delivery, for instance, or filling in with their own hands when the pumps and pipes and portals fail or, as is the case in particular disenfranchised pockets of the world, when that scaffolding is simply absent. As AbdouMaliq Simone argues, today in Africa (and, we must acknowledge, in much of the Global South and throughout the history of civilization) people often compensate for "underdeveloped, overused, fragmented, and often makeshift urban infrastructures" (2004: 425). Identifying these pockets of informal or shadow infrastructural development—practices of jury-rigging, pirating, bricolaging, and kludging—highlights the inherently splintered geography of our seemingly universal infrastructures, the political economics of access, and the infrastructural roles of biopower and human agency.

Yet in thinking across the time and scale of infrastructures, attuned to the entanglement of their hard and soft scaffoldings, we create another role for individual and collective human agency: that of the engaged, critical consumer and, perhaps more important, citizen. Media scholar Lisa Parks argues that it is our duty as infrastructural "citizen/users" to be aware of the "systems that surround [us] and that [we] subsidize and use" (2009):

> [Might we] devise . . . ways of visualizing and developing literacy about infrastructures and the relations that take shape through and around them[?] Are there ways of representing [infrastructures] that will encourage citizens to participate in sustained discussions and decisions about network ownership, development, and access?
>
> (Parks 2009)

Designers and artists have devised a number of approaches—mapping, touring, sensing, signaling, and even *playing* infrastructure—to promote infrastructural literacy (Mattern 2013b). Recent years have brought us walking tours of cell-phone antenna networks, interactive maps of transoceanic fiber-optic cables, apps leading us to the nearest public restrooms or farmer's markets, gallery exhibitions featuring photos of data centers and e-waste deposits, crowd-sourced maps of bike routes and sewage systems, and hacking and circuit-bending workshops where kids explore the guts of their iPhones. "Lines and Nodes," a Fall 2014 symposium and screening series at New York University and Anthology Film Archives examined and exhibited a variety of films, interactive projects, photo projects, and maps that make infrastructure sense-able and intelligible. All of these works promote infrastructural literacy, highlighting the value of using infrastructure as a "critical scaffolding" through which we can address important issues, including those pertaining to environmental health, the distribution of public resources, and social justice.

Many of these projects employ mapping in some form and focus on "making visible the invisible"—highlighting internet traffic, modeling data, or diagramming the "hard," material hubs and cables behind our digital infrastructures. Yet there are relatively few such projects that call attention to the human and historical dimensions of infrastructure, or that highlight the other "soft infrastructures" that Bowker and Star identify: socio-technical protocols, naming conventions, bureaucratic forms, or measurement standards. This paucity of materials to enhance *soft*-infrastructural literacy represents a great opportunity for media-makers, artists, and designers who might develop new pedagogical infrastructures for thinking *about* intellectual infrastructures. Two recent examples, however, might provide some inspiration. First, Hito Steyerl's 2013 widely exhibited and well received video, *How Not to Be Seen: A Fucking Didactic Educational .MOV File*, offers several strategies for "disappearing" oneself from surveillance technologies (I encourage you to seek out clips or stills of the video online). After addressing the protocols by which surveillance takes place, Steyerl proposes several means of evading it, some of which require a subversion of protocols or an upending of measurement standards. Those evasion techniques include camouflaging yourself, hiding in plain sight, shrinking yourself down smaller than a pixel, living in a gated community, wearing a full-body cloak, or becoming a female over 50. By referencing various marginalized populations, she undermines the position of privilege and condition of narcissism that often characterizes digital evasion strategies. Her tongue-in-cheek, yet powerfully critical, message arrives by way of a parodic form: a dark, Monty Python-esque take on the educational film—a "critical scaffolding" for thinking about soft infrastructure, with a built-in critique of established forms of instruction.

Second, Adrian Piper's *Probable Trust Registry* calls into question the ideologies scaffolded into and naturalized by our bureaucratic forms and architectures. In the gallery we find three corporate reception environments, each representing a pledge: *I will always be too expensive to buy; I will always mean what I say*; and *I will always do what I say I am going to do.* If visitors can pledge to live by these rules, they sign a contract—one copy of which is to be kept sealed for 100 years in the Adrian Piper Research Archive in Berlin, and another copy of which goes to the signatories. At the close of the exhibition, all those who have signed pledges will receive copies of all the other signed contracts for that particular pledge. These administrative formats and processes call into question what aspects of human existence can be codified in a standardized form, what ethics might be embedded in something as seemingly "neutral" and disinterested as bureaucratic paperwork, and what protocols of privacy and access should define the archive.

Artists, media-makers, designers, critical engineers, digital humanists, and their colleagues might investigate other means of highlighting both hard *and* soft infrastructures and acknowledging their entanglement. But I propose that these critical-creative practitioners' engagement with infrastructure should extend beyond the promotion of infrastructural "awareness" and intelligence. This is not to diminish the value of such literacy, but rather to recognize designers' potential to go beyond the *representation* of infrastructure to the *design* of infrastructures themselves—more efficient, effective, accessible, intelligible, and just infrastructures. Creative practitioners, I suggest, should approach infrastructure as a generative structure—a framework for generating systems, environments, and objects and cultivating subjects and communities that embody the values we want to define our society.

Infrastructure as Generative Structure

I will close by looking at a few examples of design challenges posed by infrastructure that illustrate its relevance to and applications in various fields. First, my New School colleague, anthropologist Christina Moon, is studying the global flows of resources and labor involved in "fast fashion," a relatively new industry, emblematized by retailers such as Zara and H&M, that rapidly produces inexpensive, "disposable" garments inspired by the latest runway trends. As designers increasingly concern themselves with the ethics of labor and the sourcing of material through which their designs are *made material*, Moon's work helps us to recognize the "material intimacies" of fast fashion: the everyday social and cultural practices of designers, garment workers, and wholesalers; the potentially meaningful and constructive dimensions of their work; and the potential for transnational social ties and cultural exchange *in* that work. Rewriting and nuancing the typically pejorative ways we understand "globalization" and "neoliberalism," Moon calls designers' attention to the embodied, affective aspects of creative labor, which has the potential to inspire greater cultural and ethical sensitivity throughout the interlocking infrastructures of the global fashion industry.

Second, through their Values at Play project, Mary Flanagan and Helen Nissenbaum explore the ethics and ideologies embodied in videogame design. Among designers and the games they create, Flanagan and Nissenbaum aim to instill "positive principles" like equity, empathy, diversity, generosity, humility, and negotiation (Values at Play 2005; Flanagan & Nissenbaum 2014). They have conducted interviews with game designers and created a curriculum to encourage designers to critically reflect on the social values that *are* embodied—and perhaps *should* be embodied—in their work in various dimensions: through the game narrative, its mechanics, its interface design, and, echoing Moon's work, the labor practices and creative processes in the game industry. Again, the multiple interlocking infrastructures of gaming are considered in relation to one another, and Flanagan and Nissenbaum remind us that the values inherent in any one of those systems inform the values defining the other networks to which that system is tied.

Third, designers and critical engineers are developing new infrastructures for access to information resources in parts of the world that have thus far been un- or under-served, or in regions subject to barriers-to-access or government or corporate surveillance, or as a response to the noted precariousness of existing networks in the midst of natural disasters and other crisis situations. As they are extolled, mesh networks—distributed systems for providing internet access—allow for greater adaptability, resilience, and sustainability and stronger privacy protections than centralized systems offered by corporate internet service providers. As Primavera De Filippi writes in *Wired*:

> What's really revolutionary about mesh networking isn't the novel use of technology. It's the fact that it provides a means for people to self-organize into communities and share resources amongst themselves: Mesh networks are operated *by the community, for the community*.
>
> (De Filippi 2014)

Indeed, the technology is not novel: the military has been using mesh networking for years to extend and secure battlefield communication in remote and rugged terrains. The infrastructural design offers affordances that appeal to highly disparate populations, and its flexibility—in geography, scale, and network structure—opens it to a variety of applications embodying widely disparate politics.

An analog counterpart to the mesh network, and our fourth example, is the Ideas Box, a portable media and information toolkit—a mobile knowledge infrastructure—designed for deployment in humanitarian crises. A collaboration among the United National Refugee Agency; designer Philippe Starck; and the nonprofit Libraries Without Borders, the project was inspired by efforts to provide victims of the 2010 Haiti earthquake with access to library resources. Each box, which was designed to conform to the size of shipping pallets (a key infrastructure for global distribution), contains tablet and laptop computers, physical books and e-books, a satellite internet connection (or technology for 3G coverage), equipment for cinema display or projection, films, board games and videogames, and materials for classes and workshops. Here we have a physical infrastructure that is designed to facilitate its deployment through global transportation networks and intended to provide an intellectual infrastructure for access to information and the cultivation of knowledge.

Fifth, returning to our discussion at the very beginning of this chapter, we should consider the potential contributions designers can make to the creation of effective, democratic, intelligible infrastructures for our imminent "sentient cities." I have written elsewhere about the need for designers to inform the way that people interact with and experience their cities' technical infrastructures or "operating systems" (Mattern 2014). In particular, I have considered how the design of "urban interfaces"—screens, installations, and gadgets that help us orient ourselves and navigate the city's various hard and soft infrastructures, track our use of various services and resources, and grant us access to urban data—could "compel us to ask questions about what kinds of cities we want, and what kind of citizens we want to be" (2014). Such an introspective design practice requires collaboration among representatives of the myriad networks that constitute a city.

> The creation of a *better* interface—an interface that reflects the ethics and politics that we want our cities to embody—is necessarily a collaborative process, one drawing on the skills of designers of all stripes, technicians, engineers, logisticians, cultural critics and theorists, artists, bus drivers and sanitation workers, politicians and political scientists, economists, policymakers and myriad others (including women and people of color, who have been egregiously underrepresented in

> relevant debates). If our interfaces are to reflect and embody the values of *our* city, the conception and creation of those interfaces should be *ours*, too—not Cisco's, not the administrators', certainly not *mine* or *yours*. But ours.
>
> (Mattern 2014)

We see a similarly holistic, ecological, cross-infrastructural approach to design reflected in the embrace of "landscape urbanism," which advocates for looking beyond architecture, or beyond individual buildings, to acknowledge that cities are composed of intertwined ecological, political-economic, technological, administrative, and social systems and processes (Waldheim 2006). Of course, cities and media objects manifest their own distinctive infrastructural entanglements, but cities and media are productively entangled, too, both in the way we study them and in the way we generate them.

Finally, I believe it is particularly important for students to consider the infrastructures undergirding and shaping their own fields of study and practice—what we might call the "cultural techniques" for making knowledge and generating work within a field. We should consider what enables a theory to take hold, a particular theorist or designer to gain prominence, a "movement" (such as landscape urbanism, the "sharing economy," or "object-oriented" philosophies) to gain traction, or a method or process to become naturalized. Underlying our theory and design economies are particular epistemological and disciplinary values, such as "innovation" and "sustainability," academic and commercial markets hungry for branded theories and methods (and even old ideas cloaked in neologisms), PR machines, and hordes of students who are eager to discover the "new big thing," which partly fuels the global networks of conferences, tech festivals, art fairs, and TED conferences (not to mention the airplanes, travel budgets, and carbon expenditures that make those gatherings possible). These are the entangled soft and hard infrastructures that often propel "making" in our fields.

In these novel movements and among the world of celebrity theorists and designers, I find that the liberal (or "leftist") conceptions of labor, knowledge, and taste *actually embodied* in their practices sometimes fail to match their professed politics. We are so frequently advocating for more democratic, fluid, inclusive, and ethical models of making and thinking in the world, yet the theories and practices we are building to make sense of these new modes are still often *built* via "Great Man" modes of production.

Even young critical thinkers and makers in media and design have the capacity, perhaps even the obligation, to map, deeply and widely, the infrastructures—the cultural techniques—that undergird the work in their fields, particularly the work on the "bleeding edge." Recognizing the entwined infrastructures that constitute this substrate for practice will ideally cultivate a sensitivity to issues of access, diversity, inclusivity, authorship, attribution, epistemology, and other social values and ethical concerns. Recognizing what is missing in one's field's *current* infrastructural ecology might inspire him or her to contribute to the design of a discursive space or landscape of practice that embodies a political economy more in line with those social values that our theories espouse. You, as critical-creative practitioners, have the opportunity to transform criticality into generativity—to *imagine* and *construct* the hard and soft scaffoldings for tomorrow's fields of practice.

Acknowledgments

Portions of this chapter are adapted from "Ear to the Wire: Listening to Historic Urban Infrastructures," which I published in *Amodern* in 2013.

Further Reading

Larkin, B. (2008) *Signal and Noise: Media, Infrastructure, and Urban Culture*, Durham, NC: Duke University Press.

Lockrem, J. and A. Lugo (2012) "Infrastructure," Special Issue, *Cultural Anthropology* 11, retrieved from www.culanth.org/curated_collections/11-infrastructure.

Starosielski, N., B. Soderman, and C. Cheek (eds.) (2013) "Network Archaeology," Special Issue, *Amodern* 2, retrieved from amodern.net/article/network-archaeology.

Varnelis, K. (ed.) (2009) *Infrastructural City: Networked Ecologies in Los Angeles*, New York, NY: Actar.

References

Blum, A. (2012) *Tubes: A Journey To the Center of the Internet*, New York, NY: HarperCollins.

Bowker, G. C. and S. L. Star (1999) *Sorting Things Out: Classification and Its Consequences*, Cambridge, MA: MIT Press.

De Filippi, P. (2014) "It's Time to Take Mesh Networks Seriously (And Not Just for the Reasons You Think)," *Wired* 2, retrieved from www.wired.com/2014/01/its-time-to-take-mesh-networks-seriously-and-not-just-for-the-reasons-you-think.

Edwards, P. (2003) "Infrastructure and Modernity: Force, Time, and Social Organization in the History of Sociotechnical Systems," in T. J. Misa, P. Brey, and A. Feenberg (eds.) *Modernity and Technology*, Cambridge, MA: MIT Press, pp. 185–225.

Edwards, P. N., S. J. Jackson, G. C. Bowker, and C. P. Knobel (2007) "Understanding Infrastructure: Dynamics, Tension, and Design," Workshop on "History & Theory of Infrastructure: Lessons for New Scientific Cyberinfrastructures," University of Michigan, Ann Arbor, MI.

Flanagan, M. and H. Nissenbaum (2014). *Values at Play in Digital Games*, Cambridge, MA: MIT Press.

Gabrys, J. (2011) *Digital Rubbish: A Natural History of Electronics*, Ann Arbor, MI: University of Michigan Press.

Galloway, A. (2004) *Protocol: How Control Exists after Decentralization*, Cambridge, MA: MIT Press.

Graham, S. and S. Marvin (2001) *Splintering Urbanism: Networked Infrastructures, Technological Mobilities and the Urban Condition*, New York, NY: Routledge.

Graham, S. and S. Marvin (1996) *Telecommunications and the City: Electronic Spaces, Urban Places*, New York, NY: Routledge.

Lines and Nodes (2014) retrieved from linesandnodes.com.

Mackenzie, A. (2010) *Wirelessness: Radical Empiricism in Network Cultures*, Cambridge, MA: MIT Press.

Mattern, S. (2013a) "Ear to the Wire: Listening to Historic Urban Infrastructures," *Amodern* 2 retrieved from amodern.net/article/ear-to-the-wire.

Mattern, S. (2013b) "Infrastructural Tourism," *Places*, retrieved from placesjournal.org/article/infrastructural-tourism.

Mattern, S. (2014) "Interfacing Urban Intelligence," *Places*, retrieved from placesjournal.org/article/interfacing-urban-intelligence.

Mattern, S. (2015) "Deep Time of Media Infrastructure," in L. Parks and N. Starosielski (eds.) *Signal Traffic: Critical Studies of Media Infrastructures*, Urbana, IL: University of Illinois Press, pp. 94–112.

Mayer V. (2011) *Below the Line: Producers and Production Studies in the New Television Economy*, Durham, NC: Duke University Press.

Moon, C. H. (2011) "Material Intimacies: The Labor of Creativity in the Global Fashion Industry," PhD dissertation, Yale University.

Parks, L. (2005) *Cultures in Orbit: Satellites and the Televisual*, Durham, NC: Duke University Press.

Parks, L. (2009) "Around the Antenna Tree: The Politics of Infrastructural Visibility," *Flow* 6, retrieved from flowtv.org/2009/03/around-the-antenna-tree-the-politics-of-infrastructural-visibilitylisa-parks-uc-santa-barbara.

President's Commission on Critical Infrastructure Protection (1997) *Critical Foundations: Protecting America's Infrastructures*, Washington, D.C.

Simone, A. (2004) "People as Infrastructure: Intersecting Fragments in Johannesburg," *Public Culture* 16, 407–19.

Star, S. L. and G. C. Bowker (2006) "How to Infrastructure," in L. A. Lievrouw and S. M. Livingstone (eds.) *Handbook of New Media: Social Shaping and Social Consequences of ICTs*, Thousand Oaks, CA: Sage, pp. 230–44.

Starosielski, S. (2015) *The Undersea Network*, Durham NC: Duke University Press.

Steyerl, Hito (2013) *How Not to Be Seen: A Fucking Didactic Educational .MOV File*, retrieved from player.vimeo.com/video/125475136.

Values at Play (2005) retrieved from valuesatplay.org.

Waldheim, C. (ed.) (2006) *The Landscape Urbanism Reader*, New York, NY: Princeton Architectural Press.

Part IV

REMEDIATION, DATA, MEMORY

33

OBSOLESCENCE AND INNOVATION IN THE AGE OF THE DIGITAL

Kathleen Fitzpatrick

Obsolescence and *innovation* are inextricably locked together, but their logic is not dialectical. While neither term can exist without the other, they are not delicately, viciously balanced opposites. Their logic is instead lenticular, two ways of looking at exactly the same thing. They are not just mutually imbricated, but identical; not just cut from the same cloth, but two angles on exactly the same fabric. Attempting to look at each independently winds up surfacing the other in the very act of definition. Even more, attempting to look at both together produces neither synthesis nor eternal tension, but rather a kind of eversion, a turning inside-out of our assumptions about the relationship between old and new. Perhaps this eversion is symptomatic of the contemporary-in-general: it is only in the present (any present) that our relationship to past and future matters enough to uncover the complexities of *their* relationship. But perhaps there is something specific about the period since 1945 that gives us, on the one hand, a future-oriented perspective that shapes the coming past, and on the other, an experience of the past that will linger long into the future. Like a character in William Gibson's Bigend trilogy, we inhabit the immediate future, 20 seconds ahead of the leading edge of the now. Like a character in Octavia Butler's Parable series, we find ourselves balanced in the coming aftermath of apocalypse, caught in a now that is made of nothing but change. The hinge between *obsolescence* and *innovation* is the nexus point of that now. We innovate through obsolescence; we ourselves obsolesce as we innovate. We create and are haunted by new and old alike.

Obsolescence may itself have been the defining innovation of the twentieth century. Giles Slade argues in *Made to Break*:

> Deliberate obsolescence in all its forms—technological, psychological, or planned—is a uniquely American invention . . . we invented the very concept of disposability itself, as a necessary precursor to our rejection of tradition and our promotion of progress and change.
>
> (Slade 2006: 3)

Intended to promote progress in the specific form of economic development during and after the Great Depression, the notion of obsolescence in its many forms (ranging from design obsolescence, in which small regular flourishes make old models less desirable, to death-dating, in which objects are given fixed life spans at the moment of their creation) drives innovation as well as the act of consumption that links the two. Making things old paves the way for the new, but it also leaves us with the persistent detritus of past innovation.

Obsolescence is therefore not a figure for the ongoing transformation of future into past, but instead demonstrates the eternal simultaneity of the two. The scandal of obsolescence lies in the effects of this simultaneity, which does not result in the evanescence of the material form of the obsolete object, or even necessarily of its usability, but rather in the waning of its value to us, its cultural cachet. Set aside, for the moment, the peculiar case of the outdated object that is prized for that very quality (the antique, the retro); in obsolescence, the object endures while our desire for it disappears. As John Durham Peters argues, it is this persistence that defines obsolescence; the obsolete object haunts us, ever-present but unused (2015: 90). Obsolescence is in this sense less a quality of things than a quality of our relationship to those things. Obsolescence and innovation are, most literally, ideological; they are ways of thinking about the world around us that often operate invisibly, as mere common sense, and yet they have far-reaching ramifications for the objects that surround us—not to mention for ourselves.

In fact, there is a question to be raised about the relationship between our ideas about the obsolescence of things and our own eternal sense of belatedness, as many of us find ourselves having increasing difficulty, across the span of our lives, keeping up with the now. Though this sense of belatedness contains within it the inescapable, material facts of our aging, our slowing, our approaching death, it is nonetheless manufactured, like obsolescence/innovation itself, through a process that is overwhelmingly ideological. Obsolescence, as Slade details, is far from a natural phenomenon; it was rather invented as a designed component of the product lifecycle, intended to spur consumption not just through the production of the new but through the manufacture of oldness. Obsolescence is thus not simply a *reminder of*, but the actual *production of*, our sense of belatedness. Our experience of the now—the fleeting, with which one must rush to keep up—is thus similarly manufactured and marketed.

Innovation, in this sense, is both the means through which we attempt to outpace the now, trying fruitlessly to propel ourselves out of the present and into the future, and the process through which we generate the past that encroaches ever more closely.

The ramifications of obsolescence and innovation for ourselves and our things are unpredictable, and at times paradoxical, in their effect; the obsolete object can lose all value and, as Vance Packard and Giles Slade reveal, become part of the ever-growing landfill on which we increasingly build our culture—or it can transform into a collector's object, even a fetish. Vinyl records form a small portion of overall record industry revenues, and yet those sales are not merely persistent but growing—up 52 percent in 2015 over the prior year, according to a report from the RIAA (see Cox 2015). Moreover, as Gabe Bullard explores in "Restoration Hardware," a cottage industry has sprung up, focused on the repair of curiosities such as manual typewriters, hi-fi stereo systems, and the iconic Polaroid camera. We might ask ourselves what qualities promote a particular obsolete thing for rescue from the landfill, but we should also consider what in us desires the selective transformation of the old into the vintage. What combination of aesthetics and nostalgia results in the hipster's recuperation of the purposefully out-of-date?

Perhaps there is something in the fact that much of the contemporary play of obsolescence/innovation locates itself around our communication technologies. This is an area in which the forces of innovation that, depending on one's angle, either create obsolescence or are propelled by it, seem dominant. We are abandoning our land lines, cutting our cables, moving toward an always-on mode of wireless communication that permeates the very air we breathe. Our devices (see the mobile phone, the tablet, the smart watch) become smaller, and then larger, and then smaller again; they take on dimension, and then flatten; they converge into one all-powerful device, and then disambiguate into specialized devices; they are attached to us metaphorically, and then very physically. With each innovation in function or design, the devices we already own—though it is often those devices that literally *have us* under contract—become obsolete: they may still be of the same use, but are no longer of the same value. Whether all of these relentless upgrades (some of which, on the software side, demand further updates to our hardware, a situation those Depression-era economists would have adored) have actually affected our ability to communicate with one another remains, however, something of an open question. They have undoubtedly transformed our experience of the act of communication, and thus our lived sense of what it is to communicate. If there is some social relation that is being transformed by our communication technologies, then it may be in that common experience: in connecting to our connected devices, we achieve an odd state of connectedness precisely by isolating ourselves, separately wireless-ed together.

However, it is not just our devices that reflect the constant churn of innovation and obsolescence as we seek the newest, fastest mode of connection. This pattern extends itself to the platforms on which we communicate, including both our software and social networks. Systems come and go: AOL, Friendster, and Geocities now strike us as hilariously dated. But even the systems we continue to use are subject to this process. Email, Facebook, and other such systems once seemed so new and exciting to us; not only have many become sources of obligation, anxiety, *work* (a transition mapped as early as 2005 by the Pew Internet and American Life project), but they have also gathered painful generational associations. As Bob Lefsetz points out, "Facebook is for old people": "Documenting your entire life history, building a timeline, a shrine to yourself, so that the people you grew up with will be impressed? That's for baby boomers"; the kids today gravitate toward more immediate communication about the now (2013). The obsolescence of a system, in other words, may not be entirely tied to its disuse; it may have just as much to do with *who uses it and how*. In that sense, Snapchat is emblematic, both for its imperfect evanescence—the photo sent from a wireless device, meant to self-destruct in 30 seconds, but which can nonetheless be captured, disseminated, and preserved in unintended ways—and for the media narratives of its quick adoption by the young, with perfect bafflement of the old. It is possible, as Wendy Chun (2008) has suggested, that we are driven by the desire for our communication processes to take place at the speed of experience, as a hedge of sorts against our own belatedness.

Perhaps that hedge is at the root of all of our attempts to manage time, from productivity porn to slow food. In the recuperative drives of hipster culture, from 80s-era (and now, increasingly, 90s-era) fashion to fixed-gear bikes and artisanal crafts, there is the longing for a greater permanence, not just for things, but also for the self. Value is carefully crafted not just around the new, but also around the innovative rebirth of the old. What is desired in that oldness is often the signs of care that arise from use, from the patina of age; much less esteemed, but still salable, as Hanjo Berressem explores in the work of William Gibson, are manufactured versions of patina. Recent stories suggest, for instance, that there is a perverse kind of status accorded by some teens to having a cell phone with a cracked screen, to such an extent that developers are cashing in with wallpapers mimicking the effects of such brokenness. See Wax:

> [S]ome young people say a cracked screen gives you a sort of street cred, like you've been through some real-life stuff, even if it happened on the mean streets of Bethesda. It's tough, subversive and just kinda cool.
>
> (Wax 2013)

In all of this, we find a deep tension between the consumer's desire for the new and the consumer's resentment at being required to let go of the old—between the corporate seductions of innovation and the equally powerful reincorporation of consumer resistance through the innovative use of obsolescence.

Pursuing a full elaboration of an analysis such as the one I am attempting here requires something of the standpoint of the neutral observer, one who can sufficiently understand our new technologies and platforms without fully adopting, or being adopted by, them—one who can stand at enough of a remove from the machinations of capital to study them without getting caught. This, suffice it to say, is not a position I can inhabit—but then, I am not sure that it is a terribly habitable position at all in the early twenty-first century. As scholars, and particularly scholars in the critical tradition of the humanities, we rely on our ability to resist the relentless propulsion of our culture into the future, on our training, which leads us to linger, to proceed with great deliberateness, and to keep open the avenues to the past. We rely, that is to say, on our ability to think through the present moment. And yet our experiences, and our work, are as mediated by our relationships with our communication technologies as anyone's.

We need to think, as scholars, that we can think *through*, that our thought takes place outside the dynamics of neoliberalism that drive so much of the contemporary relationship to the lived world. We embrace a lifestyle that is deliberate, that understands history, that requires careful contemplation. We are slow to discard the past and cautious about the havoc that innovation may wreak on our ways of working. We try to reconcile past and future—in all ways except in the development of our ideas. There, we follow a path of innovation through obsolescence that is every bit as ruthless as that emerging from factories and boardrooms. This mode of critical production may have its most literal manifestation in the "they say/I say" mode of understanding academic writing popularized by Gerald Graff and Cathy Birkenstein. Certainly laying this form of argumentation bare can help us develop fluency in the dominant moves espoused by academic discourse, but it perpetuates a reductive mode in which the author summarizes and dismisses prior arguments rather than genuinely engaging with them. And as in specific arguments, so in the academy at large: a new idea, or a new field, emerges on the scene; it does battle against the status quo and gathers critical or institutional support; for a shockingly brief moment, it may even achieve some kind of success. Then, in a flash, it either dissolves into the quaintly retrograde or, at best, becomes the status quo against which battle is done, in which case it gathers a next generation of critics arguing against it. The new idea is inevitably consigned to the passé, the reductive, the reactionary, and the old. Very, very few scholarly ideas escape this cycle, and those that do often become so naturalized in academic discourse that their references disappear, becoming indistinguishable from common sense. Some once-discarded ideas get recovered from the ash-heap of the scholarly past to have new life breathed into them, but they are a precious few, and it is the re-reading, the recuperation, that gives them their new value. In this sense, the renewal of critical interest in the work of a figure such as Herbert Marcuse (on which, see Romano 2011; Parry 2013) is not all that different from listening to vinyl LPs or writing with manual typewriters.

If the paired terms *obsolescence* and *innovation* represent not just the lenticular logic of consumer culture, but also the lenticular logic of cultural criticism, we might begin to recognize another reason why, as Bruno Latour (2004) has asked, critique has "run out of steam"—not simply because we have been undermined by our own resistance to the notion of the unconstructed fact, but because critique as a mode of discourse necessarily generates its own obsolescence. We as scholars obsolesce not because we fail to innovate, but because critique's negativity means that we cannot help but innovate at our own expense. One might ask whether, and how, we can develop the more positive critique Latour calls for, a critique that is fundamentally about care, a critique that might value building upon the past more than rejecting it in favor of the future.

Perhaps such a reorientation of critique might find its bearings in seeking out a mode of more direct, ongoing engagement with one another, and even with a set of broader publics, that modulates the iterative innovation-through-rejection mode of scholarly discourse and instead places multiple perspectives into ongoing conversation. Conversation, in fact, may be one avenue through which we could find our way past the need to do battle with one another—to see new ideas and old in an endless cycle of Oedipean combat—allowing us instead to create a space within which we can keep critique alive and renewed precisely by keeping old and new in active dialogue.

If we are to build such critical conversation, we must think carefully about our uses of the increasing range of technologies of inscription and dissemination that we have for connecting with one another, and for reaching out to other engaged publics. Certain of our technologies—the book, most particularly—seem to demand both a relentless production of critical innovation (in order for a publisher to be willing to invest in its dissemination) and an equally relentless resistance to future conversational forays (in the form of the text's finality, fixity, and closure, all of which leave it un-updatable, death-dated, and inevitably obsolete). Others of our technologies—at the moment, one might place Twitter in this category, though I am acutely aware of the ways that reference will inevitably date this very argument—create a flow so relentless that one is never quite able to catch up, unable even to sustain the fantasy of returning to the archive and rereading the conversation as it unfolded. Somewhere between the book's orientation toward the past and Twitter's relentless propulsion into the future might lie a platform—which, having come of age in the academy and the digital environment of the early 2000s, I cannot help but associate with the blog—that looks both forward and backward, that allows for an immediacy closer to that of conversation but that extends those conversations both temporally and across the networked landscape, that permits multiple voices engaged in revisiting and rethinking questions that have already been asked as well as raising new questions in a timely fashion, that keeps the now front and center while producing its own powerfully interconnected, always-available archive. (It is, of course, impossible to escape the irony in treating a platform as relatively new as the blog as a form in which we might achieve some kind of stability for the critical present. However, though the blog's obsolescence has been repeatedly pronounced over the last decade, its structures nonetheless underwrite a growing percentage of the web. The blog has become something more than itself—no longer merely a genre, but instead an engine, and one whose survival and expansion are worth paying some attention.)

We must pay careful attention to the platforms on which we stage our critical conversations, not least because of who we become when we engage with and on them. As Lisa Gitelman notes, "changes to writing and reading matter in large measure because they equal changes to writers and readers. New inscriptions signal new subjectivities" (1999: 11) The conventional wisdom unsurprisingly suggests that, the more we engage with writing and reading on new, malleable digital platforms—the more our practices of inscription give the appearance of dematerializing—the more oriented toward the ephemeral our own subjectivities become. Moreover, it would appear that we struggle with reading deeply today, as we are repeatedly exhorted to recuperate the value of slow engagements with writing in a culture that privileges speed (see Tombolini n.d.). However, as Matt Kirschenbaum's work on media forensics and the materiality of digital text might remind us, there is an extraordinary persistence to the digital, even in the midst of its malleability. Exploring the actual functioning of our inscriptive technologies—rather than the ways the technologies represent themselves as functioning, or the ways their promoters or detractors represent them—is crucial to understanding the ways that we will be able to make use of them in our own critical practices. As Kirschenbaum argues,

> electronic textual theory has labored under . . . uncritical absorptions of the medium's self- or seemingly self-evident representations. While often precisely Romantic in their celebration of the fragile half-life of the digital, the "ideology" I want to delineate below is perhaps better thought of as *medial*—that is, one that substitutes popular representations of a medium, socially constructed and culturally activated to perform specific kinds of work, for a more comprehensive treatment of the material particulars of a given technology.
>
> (Kirschenbaum 2008: 36)

Those popular representations are, in no small part, elements of the same kinds of marketing that have centralized the processes of obsolescence and innovation in contemporary media culture, not to mention contemporary critical culture. If we have adopted those representations as ways to describe our lived experiences of technology, then they only reveal the extent to which that lived experience is one which, like the technology itself, we have been sold.

Not everything new is created to be sold, of course, just as not everything old is destined to become waste or fetish. But our ways of understanding newness and oldness, speed and deliberation, ephemerality and permanence in contemporary culture are inevitably shaped by the ideological processes of obsolescence and innovation that privilege those modes of engagement with things. However much obsolescence urges us to dispose of the old and innovation presses us to buy the new, their lenticular logic reveals the extent to which each creates the other, creating a temporal paradox of sorts in which our future brings our past into being, and our past becomes the detritus of that future.

This is no less true of ideas than it is of things. It is possible that the only truly productive critical possibility is to acknowledge the force that obsolescence and innovation have in our own work, seeking some position of care within the now that requires neither a relentless pursuit of the new nor a retrenchment in defense of (or a recuperation of) the old. Whether such a position is possible—or whether it requires stopping time itself—remains to be seen.

Further Reading

Packard, V. (2011) *The Waste Makers*, Brooklyn, NY: Ig Publishing.

Slade, G. (2006) *Made to Break: Technology and Obsolescence in America*, Cambridge, MA: Harvard University Press.

Strasser, S. (1999) *Waste and Want: A Social History of Trash*, New York, NY: Henry Holt.

Thill, B. (2015) *Waste*, New York, NY: Bloomsbury.

Tischleder, B. and S. Wasserman (eds.) (2015) *Cultures of Obsolescence: History, Materiality, and the Digital Age*. New York, NY: Palgrave Macmillan.

References

Berressem, H. (2015) "'Zero History': The Poetics of Patination in the Work of William Gibson," in B. B. Tischleder & S. Wasserman (eds.) *Cultures of Obsolescence: History, Materiality, and the Digital Age*, New York, NY: Palgrave Macmillan, pp. 173–89.

Bullard, G. (2013) "Restoration Hardware," *The Magazine* 18.

Chun, W. H. K. (2008) "The Enduring Ephemeral, or the Future Is a Memory," *Critical Inquiry* 35(1), 148–71.

Cox, J. (2015) "Vinyl Sales Are More Valuable than Ad-supported Streaming in 2015," *The Verge*, retrieved from www.theverge.com/2015/9/28/9408233/vinyl-sales-ad-supported-streaming-riaa-2015-report.

Gitelman, L. (1999) *Scripts, Grooves, and Writing Machines: Representing Technology in the Edison Era*, Stanford, CA: Stanford University Press.

Graff, G. and C. Birkenstein (2010) *They Say / I Say: The Moves that Matter in Academic Writing*, New York, NY: W.W. Norton & Co.

Kirschenbaum, M. G. (2008) *Mechanisms: New Media and the Forensic Imagination*, Cambridge, MA: MIT Press.

Latour, B. (2004) "Why Has Critique Run out of Steam? From Matters of Fact to Matters of Concern," *Critical Inquiry* 30(2), 225–48.

Lefsetz, B. (2013) "Facebook Is for Old People," *Lefsetz Letter*, retrieved from lefsetz.com/wordpress/index.php/archives/2013/06/02/facebook-is-for-old-people/.

Lenhart, A., M. Madden, and P. Hitlin (2005) *Teens and Technology*, Washington, DC: Pew Internet and American Life Project.

Packard, V. (2011) *The Waste Makers*, Brooklyn, NY: Ig Publishing.

Parry, M. (2013) "Newly Discovered Draft of Marcuse Book Reveals Turn toward Pessimism," *The Chronicle of Higher Education*, retrieved from chronicle.com/article/Newfound-Early-Draft-of/141949/.

Peters, J. D. (2015) "Proliferation and Obsolescence of the Historical Record in the Digital Era," in B. B. Tischleder and S. Wasserman (eds.) *Cultures of Obsolescence: History, Materiality, and the Digital Age*, New York, NY: Palgrave Macmillan, pp. 79–96.

Romano, C. (2011) "Occupy This: Is It Comeback Time for Herbert Marcuse?" *The Chronicle of Higher Education*, retrieved from chronicle.com/article/Occupy-This-Is-It-Comeback/130028/.

Slade, G. (2006) *Made to Break: Technology and Obsolescence in America*, Cambridge, MA: Harvard University Press.

Tombolini, A. (n.d.) *Slow Reading Manifesto*, retrieved from www.slowreading.org/.

Wax, E. (2013) "Beat-up Cellphones with Cracked Screens Are Point of Pride for Some Young People," *Washington Post*, retrieved from articles.washingtonpost.com/2013–05–17/lifestyle/39333160_1_screen-iphone-lofton.

34

FUTURES OF THE BOOK

Jon Bath, Alyssa Arbuckle, Constance Crompton, Alex Christie, Ray Siemens, and the INKE Research Group

The erroneous belief that a new medium will completely replace a previous one is nowhere more evident than in discussions surrounding the emergence of electronic text. Having previously fended off the challenges of the phonograph, motion picture, radio, and television, in the early 1990s the book was seen as finally having met its match in the computer and the internet. In his 1994 book, *The Gutenberg Elegies: The Fate of Reading in an Electronic Age*, bibliophile Sven Birkerts bemoaned, "The stable hierarchies of the printed page—one of the defining norms of the world—are being superseded by the rush of impulses through freshly minted circuits" (1994: 3). Birkerts was responding to literary theorists such as George Landow (1992) and Jay David Bolter (1990) who saw the networked electronic text, with its relative ease of publishing and modification postpublication, as liberating authors and readers from the shackles of the printed book. They believed printed books would, in the near future, only be read by those "addicted to the look and feel of tree flakes encased in dead cow" (Mitchell 1995: 56). The book could not hope to compete against the computer, and its death was surely at hand. Except, as we now know, it was not.

Media critics such as Paul Duguid (1996) and Lisa Gitelman (2006) have responded to this rhetoric of supersession and shown how similar concerns about replacement and obsolescence have manifested across the history of various technologies. Similarly, book historians such as David McKitterick have looked at the last period of major media transition—the move from manuscript to print—to reveal that "each new technology does not replace the previous one. Rather it augments it and offers alternatives" (2003: 20). In this chapter, we examine the relationship between the printed book and the electronic book, but not as a progression from the old to the new. We begin by looking at how the electronic book has been shaped by understandings of printed books. Electronic text was initially created to encode pre-existing books and continues to carry traces of this materiality forward. As we reveal the depth of this influence, it becomes clear that the e-book, and the infrastructure that supports it, have been built by those with a very narrow understanding of what the "book" is; an Amazon Kindle may be a marvelous tool for reading novels, but it should be remembered that novels themselves are a fairly recent development in the book's existence. In opposition to this singular definition of the book, we provide an example, the *Social Edition of the Devonshire Manuscript*, of how a more fulsome understanding of the socially and institutionally contingent forms that books (and authors, editors, and readers) have taken can result in an e-book that respects, reflects upon, and responds to the book in all its diversity.

Digital text and the academic field of digital humanities share a common genesis story: the *Index Thomisticus* created by Father Robert Busa (Hockey 2004: 4). Busa desired to create a concordance—an index of all the words in the works of Thomas Aquinas and where exactly they were used. Concordances were nothing new. But considering that this concordance would have to cover a corpus of over 11 million words, Busa thought that perhaps he could leverage the newly emerging technology of the computer to assist in this task. In 1949, he travelled to New York to meet with Thomas Watson, head of IBM, to determine if this was feasible. Watson initially balked, arguing that computers could not process text, but Busa convinced him it was worth the effort to try. Watson agreed to give the project IBM's support for free (Busa 1980: 84). The impact of this conversation for current communication technologies is difficult to overstate. After 30 years of work, Busa's concordance was published as a book series, on CD-ROM, and then on the internet. More important, he helped transform the computer into a medium for language. As Stefano Lorenzetto stated in his obituary of Busa, "If you surf the internet, you owe it to him and if you use a PC to write emails and documents, you owe it to him. And if you can read this article, you owe it to him, we owe it to him" (translated in Priego 2011).

Others joined Busa and IBM in their efforts to adapt the computer to process text, and it is interesting to note how the influence of the printed text continues to propagate through the development of the computer during this period. For example, in 1969 Charles Goldfarb, along with Ed Mosher and Ray Lorie, developed Generalized Markup Language (GML), the precursor to Standard Generalized Markup Language (SGML) and thus HyperText Markup Language (HTML), the basic code underlying the World Wide Web. Goldfarb (1989) credits the experience of installing an early typesetting computer in a newspaper office with fundamentally changing his understanding of how text is structured, and thus the way documents are now encoded. Rather than encoding a text with specific instructions as to how a section was to be displayed, with GML the text was broken down into generic tagged sections (i.e., heading, caption), and then other external files specified what style to apply to each class of tags. The structure of the document, not its meaning, was the fundamental unit to be encoded. Similarly, in his work on the Coach House Press, John Maxwell (2009) has shown how, beginning in the early 1970s, printer Stan Bevington worked alongside computer science scholars to develop an SGML-based workflow for both authors and printers in an attempt to adapt the computer to the needs of the fine printer, an attempt that also resulted in the development of a number of tools for manipulating SGML and later XML.

If the code underlying digital text has been heavily influenced by the practice of printers, then theoretical approaches to it have been no less so—there is a strong line of influence from textual criticism, the study of the text as a material object, to digital humanities. Both Fredson Bowers and Charles Hinman (pre-eminent figures in the "New Bibliography" during the mid-twentieth century) were employed as cryptanalysts during World War II. Alan Galey suggests that, as both code-breaking and analytical bibliography relied upon technological advances to discover patterns in apparent chaos, the two men, knowingly or not, brought the influence of information theory and computerization to textual studies (2010: 299). Furthermore, given that textual scholarship is fundamentally concerned with texts in moments of transition, such as transforming an author's manuscript into a printed book, it is not surprising that textual scholars were some of the first to identify the transition from print to digital text as an area of interest for literary scholars. In 1985, D.F. McKenzie included computer files, as well as maps, films, and audio recordings, as forms of "text" that should fall under the purview of bibliography (1999: 19). With all of these connections between textual scholarship and the computer, it should come as no surprise that one of the earliest genres of digital humanities projects to gain scholarly traction was the digital edition. Kevin Kiernan's *Electronic Beowulf* (1993), Martha Nell Smith's *Dickinson Electronic Archives* (1994), *The Arden Shakespeare* (1997), and Elizabeth Salter's *The Wife of Bath's Tale* (1998) were just a few of the many digital editions to emerge during the 1990s, first on CD-ROM and then on the web.

However, this close connection between textual studies and the emergence of digital humanities has not been without its problems. In 1996 Jerome McGann declared, "We no longer have to use books to analyze and study other books or texts" (1996: 12). But, for better and worse, much work being done with and on digital text is still strongly influenced by ideas based on the print book. As Paul Duguid points out, the continued survival of technologies long after the appearance of supposedly superior alternatives can be explained by understanding that technology does not exist outside of human experience but rather within what Raymond Williams identified as the "social-material complex" (1996: 64). Writing about the emergence of various communication technologies, but particularly television, Williams argued it was a mistake to think that technologies are created *ex nihilo*. Rather, they are developed in response to a combination of societal needs (generally commercial and military) and previously developed technologies (Williams 1974: 20–21). The makers of any new technology do so in response to previously developed technologies, and generally change is incremental rather than revolutionary. For example, television may appear revolutionary when compared to radio; however, television relied on the science of signal transmission and reception pioneered with radio. The first viewers of television were already accustomed to radio programs and advertisements, thus, to avoid alienating potential consumers, the initial content developed for television differed little, with the obvious exception of its visual aspects, from that of radio.

In "Translating Media: Why We Should Rethink Textuality" (2003), N. Katherine Hayles shows how branches of textual criticism focused on discovering an ideal, uncorrupted version of a literary work have negatively influenced the development of encoding techniques for digital text. This ideal text is an abstract construct of how the work existed in the author's mind before it was exposed to the corrupting influences of people, such as editors and printers, charged with making it physical (i.e., printing it). The previously discussed development of markup language by Goldfarb and the Coach House Press shows how printers themselves were interested in minimizing this opportunity for errors, and thus maximizing profit, by separating the content of a work from the markup that determines how it will appear on the page. As yet another example, the Text Encoding Initiative (TEI) adopts these markup technologies and attempts to create a digital version of a text that can be manifested across electronic platforms. In doing so, it embeds the idea of the text as an abstract entity into the very code of any TEI-encoded document. Alan Liu (2004) argues this separation of form from content is part of a larger trend in postindustrialism toward ever greater standardization; rather ironically, the system designed for encoding literary works stifles the creative expression that made those works possible in the first place. Also diminished in this separation is the information contained in previous material features of a text, such as its layout and typeface. Rather than creating a digital facsimile, markup translates the work into a new medium and, like any translation, changes the text in the process (Hayles 2003: 270). In his analysis of the same novel published in both print and e-book, Alan Galey (2012) has shown just how different the two versions can be.

A further, and perhaps more familiar, example of how the social-material complex has influenced the development of electronic text can be seen in the commercial success of the e-reader. After a number of fits and starts, e-readers had their first commercial success with the release of the Amazon Kindle in 2007. The advertising copy for the Kindle mentions that the device could also be used to read a wide range of texts, from Wikipedia and blogs to newspapers. But the fundamental focus of the device is to read books, and Amazon had a very specific idea of what that act of reading entails:

> Lose Yourself in Your Reading
>
> The most elegant feature of a physical book is that it disappears while you're reading. Immersed in the author's world and ideas, you don't notice a book's glue, the stitching, or ink. Our top design objective was to make Kindle disappear—just like a physical book—so you can get lost in your reading, not the technology.
>
> (Amazon 2009)

As Amazon sees it, the primary purpose of the book is to be merely an unobtrusive conduit for the content it contains; the form does not matter, as long as it does not interfere with the reader's enjoyment of the text.

The social-material complex of the book is similarly evident in Steve Jobs's launch of Apple's iBooks for the iPad in 2010, when he demonstrated "what it is like to read a book" (Apple 2010). iBooks conform to traditional norms for the book by displaying your books on a virtual bookshelf and including animations for turning the pages. Jobs also points out that iBooks can contain photos, videos, and "whatever the author wants." Although he ends by mentioning that iBooks could also be used for textbooks, it is clear that the platform is really built for "popular books"; in his demo, he emphasizes novels and autobiographies. It is also probably not coincidental that, by definition, "popular" books are the best-selling ones and thus the best avenue for generating a profit.

Both the Kindle and iBooks are premised on a particular social construction of what the book is: a long-form text whose content is, or should be, controlled by an author and whose physical form should be an invisible technology for the reader. While there are strong historical precedents for seeing books in exactly this fashion, the most well-known being Beatrice Warde's declaration that a book should be a "crystal goblet" because "everything about it is calculated to reveal rather than hide the beautiful thing it is meant to contain" (1956: 11), an emphasis on linguistic content above all else does not characterize the full range of theories that define the book. Yet these entrenched beliefs may change. Lisa Gitelman writes, "Although they possess extraordinary inertia, norms and standards can and do change, because they are expressive of changeable social, economic, and material relationships" (2006: 8). For instance, while today's e-readers often demonstrate singular conceptions of book and author in their interface and design, histories of the book expose these monolithic concepts as, in fact, mutable and multiple, bringing to the fore alternate visions of the book and its futures. It is upon this vision, and its reconception of how books are authored and published that (as we shall see) *A Social Edition of the Devonshire Manuscript* is created.

If one re-thinks even a single part of the e-book's definition as a sole-authored, long-form text in an invisible container, then such re-thinking can have tremendous ramifications and afford e-books that are more than digital facsimiles of print texts. For example, what if we reconceptualize the idea of the author, a la Roland Barthes in "The Death of the Author"?

Citing such cultural giants as Baudelaire, Van Gogh, and Tchaikovsky, Barthes argues that "the image of literature to be found in contemporary culture is tyrannically centered on the author, his person, his history, his tastes, his passions" (1967: 143). The figure of the Lone Genius, the savant, has long skewed a collective vision of the production of ideas, from Addison's "Books are the legacy that a great genius leaves to mankind" to Emerson's conviction that solitude protected great authors from mediocrity (Addison 1711; Emerson 1860). This concept of the sole author has proliferated through the dominant print culture to the e-book and has been reinforced in the academy by rewards, such as tenure and promotion, for single-authored publications.

In reality, many individuals contribute to the creation of knowledge and its eventual output as an artifact, be it print, digital, material, verbal, visual, or any other format or combination thereof. In the field of book history, scholars such as McGann (1991) and McKenzie (1999) have demonstrated that knowledge products are never singular or static. McKenzie's *Bibliography and the Sociology of Texts* deftly illuminates that "the ostensible unity of any one 'contained' text . . . is an illusion. As a language, its forms and meaning derive from other texts; and as we listen to, look at, or read it, at the very same time we re-write it" (1999: 60). McKenzie's argument applies equally to the material content of texts, print and electronic alike: not only are an author's written ideas shaped by her collaborators and influences (including editors, sources of inspiration, and so on), but the print form those ideas take (including the physical materials of a given book or journal, the formatting conventions of the publishing house in which it was produced, and so on) are equally multiauthored. Texts exist in diverse instances and iterations.

More recent conversations around authorship and knowledge production refigure McKenzie's argument for the sociology of texts. Drawing upon the work of Johanna Drucker, Matthew Kirschenbaum, Hayles, and others, Gitelman suggests, "[E]lectronic texts need to be seen more as processes than as anything solid-state or as anything—another great imprecision—merely virtual" (2014: 69). The procedural, in-process quality of electronic texts is precisely what McKenzie draws attention to when he deflates the concept of the "contained" or "unified" text. Texts are fluid and perpetually in process as social artifacts engaging a number of actors: authors and readers, certainly, but also any combination of colleagues, editors, publishers, printers, research assistants, family members, and countless others. This dynamic un-fixedness characterizes both print and digital text, but the end product obfuscates the communal aspect of text production and presents a single object, thereby perpetuating the myth that the text is the product of the author alone. This raises the question: what would a book that acknowledges and embodies its social creation look like?

One attempt to explore this question is the *Social Edition of the Devonshire Manuscript* project (Siemens et al. 2015). The project offers a model of what new knowledge creation might look like by creating an edition that allows for community collaboration while explicitly building on existing resources to ensure authority (Siemens et al. 2012). It is an example of Alan Galey and Stan Ruecker's assertion that digital knowledge production, especially concerning text in the field of digital humanities, stems from book history because "the field of book history offers a perspective on the ethos of thinking through making, which informs much digital humanities research and pedagogy generally" (2010: 407). Engaging in a critical production process—what Galey and Ruecker identify as *thinking through making*—enables scholars to shape the form of knowledge production in the information age (407). The process permits editors to attend to Hayles's argument that the "materiality of the artifact can no longer be positioned as a subspecialty within literary studies" (2002: 19). In short, the book is not a transparent technology. While texts always have a material manifestation (on the printed page, in bits), electronic books do not need to imitate other book forms. Which features to translate to the screen and which to set aside are at the discretion of electronic book producers, although they may also be shaped by external factors: the limits imposed by programming languages, hardware, and distributors, for instance. Electronic book production can also make visible the material and institutional conventions that underpin knowledge dissemination, giving editors the power to consciously preserve best practices while setting aside conventions that might limit or inhibit new knowledge creation. To this end, electronic manifestations of book-like objects such as the *Social Edition of the Devonshire Manuscript* can simultaneously operate as material and institutional transformations in the processes of knowledge production, reshaping the pathways and protocols of textual knowledge such that they serve the needs of various intellectual communities rather than reinforcing the authority of a select few.

The *Devonshire Manuscript* project began with the editorial team's creation of the editorial apparatus. The manuscript itself, "BL MS Add. 17, 492," is a sixteenth-century courtly miscellany comprising some 194 poems and annotations from Henry VIII's court in the years leading up to Anne Boleyn's death. Following transcription, the team augmented the base text with scholarly introductions, witness lists, hand tables, commentary, textual notes, and a collective biography of the early modern contributors to the manuscript. This last feature is of particular import. The manuscript itself challenges the figure of the lone author, as the text was compiled by many contributors, each annotating and commenting on one another's new poems or copies of extant poems. In order to open the editing process to more contributors, in late 2011 the team moved the edition into Wikibooks, a sister project to Wikipedia. In the year that followed the text was edited by senior scholars, postdoctoral fellows, graduate researchers, programmers, members of the Wikibooks community, and self-selected members of the public, all guided by an editorial advisory group. While the social and economic conditions, and indeed literacies, that permit online collaboration are quite different from those in Henry VIII's court, the Wikibooks environment offered many advantages that mirrored the communal editing practices of the sixteenth-century contributors. While welcoming the opportunities for engagement with editorial communities outside of the academy, at the conclusion of the year the editorial advisory group suggested that the barriers for participation were too high, requiring, as they do, an understanding of the Wikimedia markup language in addition to content knowledge. They also expressed a general feeling of discomfort at the idea that anyone could remove or otherwise modify the text of the Devonshire manuscript poems from the Wikibooks edition. The edition was, in fact, subject to some vandalism in the early days of the project. This vandalism, however, was quickly reversed by members of the Wikibooks community before the core editorial team had to intervene (for a more detailed discussion of the vandalism, see Crompton et al. 2015). Nevertheless, the project team felt that this first electronic iteration of the edition would be improved if it met the needs of the scholarly community as articulated by the editorial advisory group.

The primary goal of the subsequent version of the edition was to lower the barriers to participation by members of the Early Modern scholarly community who were not in a position to take up Wikicode. Released in 2015, the next iteration was built using WordPress with the CommentPress plugin to facilitate the addition of commentary. CommentPress was created by a group at the Institute for the Future of the Book who were dissatisfied with the e-book as it was emerging from the commercial publishers as merely an analogue of the print book (CommentPress 2015). It materialized from a series of experiments to create a "networked" book and see if the blog, generally seen as a medium for short texts, could be adapted for long-form arguments.

The *Devonshire*'s editorial team also wanted to be sure those contributing to the project would see themselves as part of a network of scholars, and that the electronic edition would be in communication with other digital resources, just as print books are with other books on a library shelf. As a result, the new edition of the *Social Edition of the Devonshire Manuscript* is also a subproject of Iter Community, the social media networking space of Iter: Gateway to the Middle Ages and Renaissance. Iter Community is a new platform for digital projects, and, as a research project itself, is extending the codex form and testing mechanisms for ensuring credit-for-contribution in both social media and digital humanities contexts.

Iter Community is an especially appropriate place for this iteration of the social edition, offering not only a platform for social engagement with the text, but also the opportunity to literalize McKenzie's suggestion that any text's "forms and meaning derive from other texts" (1999: 60). The edition is enhanced with microdata that describes entities such as people, places, and things. Thus encoded, it can be part of the semantic web, a network of documents on the web that lets computers develop new knowledge and infer information by drawing on a number of microdata-encoded sites at once. Within Iter Community, the microdata-encoded version of the *Social Edition of the Devonshire Manuscript* brings the biographies section of the edition into explicit collaboration with the textual authorities we have come to trust in the humanities, resolving the identities of individual manuscript contributors to accounts of their lives from the Oxford English Dictionary of National Biography, GeoNames, and the Online Computer Library Center's Virtual International Authority File. This network of information is used, for example, to differentiate contributors to the manuscript who had the same name as other contemporary courtiers. Scholars have always relied upon the work of others, as evident in reference and citation networks, bibliographies, and footnotes. By using microdata formats, they can enlist computers as collaborators in the social production of knowledge, allowing encoded networks of information to expand beyond what any one scholar could ever hope to read.

The social edition is just one example of what the future(s) of the book may be. Instead of creating digital facsimiles based on the most profitable forms of print, we can look to alternative models of textual production that allow for more widespread and diverse creation of and interaction with cultural artifacts. We can consider how to effectively move beyond the single author, single text paradigm and embrace the multiplicity and sociality inherent to knowledge production. Social knowledge creation, as a practice, expands knowledge production by involving, and acknowledging, a broad participant base. In doing so, it repositions a theoretical engagement with authorship, reception, readership, and peer review in the realm of prototyping and production. Books are already the result of many hands and minds. We need to recognize them as such, and to extend this ethos to the sharing and dissemination of knowledge products to wide and diverse audiences. Electronic modes of knowledge production and distribution may facilitate this process, thereby extending and enriching the inherently social nature of print publications. Advocating the shift to electronic knowledge production, Kathleen Fitzpatrick (2011) argues that the print book is not dead and gone or a relic of the past, but rather remains undead, continually present in the digital age even as the modes of authority to which it is tied are changing. The recognition of knowledge artifacts as inherently social allows for digital innovations that build upon a rich tradition of knowledge production and sharing. Electronic instances of texts not only reveal the sociality, or to use

McKenzie's term, *sociology*, of textual knowledge; they also offer digital venues to extend that sociality to our present moment, and to "give writing its future" (Barthes 1977: 148).

Further Reading

Duguid, P. (1996) "Material Matters: The Past and Futurology of the Book," in G. Nunberg (ed.) *The Future of the Book*, Berkeley, CA: University of California Press, pp. 63–101.

Fitzpatrick, K. (2011) *Planned Obsolescence: Publishing, Technology, and the Future of the Academy*, New York, NY: NYU Press.

Gitelman, L. (2006) *Always Already New: Media, History, and the Data of Culture*, Cambridge, MA: MIT Press.

Hayles, N. K. (2003) "Translating Media: Why We Should Rethink Textuality," *Yale Journal of Criticism* 16(2), 263–90.

McKenzie, D. F. (1999) *Bibliography and the Sociology of Texts*, Cambridge MA: Cambridge University Press.

References

Addison, J. (1711) *The Spectator* 166. 10 September.

Amazon (2009) "Kindle Wireless Reading Device—2nd Generation," retrieved from www.amazon.com/dp/B0015T963C.

Apple (2010) "Steve Jobs Introduces iBooks for iPad," retrieved from www.youtube.com/watch?v=3G31PSNhVUM.

Barthes, R. (1977) "The Death of the Author," in S. Heath (ed. & trans.) *Image—Music—Text*, London: Fontana Press, pp. 142–48.

Birkerts, S. (1994) *The Gutenberg Elegies: The Fate of Reading in an Electronic Age*, New York, NY: Fawcett Columbine.

Bolter, J. D. (1990) *Writing Space: The Computer in the History of Literacy*, Hillsdale, NJ: Lawrence Erlbaum.

Busa, R. (1980) "The Annals of Humanities Computing: The Index Thomisticus," *Computers and the Humanities* 14(2), 83–90.

CommentPress (2015) "About CommentPress," retrieved from futureofthebook.org/commentpress/about-commentpress.

Crompton, C., R. Siemens, A. Arbuckle, and INKE (2015). "Enlisting 'Vertues Noble & Excelent': Behavior, Credit, and Knowledge Organization in the Social Edition," *Digital Humanities Quarterly* 9(2).

Duguid, P. (1996) "Material Matters: The Past and Futurology of the Book," in G. Nunberg (ed.) *The Future of the Book*, Berkeley: University of California Press, pp. 63–101.

Emerson, R. W. (1860) *The Conduct of Life*, London: Smith, Elder and Co.

Fitzpatrick, K. (2011) *Planned Obsolescence: Publishing, Technology, and the Future of the Academy*, New York, NY: NYU Press.

Galey, A. (2010) "Networks of Deep Impression: Shakespeare and the History of Information," *Shakespeare Quarterly* 61(3), 289–312.

Galey, A. (2012) "The Enkindling Reciter: E-Books in the Bibliographical Imagination," *Book History* 15(1), 210–47.

Galey, A. and S. Ruecker (2010) "How a Prototype Argues," *Literary and Linguistic Computing* 25(4), 405–24.

Gitelman, L. (2006) *Always Already New: Media, History, and the Data of Culture*, Cambridge, MA: MIT Press.

Gitelman, L. (2014) *Paper Knowledge: Toward a Media History of Documents*, Durham, NC and London: Duke University Press.

Goldfarb, C. F. (1989) "The Roots of SGML—A Personal Recollection," retrieved from www.sgmlsource.com/history/roots.html.

Hayles, N. K. (2002) *Writing Machines*, Cambridge, MA: MIT Press.

Hayles, N. K. (2003) "Translating Media: Why We Should Rethink Textuality," *Yale Journal of Criticism* 16(2), 263–90.

Hockey, S. (2004) "The History of Humanities Computing," in S. Schreibman, R. Siemens, and J. Unsworth (eds.) *A Companion to the Digital Humanities*, Oxford: Blackwell Publishing, pp. 3–19.

Landow, G. (1992) *Hypertext: The Convergence of Contemporary Critical Theory and Technology*, Baltimore, MD: John Hopkins University Press.

Liu, A. (2004) "Transcendental Data: Toward a Cultural History and Aesthetics of the New Encoded Discourse," *Critical Inquiry* 31(1), 49–84.

Maxwell, J. (2009) "Unix Culture and the Coach House," MIT6 Conference, retrieved from web.mit.edu/comm-forum/mit6/papers/Maxwell.pdf.

McGann, J. (1991) *The Textual Condition*, Princeton, NJ: Princeton University Press.

McGann, J. (1996) "The Rationale of Hypertext," *Text* 9, 11–32.

McKenzie, D. F. (1999) *Bibliography and the Sociology of Texts*, Cambridge, MA: Cambridge University Press.

McKitterick, D. (2003) *Print, Manuscript and the Search for Order 1450–1830*, Cambridge, MA: Cambridge University Press.

Mitchell, W. J. (1995) *City of Bits: Space, Place, and the Infobahn*, Cambridge, MA: MIT Press.

Priego, E. (2011) "Father Roberto Busa: One Academic's Impact on HE and My Career," *The Guardian: Higher Education Network*, 12 August, retrieved from www.theguardian.com/higher-education-network/blog/2011/aug/12/father-roberto-busa-academic-impact.

Siemens, R., K. Armstrong, C. Crompton, and the Devonshire MS Editorial Group (2015) *The Social Edition of the Devonshire Manuscript*, Toronto: Iter Community, 10 June, retrieved from dms.itercommunity.org.

Siemens, R., M. Timney, C. Leitch, C. Koolen, and A. Garnett (2012) "Toward Modeling the Social Edition: An Approach to Understanding the Electronic Scholarly Edition in the Context of New and Emerging Social Media," *Literary and Linguistic Computing* 27(4), 445–61.

Warde, B. (1956) "The Crystal Goblet or Printing Should Be Invisible," *The Crystal Goblet: Sixteen Essays on Typography*, Cleveland: World Publishing Company, pp. 11–17.

Williams, R. (1974) *Television: Technology and Cultural Form*, Suffolk: Fontana / Collins.

35

BECOMING A RAP GENIUS

African American Literary Studies and Collaborative Annotation

Howard Rambsy II

The large, growing bodies of scholarship on digital humanities (DH) have been largely devoid of African American literary studies. For instance, at the annual Modern Language Association (MLA) conferences between 2009 and 2015, approximately 336 DH-related sessions have taken place with just six of those sessions devoted to African American literary and black studies topics. In addition, relatively few articles in scholarly journals and major books on DH have concentrated on the convergence of technology and African American literary art. The absence of scholarly production diminishes our abilities to understand how scholars, teachers, and students simultaneously engage black artistic compositions and DH.

The paucity of scholarship in these regards deserves our attention, but we also benefit by considering the syntheses of technologies, media, and African American literary studies that we do have. The multifaceted writings and activities linked to Alondra Nelson's AfroFuturism listserv, for example, continually demonstrated the value of sometimes moving beyond the deficits of the so-called "digital divide." Nelson started the listserv in 1998. It brought a wide range of scholars, professors, artists, and students together to participate in conversations about technology, science fiction, and black diasporic histories. The lessons I gained teaching two literature courses, both entitled "Becoming a Rap Genius," in spring 2014 and fall 2014, allowed my students and me to make digital technologies central to our coverage of black literary texts in ways that had been uncommon at our university and perhaps in many other English departments as well. The courses I offered concentrated on artistic compositions by black writers while utilizing Genius, the suite of collaborative annotation sites known popularly as Rap Genius. The courses expanded the conventional parameters of DH by making African American literary studies a focal point. At the same time, they enhanced our offerings in black literature by highlighting collaborative annotation.

We need more scholarship on the interplay of race and technology. We also need more considerations of how new media and digital technologies can facilitate the study of African

American literature among college students. Consequently, the current chapter describes: (1) the history of Genius, (2) the production of "Becoming a Rap Genius" courses, and (3) the implications of offering students opportunities to take African American literature courses with a technological or online component. The chapter does not solve the problem of widespread neglect of African American subject matter in the scholarly discourse on DH. However, "Becoming a Rap Genius" does seek to alleviate aspects of that neglect.

What Is Rap Genius? A Brief History of Rap Genius

Launched in 2009 primarily as a site for online users to annotate rap lyrics, Genius quickly became widely popular, with millions of page views each month. Originally entitled "Rap Exegesis," the founders—Mahbod Moghadam, Tom Lehman, and Ilan Zechory—eventually changed the name to Rap Genius, and later created a group of related sites or channels such as Lit Genius, News Genius, Pop Genius, Rock Genius, Sports Genius, History Genius, and Screen Genius, each of which included corresponding content that allowed users to provide annotations. So, whereas the site was initially "a place to explain the esoteric metaphors and allusions of rap lyrics," wrote Josh Constine for *Tech Crunch*, the company "had a larger ambition to annotate all sorts of texts from legal documents to poetry to news" (2014). In the summer of 2014, Rap Genius was rebranded as Genius with the corresponding domain name, genius.com. The millions of page views that the site attracted each month led to multimillion dollar investments and increased media coverage.

In October 2012, the venture capital firm, Andreessen Horowitz, announced a $15 million investment in Rap Genius, an announcement that spurred substantial attention for the company. The site had been steadily gaining attention since its launch in 2009; however, the Andreessen Horowitz investment stimulated increased attention for the site. In a short statement explaining why he and his business partner, Ben Horowitz, invested in Rap Genius, Marc Andreessen (2012) noted that he had often wondered "how the Internet would have turned out differently if users had been able to annotate everything—to add new layers of knowledge to all knowledge, on and on, ad infinitum," and "Rap Genius finally gives us the opportunity to find out." In July 2014, the company gained even more public notice with the announcement of a $40 million investment from Dan Gilbert, the founder of Quicken Loans Inc. and majority owner of the Cleveland Cavaliers professional basketball team (Carlson 2014). The investment was joined by the announcement that Rap Genius was rebranding itself as Genius, a signal that the site would become more ambitious. "'Genius' is the new name of the grand project," wrote Lehman and Zechory, "born from rap's rib, to annotate the world—and of the platform and company we're building to enable it." (Lehman and Zechory 2014).

Since its inception, Rap Genius had grassroots appeal. Any web user could sign on to the site, offer comments on individual lyrics, and in turn edit and refine previous comments for clarity and accuracy. Dozens and sometimes hundreds of users would descend on popular songs, the lyrics of which had been posted on the site, and provide annotations. The majority of the millions of viewers who visit Genius do so to learn the meaning of hard-to-decipher lyrics. Although not every line of every song or text that appears on the site is correct, the collaborative or crowd-sourced nature of textual decoding ultimately makes the many annotations on the site remarkably reliable. In the case of hip hop, for example, Zack O'Malley Greenburg noted that the site, which could be described as the "Wikipedia of rap lyrics," can sometimes offer more extensive treatments of songs than their composers do (O'Malley Greenburg 2010).

Not long after rap enthusiasts began posting song lyrics on the site in 2009 and 2010, a different and occasional overlapping class of users realized that the Rap Genius platform was compatible not only with rap lyrics. If users could examine songs by Jay Z, Kanye West, Nas, OutKast, and literally hundreds of other rappers, then why not also post and annotate texts by Shakespeare, Jane Austen, Frederick Douglass, and F. Scott Fitzgerald? The growing regularity of users posting poems and then literary texts on the Rap Genius channel motivated site designers to launch Poetry Genius in June 2013. Poetry Genius provided "insight into everything literary, from poems, to short stories, to novels;" and unlike the popular literature study guide SparkNotes, observed Emma Greenberg, Poetry Genius "allows its users to share their thoughts and tease apart texts with others, rather than telling them what to think" (2013). Recognizing that users on the channel were uploading and annotating a wide range of literary texts, and not just poems, Genius eventually decided to change the channel title from Poetry Genius to Lit. Genius.

One of the early adopters of Genius was Jeremy Dean, a then graduate student at the University of Texas at Austin who was teaching high school English. Dean began coordinating educational activities, "adding many of the poems, stories, essays, and even novels" to Genius and having his students "annotate their reading for homework" (2015). He recognized that "the platform could be a dynamic teaching tool for the humanities." The founders of Genius became aware of Dean's activities and were impressed. So when they received funding from Andreessen Horowitz, they offered Dean a full-time job to create "a vibrant intellectual community of teachers using the site in their classes and regularly collaborating with each other in [the Genius] Educator forum on how to teach this emergent literacy skill of collaborative annotation" (2015). For the two and a half years that Dean worked with Genius, he was the driving force behind the formation of "the Education Genius community," which was comprised of "a diverse set of educators from around the world, teaching a wide variety of age groups and fields, from high school history students to undergrads in biology, to grad students in literary theory." (Dean has since moved on from Genius to become the Director of Education at Hypothes.is, a collaborative annotation site.) Dean's efforts, along with the numerous contributors to the Education Genius community, paved the way for classroom activities focusing on collaborative annotation and, in due course, nurtured the development of ideas and a support system that inspired me to teach African American literature classes concentrating on Genius.

A Tech-Based African American Literature Course

The "Becoming a Rap Genius" courses that I taught in spring and fall 2014 departed from the conventional text-based approach in African American literature classes that my colleagues and I had offered during the previous 10 years. Books usually served as the primary source materials for our courses; but for the Rap Genius class, students accessed the majority of the items online. During class discussions and informal surveys, students revealed that what initially drew them to the course was the chance to study rap music in a college class, not necessarily the possibility of sharpening their collaborative annotation skills. The course texts, accessed on Genius, included essays by W. E. B. Du Bois and Zora Neale Hurston, a speech by Malcolm X, poems by several African American poets, and rap music. While a main objective for my regular African American literature courses had been exposing students to select authors and literary texts, the Rap Genius course was principally designed to introduce students to the practice of collaborative annotation through an online portal.

The focus on web-based skills associated with collaborative annotation in an African American literature course presented students with a new alternative for engaging literary works and rap music. English courses rarely make black-authored compositions that appear on the web a central focal point. Yet, these Genius courses transformed reading African American literature into fundamentally digital activities. The processes of *becoming* a Rap Genius also meant that students would learn how to identify and compose "useful" annotations. Those annotations would include original, brief analyses of words and phrases as well as the addition of illuminating images, GIFs, and hyperlinks.

The objective of producing concise and useful annotations on Genius meant that students were prompted to take the values and interests of broad audiences into account in ways that were scarcely common for conventional literature courses. Usually, the professor is the target audience for class writing assignments; but for the Genius courses, the potential audience was far more expansive. "When you write something online," explains Clive Thompson in his book *Smarter Than You Think: How Technology Is Changing Our Minds for the Better*, "you're doing it with the expectation that someone might read it, even if you're doing it anonymously," and "audiences clarify the mind" (2013: 52). The awareness that their annotations would appear on a site visited by millions of people definitely clarified how students thought about making contributions that Genius users would find helpful. The possibility that audiences might provide favorable responses in the form of "upvotes" or "likes" to annotations also gave students added incentive to generate high quality, entertaining content.

Users on Genius gain IQ points based on their participation and the upvotes they receive from other users for the quality of their annotations. The IQ points are displayed next to usernames, thus providing audiences with a sense of user involvement and experience with annotating various texts. The use of colors—blue for staff, purple for moderators, yellow for editors, white for regular users, and green for verified artists—also indicates the levels of contributions. The gaming nature of Genius's point system provoked increased participation among many students in my African American literature courses. The prospect of receiving recognition from members of the online community reading the annotations was an important factor for keeping students actively involved and seeking ways to continually improve the kind of content that they produced.

The goal of developing our skills producing high-quality annotations led us to spend considerable time studying annotations by outstanding contributors on Genius channels. Although our class concentrated on African American literature and rap music, I encouraged the students to take note of a group of highly active Shakespeare annotators on Lit. Genius. We discussed what it meant that the desire to make Shakespeare plays more readily comprehensible to audiences had motivated those annotators to spend countless hours without compensation deciphering individual words, phrases, and passages; identifying complementary source materials, images, GIFs, and video clips; and then composing and refining remarks about the annotated lines. By observing those Shakespeare annotators and other highly active participants on Genius, the students were equipped with outstanding models and blueprints for elevating the quality of their own annotations and participation. In the process, students were learning that becoming a rap genius involved engagements with literary texts and lyrics as well as the content of skilled annotators.

The Significance of an African American, Collaborative Annotation Literature Course

At least three main developments related to the implementation of "Becoming a Rap Genius" made this African American literature course especially rewarding and significant. For one, the classes served as innovations to our ongoing course offerings in the field, and those innovations took seriously the interests of students, namely by utilizing a platform that showcased rap music. The classes embraced literary texts by black writers, while at the same time prompting students to engage those works on screen rather than only in conventional print. The emphasis on technology, and particularly collaborative annotation, provided a unique approach for the practice of African American literary studies in the context of the classroom. The courses revealed how cutting edge technology could be employed to examine historical texts such as W. E. B. DuBois's *The Souls of Black Folk*, and they demonstrated how longstanding research activities such as annotation and exegesis could be applied to the latest rap songs.

Second, the courses expanded views of what African American literary studies can entail in this contemporary moment. In the larger scholarly discourse, the focus is often on the histories of black literature. For instance, the vast majority of the more than 400 scholarly articles published since 2000 in the field's leading journal, *African American Review*, have concentrated on historical events and authors born prior to 1960. In the context of course offerings in African American literature, historical surveys—with an emphasis on the historical—have been mainstays for decades now. Further, most public knowledge and information presented in the field—in scholarly journals and books, at conferences, and on course syllabi—suggest that technology is not necessarily a widespread driving force in African American literature.

Thus, the "Becoming a Rap Genius" course was important and unusual for demonstrating the extent to which African American literary studies could absorb rap music and utilize a collaborative annotation platform. A black literature course that gives attention to compositions by Phillis Wheatley *and* Nicki Minaj, Frederick Douglass *and* Jay Z, and Zora Neale Hurston *and* Beyoncé, extends the range of what a class in the field can take into consideration, and notably pushes well beyond the tendency to privilege historical subject matter. In addition, the use of Genius as a central feature of the courses placed technology and digital humanities at the forefront of African American literary studies. Doing so signaled an important convergence between DH and the study of black artistic compositions.

Finally, the opportunity for students to strengthen their technological capabilities while pursuing African American literary studies was a particularly invaluable component of "Becoming a Rap Genius." Literature courses are often content-driven, concentrating on major authors and print-based literary texts, with some attention to a variety of critical paradigms and prominent themes. Those approaches to literary studies, which we will continue to provide at my university, are important. At the same time, the addition of a course that blends African American literary studies with the practice of online, collaborative annotation promises useful possibilities for students. These African American literature courses proved to be advantageous environments for students to produce concise analyses of texts along with illuminating images, GIFs, and videos in the context of an expansive community of fellow annotators. The use of those other modes ensured that the students in this literature course would think well beyond conventional texts. The technological skill-building that the students experienced in the courses was a productive gateway into wider realms of digital participation.

Moving forward, we could expose students to even more annotation platforms, such as A.nnotate, Hypothes.is, and Marky. Exposure to different platforms could stimulate new or alternative interests among students who might find one platform more compatible with their interests than another. An introduction combining African American literary and tech-based courses early in the careers of college students would likely fortify their abilities to recognize important connections across and within these fields. Professors of American and African American literature at different universities could also consider coordinating their efforts with students in various locales. Collaborative efforts among students from across the country annotating common literary texts would indeed provide them with a distinct understanding of utilizing African American literary studies and DH to establish far-reaching learning communities, practical skills, and diverse perspectives.

References

Andreessen, M. (2012) "Why Andreessen Horowitz Is Investing in Rap Genius," *Genius*, retrieved from https://genius.com/Marc-andreessen-why-andreessen-horowitz-is-investing-in-rap-genius-annotated.

Carlson, N. (2014) "The Inside Story of How Rap Genius Fired a Cofounder—And Just Raised $40 Million (Annotated!)," *Business Insider*, retrieved from www.businessinsider.com.

Constine, J. (2014) "Rap Genius Raises $40M, Changes Name To Genius, Launches Embeddable Annotations," *TechCrunch*, retrieved from techcrunch.com/2014/07/11/just-genius/.

Dean, J. (2015) "Introducing Hypothesis for Education," *Hypothes.is*, retrieved from hypothes.is/blog/introducing-hypothes-is-for-education/.

Greenberg, E. (2013) "Poetry Genius: This Brilliant Website May Revolutionize How Poetry Is Taught in Schools," *Mic*, retrieved from mic.com/articles/62817/poetry-genius-this-brilliant-website-may-revolutionize-how-poetry-is-taught-in-schools#.bZlVagsuj.

Lehman, T. and I. Zechory (2014) "Introducing Genius.com," *Genius*, retrieved from genius.com/Genius-founders-introducing-geniuscom-annotated.

O'Malley Greenburg, Z. (2010) "Jay-Z's Decoded Vs. Rap Genius," *Forbes*, retrieved from www.forbes.com.

Thompson, C. (2013) *Smarter Than You Think: How Technology Is Changing Our Minds for the Better*, London: William Collins.

36

TRAVERSALS

A Method of Preservation for Born-Digital Texts

Dene Grigar and Stuart Moulthrop

In 2013–14, we conducted *Pathfinders*, a research project funded by the U.S. National Endowment for the Humanities, Office of Digital Humanities (HD-51768–13). The effort explored a novel means of preserving early works of electronic literature threatened by imminent technical extinction. We call this strategy *Traversal*, the recording and documentation of interface and textual features through demonstrations performed on historically appropriate platforms. Traversals are envisioned as a strategy for the method of digital preservation called collection, whereby works are preserved on the original media devices (e.g., floppy disks and CDs) and software (Storyspace and HyperCard) and accessed on original computer hardware. As a digital preservation methodology, collection poses challenges to those who archive copies of electronic literature, what we call "born-digital" literature, due to the cost of upkeep for equipment and media. As a way to convey the cultural and historical context of a work, however, it proves highly effective. For this reason, we see Traversal as a useful way for scholars to gain an understanding of digital work without investing in multiple generations of digital resources—an investment that will inevitably become insupportable as new technologies evolve and fragile systems age.

Work on *Pathfinders* officially began in 2013, but it was based on crucial earlier efforts. Grigar had long embraced collection in her research on electronic literature. She had preserved copies of examples of this art form she had purchased from the 1990s onward and assembled a set of computers for use in experiencing them. In 2008, she mounted her first exhibit of early electronic literature while hosting the annual conference of the Electronic Literature Organization (ELO). That event served as the impetus for her decision to expand her collection. In 2011, she was provided space on the Washington State University Vancouver campus to create the Electronic Literature Laboratory (ELL) in the interest of preservation and support of scholarship.

Similar facilities have also appeared at the University of Colorado (Lori Emerson's Media Archaeology Lab), the University of Maryland (the Special Media Collection at McKeldin Library, coordinated with the Maryland Institute for Technology in the Humanities), and the Massachusetts Institute of Technology (Nick Montfort's Trope Tank facility). In addition, the digital author Judy Malloy has for some years been working on the *Authoring Software* project, a compendium of reflections by artists and designers on the social and technical conditions of early work. Malloy's efforts provided an important reference point and inspiration for our project. We can also point to ELO's *Electronic Literature Directory* and *Electronic Literature Collection*, Volumes 1 and 2, as well as the Organization's groundbreaking white papers concerning preservation, archiving, and dissemination: "Acid-Free Bits" (2002/2004) and "Born-Again Bits" (2005). In addition, the European project, Electronic Literature as a Model of Creativity and Innovation in Practice (ELMCIP), has created a Knowledge Base and an Anthology of Electronic European Literature, major efforts to archive and preserve works of electronic literature.

These efforts laid important groundwork and made it possible to undertake research to address the future of early born-digital texts. Still, as participants in and scholars of electronic literature, we were keenly aware of an archival crisis in 2012. At least one of our most widely studied examples, Shelley Jackson's *Patchwork Girl* (1995), was becoming more and more difficult to access because of changes in computer operating systems. An updated version of this work appeared in late 2014, but its momentary eclipse exposed a larger issue. Born-digital texts have sensitive dependencies on particular hardware and software. Their technical fragility is considerably greater than that of books or other written documents. They thus pose distinct problems for preservation, archiving, and dissemination—problems unlikely to be solved by a single form of response.

Considering these issues during a visit to the ELL, Anne Balsamo, then on faculty at the University of Southern California, began to think about video documentation as a means of at least provisionally recording software features and functions. She would later share this idea in a conversation with Moulthrop, who had entertained similar notions. Moulthrop and Balsamo both recognized the potential of video for capturing aspects of essentially performative texts, where an alternation between human decision and machine response unfolds in a momentary encounter. This method seemed usefully complementary to more textually centered methods prominent in current digital humanities practice. Moulthrop sought advice from NEH program officers and approached Grigar to initiate the project. What began as a spark of curiosity motivated by impending loss resulted in an effort to make available to scholars and the public the experience of complex works of literary art involving highly various levels and forms of interactivity. Though limited for experimental purposes to electronic literature and a small group of works, the project has produced substantial results, and we believe it points the way to future efforts.

Rationale: An Argument for Collection

Expanded access to personal computers in the 1970s and 1980s generated a significant wave of artistic experimentation with concrete poets such as bpNichol advancing the practice of procedural poetry; net artists such as Judy Malloy creating the first forms of networked social writing; fiction writers such as Michael Joyce, Deena Larsen, and Shelley Jackson exploring possibilities of hypertextual narrative; and multimedia storytellers such as M.D. Coverley and John McDaid breaking new ground in multimodal and artifactual storytelling. These preweb works were published or made available, in some case, over the internet or on various types of removable disk. Some appeared on CD-ROM just as web browsers gained wide use and prompted the migration of electronic literature to online contexts.

The works of these pioneering artists are keenly exposed to obsolescence, threatening a loss of intellectual and artistic heritage and, at the same time, registering a problem that will eventually affect most works of culture in the digital age. Technological progress rapidly displaces contexts of access and support.

The loss of key electronic texts is sometimes addressed by preservation strategies called emulation and migration. The original author or later actors may attempt to duplicate key aspects of the work in a new system, as in the GW-BASIC version of Malloy's *Uncle Roger* produced for Windows systems in 1988, or re-present the work in a new operational context, as in the recent update of *Patchwork Girl* by its publisher, Eastgate Systems, Inc. While undeniably useful, these strategies have some limitations and drawbacks. Emulation and migration efface the original context and experience of operation and may introduce shifts and distortions even when carefully done. For instance, the first version of Malloy's *Uncle Roger* (1986–7) was produced with a 50-character constraint in mind, but the lines broke very differently for Versions 2–4 (1987–88), created for platforms with a 40-character constraint. Version 5 (1995), produced in HTML for the web, returned the lines to the original line breaks, but Version 6 (2012), which Malloy considers the authorized version of her work, emulates Version 4 and so retains the visual phrasing of the broken lines. Some works are not well suited to either emulation or migration. *Uncle Buddy's Phantom Funhouse* (1992) and Coverley's *Califia* (2000) rely on systems so closely integrated with their original computing platforms that any new versions would require extraordinary efforts in design and production. To the extent the original works depend on proprietary code or software features, emulation and migration become difficult or impossible. The tendency toward complexity in digital art works further complicates this problem. From its earliest moments, electronic literature has embraced mixed and multiple mediation, as in the cassettes and offprints that form parts of *Uncle Buddy's Phantom Funhouse*, or before that, the artifacts called *feelies* included with interactive fiction titles such as Douglas Adams and Steve Meretzky's *Hitchhiker's Guide to the Galaxy*. As literary practices move away from direct remediation of the printed page, the work of preservation and dissemination becomes correspondingly fraught.

To be sure, technical obsolescence is both ultimately inevitable and culturally determinative. All work will eventually be lost, and only the most salient or important aspects can be even temporarily preserved. Why not let these nearly forgotten texts go the way of all bits? Following Lori Emerson's perspective, we believe early born-digital work is worth saving when it is "a work that self-consciously uses its own text, distributed across different media, to comment on these media and on the nature of our interactions with the text as it is mediated by these particular reading/writing technologies" (Emerson 2014: 76). Such texts represent crucial points of inflection, forks in the path of software development—whose history, Emerson notes, has increasingly bent away from complex manipulability and overt complexity of mediation toward a seamless transparency.

By capturing particular intersections of platform and expression in born-digital texts, we may preserve moments of possibility from which the mainstream of technical development has departed. This was a major objective of *Pathfinders*. In *Uncle Buddy's Phantom Funhouse*, a complete encounter with the text may involve elements that must be extracted from the data structure by a kind of first-order hacking. Contrast this with iPad apps or mobile games of today. These products are conceived not as texts open to examination, but as software commodities or services delivered under strict conditions of use. As Emerson points out, hidden features and concealed data are strictly forbidden, at least in the Apple publishing regime (2014: 33–34). To be sure, the admittedly polemical division we adopt here has important limits. The ever-so-slick world of mobile apps contains examples like Tom Phillips *Humument App* (2010) and Dave Morris's Inkle version of *Frankenstein* (2012), both of which play fast and loose with notions of textual integrity, if not intellectual property. The unruly experimentalism of electronic literature is far from dead. As Markku Eskelinen suggests, rejection of the "textual whole" may be a major if not primary impulse of electronic literature (2012:

70–71). Early examples of this critique may prove radical in two senses: both strongly divergent and root-making or foundational.

Name and Concept

In the 1990s, Michael Joyce called any particular reading of a hypertext a "traversal" (1997: 581), adopting the term from directed-graph theory and perhaps also from Espen Aarseth's "traversal function," the procedure or mechanism by which certain elements of a systematic text are presented in a specific encounter or reading (1997: 62). Our sense is closer to Joyce's than Aarseth's, in that our kind of Traversal always involves human agency even though it may be strongly inflected by program logic or machine operations.

We define a Traversal as a reflective encounter with a digital text in which the possibilities of that text are explored in a way that indicates its key features, capabilities, and themes. When undertaken by authors, Traversals resemble a software demonstration or a walk-through of a computer game: creators evoke and explain salient features in a guided tour of their systems. Because we ask participants to vocalize their interactions with the text, Traversals can also be compared to the talk-aloud protocols utilized in usability testing. For us, though, there is always an important element of oral history in the Traversal, as we encourage authors to reflect on the circumstances and design thinking behind key aspects of the work. This reflection begins in the Traversal itself and continues in a follow-up interview.

In a sense, any extended or substantial encounter with a digital text can constitute a Traversal. Any reader is eligible, not just the author. Therefore our project also includes nonauthor Traversals, conducted whenever possible by people with diverse backgrounds and histories. In the case of nonauthor Traversals, the activity takes on some aspects of user-experience study, though we do not adopt a strict methodology from that field. In both author and nonauthor Traversals, our method was more exploratory than indexical or evaluative. Though we prepared all participants with a standard set of instructions, we were less interested in common or repeated behaviors than in notably idiosyncratic patterns of use.

Method

As we define it, a Traversal must take place on equipment as close as possible in configuration to the system the author used to create her work or on which she might reasonably have intended the work to first appear (see Figure 36.1). As our test for efficacy of the Traversal strategy, we used Moulthrop's *Victory Garden* (1991), produced with a prerelease version of Storyspace and published by Eastgate Systems, Inc. on 3 ½-inch diskette. The work was largely created on a Macintosh SE (1987–90), one of the original all-in-one Macintosh models, featuring a 9-inch monochrome display. We used a similarly configured Macintosh Classic (1990–92) for Traversals of this work because, when *Victory Garden* was released in 1991, the Classic had already been on the market for 2 years and had gained popularity for its reasonable price ($1000 compared to the $3000-$4000 SE).

Following this preparation, we moved to four additional works. Version 3 of Judy Malloy's *Uncle Roger* was programmed in AppleSoft BASIC and Narrabase (a unique authoring system she invented) and sold through the *Art Com* catalog (beginning in 1988) as a box of three 5 ¼-inch floppy disks. It required an Apple IIe (1983–93) for Traversals. John McDaid's *Uncle Buddy's Phantom Funhouse* (1992) was created with HyperCard 2.0 and published by Eastgate Systems, Inc., initially on 3 ½-inch diskettes and later on CD-ROM. Much of McDaid's production took place on second-generation Macintosh II models, but for the

Traversals we utilized an Apple LC 580 (1995–96), which would have been used by many readers at the time of the work's circulation. Shelley Jackson's *Patchwork Girl* (1995) was created with early versions of Storyspace on first- and second-generation Macintosh systems. It was published by Eastgate Systems, Inc. in an initial run on 3 ½-inch diskettes, afterward on CD-ROM (and since 2014, on removable chip drive). The Traversals took place on a PowerMac G4 produced in 2003. In this case, we slightly compromised our principle of platform similarity because the somewhat newer machine allowed us to project the display image onto a screen for better video recording. The PowerMac's system software is legitimately comparable to the original release context for the CD edition. Bill Bly's *We Descend* (1997) was created with various versions of Storyspace and published by Eastgate Systems, Inc. simultaneously on 3 ½-inch diskettes and CD-ROM. Traversals of this work, which were performed at the Maryland Institute for Technology in the Humanities (MITH), utilized a Macintosh SE produced in 1987. The author verified that he began the work on this type of computer before moving to a Mac IIsi and completing it on a Powerbook 520.

Using these vintage machines allowed us to document primary aspects of the technical environment: the basic operation of the texts themselves and their relationship with encapsulating structures, such as Malloy's Narrabase, Apple's HyperCard, and Eastgate Systems, Inc.'s Storyspace. We were also able to observe subtle but important aspects of the original experience, including the characteristic chug and clatter of the Apple floppy drive and the prolonged load-in cycles of early Storyspace texts—features that tend not to be preserved in emulation.

In all Traversals we maintained the same general protocol for the activity. We imposed no absolute requirements on the participants in terms of time spent or screens visited. Authors seemed to aim for a full characterization of their work, sometimes making repeated attempts with different reading or demonstration strategies. Nonauthor participants tended to persist

Figure 36.1 John McDaid in his Traversal of *Uncle Buddy's Phantom Funhouse*.

Source: Image care of the authors.

in a single engagement until they encountered significant perplexity or ran out of interest. Author Traversals ranged from 45 minutes to a bit more than an hour. Some nonauthor Traversals were of similar length, while some were shorter, around 30 minutes.

We did not require authors to prepare a demonstration strategy in advance, though some apparently did. Authors were provided with a brief set of suggestions (Grigar & Moulthrop 2013b). Nonauthor subjects were given a shorter version of the briefing orally at the start of their sessions. We asked both types of participant to read aloud any text associated with a current state of the system and comment on the experience as they went. In particular, we asked readers to announce hypertext link words or other transitional mechanisms whenever they triggered a significant change in the system.

Traversals were recorded with multiple cameras: minimally, one camera on the subject and a second on the computer screen. For some Traversals, a hand-held camera was also used to capture moments of emergent interest.

Registering readable screen images proved challenging. Because most of the vintage computers we used did not allow for screen capture technology, we attempted to videotape the monitors to record the artists' and readers' activities. At first, this approach resulted in screen rolls and flickers because the refresh rate of the monitors was out of sync with the frame rate of the video camera. For the Jackson Traversal, we found a way to record a wall-projected screen image, allowing us to capture expressive mouse movements as well as static images. For other projects, we added to the video recording static screenshots representing key states of the system. Transferring data from twentieth-century computers to our editing platforms was a nontrivial task, but fortunately Apple decided in the late 1990s to include a personal HTTP server in its basic software suite. Since graphics in the JPEG format have been sup--ported from the early days of the web, it was possible to convert images in PICT, the native Apple screenshot format, to JPEG using an early version of Adobe Photoshop. We could access the resulting files with a web browser on a modern system connected to the vintage machine via local-area network.

Following each Traversal, we conducted an interview with the Traversal subject. A set of basic questions were available to the interviewers for both the artists (Grigar & Moulthrop 2013a) and the readers (Grigar & Moulthrop 2013c), though questions and answers tended to evolve as we went, especially in the author Traversals. The interviews were also recorded using multiple camera angles. We experimented with various orientations, including shots of the subjects' hands and various angles on the face and upper body. Keyboard shots allowed us to at least indicate alphabetic input, an important feature of the Malloy and McDaid Traversals. Shots focused on the face helped document intonation, expression, and gesture, which were particularly evocative in all four Traversals.

With student assistants, we analyzed and indexed the resulting video files. The Traversals were shaped into segments of about 10 minutes for convenient internet streaming. We edited conservatively, making cuts only for continuity and cutting between camera angles only when required for understanding. Considerable postproduction effort was spent improving the sound. Particularly in author Traversals, vocal performance was a crucial feature. Phrasing, intonation, and emphasis were of obvious interest, though these effects were often obscured by noise from computer fans and other ambient sources. Efforts by ELL technicians to produce clean audio tracks made a considerable difference in the final product.

More than 25 Traversal video segments were made quickly available from the project website (Grigar & Moulthrop n.d.), along with selections from the interviews and extensive curatorial and background material. This core material has been combined with interpretive commentary in an open-source, multimedia book (Grigar & Moulthrop 2015) using Scalar, the hypermedia authoring system from the Alliance for Networking Visual Culture (ANVC) at the University of Southern California. The final tally of video clips that make up *Pathfinders* is 102, in itself a large archive of rich cultural and historical data. In its first 4 months of availability, this resource has received more than 13,000 visits. The resources from which the *Pathfinders* e-book was constructed (alternative video and audio recordings, photographs, planning documents, and other items) remain in the collection of the ELL.

Experience

The Traversal videos constitute a reasonably durable and at least minimally transmissible record of threatened or obsolete works. These recordings have obvious limitations. While some of the Traversals, both by authors and other readers, offered multiple encounters with the texts—Malloy's and Jackson's Traversals in particular—some did not. Future efforts might assume or require multiple performances to better demonstrate the signifying potential of the art works. Video recordings are also not immediately accessible to indexing or analytical mechanisms, although presentation of the Traversals and interviews in the e-book include searchable prose summaries for each segment, and workers in the ELL are currently compiling transcripts for all the interviews.

Beyond providing a stopgap measure against the loss of important works, the demonstrations and accompanying interviews open up significant perspectives on early contributions to electronic literature:

- In her Traversal of *Uncle Roger* and the *Blue Notebook*, Judy Malloy explains how the random-access Narrabase structure of her stories proceeds from the file-sharing practices of the Whole Earth 'Lectronic Link (the WELL), which was in many ways a crucial forerunner of today's social networks.
- Traversing *Patchwork Girl*, Shelley Jackson calls attention to the Quilt, a part of the work that has received relatively little treatment in critical writing and offers extensive commentary on her understanding of the work and its interface. In the accompanying interview, Jackson reveals that the published version of *Patchwork Girl* is a second draft, set in place of an original version that featured a large (and problematic) profusion of links.
- John McDaid catalogs and comments on the various artifacts (page proofs, audio cassettes, and instruction manuals) that accompany the disk contents of *Uncle Buddy's Phantom Funhouse*. His Traversal offers a comprehensive tour of the work, including several documents hidden in the file structure of the HyperCard stacks. Nowhere else is there a complete list of the objects packaged as the *Funhouse*. In such a multifarious work, a comprehensive tour provides a first-order basis for understanding the text.

Reader Traversals were equally revealing. We had selected two for each work, choosing people with a wide range of ages and variety of experience with computers and electronic literature. Some readers, for example, had little to no training in using a Macintosh, much less a vintage one. Others had never been exposed to electronic literature. Still others were completely adept with using the machines and reading electronic literature. In general, we learned that, no matter the platform or hardware, readers could make their way through the works and understand the interface. Remembering the struggle many new readers of hypertext had at the time of these works' release, we were intrigued by the level of digital literacy among our readers.

Demonstrating the basic structure and function of these works through our recorded Traversals ensures that future artists and designers will be able to use their precedents at least as inspiration or points of departure. Beyond this, insights into unnoticed or undivulged aspects of the works suggest new avenues for analysis and critical understanding. In some cases, for instance, McDaid's demonstration of concealed text files buried within the code of the *Funhouse*, these insights suggest the need for deeper investigation into the materials and structure of these works, an effort our archives of performance and experience can only instigate, not fully enable. Traversals are clearly not a comprehensive solution for the preservation of creative software projects, though we think they have a certain value even with their limitations.

Contribution

As a concept, *Pathfinders* raises questions of purpose and identity: What does one call an initiative to keep a work alive by documenting its existence, dynamism, and experience? While *Pathfinders* is intended as a kind of digital preservation project, is it actually preserving work when it does not migrate or emulate, for example, one single node or path of the works it addresses? Even as *Pathfinders* features authors' performance of their works, collected along with vintage computers needed to read it, we can ask if *Pathfinders* in fact constitutes preservation by collection. The answer is, on the one hand, *not exactly*. At its core, *Pathfinders*' purpose is to make it possible for scholars and the reading public to experience a work of digital literature in a context as close as possible to the original by showing videos of people—the artist, other readers—experiencing works in original formats and on original computers used for their production and presentation. This is a vicarious pleasure, indeed. However, libraries and other venues that house early digital literature, but cannot or do not want to collect computers on which to access it, are also limited in their capabilities to present the work. They may enable us to hold Judy Malloy's hand-made box for *Uncle Roger* but leave us wondering about the work it contains. With *Pathfinders*, students and researchers can now see a video of Malloy performing her work—on the computer it was intended for at the time she produced it. In this way, those studying the work can see and hear the way it functioned in 1987 on the Apple IIe and are thereby able to tease out unique characteristics that may be lost in migrated versions. To be sure, no media object can ever be a time machine (a possibility with which all four authors flirt in one way or another). Duplicating the technical milieu of 1987 in a twenty-first-century context does not afford direct access to the earlier moment, but there is something to be said on the side of the derivative or indirect.

On the other hand, a second answer to our earlier question about preservation by collection is, *in a way*. The works and vintage computers make up a collection at Grigar's ELL where three of the five artists conducted Traversals and interviews. Indeed, people can travel to Vancouver, Washington, visit ELL, and experience the collection. But for those who cannot, *Pathfinders* may be a helpful alternative because it documents the collection as a way of disseminating a particularly detailed or intimate body of information about the work, thereby preserving the cultural and historical context about, and providing access to, early digital literature that is in danger of being forgotten. As we have said elsewhere, we wish we had a video of Sappho performing one of the many poems she is purported to have written but are today lost to us. So much richer would our culture be for it.

It might also be objected, as we have already suggested, that recorded Traversals can only ever capture partial impressions of works that are designed to produce many thousands of distinct experiences. Granting much to this critique we nonetheless recur again to classical antiquity, where it is understood that some works will survive only as fragments or in second-hand accounts from those who heard or read them. How many tellings of Homer's *Odyssey* were there *really*? We will never know. But the two versions left to us show that tellings may have varied radically from one another. In the case of digital works, not every work can be emulated or migrated. Recording Traversals allows us to significantly extend the range of works added to the historical record and the accessibility of those works. Like the artists who designed these complex works—and it is probably significant that we are ourselves digital artists—our efforts are bent toward approximation, not complete solutions. As the editor of this volume suggests, we "adopt principles of forensics without feeling compelled to point to a cause"—which seems a remarkably good way to describe our intention for *Pathfinders* (Sayers 2015).

There is much to be said about the future of the book and what constitutes reading in rich media environments like *Pathfinders*, especially in light of what we have witnessed in the evolution of digital platforms during the last 25 years. Floppy disks, CDs, flash drives, and cloud technology all speak to great innovations in digital technologies taking place in a very short period of history. In 1993, David Kolb published possibly the first (and certainly a very early) example of philosophical hypertext, *Socrates in the Labyrinth*. Knowing that the public can no longer experience this work because it was published on a 3 ½-inch diskette and thus requires a vintage computer for access, we become concerned about a great many works of similar innovation disappearing from our collective knowledge. Therefore, documenting just five of many, many more that need to be preserved is a small attempt in a grand gesture. There is an obvious irony in using digital formats to conduct our research about works in danger of obsolescence due to evolving digital technologies. However, through our combined 60 years of experience with electronic media, we have observed that, to date, the two most stable platforms remain the world wide web and digital video. For that reason, we have opted to trust these standards and formats, at least provisionally, to begin this project. No longer can we afford the luxury of waiting to preserve the valuable resource that is early digital literature. We hope to inspire others to do the same. Just recently, Grigar's research assistant for the *Pathfinders* project, Madeleine Brookman, applied the Traversal methodology to document the Japanese role-playing game (RPG), *Chrono Trigger*, a project resulting in the creation of the multimedia eBook, *Chronicles: Documenting the Articulation of Culture in Video Games*. We see this effort as the beginning of many future efforts to preserve media artifacts like virtual worlds, experimental digital writing, and virtual reality environments, among others.

Our strategy of Traversal has the potential of making collections come alive. For example, Malloy's *Uncle Roger* is archived at Duke University's David M. Rubenstein Rare Book and Manuscript Library where the *Judy Malloy Papers* are collected. Currently, scholars wishing to experience the work cannot do so because the library does not have an Apple IIe on hand with which to access it. However, the library can make the *Pathfinders* Traversals available via a tablet or desktop or allow scholars to use their own computing device while studying the materials in the collection. In this way, the innovation that *Pathfinders* spawned is an important intellectual tool for the study of electronic literature, one that can be easily applied to all media forms. Our vision is to not only continue to preserve early digital literature but also assist other media scholars with the preservation of their media objects.

Acknowledgments

The authors gratefully acknowledge the National Endowment for the Humanities for its support of the research described here.

Further Reading

Baldwin, C. (2015) *The Internet Unconscious: On the Subject of Electronic Literature*, London: Bloomsbury.

Barnet, B. (2012) *Memory Machines: The Evolution of Hypertext*, London: Bloomsbury.

Bell, A. (2010) *The Possible Worlds of Hypertext Fiction*, New York, NY: Palgrave Macmillan.

Drucker, J. (2009) *SpecLab: Digital Aesthetics and Projects in Speculative Computing*, Chicago, IL: University of Chicago Press.

Fitzpatrick, K. (2011) *Planned Obsolescence: Publishing, Technology, and the Future of the Academy*, New York, NY: NYU Press.

Funkhouser, C. T. (2007) *Prehistoric Digital Poetry: An Archaeology of Forms, 1959–1995*, Tuscaloosa, AL: The University of Alabama Press.

Greco, D. (1995) *Cyborg: Engineering the Body Electric*, Watertown, MA: Eastgate Systems.

Grigar, D. (2009) "Electronic Literature: Where Is It?" *Electronic Book Review*, retrieved from www.electronic bookreview.com/thread/technocapitalism/invigorating.

Harpold, T. (2008) *Ex-Foliations: Reading Machines and the Upgrade Path*, Minneapolis, MN: University of Minnesota Press.

Hayles, N. K. (2008) *Electronic Literature: New Horizons for the Literary*, Notre Dame, IN: University of Notre Dame Press.

Kirschenbaum, M. (2008) *Mechanisms: New Media and the Forensic Imagination*, Cambridge, MA: MIT Press.

Liu, A., D. Durand, N. Montfort, M. Proffitt, L. R. E. Quin, J. Réty, and N. Wardrip-Fruin (2005) "Born Again Bits: A Framework for Migrating Electronic Literature," *Electronic Literature Organization* 1(1), 5 August, retrieved from eliterature.org/pad/bab.html.

Moulthrop, S. (2013) "Lift This End: Electronic Literature in a Blue Light," *Electronic Book Review*, retrieved from www.electronicbookreview.com/thread/electropoetics/blue%20light.

Moulthrop, S. and D. Grigar (2017) *Traversals: The Uses of Preservation for Electronic Literature*, Cambridge, MA: MIT Press.

Paul, C. (2007) "The Myth of Immateriality: Presenting and Preserving New Media," in O. Grau (ed.) *MediaArt-Histories*, Cambridge, MA: The MIT Press.

Pressman, J., M. Marino, and J. Douglass (2015) *Reading Project: A Collaborative Analysis of William Poundstone's Project for Tachistoscope {Bottomless Pit}*, Iowa City, IA: University of Iowa Press.

Salter, A. (2014) *What Is Your Quest? From Adventure Games to Interactive Books*, Iowa City, IA: University of Iowa Press.

Wardrip-Fruin, N. (2009) *Expressive Processing: Digital Fictions, Computer Games, and Software Studies*, Cambridge, MA: MIT Press.

References

Aarseth, E. (1997) *Cybertext: Perspectives on Ergodic Literature*, Baltimore, MD: The John Hopkins Press.

Balsamo, A. (2011) *Designing Culture: The Technological Imagination at Work*, Durham, NC: Duke University Press.

Bly, B. (1997) *We Descend: Archives Pertaining to Egderus Scriptor*, Vol. 1, Watertown, MA: Eastgate Systems.

Brookman, M. (2016) *Chronicles: Documenting the Articulation of Culture in Video Games*, retrieved from scalar.usc.edu/works/chronicles.

Coverley, M. D. (2000) *Califia*, Watertown, MA: Eastgate Systems.

Emerson, L. (2014) *Reading Writing Interfaces*, Minneapolis, MN: University of Minnesota Press.

Eskelinen, M. (2012) *Cybertext Poetics: The Critical Landscape of New Media Literary Theory*, New York, NY: Continuum.

Grigar, D. and S. Moulthrop (2013a) "Artists' Interview Questions," *Pathfinders*, retrieved from scalar.usc.edu/works/pathfinders/interview-questions?path=introduction.

Grigar, D. and S. Moulthrop (2013b) "Artists' Traversal Protocol," *Pathfinders*, retrieved from scalar.usc.edu/works/pathfinders/artist-traversal-protocol?path=introduction.

Grigar, D. and S. Moulthrop (2013c) "Readers' Interview Questions," *Pathfinders*, retrieved from scalar.usc.edu/works/pathfinders/readers-interview-questions?path=introduction.

Grigar, D. and S. Moulthrop (2015) *Pathfinders*, Scalar Web Site, retrieved from scalar.usc.edu/works/pathfinders/.

Grigar, D. and S. Moulthrop (n.d.) *Pathfinders*, retrieved from dtc-wsuv.org/wp/pathfinders/.

Jackson, S. (1995) *Patchwork Girl*, Watertown, MA: Eastgate Systems.

Joyce, M. (1997) "Nonce Upon Some Times: Rereading Hypertext Fiction," *Modern Language Studies* 43(3), 579–97, retrieved from yin.arts.uci.edu/~studio/readings/joyce-nonce.html.

Kolb, D. (1994) *Socrates in the Labyrinth: Hypertext, Argument, Philosophy*, Watertown, MA: Eastgate Systems, Inc.

Malloy, J. (1991) "'Uncle Roger,' an Online Narrabase," *Leonardo* 24.2 Connectivity: Art and Interactive Telecommunications, 195–202.

Malloy, J. (2012) *Uncle Roger*, Version 6.0, retrieved from www.well.com/user/jmalloy/uncleroger/uncle.html#basic.

Malloy, J. (ed.) (2016) "Authoring Electronic Literature" content | code | process project, retrieved from www.narrabase.net.

McDaid, J. (1992) *Uncle Buddy's Phantom Funhouse*, Watertown, MA: Eastgate Systems.

Montfort, N. and N. Wardrip-Fruin (2004) "Acid-Free Bits: Recommendations for Long-Lasting Electronic Literature," *Electronic Literature Organization* 1(0), 14 June, retrieved from eliterature.org/pad/afb.html.

Morris, D. (2012) *Frankenstein*, Cupertino, CA: Apple.

Moulthrop, S. (1991) *Victory Garden*, Watertown, MA: Eastgate Systems.

Phillips, T. (2010) *A Humument App*, Cupertino, CA: Apple.

Sayers, J. (2015) Email correspondence with the authors, 26 August.

37
NEW MEDIA ARTS
Creativity on the Way to the Archive

Timothy Murray

In the early 1980s, the appearance of a magical portable box bearing the logo of an Apple altered the scene of the experimental media arts. When the Experimental Television Center (ETC) in Owego, New York added an Apple computer to its crowded workshop of electronic tools, it dramatically altered the options available to artists for the creation of video art. Initially, the residential artists of ETC, founded in 1971, experimented with electronic signals derived from its analog video synthesizers created by Nam June Paik, Daniel Sundin, David Jones, and Ralph Hocking. The pop and verve of electric colors, composited imagery, flying wedges, and synthetic sounds wrapped the realistic visions of television and documentary in a creative skin whose dazzling form performed the new content of conceptual video. The works challenged the televisual dominance of patriarchy, the commercial comfort with capitalism, the hegemonies of white culture, the planned obsolescence of technology, and traditional media indifference to expansive theorizations of time, color, motion, and sound. With the digital turn in the late 1980s, the portable computer permitted additional flexibility to ETC as it could provide its residential creators with a fully integrated spectrum of digital and analog tools with which to work.

The rapid development of miniaturized chips, expansive RAM, and the growing capacities of portable home computers extended the range of data available to artists for their experimentation with ETC's incomparable tools for creative video mixing. With the explosive availability of portable systems, the artists working at ETC and similar centers throughout the world began to realize the added archival capacity of their creation tools. They could not only experiment with form but also build and dialogue with their own archives. In this and other artistic workshops, artists enthusiastically embraced the creative and archival dynamics of the digital interface. Artistic production and reception reached across the globe in an expanding network of creative formats, exhibition portals, and discursive practices. At a turning point during the early 1990s, the marriage of analog and digital media created something of a utopian fervor.

From CD-ROM to Net.Art

The initial creative impact was a development of complex interactive artistic performances and installations, on the one hand, and more portable works created on optical disks or

CD-ROMs, on the other. For instance, Laurie Anderson joined with digital specialists to create special effects for her tour of the album, *Bright Red*. With designer, Hsin-Chien Huang, she then partnered with Voyager publishing to produce an interactive CD-ROM, *Puppet Motel* (Anderson & Huang 1995), which permitted home users to interact with virtual sets, musical archives, and digital imagery. In transforming the passive reception of Anderson's productions into an interactive engagement with its details and interfaces, *Puppet Motel* even provided a link to her website. The ongoing publicity for *Puppet Motel* now focuses on the artist's reliance on participant activity for the realization of her artistic vision: "Navigating PUPPET MOTEL is a challenge in itself; the map is your memory of what you've already seen, with objects functioning as signposts" (Amazon 2017).

Memory as the paradigm for the combination of participant practice and archival site became key to the proliferation of digital art since the early 1990s. While individual artists collaborated with programmers and designers to expand the limits of artistic expression, emergent arts organizations and archives worked with artists to develop portable platforms for their artworks, often combining installation and CD-ROM. Most of these pieces were designed on Macs with the accessible software, Director. Their artists teamed up with designers, engineers, and other artists to tweak and experiment with the software by creating sophisticated sound roll-overs and varying tempos of sound tracks, composited digital imagery, elegant composite imagery and montage, and innovative trackball interfaces permitting users to pull images left and right, up and down, if not also in and out.

Most notable in these projects was the artists' attraction to the archival capacity of the CD-ROM, where they could mix the presentation of databases with emergent forms of expression and the theoretical frameworks sustaining them. For her interactive performance of feminism and lesbian erotics in *Cyberflesh Girl Monster* (1995), Linda Dement morphed hybrid monsters from her collection of abstracted images of female body parts, donated by women who scanned their flesh at the Adelaide Festival of the Arts. In the U.K., Simon Biggs wove eerie electronic imagery into slow moving, interactive conceptual essays, which he published with his artist books, *Book of Shadows* (1996) (CD-ROM, artist book) and *The Great Wall of China* (1997) (CD-ROM, artist book). Chinese artist, Qui Zhijie, capitalized on the nonlinear format of hypertext narrative and the widely available PowerPoint software to mount video clips for his CD-ROM critique of "The West" (1999). In the United States, Reginald Woolery in *Million Man March/World Wide Web* (1997) and Leah Gilliam in *Split* (1999) experimented with digital technologies to cull footage from Hollywood and family archives to theorize racial disparities in America. Such a reconsideration of the family archive was influenced by George Legrady's pioneering piece, *An Annotated Archive from the Cold War* (1994a). Legrady built a virtual museum of his personal collection of Cold War artifacts, including family mementos and Communist Party documents from Hungary, identity cards, sound recordings, and socialist propaganda, which he organized into eight rooms superimposed on the original floor plan of the "Workers Museum" in Budapest (the official propaganda museum of the Communist Party). This collection makes public the private archive of the artist, while juxtaposing seemingly unrelated items to open unanticipated links of artifact, affect, and analysis. Regarding his creation of the "virtual museum," Legrady emphasized that the architectonics of the site "reminds us of the museum's cultural function, as a site of memory for the inscription of the social collective imagination and as a site of representation and power" (1994b). For the award-winning CD-ROM, *Shock in the Ear* (1998), the Australian artist, Norie Neumark, teamed with designers and engineers to program an artistically rich and interactive archive of interviews with victims of shock (e.g., torture, war, shock treatment, and accident trauma), electric sound files, and digital imagery.

The beauty of this work is that its code permits for unusual interactivity yet frustrates the participant who must unlearn the literary habit of imagining that she can easily return to passages she most enjoyed. The unexpected and unanticipated user experience enhances the texture of shock in this work. These mnemonic projects challenge habits of viewing culture electronically by disrupting passive reception with the demand for interaction. We might also ask whether they work to expand the interface of the screen and the archival database by posing sharp questions about assumptions of dominant cultural expression and archival authority. Whose archive, whose representation, and whose self-reference?

The CD-ROM also built upon the precedent of a vast array of electronic and hypertext literature for which the advantage of hypertext and embedded multimedia stretched the conventions of print literature. N. Katherine Hayles describes the 1987 hypertext fiction, *afternoon, a story*, by Michael Joyce:

> [T]here is no central representation. Whereas in a novel like Faulkner's *The Sound and the Fury* it is possible to coordinate the different narrative voices to arrive at a coherent picture of what happened, the diverse pathways in *Afternoon* do not resolve into a unified account.
>
> (Hayles 1999: 214)

The conventions of literary narrative were pulled and stretched further by the artists of the CD-ROM era. For her digital adaptation of Nicole Brossard's 1987 experimental Quebecois novel, *Le Desert mauve*, artist Adriene Jenik transformed the experimental patterns of hypertext, in her CD-ROM, *Mauve Desert* (1997), into a multimedial experience that permits users to join Brossard's protagonist in elicit joy rides, this time across the Southwestern U.S. In a move to bring the literary past forward through the marvels of digital technology, French artist, Jean-Louis Boissier (2000), worked with Editions Gallimard to create an interactive CD-ROM version of texts by Jean-Jacques Rousseau. Embedded in Rousseau's text are links to clips of Boissier's video restaging of Rousseau's visions. Boissier capitalized in the mid-1990s on the imaginations of artistic creation to cross timelines and make readily available the delights of fantasy and erotics that permit users to experience the multiple temporalities of historical literary culture gone digital. The act of reading across the digital platform activates the archival fantasies of literary imagination into interactive events of critical creation. Rather than adhere to well-established artistic genres such as documentary, adaptation, or realistic narrative that set the parameters of aesthetic resemblance, the kind of digital interactivity promoted by these media positions the artist, spectator, and researcher on the common threshold of the virtual. As put succinctly by Pierre Levy, the image "abandons the exteriority of spectacle to open itself to immersion" (1997: 179, my translation). The added premise of the artistic CD-ROM was that its enhanced databases, complex multimedial platforms, and zones of interactivity easily enabled users to collaborate with the creative dimensions of the artwork in the projection or simulation of their own associations, fantasies, and memories.

In the context of artistic community building, the CD-ROM placed artists separated by geographical and cultural distance right at the epicenter of the exchange of both old and new public information and entertainment systems. Reception of their works was no longer limited to the user's physical visit to the geographically isolated gallery or studio. Instead of pandering to the habitual rituals of gallery spectatorship and the contemporary corollary of accruing art capital, the CD-ROM contributed to the rejuvenation of what Walter Benjamin called the "other function" of art: "politics" (1969: 224). Frequently working in the independent spaces of their homes, schools, and cooperative art centers, these cultural workers profited from the deep memory and fluid interface of digital technology to represent the political divides of global capitalism and sometimes even the paradox of new media's own "digital divide."

From the earliest days of interactive art, the challenge of audience access tested the growth of the media. Initially, complex installations requiring networks of multiple computers, projectors, and monitors were confined to the exhibition spaces of a very small set of international institutions, such as the NTT InterCommunication Center in Tokyo, the Museum of Contemporary Art in Australia, SOHO Guggenheim Museum in New York, the Walker Art Museum in Minneapolis, the Wexner Center for the Arts at Ohio State University, the Kiasma in Helsinki, and the Center for Art and Media Technology (ZKM) in Karlsruhe, Germany. Indicative of the attraction to alternative formats and artistic communities, the first generation of new media artists relied on festivals and digital centers for the exhibition and dissemination of their work. Early impetus was provided by the annual exhibit of the Prix Ars Electronic, begun in 1987 in Linz, Austria, and the inclusion of new media art by the Ars Electronica Festival, also in Linz, Austria, as well as the Berlin Transmediale Arts Festival, which first began to foreground video art in 1979 and 1988, respectively. Also crucial to the growth of new media exhibition was the international gathering of electronic artists, ISEA, which was founded in 1991 and continues annually. Artifices at St. Denis, one of the first annual festivals dedicated to new media art, was curated by Jean-Louis Boissier and Anne-Marie Duguet (1991–94). Other renowned festivals, such as Microwave in Hong Kong, File in Sao Paulo, the Boston Cyberarts Festival, Impact Festival in Utrecht, and MAAP (Multimedia Art Asia Pacific), have followed since the beginning of the new millennium.

The most complex institutional projects were sponsored by the ZKM in Karlsruhe. Founded in 1987, it expanded in a newly refurbished factory building in 1997 that included the ZKM Museum of Contemporary Art and the creative division, ZKM Institute for Visual Media, directed by Jeffrey Shaw. Recognizing the opportunities provided by the CD-ROM, the ZKM published the interactive media journal, *artintact*, from 1995 to 1999, which combined a CD-ROM of interactive artworks produced at the ZKM with a bilingual (German and English) book of critical essays on digital theory and criticism. The five editions of *artintact* stand as an important digital benchmark in the parallel histories of interactive installation, the book, and new media theory. From interactive installations of touch and movement to digital archives of sound, image, and text, *artintact* ushered in a new era of multimedia publishing. From a social point of view, the works of *artintact* and accompanying essays by influential theoreticians of digitality, from Timothy Druckrey and Anne-Marie Duguet to Erkki Huhtamo and Jean Gagnon, elaborated on CD-ROM art and theories of memory and archives while also positioning the ZKM's nurturing of international artists to enhance understanding of global artistic citizenry. At stake were not only cool projects of multimedial art, but also searing commentaries on the relation of art to global politics, from the cultural impact of the network to international perspectives on gender, sexuality, class, and commodification.

In a related vein, Duguet featured the political multimedia artist, Antoni Muntadas, in launching the ongoing Anarchive Project at the University of Paris 1. Muntadas reflects on the variables of "translation" in understanding the place of media in politics, culture, and capital. For the inaugural Anarchive, Duguet combined a critical book and CD-ROM, before moving the project to DVD and now the internet and augmented reality. Anarchive collaborates with featured artists—Muntadas, Michael Snow, Nam June Paik, Thierry Kuntzel, Jean Otth, Fujiko Nayaka, and Masaki Fujihata—to design a catalogue raisonné in the form of an interactive artwork. Here, the database of artist drawings, writings, projects, and accompanying theoretical essays expands the aesthetic parameters of the individual artwork to provide users with the network of archival data informing the artist's oeuvre. The aim here is to destabilize the boundaries and territories of the artistic archive as it seeps into the ephemeral zones of installation and interactive reception.

In contrast to Anarchive's emphasis on fluid archives of the individual artist, the expanding power of the internet and informal international networks of new media arts provided unanticipated opportunities for building broad and diverse artistic collectives. Three early exhibitions of CD-ROM art created venues for connecting international artists who had been working with the same creative suite in relative isolation. In 1996, Mike Leggett teamed with the Museum of Contemporary Art, Sydney, to curate a grouping of 30 CD-ROMs for the first international exhibition of the genre, "Burning the Interface <International Artists' CD-ROM>." In 1998, the Ecole régionale des beaux-arts de Rennes collaborated with the University of Rennes 2 to host an exhibition of CD-ROMs by 25 international artists, curated by Bertrand Gauguet. An international call for participation I posted on the Rhizome listserv, created by Mark Tribe in 1996, resulted in the submission of some 130 international artworks for my exhibition, *Contact Zones: The Art of CD-ROM*, which I curated from 1999 to 2003. *Contact Zones* included 95 artists from nineteen countries and toured from 1999 to 2004, with access to the first bilingual (English, Spanish) online art catalogue.

The rapid development of the multimedial capacities of the internet for gathering together communities of artists and critics through listservs such as Rhizome and -empyre- also generated yet another stream of mobile art practice that expanded the creative field of new media art. Profiting from the flexibility of the Adobe Flash software platform, which displays text, vector, and raster graphics for animations and interactives, net.art attracted a broad network of international, low bandwidth users across generations. The growing capacity of home computers, the expansion of the internet, and the availability of affordable software packages provided emergent artists with opportunities to make a bold statement in this new field by creating low memory, high impact pieces. But as artists began to post individual artworks for wide reception, it became apparent that access to these works was limited by the structural hierarchies of the major search engines, which reinserted into digital art a restrictive gateway that emulated the gallery-museum nexus. One response was the development of online exhibitions and archival sites dedicated to net.art. The longest running sponsor of internet art, Turbulence, began commissioning and curating digital works in 1996 until 2016, with Rhizome also hosting net.art since 1998. On a front more targeted to political and conceptual works, I joined with Arthur and Marilouise Kroker to produce *CTHEORY Multimedia* in the Cornell Library from 2000 to 2004. Building on the success of the Kroker's first issue on "Digital Dirt" in 1998, we designed and published issues of net.art that addressed political themes important to the digital age, such as genomics, terrorism, ethnic paranoia, and sound. The explosion of social media over the past decade then expanded the options of individual artists to explore the artistic dynamics of mobile screen devices, app artworks, and social networks, while critiquing the very same infrastructure that simultaneously enhanced surveillance and tracking and remained indifferent to the dynamics of race and sexuality.

Archives and Preservation

Archived on the Cornell Library server, *CTHEORY Multimedia's* collection of 50 works of net.art, along with the CD-ROMs gathered for *Contact Zones*, then provided the critical mass for the establishment of the Rose Goldsen Archive of New Media Art, which I founded in

2002 in the Cornell Library. Meant to carry on the collaborative and amateur legacy of the rise of new media art, the Goldsen Archive focuses on including materials by an expansive range of emergent international artists, art centers, and collectives, such as the ZKM, Anarchive, subRosa, Dongtai Academy of Art in China, and Experimental Television Center. Designed as a center of research and creativity, the Goldsen Archive emphasizes broader sets of artworks and ephemera grouped around media genre and international sponsors, such as 400 dossiers of American artists nominated for the Renew Media/Rockefeller Foundation Fellowships in New Media, 8,000 digitized images of Taiwanese installation and new media art in the Yao Jui-Chung Archive of Contemporary Taiwanese Art, Wen Pulin's 360 hours of digitized video of contemporary Chinese art, the archives of net.art from Computerfinearts and Turbulence, and the archives of the New York State Council on the Arts' competition in Electronic Media and Film. Goldsen also collaborates on conceptual experimentation and archival strategies with international curatorial and fellowship projects, from the Taishin Bank Foundation for Arts and Culture in Taiwan to the National Endowments for the Arts and Humanities in the United States.

Whether established as research archives or museum collections, the institutional hosts of new media art collections faced serious decisions in direction and purpose as new media art developed and matured. Primary was the question of whether (1) to collect the oeuvre of single well-established artists, as was the direction taken by the Langlois Foundation Archive when investing in the archive of the Vasulkas and by the Walker, Whitney, and Berkeley Art Museums in collecting a select number of artists for promotion; or (2) to feature broad collections of artists and ephemera across the media to make accessible to users the collaborative context and collective spirit of new media art. Emphasizing archive over exhibition, the Goldsen Archive is situated in the Division of Rare and Special Collections of the Cornell Library to permit it to host very large sets of collections that might provide artists and researchers with access to collections of video art as well as to the range of materials now known as new media art. The decision to eschew singular artistic fame for medial depth placed less emphasis on the celebrity of the artist and more on the contribution of the artwork to the broader network of media creation to which it belonged. While the deep data sets of much of Goldsen's collection on CD-ROM and interactive media require on-site access for Goldsen materials, Goldsen joined other international archives in building repositories of portable collections for access online, notably the Langlois Foundation (Montreal), ZKM (Karlsruhe), Asia Art Archive (Hong Kong), ADA: Archive of Digital Art (Krems, Austria), ICC Online Archive Zone (Tokyo), Rhizome (New York), and V2_Institute for the Unstable Media (Rotterdam). It also took the additional step of fostering the theoretical discourse of new media by hosting the international new media listserv, -empyre-, a soft-skinned space.

Regardless of their scope of acquisition, institutional participants in the promotion of new media art came to the realization that access and durability would become a leading focus of their institutional missions. In recognition that digital formats were far less stable than initially imagined, preservation developed into a predominant concern of new media art curators, often in tension with the new media community's enthusiasm for the embrace of unpredictable and unstable formats and its affection for the artistic ephemerality associated with performance, installation, and online interaction. A number of technical issues came to the forefront. With net.art, the challenges of initial design issues became endemic: overall design for multiple browsers, dead internal links, increased RAM speeding up prior interfaces designed to be slow, the freezing of ongoing online archival projects for archived net.art pieces, and, most recently, the promise of browsers to eliminate access to Flash (riding the wave of Apple's earlier decision to do so for the iPad and iPhone). Work created on CD- and DVD-ROM faced a myriad of other archival challenges, such as Apple's refusal to provide backwards compatibility with earlier versions of QuickTime, broken links to active websites embedded in CD-ROMs (in the case of Laurie Anderson and Muntadas), obsolete software such as early VRML packages, scratched or damaged optical disks, data degradation or bit rot, and, most seriously, planned obsolescence as a result of Apple's 2005 adoption of Intel for OSX, which promised to render inaccessible the hundreds of artistic CD-ROMs created on "Mac classic" in the 1990s. Ironically, the archival celebration of memory, interactivity, and digital durability that propelled artistic creation in the early 1990s became the new millennial threat to new media's archival future.

It should be no surprise that the response of curators and artists to this challenge tended to reflect their initial strategies in building museum collections or research archives of new media art. From 2005 to 2010, the international collective DOCAM (Documentation and Conservation of the Media Arts Heritage, sponsored by the Langlois Foundation) identified and implemented five research axes that contributed to the preservation of the media arts heritage: conservation, documentation, cataloguing, history of technologies, and terminology. Conservation entails the preservation of original materials and/or translation of original digital standards (code and software configurations) into contemporary, operable equivalents. For deposit in large library and museum collections, novel strategies of defining and describing new media projects were required for documentation and cataloguing. Accounts of the histories of hardware and software enabled curators to plan for the closest proximity of original exhibition conditions. And new sets of standardized terminologies for emergent formats permitted artists, curators, and preservationists to communicate effectively. Contributing to these goals was the emphasis placed on the artist by the Variable Media Network, which was coordinated by Alain Depocas of Langlois and Jon Ippolito then at the Guggenheim and now a principal architect of the Forging the Future Initiative at the University of Maine. As described on the Forging the Future website, The Variable Media Paradigm

> explores both new and proven concepts of preservation by concentrating on the behaviors, rather than solely the material, of contemporary artifacts made in ephemeral mediums. A second approach centers on a work's creator rather than its medium. The variable media paradigm asks creators themselves, rather than just technicians and conservators, to imagine ways to outwit the obsolescence that often besets technological and other ephemeral art forms. This approach proposes that the best way to preserve works in ephemeral formats, from stick spirals to video installations to Web sites, is to encourage their creators and users to describe their own works.
>
> (Variable Media Paradigm n.d.)

Via its development of the Variable Media Questionnaire, this approach focuses best practices around artist preferences for ideal exhibition conditions. Questions range from "how should the limitations of the original rule set implementation be represented in future implementations (e.g., the effect of processor speed on an algorithm)?" to "can this be displayed on other screens and with other resolutions?" and "can a plasma screen be used?" This emphasis on variable media led both the Guggenheim and Berkeley Art Museum to focus on a small, select group of artists for collaboration in the preservation of their media works. Although this focus has resulted in successful results of migration to new formats for particular works, it also has been circumscribed by some of the more traditional principles of building museum collections around the works of successfully monetized artists. Nevertheless, the Variable Media Questionnaire has provided a model for involving the expertise of creators in much broader preservation projects of first generation, digital interactive art.

Since the Goldsen Archive has been a central participant in these efforts, I will conclude these reflections on "Creativity on the Way to the Archive" by focusing on approaches to the collection and preservation of net.art and CD-ROM art that have been important to Goldsen. From the outset, net.art was constrained by two limitations to access: (1) the lack of adequate bandwidth for home users to access complex works—a result of the "digital divide" that empowers some communities technologically while leaving less privileged populations behind; and (2) the action of hosting sites that might take its collections offline, often as a result of economic constraint. A net.art exhibition I curated in 2000 with Teo Spiller in Slovenia responded to both of these challenges while also providing the paradigm that Goldsen has followed for its collection and preservation of net.art. For this show, we distributed a competition call for completed works of net.art that we could print on a single CD-ROM and distribute free and offline to participants at Slovenia's annual technology fair, INFOS 2000, as well as to international arts and cultural organizations lacking the proper bandwidth to screen new media art online. While remaining sensitive to the concern that this exhibition paradigm could be understood to betray the ephemeral spirit of networked art, Goldsen has adopted this strategy of archiving large sets of net.art offline. While this approach will not solve the dilemma of broken internal links or browser abandonment of Flash, it provides the Goldsen team with access to the raw data of extensive collections of net.art for future preservation research.

A more recent preservation project on CD-ROM art has provided the Goldsen team with a promising approach that might also become applicable to net.art. The preservation community's initial approach to providing "best-feasible" access to artistic CD-ROMs was to focus on migration from one container to another with the expectation that preservation of the raw data would enable preservation of the interactive artwork. With this aim, Goldsen began by making disc images of the artworks. But we soon realized that *the migration of information files to another storage medium fails to preserve their most important cultural contents.* For it is the unpredictability of interactivity built into the code of many first generation CD-ROMs that distinguishes the creativity of their user experience from the passivity of conventional progression through linear narratives. The most successful CD-ROMs depended on the cultural habits and intellectual toolkits of user interaction for movement from one link to another, with no guarantee of repetition or outcome for subsequent use. For instance, Neumark's *Shock in the Ear* includes a database of five narratives of shock, each spoken by five different voices. Their random rotation during different journeys through the interface confronts users with an appreciation for the depth and breadth of shock trauma. Even the most comprehensive set of disk images could not migrate these kinds of playful and unpredictable characteristics of user interactivity.

As a counter strategy, the Goldsen research team quickly turned to the promise of operating system emulation as a strategy that could provide fully interactive access to obsolete artworks at very reasonable quality. One initial access strategy was simply to retool the code of a particular artwork for rough compatibility with more recent systems (for example, a number of artists redesigned their CD-ROMs from "Mac Classic" [System 9 down] to Mac System 10, which was compatible with newer generations of PowerMacs prior to Mac's migration to the Intel chip). But this time-consuming and expensive approach was only applicable to the most successful artists or well financed archives. In contrast, system emulation seeks not to refashion the artwork but, much more basically, to emulate the initial system software itself, thus providing access to all CD-ROMs on the broadest number of computers (Mac, PC, etc.) with one interface. As a result of the Goldsen team's research of compatible emulators, we were able to provide artists in the collection with the ability to access their own CD-ROM artworks for the first time in years. Even though the adoption of emulation as an archival access strategy will require us to preserve emulators as well as artworks, we feel that the motivation of preserving the unpredictable creativity of the CD-ROMs overshadows our initial strategy of aiming for the more hermetic duplication of disk imagery.

That said, the emphasis on emulating operating systems remains controversial from the perspective of forensic approaches that value the museum standards of best exhibition quality in contrast to Goldsen's archival ambitions of "best-feasible" access. Emulation remains suspect for its propensity to mask the material historical contexts in which and for which digital artworks had been created. This part of the artwork's history could be understood as an element of its authenticity, which the museum institution must preserve to the best of its ability. However, the Goldsen team determined that the broadest cultural access to interactive creativity trumped the more traditional and material values of forensic authenticity. In contrast to the high exhibition standards sought by most museums to show individual works, wed to the specifics of the Variable Media Questionnaire for presentational purposes, Goldsen's aim is for the broadest access in the research setting of the archive to the most CD-ROMs in its collection—with best achievable quality for scale.

Returning us to the early days of ETC's mixing of analog video and digital tools, the Goldsen Archive continues to be guided first and foremost by the principles of creative archivization that fueled the early mnemonic delights of new media creation.

Further Reading

Chun, W. H. K. and K. Thomas (eds.) (2015) *New Media/Old Media: A History and Theory Reader*, New York, NY: Routledge.

CTheory.net. (n.d.) retrieved from ctheory.net.

-empyre-soft-skinned space. (n.d.) retrieved from empyre.library.cornell.edu.

High, K., S. Miller-Hocking, and M. Jimenez (eds.) (2014) *The Emergence of Video Processing Tools: Television Becoming Unglued*, 2nd vol., London, U.K.: Intellect.

Kroker, A. and M. Kroker (eds.) (2013) *Critical Digital Studies: A Reader*, Toronto, ON: Toronto University Press.

Murray, T. (2008) *Digital Baroque: New Media Art and Cinematic Folds*, Minneapolis, MN and London, U.K.: Minnesota University Press.

Murray, T. (2016) *Signal to Code: 50 Years of Media Art in the Rose Goldsen Archive*, retrieved from rmc.library.cornell.edu/signaltocode/.

Parrika, J. (2012) *What Is Media Archaeology?*, London, U.K.: Polity.

Paul, C. (2015) *Digital Art*, London, U.K.: Thames & Hudson.

Rinehart, R. and J. Ippolito (2014) *Re-collection: Art, New Media, and Social Memory*, Cambridge, MA: MIT Press.

Shanken, E. (2014) *Art and Electronic Media*, London, U.K.: Phaidon.

Shaw, J. and P. Weibel (eds.) (2003) *Future Cinema: The Cinematic Imaginary after Film*, Cambridge, MA: MIT Press.

References

Anarchive (n.d.) retrieved from anarchive.net/.

Anderson, L. with H. Huang (1995) *Puppet Motel* (CD-ROM), New York: Voyager.

Amazon (2017) "Puppet Motel by Laurie Anderson," retrieved from www.amazon.com/Puppet-Motel-PC-Mac-CD-ROM/dp/1581250401.

Benjamin, W. (1969) "The Work of Art in the Age of Mechanical Reproduction," in H. Arendt (ed.) *Illuminations: Essays and Reflections*, 217–52, New York, NY: Schocken.

Biggs, S. (1996) *Book of Shadows* (CD-ROM, artist book), London, U.K.: Ellipsis.

Biggs, S. (1997) *The Great Wall of China* (CD-ROM, artist book), London, U.K.: Ellipsis.

Boissier, J. (2000) *Moments de Jean-Jacques Rousseau, Confessions et Rêveries* (CD-ROM and artist book), Paris, France: Gallimard.

Brossard, N. (1987) *Le Desert mauve*, (CD-ROM), Montreal, QC: Hexagone.

CTHEORY Multimedia (n.d.) retrieved from ctheorymultimedia.cornell.edu.

Dement, L. (1995) *Cyberflesh Girl Monster* (CD-ROM), Sydney, Australia.

Forging the Future (n.d.) retrieved from forging-the-future.net.

Gauguet, B. (1998) *COMPACTS. Oeuvres numériques sur CD-ROM: Digital Works of Art on CD-ROM*, Ecole régionale des beaux-arts de Rennes and Station Arts Electroniques—Université Rennes 2, Rennes, France.

Gilliam, L. (1999) *Split* (CD-ROM), New York, NY.

Hayles, N. K. (1999) "Artificial Life and Literary Culture," in M. Ryan (ed.) *Cyberspace Textuality: Computer Culture and Literary Theory*, Bloomington, IN: Indiana University Press, pp. 205–23.

Jenik, A. (1997) *Le Desert mauve* (CD-ROM), Los Angeles, CA: Shifting Horizons Productions.

Joyce, M. (1987–91) *afternoon, a story*, in P. Geyh, F. G. Leebron, and A. Levy (eds.) *Norton Anthology of Postmodern American Fiction*, New York: W.W. Norton, 1997, retrieved from www.wwnorton.com/college/english/pmaf/hypertext/aft/index.html.

Leggett, M. (1996) "Burning the Interface <International Artists' CD_Rom>," retrieved from www.mikeleggett.com.au/projects/burning-interfaceinternational-artists-CD-ROM.

Legrady, G. (1994a) *An Annotated Archive from the Cold War* (CD-ROM), Toronto, ON.

Legrady, G. (1994b) "Notes on An Annotated Archive from the Cold War," retrieved from contactzones.cit.cornell.edu/artists/legrady.html.

Levy, P. (1997) *Cyberculture: Rapport au Conseil de l'Europe dans le cadre du project 'Nouvelle technologies: Coopération et communication*, Paris, France: Odile Jacab.

Murray, T. (1999) *Contact Zones: The Art of CD-ROM*, retrieved from contactzones.cit.cornell.edu/index.html.

Murray, T. (2008) *Digital Baroque: New Media Art and Cinematic Folds*, Minneapolis, MN and London, U.K.: University of Minnesota Press.

Neumark, N. (1998) *Shock in the Ear* (CD-ROM), Sydney, Australia.

Rieger, O. , T. Murray, M. Casad, D. Dietrich, J. Kovari, L. Muller, and M. Paolillo (n.d.) "Preserving and Emulating Digital Art Objects," retrieved from ecommons.cornell.edu/handle/1813/41368.

Rose Goldsen Archive of New Media Art (2002) retrieved from goldsen.library.cornell.edu.

Turbulence (n.d.) retrieved from turbulence.org.

Variable Media (n.d.) retrieved from variablemedia.net/.

Woolery, R. (1997) *Million Man March/World Wide Web*, (CD-ROM), New York, NY.

Zhijie, Q. (1999) "The West," retrieved from qiuzhijie.com/worksleibie/hudong/e-The%20West.htm.

38

APPREHENDING THE PAST

Augmented Reality, Archives, and Cultural Memory

Victoria Szabo

Background

"Digital heritage" is a term used to describe the confluence of digital technologies with cultural heritage initiatives. This emergent field includes a wide range of practices, such as virtual reality, 3-D modeling, interaction design, simulation, geographical information systems (GIS), statistical content analysis, and historical reconstruction. It refers to both digitized historical materials and the born-digital content designed to represent and interpret them and their referents. Central concerns for digital heritage include scholarly preservation and analysis, sustainability, and public access. The 2013 Digital Heritage International Congress in Marseille, France used the term "Built Heritage" to describe "sites to cities, towns, and cultural landscapes, i.e., World Heritage" as a key area in its call for proposals. Built heritage sites are increasingly a focus for mobile augmented reality applications (DHIC 2013).

Media studies brings to digital heritage an awareness of the critical implications of, and creative possibilities for, digital media authorship. Value-based choices inevitably inhere in any kind digital re-presentation of cultural objects, whether a digital version of a material object or a provision of framing materials. What is the basis of our decision-making about what to include in a reconstruction or exhibition? How can we ensure that the traces of our choices remain visible in a digital project? What role does access to archival resources play in understanding a specific location or object in situ? How can we engage users in meaning-making within the hybrid reality system we create?

The term "augmented reality" (AR) refers to the use of digitally delivered overlays or supplements to existing material environments. AR content is associated with a specific object or location. Users trigger access to AR resources through the use of downloadable smartphone applications or headsets. AR is distinguished from virtual reality by the fact that it supplements, rather than replaces, a field of view. Mobile AR systems have the potential to help users create situated knowledge by bringing scholarly interpretation and archival resources in dialog with the lived experience of a space or object. This approach builds upon a number of historical traditions of annotation and representation, and of interpreting urban experience.

Since they are meant to be experienced in real space and real time, the resulting digital heritage projects can be understood as "hybrid reality systems." They combine material elements with virtual components to create a zone of interactive engagement. That zone can exist in museum contexts, in designated cultural heritage sites, and in the wider world.

Comprehension and Apprehension

A "comprehension" model for learning is one way to convey historical information about a built environment. The visitor *comprehends* the significance of a site or object as part of a historical phenomenon, or as an exemplar of aesthetic or technical achievement. Such an approach typically implies historical distance and appreciative observation. This stance is familiar as the educated user's approach to heritage sites and is reflected in many of the materials that help us interpret those sites. However, on-site applications also lend themselves to *apprehending* the past. The term "apprehension" conveys multiple relevant meanings. According to the *Oxford English Dictionary* (OED), apprehension's original meaning is to physically grasp, a concept that extends to mental prehension. Apprehension also suggests a state of anxious uncertainty, as well as seizure by an authority. (The police "apprehended" the criminals.) All of these meanings convey an aspect of AR design for digital heritage. By combining an intellectual approach to historic content with a visceral one, the hope is to create a more nuanced and immediate sense of the presence of the past in our lives today. The anxious uncertainty comes from recognition that we can never fully know the past, yet we reconstruct it to serve our own interests from a present-day perspective. In this sense, we potentially bind and contain the past as we make it our own.

As David Kolb (1984) and others have suggested, in experiential learning theory the difference between comprehension and apprehension is the difference between acquisition of abstract knowledge and experiential knowledge of a subject. Or, as Dieleman and Huisingh describe it:

> experience grasped through apprehension relies on the tangible and felt qualities of the immediate experiences. That refers to the kind of learning processes one goes through while exploring things, looking at them and touching, feeling, smelling, tasting and hearing them. It relies upon intuition, feeling, emotion and insight that are lateral processes of thought . . .
>
> (Dieleman & Huisingh 2006: 837)

Such tangible, lateral, intuitive elements are part of what we bring to bear through on-site engagement with digital resources. When coupled with intention ("an internal process that is achieved through reflection on an experience") and extension ("an external process that is achieved through active experimentation"), a transformation in learning combines comprehensive and apprehensive knowledge production (Sewchuk 2005: 1312). While all abstract knowledge is necessarily embodied or experienced in some way, the shift here is toward consciously crafted, combined effects. Transformation occurs when the learner integrates these elements into an alternate worldview and reflexive understanding of the self within it.

Such a transformative approach to built heritage, one that relies upon both intellectual and affective experiences, cannot rely on a mirror world or isomorphic map of everything, as Borges famously described it in his satiric short tale, "On Exactitude in Science" (1999 [1960]). Rather, it is to create a memory palace that overlays the world. It is a conscious construction of *selected elements* designed to enrich our experience and deepen our understanding—on site, and on location. And by being in the presence of a place or material object, we introduce potential counter-narratives to abstraction and isomorphism.

Theories of Annotation

With AR, the designer creates digital content that is meant to be paired with an object or location. This content is accessible through a smartphone, headset, or other device and is triggered by either image recognition through the device camera or a GPS location match. The application that matches trigger with referent will display content that might include an image, a sound file, a 3-D object, a video, a web link, or a link to another AR track. AR can also trigger external applications, such as the device phone or Twitter.

In "A Look at the Museum of the Future," the *Wall Street Journal* identified AR as one of several types of *digital interventions* that are becoming more commonplace in art and cultural heritage museums. AR in this context occurs on a continuum with virtual reality; the sites themselves are curated experiences. With AR, institutions such as the Metropolitan Museum of Art are moving beyond existing marker-based technologies like QR codes to image recognition of paintings and objects as well as beacon-assisted geolocation. These sites can be seen as incubators for future interventions into apprehensions of the past (Gamerman 2015). Yet, this kind of immediate intervention has made substantive inroads outside the museum or designated heritage site context as well, as seen in apps like *London Street Museum*, with its AR overlays of historic images upon contemporary street scenes (Museum of London 2015). Such interventions often build upon previously existing content.

There are two main types of AR annotation relevant to built heritage interventions. First, a *documentary annotation* is directly related to, and representative of, the history or attributes of the object of inquiry—for example, an historic photo of a current site or a 3-D model documenting vanished architectural detail. Such annotations could be thought of as virtual palimpsests, or traces, of earlier "writing" on the fabric of the annotated object. Annotations can be triggered by a specific image or object, or in reference to a specific location. For instance, consider the *Digital Durham* AR app, which reframes Preservation Durham's walking tours of Durham, North Carolina as augmented Tobacco Heritage and Civil Rights AR experiences with both historic imagery and audio tracks (Digital Durham 2015). For these kinds of projects, geolocation serves as the trigger linking the physical location to the virtual trace. Users access these annotations by activating a mobile application layer that pulls up different images, 3-D models, or sound files based on GPS coordinates. The world becomes the "Museum Without Walls," a concept that CultureNOW describes as "celebrating our vast cultural environment as a gallery that exists beyond museum walls through cultural tourism and arts education" (Museum Without Walls 2015). A primarily visual experience might be complemented by audio, for example, or related materials about authors, audiences, and effects. Contextual data, informational graphics, network diagrams, and other framing devices might offer just-in-time information with greater impact. The digital difference is that these annotations can appear on location, and they can themselves be triggered and sometimes manipulated by users. These interactive elements may prompt the apprehensive qualities of the experience by introducing a degree of openness and user interpretation.

A second type of AR intervention, the *interpretive annotation*, is less about a one-to-one correspondence between material objects and their virtual analogues, and more about adding a complementary, interpretative layer to the experience. These annotations might be archival, historical, or contextual framing. They might be fanciful or personal. They might also include games and other add-on activities to enrich the experience. Such experiences might draw upon sensory modes that complement, rather than compete with, the primary sense organs in play. Synecdochic and synesthesia effects might facilitate informational overlay at an associative or even subconscious level of experience design. For instance, the New York Public Library has created several AR experiences that move beyond direct, documentary annotation, most ambitiously with the "Unveiling Visions: The Alchemy of the Black Imagination" exhibition in 2015, which combined AR elements with existing artwork in a critically engaged intervention about Afrofuturism (Frederick 2015).

Returning for a moment to the Museum Without Walls, these two types of annotation are so powerful because they happen outside of the museum or other controlled settings. The unique object or location becomes the gateway into the wider, hybrid reality world. With AR image recognition and location-based content provision, material intervention may not even be necessary to create a hybrid reality environment, either. In fact, the social and cultural implications of a GPS, satellite-reliant culture may become the subject of apprehension itself. Consider recent work by the Manifest.AR collective at the Museum of Modern Art and the Venice Art Biennale, for example (Sterling 2010). ManifestAR artist, Tamiko Thiel, interjects gold AR silhouettes of censored artists, suggesting that each "erased silhouette stands for countless unknown or lesser known artists who face censorship or persecution with no public support" (2011). AR itself can be controversial as a medium. In 2012, the Collaborations: Humanities, Arts and Technology Festival at Duke University included AR triggers scattered around campus to highlight artwork and programs featured in the museum and temporary exhibitions (CHAT Festival 2012; Ferreri 2012). The application creator faced more trouble getting permission to inject AR into the museum space than in allowing projection mapping onto the façade of the museum itself.

Historical Precedents

Designs for digital heritage applications for on-site experience derive in part from traditional, analog forms of spatial and contextual communication. One could trace a trajectory of location-based annotation back to centuries of travel guides, for example. We might also take inspiration from older, "detached" representations of place—comprehensive approaches to seeing an environment with some critical distance from the object of inquiry—such as eighteenth-century zogatropes (Blake 2003) or nineteenth-century stereoscopes (Schiavo 2003). Contemporary analog models for AR might include guidebooks, annotated maps, tours (human-led and audio-guided), documentaries, and books with acetate layers showing before-and-after renderings.

With these media in mind, three key approaches to AR are *layering* (as in the case of overlays and maps), *scaling*, and *one-to-many approaches* to knowledge sharing. Scaling occurs on both spatial and temporal levels. Annotations might draw upon the tradition of museum maquettes or architectural building models that show how a building might have looked in another time. This use of scale gives people a sense of the whole construction via miniaturization. Similarly, image-based juxtapositions participate in a long history of recapture photography, employing a temporal dimension mapped onto an implicit z-axis, where images from the past are juxtaposed or overlaid directly upon contemporary scenes. They might also draw upon existing one-to-many experiences, as in the case of amateur photographers recapturing iconic sites photographed by famed photographer, Ansel Adams (Ansel Adams Gallery 2015). A single photograph may produce many derivatives or versions, as people mimic historical works and styles.

For historical precedents to apprehensive annotation, we might turn to creating sketches, writing postcards, or journaling about a place. More recently, we might create metalayers of participatory conversations through microblogging, group mapping, and digital graffiti with AR tags. These activities may facilitate a sense of collectivity or membership within a city or similar environment. In all of these, we mediate and remediate experience with the aid of digital media forms, such as games, which naturally lend themselves to participation. In 2011, the New York Public Library made headlines when Jane McGonigal created a game there; it was called *Find the Future* and relied upon students to find QR codes associated with historic objects and then write their own associated content (Terdiman 2011). More recently, the Google startup, Niantic Labs, created a game called *Ingress*, which, in 2015, engaged over a million users per day in searching for real-world landmarks as part of a contest between two "opposing forces" (Tatera 2015).

For more object-specific annotations, we might look to museums and their use of exhibition signage, dioramas, panoramas, and handheld guides, not to mention the layouts of museums themselves as interpretive contexts. Christopher Jones traces a trajectory of museum supplements, from audio tours and mobile websites to QR codes, apps, and games, to suggest how an object's meaning and significance are understood. He highlights AR interventions in the Tate, the Louvre, and the Uffizi as key new developments and approaches (2015: 190). Elsewhere, QR codes are already found in many heritage sites, once again reinforcing the idea of the world as a museum or exhibition. QR codes are popular because they provide accessible web links to online resources and can be created quickly and easily.

With AR, we can also move beyond transmitting historical tidbits about objects and environments into curating experiences of specific sites that both support and challenge traditional narratives. A simple way to do this is to create the potential for multiple viewpoints to exist simultaneously in a given location or situation. For example, the Soundwalk tours originating in New York during the 2000s describe their work as "an exclusive and poetic discovery of a city, on the bridge between Baudelairian stroll and cinematic experience" (Soundwalk 2015). Here, history is not a given. It is not merely transmitted to a listener. Instead, it is a collection of different sounds and various voices that contextualize a landscape. People do not look at it; they stroll through it.

Place, Space, and the Architecture of Apprehension

Apprehending the past through AR goes beyond an emphasis on learning styles and annotation to also suggest an *apprehensive stance* toward the very project of digital heritage or historical-place-making. For insight into critical engagement with the construction of place, space, and everyday life, many theorists build upon the work of Henri Lefebvre. In *The Production of Space* (1992 [1974]), he famously describes three registers of space-making. Perceived space is the space of everyday experience, while conceived space is the space of urban planners and map-makers. Lived space bridges these two modalities. It is into the context of enriching lived space that AR projects intercede. They rely upon both the sensory affordances of the physical location in question and the abstract information rendered accessible through the mobile platform (Lefebvre 1992: 38–39). Human experience completes the process of placemaking.

As human geographer Yi-Fu Tuan points out, "place is whatever stable object captures our attention" (2001: 162). On the topic of heritage objects and sites, Tuan suggests that, "[i]f a piece of sculpture is an image of feeling, then a successful building is an entire functional realm made visible and tangible" (164). The life-world implied in a monument or built structure creates the observer and the observed. There is a danger here, however. Tuan also notes that the production of cultural heritage sites is itself a sign of willed comprehension and critical distance. It "annul[s] the past by making it all present knowledge" (198). While AR might arguably afford opportunities for richer, transformative engagement with historic sites, is it done so at the expense of the history and lifeworlds of actual inhabitants, past and present? Could a solipsistic interest in creating "user experiences"—in drawing upon apprehensive responses as well as comprehensive strategies—turn the world into a personal theme park? Is there a way to prevent our overlaid experience design from negating what came before? Does AR privilege a presentist response to the past? We must be apprehensive about our interventions and aware of the extent to which, as designers of digital heritage applications, we are imposing a convenient fiction upon a place, even as we co-create a new one.

How, then, do we begin to understand our sites of annotation and architect the museum without walls? As noted earlier, layers, models, and one-to-many relations become critical features for organizing annotations. But, to take full advantage of the medium's possibilities, we also need to understand how users experience space. In *The Image of the City* (1960), urban planner, Kevin Lynch, famously studied the ways in which individuals engaged in urban wayfinding through surveys and studies of their behaviors. Lynch introduced the idea of place legibility, or *imageability*. He identified features of the city familiar to mapmakers (the paths, edges, districts, nodes, and landmarks of Lefebvre's conceived space), described how those features become relevant to users in perceived space, and explained how they also contribute to the collective conception of the city—to the transformative space of lived experience. His insights can help designers understand both how urban spaces are constructed and experienced and how they might choose their own objects of augmentation. For instance, his identification of geographic primitives, or the vector-friendly attributes of the map that translate into how people navigate the world, can serve as a first step for creating points, paths, and regions of activity for users. The "image of the city" is constructed of these elements. The *Visualizing Venice* AR app built upon this idea when it used the Venetian network of over 4000 cisterns as a starting point for understanding Venetian architectural history. As geolocated points on a map, the individual cisterns became landmarks within the individual plazas constructed around them (Lanzoni, Szabo & Olson 2015).

For most location-based AR, reliance on the map substrate for information management and presentation is part of the operating system (wireless beacons are sometimes used in more enclosed spaces like museums and exhibitions). The underlying grid of X and Y coordinates necessarily undergirds the construction of location-based markers, regions, and zones in a GPS-dependent system. Planned spaces are often built from maps and blueprints. Maps in this sense have generative power. They are also used for interpretation and representation. And we rely upon their conventions, especially when using GIS to create a location-based AR project. GIS software is designed to help users create points, lines, paths, and regions. We can then explore these features in digital environments and use them as a basis for AR authorship. The map becomes a necessary precondition for this engagement, and the layered map becomes a conceptual framework for situating annotations. Assumptions about the importance of geographic features, which can be located on a map as vector data, are embedded in the conventions of GIS software itself. The familiar points of interest found in guidebooks and tourist maps translate into Points of Interest (POIs) in the system. POIs are a geometric fiction brought to life in an ambient zone of temporal and spatial experience; we realize and inhabit that fiction in our AR scenarios. However, as in GIS software, which has to accommodate the reality of image-based historic maps by allowing for georectification (or association between points on an historic map and the contemporary grid), AR designers can complicate this picture. By making maps more interactive through AR, and by encouraging a sustained engagement with the complexities of their referents through lived experience on site and on location, designers can draw upon the vector-driven sense of their importance alongside a "raster," or uniquely qualitative sense, of their specificity.

Critical cartographers engage with this facticity of map-making, their rhetorics, and their cultural power; from leaders in the field, such as John Pickles (2003), Denis Wood and colleagues (2010), and J. B. Harley and P. Laxton (2002), AR designers learn how map-makers operate. Mark Monmonier (1996) discusses *How to Lie with Maps* by helpfully decoding mapping conventions, while Pickles draws our attention to counter-mapping practices, or mapping focused not on geometric bases alone, but on time, ideas, activist goals, intellectual associations, and community values. Tensions between what was designed and what is experienced could be important moments for an AR intervention. Map artists, such as those found in *The Map as Art: Contemporary Artists Explore Cartography*, suggest other creative models as well (Harman & Clemens 2010).

Experience Design

Just as annotation systems draw upon earlier inspirations, so, too, does the experience design of AR systems. Such design can include the more obvious documentary elements noted earlier, but also encourage apprehensive elements: the affective and sensory engagement with the real and virtual worlds combined through AR. From Edgar Allan Poe's "Man of the Crowd" (1840), which suggests focused (if monomaniacal) attention to the one in the many, to Baudelaire's sauntering flâneur reveling in the crowd, we can take inspiration from literary wanders and wanderers to shape user positionality. In *The Arcades Project* (2002), Walter Benjamin discusses Baudelaire and nineteenth-century Paris while identifying a key tension between the shock and enjoyment of urban experience. How might we foreground that tension?

In experience design for AR, heightening existing phenomena or reading against the grain of what the city "wants" can create productive contrasts. The field of psychogeography describes "specific effects of the geographical environment (whether consciously organized or not) on the emotions and behavior of individuals," as Guy Debord suggested in 1955 (1). The Letterists, the Situationists, and the Surrealists before them, all focused on the individual and collective experiences of the city. Debord introduces the dérive as the "playful-constructive" movement through the city—a drift—by a small group of people alert to "the attractions of the terrain and the encounters they find there" (1958: 62). This alertness on the part of the designer could result in enriched experience for users. In "Walking in the City," Michel de Certeau (1980) distinguishes the city produced by "strategies" from the individual who uses "tactics" to move within the city. Suggesting we learn from these precursors, Merlin Coverley's *Psychogeography* (2010) explores "new ways of apprehending our surroundings, transforming the familiar streets of our everyday experience into something new and unexpected" (cover). The designer of an AR system may become part producer and part consumer advocate, helping to introduce a third space in which design suggests possibilities and creates suggestions, as users enact them in their own ways. This combination of comprehension and apprehension is reflected in the idea of "algorithmic walking": a preset series of steps and turns to take, without reference to a map, to see what they reveal. Such "generative psychogeography" is updated for the contemporary age by groups such as Psy-Geo-conflux (Hart 2004).

While Lynch helps us comprehend how people experience urban space in terms of geometric forms, and the psychogeographers help us develop tactics for recognizing our own agency in apprehending our environments, Grant Hildebrand (1992) explores dimensions of how we experience natural and architectural spaces in light of human survival instincts and the pleasures of peril, hazards, and heroic quests. In *The Origins of Architectural Pleasure*, he bases his work on the English geographer Jay Appleton, and cites Stephen Kaplan, who "has empirically validated" preferences for landscape scenes that "either contained a trail that disappeared around a bend or . . . depicted a brightly lit clearing partially obscured from view by intervening foliage" (Kaplan qtd. in Hildebrand 1992: 52). Mystery and enticement, Hildebrand suggests, are products of a controlled and controllable environment. With novelty, there are limits; for "there is a sense of control, a sense that the rate of exposure to novelty is at the discretion of the viewer" (53). Information architects, Stan Ruecker, Milena Radzikowska, and Stéfan Sinclair (2011), also draw upon Appleton's ideas in "I See What I Can Do: Affordances of Rich Prospect Browsing." An urban landscape to explore might be mirrored conceptually with an annotated, augmented world. Similarly, as Wendy Chun remarks in *Programmed Visions*, part of the appeal of computer mediated experience lies in its ambiguity, in not knowing what lies beneath the surface of the interface (2011: 2).

Hybrid Reality and Games

Such rich prospects might extend to alternate and hybrid realities. For instance, the *Reacting to the Past* (2015) paper-based games encourage students to role-play historical events. Of course, many attempts have been made to create historically based videogames, too, from *The Oregon Trail*, which was first available in 1971 and taught an entire generation of schoolchildren about U.S. settlement of the west, to the *Assassin's Creed* games, which have relied on elaborate reconstructions of historic Florence, Jerusalem, and London, among others. Though not always accurate as models, as Nicholas Trépanier points out, "video games [are] a very efficient way to let undergraduates engage with historiography and leave them with a sophisticated, critical perspective that is likely to remain alive long after they graduate" (2014). The *Hidden Florence* AR app uses this rationale, employing a fictional character, the 1490s woolworker "Giovanni," to draw users through the Renaissance city (Hidden Florence 2015). Engagement with the character leads to greater compression of the urban context.

Alternate reality games, or ARGs, also provide models for how historical, participatory, and social elements could be combined to create engaged experiences of heritage locations. Frans Mäyrä and Petri Lankoski describe hybrid reality in relation to gamespace. Complicating the well-known "magic circle" (a term first defined by Johan Huizinga) as a separate, consensual space for games, they consider how location-based games unfold within the context of everyday life (Mäyrä & Lankoski 2009: 131; Huizinga 2014 [1944]). Their idea of the "gaming frame" provides a useful way of understanding the ambiguous nature of interaction between the virtual world implied by the existence of AR and the material world of lived experience. Mäyrä and Lankoski also describe a "playability zone" in which users interact between a spirit world and a physical world when logged into the system. This middle zone, the "mixed world," becomes the site of interaction. This concept inspired the "InnerSpace Adventure" AR experience (see Figure 38.1), a temporary AR art installation at a conference at the New York Hilton in 2013. Participants were posited as academic conference-goers engaging with an imaginary site as well as context-specific conundrums as they moved through the hotel's public spaces (Rudinsky & Szabo 2013).

Figure 38.1 InnerSpace Adventure augmented reality game presented at the College Art Association Conference in New York City, February 2013, as part of the AR2View show. Created by Joyce Rudinsky and Victoria Szabo.

In Jorge Luis Borges's, "The Garden of Forking Paths" (1991 [1941]), with its alternate histories simultaneously unfolding, we can find inspiration in literature for how to situate users and create new experiences as well. The idea of what was not built, or what did not happen, could be the starting point for a game-based approach to digital heritage AR. Explorations of the unbuilt world might highlight architecture, but also alternate outcomes for conflicts, migrations, and crises. The options are not completely open-ended, but rather curated, and can include considerations of operations before, during, and after a site visit. Then again, true interactivity might necessitate shutting down the system entirely.

The Digital Heritage Ecosystem

AR projects for digital heritage can grow out of and complement digital mapping, archival, and virtual world projects in how they take advantage of the affordances of digitality. They can be quantitative and qualitative and also incorporate both near and far perspectives (zoom in/zoom out) in how they engage users. They can address dissatisfaction with computer simulations as well as the abstractions of mapping by oscillating between these two modalities of hybrid reality systems; they can also inhabit a heterogeneous third space that combines the two. They can make access to archival materials meaningful in context while integrating game elements to encourage active engagement. As Ole Kjaer Mansfeldt, Ellen Marie Vestager, and Marie Baek Iversen point out in their 2007 study, *Experience Design in City Tourism* for Scandinavia, only 16 percent of tourists are actually motivated to travel by learning history (2008: viii). Yet, they want to be more than tourists—to go off the beaten path and meet the locals—and are attracted by "atmosphere"—by the desire to know the architecture, art, and history of the places they visit (38). These results are suggestive for future AR design. The goals of a city-wide AR project might be to reconnect lived experience of the city to the enriched information we share about its history, culture, and people; to highlight palimpsestic architecture and the practices of diverse communities; and to instantiate frames of reference that operate within the city itself. They might surface contradictory uses, flows, and networks within the city that transcend or cut across point-based annotations and peel away the fabric of the present to help users apprehend change over time—to enrich experiences of the unfolding now.

Further Reading

Acceleration Studies Foundation (2009) *The Metaverse Roadmap: Pathways to the 3D Web*, retrieved from www.metaverseroadmap.org.
Coverley, M. (2010) *Psychogeography*, Harpenden, UK: Oldcastle.
de Souza e Silva, A. and D. M. Sutko (eds.) (2009) *Digital Cityscapes: Merging Digital and Urban Playspaces*, New York, NY: Peter Lang.

References

Ansel Adams Gallery (2015) *Photography Education*, retrieved from www.anseladams.com/photography-education.
Benjamin, W. (2002 [1923–1940]) *The Arcades Project*, trans. H. Eiland and K. McLaughlin, Cambridge, MA: Belknap Press of Harvard University Press.
Blake, E. (2003) "Zograscopes, Virtual Reality, and the Mapping of Polite Society in Eighteenth-Century England," in L. Gitelman and G. B. Pingree (eds.) *New Media, 1740–1915*, Cambridge, MA: MIT Press, pp. 1–30.
Borges, J. L. (1999 [1941]) "The Garden of Forking Paths," in *Collected Fictions*, trans. A. Hurley, New York, NY: Penguin, pp. 119–28.
Borges, J. L. (1999 [1960]) "On Exactitude in Science," in *Collected Fictions*, trans. A. Hurley, New York, NY: Penguin, p. 325.
Chun, W. H. K. (2011) *Programmed Visions: Software and Memory*, Cambridge, MA: MIT Press.
Collaborations, Humanities, Arts and Technology (CHAT) Festival (2012) retrieved from chatfestival2012.org.
Coverley, M. (2010) *Psychogeography*, Harpenden, UK: Oldcastle.
de Certeau, M. (1980) "Walking in the City," in *The Practice of Everyday Life*, trans. S. Rendell, Berkeley, CA: University of California Press, pp. 91–110.
Debord, G. (1955) "Introduction to a Critique of Urban Geography," *Les Livres Nues* 6.
Debord, G. (2006 [1958]) *Situationist International Anthology*, trans. K. Knabb, Berkeley, CA: Bureau of Public Secrets.
Dieleman, H. and D. Huisingh (2006) "Games by which to Learn and Teach about Sustainable Development: Exploring the Relevance of Games and Experiential Learning for Sustainability," *Journal of Cleaner Production* 14, 837–47.

Digital Durham (2015) retrieved from web.duke.edu/digitaldurham/.

Digital Heritage International Congress (DHIC) (2013) retrieved from www.digitalheritage2013.org/thematic-areas.

Ferreri, E. (2012) "A Glimpse of Art's High Tech Future," *Duke Today*, retrieved from today.duke.edu/2012/02/chatnasher.

Frederick, C. (2015) "Art, Futurism, and the Black Imagination," *New York Public Library*, retrieved from www.nypl.org/blog/2015/09/29/art-futurism-black-imagination.

Gamerman, E. (2015) "A Look at the Museum of the Future," *Wall Street Journal*, retrieved from www.wsj.com/articles/alookatthemuseumofthefuture1444940447.

Harley, J. B. and P. Laxton (2002) *The New Nature of Maps: Essays in the History of Cartography*, Baltimore, MD: Johns Hopkins.

Harman, K. and G. Clemans (2010) *The Map as Art: Contemporary Artists Explore Cartography*, Princeton, NJ: Princeton Architectural Press.

Hart, J. (2004) "A New Way of Walking," *Utne Reader* (July/August), retrieved from www.utne.com/community/a-new-way-of-walking.aspx.

Hidden Florence (2015) retrieved from hiddenflorence.org/.

Hildebrand, G. (1992) *The Origins of Architectural Pleasure*, Berkeley, CA: University of California Press.

Huizinga, J. (2014 [1944]) *Homo Ludens: A Study of the Play-Element in Culture*, Eastford, CT: Martino.

Jones, C. (2015) "The Future of History Is Mobile: Experiencing Heritage on Personal Devices," in H. Din and S. Wu (eds.) *Digital Heritage and Culture: Strategy and Implementation*, Singapore: World Scientific, pp. 177–94.

Kolb, D. A. (1984) *Experiential Learning: Experience As the Source of Learning and Development*, New York, NY: Prentiss-Hall.

Lanzoni, K. H., M. J.-V. Olson, and V. E. Szabo (2015), "Wired! and Visualizing Venice: Scaling Up Digital Art History,"*Artl@s Bulletin* 4(1), retrieved from hep://docs.lib.purdue.edu/artlas/vol4/iss1/3.

Lefebvre, H. (1992 [1974]) *The Production of Space*, New York, NY: Wiley-Blackwell.

Lynch, K. (1960) *The Image of the City*, Cambridge, MA: MIT Press.

Mansfeldt, O. K., E. M. Vestager, and M. B. Iversen (2008) *Experience Design in City Tourism*, Norway: Wonderful Copenhagen, Nordic Innovation Centre.

Mäyrä, F. and P. Lankoski (2009) "Play in Hybrid Reality: Alternative Approaches to Game Design," in A. de Souza e Silva and D. M. Sutko *Digital Cityscapes: Merging Digital and Urban Playspaces*, New York, NY: Peter Lang, pp. 129–47.

Monmonier, M. (1996) *How to Lie with Maps*, Chicago, IL: University of Chicago Press.

Museum of London (n.d.) retrieved from www.museumoflondon.org.uk/Resources/app/you-are-here-app/home.html.

Museum Without Walls (2015) *Museum Without Walls Mission* retrieved from www.culturenow.org/mission.

Pickles, J. (2003) *A History of Spaces: Cartographic Reason, Mapping, and the Geo-Coded World*, New York, NY: Routledge.

Poe, E. A. (1840) "The Man of the Crowd," retrieved from www.gutenberg.org/files/2151/2151-h/2151-h.htm.

Reacting to the Past (n.d.) retrieved from reacting.barnard.edu.

Rudinsky, J. and V. E. Szabo (2013) "Innerspace Adventure," *AR2View*, retrieved from v1b3.com/art2view/ARCAAFINAL.pdf.

Ruecker, S., M. Radzikowska, and S. Sinclair (2011) "I See What I Can Do: Affordances of Rich Prospect Browsing," in *Visual Interface Design for Digital Cultural Heritage: A Guide to Rich-Prospect Browsing*, Farnham, U.K.: Ashgate, pp. 29–57.

Schiavo, L. B. (2003) "From Phantom Image to Perfect Vision: Physiological Optics, Commercial Photography, and the Popularization of the Stereoscope," in L. Gitelman and G. B. Pingree (eds.) *New Media, 1740–1915*, Cambridge, MA: MIT Press, pp. 113–38.

Sewchuk, D. (2005) "Experiential Learning—A Theoretical Framework for Perioperative Education," *AORN Journal* 81(6), 1311–18.

Soundwalk (2015) retrieved from www.soundwalk.com.

Sterling, B. (2010) "Augmented Reality: Invading the Museum of Modern Art," *Wired*, retrieved from www.wired.com/2010/10/augmented-reality-invading-the-museum-of-modern-art.

Tatera, K. (2015) "Virtual Reality Turns Your City into a Game Board," *The Science Explorer*, retrieved from thescienceexplorer.com/technology/virtual-reality-turns-your-city-game-board.

Terdiman, D. (2011) "Jane McGonigal Hits New York Public Library in New Game," *C-Net*, retreived from www.cnet.com/news/jane-mcgonigal-hits-new-york-public-library-in-new-game.

Thiel, T. (2011) "Tamiko Thiel @Venice Biennial 2011," *ManifestARBlog*, retrieved from manifestarblog.wordpress.com/thiel_venice-2011.

Trepanier, N. (2014) "The Assassin's Perspective: Teaching History with Video Games," *Perspectives on History* 52(5), retrieved from www.historians.org/publications-and-directories/perspectives-on-history/may-2014/the-assassin%E2%80%99s-perspective.

Tuan, Y-T. (2001) *Space and Place: The Perspective of Experience*, Minneapolis, MN: University of Minnesota Press.

Visualizing Venice (2016) retrieved from www.visualizingvenice.org.

Wood, D., J. Fels, and J. Krygier (2010) *Rethinking the Power of Maps*, New York, NY: Guilford Press.

39

EXPERIENCING DIGITAL AFRICANA STUDIES

Bringing the Classroom to Life

Bryan Carter

Digital humanities is one of my many passions and has been so since 1997, before I even knew what the term was or meant. Although there is no one clear definition of digital humanities, I believe it can be generally agreed that they are a set of theories that explore how various technologies can be used to help understand the human condition. Equally as interesting to me is how a variety of technologies can be used in the classroom to help an instructor engage the learning environment. Likewise, this sort of learning environment helps students become connected to the content differently than with traditional modes, by assisting them in expressing their understanding of course content in meaningful, creative, humanistic, and knowledgeable ways. I am committed to exploring not only how technology can be used to enhance the humanities, but also how the humanities can inform new technological directions. A good example of this idea is how novelist William Gibson (who coined the term, "cyberspace") wrote in *Neuromancer* (1984) about what we now call the internet and inspired a generation of computer programmers to build virtual environments. Because of my research specialty—African American literature of the early twentieth century, specifically the Harlem Renaissance—and my position in an Africana Studies department, I am particularly interested in how new technologies can be used in my Africana Studies courses.

A colleague of mine, Dr. Howard Rambsy, also found in this Companion, has mentioned on a number of occasions that new technologies are interesting in Africana Studies because he believes students of color *do* technology differently when given the opportunity. While I agree that many African American students and students of color have less exposure to cutting edge media technologies, an increasing number of them are fairly well versed with a variety of social media and productivity tools, many of which are not the traditional ones used in the classroom (Lenhart 2015). It has been my experience as well that, in addition to students of color adding a certain flare to creative research projects after becoming familiar with new technologies, *all* of my students exhibit what I call a "4-D expression" of their understanding of specific course content dealing with Africana Studies. I suggest that 4-D expression is a combination of Africana content with an increased understanding of the human condition, along with an introduction to, and fascination with, new media technologies, which tend to heighten empathy and appreciation in course content that is manifested through creative course projects. Perhaps, to the ongoing conversation about technology and the future regarding people of African descent, we should add an introduction to, and examples of, *Digital Africana Studies* and how they bring the classroom to life.

Closely aligned with digital humanities, Digital Africana Studies are also informed by a number of theories, including Afrofuturism (Nelson 2002) and eBlack Studies (eBlack Studies Workshop 2008). While these important discussions help include people of color in conversations about both the future and tools to understand the past, the pedagogical and methodological parts—or how Africana content can be made differently accessible, understood, appreciated, and expressed in the classroom by everyone—are often missing. As a 4-D experience, Digital Africana Studies is a specific conversation about what happens in the Africana classroom that is directly informed by Afrofuturism and eBlack Studies. Therefore, my research in Digital Africana Studies inherently intertwines research, pedagogy, *and* methodology, as they each inform one another, inspiring new avenues of creative and critical inquiry; in my mind, one does not exist without the other.

Bringing the classroom to life is no easy task. As most will admit, engaging students can be challenging, and doing so while simultaneously incorporating new technologies can sometimes be overwhelming. When considering the use of technology in the classroom, there are a few givens, some uncertainties, and a number of crucial questions that must be answered. First, it is a given that an instructor has researched extensively and is a content expert in the classroom, has considered a number of ways to present that content to students, and has designed a variety of ways to assess learning. What may be less certain are the types of technology that might be helpful in the classroom, the tools to which students have access, or the operating systems that are necessary before making any choices. However, the fundamental questions an instructor must first address include: What technological, pedagogical, methodological, and research problems need to be engaged in the classroom? What is my comfort level with technology? My students' comfort level? What basic tools are available in the classroom? What tools are accessible to me and my students outside of the learning environment? If these issues are not first addressed, and some discussion is not held with students on the interrelatedness of tools with learning, then any use of technology will almost always result in frustrations for everyone involved.

I was very fortunate that, at the beginning of my foray into digital humanities and Digital Africana Studies (before I even knew I was venturing into either field), colleagues primed me to address these very issues up front. What problems did I want to address in the classroom? I wanted to engage students enrolled in my African American literature classes differently. I wanted to experientially, visually, and tactilely connect them to a period in African American life and culture in ways that I hoped would help them connect differently, through the literature we studied, an engagement with the past, and their own perspectives and understanding. I considered my comfort level with traditional technologies to be rather high, but, in 1997, virtual reality (VR) was an entirely new thing for me and many other people in academia. Working with the Advanced Technology Center at the University of Missouri-Columbia solved much of that problem, as well as issues related to access. This new unit on the Missouri-Columbia campus was tasked with developing VR projects and introducing a new level of advanced visualization to the university community. The Virtual Harlem Project was one of three projects selected as testbeds for this technology.

At this time, I also began considering ways to assess aspects of using VR in the classroom. Early on, I gravitated toward comparative analysis, looking at differences in oral and written expression between those enrolled in a class using VR and those who were not. This analysis was important because VR and the use of similar technologies, such as videogames, were so new that many of us had to conduct research to justify using them, explaining why we were putting so much time, money, and effort into this sort of experience. Even as comparisons were done that demonstrated higher levels of description, awareness of one's surroundings, and aural interpretation of a literary context, I became aware of new, emerging questions that were not before possible—new areas of inquiry only made visible by immersing oneself within a content-rich, participatory environment. So it was at the University of Missouri-Columbia, specifically through the development of the Virtual Harlem Project, that Digital Africana Studies was born, before words were there to adequately describe the field of research.

The overall vision of Virtual Harlem was to create a visually and even tactilely rich 3-D environment that would allow visitors to experience what may have helped inspire the creative works of the Harlem Renaissance, circa the 1920s. I did not realize how complex this vision was until well into the first year of researching visual and aural content for the construction of the 3-D space. This complexity not only included the technical details of Virtual Harlem, but also the pedagogical and methodological aspects of creating an environment reminiscent of an actual historic location (Sosnoski, Harkin, & Carter 2006). Critically considering facets of the environment that should or should not be included, and why, became an integral part of planning meetings before construction even began. Also of primary importance, and related to our discussion in this chapter, was how the environment was to be used in class: not just how *I* would use it, but also how I envisioned *students* using it and why they may tend to use it in one particular way or another. Thus, research, methodology, and pedagogy were all a part of Virtual Harlem from its inception.

As the project evolved, became larger (e.g., incorporating Virtual Montmartre, the eighteenth Arrondissement in Paris, France and popular destination of rich and famous jazz lovers during the 1920s), more intricate, and situated on a variety of platforms, the research questions also evolved and became more complex. This complexity intensified as the technologies supporting the project advanced, network speeds increased, and more was expected by both students and researchers, all while dealing with fewer research funds available for projects dealing with virtual worlds. Thus, over a multiyear period, Virtual Harlem has existed on high-end supercomputers and in proprietary and distributed virtual worlds. It is currently being developed with the Unity 3-D platform. Through this third iteration of the project, lessons learned from earlier versions are being addressed and additional innovations incorporated.

When one considers working within digital humanities, rarely is there a sustained discussion about maintenance or evolution of projects as technology advances. Graphics are getting better, data transfer rates are increasing, processors are getting faster, and mobile devices are being introduced at an alarming rate. So where does this leave a project developed using one platform, technology, or "location"? Do we consider where the project will be 3, 5, or even 10 years down the road? Maintenance is one of the new questions generated as we explore the use of virtual worlds. As digital humanists, we must not only learn to visualize the present development and use of our projects but also have a view of the future as part of our overall vision. This way, proper plans can be put in place at the beginning. Virtual Harlem 1 was developed on rather high-end, silicon graphic supercomputers and encompassed approximately ten blocks of a portion of Harlem, New York as it existed during its Renaissance of the

1920s. Throughout the life of the first version, the primary focus was on access to content and navigation through the space. Limitations included less than perfect placement of historic locations and less than stellar graphic performance. In 1997–98, there was still the perceived expectation that VR was going to deliver much more than was possible on most computers. Try as we may, the massive virtual worlds suggested by Gibson's cyberspace (1982) or Stephenson's Metaverse (1992), where individuals could interact with one another through various personae from any location, were way before their time, until, that is, the introduction of Second Life.

When Virtual Harlem evolved into Second Life in 2005 (Harlem 2), predictions by VR advocates during the 1980s and 1990s were apparently coming true: massive numbers of individuals interacted with one another while being physically located anywhere in the world where there was a stable and fast network connection. Voice, interactivity, animations, and commerce were all part of Harlem 2 when the project moved into Second Life. However, because of the proprietary nature of asset development that did not conform to industry standards, as well as a number of business decisions regarding ownership and copyright of those assets by Linden Lab (the parent company of Second Life), the Harlem 2 environment flourished and then stalled, unable to keep pace with the rapid graphic and interactive evolution of the videogame industry.

Virtual Harlem evolved, grew, and then shrank in Second Life, and later in its parallel open source platform, Open Simulator, for 7 years. During this time, a number of courses were taught fully within Virtual Harlem, and countless collaborations also occurred and evolved between faculty, students, and people outside of academia who were interested in the period and potential of the project. The results of these collaborative efforts brought the classroom to life through performance, content development, experiential learning, role playing, machinima, and new, creative modes of presentation and research (Carter 2009). Unfortunately, the limitations inherent with these platforms became more glaring as 3-D assets became more complex, the ability to interact with increasing numbers of simultaneous users was limited, and access from mobile devices and game consoles was never realized. As a result, development of Harlem 3 began in 2012 on a platform designed to address most, if not all, of the aforementioned concerns.

Unity 3-D is a platform for creating virtual worlds and games that accepts 3-D assets (or models) saved in Open Standards format, meaning nearly any 3-D modeling tool can be used to create assets before they are imported into the platform. This environment also enables people to build assets once and render them to a variety of sources (e.g., PC, tablet, game console, or mobile devices). Finally, Unity allows users to connect using a variety of 3-D immersive headsets (e.g., Oculus Rift or HTC Vive). The design and engagement plan for Harlem 3 takes advantage of the enhanced capabilities of Unity 3-D to incorporate higher resolution graphics, nonplayer character animations through motion capture, increased accuracy of user movement, and a wider variety of realistic avatars, to name a few. We also have two plans for increasing the number of simultaneous users who can access Virtual Harlem. The first option will be through Unity Web, which deploys a web version of the environment. For this option, users only need the Unity 3-D plugin, which works in most browsers. Limitations on the number of simultaneous users are based on bandwidth and the RAM of the host server. The second option involves our work with Virtual World Web. This company built a 3-D web browser called Curio, which enables navigation through both the 2-D web and 3-D environments with one interface. Virtual World Web has also patented a technology that enables hundreds of avatars to populate the same space with no noticeable degradation in performance, all while using Unity 3-D as the underlying runtime engine. The revamped version of Virtual Harlem will be deployed using both of these platforms. Recent internal funding from the University of Arizona has also allowed a total revision of the Virtual Harlem Project to place significant buildings in their historically accurate locations using OpenStreetMap. Once finished, this revision will enable new methods, including geographic information systems (GIS) data and augmented reality, to be employed in Virtual Harlem.

Related to VR, augmented reality (AR) is a relatively new technology where virtual content is layered over the real world in a variety of ways. A good example is the Berlin Wall 3-D project, where users of an AR application can point their camera phones where the Berlin Wall once existed and actually "see" the wall on their screen. Layered on top of the real world, this virtual wall is supplemented with other content, such as video narratives, textual information, and audio narration.

When considering the use of AR in my Africana Studies courses, I contemplated not only how to do it but, most importantly, *why*. Soon, much of our lives will be augmented in some way or another. Caitlin Fisher and her work with the Augmented Reality Lab at York University are demonstrating the relevance of AR through a variety of projects. John Pavlik's work on AR as storytelling is also an example of this innovation's effective use in the classroom (Pavlik & Bridges 2013). Automobiles are already incorporating heads-up displays, augmenting the road ahead with a variety of information. Google Glass 1, which has been removed from the market (but is being revised by Google), and other wearable technologies are being introduced, enabling users to obtain additional information about their environments, perform basic communication tasks such as email and social networking, and easily record the world right before their eyes. Magazines and newspapers are developing AR content, enhancing the interactivity of what was once considered a passive mode of information display. To justify using this technology in my classes, I suggest to both students and peers that AR is a part of our collective future; and, for Africana Studies to be a part of that conversation, good examples of AR in the Africana Studies classroom are necessary. Part of the planning also includes finding a cross-platform development tool that is free for students, faculty, or nonprofit organizations, explaining to students how and why this tool is being used, showing them examples of AR in the context of our class, and helping them create augmented experiences of their own.

I selected two AR applications to introduce to my students in my course, "When African Americans Came to Paris." This course explores the African American expatriate presence in Paris from just before the turn of the twentieth century through the 1960s. One of its highlights is a short-term study abroad trip to Paris, where students experience what we research throughout the term. It made sense to me that AR could be employed during our trip and throughout the term. VR was not feasible in this instance, but most students had smart devices of some sort and the accessibility of AR was becoming more apparent. The AR application I chose was selected not only for its usability but also because it has a cross-platform viewer and web-based development interface. Layar offers students, faculty, and nonprofit organizations a number of free "pages" or "augments" that stay active for one year, with the option to extend them for an additional period. According to their website, Layar was founded in 2009 and quickly gained international attention as one of the first mobile, augmented reality browsers to hit the market. It touts itself as a global leader in AR and interactive print, helping to bridge the gap between print and digital worlds. The company has a sponsored program that offers credits to educators and students. Layar Creator is one of the primary reasons I selected Layar, mostly because of its ease of use and functionality.

It is web-based, and, after logging in, prompts users through the process of creating their first augmented experience. After uploading a "trigger image," users are then instructed to identify or upload interactive elements that will appear on top of the trigger image when it is scanned by Layar on a mobile device.

In class, this application was used by a number of students during "topic discussions," an assignment that is similar to a presentation but more interactive and engaging. During a topic discussion, images are placed around the room. After downloading and installing Layar on their mobile device, students walk around the room scanning the various images, use Google Docs to collaboratively document and describe the images, and engage one another both face-to-face and through a Twitter feed. Using Layar in Paris involved students augmenting a number of points along a tour route related to African American expatriate Paris with additional information. This example of authentic experiential learning through augmented reality included image carousels, audio files, short video clips, links to websites, and Twitter feeds. Advanced visualization fit well in this case because Paris is a very visual city, but also because the period we were studying produced a wide variety of visual media. Using AR also encouraged students to consider issues related to visualization, visuality, and the gaze, combining these ideas with those presented through the novels, poetry, and essays assigned throughout the term. The use of AR to explore these ideas became just as seamless and normalized as the ways in which visuality played, and still plays, a crucial aspect in our society.

Unfortunately, few projects related to Africana culture use AR or VR technologies. A logical new direction for research is to explore how these or other advanced tools can be used to not only explore and inform users about Africana life and culture, but also immerse them within those cultures. Additionally, they can be used to attract other students who were not expecting to learn anything about the subject matter to become intrigued by it and want to learn more. In addition to this, I am keenly aware of how much of an impact on our culture gaming has and will continue to have. The edutainment aspect of the Virtual Harlem Project, as well as my current research projects in AR, are efforts to capitalize on the curiosities of a new generation of young people who may be interested in gaming, advanced visualization, and interactive tools and, through those media, may ultimately become more informed about various aspects of Africana culture. The wonderful thing about using these tools and connecting their use with historical moments like the Harlem Renaissance is the reflexivity related to both. During the Renaissance, entertainers, artists, intellectuals, and activists traveled around the world, exchanging ideas and techniques, learning from one another, and later incorporating those new methods into their own modes of expression. The same is true with digital technologies. By using them, the Africana Studies scholar not only learns new methodologies and techniques but also informs the development of new environments, code, or modes of interaction that address specific aspects of Africana Culture, thus inspiring coders to both learn about the culture and move in one direction or another based on need or desire. Bringing the classroom to life can take many forms, and the two methods outlined above are examples of the many interactive technologies employed in my Africana Studies courses.

So, what do these developments in AR and VR offer the Digital Africana scholar? I believe they offer five very real and distinct possibilities. First, VR offers the opportunity to fully immerse oneself into a collaborative, participatory, engaging environment focusing on moments in Africana Culture. Second, VR offers the opportunity to explore aspects of personae, passing, alternate realities, out of body performances, and the gaze, where new questions about the self and how one views others and is viewed by them are the primary area of focus. Third, AR offers the opportunity to enhance our existing environments with relevant, accurate, useful, and culturally oriented information and experiences. Furthermore, AR encourages new questions about authenticity, inclusion, and ownership to be considered differently. Finally, and perhaps most exciting, the combination of VR with AR creates compelling experiences in the real world. Yet, to help shape those powerful experiences into something which is not based on traditional stereotypes, Digital Africana Studies scholars must be aware of such technological advances and familiar enough with them to tell our own stories within new digital spaces.

Acknowledgments

I would like to thank the Confluence Center for Digital Inquiry, Innovative Classroom Spaces, and the Africana Studies Program at the University of Arizona for supporting this research.

Further Reading

DeFrantz, T. (2003) "Believe the Hype: Hype Williams and Afrofuturist Filmmaking," *Refractory: A Journal of Entertainment Media*, retrieved from refractory.unimelb.edu.au/2003/08/27/believe-the-hype-hype-williams-and-afrofuturist-filmmaking-thomas-f-defrantz.

Nelson, A. (2002) "Introduction: Future Texts," *Social Text* 71, 20(2), 1–15.

Rockeymoore, M. A. (2002) "What Is Afrofuturism?" *AuthorsDen.com*, retrieved from www.authorsden.com/visit/viewarticle.asp?id=4308&AuthorID=7174.

References

Augmented Reality Lab (n.d.) York University, retrieved from ar.lab.yorku.ca/.

Carter, B. (2009) "Enhancing Virtual Environments," in J. Molka-Danielsen and M. Deutschmann (eds.) *Learning and Teaching in the Virtual World of Second Life*, Norway: Tapir Academic Press, pp. 103–14.

eBlack Studies Workshop (2008) "The Next Movement in Black Studies: 'eBlack Studies,'" Department of African-American Studies, University of Illinois at Urbana-Champaign, retrieved from eblackstudies.org/workshop/.

Gibson, W. (1982) "Burning Chrome," *Omni* 4 (July), 72–77, 102–04.

Gibson, W. (1984) *Neuromancer*, New York, NY: Ace.

Lenhart, A. (2015) "Teens, Social Media & Technology Overview 2015," *Pew Research Center: Internet, Science, & Tech*, retrieved from www.pewinternet.org/2015/04/09/teens-social-media-technology-2015.

Nelson, A. (ed.) (2002) *Afrofuturism: A Special Issue of Social Text, Social Text* 71, 20(2), Durham, NC: Duke University Press.

Pavlik, J. V. and F. Bridges (2013) "The Emergence of Augmented Reality (AR) as a Storytelling Medium in Journalism," *Journalism & Communication Monographs* 15(1), 4–59, retrieved from jmo.sagepub.com/content/15/1/4.short?rss=1.

Sosnoski, J. J., P. Harkin, and B. Carter (2006) "Configuring History: Teaching the Harlem Renaissance through Virtual Reality Cityscapes," in S. Jones (ed.) *Digital Formations*, New York, NY: Peter Lang.

Stephenson, N. (1992) *Snow Crash*, New York, NY: Bantam Books.

40

ENGAGEMENTS WITH RACE, MEMORY, AND THE BUILT ENVIRONMENT IN SOUTH AFRICA

A Case Study in Digital Humanities

Angel David Nieves

Today, digital reconstructions of historical environments "seem to be everywhere," notes architectural historian Diane Favro—who has, for two decades now, argued for the use of 3-D models in helping researchers to understand Ancient Rome (2012: 273). With their hyper-realistic CGI (computer-generated imagery) of buildings and landscapes, popular films such as *Gladiator* (2000), *Pompeii* (2014), and *Exodus: Gods and Kings* (2014) have also helped to increase public interest in digital reconstructions (Farvo 2006; Gill 2009; Snyder 2012). Much of this work, however, fails to provide the public with a more complex understanding of a building's history over time and its symbolic or material importance to a variety of constituencies. My experience documenting memory and the built environment in postapartheid South Africa suggests a model that could animate practice in the U.S. and elsewhere as well.

As an American activist digital humanities scholar of both the built environment and the African Diaspora, I was compelled to focus on South African history while researching African American women activists during the Jim Crow era of the United States. Among these women's peers was a South African named, Charlotte Maxeke, who had graduated from Wilberforce College in Ohio (now Wilberforce University) in 1908. Maxeke returned to South Africa and became active in the promotion of Methodist Church boarding and day schools for black South Africans as educational opportunities for Blacks were being chipped away under the dominant apartheid regime. By following the trail to South Africa, I became interested in the web of connections among the black, colored, and white South Africans who were resisting apartheid at that time. Eventually, I was determined to lay a theoretical groundwork for my research into the racialized space of apartheid-era Soweto in Johannesburg, South Africa. As such, my work has brought together historical reconstructions and digital ethnography as tools to expose gross human rights violations and forms of spatial resistance against the apartheid state.

Today, my research into the events of Soweto and South Africa's Student Uprisings of 1976—now in a process of recovery and memorialization—remains grounded in contested history.

It is without dispute that the morning of June 16, 1976, which marks the beginning of the Soweto Uprising, is an exemplary moment in the "common officializing memory" of South Africa's black townships. Then, black African students marching to protest the adoption of Afrikaans as the primary language of instruction for schools in Johannesburg's "South Western Townships" (SO-WE-TO) were gunned downed by members of the South African police and security forces. The physical backdrop to these events, the so-called "model native township" of Soweto, was made up of a series of systematically planned, would-be South African garden cities with the primary purpose of reinforcing the powers and capacities of the state system of apartheid. Physical spaces such as these, built under apartheid, have provided the social, political, and economic context for black urban life since the founding of Johannesburg in 1886. However, few studies have considered the historical significance of these townships as extant physical artifacts of a difficult past. This lack of scholarship is particularly timely as townships now face complex heritage issues and the concurrent pressures of the international tourist market.

Microhistorical Reconstruction: *Digital Townships*

Readers of this volume might be aware of the many contested definitions of digital humanities (DH). Classic uses of DH include data mining, crowdsourcing, and various GIS strategies, including deep mapping, explorations in literary geography, the use of LIDAR technology, and 3-D reconstructions while attempting to answer humanities-based questions. DH can also act as a set of research practices employing the organization and analysis of "big data" in the service of humanities inquiry. In light of both the current limitations and boundless possibilities of computer programming, as well as the present day state of historical recovery and the monumental task of inputting data, DH will often find itself researching macro and micro worlds—both extant or erased, as in the case of South Africa. A macrohistory may privilege the prominent changes over time, such as construction, destruction, and shifts in the physical structure of a location. Meanwhile, a microhistory invests in more specific contextual details, including stories of relevant events and the everyday roles of people involved in the construction or history of the location. My own work is what you might call *microhistorical reconstruction*: the project of virtually re-creating the detailed histories of the local, domestic, or residential. Imagine, for example, the forensics of resistance in a local shebeen or tavern, as it were, or at a small farm in the outskirts of Rivonia, Johannesburg. DH at this scale permits a reconstruction of "real life" unthinkable in other kinds of spatial historiography.

My work with microhistorical reconstruction began with a prototype for *Soweto '76: A Living Digital Archive*, where I served as a faculty fellow at the Maryland Institute for Technology in the Humanities (MITH) at the University of Maryland, College Park. *Soweto '76* is a prototype for an online multimedia archive of the holdings of Johannesburg's Hector Pieterson Memorial and Museum. Using existing oral histories, testimonies, photographs, video footage, material objects, and sound recordings in the collections of the Hector Pieterson Memorial and Museum, the work seeks to redress the existing portrayal of the lives of township residents in the mainstream or "official" historical record. The prototype was completed in 2008, followed by the development of *The Soweto Historical Geographic Information System* (SHGIS) and *The Social Justice History Platform*. The SHGIS examines the micro-geography of resistance on the part of South Africa's township residents and the layering of meaning and action engendered in built form during the former apartheid regime there. More generally, *The Social Justice History Platform* is designed to represent geographic and spatial data within an enhanced interface that contextualizes locations and objects alongside primary source documents to provide historical narrative. As a virtual reality-enabled 3-D platform (built atop the Unity engine), *The Social Justice History Platform* is able to represent both 2-D geospatial information (such as maps, photographs, and records) and 3-D representations of landscapes and locations, together with 3-D models of historical buildings and objects. The platform also lets users explore changes to those locations or objects over the course of a defined timeline of its history, allowing for an interactive view that lets users step backward or forward through a location's changes over time.

And yet another project, *Digital Townships*, builds on both *Soweto '76* and SHGIS to build a historical GIS database drawn from a collection of 39 largely unseen maps, architectural plans, and drawings discovered at the National Archives of South Africa. These documents—dating from the 1890s to the 1960s and developed by architects, engineers, and city planners—provide great insights into the design and construction of model township communities for the City of Johannesburg during the apartheid era. That these existing idealized township designs were never realized for a variety of political, social, and economic factors is a topic that no researcher has yet to discuss in the fields of historical GIS and historical geography. The *Digital Townships* project proposes the (real-time) 3-D visualization of historical GIS in a virtual world and addresses questions of power and reconciliation by using gaming conventions to represent indigenous cultures, particularly in South Africa, as they relate to racial segregation, colonialism, and resistance against the state through the built environment.

The first conceptual model for the *Digital Townships* project involves converting existing 2-D map and satellite/aerial photography data into a 3-D representation of the Soweto region. (*Digital Townships* is, in part, an effort to start an online encyclopedia of townships across South Africa, much like Jan Reiff's *Encyclopedia of Chicago*.) This portion of our work hopes to achieve an expansion of the geo-rectification efforts begun in our partnership with Middlebury College, further enhancing these maps to include a third dimension including both topography and the built environment. Thematically, a central goal of this project is the communication of the contrasts between the plans and the realities of urban planning in such regions. By utilizing a 3-D environment and visualizing these differences, a striking and effective communication of the project's messages will show at once what was built within the township and, perhaps equally important, what was not. Moreover, as a largely historical project, the changes to this region over time will be a central goal of the 3-D environment, leveraging its dynamic capabilities to show the township in various states of construction and change over the last 120 years. We believe it will prove equally compelling to compare the original construction plans against both the evolving and the modern states of the townships.

Finally, and perhaps most importantly, in continuing with the theme of historic data, we plan to utilize this 3-D environment as an access point for our vast holding of archival media related to the area, its people, its government, and its history. We envision a unique kind of geo-located archive, where our digital multimedia assets (such as images, audio interviews, video clips, and newspaper articles) can be tagged with geographic coordinates but (as interactive elements of the virtual model) are also associated with individual 3-D features such as buildings, city blocks, and regions. By coding this archive and its materials according to both location and time, this kind of interactive cityscape would allow the archive's users to watch the city both grow and play out as an historical narrative, all enhanced and enlivened by the ability to reach down into the city at any historic moment and explore its historic state and the voices of its people and history itself.

Despite abundant 3-D virtual environments for historic sites that have emerged over the past decade, the impact of historical character modeling in digital humanities has received little scholarly attention. Instead, when characters (or avatars) are used in virtual environments, the emphasis often tends to be on the constructed space—with less attention paid to the modeling of the characters themselves—and how these virtual embodiments impact the viewer/player. While this lapse may be due, in part, to a lag in technology, avatars now have the potential to become increasingly realistic. This presents us with many conceptually significant choices as we create avatars, each with important cultural and historical implications, and we need to think about how to make those choices.

In order to assess that work and its applicability elsewhere in digital humanities, it will be important to develop an inter- and-multidisciplinary framework of analysis that includes models for both theory and practice. As I suggest throughout this chapter, much of this work may be informed by black feminist praxis and intersectional theories and methods as applied to the spatial humanities (Gunew 2013: 23).

Black Feminist Praxis and Intersectionality as Methods for 3-D Virtual Heritage

Academic disciplines are somewhat staggered by the emerging opportunities for researching documentation with respect to GIS and neogeography, given the sheer amount of data now flooding into servers and awaiting analysis and interpretation. "Landscape turns" and "spatial turns" remain buzzwords in the academy. An architect by training, I cannot fail to recall how the act of creating architecture is hugely expensive and, typically, an elitist enterprise; but, as an activist by nature, and as a researcher committed to feminist inquiry, I am also intrigued by how the space of architecture accommodates, inspires, and mobilizes people. So, I pose the question, "Can one join a spatial turn to activist, feminist academic inquiry?"

Today, hallmarks of feminist inquiry include nonhierarchical models of knowledge construction and formation. The "subjects" of patriarchal scholarship may indeed be welcomed as partners in the research process, with the researcher becoming an advocate for community engagement. The feminist researcher embraces an inclusive model of sexuality and does not privilege certain sexual orientations and identities over others. The feminist researcher may also become a facilitator and act as a conduit to institutional structures, using these same structures for the benefit of the community being researched, as opposed to the benefit of the onlooker community. By doing so, the feminist researcher recognizes systems of power and privilege, intending that persons inside and outside the community realize how privilege and patriarchy shape how one thinks and moves in the world.

A recent symposium at the University of Michigan, the "Black Feminist Think Tank," sought to "map key questions, concepts and debates regarding Black feminism's theoretical breadth and political and social praxis," but seemingly overlooked the need for more scholarly work on the internet and the recent emergence of a strong form of "internet feminism," where young black women of color can hold an inordinate amount of power and influence (Poniewozik 2014). As some have argued about the kinds of internal clashes between black and white feminists most recently,

> White women's feminisms still center around *equality* . . . Black women's feminisms demand *justice*. There is a difference. One kind of feminism focuses on the policies that will help women integrate fully into the existing American system. The other recognizes the fundamental flaws in the system and seeks its complete and total transformation.
>
> (Cooper 2014; see also Traister & Schulevitz 2014)

I would instead argue that we have allowed the neoliberal state—i.e., global American capitalism working in tandem with the rump projects of the New Deal and Great Society—with all its many false promises, to divide our politics of solidarity and radical antiracist, feminist knowledge production along these two "camps" (equality vs. transformation), when, in fact, working in collaborative ways to dismantle state-based institutions is our feminist praxis.

My work in South Africa is also very much a project in *media archaeology*, as a kind of methodology in critical media studies where, if we are to understand the current state of the postcolonial archive in South Africa, the centrality of the archive is of utmost importance. It is also important to remember that among Michel Foucault's (1969) contributions to the archaeology of knowledge and culture was his emphasis on it as a methodology for excavating conditions of existence. The series of projects I have been involved with over the past decade have very much been an excavation of material objects in the archive, produced by technologies of the apartheid state and (as I have argued elsewhere) reflective of the spatial locations of resistance in response to state-sponsored terrorism and countless human rights violations.

The Specific Case of the Mandela House

As historian Elizabeth Elbourne points out,

> ideas about domesticity [in South Africa] were frequently used as a weapon in the colonial power struggles between and among Europeans and Africans . . . Ways of talking about houses and domesticity were also, then, ways of talking about the justification for conquest.
>
> (Elbourne 2002: 27–28)

For South African Women's Studies scholar Gabeba Baderoon, the history of "the South African household—both black and white—has been a shadowed one" (2014: 178). Drawing on the work of Jacklyn Cock, she writes, "'the veiled and hidden abode of reproduction—the household'—made possible 'the ultra-exploitability of domestic workers'" (Cock in Baderoon 2014: 178). Interactions both public and private were deeply structured in space, marked by ritualized practices and entrenched inequality. Some have even argued that, because of the sheer scale of the challenges imposed by apartheid's policies over space (architecture and city planning, for instance), South Africans "have," to quote Njabulo Ndebele, "yet to arrive at home" (in Baderoon 2014: 178).

My work shows that the domestic sphere for black women in the townships was home, despite attempts by apartheid's engineers, who sought the active destruction of the family structure through the creation of "dormitory enclaves" designed "to export their energies" (Ndebele in Baderoon 2014: 178). On the contrary, single sex hostels and townships could be self-sustaining areas if we were to begin analyzing them as more than what Belinda Dodson calls "fundamentally a geographical project" (in Baderoon 2014: 179). We have yet to fully explore the "intimate geography" of the house and its many complexities in the township

(179). In particular, recasting microhistory (von Lunen 2013: 221), popularized in the 1970s, into a kind of *spatial microhistory* could build a bridge between *historical GIS* and *historical studies using GIS*, including qualitative data from digital ethnographies. A *spatial microhistory* works from the premise that both the social and cultural history of everyday individuals can be inferred through the use of various interdisciplinary research methods, including feminist geography, critical race theory, and feminist GIS. This approach might allow us to begin understanding the network of individuals from across the various townships who participated in the student uprisings of 1976 and how those activist networks were embedded into the physical geography and architecture of individual houses. Examining forms of resistance at various scales, from the micro to the macro, will also allow us to document the ways in which activists such as Steve Biko came to Soweto from the Eastern Cape. Much of my work in the spatial humanities as a field "relies upon powerful geospatial technologies and methods to explore new questions about the relationship of space to human behavior and social, economic, political and cultural development," which I will discuss in more detail later (The Polis Center 2016).

My work on the Nelson Mandela House materials is evidence of an intimate geography in a very particular township home. Several video clips I have been working with are part of a series of interviews conducted in 2008 with members of the Mandela family. The interviews were conducted as part of a comprehensive tourism planning and heritage re-development project that included the Mandela House. Many of these heritage projects were in preparation for the 2010 FIFA World Cup that was to be held across South Africa (Walker et al. 2013). Then, Haley Sharpe, an international tourism, heritage, and visual communications management solutions company was appointed by the Soweto Heritage Trust to undertake the research and restoration of Mandela's family home at 8115 Vilakazi Street, Orlando West, Soweto. Haley Sharpe was also asked to include plans for the design and construction of new visitor facilities and an interpretation plan. Many of these interviews remain unseen and will comprise part of a forthcoming Omeka/WordPress online archive and publication entitled *8115 Vilakazi*. The interviews include Winnie Madikizela-Mandela, her two daughters Zenani (b. 1959) and Zindziswa (b. 1960), and the documentary photographer Alf Khumalo. Zenani was age four when her father was sent to prison, and she was not able to visit him in prison until 1974, when she was a teenager. Zindziswa Mandela (or Zindzi) is the younger of his two daughters.

While I am not trying to reify the heroine figure through my discussion of Madikizela-Mandela—something that would repeat the trappings of the officializing, state-sponsored meta-narrative—I understand that hers is an incredibly complicated narrative that, as I see it, helps us/me frame a number of entry points for telling complex histories, including LGBTQi histories, which move us beyond the typical historiography of the period. The denial of a more complex layering of history—including the killing of a queer youth in Mandela's home—is perhaps one of the most glaring examples where the queer and activist community there was suppressed or erased. However, the technologies now at our disposal can allow us to layer the story using multiple tools for mapping, text mining, and 3-D visualizations so that Winnie Mandela's narrative serves as a necessary transition into a difficult queer history that acts as more than the officializing memory of social justice and human rights. Digital humanities may actually help us sort through these issues and can also help both reconstruct and recover a history that is still very early in the telling, despite what we think we know about the liberation struggle (particularly due to the "liberation struggle industry"). The layering of many narratives also helps lay bare the messiness of archive making, the methodologies of digital ethnography, and the endangered nature of archives across South

Africa. I know how very charged the history of Soweto is, particularly that surrounding Madikizela-Mandela, a history which has still not been fully told. There is also value in what we find in the post-apartheid, South African state's Truth and Reconciliation Commission's (TRC) memory-making process when we are facing the "disappearance" of records from the National Archives. Telling these stories requires not only a careful, feminist, and gender-based praxis of collaboration but also working in community-based organizations.

The Mandela House at 8115 Vilakazi is not "a typical township house, in an ordinary township" as Madikizela-Mandela suggests in an interview (Haines & Mandela 2008). She is perhaps hinting that any other house in Soweto could have been substituted for hers, but hers was, indeed, the headquarters for most of the planning behind the student uprising in June of 1976. In another portion of the interview, she finally makes clear that

> [the house] *was headquarters for every activity that took place in the country* and some of the stuff I can't tell you of course, otherwise I'll revive terrible memories to those we were fighting with. Ja, no, *it was the headquarters, all decisions were taken even part of the 1976 uprising, the consultations took place there, so it was a hive of activity . . . Meetings took place right there, because they never thought we would meet there.*
>
> (Haines & Mandela 2008, emphasis added).

Resistance occurred under the guise or cloak of the domestic sphere, in this "ordinary house," as opposed to a kind of resistance resulting from a patriarchal imagination.

Madikizela-Mandela was the victim of incarceration, physical violence, banning, and systematic harassment at the hands of the South African authorities while her husband, Nelson Mandela, remained jailed for 27 years. She was detained and tortured by security forces, in part for her support of the Soweto uprisings of 1976. Madikizela-Mandela, "like many other women involved in political struggles against colonial regimes, has been the target of ongoing state violence and of state and media efforts to depict her as a 'wicked' woman" (Pohlandt-McCormick 2000: 586). Through the mid-1980s, she became a vocal proponent of the African National Congress' use of strategic violence, a position she defended in a 1985 speech:

> I will tell you why we are violent. It is because those who oppress us are violent. The Afrikaner knows only one language: the language of violence . . . all that is left to us is this painful process of violence.
>
> (Phillips & Reyes 2011: 141)

In 1986 she was influential in bringing resolution to a conflict within the Orlando West branch of the Soweto Youth Congress (SOYCO); it resulted in the formation of the Mandela United Football Club (MUFC) (*The Independent* 1998). A number of the youths involved in this conflict moved into the outbuildings of the Mandela home and were later implicated in a series of killings.

Madikizela-Mandela's fall from "Mother of the Nation" (or Mama Wetu) to deviant "Mugger of that Nation" began in 1986 with her infamous statement regarding the necklacing of her opponents (immolation with gasoline and flaming rubber tires around the neck): "Together, hand in hand, with our boxes of matches and our necklaces we shall liberate this country" (Phillips & Reyes 2011: 142). Just two years later, Nelson Mandela, while still at Poolsmoor Prison, requested that the Soweto community call upon the Crisis Committee to investigate the abduction of four youths who were being held by the MUFC. The first in a series of incidents began as far back as May 1987, when two brothers, Peter and Philip Makhanda, were taken by force to the back rooms of the Mandela home and assaulted. One of the victims was fourteen-year-old Stompie Moeketsi Seipei (allegedly gay and, Winnie's partisans allege, an informer for security forces of the apartheid regime), who was later found on an open piece of land between New Canada and Soweto, dead of stab wounds and severe injuries to his skull. For over 18 months between August 1988 and the end of February 1989, occupants of the Mandela household at 8115 Vilakazi Street and the house in Diepkloof Extension were implicated in a range of criminal incidents including assaults, abduction, and the attempted murder of over a dozen individuals. Madikizela-Mandela's team of bodyguards from the MUFC were charged with kidnapping four youths (including Seipei) from a gay white Methodist minister's home in Soweto and taking them to her house, where they were savagely beaten.

If the house at 8115 Vilakazi was re-interpreted—to include not only the officializing narrative of the TRC (that it currently depicts), but also a multilayered spatial microhistory, displayed or rendered visible through virtual technologies—we could easily imagine a radical queer politics and feminist analysis for understanding the contributions of South Africa's LGBTQi community to its liberation history (something severely lacking in the historiography of the period). Indeed, would it be possible to tell a queer history of that "typical township house" at 8115 Vilakazi?

We know that the "blanket" amnesty afforded by the TRC has been chipped away at, with some cases being re-opened or re-examined to make possible individual prosecutions for grievous acts. In her interview, Madikizela-Mandela seems very cognizant that she and other former activists or students could easily be put back into jeopardy. Later in that same interview, she says that the others (those who were a part of the 1976 uprisings) will have to tell their own stories and that she will not be so presumptuous as to do it for them. The TRC eventually found her

> politically and morally accountable for the gross violations of human rights committed by the MUFC. The commission finds that Ms. Madikizela-Mandela failed to account to the community and political structures. The commission finds that Madikizela-Mandela was responsible, by omission, for the commission of gross violations of human rights.
>
> (Pohlandt-McCormick 2000: 585)

The contentious public memory generated by the TRC allowed South Africa to advance to a democratic praxis because it laid bare the many inconsistencies in values and goals.

Public Memory and Matters of Representation

Public memory, like other forms of memory, exists on a broad spectrum between memory as object and memory as process. At times, memory becomes more fixed in the public imaginary; and at other times, it primarily consists of contestation over how to remember the past (Phillips & Reyes 2011: 135). The TRC's state-sanctioned status enabled them to transform what is widespread knowledge into formally recognized "truths." This process allows the state to acknowledge its misdeeds. Fortunately, this process has not, however, made certain that the state-sanctioned official narrative of events becomes circumscribed in all of the extant physical locations of the liberation struggle. Alex Boraine, deputy chairperson of the commission, describes the commission as a "third way" of dealing with the past, one that prioritized truth gathering and reconciliation over retributive justice. For Boraine,

> South Africans desperately needed to create a *common memory* that can be acknowledged by those who created and implemented the apartheid system, by those who fought against it, and by the many more who were in the middle and claimed not to know what was happening in the country.
>
> (Boraine 2006: 312)

This production of a "common memory" of the apartheid past constituted a multifaceted effort to create a new democratic South Africa. It has meant that a multilayered, complex, and often contradictory public history narrative does not exist in museums, heritage sites, or state-sponsored programs. An unstable or flexible, highly iterative process for collecting and interpreting those histories therefore cannot exist unless we begin to make digital interventions—across multiple platforms and interfaces—accessible to a wide public audience.

In the early days of the internet, some scholars imagined it would function as a virtual space where people would go to free themselves of their embodied racial and gender identities. In the 1990s, Sherry Turkle, Nicholas Negroponte, and other scholars saw "a new horizon of possibilities awaited where visual appearance and 'otherness' were not as apparent as in 'real life'" (Jenson et al. 2015: 860). Some saw the internet as a "utopia" where there is "no race, no gender." The reality (or virtual reality) that has emerged is quite different; race and racism persist in ways that are unique to the internet while also recapitulating centuries-old beliefs and stereotypes. I would argue that the internet holds serious implications for not only understanding whiteness, but also engaging in more critical discourses informed by feminist and queer theory about representation.

Character Modeling, Race, and Avatars

In the spring of 2014, colleagues from five different institutions and I were awarded a National Endowment for the Humanities (NEH) Office of Digital Humanities (ODH) Start-Up Grant (Gill 2014). For this project, entitled "Dangerous Embodiments: Theories, Methods, and Best Practices for Historical Character Modeling in Humanities 3-D Environments," we are working toward the development of a comprehensive typology for avatar (i.e., virtual digital persons) creation—an essential, new, and potentially valuable contribution to the field—and the deployment of different possible avatars in two virtual "difficult heritage" environments: Soweto, Johannesburg and the Jerome Japanese Internment Camp in Arkansas from World War II. We intend to study viewer responses to different avatars within these environments using tools drawn from experimental philosophy, and to publish the results with interpretation by scholars across a diverse array of fields. Also, in my capacity as co-PI on the grant, I am particularly sensitive to my situation as the sole person-of-color on the project and as someone who continues to make both race and gender part of an intersectional framework in their scholarship, teaching, and practice. As new technologies emerge, we are testing all available possibilities and alternatives for user interaction but are remaining cognizant of the continuing chasm of the digital divide.

As 3-D environments proliferate, the creation of a comprehensive typology for avatars and publication of the consequences of certain choices that we make when creating avatars in these environments are needed. The preamble to the *London Charter for the Computer-based Visualization of Cultural Heritage* notes that "a set of principles is needed that will ensure that digital heritage visualization is, and is seen to be, at least as intellectually and technically rigorous as longer established cultural heritage research and communication methods," and yet the London Charter does not make mention of characters or avatars (Denard 2009). Identity and performance in online spaces matter for marginalized groups who are, as Adrienne Shaw argues in *Gaming at the Edge* (2015), "forced to interact in digital spaces where white and male are often the unmarked norm" (2015: 188). When issues of race, gender, and sexuality are considered unimportant online, it is with the assumption that everyone is heterosexual, white, and gendered male—race, gender, and sexuality are unimportant to those people who never have to face violence based on those identities. Shaw makes clear that, "People of color, queer people, women, gender queer people, transgender people, and others never have this privilege" (2015: 189).

The dangers of iconic representations and the powerful sway images exert over us have long been recognized by scholars working in the humanities, with Brian Molyneaux in *The Cultural Life of Images* eloquently noting that, "The reinforcement of ideas in some images is very powerful . . . Pictures and other visual representations . . . have a tremendous inertia, or staying power, that may persist long after the ideas behind the images have gone out of fashion" (1997: 6). And, as the Shape Modelling Group's Michela Mortara et al. have shown in their work on serious games,

> [e]mpathy with a game character and plot may be very helpful for understanding historical events, different cultures, other people's feelings, problems, and behaviours, on the one hand, and the beauty and value of nature, architecture, art and heritage, on the other one.
>
> (Mortara et al. 2014: 7)

But for the eventual employment of 3-D immersive virtual environments, coupled with the documentary evidence of racial hatred as experienced in the built environment of South Africa, the memory of former all-black townships could easily be erased or destroyed in the face of ill-conceived tourism initiatives, irresponsible local politicians, or simple neglect. And, as I have argued elsewhere, I anticipate that through historical recreations these sites of tragedy and dissonant heritage, like so many others related to the Soweto uprisings of 1976, will withstand time and forgetfulness and will continue to be used as models for community-based education and renewed political and social inclusion (Nieves 2009: 199).

In the U.S. alone, the internet has been widely harnessed for political change during the last few years—the Black Lives Matter digital groundswell (#BlackLivesMatter) bears testament to this—to document racial violence and past injustices in urban communities and elsewhere. In particular, young women of color can articulate a broad, black feminist political agenda, as in the 2014 events of Ferguson, Missouri and elsewhere, through their online digital activism. Similarly, in South Africa, students have made significant inroads in dismantling the physical and social remnants of colonial power in the #RhodesMustFall and #FeesMustFall movements. And it will soon be feasible for minority communities across South Africa and elsewhere to employ digital technologies to tell their difficult histories through collaborative and grassroots-based forms of restorative social justice.

Further Reading

Comes, R., Z. Buna, and I. Badiu (2014) "Digital Archaeology: Creation and Preservation of Digital Cultural Heritage," *Journal of Ancient History and Archeology* 1(2), 50–56.

Gomes, L., O. R. P. Bellon, and L. Silva (2014) "3D Reconstruction Methods for Digital Preservation of Cultural Heritage: A Survey," *Pattern Recognition Letters* 50, 3–14.

Guidi, G., M. Russo, and D. Angheleddu (2014) "3D Survey and Virtual Reconstruction of Archaeological Sites," *Digital Applications in Archaeology and Cultural Heritage* 1, 55–69.

Mortara, M., C. E. Catalano, F. Bellotti, G. Fiucci, M. H. Panchetti, and P. Petridis (2014) "Learning Cultural Heritage by Serious Games," *Journal of Cultural Heritage* 15(3), 318–25.

References

Baderoon, G. (2014) "The Ghost in the House: Women, Race, and Domesticity in South Africa," *The Cambridge Journal of Postcolonial Literary Inquiry*, 1(2), 173–88.

Boraine, A. (2006) "Truth and Reconciliation Commission in South Africa Amnesty: The Price of Peace," in J. Elster (ed.) *Retribution and Reparation in the Transition to Democracy*, Cambridge: Cambridge University Press, pp. 299–316.

Cock, J. (1989) *Maids and Madams: Domestic Workers under Apartheid*, New York, NY: Women's Press.

Cooper, B. (2014) "Feminism's Ugly Internal Clash: Why its Future is Not up to White Women," *Salon*, retrieved from www.salon.com/2014/09/24/feminisms_ugly_internal_clash_why_its_future_is_not_up_to_white_women.

Denard, H. (2009) "A New Introduction to the London Charter," *London Charter*, retrieved from www.londoncharter.org/introduction.html.

DHInitiative.org (2016) Soweto Historical GIS Project, retrieved from dhinitiative.org/projects/shgis.

Dodson, B. (2013) "Reconfiguring Space, Reimagining Place: Post-Apartheid Geographies of South Africa and Its Region," *Canadian Journal of African Studies* 47(1), 1–8.

Elbourne, E. (2002) "Domesticity and Dispossession: British Ideologies of 'Home' and the Primitive at Work in the Early Nineteenth-Century Cape," in W. Woodward, P. Hayes, and G. Minkley (eds.) *Deep Histories: Gender and Colonialism in Southern Africa*, Amsterdam: Rodopi, pp. 27–54

Favro, D. (2006) "In the Eyes of the Beholder: Virtual Reality Re-creations and Academia," *Journal of Roman Archaeology Supplementary Series* 61, 321–34.

Favro, D. (2012) "*Se non èvero, èben trovato* (If Not True, It Is Well Conceived): Digital Immersive Reconstructions of Historical Environments," *JSAH: Journal of the Society of Architectural Historians* 71(3), 273–77.

Foucault, M. (1972 [1969]) *The Archaeology of Knowledge*. New York, NY: Routledge.

Gill, A. (2009) "Digitizing the Past: Charting New Courses in the Modeling of Virtual Landscapes." *Visual Resources: An International Journal of Documentation*, 25(4), 313–32.

Gill, A. (2014) "NEH Digital Humanities Start-Up Grant (2014): Dangerous Embodiments: Theories, Methods, and Best Practices for Historical Character Modeling in Humanities 3D Environments," retrieved from www.academia.edu/7082354/NEH_Digital_Humanities_Start-Up_Grant_2014_Dangerous_Embodiments_Theories_Methods_and_Best_Practices_for_Historical_Character_Modeling_in_Humanities_3D_Environments.

Gunew, S. (2013) "Feminist Knowledge: Critique and Construct," in S. Gunew (ed.) *Feminist Knowledge (RLE Feminist Theory): Critique and Construct*, Abingdon, UK: Routledge, pp. 13–35.

Haines, S. and W. Mandela (2008) Interview with Winnie Mandela, joburg.org.za/index.php?option=com_content&id=2978&Itemid=203.

The Independent (1998) "Truth and Reconciliation Commission: A Mirror on Apartheid's Violent History," retrieved from www.independent.co.uk/news/truth-and-reconcilitation-commission-a-mirror-on-apartheids-violent-history-1181541.html.

Jenson, J., N. Taylor, S. de Castell, and B. Dilouya (2015) "Playing with Our Selves," *Feminist Media Studies*, 15(5), 860–79.

Molyneaux, B. (1997) *The Cultural Life of Images: Visual Representation in Archaeology*, London, UK: Routledge.

Mortara, M., C. E. Catalano, F. Bellotti, G. Fiucci, M. H. Panchetti, and P. Petridis (2014) "Learning Cultural Heritage by Serious Games," *Journal of Cultural Heritage* 15(3), 318–25.

Ndebele, N. (2010) "Arriving Home? South Africa beyond Transition and Reconciliation," in F. du Toit and E. Doxtader (eds.) *In the Balance: South Africans Debate Reconciliation*, Johannesburg: Jacana, pp. 55–73.

Nieves, A. D. (2009) "Places of Pain as Tools for Social Justice in the 'New' South Africa: Black Heritage Preservation in the 'Rainbow' Nation's Townships," in W. Logan and K. Reeves (eds.) *Places of Pain and Shame: Dealing with Difficult Heritage*, London, UK: Routledge, pp. 198–214.

Phillips, K. R., and G. M. Reyes (2011) *Global Memoryscapes: Contesting Remembrance in a Transnational Age*, Tuscaloosa, AL: University of Alabama Press.

Pohlandt-McCormick, H. (2000) "Controlling Woman: Winnie Mandela and the 1976 Soweto Uprising," *The International Journal of African Historical Studies* 33(3), 585–614.

Polis Center (2016) *Spatial Humanities*, retrieved from thepoliscenter.iupui.edu/index.php/spatial-humanities.

Poniewozik, J. (2014) "Misogynist Online Abuse Is Everyone's Problem—Men Included," *Time*, 16 October, retrieved from time.com/3512896/gamergate-misogyny-men-anita-sarkeesian.

Shaw, A. (2015) *Gaming at the Edge: Sexuality and Gender at the Margins of Gamer Culture*, Minneapolis, MN: University of Minnesota.

Snyder, L. (2012) "Virtual Reality for Humanities Scholarship," in B. Nelson and M. Terras (eds.) *Digitizing Medieval and Early Modern Material Culture*, Tempe, AZ: Arizona Center for Medieval and Renaissance Studies, pp. 395–428.

Soweto76Archive.org (2016) *Soweto '76*, retrieved from www.soweto76archive.org.

Traister, R. and J. Shulevitz (2014) "Feminism Has Conquered the Culture. Now Comes the Hard Part: A Debate on this Unprecedented Opportunity," *New Republic*, retrieved from www.newrepublic.com/article/119412/feminisms-future-debate.

von Lunen, A. (2013) "Tracking in a New Territory: Re-imaging GIS for History," in A. von Lunen and C. Travis (eds.) *History and GIS: Epistemologies, Considerations, and Reflections*, Dordrecht, NLD: Springer, pp. 211–40.

Walker, M., K. Kaplanidou, H. Gibson, B. Thapa, S. Geldenhuys, and W. Coetzee (2012) " 'Win in Africa, With Africa,' Social Responsibility, Event Image and Destination Benefits," *Tourism Management* 34, 80–90.

41

RELATIONSHIPS, NOT RECORDS

Digital Heritage and the Ethics of Sharing Indigenous Knowledge Online

Kimberly Christen

> Archive: from Gk. *ta arkheia* "public records," pl. of *arkheion* "town hall, public building," from *arkhe* "government," literally "beginning, origin, first place," from Gk. *arkhon* "ruler, commander, chief, captain," present participle of *arkhein* "be the first," also "to rule" (Online Etymology Dictionary 2001–17)

The etymological roots of the term *archive* highlight the relationship between archives, state institutions, and public policies. The origins of modern archives are intimately linked to colonial logics of vanishing races, imperial projects of collection, and colonial nation-making strategies. Colonial expeditions displayed national treasures collected from around the world and also standardized knowledge based on their own interpretations and uses of those materials. Consider the state-sponsored anthropologists taking photographs of Indigenous peoples' rituals or artifacts; or, the botanist traveling with colonial expeditions, documenting and collecting flora and fauna along with Indigenous names and uses for them; or, the missionaries simultaneously documenting Indigenous languages and defining the "savage" religious practices of Indigenous peoples. The archive was simultaneously a physical place to store Indigenous materials and a political representation of policies of displacement and destruction of Indigenous cultural practices, languages, and ways of life.

Archives are physical reminders of colonial practices that once promoted the exclusion of minority and subaltern voices (Foote 1990; Mifflin 2009). While archives grapple with this history and archivists make strides in creating a new basis for archival work, archives still often engender ambivalent feelings among Indigenous peoples who see them as testaments to the hyper-surveillance of their lives and marginal status in the nations in which they live as well as potential sources for recovering lost histories, reconnecting with family members, and finding evidence of their legal claims to land and resources. Collected, collated, and curated for a non-Indigenous audience and used to build cases for territorial dispossession and historical erasure, the documents, maps, ledgers, photos, and ephemera in modern archives are simultaneously part of the colonial past and an anchor for present reconfigurations of history, memory, identity, and sovereignty. The materials collected can be, and indeed are being, repurposed for uses not originally intended or desired.

Archives have always been home to humanists; they are places where voices are recovered from long quiet pages. Marginal notes inspire new historical insights, and government documents unearth untold national trajectories. Archives inspire. They can also silence by directing viewers to partial or incomplete records or records compiled from one perspective. Archival standards provide categories for searching, subject headings for linking materials, and classification systems for arranging materials, all defined through dominant western histories and logics. Archivists choose what to accept, accession, describe, catalogue, and document. These are not neutral or nonbiased acts. Defining collections, annotating items, and providing finding aids all require interpretive work and choices about what gets included and what gets left out. Interpretation does not necessarily mean that a bias results in erasure, but it does leave archival practices open to cultural criticism and the creation of multiple sets of records to fully define histories of material.

Physical documents detailing the attempted erasure of Indigenous peoples remain, at least selectively, open in archives. But these repositories have often been "largely inaccessible to indigenous owners" (Dyson & Hendriks 2007: xvi). Physical distances, educational and linguistic barriers, and high levels of poverty have all made archives unapproachable places for Indigenous communities, whose cultural materials and institutional histories are preserved within them. In the last 30 years, Indigenous activism has spread to archives, and there has been a simultaneous growth of Indigenous-run archives on Indigenous lands and the insertion of Indigenous systems of knowledge production and information management into archival policies and practices (Christen 2011; O'Neal 2015). Many archives in Australia, for example, now offer services for Indigenous community members to aid in finding relatives who were part of the Stolen Generation (e.g., children taken by the government to boarding schools). The Australian Institute for Aboriginal and Torres Strait Islander Studies provides a range of archival policies geared toward Aboriginal cultural values—keeping culturally sensitive materials from public view and requiring community permissions to access some sacred materials (Nakata 2005). Similarly, in the United States, the First Archivists Circle created the Protocols for Native American Archival Materials as a set of guidelines for non-Native archivists to consult during the process of archiving Native materials to ensure cultural values and ethical concerns are addressed at all steps of the archiving process, from acquisition to cataloguing (O'Neal 2014). Jeffrey Mifflin suggests that:

> There is no real neutrality in either historical research or archival science. Mediation inevitably occurs when researchers come to an archival repository to study materials. Access policies, the level of detail and characteristics of finding aids, the physical condition or format of materials, the helpfulness of staff, and the specialized insights of archivists are all variables. How should this affect archivists who administer Native American or other indigenous collections? There are no ready answers, and perhaps the most honest and sensitive approach would be to confer with representatives of the cultures most affected before devising (or revising) policies and procedures.
>
> (Mifflin 2009: 381)

Taken together, there is a quickly emerging consensus around these trends in archival practices that are becoming normalized as best practices for handling Indigenous materials in all types of repositories and collecting institutions. As old practices shift, it is helpful to examine how new ones are planned, defined, and put into action, as well as what they signal in terms of our academic and ethical values.

Cultural Checks: Digital Heritage Stewardship

Digital technologies have made new types of access and modes of curation possible and provide one avenue for examining archival openness, access policies, and how values are embedded in archival acts. Over the last 10 years—with digital tools and platforms that rely on and privilege user-generated content and curation growing in popularity—curation as imagined within the digital landscape has been linked to outward-facing export processes and practices. Curation at its base is about organizing a set of materials in a meaningful way. Where once curation was seen as the job of archivists, librarians, or museum professionals, it is now more commonly seen as a creative act that anyone can perform. In fact, social media platforms encourage it; we are prompted to curate our own content—photos, scanned images, audio clips, video files—to engage with friends, share memories with family, or promote ourselves to potential employers or partners. The read/write or import/export model of content curation is undone through these emergent practices of digital curation, where viewing, displaying, arranging, and remixing content become more visible and saving or storing becomes less visible. In 2014, *every 60 seconds* there were 120 hours of video uploaded to YouTube, 1380 blog posts published on Wordpress blogs, 41,000 photos uploaded to Instagram, and 3.3 million Facebook posts. Each of these could be considered an act of digital curation (CLT 2014). With all this content, curation becomes a more everyday act, one worthy of understanding and exploration for what it reveals as well as what it may conceal.

Typical models of digital curation follow a framework of (1) getting/finding, (2) arranging, and (3) sharing content. One need only Google "digital curation" to find a wealth of graphics showing various workflow scenarios. Even detailed workflows all start with finding or getting content. The workflows suggest a process that begins with a notion of discovery that replays a colonial collecting paradigm, where content is imagined as unhinged from peoples and cultures and free for the taking (Christen 2012; Hennessy 2013). One can quite easily get content from a Google image search, scrape it from a website, or download it from an academic digital archive. The process is imagined as a neutral act—one of taking something that is already offered up for consumption. The term "data mining" offers a telling example of how colonial legacies of collecting physical materials from local places and peoples are grafted onto digital content. Content is imagined as open, reusable, and unhinged from communities, individuals, or families who may have intimate ties to the materials.

Once content is found, the process of curation can take on many meanings. In the current technical landscapes, curation may mean a playful remix of images and sound to mock a world leader or an ironic arrangement of videos and text to make a social intervention. Or, it could simply gesture to making lolcat GIFs. In any case, curation implies a conscious effort to put materials in relation to one another to form something new—whether that be for commercial, academic, entertainment, or other purposes. This process—as generally imagined—does not necessarily involve providing cultural, historical, or political context for collections in relation to local communities of origin. Additionally, generally accepted approaches include academic research practices that have not been historically open to subaltern voices, and popular trends in digital curation do not suggest an ethical commitment to maintaining the integrity of collections or providing the familial or community-based links to and narratives of these items.

One of the foundations of archival practices is providing metadata, "information about information," for all materials. In physical archives, this once meant accession documents, card catalogues, finding aids for entire collections (brief summaries with larger chunks of information), and item level metadata such as date, creator, publisher, subject, and a unique identifier (an alphanumeric string assigned to each item). While metadata has often been viewed as neutral information ("facts"), its status has been re-evaluated, showing that the creation of metadata, like other forms of information, is influenced by social, cultural, and political values and norms. The notion of a single creator or author of a work is prime example. In western settings (and legal contexts) the author is seen as the sole creator of a work, and legal as well as financial rights may be assigned to that person. In many Indigenous communities, however, the notion of a single creator of a song or author of a narrative is undone by value placed on community production, ancestral creation of stories, or other forms of cultural and artistic content. A design on a Zuni mask, for example, may belong to one family or clan, and the songs associated with its performance may belong to another. No one person can or would assert authorship or ownership of these materials (Torsen & Anderson 2010).

Finally, in normative workflows for digital curation, sharing with an unidentified public across multiple platforms is presumed to be not only a best practice but also a de facto public good. Current social media platforms and online display tools work across one another so that sharing may mean a post on Facebook, a collage on Instagram, 140 characters on Twitter, an online exhibit, or a multimodal book display. The possibilities for curation have been extended through digital tools that allow for both weaving together many types of digital objects in one space and the connections one can make across the digital landscape. While openness may seem to be a neutral and homogenous term and standard for access, it is in fact a culturally determined and political act. Making digital content open to all, to do with what they will without question, is very rarely what proponents of open access mean.

Access and openness are almost always more complicated, more nuanced, and conditional. If we take away the utopian allure of openness and look at how people share, access, and circulate information, then we see a range of ways to do so, and only very few are oppressive or opportunistic. If we take away the extremes, then we see that sharing content and defining access can relate to historical circumstances, political realties, personal safety, community growth, and varied educational needs. This basic model of curation can be expanded for the sake of sustainability, preservation, and discoverability of metadata, but its foundation in practices of discovery or collection implies unfettered access as the norm and description and sharing without cultural, historical, or political context (Phillips 2005; Lonetree 2012).

Indigenous cultural production in archiving and curation provides a counterbalance to these workflows and gives us different models for sharing, arranging, and circulating knowledge. In Australia, Aboriginal practices of masking, deleting, and hiding images, objects, and artifacts are quite common. In museum exhibits, online archives, and virtual exhibits, there are often warnings that these physical or virtual spaces contain images and names of deceased people—for example, the National Museum of Australia may "cause sadness and distress to Aboriginal and Torres Strait Islander people." In Vancouver, Canada, the Musqueam Indian Band's online place name archive requires visitors to accept certain terms for viewing Musqueam places and hearing Musqueam stories and the hən̓q̓əmin̓əm̓ language. Only upon accepting these terms, which include being "respectful" and "not reproducing any portion of the site without permission," can one enter the site; view some of the content, videos, and maps; and hear the language. Thus access and use are conditional on making an ethical commitment to act responsibly as opposed to standard online click-through agreements that generally emphasize commercial and legal interests.

Similarly, the Blackfoot people's Blackfoot Digital Library has a terms of service (TOS) statement and conditions of use policy on their website that includes this statement on knowledge acquisition and use: "You are not considered a member of any Blackfoot tribe nor are you considered a Shaman/Medicine person because you learned something on this site. This site is not for recreating Blackfoot ceremony by non-Blackfoot people." With this very direct statement, the Blackfoot undo the common notion that information online can and should be used freely for individual purposes. Grounded in a long history of appropriation of Native peoples' religious and ceremonial practices, the Blackfoot TOS are a *cultural intervention*: a clear set of terms for what *not* to do with the site's content. The Blackfoot TOS can be seen as an invitation for all viewers and site users to engage ethically, regardless of legal terms.

In the Inland Pacific Northwest at the Northwest Museum of Arts and Culture, many Native American collections are kept separate, and public access to these objects is restricted. The Museum has a private room for sacred materials set apart from the general collections area. Tribal community members and elders can view, touch, and interact with their cultural belongings at the Museum, but the general public cannot. This policy is a reminder that not all objects are ripe for inspection, documentation, and use.

All of these examples are reminders of tactile, material, and embodied ethical practices of curation that disrupt the continued disavowal of Indigenous histories, knowledge systems, and sovereignty. They promote a type of curation that relies on histories, relationships, and the social life of information to define strategies of collection, arrangement, and sharing. If we take the general "get it, curate it, share it" model and expand it to include *cultural, ethical, and historical checks* at each step, then we get a workflow that encourages collaboration, relies on historical specificity, and has ethical considerations embedded at every step. Finding or discovery should not be guided by a search paradigm that disregards the colonial histories of collection or upholds notions of access that privilege the public domain. It takes a bit of historical amnesia to forget that the public domain has never been a very welcoming place for Indigenous peoples, whose cultural materials found their way into both public and private collections by dubious and often violent means (Phillips 2005; Lonetree 2012).

By disregarding this historical context, the default for digitization and curation becomes mired in competing notions of open access and the public good, where accessibility is synonymous with "open to all" without regard for cultural, social, and historical conditions. But, if we add in *cultural checks* prior to curation or sharing, then we are compelled to think through the implications of curating a set of belongings (not objects). Is it appropriate to display images of deceased people? Is imposing a Native design on unrelated materials a type of intellectual violence? How might it affect contemporary Indigenous peoples to have their personal records in a searchable database? Inserting these checks slows down the process and in that process invites conversations between various sets of stakeholders. Emphasizing cultural checks broadens the notion of curation beyond the individual item or collection by locating it within a history, social relations, and ongoing political situations that move between the past and present and multiple groups of people.

We can think about this slow process as one of *digital heritage stewardship*. Shifting from collecting to stewarding undoes the colonial model and inscribes a relational model built on obligations that one has to care for, maintain, and preserve a variety of belongings. Building specifically from Indigenous systems of relation, obligations to act are meaningful commitments to one's kin—human or other-than-human—including the physical landscape. Digital heritage stewardship is based on a model of *collaborative curation*—a set of practices that redefine and interrupt the standard workflow of the digital content lifecycle, where content often seems devoid of context or culture and processes of discovery and re-use do not always account for colonial collecting practices, current political situations, and the biased classification systems that permeate curation models.

Collaborative Curation: The Plateau Peoples' Web Portal

At the core of engaging in collaborative curation is grounding all parts of the work—technological, archival, design, and production—in a give-and-take between all sets of stakeholders. Community members should be involved from the inception of the project. The "build it, and they will come" model of software design and/or collections management disregards individual- or community-level needs, desires, and goals. While no community is homogeneous, and there will always be more than one way to curate a collection, open dialogue from the beginning undoes the traditional expert role of academics, archivists, and technologists and begins with an understanding that the process of curation entails many voices from each local community and from within and beyond the academy (Barber 2013; Mifflin 2014; McCracken 2015).

The Plateau Peoples' Web Portal (Portal), a project I direct at Washington State University (WSU), is an online archive of Plateau peoples' cultural materials that is collaboratively curated and reciprocally managed by representatives from six tribes—the Colville, Coeur d'Alene, Spokane, Umatilla, Yakama, and Warm Springs, with whom WSU holds a Memorandum of Understanding (MOU)—and the WSU Libraries' Manuscripts, Archives, and Special Collections team. Creating the Portal grew out of the expressed needs of the tribes, who wanted an online space where tribal members could both access and participate in narrating records from the WSU libraries. I first met with tribal representatives in 2008 to discuss their needs and vision for the Portal. Being dispersed across three states, the tribes wanted a way to access collections related to their communities without having to go to the WSU campus, they wanted to take part in the management and curation of their cultural materials, and they wanted some assurances about the long-term storage and security of those materials. To this end, we worked together to both technically and philosophically make tribal knowledge central to every aspect of the Portal. We made individual MOUs available to each tribe to define their specific goals, needs, and project parameters. This may seem like an unnecessary step; however, creating an MOU or another document that clearly states the contours of engagement, sharing, and partnership empowers each set of partners and encourages collaboration that goes beyond good intentions by defining goals, outcomes, and resources. Similarly, at the institutional level, we secured server space in perpetuity for the Portal content and ensured the longevity of the project by locating it physically within the WSU Libraries and within the overall scope of the Library's duties (not one individual). Thus, at every stage, we sought to strike a balance between the informational needs, sovereign rights, and ethical concerns of the tribes and the professional concerns and institutional standards of librarians, archivists, and other information specialists.

The Portal starts from a position that recognizes and respects the fact that tribal cultural protocols define a range of access parameters, of which "open" is only one among many. It is possible that an image may only be viewable to family members because someone in the picture is recently deceased and the community's cultural protocols do not allow nonfamily members to view the images. Or, it could be that a map depicting sacred burial grounds may only be open to elders in the tribe because the location of the grounds needs to be protected. It could also be that an audio file may only be accessible to specific ritual participants due to the sensitive nature of the materials. There are many scenarios in which individuals and communities wish to define access based on their own histories, social systems, and cultural norms. Allowing communities to define their own protocols for access and circulation respects these differences, and good design and technological architecture should support, not suppress, such differences.

During the production of the Portal, our WSU team and tribal partners worked together to make decisions about design, technical functions, and collections needs. A prime example of using design to embed cultural and historical values is the Portal's main page. The design of the Portal recognizes the sovereignty of each tribe as well as what unites them across time and space. The tribal representatives chose an image of the Columbia River to signify the uniting body of water that flows through all tribal boundaries, and each tribe also has their own "tribal path" in the Portal with an image, welcome audio and text, and their own tribal links. Importantly, on the backend they can change any of this design at any time on their own with no permission required from the WSU team. Similarly, the Portal's metadata fields are grounded in tribal priorities. We sought to expand traditional standard metadata fields to include an emphasis on local knowledge, values, and sensibilities. For example, while Library of Congress (LOC) standard subject headings are an option within the Portal for records search, the main browse and search interfaces and selection choices are driven by tribally generated categories, subjects, and keywords. The twelve main browse categories were chosen by tribal representatives and can be expanded or updated at any time.

In addition, at the individual item level, tribal members can add tribal knowledge and cultural narratives to each record. The scholarly record is not erased, but enhanced with tribal voices. For example, one photograph titled "3 Yakama Women" from WSU's L.V. McWhorter collection was chosen by the Yakama tribal representatives for digitization and inclusion in the public view of the Portal. The metadata for the record from WSU—the scholarly record—includes an approximate date the photo was taken (1911) and a description of the photo: "A photo of 3 Yakama women in regalia (1911)." Beyond that, there is no more information about the photo, the women, the regalia, the Yakama people and culture, the historical circumstances, why the photo was taken, or if the women gave their permission.

However, because the Portal allows multiple records for one piece of content and tribal community members provide those records, we now have a more nuanced understanding of the photo. Jolena Tillequets and Vivian Adams, both Yakama women, added their own narratives to the image. Tillequets writes:

> The ladies in this picture are all very unique in their style of dress. They may have helped in the creation of their dresses'. With the skinning and tanning of the buckskin, to the beadwork to their dress and accessories. The wampum necklaces were usually passed down to young woman as part of their dowry. As you see the first lady on the left has many strands of wampum while the third has one but has the two eagle feathers.
>
> ("3 Yakama Women" 2014)

Adams adds:

> Historically, hide dresses were worn daily, many undecorated because they were "work" clothes, although some form of decoration might be added. More highly decorated hide dresses were made to be used in rite-of-passage ceremonies including important family or tribal gathering events. Hide dresses were once decorated with

> natural color-dyed porcupine quills and when beads were introduced circa early 1800s, they were much easier to use in curilinear designs and became plentiful as fur traders and settlers began moving westward and trades increased with them. Dresses still use shells, elk teeth, hide fringes, wampum bone beads, tiny bells or coins and whatever else may add to the aesthetics of the dress. The hide dresses these young ladies wear don't seem to have the original animal tail as part of the neck decoration. The tail was often used not only as an aesthetic enhancement but also as a show of respect and thanks to the animal for giving its life for the hide dress, food and utility tools made from its remains. The dresses do have beaded geometrical motifs which stand in place of the animal tails and these are beaded center front and back of the dress, so the form of thanks and respect is still given in this newer method of decoration.
>
> ("3 Yakama Women" 2014)

This added knowledge expands the public record and invites viewers to understand more about the Yakama, their history, and their cultural practices. Importantly, it also undoes the taken-for-granted viewing of Native peoples out of historical and social context.

Collaborative Stewardship: Some Practical Steps

For those of us working in universities, at collecting institutions, or on digital humanities or media projects that engage with content by or about Indigenous communities, it is important to be cognizant of histories of exclusion and how our technologies can reproduce imbalances. There are a few steps I have learned through these projects that are helpful in building an ethical and reciprocal framework for collaborative curation.

- First, engage. Projects should begin with engagement with all stakeholders: tribal nations representatives, community members, library staff, IT staff, and graphic designers, for example. Do not start with technologists assuming that a "digital" project has its roots in zeros and ones. Instead, projects should grow from stated needs, issues, challenges, and scenarios already in play.
- Second, talk. Start by talking face-to-face with all interested parties. And then talk some more, and talk a little bit more. Often specific needs will unfold over the course of several in-person gatherings, and it is important to build trust, especially with communities and user groups who have been historically shut out of these conversations. Be open to talking with multiple groups within tribal nations and collecting institutions. If you work at a non-Indigenous library, museum, university, or institution, go to the communities you want to engage, attend their public meetings, and do not have all your interactions in a university setting. Power rests in places.
- Third, help. Projects have an arc, and it is important to help people at every step to determine the specific needs for certain tasks. Note which partners need which kind of technology support and training, and define what type of help is best suited for each. Highlight your strengths as well as the strengths of stakeholders. Do not replay a victim model, where others need outside researchers and experts to come and save them. In a collaborative project, all stakeholders bring something to the table.
- Fourth, invest. Research-driven projects often have timelines defined by tenure clocks, grant funding cycles, and other non-community-based concerns. However, when partnering with communities who have been displaced and whose resources and

knowledge have been used and abused by researchers, it is important to take the time to build relationships by investing in resources. Digital equipment, infrastructure, and educational tools are only some types of investments. Building up both technical and human resources shows a commitment to the long term, not to a one-off project that benefits only outsiders.
- Fifth, create. For the types of archival, linguistic, and cultural projects Indigenous communities may wish to produce, creation might mean building new tools and platforms or finding ways to tweak existing ones. Instead of asking Indigenous peoples to bend to your technology, be willing to bend the technology to their needs, goals, and priorities.
- Finally, support. Provide ongoing and uninterrupted support for tribal partners including (but not limited to) technical and educational opportunities. After the platform is built or the archive is programmed, there is much more to be done. Providing ongoing support is the thread that runs through the project and will lead to a long-lasting relationship.

Taken together, these steps comprise an ETHICS (Engage, Talk, Help, Invest, Create, Support) for archival practices. Choosing to follow this path will not guarantee success, but ETHICS does set a framework for respectful digital archiving projects that create not just records, but relationships.

Acknowledgments

This work has been funded by the American Council of Learned Societies, the National Endowment for the Humanities, and the Institute for Museum and Library Services. None of the work on the Portal would be possible without the partnerships between Washington State University and the Spokane Tribe of Indians, the Confederated Tribes of the Colville Reservation, the Confederated Tribes of the Umatilla Indian Reservation, the Coeur d'Alene Tribe of Indians, the Confederated Tribes of Warm Springs, the Nez Perce Tribe, and Yakama Nation. Finally, a debt of gratitude to my generous, hard-working, and talented colleagues at the Center for Digital Scholarship and Curation at WSU.

Further Reading

Coombes, A. E. and R. B. Phillips (eds.) (2015) *The International Handbooks of Museum Studies: Museum Transformations*, Hoboken, NJ: John Wiley & Sons, Ltd.

Ess, C. (2009) *Digital Media Ethics*, Cambridge, MA: Polity Press.

Metoyer, C. and A. Doyle (eds.) (2015) *Cataloging & Classification Quarterly*, Indigenous Knowledge Organization Special Issue 53(5/6).

O'Neal, J. and D. G. Lewis (eds.) (2015) *Journal of Western Archives*, Native American Archives Special Issue 6(1).

Vermeylen, S. and J. Pilcher (2009) "Let the Objects Speak: Online Museums and Indigenous Cultural Heritage," *International Journal of Intangible Heritage* 4(4), 60–78.

References

3 Yakama Women (2014) Plateau Peoples' Web Portal, retrieved from: plateauportal. libraries.wsu.edu/digital-heritage/3-yakama-women.

"archives (n.)" (2001–17) in D. Harper (ed.) *Online Etymology Dictionary*, retrieved from www.etymonline.com/word/archives.

Barber, K. (2013) "Shared Authority in the Context of Tribal Sovereignty: Building Capacity for Partnerships with Indigenous Nations," *The Public Historian* 35(4), 20–39.

Blackfoot Digital Library (2015) retrieved from www.blackfootdigitallibrary.com/.

Centre for Learning and Teaching (2014) "What Happens Online in 60 Seconds?" 3 November, retrieved from clt.vtc.edu.hk/what-happens-online-in-60-seconds/.

Christen, K. (2011) "Opening Archives: Respectful Repatriation," *American Archivist* 74, 185–210.

Christen, K. (2012) "Does Information Really Want to be Free? Indigenous Knowledge and the Politics of Open Access," *The International Journal of Communication* 6, 2870–93.

Dyson, L. and G. Hendriks (2007) *Information Technology and Indigenous People*, Hershey, PA: IGI Global Press.

First Archivists Circle (2007) *Protocols for Native American Archival Materials*, retrieved from www2.nau.edu/libnap-p/protocols.html.

Foote, K. (1990) "To Remember and Forget: Archives, Memory, and Culture," *American Archivist* 53, 378–92.

Hennessy, K. (2013) "The Inuvialuit Living History Project: Digital Return as the Forging of Relationships between Institutions, People, and Data," *Museum Anthropology Review* 7(1–2), 44–73.

Lonetree, A. (2012) *Decolonizing Museums: Representing Native America in National and Tribal Museums*, Chapel Hill, NC: UNC Press.

McCracken, K. (2015) "Community Archival Practice: Indigenous Grassroots Collaboration at the Shingwauk Residential Schools Centre," *American Archivist* 78(1), 181–91.

Mifflin, J. (2009) "'Closing the Circle': Native American Writings in Colonial New England, a Documentary Nexus between Acculturation and Cultural Preservation," *American Archivist* 72(2), 344–82.

Mifflin, J. (2014) "Regarding Indigenous Knowledge in Archives," in M. Caldera and K. Neal (eds.) *Through the Archival Looking Glass: A Reader on Diversity and Inclusion*, Chicago, IL: Society of American Archivists Press, pp. 61–89.

Musqueam Place Names Web Map (2011), retrieved from www.musqueam.bc.ca/musqueam-our-history-web-map.

Nakata, M. (2005) "Indigenous Knowledge, the Library and Information Service Sector, and Protocols," in M. Nakata and M. Langton (eds.) *Australian Indigenous Knowledge and Libraries*, Sydney, Australia: UTSePress.

National Museum of Australia: First Australians (n.d.) retrieved from www.nma.gov.au/history/aboriginal-torres-strait-islander-cultures-histories.

O'Neal, J. (2014) "Respect, Recognition, and Reciprocity: The Protocols for Native American Archival Materials," in D. Daniel and A Levi (eds.) *Identity Palimpsests: Archiving Ethnicity in the US and Canada*, Sacramento, CA: Litwin Press, pp. 125–42.

O'Neal, J. (2015) "The Right to Know: Decolonizing Native American Archives," *Journal of Western Archives, Native American Archives Special Issue* 6(1), retrieved from digitalcommons.usu.edu/westernarchives/vol6/iss1/2/.

Phillips, R. (2005) "Re-Placing Objects: Historical Practices for the Second Museum Age," *Canadian Historical Review* 86(1), 83–110.

Plateau Peoples' Web Portal (n.d.) retrieved from plateauportal.libraries.wsu.edu/.

Torsen, M and J. Anderson (2010) *Intellectual Property and the Safeguarding of Traditional Cultures: Legal Issues and Practical Options for Museums, Libraries and Archives*, Geneva, Switzerland: World Intellectual Property Organization.

42

SEARCHING, MINING, AND INTERPRETING MEDIA HISTORY'S BIG DATA

Eric Hoyt, Tony Tran, Derek Long, Kit Hughes, and Kevin Ponto

The writing of film and media history is driven by questions. Many of these questions pertain to the aesthetic and stylistic dimensions of media forms: How has the pace of television editing changed over time? When did the close-up gain prominence in film storytelling? Such questions can only be answered by studying the audiovisual productions themselves; and in the last decade, scholars such as Kuhn et al. (2012), Manovich (2012), Butler (2014), Cutting (2014), Casey and Williams (2014), and Ferguson (2015) have sought to apply computational approaches to these questions of stylistic stasis and change at scale. However, even a very basic question about style—for example, why does the *Mary Tyler Moore Show* look and sound the way it does?—requires us to go beyond the screen image and consult primary and secondary sources, such as technical journals for the 1970s U.S. television industry and the scripts of the show's production company, MTM that are archived at the Wisconsin Center for Film and Theater Research. Moreover, recent exciting works in film and media historiography have asked questions that, as Smoodin argues, "demonstrate the possibility for film scholarship without films; for using primary materials other than films themselves for examining the history of the cinema in the United States" (2007: 2). Questions about how and why media industries produce content, or how audiences encounter and experience that content, cannot be answered solely through an analysis—close or distant—of films and television as "texts." In fact, *most* film and media history research questions cannot be answered by analyzing the audiovisual texts alone.

Online resources have greatly aided researchers in the exploration of media history beyond the analysis of films and broadcast programs. For example, the Media History Digital Library (MHDL) has made available over 2 million pages of trade papers, fan magazines, books, and other publications related to the histories of film and broadcasting, while David Gleason's remarkable library, AmericanRadioHistory.com, has digitized more than 3 million pages related to broadcasting history. This growth in online searchable collections has enabled scholars to augment traditional research methods and leverage computational approaches toward writing media history. This chapter discusses some of the opportunities and challenges of doing this type of work, focusing on the research potential of digitized collections of newspapers, magazines, and trade papers. We expect that you, the reader, already have some experience running keyword searches through these collections. By the end of this chapter, however, we hope you will return to those searchable collections with a better understanding of their strengths, limitations, and—most fundamentally—how they work.

This chapter introduces you to Scaled Entity Search (SES), an alternative method to traditional keyword searching. SES is a method of performing searches and a critical framework for interpreting their results. It allows users to search simultaneously for multiple entities (e.g., actors, film titles, and production companies) across a large body of documents called a "corpus." The SES process highlights relationships between entities while also contextualizing the trending of entities across the whole corpus. Using SES as an effective search approach requires pairing the *technical method*, or the understanding of how particular search platforms operate and are organized, with an *interpretive method*, which considers relationships between the entities, the corpus, and digital technology.

We also introduce you to Arclight, a software platform for applying SES to media history sources. Arclight allows you to visualize and examine how entities trend across the MHDL's 2-million-page corpus. In this chapter, we use Arclight to track the popular Japanese American silent film actors, Sessue Hayakawa and Tsuru Aoki, within the MHDL. As we elaborate later, Hayakawa and Aoki, as both historical figures and digitally defined entities, allow us to illustrate and emphasize the key aspects and contexts you should consider when using SES and interpreting your Arclight results. Through this celebrity couple, we also demonstrate how SES and Arclight can be productively applied to new historical questions and confirm and enrich existing historical scholarship. Arclight was developed at the University of Wisconsin-Madison in collaboration with a team, led by Charles Acland, at Concordia University in Montreal. Our research and software development was made possible thanks to the support of an international Digging into Data grant, sponsored by the Institute of Museum and Library Services (IMLS) in the U.S. and the Social Sciences and Humanities Research Council (SSHRC) in Canada.

Searching Magazines and Newspapers

While internet access and digital literacy are not universal, it is undeniable that digitized collections have permitted historical materials to be more easily read and processed by a diverse set of users, from history enthusiasts to academic researchers. Materials that were once constrained to a limited number of physical archives and libraries are now more accessible than ever before. Beyond access, the ability to search these large collections has also altered how users move through historical documents, allowing them to efficiently peruse and filter materials to find relevant information.

Considered in terms of convenience and efficiency, the digital availability of these materials has been a tremendous boon for researchers. However, we must remain aware of the underlying technical dimensions that frame the practice of searching digital collections. Search engines are pervasive in our everyday lives; they play a crucial role in mediating and sorting our experiences and encounters (Van Couvering 2008; Halavais 2009). Additionally, their ubiquity has rendered their functions and influences on the practice of media history increasingly invisible. In recognizing the roles search engines play in shaping our research, we can remain critical and reflexive in our methods to better consider how we find and produce historical knowledge in an age of digitized and searchable collections. To fully harness the potential—as well as the capabilities, limitations, and blind spots—of using search engines to explore media history, we must first understand some of their key technical aspects.

The technical aspect of search engines that we most often hear researchers talk about—or perhaps more accurately, complain about—is optical character recognition (OCR). After a book, magazine, or microfilm reel is digitally scanned, OCR software turns the scanned images into computer-readable text. The software makes a lot of guesses about particular words, characters, and languages and, for the most part, guesses correctly (Holley 2009). But no automated process can completely account for the innumerable forms of physically printed text, with its varying scripts, typefaces, smudges, speckling, and distortion through normal wear and tear. As a result, the software can make mistakes (e.g., an "e" in Latin script becomes a "c") and obscure text from search engines. Bad OCR appears in full view of researchers when a search retrieves a text snippet. Less visible to researchers, however, are the approximate string matching algorithms that make probabilistic guesses, break apart words, and help mitigate imperfect OCR (Navarro 2001). These computational gymnastics affect returned results as much as, if not more than, the OCR process. Good OCR matters, but it is far from the whole story about how search works.

An even more important technical point to understand is that, when a researcher performs a keyword or SES search, he or she is always searching an index, not the actual content. A search index is a lot like the index at the back of a book: it organizes information in a special way to help readers find more quickly what they are looking for. Similarly, a search engine, such as the popular open source index, Solr, takes a document and breaks it into small bits, arranging it in specific ways so that a computer can quickly search it without reading the entire text from start to finish. Solr is optimized to work in a particular way; and in the case of the MHDL's search platform, Lantern, as well as most newspaper search platforms, Solr comes loaded with the search algorithms that do most of the heavy lifting. As software developers, however, we can guide Solr in the kinds of information we want our index to prioritize. We select the metadata fields, such as year and title, we want to include in the index (typically, the metadata itself is edited and stored elsewhere—in a relational database or XML documents, for example). We also provide Solr with a schema that defines the data types for the metadata fields (e.g., year is an integer; title is a string). Although selecting the metadata fields and constructing the schema may seem like merely technical steps, they are extremely important and determine how users can filter and sort results. Want to arrange results chronologically by year? Or filter out books from a list of results? If the metadata and schema do not define these categories, then you cannot do so.

The affordances of search engines have made some aspects of research more efficient, but they have also changed the processes of how we discover information. While seemingly inefficient, there is much to be gained from the organic process of physically combing through boxes of documents, or even skimming reels of microfilm. We are reminded of the tactile and fragile nature of history—often shocked by the sheer size of newspapers when compared to how they appear on our laptop screens—as well as given a tangible context for our discoveries. By highlighting and pointing us to the exact keyword we wish to find, digital search can seduce us with its efficiency, placing blinders on us that take our attention away from the broader contexts and documents that surround our keyword.

Due to their widespread use, several digital humanists have been critical of search engines. Matthew Jockers calls for a move "beyond search," arguing that, while single keyword searches are still useful for uncovering individual nuggets in the twenty-first century digital library, they are ineffective at mining deeper veins of knowledge and evidence that exist throughout the library (2013: 9). Ted Underwood labels full-text search in the humanities a "Boolean fishing expedition," whereby researchers repeat combinations of keywords until the desired result is produced at the top of search results (2014: 64). As Underwood points out, it is easy to forget that full-text search is not a neutral tool; it has underlying algorithms that make independent—and often invisible—decisions about the ranking and filtering of results. For Underwood, the consequence of full-text search is that scholars cite a few select sources—often cherry-picked from large collections—that reaffirm a researcher's pre-existing beliefs and hypotheses rather than potentially challenging them.

Certainly, keyword searches present major methodological issues that should not be ignored. However, we argue against the dismissal of search as a method of historical research at scale. As mentioned above, search has become a central component in our lives, and in many ways it has helped to produce and spread historical knowledge. As a largely intuitive mode of digital scholarship, search allows users to quickly dive into a document corpus and learn its strengths and weaknesses in an iterative, self-correcting way. The real question is this: How do we take advantage of the efficiency and familiarity that search brings to research while also addressing and minimizing its limitations? To begin answering this question, we turn to SES and Project Arclight.

Scaled Entity Search and Project Arclight

SES is a technical and interpretive method for searching large digital collections. As a technical method, it allows and encourages users to search for multiple entities (rather than a single keyword or phrase) and track those entities in a transparent manner across a large corpus. In doing so, it restores some of the context lost when we only search for individual keyword "nuggets" by mapping how these nuggets comprise broader veins of data. By looking at how entities trend over time and in relationship with each other, we can begin to situate our results and close readings of sources within larger contexts and also measure our historical claims.

To put this into practice, we have developed Arclight, a web-based tool informed by the SES technical method that allows users to quickly search and visualize how entities trend across time within the MHDL's corpus of 2 million pages. To be as transparent as possible in our search functions, Arclight utilizes an open source Apache Solr search index. While many humanities researchers have neither the time nor the training to fully understand the workings underlying most search algorithms, Solr mitigates this "black box" problem by making its documentation and search functions open and freely available for users who wish to investigate further. Indexed within Arclight are roughly 2 million discrete XML documents, each representing an individual page from the thousands of periodicals and books related to theater, film, broadcasting, and recorded sound digitized in the MHDL (Hoyt et al. 2014).

When users enter a query in Arclight, the software returns a visualization that graphs the number of pages per year in which the query appears. From this visualization, we can quickly see how an entity trended within the MHDL over time, including when it begins to appear in the corpus, the years that it peaks, and when it begins to disappear. Arclight also has the ability to search multiple entities at the same time, allowing us to produce comparative views of media history with large entity lists. With a simple search, we can see the trending patterns of several entities at once, raising possible questions about their relationships and intersections. In addition to the graph, the data produced by searches can be downloaded in the form of comma-separated value (CSV) files, which can be viewed and analyzed as Excel spreadsheets.

While distant reading can help us consider the bigger picture, we do not want to eliminate the detail and richness that come from close readings of documents. As users move their cursors over the graph lines, Arclight provides them with more information, such as the dates, titles, and types of the periodicals represented, in the same interface. Additionally, users can click through to Lantern, the MHDL's search platform, allowing them a choice between either a "mid-level" view of the search results or a close-up look at the actual page. This process combines abstraction and granularity; users can read fine details while situating them within the larger corpus and in relation to other entities.

While Arclight produces data and visualizations at an amazingly fast speed, it is important to situate these results within a framework that helps us remain critical of them, mitigating as much as possible the criticisms of search discussed above. To this end, we offer the interpretive side of SES as a method to better understand and contextualize our searches and results. We focus on three key elements that shape the processes of Arclight—the entities, the corpus, and the digital—in a triangulated framework that encourages critical awareness of these elements and the relationships between them.

For the entities, SES asks you, the user, to reflect on how your entity list was developed and formed. Why did you select or omit these specific terms? What sources did you use to generate this list? How do these factors limit or enhance returned results? As we know, the most crucial element in search is the human being behind the keyboard; the exact terms that we search (and do not search) play a huge role in our results. We also need to reflect on our corpus: What is its size and scope? Who created it, and why? What are its strengths and weaknesses when it comes to the periodization and diversity of its contents? In other words, what silences and lacunae must we consider? And lastly, it is important to examine what we call *the digital*—the technologies, conventions, and processes that come into play and influence the results. What schema, fields, and other metadata categories were accounted for, and how reliable is that metadata? What do we lose and gain when historical materials and experiences are processed digitally? What technical settings were used to transform physical materials to digital form? How does digitizing materials and making them machine-readable (using OCR) influence our research process?

In asking questions about these three elements, we must also understand how they relate to each other. How does the entity list work with the corpus? How does the corpus change when it becomes digital, and how does this process interact with our entity list? In the context of our own corpus (the MHDL, which focuses on twentieth-century U.S. media), it might be limiting to search for a list of botany terms. However, we should not allow corpus limitations to restrict research questions, and playing only to the strengths of a corpus can also limit our ability to ask new and surprising questions. Since our corpus is heavily focused on U.S. media, a list of foreign films may have low results. But with Arclight, we can see which and when foreign films or filmmakers began appearing in our corpus and start to ask ourselves why certain entities are showing up in a corpus that is not oriented toward that list. Though exploratory in nature, such questions can reveal surprising patterns and unexpected turns for which a researcher's initial query may have never accounted.

Understanding the temporal scope of our corpus in relation to the entity list is also important to analyzing our results. Instead of assuming that a visualized trend indicates that a certain actor or actress lost popularity in the 1940s, we should also consider that many of the trade papers and fan magazines in the MHDL only go up to the 1940s. Limitations and blind spots in a corpus might result from a variety of factors: copyright and budget restrictions, access, and/or content availability, all of which affect the relationship between the corpus and the digital. Additionally, we must think about how our entity lists can produce misleading results through digital search. For example, an Arclight search for "First National" returns hits for the First National Bank building in Chicago and the "first national motion picture exposition" of 1916 in addition to the hits for the film distributor.

In thinking critically about these elements and their relationships to each other, SES provides users with multiple ways to interpret and contextualize their Arclight results as well as develop new questions about media history. To demonstrate the SES method and Arclight in action, we turn to our case study of two early Hollywood stars: Sessue Hayakawa and Tsuru Aoki. After briefly reviewing the existing literature on the actors, we present our Arclight results for them as a concrete example of the potentials and pitfalls of the software and the SES process.

Hayakawa, Aoki, and Arclight: Revisiting the Trajectory of an Early Hollywood Power Couple

As Miyao illustrates, by 1917 Sessue Hayakawa achieved a stardom on par with (and at times even greater than) his contemporaries, Charlie Chaplin and William S. Hart (Miyao 2007: 3). During the late 1910s, Hayakawa and his wife, actress Tsuru Aoki, were a bona fide celebrity couple. Often featured in fan magazines, Hayakawa was commonly viewed as a cosmopolitan sex symbol, while Aoki was often positioned in a lesser role as the all-American domestic wife (albeit with an Orientalist tinge). Their presence as major film stars in the early studio system is almost perplexing given the nativist attitudes of the time, not to mention the continued lack of Asian and Asian-American leading actors in Hollywood (Ono & Pham 2009). Despite their contemporary popularity, Hayakawa and Aoki have been mostly forgotten, even among film scholars. While Ross (2005) and Miyao (2007) produced persuasive works on Aoki and Hayakawa, respectively, the Japanese-American couple has not received the same treatment or attention as other figures from American cinema in the 1910s.

Thus, Hayakawa and Aoki present an interesting case study in the ways that Arclight and the SES process can help confirm existing scholarship, nuance historical narratives, and raise exploratory questions. In addition to being understudied, Hayakawa and Aoki are ideal subjects for Arclight because—as is the case for many silent cinema stars—most of their films, including *The Chinatown Mystery* (Mutual, 1915), *Alien Souls* (Paramount, 1916), and *Locked Lips* (Universal, 1920), are lost, forcing us to think about their place in film history beyond their films. Furthermore, excluding Ross and Miyao, much of the scholarship on Hayakawa and Aoki focuses on their on-screen images, often using them as examples of the "yellow peril" or "lotus blossom" stereotypes. While such representations are real and have had an impact on understandings of race and ethnicity, defining Hayakawa and Aoki only in terms of these stereotypes denies their agency as professionals working to survive in a racist Hollywood structure and society. It also obscures the intricate and contradictory relationship between their on-screen images and the fan-favorite, all-American personas crafted in the trade press and fan magazines. Using Arclight to map Hayakawa and Aoki's trending through the MHDL corpus can unveil different ways that media historians might view them.

Hayakawa and Aoki also perform well as search entities. To put it bluntly, their names are unique within the context of American film, making false positives in the search results quite unlikely. However, this does not mean that their names are unambiguous. Tsuru Aoki's first name has occasionally been misspelled as "Tsura" and "Tsuri," and she is also sometimes referred to as "Mrs. Sessue Hayakawa," skewing the results for both her and her husband. The misspellings were easily addressed; our entity list simply included "Tsura Aoki" and "Tsuri Aoki" in addition to the correct spelling, and those results were combined. The use of

Hayakawa's name to refer to Aoki was a more difficult issue, as Arclight is unable distinguish between these labels. Based on preliminary scans of the results, "Mrs. Sessue Hayakawa" did not occur often enough to significantly impact our discussion here. Nevertheless, this issue highlights the importance of users' attention to the broader contexts and semiotics of their entities—in this case, the gendered descriptions of married women.

It is also important to consider the periodization of our search. Regardless of whether a researcher focuses specifically on a certain period or arbitrarily chooses a time frame, she must consider how time parameters interact with both the entities and the corpus in SES. For two reasons, we chose to focus our search of Hayakawa and Aoki on the period 1913–1922. First, this range encompasses the start of their careers in early Hollywood, their eventual peaks as silent cinema stars, and the end of their status as leading actors. Second, it plays to the strengths of our corpus; the MHDL has lengthy runs of film industry papers and magazines, including *Moving Picture World*, *Motion Picture News*, *The Film Daily*, *Variety*, *Photoplay*, and *Motion Picture Magazine*, that extensively cover this period.

With our complete entity list—consisting of both actors' names as well as variants and misspellings—and time frame selected, we were ready to begin our search. From a distant view, the resulting final graph (see Figure 42.1) of Hayakawa and Aoki's trajectory through the MHDL confirms the overall narrative of the couple established by Ross and Miyao.

Aoki, who started her Hollywood career before Hayakawa did, begins trending before him, in 1913. By the time Hayakawa appears in the corpus the following year, Aoki's hits double his numbers. However, Miyao contends that, after their marriage in 1914 and Hayakawa's instant stardom with *The Cheat* (1915), Aoki played an important but ultimately subordinate role in the construction of Hayakawa's star text (2007: 142). In Miyao's account, Aoki was mostly linked to her husband, hence the use of "Mrs. Sessue Hayakawa" (143). Painted by the studios and fan magazines as a background character in the ideal Victorian family image constructed for the couple, Aoki stopped playing lead roles by 1916.

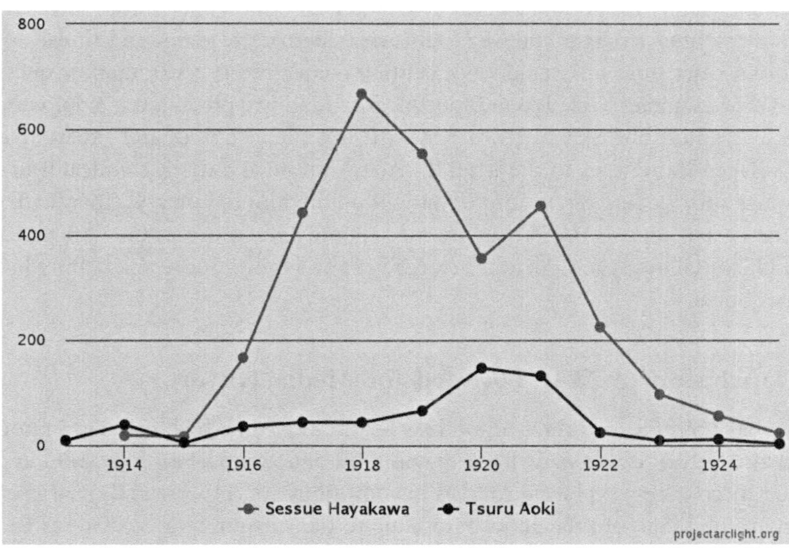

Figure 42.1 Total number of page hits for Hayakawa and Aoki in Media History Digital Library, 1913–1925.

Our Arclight results mostly support Miyao's account; after 1915, the quantity of Aoki's page hits never surpasses her husband's, averaging only about 38 pages a year compared to Hayakawa's yearly average of 232 pages. However, an additional benefit of using SES and Arclight is the ability to see relationships between entities. Miyao's contention that Aoki was purely subordinate and largely linked to her husband suggests that Aoki's trending patterns would closely reflect Hayakawa's, and this is mostly true—except for 1920. After Hayakawa peaks in 1918, he steadily declines into the 1920s, dropping about 25 percent each year; however, Aoki actually peaks in 1920, tripling her page hits from 1919. This increase forces us to reconsider the trajectory of Aoki's stardom; if her role was secondary to Hayakawa's, then why does she trend sharply upwards as her husband declines?

While space constraints limit our exploration of this question, a mid-level analysis of her hits in the year 1920 shows that about 75 percent of the pages are related to either her new Universal Films contract or the resulting films. While she was never advertised on the level of her husband, the Arclight results reveal that Aoki was still active in the industry as an actress after 1915 and even promoted as a lead in 1920. Another surprising discovery is the location of these pages. In demonstrating Aoki's dominant and complex image as a domestic figure, Ross and Miyao both heavily rely on sources from fan magazines, leading us to expect that Aoki's peak in the MHDL would occur in those magazines. However, only 13 percent of the pages in 1920 come from fan magazines; the rest are located in industry trade papers, such as *Exhibitor's Herald*, *The Film Daily*, and *Motion Picture News*. Mentions and representations of Aoki thus ebb and flow in very different ways depending on whether they are situated in the context of fan or industry coverage.

To be clear, these results are not meant to disprove Ross or Miyao. As discussed above, Arclight confirms a lot of their work. We should not take these results as some sort of definitive quantitative answer, either; there is always a degree of error in the trend numbers (as a result of imperfect OCR and ambiguous entities such as "Mrs. Sessue Hayakawa," for instance). Additionally, although these entities pair well with the corpus, both the corpus and the results only represent a specific subset of the many texts discussing contemporary American culture; different narratives and results would likely come to the fore in other collections. However, our example does show how Arclight and SES can reveal alternate readings and threads of information that can nuance our understanding of existing media history, creating new questions in the process. For example, while it is indisputable that Aoki was presented as a domestic figure within fan magazines, our SES helps to contextualize these sources and situate that reading quantitatively: in some years in the MHDL, Aoki's image as a domestic ideal is not the *dominant* discourse surrounding discussions of her within the film industry. Rather, at her highest point in the corpus, Aoki's name is mentioned significantly more in the film trades and in relation to Universal, suggesting that her career in early Hollywood was anything but linear or one-dimensional.

Conclusion: A Way Forward for Media History

In this chapter, we have put forward three arguments for the ways in which our conception and practice of media history can benefit from digital tools and approaches. First, film and media history need to continue exploring sources beyond films and other audiovisual productions, broadening the scope of their inquiry to explore the surrounding ecosystems and discourses that influence how productions are created, circulated, and received. Second, search can be a powerful and efficient tool, but taking full advantage of the twenty-first century digital library requires that researchers thoroughly understand how search algorithms and indexes mediate our experience of search. Finally, we have offered a specific software tool (Arclight) and an interpretive method for using it or similar methods that afford contextualized search at scale.

Digital methods such as SES and software tools such as Arclight will never replace traditional approaches to historiography. No matter how comprehensive our collections of digitized documents or how fast our search indexes, historical knowledge will continue to be produced—and in most respects, can *only* be produced—by means of closely reading primary sources and constructing empirically verifiable interpretations. However, the strength of these traditional approaches lies in how they provide for revision in light of new evidence, and the new availability of vast swaths of such evidence in digital form suggests that many new revisions will be made in the coming years. Beyond simple access, digital methods also allow for historical revision in another way—not in directly feeding researchers with new *answers* (which in some ways continues to be the utopian dream of digital humanities), but in prompting them to ask new *questions*. The true strength of computational approaches is encouraging researchers to read their evidence in different ways—in quantitative ways, yes, but also ways that highlight the marginal, the unexpected, and the forgotten.

Acknowledgments

Arclight was developed at the University of Wisconsin-Madison in collaboration with a team, led by Charles Acland, at Concordia University in Montreal. Our research and software development was made possible thanks to the support of an international Digging into Data grant, sponsored by the Institute of Museum and Library Services (IMLS) in the U.S. and the Social Sciences and Humanities Research Council (SSHRC) in Canada.

Further Reading

Acland, C. and E. Hoyt (eds.) (2016) *The Arclight Guidebook to Media History and the Digital Humanities*, Falmer: REFRAME/Project Arclight, retrieved from projectarclight.org/book.

Holley, R. (2009) "How Good Can It Get? Analyzing and Improving OCR Accuracy in Large Scale Historic Newspaper Digitization Programs," *D-Lib Magazine* 15(3/4).

Hoyt, E., K. Hughes, D. Long, T. Tran, and K. Ponto (2014) "Scaled Entity Search: A Method for Media Historiography and Responses to Critiques of Big Humanities Data Research," *Proceedings of IEEE Conference on Big Data*, pp. 51–59.

Hughes, K., E. Hoyt, D. Long, K. Ponto, and T. Tran (2015) "Hacking Broadcasting History's Data: Station Call Signs, Digitized Magazines, and Scaled Entity Search," *Media Industries Journal* 2, no. 2 (2015), retrieved from mediaindustriesjournal.org/index.php/mij/article/view/128/182.

Miyao, D. (2007) *Sessue Hayakawa: Silent Cinema and Transnational Stardom*, Durham, NC: Duke University Press.

References

Arclight (n.d.) retrieved from search.projectarclight.org.

Butler, J. (2014) "Statistical Analysis of Television Style: What Can Numbers Tell Us About TV Editing?" *Cinema Journal* 54(1), 25–44.

Casey, M. and M. Williams (2014) "Exploring Film Auteurship with the ACTION Toolbox," paper presented at *Society for Cinema and Media Studies Annual Conference*, Seattle, WA.

Cutting, J. E. (2014) "Event Segmentation and Seven Types of Narrative Discontinuity in Popular Movies," *Acta Psychologica* 149, 69–77.

Ferguson, K. (2015) "Volumetric Cinema," Video Essay, *[in]Transition*, retrieved from mediacommons.futureofthebook.org/intransition/2015/03/10/volumetric-cinema.

Gleason, D. (ed.) (n.d.) *AmericanRadioHistory.com*, retrieved from americanradiohistory.com

Halavais, A. (2009) *Search Engine Society*, Cambridge, MA: Polity Press.

Holley, R. (2009) "How Good Can It Get? Analyzing and Improving OCR Accuracy in Large Scale Historic Newspaper Digitization Programs," *D-Lib Magazine* 15(3/4).

Hoyt, E., K. Hughes, D. Long, T. Tran, and K. Ponto (2014) "Scaled Entity Search: A Method for Media Historiography and Responses to Critiques of Big Humanities Data Research," *Proceedings of IEEE Conference on Big Data*, pp. 51–59.

Hughes, K., E. Hoyt, D. Long, K. Ponto, and T. Tran (2015) "Hacking Broadcasting History's Data: Station Call Signs, Digitized Magazines, and Scaled Entity Search," *Media Industries Journal* 2, no. 2 (2015), retrieved from mediaindustriesjournal.org/index.php/mij/article/view/128/182.

Jockers, M. L. (2013) *Macroanalysis: Digital Methods and Literary History*, Urbana, IL: University of Illinois Press.

Kuhn, V., R. Aurora, A. Craig, K. Franklin, M. Simeone, D. Bock, and L. Marini (2012) "Large Scale Video Analytics: On-demand, Iterative Inquiry for Moving Image Research," in *Proceedings of the IEEE eScience Conference*.

Lantern (n.d.) retrieved from lantern.mediahist.org.

Manovich, L. (2012) "How to Compare One Million Images?" in D. M. Berry (ed.) *Understanding Digital Humanities*, New York, NY: Palgrave Macmillan, pp. 249–98.

Media History Digital Library (n.d.) retrieved from mediahistoryproject.org.

Miyao, D. (2007) *Sessue Hayakawa: Silent Cinema and Transnational Stardom*, Durham, NC: Duke University Press.

Navarro, G. (2001) "A Guided Tour to Approximate String Matching," *ACM Computing Surveys* 33(1), 31–88.

Ono, K. and V. Pham (2009) *Asian Americans and the Media*, Malden, MA: Polity Press.

Ross, S. (2005) "The Americanization of Tsuru Aoki: Orientalism, Melodrama, Star Image, and the New Woman," *Camera Obscura* 60, 20(3), 129–58.

Smoodin, E. (2007) "Introduction: The History of Film History," in J. Lewis and E. Smoodin (eds.) *Looking Past the Screen: Case Studies in American Film History and Method*, Durham, NC: Duke University Press.

Underwood, T. (2014) "Theorizing Research Practices We Forgot to Theorize Twenty Years Ago," *Representations* 127, 64–72.

Van Couvering, E. (2008) "The History of the Internet Search Engine: Navigational Media and the Traffic Commodity," in A. Spink and M. Zimmer (eds.) *Web Search: Multidisciplinary Perspectives*, Berlin: Springer, pp. 177–206.

43
THE INTIMATE LIVES OF CULTURAL OBJECTS

Jeffrey Schnapp

Big data is big. Big in as much as it has become a dominant feature of the public conversation regarding the knowledge economy. Big also to the degree that it is the focal point of major investments in organizations of every kind, from government to business and media to universities. In this context, the adjective "big" has tended to become commensurate with adequacy and completeness.

Small data is small. Small in as much as there is much less public discourse about small data sets, even though the great majority of data sets fall into that category. In the big data conversation, the adjective "small" has become associated with inadequacy and incompleteness, even insignificance.

There is, of course, no consensus on what counts as big or small, because data scales are a moving target and data densities do not always correlate with data volumes or the size of a given source. The big data of yesteryear are all too readily the small data of today. And the sensor systems embedded in the traffic lights at a city crossroads may produce torrents of information that, from a computational standpoint, are "small" because their simple structure makes them easy to process.

Such inherent ambiguities aside, there are, of course, some agreed-upon, conventional understandings regarding what counts as big. They run something like the following:

> Big data implies not just *size* but also *complexity*, attributable to the confluence of a variety of independent data sources that cannot readily be analyzed or managed with standard tools and techniques, this due to the unpredictability or shifting nature of their permutations and combinations. When brought together, significant size and complexity create the distinctive challenges and opportunities that define the field of big data.

Much of the public conversation around big data has, in reality, been about the present and future of big business or, sometimes, big cities—about the accelerated processing of real-time data streams, particularly the data produced by social media, for purposes of monitoring, management, or forecasting the behavior of complex systems.

A good deal of this conversation seems to me of only oblique interest to the humanities, that is, unless real-time historiography and trendcasting were to suddenly bubble up and reinforce the hold—some would say the *stranglehold*—of presentism over the contemporary humanities. This said, the question of designing and building "animated archives" that document contemporary culture and history—particularly *emergent* cultural forms and *emergent* historical events—is surely apropos, implying, as it does, size, complexity, and the unpredictability engendered by large volumes of highly diverse media as well as heterogeneous user populations. One case in point is the Digital Archive of Japan's 2011 Disasters, which metaLAB played a key role in prototyping what my colleagues and I like to call "live crisis archiving." Known as the JDA, the project expands the compass of how memories are built in, attend to, and serve the *present* while, at the same time, ensuring the transmission of the past to future generations much as archives have always done. Participatory in character, federative in its design (involving partners from Yahoo! Japan to the National Diet Library), encompassing media types from tweets and photographs to testimonials generated on-site to websites and video, the JDA is made up of not only documents but also and most especially the beehive-like curatorial and interpretive activities of the community that animates it: a community that includes everyone from victims and activists to policymakers and journalists to students, scholars, and environmental scientists. And what is perhaps transformative is that the diverse time horizons of this varied user population are matched by the ability of the archive itself to permit users to analyze the events associated with the March 2011 earthquake and tsunami on time scales that extend from hundredths of seconds to months and years and eventually decades. (As a cultural historian, I am usually excited when I can track an event down to the scale of years or months. The notion of being able to excavate events on the scale of tens of seconds seems as daunting as it is exhilarating.)

Other portions of the public conversation regarding big data seem to me more directly pertinent to future work in cultural-historical fields: fields where open and linked data infrastructures analogous to the Global Biodiversity Information Facility may one day allow for the aggregation and analysis of data sets in the form of bibliographies, collections, inventories, demographic databases, text repositories, and social and economic surveys across institutions. The promise tendered by such infrastructures to future generations of scholars is multiple: the promise of being able to reconstruct forgotten, ignored, and invisible histories—histories including not just texts and images but also sound and the tangible world; the promise of enhanced reach, rigor, and precision in humanities research findings; the promise of being able to tell stories about culture on unexpected scales by, for example, providing moment-by-moment, "picture-perfect" time slices of the evolution of communities and cultural institutions, or exploring local or global entanglements between economic, social, and cultural trends over time scales, from hours and days to centuries and millennia. Perhaps there is even space here for a quantitative humanities that would build bridges with or critique the quantitative social sciences.

Whatever the case may be, fulfillment of these promises depends upon the quality, consistency, and design of individual records. Big data, however defined, are built out of small data, and even the smallest of data are hardly *given* or *captured* (as the Latin *datus* and *captus* misleadingly suggest). Rather, data are *constructed*; and, when captured, it is these *constructs* that are seized. Data are, of course, constructed according to institutionally inflected schemes that presuppose assumptions regarding value, significance, and use; they are also shaped as a function of information architectures, tools, and techniques. All of which is a roundabout way of saying that, when it comes to data (as in the case of complex systems like those of the natural world), the big is fatally entangled with the small and the small with the big in ways that enable the kinds of stories, big or small, we can tell with them. So the deeper question, in my mind, is not *big or small*, but rather *big and small*, or how we *design* the webs of interconnection, the zooming spaces, between different scales and points of entry.

I would now like to drill down to the level of core records to then wrap up with consideration of some work related to my interest in museums as sites where academic research has the potential to speak to expert and nonexpert audiences alike. In so doing, I would like to examine the relation of these core records to the cultural objects from which they emanate like a kind of virtual projection or aureole to ask *how expanded modes of registration, record-making, and linking might thicken and enrich those virtual projections, whether from a social and informational standpoint or the standpoint of the sensory data they convey.* Every such data halo is, of course, at once a description and an abstraction, a set of representations and reductions. Irrespective of whether the object at hand is a Japanese woodblock print, a native Hawaiian feather headdress, a two-ton Assyrian monolith, or a mid-twentieth-century stovetop coffee maker, to extend its objecthood into the realm of data and digital media is to enact a metaphoric displacement and create a new set of objects that have their own materiality, affordances, expressivities, and even poetry: so-called "digital surrogates." The elements that compose the world of objects and render them meaningful sources of experience and vectors of human sense-making encompass senses (touch, taste, vision, and hearing) that are not readily reducible to snapshots, verbal descriptions, or data schemes. No record, no matter how exact or exhaustive, constitutes a perfect replica; discoverability, portability, and exchangeability are all achieved by stripping *some data* away in the name of *other data.* And the stories that objects, however small, tell often turn out to be not small at all, whether from the standpoint of data or their importance. The verse, "To see a World in a Grain of Sand," from the opening of William Blake's *Auguries of Innocence* comes to mind, as does the Zen parable of the monk who sees a landscape filled with mountains, rivers, and prairies on the apparently "blank" surface of a bean.

The humanities disciplines bring a unique set of skills to the table when it comes to the arts of observation, description, classification, and interpretation. Close attention to texts and artifacts (in particular, to their polyvalences and ambiguities), critically informed reflection on taxonomical practices, and nuanced thinking about power, shifts in media, and sociohistorical context are all hallmarks of humanistic thought. So my question here is how we might bring this skill set to bear on the design of cultural records, not to mention the platforms that they support and depend upon in turn. Poets, in particular, have mused deeply and sometimes movingly about the question of what it means to coax objects to yield themselves up in the form of words and how the necessary "failure" of all such metaphoric transfers is generative, yielding new forms of experience, thought, and even beauty. Among them, I am fond of Mark Doty, who has recently written of perception that it is:

> [S]imultaneous and layered, and to single out any aspect of it for naming is to turn your attention away from myriad other things, those braiding elements of the *sensorium*—that continuous, complex response to things perpetually delivered by the senses, the encompassing sphere that is such a large part of our subjectivity.
>
> (Doty 2010: 3)

As Doty goes on to note, this shifting, ever provisional field of experience forms "a seamless web of information—but *information* is the driest and least revealing of essential twenty-first century words, and the data the senses offer every waking moment is anything but that" (4).

The data of the senses may be elusive, wet, and subjective, with one sense spilling over into the next; and information may be cut and dry, unrevealing, and institutional, much as

Doty would have it. But there is an in-between space worthy of exploration that places the powers of the first in productive tension and dialogue with the second, and I would like to explore that in-between space with three convergent aims. First, to think about some modes of "sensory translation" that are more portable and less local or momentary than Doty's normative body-to-body encounter between a given person and a given thing: what are the traces of otherwise difficult-to-represent sensory data—texture, smell, temperature, timbre, grain—that could conceivably be (indirectly) captured, described, or transplanted to the database or screen? How might we get "closer" to objects, so to speak, even as we translate them into the realm of information? Second, I would like to think about how platforms built to leverage the power of expanded modes of description might enable users to interpret, analyze, curate, narrate, and/or experience cultural objects in some novel ways. Third, I would also like to think about the expressive potential of the metadata and media associated with objects and collections as *cultural materials in and of themselves*, particularly as these grow in scope and complexity: what are the braiding, medium-specific elements that make up the *sensorium* of information? Or to put it otherwise, where might the stuff of poetry lie in the metadata and media? And how might these be sculpted into meaningful, freestanding experiences?

* * *

A world of purely autotelic analog objects has never existed. Objects have always been *social* in the minimal sense of being interconnected in the natural environment (even before the arrival of human agents to manipulate them) and, more often, in the maximal sense of becoming units of accumulation, exchange, and modification. As, many centuries ago, collections—be they collections of tablets, scrolls, books, legal records, or art objects—scaled up to proportions that exceeded the cognitive ability of individuals to manage them without inventorial systems, the question of exactly *what* such records should record and *how* they should be tethered to the objects collected has remained an abiding question *internal* to culture.

Symptomatic of this fact is one of the founding moments in the western poetics of metadata: the publication of the 120 tablets of the *Pinakes*, authored by the third-century BC epigrammatist, Callimachus, in quantitative verse, in which the poet inventoried the 400,000 scrolls of the Alexandrian library, parsed by discipline, author, and genre. In the tens of centuries that followed the era of Callimachus, schemes for texts, art works, objects, and other socially or culturally significant items have evolved and eventually gelled into the standardized schemes that structure our bibliographical and collections databases.

So how to describe the things and, in turn, the aggregates of things known as collections, with whose care today's librarians, registrars, curators, and scholars are entrusted? And how do we do so in ways that make them not just accessible to computational analysis but also engaging, if not sensorially, then in other ways? The conventional response, a response codified in the course of many centuries of inventorial, curatorial, and bibliographic practice, remains the most powerful option: to follow the conventions that reduce a given object to a series of fields: title, creator, date, place of creation, medium, and provenance, plus associated inventorial data—object and accessions number, condition report, and location code, for instance. Add a still photograph or two, and a record is born: the standard record we now routinely experience (at least partially) exposed on museum websites. But how adequate are such descriptions given the range of descriptive techniques and media available to us?

By whom and for whom ought they be produced? And how to confront the endemic problem faced by every taxonomical scheme: namely, that objects are blithely indifferent to human categories? Even a book can be a multitude of things: a sequence of letters and words organized into pages, a jewel-encrusted object whose significance is associated with its binding, a secret notebook in which readers transmit messages to future readers, or the sole surviving object documenting a shipwreck. Likewise, 190 fifth-century BC pottery shards or *ostraka*, like those found in a pit on the northern slope of the Athenian Acropolis, may be described correctly as the remains of broken urns and pots. But they may also form a corpus of deliberately falsified voting ballots authored, not by hundreds of citizens, but by the four conspirators who sought to have the Athenian leader, Themistokles, ostracized and sent into exile as part of a political plot (American School of Classical Studies n.d.).

For most of the history of modern cultural institutions—let us continue to limit ourselves to art museums—the conventional acts of reduction to title, creator, date, medium, and place of creation were viable because the data were visible only on the inside. Collections data served the needs of inventory management and were the near-exclusive province of museum staff—registrars, conservators, curators, and educators—exposed to outsiders only in the form of wall labels and captions. But as catalogues and inventories have migrated out into public view on the world wide web, the situation has changed. The visit that once began and ended at the museum's door has dilated into a before, during, and after, with telepresence governing the before and after and sometimes infusing even the *during*. Yet the modes of description and representation in online catalogs remain much as they were in the predigital era: top down, tethered to standardized schemes, based upon atomized approaches to objects. Collections are made visible only as assemblages of individual objects; and, even at the level of individual records, the majority of fields are routinely stripped away.

As a case in point, let us compare how the New York MoMA and Amazon.com describe the same item online: the Bialetti Moka Express—a design artifact born in the 1930s, industrialized in the 1950s, and now a ubiquitous household object (Schnapp 2001).

The MoMA description strips the object of any trace of commerce to elevate it into the ether of blue chip design. It assigns the title of "creator" to Alfonso Bialetti; in point of fact, he was an inventor who, knowing nothing about design, stole the Moka's look from contemporary Parisian silver coffee sets. It provides a date of creation, but the object photographed does not correspond to that date: it is not the original mid-1930s Moka, but rather one from a late twentieth-century production run. It reduces the object to a single photographic image in which the coffeemaker has been rotated to conceal the pressure valve, the mechanical stamp along the object's waist, and the Bialetti logo, with its moustachioed cartoon of Alfonso Bialetti, created in the 1950s. The record provides no data regarding manufacturer, materials, size, and source. Nowhere does it hint that this is one in a vast series, that it is composed of three main components, or even that it is a stovetop coffee maker. (The existence of related products at MoMAstore.org is tastefully relegated to a link.)

The Amazon description is richer, more accurate, and opens up a space for engagement and collaborative description. It includes text, photographs, and video. It situates the object within a multilayered series of fields that show the size range of the device (from one to 40 cups); the families of variations and imitations it has engendered; the uses to which it can be put; the other objects, products, and processes with which it is associated; and its constituent parts and weight. There is no embarrassment regarding the logo, the steam release fitting, or the mechanical stamp: they move front and center in the midst of a plurality of story lines that crisscross the object. There is a cacophony of voices: the Bialetti company's; various distributors, sellers, and advertisers; Amazon itself; the buzz of critical citizen-consumers. In short, Amazon treats the Moka as much a *network* as a *product*.

Amazon's descriptions are hardly perfect. As one might expect, they show little interest in data that are not associated with use-value or consumption. They tell us little about the materials that make up the device, how or where it was fabricated, or the mutations that its design has undergone in the course of its 70-year history. But they hint at the potential for multifaceted, striated regimes of description that both expand the nature of the descriptors themselves and build them from the ground up, tapping into a plurality of communities of interest and expertise. Most of all, they approach the act of description as interpretive: curation and interpretation begin at the moment of accession, not in some distant afterlife.

In thinking beyond the Amazonian model, might not the design question for digital humanities be how to layer a diversity of representations on top of the standard descriptors so as to better approach the full sensorium—the weight, the texture, the feeling—of a cultural object? And how about unjamming the data resources through open APIs and linked data environments to create virtual realms of curation where researchers can work with open collections data and stories can be told through individual objects (excavated down to the nano scale) as well as with collection-sized aggregates, even *very* large aggregates? There are close to 14 million analog photographs currently housed at the United States Library of Congress, far too many to examine in the course of a lifetime. Yet they document twentieth-century American experience more thickly and richly than any competing repository. To render them accessible in digital form, while invaluable, does little in and of itself; it is only by making them usable with analytical and interpretive tools, which render them viewable and navigable as both aggregates and individual items, that we can begin to unlock their potential as engines of cultural argument on the micro, meso, and macro scale.

* * *

What might a world look like where every object is understood as a collection and every collection understood as a social network of things? There is of course no single answer. But one provocative, platform-level response that I admire is James Bridle's *Hyper-Stacks* project, recently on exhibit at the Victoria and Albert Museum (V&A) (Bridle 2015b). The hyper-stacks in question are networks of objects belonging to the V&A, whose records, accessed via their API, have been analyzed using Open Calais to extract the swarm of tags from which collection maps are in turn generated. These maps are displayed in the V&A gallery as physical stacks and online as force-based network graphs and tag and inventory lists, which can be reshuffled and modified by means of user input (Bridle 2015a).

Bridle is, of course, working with the V&A's records as they stand. So to return once again to the question of what exactly an *expanded core record* might look like, it is perhaps worth mentioning a few high-end techniques currently being employed for research purposes that could also be used to capture traces of Doty's "braided sensorium" and enable experiences of an object's morphology or viscera. Two particular techniques fascinate me: one external—the use of computational photography tools such as RTI (Reflectance Transformation Imaging) and Algorithmic Rendering—and the other internal—micro-CT (Computed Tomography), a nondestructive technique for the full-volume scanning of an object's physical structure (Cultural Heritage Imaging n.d.). RTI has been used to expose processes of overwriting in stone inscriptions and medieval manuscripts as well as analyze decorative features of seventeenth-century bindings. Thanks to RTI, highly attenuated threshold attributes, such as the grain of an item, invisible to a conventional camera lens or the naked eye but available to the sense of touch, can be represented Micro-CT instead plumbs depths that can be, at best, intuited; it has been fruitfully employed for the study of mummies, the restoration of statues, and the study of antique furnishings (Re et al. 2014). Tomography tells us about the way that things are made, the secrets they harbor; it allows us to experience features of an object that may have been inaccessible even to its creator. For the moment, both are expensive technologies. But there exists a growing array of low cost, "rough and dirty" techniques from open source, automated image analytics and photogrammetry to the recording of object sound files (what does a vase sound like when it is tapped?), animated GIFs (what does it look like in the round?), high magnification photography (what is its texture?), and video (how does one manipulate it?), all of which produce data objects that can increasingly be analyzed and rendered searchable thanks to tools such as image and acoustical search engines and speech recognition software. And let us not ignore the registration of simple aspects of physicality, like an object's texture or weight, that are still frequently omitted from data schemes.

An approach of this kind was sketched out in *Teaching with Things* (see Figure 43.1), a project I developed a couple of years back with my colleagues, Matthew Battles and Yanni Loukissas (now at Georgia Tech). In *Teaching with Things*, the point of departure was to enrich inventory records by adding multimedia elements to the standard core: an "anchor" representation in the form of a quick-and-dirty 3-D model produced via photogrammetry and a library of video clips developed in the act of processing the object. The latter might typically

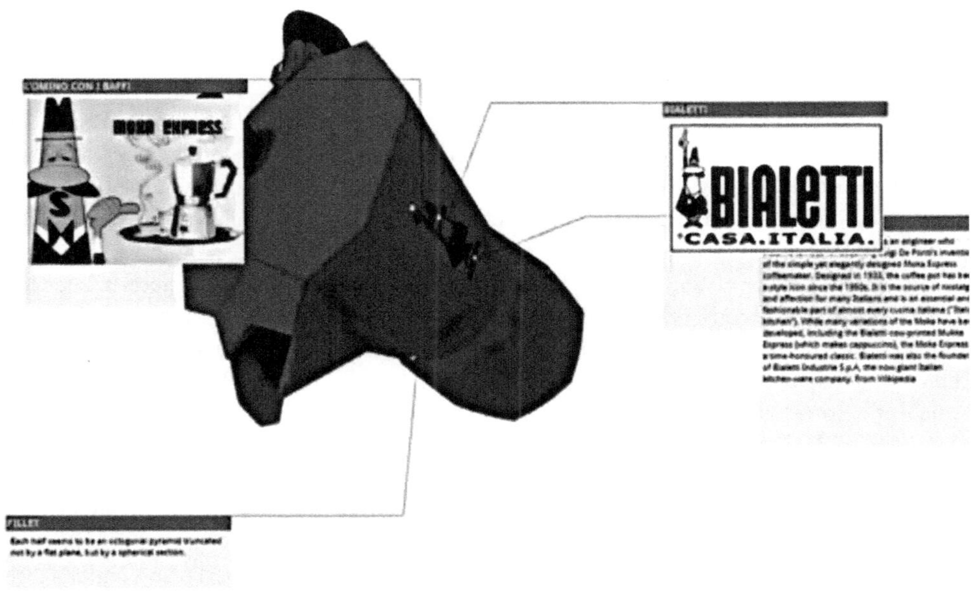

Figure 43.1 Screenshot from metaLAB (at) Harvard's *Teaching with Things* (2013) showing an "artifactual interface" in which annotations are pinpointed directly onto the surface of a 3-D model. In this particular case, the object in question is a Bialetti Moka Express.

Source: Matthew Battles, Yanni Loukissas, and Jeffrey Schnapp

include documentation of the object's scale and weight, its acoustical properties, its component parts, and any details that are significant from the standpoint of its use or meaning. These base elements were supplemented with forms of capture that expose otherwise imperceptible features: things you could not see even if the object was sitting right there in front of you—high magnification views of surfaces or hidden contours; slices of the object's geometry based on 3-D scans. In other words, describing an object and building its record were understood as interpretive processes that result in a multimedia composite. In addition to the core record, there is an anchor model, which is little more than a working model. No one representation, whether text or video clip or photograph or sound file, puts itself forward as the definitive portrait. Rather, each and every object is treated as a collection, a mosaic, an aggregate of characteristics.

Step two in *Teaching with Things* was to transform this standard record plus multimedia composite into a node that supports an array of interpretive activities, from annotations and commentary to links across the collection and beyond. Such annotations, whatever their medium, can be "pinned" to any location on the 3-D anchor model or to the model as a whole. They can be displayed in one of two forms. The first is as a set of windows radiating outward from the model that serves as an "artifactual interface." Much as you explore an object in the physical world with your hands, you are able to explore clusters of annotations without ever entering a keyword: by simply rotating and zooming in and out of the anchor model. The second form involves a split-screen representation in which the core record of an anchor model plus a multimedia description appear on the far left, while on the right appears the accumulated stratigraphy of forms of analysis, cross-reference, argument, and commentary that, considered together, tell a full but still unfolding story of a given object, its family relations, its meanings as construed by various communities of interpreters. Much like Bridle's *Hyper-Stacks*, the aim is to model a world where, instead of being treated as singularities, cultural objects appear enmeshed in the networks that confer meaning upon them.

If the overall aim of *Teaching with Things* was to explore the webs of relations that animate a given cultural object in the digital environment, then the final destination places those webs in direct dialogue with physical originals. By way of a conclusion, I would like to demo an installation project that builds an experience of a collections database into the very site where the source materials are housed.

On the top floor of the recently inaugurated Harvard Art Museum, there is a leftover space between the conservation labs and the glass-enclosed central courtyard where the nineteenth-century Fogg Museum merges with Renzo Piano's new glass and steel structure. This otherwise useless space is too bright for paper objects, too small for exhibits, and too much of a corridor for the silent contemplation of artworks. The result was its recasting as the so-called Lightbox Gallery, with a wall of monitors on one side and a set of networked projectors on the other that cast their images onto semiopaque shades (Harvard Art Museums n.d.). Deployed as a space for multimedia events, media artworks, and media-augmented micro-exhibitions, its default identity was developed by a student team led by my colleagues, Jessica Yurkovsky, Krystelle Denis, and James Yamada, as part of the Berkman Center's 2014 Digital Problem-Solving Initiative. Their work assumes the following form. Upon entering the gallery, you are greeted by an object map made of thumbnails for every single item installed on the floors below: some 1,800 items from ancient coins to works of contemporary art. Displayed on the wall of monitors, these thumbnails are called by a JavaScript program via the museum API. When a visitor points an air mouse at any of the thumbnails and clicks on it, the item is pulled to the center of the object map and surrounded by an overlay, which exposes the entire database record as well as the stack of surrogates that accompany it: x-ray images, an analysis of color saturation and balance, other copies of the work, related objects in storage . . . you name it. If the visitor moves the cursor over any of the data fields, then the field lights up as if to say, "click on me." When one accepts the invitation, the entire object map is reshuffled in accordance with the filter applied. Perhaps the visitor wants to see the entire collection organized by material, the frequency of online visitors, or date of accession. All of these actions have a secondary effect: they activate the projection system, which produces a variety of data visualizations that allow visitors to see where the object they have selected ranks in that given category (date of accession, medium, or provenance, for instance). By toggling between these two modes of viewing, you will get a general sense, I think, of how the Lightbox works.

The Lightbox Gallery is designed to productively entangle the small with the big and the big with the small in two complementary but divergent ways. On the one hand, it seeks to add value to the visitor's experience of the physical originals: visitors arrive at the Lightbox *after* they have completed their visit to the exhibition floors below, and many return downstairs to view the originals experienced in digital form via the Lightbox. On the other hand, the gallery is designed as an immersive database theater where—emancipated from referential obligations—metadata and digital media are free to dance at the visitors' commands, making a show of a mutability, scalability, and zoomability that is theirs alone (i.e., not shared with their physical counterparts). There is even a geeky wink here to the developer community: Lightbox is the JavaScript library that dims out a web page as an image or video fills the center of the screen.

The project's point is easy enough to sum up: the addition of a "virtual" gallery like the Lightbox is not an either/or proposition with respect to understanding a museum as an institution dedicated to the stewardship of collections of things. Here it is not surrogates *or* originals, but surrogates *and* originals working side by side, sometimes as individual entities, sometimes as members of a larger whole.

Further Reading

Borgman, C. L. (2015) *Big Data, Little Data, No Data—Scholarship in the Networked World*, London and Cambridge, MA: MIT Press.

Sterling, B. (2005) *Shaping Things*, Mediaworks Pamphlets, Cambridge, MA: MIT Press.

References

Alpers, S. (1983) *The Art of Describing: Dutch Art in the Seventeenth Century*, Chicago, IL: University of Chicago Press.

American School of Classical Studies (n.d.) "Factional Politics: The Ostracism of Themistokles," retrieved from www.agathe.gr/democracy/factional_politics.html.

Bowers, F. (1994) *Principles of Bibliographical Description*, New Castle, DE: Oak Knoll Press.

Bridle, J. (2015a) "Five Eyes," retrieved from shorttermmemoryloss.com/portfolio/project/five-eyes—hyper-stacks.

Bridle, J. (2015b) "Hyper-Stacks," retrieved from hyper-stacks.com.

Cultural Heritage Imaging (n.d.) "Overview of CHI Technologies," retrieved from culturalheritageimaging.org/Technologies/Overview.

Digital Archive of Japan's 2011 Disasters (n.d.) retrieved from www.jdarchive.org/ja/home.

Digital Problem Solving Initiative (2013) "Category Archives: Lightbox Gallery," retrieved from blogs.law.harvard.edu/dpsi/category/teams/museums-team-2013.

Doty, M. (2010) *The Art of Description: World into Word*, Minneapolis, MN: Graywolf.

Harvard Art Museums (n.d.) retrieved from www.harvardartmuseums.org.

Mayer-Schönberger, V. and K. Cukier (2013) *Big Data: A Revolution that Will Transform How We Live, Work, and Think*, Boston, MA: Houghton Mifflin Harcourt.

McKitterick, D. (2013) *Old Books, New Technologies: The Representation, Conservation, and Transformation of Books since 1700*, Cambridge, U.K.: Cambridge University Press.

Nicholson, M. H. (1928) *The Art of Description*, New York, NY: F. S. Crofts.

Re, A., F. Albertin, C. Avataneo, R. Brancaccio, J. Corsi, G. Cotto, S. De Blasi, G. Dughera, E. Durisi, W. Ferrarese, A. Giovagnoli, N. Grassi, A. Lo Giudice, P. Mereu, G. Mila, M. Nervo, N. Pastrone, F. Prino, L. Ramello, M. Ravera, C. Ricci, A. Romero, R. Sacchi, A. Staiano, L. Visca, and L. Zamprotta (2014) "X-ray Tomography of Large Wooden Artworks: The Case Study of 'Doppio Corpo' by Pietro Piffetti," *Heritage Science* 2(19), retrieved from www.heritagesciencejournal.com/content/2/1/19.

Schnapp, J. (2001) "The Romance of Caffeine and Aluminum," Special issue on "Things," *Critical Inquiry* 28(1), 244–69.

Teaching with Things: Curation, Hybrid Multimedia, and Object-Oriented Pedagogy (n.d.) retrieved from hilt.harvard.edu/pages/teaching-things-curation-hybrid-multimedia-and-object-oriented-pedagogy.

44

TIMESCAPE AND MEMORY

Visualizing Big Data at the 9/11 Memorial Museum

Lauren F. Klein

For visitors to the 9/11 Memorial Museum in New York City, the dominant experience is one of sensory and emotional overload. Set deep in the ground at the site of the former World Trade Center, the museum is explicit about its desire to "convey the scope and scale of loss" experienced on September 11, 2001, to its millions of guests—most of whom did not directly witness the events of the day ("The Museum's Exhibitions" 2014). As visitors proceed through the Historical Exhibition, as the permanent collection is known, they encounter an array of physical artifacts: a fire truck reclaimed from Ground Zero, grotesquely disfigured from the blaze; the antenna from the North Tower, toppled on its side; documentary photographs, news footage, audio recordings, and a range of other media objects that, taken together, reproduce the initial trauma of the terrorist attacks. By deliberately placing this "collection of monumental and authentic artifacts" on display, the museum seeks to convert individual affective response into national cultural memory ("About the Museum" 2014).

But the enduring effects of 9/11, both political and affective, are far more difficult to put on display. Of this challenge, too, the museum's designers and curators seem keenly aware. Upon exiting the Historical Exhibition into the stark surrounds of Foundation Hall, visitors encounter two additional artifacts, each purposefully constructed to evoke the lasting impact of the attacks. To the left stands the original retaining wall from the North Tower, resurfaced and reengineered to serve as the room's southwest side. With its exposed concrete, punctuated by steel tiebacks, the wall bears the symbolic weight of two messages: the first of the permanence of the events of September 11, 2001, and the second of the city's strength and resilience. In the hall to the right, projected across 34 feet of sanded concrete, is *Timescape*, a data visualization of 9/11 in the news. An artifact no less engineered than the retaining wall, *Timescape* (see Figure 44.1) remains far more difficult to interpret on the basis of its surface alone.

Visualization has long been recognized for its ability to bring the "big picture" of a particular dataset into view (Shneiderman 2014: 730). As early as 1786, William Playfair, the Scottish political economist often credited as the "inventor" of modern data visualization, remarked upon the power of statistical charts to "giv[e] form and shape, to what otherwise would only have been an abstract idea" (Playfair 1786: 9; Tufte 2001: 32). Today, we can describe the

Figure 44.1 *Timescape* as installed in the 9/11 Memorial Museum's Foundation Hall.

Source: Photo by Jin Lee, courtesy of the 9/11 Memorial.

benefits of data visualization more precisely: visualization enhances human understanding by "offloading" the basic tasks associated with data processing from cognitive to perceptual systems, abstracting individual data-points into recognizable shapes and patterns, and facilitating more advanced interactions with the dataset as a whole (Card et al. 1999: 16). We now encounter visualizations of data all around us—think of an interactive map of election returns, a network diagram of celebrity tweets, or even a basic bar chart that you might create for a lab report using Microsoft Excel. As these examples show, data visualizations can serve different purposes: a visualization can provide a pathway to insight, as in the case of an interactive map; or offer proof of results, as in the case of an Excel chart. In all cases, however, visualizations must be interpreted so as to better understand the assumptions and arguments embedded in their construction. In bringing these assumptions and arguments to light, a media studies approach to data visualization—that is, an approach that considers a visualization's formal features as well as its technical design—helps us better understand how visualizations facilitate the production of new knowledge at the same time that they render visible a particular view of the data themselves.

The knowledge produced by data visualization is always partial, as the example of *Timescape* in the 9/11 Memorial Museum makes plain. No quantity of data, however large, and however it might be visualized, can be made to represent the global impact of 9/11 in a single view. *Timescape*'s designers, the design consultancy, Local Projects, working in collaboration with media artist, Ben Rubin; data journalist and statistician, Mark Hansen; and artist/designer, Jer Thorp, faced an impossible task: to portray an event that, to most, still feels unimaginable—too traumatic to ever fully comprehend. But as an event characterized by extremity—a term valuably theorized by Paul Benzon elsewhere in this book (see Chapter 31)—9/11 becomes a limit case for thinking through the issues of scale that pervade all aspects of life in the twenty-first century. The global media networks that enabled the collective experience of the trauma of 9/11 represent one instance of this amplified scale, and the rise of big data that enabled the creation of *Timescape* represents another. Considering *Timescape* as a work in which affective and quantitative scales align helps to expose how data and their visualization, in the contemporary moment, are always implicated in issues of politics and power.

To identify these issues, and to be able to critique them "*in and through* our objects of study," as Tara McPherson has advanced, we must understand how data visualization produces knowledge on multiple fronts (2009: 120). In the pages that follow, I work through three levels of meaning-making that are on display in *Timescape*: (1) the level of the data-image: in other words, what the viewer sees; (2) the level of data-processing: that is to say, the underlying algorithms and their implementation in software; and (3) the level of the dataset itself: that is, the dataset's contents and structure, as well as any preprocessing involved in preparing the dataset for use. By exposing and interpreting the multiple layers of *Timescape*, this chapter demonstrates how humanistic inquiry must stand alongside data visualization and related computational practices if we are to most fully address the scale and complexity of life in the digital age.

The Story as Seen: *Timescape*'s Data-Image

"Historical museums typically serve as a way to tell the official story of something that happened and what it means," explains Cliff Kuang (2014), a journalist who reported on the opening of the 9/11 Museum for *Wired* magazine. But, he continues, "this one is different." Kuang's sense of the "difference" of 9/11 seems to derive from an awareness, echoed in the design of the museum itself, of how the impact of September 11, 2001, continues to reverberate across the globe. Kuang's observation also underscores how the meaning of 9/11 ranges widely, depending on both personal consequences and political stakes. For the victims' families, for instance, 9/11 is most likely synonymous with tragedy and loss. For the additional persons who witnessed the attack first-hand—some but not all of whom lost loved ones—9/11 might summon somatic as well as psychological trauma. At the level of national affiliation, consider how, for certain U.S. citizens, 9/11 became a literal call to arms, a recommitment to the nation's founding ideals through military engagement, and a renewal of centuries-old geopolitical, religious, and sectarian conflict. By contrast, for many of those in the Middle East, 9/11 was equally catalyzing, but for a different range of reasons and to various other effects. In attempting to acknowledge this complexity, the museum's designers and curators realized that "conventional narrative wouldn't cut it," as Alice Greenwald, the director of the museum, explains (in Kuang 2014). The idea of an algorithmically generated data visualization held appeal because it could convey the desire for—if not the reality of—an objective curatorial stance.

Timescape consists of an approximately 10-minute cycle of three "scenes" in which clusters of keywords related to 9/11 are traced through an ever-expanding dataset of newspaper articles from 2001 to the present day. The current article count is nearly four million, according to Jake Barton, Principal at Local Projects (2015). The first scene, "9/11 in the News" (see Figure 44.2), begins with a note on method:

> Every day, this database of millions of news articles from September 11, 2001, to today is updated with new content. An algorithm searches the database for related key terms and groups them into timelines that demonstrate 9/11's ongoing impact.
>
> (Local Projects 2014)

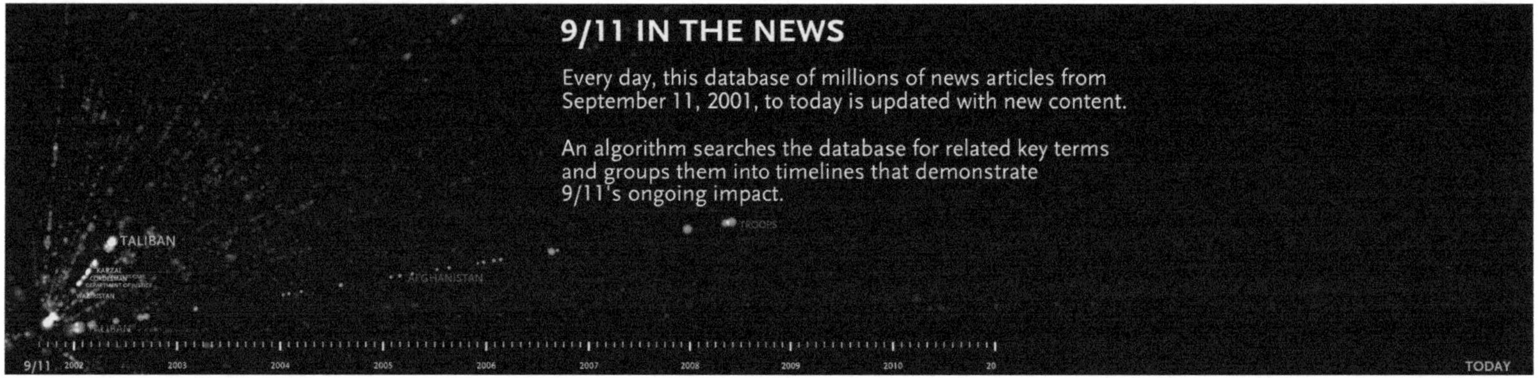

Figure 44.2 The first "scene" of *Timescape*, "9/11 in the News," displaying a note on method and a visualization of clusters of statistically significant terms.

Source: Image courtesy of the 9/11 Memorial.

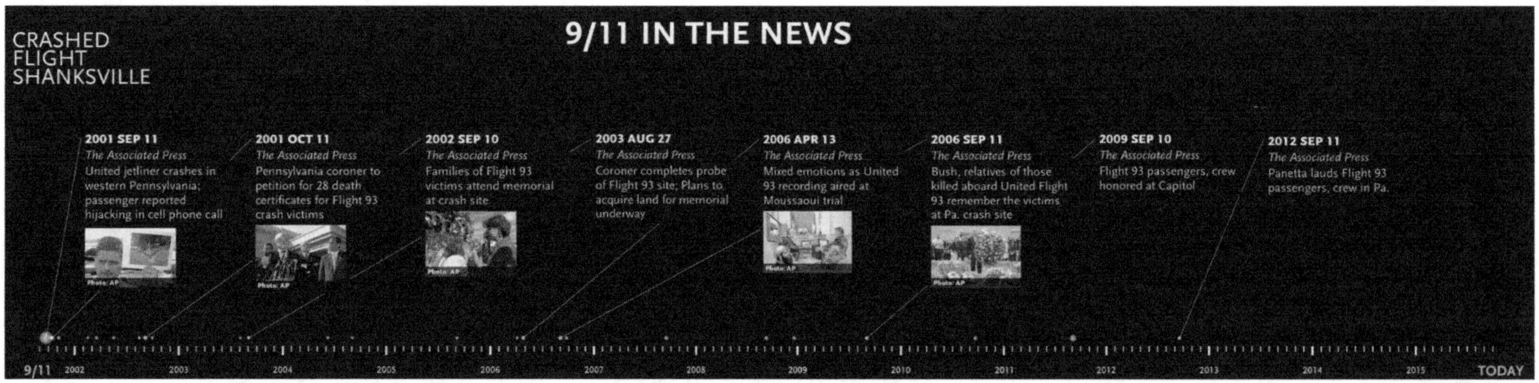

Figure 44.3 A timeline scene from *Timescape*, displaying newspaper headlines from 2001 to the present that contain the terms "crashed," "flight," and "Shanksville." Some headlines are accompanied by photos.

Source: Image courtesy of the 9/11 Memorial.

Figure 44.4 The third scene of *Timescape*, "9/11 and Today," displaying recent newspaper coverage of 9/11.

Source: Image courtesy of the 9/11 Memorial.

The clarity of the explanation, underscored by the simple sans-serif font in which it is displayed, enforces the sense of objectivity that the museum's designers and curators seem intent to convey. With the text remaining on the wall, the date "9/11" appears in the lower left corner of the frame, followed by the word "today," which then appears in the far right. A standard timeline fades into view from left to right, followed by a nebula-like cluster of translucent dots of varying size, numbering in the hundreds. The dots emerge from the "9/11" at the lower left, floating up and across the timeline. As they move farther from the origin, their arrangement becomes clear: lines, loosely structured, each indicating the temporal trajectory of a particular set of terms (e.g., "passengers," "airport," and "Transportation Security Administration"). Visually, the image most closely resembles a spray of lens flares, radiating from a central source. The monochromatic color palate keeps the viewer centered on the visualization's formal features and temporal flow, each of which accentuate the continually expanding albeit increasingly diffuse impact of the events of 9/11 on the present day.

No sooner do the lines cohere than they begin to fade. In the end, all that remains visible is a single set of dots corresponding to a single set of terms. The dots slowly sink toward the bottom of the frame, as if to anchor the abstraction of the image and its associated terms in recorded time. Shifting from abstract visual imagery to more recognizable graphical typologies, *Timescape*'s designers employ the associations of the timeline—horizontal, with a single axis, punctuated by events—to convey the very real impact of this penumbra of effects. As Daniel Rosenberg and Anthony Grafton observe, the timeline "seems among the most inescapable metaphors we have" (2010: 14). And yet, it represents a relatively recent innovation in the long history of visual display, one that advances a very particular view of the unfolding of time: its "uniformity, directionality, and irreversibility" (19). Compared to the circular shape and motion of the clock, for instance, the linear form of the timeline suggests a conception of history as progressing from past to present. The effects of 9/11 may be multiple, *Timescape*'s cyclical structure suggests, but any single effect is irreversible—the result of a single event on a single day that forever changed the world.

This conception of the inevitable forward progression of history is enforced through *Timescape*'s second scene, "Through the Lens of 9/11." It begins with a bar of white light that scrolls from left to right like the bright light of a flatbed scanner, separating past from present. As in the final phase of the previous scene, the three terms that rest on the timeline appear in much larger type in the upper left of the frame. Trailing the vertical bar of light, diagonal lines sprout from the timeline, connecting the terms to a set of newspaper headlines, sometimes accompanied by photos, in which the terms appear (see Figure 44.3). Again, abstraction gives way to text and image and translucence to solid form. Here and throughout *Timescape*, opacity serves as a visual metaphor that underscores the conceptual shift that the scene enacts: from general impact to specific consequences, sharply felt, as evidenced through the coverage of 9/11-related terms in the news.

In the third scene, "9/11 and Today" (see Figure 44.4), the same visual template is applied in reverse, as lines project backwards from the timeline's endpoint of "Today." Instead of articles (presumably) selected randomly from the years between 9/11 and today, the articles displayed are selected only from a set of more recent news. Rather than print the headlines, as in the previous scenes, the articles are labeled according to how long from the present moment they were published (e.g., "8 hours ago," "11 hours ago," and "17 months ago"). The scene thus reorients the viewer's perspective through text as well as image. It appears less frequently than the first two scenes, which alternate several times before moving on. The relative frequency of the first two scenes places the emphasis of the piece on the continually unfolding implications of the events of September 11, 2001, rather than the retrospective view encouraged by this particular scene. Like the museum itself, *Timescape*'s primary goal is to encourage an eternal return to the events of the day. The present meaning of 9/11, the piece suggests, is best understood—and experienced—by reliving the events of the past.

The Story as Constructed: Engineering and Reverse Engineering *Timescape*

As the dynamically generated timeline indicates with its relative endpoint of "Today," *Timescape* was designed to be open-ended. But more than a representation of the unfolding nature of the interpretive process, the museum's designers and curators, in commissioning *Timescape*, sought an expression of objectivity—an indication of the suspension of judgment they believed was enforced through the algorithms that determined the terms and images projected on the wall. Describing the various document-clustering algorithms that were synthesized to identify the terms related to 9/11, and then the natural language processing techniques applied post hoc to pull up the relevant news stories. Barton explains that the algorithmic basis for the system "lets the curators say they haven't set an agenda" (Kuang 2014). Greenwald confirms this view. "We're still living in the aftermath of this event. It's not something that happened 50 years ago, or 150 years ago and we know the consequences of that event," she reports to NPR. "So we weren't, from a curatorial point of view, able to wrap things up" (in Shahani 2014).

The installation's algorithmic basis has yielded some insightful results, as the developers themselves have observed. "You have some expected answers, like Pakistan and Osama bin Laden or Afghanistan, George W. Bush," Barton explains in a video interview in the *Wall Street Journal*:

> But then you have these very unexpected timelines like the airlines industry, or a terrorist event in Bali, or looking at the arc of Dick Cheney as it begins with that moment and then goes toward the end of his career. And that's what's been interesting about it, is that the *Timescape* has both cut down on some of the work and labor that the museum might have to do to tell the post-9/11 world story. But frankly it's produced insights that I don't think anyone expected. Certainly not us. And as we were working on it there's a funny way in which we ourselves would be surprised and say, "Woah, there must be some mistake here!" And then we'd say, "Oh no, this is right, because you can basically trace this back to this original cluster from the day itself, and see how it evolved over time."
>
> (Weiss 2014)

Barton's account of the development process accentuates many of the ways that visualization is thought to lead to insight: the reduction in human labor and processing time, the unexpected connections forged by automated pattern recognition techniques, and the way in which automated results can be reverse-engineered, so to speak, to more fully understand how they came to be.

But while reverse-engineering, as Nick Seaver has observed, "might be a useful strategy for figuring out how an existing technology works, it is less useful for telling us how it came to work that way" (2014). Seaver's primary example is Ian Bogost and Alex Madrigal's attempt to reverse-engineer the Netflix movie classification algorithm. In his analysis, Seaver identifies how reverse-engineering, as an interpretive technique, "fails to piece together how engineers imagine and engage with culture." The same might be said of reverse-engineering the output of *Timescape's* algorithms or, for that matter, reverse-engineering *Timescape's* algorithms themselves. In other words, reverse-engineering might indeed allow us to better understand the algorithmic processes by which *Timescape* "produces the knowledge it draws," to borrow a phrase from Johanna Drucker, but it cannot be made to reveal the social or cultural conditions of its making (2014: 5). Rather, some of what is revealed through the process of reverse-engineering, or of interpretation more generally, is how we ourselves construct knowledge about the images, objects, and events that we encounter in the present. When interpreting an image, derived from data or otherwise, we must therefore remain attentive to what gaps in the technical process—in the surrounding social or cultural context, or in our own knowledge—we might also expose when our ability to reverse-engineer falls short.

From a blog post by Andreas Borg (a member of the development team), we know that *Timescape*'s algorithm for selecting the featured terms relies upon a metric known as "term frequency-inverse document frequency" (TF-IDF) to generate the "original cluster [of terms] from the day itself" (n.d.). TF-IDF is a method by which individual terms in a set of documents are assigned a numerical value that corresponds to their statistical significance in the document set. The significance increases in proportion to the frequency with which the term appears in a particular document, but it is offset by the frequency with which the term appears in the entire document set—its "inverse document frequency." In a set of news articles from September 11, 2001, "Osama bin Laden," for example, would likely have a high TF-IDF value, while "plane"—because of its more varied general use—would have a lower value. An even more common word such as "and" or "the" would have a TF-IDF value so low as to be negligible. But we do not know how the set of documents "from the day itself" was assembled, nor do we know whether the "clusters" that are displayed in the installation were determined by comparing all of the news articles from 9/11 with a larger set of articles, or whether another term-selection algorithm—Borg suggests Named Entity Recognition, a computational technique for automatically identifying the names of people and places that occur in a set of documents—was used to select the terms from a dataset consisting of only news articles from the day.

Questions of reverse-engineering aside, the composition of the dataset itself raises questions. Art historian, Mary Anne Staniszewski, observes that, since the news articles appear to be English-language only, they reflect an "'American point of view'" (in Shahani 2014). This may well be true, although without any detailed knowledge of the dataset's sources, it is impossible to determine the validity of this or any content-based claim. We do know that issues of access influenced the composition of the dataset, however. Barton himself admits that securing access to the data, not only of the day's events, but in perpetuity, was a challenge in itself. "The algorithms are a tour de force," he states, "but the legal agreements have just been incredible" (Manaugh 2014). In an interest of scale quite common in digital humanities, Barton (2015) admits to employing "everyone we could license." But in spite of its massive size, the dataset remains radically incomplete. In other words, while it is easy to conflate "big data" with "all data," the two are not one in the same. Visualizing the former may confer insights that could not otherwise be perceived. However, those insights must always be measured against what the dataset does not or can never contain.

The insights of *Timescape* relate to its particular perspective on the mainstream news—one that, under the auspices of the emerging field of "data journalism," has become increasingly prevalent everywhere from BuzzFeed to the lobby of *The New York Times*. But data journalism, like any other form of journalism, is not bias-free. The dataset itself presents a particular perspective on the coverage, not only because of its Anglo-centric focus, but also because of the various factors—the financial flexibility associated with a major news organization, the legal counsel required to negotiate such an agreement, the willingness for original reporting to be repurposed without editorial oversight—that led the particular news sources to be included in the dataset. There is no way for *Timescape*'s viewers to determine what sources go into the dataset, and yet it is presented in an institutional context where it is interpreted merely as "the news."

TF-IDF is also not a bias-free method of determining significance, as it is able to identify individual words (e.g., "terrorism") with more readiness than larger concepts or ideas (e.g., global religious strife). Named Entity Recognition, mentioned above, which is also incorporated into *Timescape*'s underlying algorithms, is similarly non-neutral; as the name suggests, it identifies only proper nouns (e.g., "bin Laden") and cannot identify unnamed individuals or groups (e.g., "firefighters") who influenced the narrative of 9/11. It is a fundamental irony of the post-9/11 world, characterized as it is by geopolitical alliances that transcend nations and cultures, conflicts that emerge from no single point of origin, and increasingly inchoate notions of what we mean by "enemy," "warfare," and "threat," that the quantitative methods that we increasingly rely upon for analyzing big data are so poorly equipped to identify this complexity on a global scale.

While the 9/11 Museum has chosen to emphasize the sense of objectivity associated with the idea of an algorithm, Barton himself acknowledges the complexity of the picture that *Timescape* presents: "We wanted to focus the design on something that wouldn't render it overly simply, but would tell the story of both the data and how we were deriving the individual timelines" (Rosenthal 2014). The "story" of *Timescape*, it seems, is of the interpretive process, one that involves data and algorithms, to be sure, but also acknowledges that data are created and assembled by people, and that algorithms are designed and implemented by people as well. As such, *Timescape*—indeed, all visualizations—must be analyzed through a composite lens, one that takes into account both materials and makers, as well as the limits of each.

Timescape as Media Event

9/11 has come to be theorized as a media event, both for how it confirmed the uneasy kinship between terrorism and the media coverage required for its impact, and for how it exemplified a new form of collective trauma made possible through the media's global reach. In point of fact, most of the world experienced the events of September 11, 2001 through media, and the same media coverage that accorded 9/11 its initial collective impact soon became the medium—that is to say, the news—through which the world would process its implications. Thus *Timescape* does not only produce knowledge in the particular terms that its algorithms identify and visualize; it also represents the more general process of twenty-first century knowledge production. Its location in the 9/11 Memorial Museum, itself situated in the footprint of the original Twin Towers, accentuates the site-specific nature of the knowledge that it brings to light. The three Christie projectors, two Nvidia graphics cards, one top-of-the-line Dell computer, and a rack-mounted server that together work to generate *Timescape* emphasize that all data-driven knowledge is social, cultural, and, at some level, material. *Timescape*'s messages are determined by issues of access and authority as well as by who is empowered both financially and politically to present those messages to the public. None of this is to say that data visualizations should not appear in sites such as the 9/11 Memorial Museum, nor that we should cease to design them. Rather, we must continue to insist upon a rigorous interpretation of the images we see and the interactions we explore. As we increasingly seek to create visualizations that do more than merely "reveal" knowledge, we must more fully account for the multiple layers—formal, technical, and political—through which data visualization produces meaning, advances arguments, and performs critique (Coopmans 2014: 38).

Acknowledgments

Thanks to Paul Benzon, Amy Klein, Yanni Loukissas, Jentery Sayers, and Gregory Zinman for their comments and suggestions on earlier drafts of this piece.

Further Reading

Coopmans, C., J. Vertesi, M. Lynch, and S. Woolgar (eds.) (2014) *Representation in Scientific Practice Revisited*, Cambridge, MA: MIT Press.

Drucker, J. (2014) *Graphesis: Visual Forms of Knowledge Production*, Cambridge, MA: Harvard University Press.

Gitelman, L. (ed.) (2013) *Raw Data Is an Oxymoron*, Cambridge, MA: MIT Press.

Tufte, E. (2001) *The Visual Display of Quantitative Information*, 2nd ed., Cheshire, CT: Graphics Press.

Wright, A. (2007) *Glut: Mastering Information through the Ages*, Ithaca, NY: Cornell University Press.

References

"About the Museum" (2014) *9/11 Memorial*, retrieved from www.911memorial.org/about-museum.

Barton, J. (2015) Email correspondence with the author, 19 May.

Borg, A. (n.d.) "9/11 Timescape (NYC): Designing with Random," retrieved from crea.tion.to/911-timescape-designing-with-random.

Card, S. K., J. D. Mackinlay, and B. Shneiderman (eds.) (1999) *Readings in Information Visualization: Using Vision to Think*, Burlington, MA: Morgan Kaufmann.

Coopmans, C. (2014) "Visual Analytics as Artful Revelation," in C. Coopmans, J. Vertesi, M. Lynch, and S. Woolgar (eds.) *Representation in Scientific Practice Revisited*, Cambridge, MA: MIT Press, pp. 37–59.

Drucker, J. (2014) *Graphesis: Visual Forms of Knowledge Production*, Cambridge, MA: Harvard University Press.

Kuang, C. (2014) "The Near Impossible Challenge of Designing the 9/11 Museum," *Wired*, retrieved from www.wired.com/2014/05/911-museum-3/.

Local Projects (2014) *Timescape* (installation), New York, NY.

Manaugh, G. (2014) "The Algorithms at the Heart of the New September 11 Memorial Museum," *Gizmodo*, retrieved from gizmodo.com/the-algorithm-at-the-heart-of-the-new-september-11-memo-1576067926.

McPherson, T. (2009) "Media Studies and Digital Humanities," *Cinema Journal* 48(2), 119–23.

"The Museum's Exhibitions" (2014) *9/11 Memorial*, retrieved from www.911memorial.org/museum-exhibitions.

Playfair, W. (1786) *The Commercial and Political Atlas*, London: J. Debrett.

Rosenberg, D. and A. Grafton (2010) *Cartographies of Time: A History of the Timeline*, Princeton, NJ: Princeton University Press.

Rosenthal, E. (2014) "Haunting Data Visualizations Display the Aftermath Of 9/11," *The Creators Project*, retrieved from thecreatorsproject.vice.com/en_uk/blog/haunting-data-visualizations-display-911.

Shneiderman, B. (2014) "The Big Picture for Big Data: Visualization," *Science* 343(6172), 730.

Seaver, N. (2014)"On Reverse Engineering," *Anthropology and Algorithms*, retrieved from medium.com/anthropology-and-algorithms/on-reverse-engineeringd9f5bae87812.

Shahani, A. (2014) "An Algorithm Is a Curator at the Sept. 11 Museum," *NPR*, retrieved from www.npr.org/sections/alltechconsidered/2014/06/30/326954812/an-algorithm-is-a-curator-at-the-sept-11-museum.

Tufte, E. (2001) *The Visual Display of Quantitative Information*, 2nd ed., Cheshire, CT: Graphics Press.

Weiss, J. (2014) "'Timescape' Exhibit Reads the News Since 9/11," *The Wall Street Journal*, retrieved from www.wsj.com/video/timescape-exhibit-reads-the-news-since-911/42952861-CA78-4C2A-9385-85CB460FA69C.html.

Part V

MAKING, PROGRAMMING, HACKING

45
PROGRAMMING AS LITERACY

Annette Vee

Connections between writing and programming have long been commonplace in certain areas of computer science (Knuth 1992; Abelson et al. 1996). In fact, almost as soon as computers arrived on college campuses in the United States, computer programming was proposed as a burgeoning literacy akin to reading and writing. In 1961, computer scientist Alan Perlis (1962) argued that undergraduates should be taught programming just as they are taught writing in first-year composition courses. Shortly afterward, mathematicians John Kemeny and Thomas Kurtz developed the BASIC programming language, which was widely taught in schools in the 1970s and installed on many of the first home computers to hit the U.S. and U.K. in the 1980s. In U.S. schools in the 1980s, Logo promised to introduce programming on a wide scale, preparing the next generation to fight in the Cold War. Educational approaches to "computer literacy" shifted away from programming and toward usage in the 1990s, as operating systems began offering graphical interfaces and the commercial software market expanded. But, as computers have become even cheaper, more accessible, more ubiquitous, and more relevant to contemporary communication practices, the link between programming and literacy has been revived (Prensky 2008; Rushkoff 2010). Supposedly, "everyone should learn to code." What is it about programming that prompts these persistent connections to literacy and writing, and what do these connections mean?

The humanities can help to answer these questions. While computer science can tell us about what programming can do, approaches to programming from the humanities can tell us about programming's significance in developed societies: what it means for people to program computers and for programmed computers to increase their roles in our everyday lives. In particular, literacy studies has much to say about these questions because literacy research has long grappled with how people work with socially situated, technological systems of signs. As programming is tracing a trajectory similar to that taken by reading and writing in society, the theoretical tools of literacy studies aid us in understanding the history and future of the who, what, and why of programming.

With help from literacy studies, we will dive more deeply into the complex relationship between programming and writing. Programming has been rhetorically framed as writing when it is discussed as a potentially widespread ability like literacy. Its relationship to writing is under consideration when its status is debated in the law. This chapter explores the relationship between programming and writing, and what that relationship means for contemporary literacy, by introducing several influential projects that have posited programming as a literacy and then outlining some of the strange borders between writing and programming that certain legal cases have highlighted. It concludes by pointing to several ways the humanities have already and can contribute to our understandings of computer programming as part of the environment in which humans now dwell and communicate.

The Rhetoric of Programming as a Literacy

Coding is currently a male-dominated practice. Because of historical, social, and economic barriers, women and certain minority populations are underrepresented in the population of people who can code (Ensmenger 2010). There are now countless initiatives aimed at making coding more inclusive: Code.org, Made with Code, #YesWeCode, Black Girls Code, and many more. Inertia behind these initiatives is so strong that they are often thought of as constituting a "coding for everyone" movement. They frequently select from the history and characteristics of mass literacy to frame their goals. Strategically, this framing makes sense: literacy, like programming, is a complex communicative ability facilitated by technology. Since textual literacy is much more prevalent than the ability to program, the analogies the movement makes are aspirational: "coding for everyone" is still a dream.

However, the project of mass literacy was similarly ambitious: the idea of getting *everyone* to read and write. We have naturalized these skills, but the truth is that reading and writing are complex—no more or less complex than programming. Literacy is still unevenly distributed: rates are generally lower among women worldwide, and in poor countries or among people of lower classes in richer countries. And literacy campaigns have been handmaidens to larger projects of cultural homogenization, such as "Americanization" in the early twentieth century. So there are obvious problems with holding literacy up as an ideal for the coding campaigns. Yet literacy rates exceed 95 percent in all industrialized countries, and the worldwide literacy rate is around 85 percent. Almost 90 percent of men and over 80 percent of women in the world can read and write by the time they are fifteen (UNESCO Institute for Statistics 2015). The dream of mass literacy has largely come true, although people's opinions differ on what it looks like and how to measure or teach it. Still, governments and citizens almost universally support literacy as a concept and as a moral good. While computer science educators can debate how we might teach "coding for everyone," the humanities are situated to ask different questions, including whether the "coding for everyone" movement *should* follow the path of mass literacy.

To help us consider this question, we can look to the historical treatment of programming as a literacy (Vee 2013). The rhetoric of programming as a literacy begins in 1961 with an address by computer scientist, Alan Perlis, at a conference at MIT. Perlis (1962) argued that all undergraduates should be taught programming just as they are taught writing in first-year composition courses. First-year composition courses were (and largely still are) seen as service courses to the rest of the university, venues for imparting the written communication skills that are essential to success in college and beyond. Perlis's argument that programming was similarly essential to undergraduate education implies that it would become foundational to many different disciplines and to civic life more generally. His vision is particularly striking given the state of computers at the time: when he gave his address, only a few college campuses had mainframe computers. But computers were increasingly important to large-scale business and government, including defense. His emphasis on broad undergraduate education in programming suggested that future leaders of America should know something about how to write for these machines.

Perlis's vision was at least partially realized with the BASIC programming language, designed at Dartmouth during the early 1960s by John Kemeny and Thomas Kurtz. Like

Perlis, Kemeny and Kurtz (1968) saw the computer as universally relevant. They designed BASIC to be accessible to undergraduates in the liberal arts as well as those in engineering or hard sciences. Kemeny (1983) in particular was concerned that future leaders trained at Dartmouth should know something about computation, given its increasingly important role in national infrastructure. BASIC was successful. By the 1968 fall term, 80 percent of Dartmouth undergraduates, plus several hundred faculty, had learned how to write computer programs (Kemeny & Kurtz 1968). In part because Kemeny and Kurtz made BASIC and their time-sharing system free, the programming language spread across college campuses during the 1960s and has enjoyed a long life afterward as well.

During the 1960s, efforts to teach programming broadly were focused on undergraduates, since computers could be found only in government offices, large corporate centers, and some college campuses. But, as the technology and culture of computing spilled out of college campuses in the 1970s and West toward California, the impetus to promote programming to the masses seems to have taken the same direction. West coast programming initiatives were imbued with post-60s San Francisco area politics: hobbyists and hackers thrived, typified by the Homebrew Computer Club, the People's Computer Company, and Ted Nelson's manifesto *Computer Lib/Dream Machines*. Nelson argued, "If you are interested in democracy and its future, you'd better understand computers" (1987 [1974]: 5). In the 1970s, computer programming—usually in BASIC—was widely taught in high school after-school programs and accelerated math classes.

By the mid-1980s, computers became cheaper and easier to use as well as more common in middle-class American households, businesses, and schools: U.S. computer ownership almost doubled from 1984 to 1989, from 8.2 percent to 15 percent, according to the U.S. Census Bureau. Affordable and accessible personal computers, such as the Commodore 64 and Apple II, meant that, for the first time, computers became available to children. The idea of computers as tools for children owes much to educational research done in the 1970s, especially by Seymour Papert and Alan Kay. Papert's team developed the Logo programming language in the U.K. and piloted it in classrooms during the late '60s and '70s. A student of Jean Piaget, Papert (1980) argued that programming could scaffold young children to work with concepts often considered too complex for their age. At Xerox PARC in the 1970s, Alan Kay led a team of researchers to prototype the Dynabook laptop as well as the programming language Smalltalk, both of which were designed to make computing and programming more accessible to children (Kay 1993; Kay & Goldberg 2003 [1977]). This research preceded the home computer revolution and provided a frame that allowed computer programming and computer usage (largely still fused at this point) to be considered general rather than specialized skills.

Efforts to widen access to computers and programming in America were focused on K-12 education in the 1980s, because of not only the efforts of people like Papert and Kay, but also the heightening of the Cold War. American schools adopted programming in Logo or BASIC as part of their curriculum, funded by Cold War initiatives for math, science, and technology preparation. These initiatives imagined the front lines on the grounds of both nuclear and computational technologies, and so children's literacy with programming was seen as critical to national defense and health during the 1980s. The term "literacy" becomes more common in the rhetoric surrounding mass programming education at this point, perhaps because literacy is often thought of as a primary goal of elementary education and, since the nineteenth-century mass education movement, children have often been the site where literacy is measured.

While the "computer literacy" movement went mainstream in the 1980s, a shift in computer technology that followed the wave of home computers began to fundamentally change what it meant. The commercial software era severed computer programming from computer usage. Because people no longer needed to know how to program in order to use computers, the idea of computer literacy came to mean knowledge of file structures, saving work to disks, and menu operations (diSessa 2000). This utilitarian and skills-based idea of computer literacy stripped it of the optimism associated with earlier initiatives. Moreover, Papert's Logo pilot program did not scale well: uneven resources and support for teachers deflated the program's efficacy. Critics pointed to a lack of promised gains in children's cognitive abilities (Pea & Kurland 1984); and, despite Papert's open disappointment in the implementation and lack of follow-through, most programming initiatives in elementary schools were eventually phased out.

In the 1990s, the energy behind the mass programming movement shifted from elementary schools to the new World Wide Web, which once again widened access to programming. The architect of the web, Tim Berners-Lee, insisted on technical and organizational protocols that would enable it to be accessible and programmable by everyone (Berners-Lee & Fischetti 1999). For their introduction to programming, many people today credit HTML, the simple markup language on which the web is built. HTML does not have the computational capabilities of BASIC. However, BASIC inspired it, and it shares BASIC's accessibility and ubiquity. As the authors of *10 PRINT* (a collaborative book based on a BASIC maze program widely circulated during the 1980s) write, "HTML . . . copied BASIC's template of simplicity, similarity to natural language, device independence, and transparency to become many users' first introduction to manipulating code" (Montfort et al. 2012: 192). The possibilities of HTML and its ease of use, plus the fact that it led users to other more extensive languages, such as JavaScript, Perl, and PHP, enacted that gentle novice-to-expert climb that Kemeny and Kurtz sought for BASIC. However, even with most web browsers' capability to show the source code for any webpage, people are not automatically exposed to code now in the same way that they were on their Commodore 64s in the 1980s. Many mass programming advocates have pointed to this lack of exposure as a problem (why the lucky stiff 2003). While people enjoy What-You-See-Is-What-You-Get (WYSIWYG) interfaces, any interface makes assumptions about its uses and users. People learn to use menus with these assumptions embedded, rather than thinking about or creating alternative kinds of software.

The 2000s took the "coding for everyone" movement into diverse online communities with little connection to formal computer science and institutions. In his 1999 DARPA grant application, Guido van Rossum, the designer of the Python programming language, tapped into the positive cultural associations of literacy to secure funding for his dream of coding for everyone:

> We compare mass ability to read and write software with mass literacy, and predict equally pervasive changes to society. Hardware is now sufficiently fast and cheap to make mass computer education possible: the next big change will happen when most computer users have the knowledge and power to create and modify software.
>
> (van Rossum 1999)

His initiative was only funded for a year, but it signaled a burgeoning online education movement where people could learn programming by downloading copies of language compilers and developing environments, asking questions on forums such as Slashdot and Usenet, contributing to open source projects and getting feedback on SourceForge, and watching videos or reading blogs posted by people motivated to teach programming for fun, exposure, or profit. Resources for learning programming outside of computer science had never been greater. The growth of the web allowed for ready circulation of open source programming languages, such as JavaScript, Python, Perl, PHP, and Ruby, some of which augment the computational possibilities of HTML and echo BASIC's appeal to novices.

In the 2010s, the decentralized culture of how-to videos and forums online have become consolidated by programming-promoting organizations such as Code.org, Khan Academy, and Codecademy, which feature video lessons, e-books, interactive online code-checking, and a wealth of other resources helpful to anyone wanting to learn programming. These groups echo more general interest in mass online education, typified by Lynda.com, TED Talks, and free lectures from universities through edX, as well as massively open online courses (MOOCs) through for-profit entities like Coursera. Motivations for these groups vary from profit to social justice, although all reflect an emphasis on education outside of formal programs and institutions and position students as "neoliberal" workers "both empowered and wanting (e.g., always in need of training)" (Chun 2011: 59).

The rhetoric of the current "coding for everyone" movement echoes the "empowerment" of earlier efforts. In popular commentary, Douglas Rushkoff says that learning programming gives people "access to the control panel of civilization" (2010: 1), and Marc Prensky argues "[a]s programming becomes more important, it will leave the back room and become a key skill and attribute of our top intellectual and social classes, just as reading and writing did in the past" (2008). Code.org, a nonprofit launched in 2013 and supported by Mark Zuckerberg and Bill Gates, showcases on their website a litany of quotes from educators, technologists, and public figures claiming that learning to code is an issue of "civil rights," the "4th literacy," and a way to "[c]ontrol your destiny, help your family, your community, and your country." Black Girls Code reflects literacy ideologies of wider access and "mastery" in their mission statement: "By promoting classes and programs we hope to grow the number of women of color working in technology and give underprivileged girls a chance to become the masters of their technological worlds" ("About us" 2014). Black Girls Code and Code.org are very different organizations with different funding structures and goals, making it especially interesting that they both draw on the tropes of literacy empowerment to promote programming education to a wider population. While some of the other initiatives discussed here do not use the term "literacy," they often draw on a similar profile of empowerment, social justice, citizenship, and productivity.

As this brief history of the "coding for everyone" movement demonstrates, programming has long been touted for its artistic possibilities as well as its utility for workers, businesses, and government applications. These attributes are also often ascribed to literacy and have been leveraged in mass literacy campaigns connected to democracy, defense, and mass schooling. References to literacy in the promotion of programming can help to convey individual as well as collective goals and responsibilities because literacy is an individual skill, but one which gains meaning and value in social contexts. Literacies purportedly help workers and boost national productivity. It is for these reasons that Code.org could recruit both U.S. President Barack Obama and a political rival, House Majority Leader Eric Cantor, in 2013 to make video statements in support of their project: programming, like literacy, is good for the country.

How Is Programming Like Writing?

The promotion of programming on a wide scale borrows from the ideas of mass literacy movements. Underneath this rhetoric, the parallels between programming and writing are quite apt. Written text and code are both symbolic systems operating through an inscribed language and social contexts. Symbolic systems such as text and code can be distinguished from other important technologies, such as carpentry, because they are "media machines" that "process texts, images, and sound" (Poster 2011: x). Because of the ways that code can process infinite forms of information, programming is the language that transforms computers into what Alan Turing called the "universal machine."

One way for us to explore how programming is like writing is to look at the ways programming is treated like writing in United States law. (While the legal history I provide here is specific to the U.S., international copyright agreements such as the Berne Convention mean that the effects of U.S. law are similar across most developed countries.) In 1980, the U.S. Congress amended the 1976 Copyright Act to define computer code as a "literary work" and a "form of writing" when it was seeking a way to protect the intellectual property of the growing software industry. This amendment and its surrounding debate cemented computer programming as a form of creative expression. By 1994, prominent legal scholars noted, "virtually all nations have recognized the textual character of program code in deciding to use copyright law to protect it" (Samuelson et al. 1994). Somewhat controversially, copyright protection extends not only to source code (the code generally written by and for programmers to read) but also object code (the code that the computer reads). In other words, programming produces copyrightable "writing" addressed to people as well as computers (Vee 2012).

If programming produces "literary" writing, then it can be protected by First Amendment or "free speech" rights in the United States. Activities protected as "speech" under the First Amendment include oral communication, textual writing, methods of dress, gestures, visual art, and computer code. "Speech" is unprotected when it verges on conduct, such as yelling "fire" in a crowded theater. Since code is both conduct and writing—it *does* things as well as *says* things—it occupies a liminal space in these laws. Testing this boundary in U.S. courts was a series of cases involving cryptographic code written by a PhD student, Daniel Bernstein, that the U.S. State Department argued should be regulated as a "weapon." In its decision, the court rejected the State Department's argument that speech that performed a function was not entitled to protection: recipes and sheet music were clearly protected speech, yet they enabled people to do something. No form of communication can be divorced from its function, argued the court; and so computer programming, while it does *do* things, also *says* things: code is, therefore, a protected form of writing or speech.

The *Bernstein* case tested the lines between code's status as creative expression and a potential weapon. A new case involving plans for a 3-D printed gun pushes this debate further. "Wiki weapon" designer, Defense Distributed, uploaded plans to the internet that would allow a 3-D printer to produce a working handgun. When the State Department pursued them with the same weapons law used against Bernstein, they argued that their First Amendment rights had been violated. Their founder, Cody Wilson, asks: "If code is speech, the constitutional contradictions are evident . . . So what if this code is a gun?" (Greenberg 2015). Here, as in *Bernstein*, the question about how programming is related to writing is more than just academic. If sticks and stones rather than words break bones, then what does an executable blueprint for a gun do?

Writing has always been a potentially dangerous activity, Deborah Brandt (2014) argues, and it has consequently enjoyed fewer legal protections than reading. Is the situation different for programming? Because code does things, it is currently regulated by patent law; because it is writing, it is also governed by copyright law; and because it is creative expression, it is protected by law against censorship. If we think of programming as literacy, what kinds of legal protections *should* pertain to the writing or reading of code?

Conclusion

As these border cases demonstrate, programming is not separate from writing or any other form of human communication. Algorithms interoperate with our lives, including our music and movie tastes and even the heating of our homes (e.g., Pandora, Netflix, and the Nest thermostat), and necessarily combine both computational and human procedures to do their work. Self-taught algorithms take in and respond to analog input, leading to levels of complexity neither computers nor humans can fully understand alone (Hayles 2005; Aneesh 2006). Moreover, computational and programmable devices are now joining a panoply of other read-write tools to form a new matrix of social practices and technologies that constitute literacy. Programming plays a supportive role in traditional writing through word-processing programs, and it facilitates new forms of written communication such as tweets, texts, Facebook posts, emails, and instant messages. It also remaps communication when it contributes to what A. Aneesh (2006) calls "algocracy" (rule by algorithm) or acts as a blueprint for printed objects such as guns. Programming is a kind of writing, *and* it is bound up with traditional writing, *and* it exceeds historically assumed boundaries of writing. Popular discourse about "programming as a new literacy" as well as legal cases debating the nature of code reflect the complicated relationship between writing and programming.

Writing and programming are both/together inextricable and important forms of composition and communication. If *literacy* implies an ability to wield the dominant tools of communication in a society, then in contemporary networked societies it includes some degree of facility with computer programming. But literacy to what degree? For whom, and why? How might people go about learning this new kind of literacy? And how should the activities of literacy be protected through our social and legal institutions? These value-laden questions have been considered by literacy studies in terms of textual writing and reading. In terms of programming, they are currently being considered by fields such as digital rhetoric, digital humanities, and software studies, which are developing theoretical tools to consider the material and social affordances of digital technologies in human lives. While computer scientists have considered the unique challenges in teaching novice programmers (Soloway & Spohrer 1988) and what education in computational literacy might look like (Wing 2006; Guzdial 2008), approaches to these questions from the humanities can help us consider questions of politics and identity embedded in *who* learns computational literacy and *why*.

Further Reading

Brandt, D. (2014) *The Rise of Writing: Redefining Mass Literacy*. Cambridge, U.K.: Cambridge University Press.

Chun, W. H. K. (2011) *Programmed Visions: Software and Memory*, Cambridge, MA: MIT Press.

diSessa, A. (2000) *Changing Minds: Computers, Learning and Literacy*, Cambridge, MA: MIT Press.

Guzdial, M. (2015) *Learner-Centered Design of Computing Education: Research on Computing for Everyone*, San Rafael, CA: Morgan & Claypool Publishers.

References

Abelson, H., G. Sussman, and J. Sussman (1996) *Structure and Interpretation of Computer Programs*, 2nd edn. Cambridge, MA: MIT Press.

Aneesh, A. (2006) *Virtual Migration: The Programming of Globalization*, Durham, NC: Duke University Press.

Berners-Lee, T. and M. Fischetti (1999) *Weaving the Web*, New York, NY: HarperBusiness.

Black Girls Code (2014) "About Us," retrieved from www.blackgirlscode.com/what-we-do.html.

Bolter, J. D. (1991) *Writing Space: Computers, Hypertext, and the History of Writing*, 1st edn. Hillsdale, NJ: Lawrence Erlbaum.

Brandt, D. (2001) *Literacy in American Lives*, Cambridge, U.K.: Cambridge University Press.

Brandt, D. (2014) *The Rise of Writing: Redefining Mass Literacy*, Cambridge, U.K.: Cambridge University Press.
Chun, W. H. K. (2011) *Programmed Visions: Software and Memory*, Cambridge, MA: MIT Press.
Code.org. (2013) "Leaders and Trend-setters All Agree on One Thing." retrieved from www.code.org/quotes.
diSessa, A. (2000) *Changing Minds: Computers, Learning and Literacy*, Cambridge, MA: MIT Press.
Ensmenger, N. (2010) *The Computer Boys Take Over*, Cambridge, MA: MIT Press.
Greenberg, A. (2015) "3D Printed Gun Lawsuit Starts the War Between Arms Control and Free Speech," *Wired*, retrieved from www.wired.com/2015/05/3-d-printed-gun-lawsuit-starts-war-arms-control-free-speech/.
Guzdial, M. (2008) "Education: Paving the Way for Computational Thinking," *Communications of the ACM* 51(8), 25–27.
Hayles, N. K. (2005) *My Mother Was a Computer*, Chicago: University of Chicago Press.
Kay, A. (1993) "The Early History of Smalltalk," *ACM SIGPLAN Notices* 28(3), 69–95.
Kay, A. and A. Goldberg (2003 [1977]) "Personal Dynamic Media," in N. Wardrip-Fruin and N. Montfort (eds.) *The New Media Reader*, Cambridge, MA: MIT Press, pp. 393–404.
Kemeny, J. (1983) "The Case for Computer Literacy," *Daedalus* 112(2), 211–30.
Kemeny, J. and T. Kurtz (1968) "Dartmouth Time-Sharing," *Science* 162(3850), 223–28.
Knuth, D. (1992) *Literate Programming*, CSLI Lecture Notes, United States: Center for the Study of Language and Information.
Montfort, N., P. Baudoin, J. Bell, I. Bogost, J. Douglass, M. C. Marino, M. Mateas, C. Reas, M. Sample, and N. Vawter (2012) *10 PRINT CHR$(205.5+RND(1)); : GOTO 10*, Cambridge, MA: MIT Press.
Nelson, T. H. (1987) *Computer Lib / Dream Machines*, Redmond, WA: Microsoft.
Ong, W. (1982) *Orality and Literacy*, London: Routledge.
Papert, S. (1980) *Mindstorms: Children, Computers, and Powerful Ideas*, New York, NY: Basic Books.
Pea, R. D. and D. M. Kurland (1984) "On the Cognitive Effects of Learning Programming," *New Ideas in Psychology* 2(2), 137–68.
Perlis, A. (1962) "The Computer and the University," in M. Greenberger (ed.) *Computers and the World of the Future*, Cambridge, MA: MIT Press.
Poster, M. (2011) "Introduction," in Flusser V. *Does Writing Have a Future?* Minneapolis, MN: University of Minnesota Press.
Prensky, M. (2008) "Programming Is the New Literacy," *Edutopia*, retrieved from www.edutopia.org/literacy-computer-programming.
Rushkoff, D. (2010) *Program or Be Programmed: Ten Commands for a Digital Age*, OR Books. Kindle file.
Samuelson, P., R. Davis, M. D. Kapor, and J. H. Reichman (1994) "A Manifesto Concerning the Legal Protection of Computer Programs," *Columbia Law Review* 94(8), 2308–2431.
Soloway, E. and J. C. Spohrer (eds.) (1988) *Studying the Novice Programmer*, London: Psychology Press.
UNESCO Institute for Statistics (2015) "Adult and Youth Literacy," *United Nations Educational, Scientific and Cultural Organization*, UIS Fact Sheet 32, retrieved from www.uis.unesco.org/literacy/Documents/fs32–2015-literacy.pdf.
U.S. Census Bureau (2009) *Households with a Computer and Internet Use 1984–2009*, retrieved from www.census.gov/hhes/computer/.
van Rossum, G. (1999) Computer Programming for Everybody (Revised Proposal), Reston, VA: *Corporation for National Research Initiatives*, retrieved from www.python.org/doc/essays/cp4e.
Vee, A. (2012) "Text, Speech, Machine: Metaphors for Computer Code in the Law," *Computational Culture* 2, retrieved from computationalculture.net/article/text-speech-machine-metaphors-for-computer-code-in-the-law.
Vee, A. (2013) "Understanding Computer Programming as a Literacy," *Literacy in Composition Studies* 1(2), 42–64.
why the lucky stiff (2003) "The Little Coder's Predicament," retrieved from viewsourcecode.org/why/hacking/theLittleCodersPredicament.html.
Wing, J. (2006) "Computational Thinking," *Communications of the ACM* 49(3), 33–35.

46

EXPRESSIVE PROCESSING

Interpretation and Creation

Noah Wardrip-Fruin

Background: Software Studies

There are many things that a computer is not. It is neither an interactive movie projector, nor an expensive typewriter, nor a giant encyclopedia. Instead, it is a machine for running software, which can enact processes, access data, communicate across networks, and, as a result, act like a movie projector, typewriter, encyclopedia, and many other things.

Outside engineering and mathematics, most studies of software have considered software in terms of what it acts like and how that behavior is experienced outside the system. But some authors have consistently written about software as software. This approach includes considering software's internal operations (as my work does), examining its constituent elements (e.g., the different levels, modules, and even lines of code at work), studying its context and material traces of production (e.g., how the workings of money, labor, technology, and the market can be traced through whitepapers, specification documents, version control system archives, beta tests, patches, and so on), observing the transformations of work and its results (from celebrated cases such as architecture to the everyday ordering and movement of auto parts), and, as the foregoing implies, a broadening of the types of software considered worthy of study (not just media software, but also design software, logistics software, databases, office tools, and so on).

These investigations form a part of the larger field of "software studies"—a field that had its start long before scholars began using the term. Often this field is positioned as part of digital humanities, and we can see why this might be the case. First, much of software studies involves the interpretation and critique of digital objects and culture that are common in digital humanities. Other software studies work, such as Warren Sack's forthcoming *The Software Arts*, involves making novel software inspired by (or enacting) a critical interpretation of software's specifics. This method fits relatively comfortably with the parts of digital humanities that engage making through scholarly communication. Third, there is another set of software studies work—such as the "cultural analytics" collaborations of Lev Manovich, Jeremy Douglass, and William Huber—that continues the quantitative humanities computing tradition (now sometimes positioned as the "big data" of the humanities) (Manovich, Douglass, & Huber 2011).

But if I examine my own route into software studies, the picture looks quite different. Some books that influenced me—such as Paul Edwards's *The Closed World* (1997), a history that fits within humanistic study of software objects and institutions—could be positioned within digital humanities. But other books that influenced me cannot. Consider Lucy Suchman's *Plans and Situated Actions* (1987). This is a work of social science, applying ethno-methodological concepts to understanding software and how we interact with it. Not only does this move into the social sciences take us outside digital humanities, but Suchman's book is also explicitly positioned as a piece of thinking about how software is *designed*, and should be designed. Such research is software studies as part of a practice of making software (rather than making software as part of a practice of software studies). Or consider Phil Agre's *Computation and Human Experience* (1997). It uses humanistic approaches to expose conceptual problems in approaches to artificial intelligence (AI) and identify alternative conceptualizations. Then it describes actual architectures—that is, computer science research—that result from this inquiry. In other words, in Agre's book, software studies is a method of computer science. Finally, teaching software studies also leads me to believe that software studies is a route to thinking critically about software models—their histories, commitments, and potentials. Software studies is a route to "procedural literacy" (Mateas 2005).

Procedural literacy is one of the core aims of what I suspect is the first software studies book: Ted Nelson's *Computer Lib / Dream Machines* (1974). Published the year before the arrival of the first kit for assembling a personal computer, Nelson's book contains much that could be seen as purely informational, including introductions to different types of computers and programming languages. But it also contains much that is clearly the critical interpretation of software, connecting the technical level to the cultural one—ranging from discussing the "drill and practice" assumptions built into the Tutor programming language to exposing the surprisingly simple workings of *Eliza* and other systems used to market artificial intelligence ideas (Nelson 1974: DM27, DM14). Nelson's book introduced critical thinking about software as a basic part of understanding computing.

Given all this, my view of software studies includes all investigations that use humanities and/or social science methods and encompass the specific operations of particular software, for purposes ranging from understanding digital culture and software society to the development of procedural literacy and inspiring, guiding, and evaluating how novel software is made.

The phrase "software studies" was coined by Manovich in his widely read book *The Language of New Media* (2001). Manovich characterized software studies as a "turn to computer science," perhaps analogous to the "linguistic turn" of an earlier era. In his book, software studies operates analytically through programmability (rather than, say, signification). In 2003, Matthew Kirschenbaum offered his own expansion of Manovich's term, one influenced by Kirschenbaum's background in bibliography (the study of books as physical objects) and textual criticism (the reconstruction and representation of texts from multiple versions and witnesses). Kirschenbaum argued that in the field of software studies—as opposed to the rather loose, early "new media" field—"the deployment of critical terms like 'virtuality' must be balanced by a commitment to meticulous documentary research to recover and stabilize the material traces of new media" (2003: 150). Kirschenbaum's *Mechanisms* made good on this assertion in 2008, which also saw the publication of the field's first edited volume: *Software Studies: A Lexicon* (Fuller 2008). Soon after, the MIT Press established the first book series for software studies. All this helped create the conditions of possibility for my book, *Expressive Processing* (2009), which I see as an example of software studies.

Expressive Processing

I am drawn to software studies, in part because it brings together currents of work in computer science, humanities, social sciences, and the arts. In computer science, there is a long tradition of those who see their work on software in terms of culture—from Don Knuth's "literate programming" (1984) to Phil Agre's "critical technical practices" (1997). Similarly, in other fields there are those who have felt a need to engage the specifics of software in the course of their research and creation, in areas ranging from computer games to software art to multinational firm organization. My *Expressive Processing* focuses on software studies for computational media, especially games and fictions. I use the term "expressive processing" to point toward two important critical issues.

First, "expressive processing" encompasses the fact that the internal processes of computational media are designed artifacts; in this sense, they are like buildings or transportation systems. As with other designed mechanisms, processes can be seen in terms of their efficiency, their aesthetics, their points of failure, or their (lack of) suitability for particular purposes. Their design can be typical or unusual for their era and context. The parts and their arrangement may express kinship with, and points of divergence from, design movements and schools of thought. They can be progressively redesigned, repurposed, or used as foundations for new systems—by their original designers or others—all while retaining traces and characteristics from prior uses.

Second, unlike many other designed mechanisms, the processes of computational media operate on, and in terms of, elements and structures meaningful to humans. For example, a natural language processing system (for understanding or generating human language) expresses a miniature philosophy of language in its universe of interpretation or expression. When such a system is incorporated into a work of computational media such as an interactive fiction, its structures and operations are invoked whenever the work is experienced. This invocation selects, as it were, a particular constellation from among the system's universe of possibilities. In a natural language generation system, this invocation might be a particular sentence shown to an audience in the system output. From looking at the output sentence alone, it is not possible to see where the individual elements (e.g., words, phrases, sentence templates, or statistical language structures) once resided in the larger system. It is not possible to see how the movements of the model universe resulted in this constellation becoming possible—and becoming more apparent than other possible ones.

To put it another way, in the world of computational media, and perhaps especially for computational games and fictions, we have as much to learn by examining the model that drives the planetarium as by looking at a particular image of stars (or even the animation of their movement). This is because the model universes of these works are built of rules for character behavior, structures for virtual worlds, techniques for assembling human language, and so on. They express the meanings of their fictional worlds through the design of every structure, the arc of every internal movement, and the elegance or difficulty with which the elements interact with one another.

Trying to interpret a work of computational media by looking only at the output is like interpreting a model solar system by looking only at the planets. If the accuracy of Mars's surface texture is in question, then looking only at planets is fine. But it will not suffice if we want to know if the model embodies and carries out a Copernican theory—or, instead, places Earth at the center of its simulated solar system. Both types of theories could produce models that currently place the planets in appropriate locations, but examining the models' wires and gears will reveal critical differences, probably the most telling differences.

That is, the processes of computational media can themselves be examined for what is expressed through their selection, arrangement, and operation. As I have just discussed, a system operating on language (or other elements meaningful to humans) can be interpreted for what its design expresses. However, expressive processing also includes considering how the use of a particular process may express connection with a particular school of cognitive science or software engineering; or how the arrangement of processes in a system may express a very different set of priorities—or capabilities—from authorial descriptions of the system; or how understanding the operations of several systems may reveal previously unrecognized kinships (or disparities) between them. Recognizing such things can open up important new interpretations for a computational media system, with aesthetic, theoretical, and political consequences.

Interpreting: The Goldwater Machine

In *Expressive Processing*, one of the systems I interpret is the earliest explicitly political project in computational media, best known by its nickname: "The Goldwater Machine." I analyze it at the time of a 1965 paper by Robert Abelson and J. Douglass Carroll (Abelson & Carroll 1965), though it is a project that Abelson and his students had pursued since the late 1950s and would continue to pursue into the 1970s. At the point of their 1965 paper, the "ideology machine" consisted of an approach to belief structures and a number of operations that could be performed on such structures. Sample belief structures from the paper range from common Cold War views ("Russia controls Cuba's subversion of Latin America") to absurd statements ("Barry Goldwater believes in socialism") and also include simple facts ("Stevenson ran for President").

As these examples foreground, the Goldwater Machine is a system built in the midst of the Cold War. The Cuban Missile Crisis, President Kennedy's assassination, and the Gulf of Tonkin Resolution were all recent events. The world seemed polarized to many, and, within the United States, names such as Adlai Stevenson and Barry Goldwater did not simply indicate prominent politicians with occasionally differing philosophies. As the Republican nominee for President of the United States in 1964, Goldwater was an emblematic believer of the idea that the world's polarization was an inevitable result of a struggle between good and evil—a position that would be echoed by his ideological descendants (e.g., Ronald Reagan's "evil empire" and George W. Bush's "axis of evil"). On the other hand, Stevenson—who was the Democratic candidate for president in 1952—was emblematic of those with a more nuanced view of world affairs and a belief in the potential of international cooperation. He was publicly derided for this view and belief by those with more extreme views.

Interaction with the Goldwater Machine consisted of offering the assertion that a particular *source* (e.g., an individual) has made the claim that a *concept* (e.g., a particular nation) has the stated relation to a *predicate* (generally a verb and an object). For example, "Stevenson claims Cuba threatens Latin America." The statement was evaluated, and a response was generated. For example, if a "good" actor was asserted to be engaged in a bad action, then the system would attempt to deny the alleged fact or that the assertion was made. On the other hand, if a "bad" actor was asserted to be engaged in a good action, then the system would attempt to rationalize the alleged fact or the making of the assertion.

The Goldwater Machine system was presented as a structure and set of processes for modeling human ideology. Abelson and collaborators suggested it could then be populated with data (belief structures of the sorts mentioned above) to represent a particular ideology. If they had succeeded in building such a system, then the machine's processes would be ideologically neutral; only the data would carry a particular position. In the absence of an expressive processing analysis of the system, there would be no reason to question this claimed underlying neutrality.

However, if one undertakes such an analysis, looking at the specifics of the system's operations, then they can reveal that the Goldwater Machine's ideology is also encoded *in its processes*. This encoding begins at the center of its operations, with the system motivated to dismiss any statement by a negatively viewed source, even a statement with which the system data agrees. It is also found in the design of the processes for denial and rationalization, which are predicated on a world divided into "good actors" and "bad actors." Further, in addition to being designed to operate in terms of good and bad, the primary processes for interaction are dedicated to finding routes to deny even the smallest positive action by the bad actors and seeking means to rationalize away even minimally negative actions by the good actors on the basis of paranoid fantasies, apologetic reinterpretations, and misdirections.

This is not a general model of ideology. It is a parody of one particular type of ideology, one that depends on fear to gain power. One can imagine Stevenson being critiqued exactly because his ideology operated by processes rather different from those encoded in the Goldwater Machine. As a result of this difference, it would be impossible to create a "Stevenson Machine" simply by providing a different set of concept-predicate pairs. Yet, without an examination of its processes, we would have had no reason to question its creators' claims to the opposite.

We live in a world in which software processes play increasingly consequential roles in our lives. We are generally asked to take at face value the claims of software creators about what their systems do and to treat those systems as ideologically neutral unless explicitly positioned otherwise. We cannot afford to do this. But to enact an alternative, we must have practice critically interpreting computational processes and must also develop knowledge of different software approaches in a context that makes them legible (rather than deliberately murky or obfuscated, as with high stakes areas such as voting machine systems and terrorist watchlist generators). I believe works of computational media provide some of the most legible and interesting examples for developing this ability, this kind of procedural literacy, as well as for understanding how such media influence our culture—and my approach to these examples is one aspect of what I mean by "expressive processing." The next section of this chapter explores another aspect.

Guiding: Prom Week

Expressive processing is not just an approach that helps us interpret computational media that already exist. It can help us guide the creation of new works. And we need approaches that can help us create, because applying existing criteria for guidance and evaluation (e.g., a technical focus on efficiency or maintainability, or an arts critique honed for fixed media) is not enough as we explore the new computational media experiences that matter.

Just as we are in a period in which software increasingly shapes our lives in a broad sense, we are also in a period of computational media growing in its scope and connection with our lives—from videogames to social media to smartphone apps. Yet we have a paucity of technical and design approaches for making computational media that engages with the things that matter most, from social relationships to ideology to storytelling. We need means to guide ourselves as we seek new uses for existing tools and, perhaps even more, as we seek to invent means to broaden what computational media can meaningfully address.

The three "effects" I outline in *Expressive Processing* might guide computational media creators. The first, the "*Eliza* effect," was already widely discussed before the book. It is what happens when a piece of software (like *Eliza/Doctor*) tries to fool audiences into thinking it is significantly more complex than it is. The results are interactions that can succeed based on initial expectation, but that suffer eventual breakdown (determined by the underlying system's shape) unless interaction is severely restricted. The second, which I call the "*Tale-Spin* effect," is what happens when the system's complex internal processes are never apparent to the audience. The result is that the systems contribute little to audience experience, usually only revealing their interest in moments of breakdown. The third, which I call the "*SimCity* effect," is what happens when software is designed to transition audiences (often through experimentation and feedback) from their initial expectations to an understanding of the underlying system's shape. This is an effective route for making novel processes the center of audience experiences, opening new possibilities for the issues and situations that computational media can address interactively.

I have attempted to use expressive processing as an approach to guide the creation of particular computational media works, and in this section I will briefly describe the attempt to do so with the experimental game *Prom Week* (2012), a social simulation set in the time leading up to an end-of-year dance at a U.S. high school. Each character in *Prom Week* has their own personal characteristics and desires, but these are defined against an elaborate set of rules and beliefs that determine "normal" behavior in the game's fictional high school. Players interact with *Prom Week* by selecting pairs among the characters, examining what actions they most wish to take with one another, and choosing which actions to attempt (see Figure 46.1). Each action is an attempt to change the social state in some way—one desired by the initiating character—which may succeed or fail. In either case, each attempt results in a short scene, which will play out differently depending on the specifics of the world history and character relationships, as well as a number of effects. These effects include changing the characters' relationships with each other, giving one or both characters temporary statuses that may change how future exchanges unfold (e.g., "embarrassed" or "angry at" a particular character), recording events in the ongoing history of the world, and triggering events based on patterns in the world state and character relationships. As a result, players can explore a wide range of possible social worlds, make important events happen in the lives of the characters, and fulfill (or ignore, or subvert) some of the character-specific goals presented at the start of each level—the last of which determines the ending of that character's story.

My interest in helping create *Prom Week* goes back to a question I pose on page 317 of *Expressive Processing*: Given how *The Sims* succeeds through the *SimCity* effect, "[c]an we find similar success with characters more complex than eight mood meters, and fictions more well formed than *The Sims*' implied progression through possessions and careers?" I was excited when, shortly after my arrival at UC Santa Cruz, there was a critical mass of student and faculty interest in pursuing a game of this sort. Josh McCoy was spearheading work on a new AI system that would allow characters to have motivations much more complex than Sims have—and also for characters to be caught up in systems of social expectation that, at that point, games had largely ignored (McCoy & Mateas 2009). Over the course of the project, the game evolved considerably, as we were guided by an expressive processing approach (for the final shape, see McCoy et al. 2013, 2014).

In particular, while we developed *Prom Week* and its underlying AI system, we regularly had meetings during which we stepped back and tried to ask two questions. First, is the design of the system expressing the ideas we have for *Prom Week*? Second, what are we building

Figure 46.1 In this image from *Prom Week*, a player has selected Oswald and is examining other characters from his perspective. Currently, the game shows what social actions Oswald most wants to initiate toward Doug, as well as high-level summaries of how Oswald and Doug feel about each other in terms of friendship, romance, and coolness.

into the system to communicate its design to players, so they can see their opportunities for creativity and play and get appropriate feedback? Obviously, these two questions are deeply connected, especially for a system, like a game, that only comes to mean through play. For example, much of the *Prom Week* system is designed to make the world function like a fictional high school when everything is "happening normally." The shy people do not get up the nerve to tell people how they really feel. Mean, popular people hold sway in the hallways. No one breaks out of their stereotypes.

In nonplayable media, we see the world working this way and then someone (the main character, usually) decides not to play along. We then see the world change. In *Prom Week*, the player not only gets to see how the world operates through depiction, but also experiments with it and gains a sense of its rules, and then decides which characters to nudge (or even use "social influence points" to nudge harder) and push out of their comfort zones—to make things happen that would not otherwise. This is tricky because a lot of what the system does, a lot of what its rules seem to express, is only part of what we want a play session to look like. We use the system's rules and initial scenario to not just express the way the world works but also show *the way the world does not have to be and help the player learn how to make a different world.* A player who understands the game can make radical shifts in the social landscape—one beta test player joyfully reported inverting the high school's entire popularity structure. It is that experience of changing the world, and of coming to understand some of the many ways the world could change, that is (hopefully) the core experience of *Prom Week.*

While through approaches such as playtesting (which we employed) we can gather some insight into whether an experience like *Prom Week* is succeeding, players only see the surface of a game. Playtesting might tell us that the underlying ideas we intend to express through system design are not coming through, but it will not help us press, critique, or even understand those underlying ideas. For instance, I think *Prom Week* is a better game for the critical discussions we had about issues such as how "popularity" should function in a game, and how popularity should be expressed to players. Perhaps counterintuitively, some of our most important decisions were about what we chose *not* to encode in our processes and how this absence was communicated to players. While *Prom Week*'s simulated school encodes many stereotypes and biases, it does not include, for example, racism and heteronormativity. The second of these proved particularly difficult for some players to understand, even though the first nontutorial level is designed to encourage players to discover it. (This level focuses on Oswald, a character who wants a date for the prom. His level is populated by a number of female characters with whom he has little connection, as well as by Nicholas, a "frenemy" with whom there is a lot of potential. But, despite the nudging of the level introduction, this potential proved difficult for some players to discover, or to accept.) In short, we learned that the power of initial audience expectation—which is key to both the *Eliza* and *SimCity* effects—must not be underestimated. Computational media that means to challenge, invert, or even leave out biases of the audience faces a particular challenge when pursuing the *SimCity* effect.

More broadly, I think an expressive processing approach could help many computational media creators give their processes the attention they deserve. We need to ask questions beyond, "Does this work?" and "Is this fun?" We need to ask questions such as, "If this part of the system were taken as an idea, then is it what you would want your audience to understand?" and "If so, then how does the system help them understand the idea through interaction?"

Further Reading

Wardrip-Fruin, N. (2009) *Expressive Processing: Digital Fictions, Computer Games, and Software Studies*, Cambridge, MA: MIT Press.

Wardrip-Fruin, N. (2011) "Digital Media Archaeology: Interpreting Computational Processes," in E. Huhtamo and J. Parikka (eds.) *Media Archaeology: Approaches, Applications, and Implications*, pp. 302–22.

Wardrip-Fruin, N. (2015) "We Can and Must Understand Computers NOW," in D. R. Dechow and D. C. Struppa (eds.) *Intertwingled: The Work and Influence of Ted Nelson*, New York, NY: Springer International Publishing, pp. 105–12.

References

Abelson, R. P. and J. D. Carroll (1965) "Computer Simulation of Individual Belief Systems," *The American Behavioral Scientist (pre-1986)* 8(9), 0–24.

Agre, P. (1997) *Computation and Human Experience*, Cambridge, UK: Cambridge University Press.

Edwards, P. N. (1997) *The Closed World: Computers and the Politics of Discourse in Cold War America*, Cambridge, MA: MIT Press.

Fuller, M. (2008) *Software Studies: A Lexicon*, Cambridge, MA: MIT Press.

Kirschenbaum, M. G. (2003) "Virtuality and VRML: Software Studies after Manovich," in M. Bousquet and K. Wills (eds.) *The Politics of Information*, Alt-X Press, pp. 149–53.

Kirschenbaum, M. G. (2008) *Mechanisms: New Media and the Forensic Imagination*, Cambridge, MA: MIT Press.

Knuth, D. E. (1984) "Literate Programming," *The Computer Journal* 27(2), 97–111.

Manovich, L. (2001) *The Language of New Media*, Cambridge, MA: MIT Press.

Manovich, L., J. Douglass, and W. Huber (2011) "Understanding Scanlation: How to Read One Million Fan-translated Manga Pages," *Image & Narrative* 12(1), 206–28.

Mateas, M. (2005) "Procedural Literacy: Educating the New Media Practitioner," *On the Horizon* 13(2), 101–11.

McCoy, J. and M. Mateas (2009) "The Computation of Self in Everyday Life: A Dramaturgical Approach for Socially Competent Agents," in *Papers from the AAAI Spring Symposium: Intelligent Narrative Technologies II*, pp. 75–82.

McCoy, J., M. Treanor, B. Samuel, A. A. Reed, M. Mateas, and N. Wardrip-Fruin (2012) "Prom Week," Center for Games and Playable Media, UC Santa Cruz, retrieved from promweek.soe.ucsc.edu.

McCoy, J., M. Treanor, B. Samuel, A. A. Reed, M. Mateas, and N. Wardrip-Fruin (2013) "Prom Week: Designing Past the Game/Story Dilemma," in *Proceedings of the Foundations of Digital Games*, pp 94–101, retrieved from games.soe.ucsc.edu/prom-week-designing-past-gamestory-dilemma.

McCoy, J., M. Treanor, B. Samuel, A. A. Reed, M. Mateas, and N. Wardrip-Fruin (2014) "Social Story Worlds with Comme il Faut," *Computational Intelligence and AI in Games, IEEE Transactions* 6(2), 97–112.

Nelson, T. H. (1974) *Computer Lib / Dream Machines*, independently published.

Suchman, L. A. (1987) *Plans and Situated Actions: The Problem of Human-Machine Communication*, Cambridge University Press.

Wardrip-Fruin, N. (2009) *Expressive Processing: Digital Fictions, Computer Games, and Software Studies*, Cambridge, MA: MIT Press.

47
BUILDING INTERACTIVE STORIES

Anastasia Salter

We live in an age of electronic literature: e-book readers are being supplanted by the tablets and smartphones that most of us already carry, with whole libraries, such as Project Gutenberg's collection of public domain texts, available on demand while web comics and digitized comics, such as Marvel Unlimited, bring archives into our phones. However, much of this electronic literature is not meaningfully digital, and in most cases even the term "electronic book" is a misnomer: the stories we consume on digital devices are often simply wrappings for a print codex. Some works take technology a step further and meaningfully use the digital to afford interaction: videogames are the most popular example. Electronic books have the potential to make use of the interactions digital technologies allow. In the age of iPads, tablets are filled with interactive picture books (including adaptations of the works of Dr. Seuss and Lewis Carroll) and digital texts. For instance, the inkle studios app, *Frankenstein* (Morris 2012), allows the reader to explore the experience of the Creature through a choice-driven narrative, although the tragic outcome is predetermined. Reviewer, Laura Miller, notes the satisfaction this exploration offers even as the reader cannot "save" the Creature:

> The great insight that writer Dave Morris brings to this adaptation of the novel is that while a reader cannot significantly change the outcome of the story, the interactive element *can* change the shading and flavor of the tale. It can be mournful and reflective or action-packed. The creature and his creator can show greater or lesser ambivalence about their own behaviors.
>
> (Morris 2012)

Such works are examples of interactive stories: works that communicate a narrative through a system that allows for readers to take a range of actions to explore or direct the experience.

The integration of interactive stories into digital humanities practice has taken several forms. Interactive stories are certainly an object of study, and the intersection of digital humanities with media and game studies (as well as communities dedicated to making and studying interactive stories, such as the Electronic Literature Organization, which released *Electronic Literature Collection* 1, 2, and 3) has assisted our understanding of what interactive stories might accomplish. A growing interest in games in the classroom has also focused attention on serious and educational games, which often use interactive storytelling as one means to build an experience. (Significant examples include Jane McGonigal's *Evoke*, an alternate reality game encouraging players to collaborate and address world hunger and water shortages, and *Play the Past*, a nondigital role-playing game system for character-based play in history courses.) By building interactive stories, we can communicate complex ideas that change our relationship to texts and have the potential to serve as textbooks, persuasive works, thought experiments, and personal narratives. In this chapter, I first position and define interactive stories as a medium, placing the form in its contested space in scholarship. Then I survey exemplars, design principles, and platforms for building interactive stories.

Defining Interactive Stories

When we discuss interactive stories, the examples that come to mind are usually digital: an interactive picture book on the iPad, an adventure game, a hypertext novel. Defining interactive stories by their use of digital media can seem like an alluring place to start. Bryan Alexander defines digital stories as "narratives built from the stuff of cyberspace" (2011: 3), a definition that can be broadly interpreted and recalls some of the challenges of defining digital humanities. This definition can make it difficult to decide where the category ends: Alexander suggests using the "born digital" test to focus on works designed for the affordances of the web (15). We can understand affordances as those things a digital media environment offers that are significant capabilities of the form: for instance, the ability to encode hyperlinks and create meaning through nonlinear connections, or the ability of a system to take input, evaluate it based on a set of procedures, and respond.

However, nondigital systems can include elements of these affordances. *Choose Your Own Adventure* novels offer prescriptive systems for allowing decision-based narratives navigated through multiple paths, while Oulipian texts such as Raymond Queneau's *A Hundred Thousand Billion Poems* (1961/1998) offer paper-based algorithmic poetry generators. Queneau's poetry-generator uses the physical book to bind the lines of potential poems together, but each line is its own page, allowing the reader to combine the pieces to form new works. Such systems fall into the broader definitional rubric Espen Aarseth offers as "cybertext":

> [A] machine for the production of variety of expression. . . . [W]hen you read from a cybertext, you are constantly reminded of inaccessible strategies and paths not taken, voices not heard. Each decision will make some parts of the text more, and others less, accessible, and you may never know the exact results of your choices; that is, exactly what you missed.
>
> (Aarseth 1997: 3)

In physical media, the paths not taken might be easily mapped, as anyone who has marked the page of their last choice while reading a *Choose Your Own Adventure Book* is aware. In digital systems, like in Queneau's generator, the paths not traveled are often too numerous to easily explore. Aarseth's definition thus complicates the easy association of the medium with the technology.

This interdisciplinary discourse and range of media leads us to find discussions (and definitions) of interactive stories in a range of spaces. Hartmut Koenitz, Gabriele Ferri, Mads Haahr, Digdem Sezen, and Tonguc Ibrahim Sezen recently summarized the history of what they term "interactive digital narrative" as originating with text-based games in the 1960s and following three evolutionary paths: "text-based, cinematic/performative, and ludic/experimental" (2015: 11). These trajectories are useful for resolving the multitude of disciplinary spaces where interactive narrative is discussed and performed. Likewise, Chris Crawford defines interactive storytelling as a field that emerged in the 1980s but did not really take off until 2010:

> [L]ike the proverbial elephant, everybody perceived it from his or her own vantage point. Moviemakers see it as a form of cinema, video-game people claim it as an extension of their own field, computer scientists think of it as part of the broader field of artificial intelligence, and experts in the art of improv consider it to be the computerization of their skills.
>
> (Crawford 2012)

Ultimately, defining interactive stories hinges on understanding the role of interactivity. Marie-Laure Ryan identifies interactivity as the essential affordance digital systems bring to our ability to produce and experience narrative: "Digital media do not simply place us in front of a static text; they situate us inside a system that continually produces a dynamic object" (2004: 329–30). Janet Murray suggests that this interactivity transforms the roles of authors and readers:

> [I]n electronic narrative the procedural author is like a choreographer who supplies the rhythms, the context, and the set of steps that will be performed. The interactor, whether as navigator, protagonist, explorer, or builder, makes use of this repertoire of possible steps and rhythms to improvise a particular dance among the many, many possible dances the author has enabled. We could perhaps say that the interactor is the author of a particular performance within an electronic story system, or the architect of a particular part of the virtual world, but we must distinguish this derivative authorship from the originating authorship of the system itself.
>
> (Murray 1997: 153)

This definition yields a productive concept, the procedural author, suggesting that we can best define interactive stories through the work of their creation, including the creation of a rules-based system to communicate a narrative.

Why Not "Games?" The Ludology Vs. Narratology Debate

Defining interactive stories as procedurally authored works intersects them with games. The challenge of labeling and categorizing interactive stories reflects an ongoing debate in the field, particularly in game studies. While it might seem easy to pull the lens of game studies (and with it, the term "game") into any discussion of interactive narrative media, this tendency has been largely debated in both academia and popular discourse. Game studies is a relatively new field: Aarseth suggests that computer game studies emerged as a full international scholarly field in 2001, which saw both the first international computer game conference and the publication of the first issue of *Game Studies*. In outlining the challenges for this new discipline, Aarseth stakes out the need for computer game studies as its own discipline, noting that "games are not a kind of cinema, or literature, but colonizing attempts from both these fields have already happened, and no doubt will happen again" (2001).

These "colonizing attempts" refer to the tension between approaching games primarily as narratives (usually associated with scholars from disciplines such as literature or film) versus approaching games primarily as systems of mechanics or simulations. There have been several accounts summarizing and extending this debate over the past two decades. While the two "camps" (which is itself an oversimplification) are often labeled as ludology and narratology, they might better be understood as interaction versus narration. Michael Mateas (2002) rejects the term narratologist, which reflects a particular humanities discipline, not just the study of narrative. To recall our challenge in defining interactive stories, the tension of games with other narrative media is central to defining the uniqueness of games. Writing a few years after the publication of Aarseth's *Cybertext* (1997), Mark Barrett suggests in "Irreconcilable Differences: Games vs. Story" that "not only are story and game achieving their emotional power through uncertainty of outcome in exactly opposite fashions, but the power derived from one method destroys the power of the other" (Barrett 2000). This opposition seems to set up a hard binary that is difficult to traverse, and indeed a few years later Gonzalo Frasca (2003a) summarized the debate as one driven by false binaries, suggesting that, while the characteristics of games may not seem to fit all definitions of narrative, re-defining narrative might shed new light on both games and stories. Frasca elaborates on this incompatibility in "Simulation vs. Narrative," with another analysis of the binary conflict: "simulation cannot be understood just through its output. This is absolutely evident to anyone who played a game: the feeling of playing soccer cannot be compared to the one of watching a match" (2003b: 224). These debates ask us to reconsider what is important in the experience of the interactive story: Is there something new about being able to press buttons or touch a screen to change a story's path? Or are these narratives better understood as drawing on the history of literature, film, and poetry? Our answer might well vary with each piece we explore—a videogame's frantic pace draws the focus to interactivity, while a digital work of poetry heralds back clearly to literary narrative traditions. Thus it is unsurprising that Celia Pearce (2005) takes issue with Frasca's dismissal of the simulation-narrative debate, drawing our attention to the very different levels of narrative present in different interactive forms. A player of games such as Scrabble and Chess might later tell a story of their experience, but the game itself does not present a strong narrative.

The apparent impossibility of resolving this debate suggests that this tension is essential to all forms of interactive storytelling, including games. Narrative and play cannot help but conflict, as traditional definitions of narrative privilege authorial control, and allowing a user to play means surrendering at least some of that control. Ian Bogost recently surveyed the state of this debate given the evolution of game studies trends over the past decade:

> Not quite fifteen years after Espen Aarseth declared ["]Computer Game Studies, Year One["] . . . , ours is an improbable, fledgling discipline whose future is hardly secure. It's possible we've all made an error in isolating any media form from its kindred, particularly in the post-2008 era of austerity, where perhaps the only way for media studies to flourish is by teaming up, Voltron-style, and finally realizing that the overall project of making and critiquing media in culture needs a strong foundation atop which to develop medium-specific theories and approaches . . . Or else, or in addition: we need more and greater dispute, such that the terms and principles of various schools of thought are clearly identifiable, associated with specific individuals and institutions, clearly namable for invocation, and receptive to invocation in critical and design contexts.
>
> (Bogost 2015)

When seeking to build interactive stories, then, we might take Bogost's advice to consider the work as both part of a much broader media discourse and a clearly identifiable, separate form. While games in general must be understood as systems where narrative (broadly construed) might create one thread of the experience, interactive stories explicitly privilege narrative as output and purpose. By thinking of building interactive stories instead of building games, we also free ourselves from some of the constraints that go along with game design, such as the expectation of either a conflict for the user to resolve or a competition with a winning or losing outcome.

Designing Stories for Interaction

Distinguishing interactive stories from other forms allows us to focus our design on three essential components:

- Narrative development,
- Purpose of interaction, and
- Procedural system.

First, our interactive story needs a narrative, and that narrative needs a compelling reason for existing in an interactive form. Interactive stories can draw on any genre, from horror-inspired adventures such as *The Walking Dead* (Telltale Games 2014) to comedies such as Nick Montfort's procedural poem, "Taroko Gorge" (2009), and its many versions. The distinction between story and narrative varies by interpretation: a story is a sequence of events, while narrative encompasses the techniques and texts from which story draws. Often, interactive stories play with viewpoint and the concept of the narrator: sometimes the player is directly the actor in the story, as in the "you are the hero" model of *Choose Your Own Adventure* works, while other works invite the player-reader to engage with someone else's story, as in Shelley Jackson's hypertext, *my body—a Wunderkammer* (1997). While interactive stories might remediate existing narratives, those narratives are usually meaningfully transformed in the process (see Bolter & Grusin 2000). For instance, inkle's *Frankenstein* (Morris 2012) includes almost twice the text of the original novel to allow the reader to dive into the mindset of the Creature. By moving away from the original narrator's perspective, the reader can experience the Creature's relationships with other characters and his developing philosophy. An interactive story can also be originally written for the form, which often impacts the conceit and organization. For instance, *my body—a Wunderkammer* is fragmented around the physical interface of the human form. Stories that lend themselves to interactivity can also follow traditional patterns of branching, as in Jason Shiga's *Meanwhile*, a graphic novel adapted for iOS by Andrew Plotkin that opens with the choice of vanilla or chocolate ice cream and then launches a time travel adventure that boasts "3,856 Story Possibilities" (Shiga & Plotkin 2012). Other narratives take advantage of the simulation aspect of interactive systems to allow exploration through a virtual space. For example, *Gone Home* (Gaynor 2013) slowly reveals a family conflict through objects in an apparently abandoned house. Spatial stories are particularly common in games or physical environments such as theme parks, and they rely on what Henry Jenkins defines as environmental storytelling:

> [Environmental storytelling] creates the preconditions for an immersive narrative experience in at least one of four ways: spatial stories can evoke pre-existing narrative associations; they can provide a staging ground where narrative events are enacted;

they may embed narrative information within their mise-en-scene; or they provide resources for emergent narratives.

(Jenkins 2004: 23)

Other examples of environmental storytelling include alternate and augmented reality games, such as Google's Ingress (Niantic Labs 2012), a faction-driven, science fiction battle game that plays out in real cities.

Each type of interactive story tends to use the mechanisms appropriate to its goals. Environmental storytelling is common in games and other interactive stories where the emphasis is on the action; for instance, *BioShock* (Irrational Games 2007) uses audio messages and atmospheric posters to convey the history of a sunken city in between the player's battles with monsters. More text-driven works tend to rely on a strong organizational mechanic, whether it is based on a simple choice-driven progression, such as the decision to destroy one's surroundings and self in Pierre Chevalier's *Destroy / Wait* (2013), or a spatial metaphor turned textual, such as the exploration of caves in Crowther's original *Adventure* (1976). The choice of mechanics determines the pace and sets the expectations of the user as well as the user's role: in environmental works, the user is often cast as a player, focused on motion and progression. In text-based or poetic works, the user is instead invited into the role of reader. The integration of elements from different genres and expectations can change the pace: some text-based works incorporate timers, as in Anna Anthropy's frantically paced *Queers in Love at the End of the World* (2013), which simulates the last moments with a lover prior to the destruction of the planet.

Next in our design process, our interactive story needs clear purpose and goals for the user/reader's interactions with the system. Mark Meadows addresses the challenge of system design while also engaging the ludology/narratology debate: "The narrative's structure and the design of the interactivity should be two ingredients in a single recipe. In the best forms of interactive narrative, one can't take precedence over the other" (2002). Obviously, this remark assumes the purpose of the work is to communicate a story, which fundamentally distinguishes some genres of interactive media from others. While a story might be constructed from the play of *Monopoly* or *Tetris*, it is hardly fundamental and certainly does not play a role equal to the simulation; likewise, in a game such as *Monkey Island*, the interactions and puzzles serve primarily to advance the story.

Interactive stories use interaction in several ways, including:

- Choice: Choice-driven narratives are usually branching and allow the player to move between meaningful options. A powerful example is Porpentine's *With Those We Love Alive* (2014), a text-driven game where the player writes symbols on their arm to represent key choices while responding to a nightmarish society's demands.
- Exploration: Exploration-driven narratives can involve movement through a virtual or real space (as in environment-driven works such as *Gone Home*) or the exploration of time and context, as in Dan Waber's poetic text game, *A Kiss* (2013), which includes over one thousand passages that allow the user to delve into a relationship by moving through moments before and after a kiss.
- Obstacles and Problem Solving: Overcoming obstacles to advance a story is often associated with games, from classic text games to adventure games. Alternate reality games also rely on collaborative problem solving as in *I Love Bees* (42 Entertainment 2004), a science fiction, alternate reality game where players unravel hints to receive story fragments such as a call to a phone booth at an encrypted place and time.

Finally, the nature of these interactions and the needs of the narrative determine the system and platform we must construct or use to build the interactive story. This system cannot be separated from the narrative and goals of interaction, meaning the design and procedural layers have to be built in tandem. This is reflected in Susan H. Delagrange's assertion about interactive scholarship, a genre that often draws on the methods and tools of interactive stories: "Design is intrinsic to an argument, not decoration for it, and must be part of the writing-imaging-designing process from Day One" (2009). This intersection is productive to the design and argument of my project, "Alice in Dataland" (2015), which uses multiple platforms of interactive storytelling to remediate *Alice's Adventures in Wonderland.* Shifting through platforms allows us to recognize the strengths and affordances of each, which in turn transforms the experience of our interactive stories. Such jolts of platform or modality shift are also demanding of the reader; they require attention to changes across spaces, for instance.

Platforms for Interactive Stories

Over the past decade, digital humanities projects have benefited from the increasing accessibility of digital production tools and methods: new resources make it possible to build complex interactive systems with small teams and often without intensive programming. The impact of open source tools designed for use by "non-coders" has likewise been particularly powerful in the realm of interactive storytelling. A few of the platforms that have been widely adopted and/or offer valuable affordances include:

- ARIS: The ARIS augmented reality storytelling project was developed by a team led by David Gagnon at the University of Wisconsin-Madison. The platform allows for the development of locative games that can be played on mobile devices through the ARIS app. Building stories on this platform allows creators to employ elements of environmental storytelling, as characters and items are placed relative to real-world locations. For instance *Steel* (2013), based in downtown Madison, invites players to explore the historical steel industry and collect metal to exchange.
- Twine: Created in 2007 by Chris Klimas, Twine is a node-based system for building games that include many of the fundamental affordances of hypertext novels. Examples of Twine games include *A Kiss* (Waber 2013) and *With Those We Love Left Alive* (Porpentine 2014). Twine has proven particularly successful in bringing underrepresented voices into game development, and the subject of Twine's definition as a gaming platform has proven controversial. Twine creators typically define their works as games, inviting comparison and conversation with mainstream gaming culture, while the typical face of videogames is very different.
- Inform 7: Text adventure games remain a primary example of interactive storytelling, but the genre of interactive fiction has evolved significantly since its roots. Inform 7 is a natural language tool for building interactive stories that are centered on explorable worlds and parser-driven play (where the author anticipates the use of verbs and nouns to interact with the environment) and thus can offer a space that feels as responsive as the author's anticipation of player actions. Emily Short's *Bronze* (2011), a retelling of *Beauty and the Beast,* demonstrates Inform 7's flexibility and power while offering many variations on the fairy-tale ending.
- Adventure Game Studio: Developed by Chris Jones, Adventure Game Studio is an open source platform for building graphic adventure games. The platform features an accessible graphical interface and has seen several versions since 1997. The tool is inspired by classic

games such as *Monkey Island* and *King's Quest* and has seen several impressive independent releases, including the split-screen narrative, *What Linus Bruckman Sees When His Eyes Are Closed* (Twelve 2006).

- iBooks Author: With the introduction of the iPad as a platform for reading in 2009, more attention has centered on taking book-like experiences and enhancing them with digital affordances. Most of the outcomes of this type of development are multimodal, but rarely truly interactive: the reader might respond or act, but the system cannot react. iBooks Author has made building multimedia texts with responsive content accessible, and the less proprietary EPUB format has also been undergoing revision to allow more dynamic content. Currently, the tool is rarely used creatively and most often used for math textbooks, but the platform's capabilities are evolving.
- Unity: The Unity platform offers the tools of a production-level game engine with 3-D or 2-D graphics and an impressive range of assets for free. While most digital humanities and educational projects do not reach this level of development, Unity and similar platforms are popular choices for independent and professional interactive stories, including *Gone Home* (Gaynor 2013). Just as Twine complicates any barrier between game and interactive story, so, too, does the use of Unity remind us that the overlap between the two is extensive.

Open source platforms for building interactive stories can lower the barriers to entry for creating works that use procedural systems as their foundations. The choice of platform is essential to the feel and capabilities of a work, as different platforms better enable different types of interactions. While many of these platforms are based on minimizing the amount of coding literacy required to create interactive stories (particularly Twine and Adventure Game Studio), the development of a procedural system and the creation of rules for responding to actions are still central. The emphasis on visuals varies between platforms, with tools such as Twine and Inform 7 minimizing or eliminating the role of graphics, while Unity and Adventure Game Studio both require the development of an environment in two or three dimensions.

The choice of platform is more than aesthetic: just as the form of a book influences its content, whether subtly—through the placement of words or the division of a sentence across pages—or explicitly—as with serialized novels and their corresponding cliffhanger-based structure—so, too, does the platform's machine layer transform a work. Any interactive story relies on encoded algorithms, or decision-making rules systems, that are built into the platform. The author can set some of the rules of the system and in doing so determine the player's options for interactivity, but other rules and options are determined by the platform itself.

Building interactive stories allows us to explore the capabilities of the technologies and devices we use every day. The presence of interactive stories (and, indeed, of games) on the computers we carry in our pockets has a growing potential to change our relationship with both devices and the world around us. Through the lens interactive stories provide, we can also probe at and rethink related genres and media, from games and electronic literature to print codices and comics. Building an interactive story can also be an act of scholarship, whether covert (such as the retelling of *Frankenstein* or *Beauty and the Beast*) or deliberate (as with "Alice in Dataland" and the journal, *Kairos*). Interactive stories provide a way to communicate theories and ideas through a nonlinear form with different constraints, feedback, and expectations than an essay intended for print. By engaging with interactive stories as part of digital humanities, we can expand our methods and practice.

Further Reading

Anthropy, A. (2012) *Rise of the Videogame Zinesters: How Freaks, Normals, Amateurs, Artists, Dreamers, Dropouts, Queers, Housewives, and People Like You Are Taking Back an Art Form*, New York, NY: Seven Stories Press.

Funkhouser, C. T. (2012) *New Directions in Digital Poetry: Volume I of International Texts in Critical Media Aesthetics*, New York, NY: A&C Black.

Hayles, N. K. (2008) *Electronic Literature: New Horizons for the Literary*, Notre Dame. IN: University of Notre Dame Press.

Ryan, M. L. (2006) *Avatars of Story*, Minneapolis, MN: University of Minnesota Press.

Wardrip-Fruin, N. and N. Montfort (2003) *The New Media Reader*, Cambridge, MA: MIT Press.

References

42 Entertainment (2004) *I Love Bees*, Burbank, CA: Bungie.

Aarseth, E. (1997) *Cybertext: Perspectives on Ergodic Literature*, Baltimore, MD: Johns Hopkins University Press.

Aarseth, E. (2001) "Computer Game Studies, Year One," *Game Studies* 1(1), retrieved from gamestudies.org/0101/editorial.html.

Alexander, B. (2011) *The New Digital Storytelling: Creating Narratives with New Media*, Santa Barbara, CA: Praeger.

Anthropy, A. (2013) *Queers in Love at the End of the World*, retrieved from auntiepixelante.com/endoftheworld.

ARIS (2013) *Steel*, retrieved from arisgames.org/featured/steel.

Barrett, M. (2000) "Irreconcilable Differences: Games vs. Story," *GameDev.net*, retrieved from www.gamedev.net/page/resources/_/creative/game-design/irreconcilable-differences-game-vs-story-r887.

Bogost, I. (2015) "Game Studies, Year Fifteen: Notes on Thoughts on Formalism," retrieved from bogost.com/writing/blog/game-studies-year-fifteen.

Bolter, J. D. and R. Grusin (2000) *Remediation: Understanding New Media*, Cambridge, MA: MIT Press.

Chevalier, P. (2013) *Destroy / Wait*, retrieved from lilinx.com/destroywait.

Crawford, C. (2012) *Chris Crawford on Interactive Storytelling*, 2nd edn, New York, NY: New Riders.

Crowther, W., D. Woods, and K. Black (1976) *Colossal Cave Adventure*, computer game.

Delagrange, S. H. (2009) "When Revision Is Redesign: Key Questions for Digital Scholarship," *Kairos: A Journal of Rhetoric, Technology, and Pedagogy* 14(1), retrieved from kairos.technorhetoric.net/14.1.

Frasca, G. (2003a) "Ludologists Love Stories, Too: Notes from a Debate That Never Took Place," in *Level Up: International DiGRA Conference Proceedings*.

Frasca, G. (2003b) "Simulation Versus Narrative," in M. J. Wolf & B. Perron (eds.) *The Video Game Theory Reader*, New York: Psychology Press, pp. 221–35.

Gaynor, S. (2013) *Gone Home*, Portland, OR: Fullbright.

Irrational Games (2007) *BioShock*, Boston, MA.

Jackson, S. (1997) *my body—a Wunderkammer*, retrieved from collection.eliterature.org/1/works/jackson__my_body_a_wunderkammer.html.

Jenkins, H. (2004) "Game Design as Narrative Architecture," in N. Wardrip-Fruin and P. Harrigan (eds.) *First Person: New Media as Story, Performance, and Game*, Cambridge, MA: MIT Press, pp. 118–30.

Juul, J. (2004) "The Definitive History of Games and Stories, Ludology and Narratology," *The Ludologist*, retrieved from www.jesperjuul.net/ludologist/the-definitive-history-of-games-and-stories-ludology-and-narratology.

Koenitz, H., G. Ferri, M. Haahr, D. Sezen, and T. I. Sezen (2015) "Introduction: A Concise History of Interactive Digital Narrative," in H. Koenitz, G. Ferri, M. Haahr, D. Sezen, and T. I. Sezen (eds.) *Interactive Digital Narrative: History, Theory and Practice*, New York: Routledge, pp. 9–21.

Mateas, M. (2002) "Interactive Drama, Art and Artificial Intelligence," dissertation, Carnegie Mellon University, Pittsburgh, PA.

Meadows, M. S. (2002) *Pause & Effect: The Art of Interactive Narrative*, Indianapolis, Indiana, IN: New Riders.

Miller, L. (2012) "Frankenstein," *The Chimerist*, retrieved from thechimerist.com/post/22122232431/Frankenstein.

Montfort, N. (2009) "Taroko Gorge," retrieved from nickm.com/poems/taroko_gorge.html.

Morris, D. (2012) *Frankenstein*, Cambridge, U.K.: inkle studios.

Murray, J. (1997) *Hamlet on the Holodeck: The Future of Narrative in Cyberspace*, New York, NY: The Free Press.

Niantic Labs (2012) *Ingress*, San Francisco, CA: Google.

Pearce, C. (2005) "Theory Wars: An Argument against Arguments in the So-called Ludology/Narratology Debate," paper presented at *DiGRA 2005: Changing Views: Worlds in Play, 2005 International Conference*.

Porpentine (2014) *With Those We Love Alive*, retrieved from aliendovecote.com/uploads/twine/empress/empress.html.

Queneau, R. (1961/1998) "One Hundred Thousand Million Poems," in H. Matthews & A. Brotchie (eds.) *Oulipo Compendium*, S. Chapman (trans.), London: Atlas Press, pp. 15–33.

Ryan, M. L. (2004) *Narrative across Media: The Languages of Storytelling*, Omaha, NE: University of Nebraska Press.
Salter, A. (2015) "Alice in Dataland 2.0," *Kairos: A Journal of Rhetoric, Technology, and Pedagogy* 20(1), retrieved from kairos.technorhetoric.net/20.1/inventio/salter/index.html.
Shiga, J. and A. Plotkin (2012) "Meanwhile: An Interactive Comic Book," *Zarfhome Software Consulting*, retrieved from zarfhome.com/meanwhile.
Short, E. (2011) *Bronze: A Fractured Fairy Tale*, retrieved from inform7.com/learn/eg/bronze/index.html.
Telltale Games (2014) *The Walking Dead*, San Rafael, CA.
Twelve, V. (2006) *What Linus Bruckman Sees When His Eyes Are Closed*, *xiigames*, retrieved from xiigames.com/linus.
Waber, D. (2013) *A Kiss*, retrieved from www.logolalia.com/hypertexts/a-kiss.html#.

48

READING CULTURE THROUGH CODE

Mark C. Marino

Historically, computer source code has been treated like hieroglyphics read only by high priests or, in more mundane terms, like a highly specialized mechanism read only by technicians, even as software increasingly influences every aspect of our lives. However, in the last 10 years, reading code has become common among more and more groups, from a great variety of perspectives. In fact, 2012 was called the Year of Code, and sites such as Code Year offer online instruction in programming to the uninitiated. Courses that teach code have once again been added to elementary school curricula, to an extent not seen since the days of BASIC, Logo, and personal computing in the 1980s. In his 2016 State of the Union Address, U.S. President Barack Obama included computer science courses for all students as one of his chief priorities for the remaining days of his presidency. We are in the middle of a new wave of interest in programming, with a growing sense that programming, like mathematics and reading, is one of the core skills.

In the midst of the broader literacy movement (where "literacy" itself has been challenged as a term), I have been working with an interdisciplinary group of scholars to pursue the epistemology of code, asking whether it is more than merely a practical, utilitarian system of *encoding* and instead a form of *communication* with layers of meaning for its wide and varied audiences. We call these methods Critical Code Studies (CCS), which is the application of hermeneutics to interpret source code's extra-functional significance. Rather than treating code as the sole object and end point of this application, CCS sees it as an entryway into investigating the interactions between not only computers and humans but also code and many different kinds of systems, including software and hardware. Instead of rendering code an inevitable set of processes (such as arithmetic) or a logical extension of hardware, CCS frames code as a *cultural text*—not a fine art, but perhaps an artisanal craft. Donald Knuth (1992) coined the term "literate programming" to name the practice of writing code not merely for its function but also for its form, attending particularly to its legibility for human readers. Importantly, the act of programming does not involve the fulfillment of an obligation. Instead, it is the subjective and creative construction of an assemblage from a wide array of possibilities—an infinite array of them, in fact.

Programmers choose from various languages, programming styles, and architectures. From these selections, the programmer (alone or, more often, in collaboration with others) creates an assemblage of processes. For any given task, there are millions and millions of choices. Of course, the choice is not completely free. Each programming situation has its own constraints, including its own parameters and conventions. Hardware, time, money, social conditions, cultural norms, and the priorities of a project may also limit or structure what programmers can do. But, like the chef working on a limited budget, constraints do not necessarily imply a lack of creativity or self-consciousness. Programming can be an imaginative act and intervention.

What Is a Critical Approach to Code?

How can CCS be distinguished from any discussion of code? If the process of contextualizing code involves an ethnographic or archaeological process, then CCS also presents an ontological challenge. One might think that an approach borne of hermeneutic or literary traditions would interpret code as a work of poetry, echoing the WordPress mantra, "code is poetry" (Bigelow 2011). Yet this suggestion makes some programmers cringe. Programming is not only prosaic; code can also seem virtually illegible, especially when written by someone else. Rather than interpreting code as a literary object or presupposing a high quality of expression, approaching it as a cultural text assumes that significance arises from its history, circulation, and reception. This approach draws heavily from cultural studies, as typified by a collaborative reading of the Sony Walkman (Du Gay et al. 2013). In this sense, a "text" is less an artwork and more an everyday object of inquiry—like a building, a nail, or even a network—with a meaningful relationship to culture. To treat code as a cultural text is to examine its accrual of significance through the ways it is regarded as well as the ways people respond to and interact with it.

In the realm of computer science and programming classes, code is already more than a utilitarian medium, for it has subjective, aesthetic traits. Elegance, for example, is a subjective quality of code that is routinely praised. While I am not particularly interested in debating what makes code elegant, the fact that programmers develop a *sense of elegance* and pursue it suggests a main attribute of programming: it is not a purely functional activity, and the shape of the code is not inevitable. To make code is to engage in discourse while also recognizing that code has to function, even if it's irreducible to that functionality. Programmers speak code and code speaks, as Geoff Cox and Alex McLean (2013) put it. Code proves itself all the more discursive because it is made of signs—material signs in artificial languages—and, like any realm of discourse, this one develops rhetoric, creativity, and meaning.

In pursuing this cultural approach, CCS builds upon the practices of material culture studies, media archaeology, and science and technology studies (Spiegel-Rösing & de Solla Price 1977) by emphasizing critical intervention. Though such approaches involve a wide array of practices from scholars whose foci hardly follow a single rule, the comparison is instructive in identifying high-level differences in emphasis. For, in keeping with the historical inquiry of these three approaches, CCS seeks to recover the conditions under which code has been written, not primarily for archival purposes, but in service of inquiry into the more complex aspects of history: the assumptions behind code's creation; the negotiations of forces, social and physical, that enabled or inhibited its production; and the nature of its reception and iteration, to name a few. CCS pursues the "throughlines" of technological development, where even an artifact as young as code participates in histories that long predate it. A goal of CCS is thus *not merely to document but to question*—to ask what is this object, where did it come from, how did people develop it, how did people use it, and how was it received. While CCS demands a kind of ethnographic and, following the methods of Matthew Kirschenbaum (2008), forensic research, the term "critical" implies a challenge to conventional narratives of technological development. Rather than tracing the history of media forms for the sake of nostalgia, corporate history, or some progress narrative, CCS investigates and critiques the forces that shape technology as well as the investments and motivations of those, at times, agonistic forces. Such investigations can be equally applied to one line of code and to thousands of lines (see Montfort et al. 2013).

Still, even if some programs are as short as some poems, code cannot be completely understood by reading its text alone. Code is not simply what is seen (symbol or signifier); it shapes what is seen. Early in the development of CCS, Kirschenbaum (2011) pointed out that code cannot be read by itself, separate from its platforms and the other software with which it interacts. Without these platforms and dependencies, it will not execute. Instead, we read code in situ, in the context of its platform and interoperating software, as well as the culture of its development and circulation.

After situating code within its cultural and technological context, we determine what code does and how. Perhaps this is the biggest difference between reading code and reading other text-based semiotic objects. As part of a digital system, code has specific and predictable effects on the interoperating software as well as the hardware on which it runs. Unlike a poem or even a law, which exist with typographical errors, a line of code rarely functions with a mistake. The systems that process code are largely unforgiving of error. Code may be, as Alexander Galloway posits, "*the only language that is executable*" (2004: 165–66); it is a language that, when processed (whether compiled or executed), causes certain necessary, deterministic effects. Machines process it in a verifiable and replicable manner, with input becoming output. In CCS, the critic must know which effects code causes in the system, while recognizing that every known effect stands in for and masks a host of other effects. Here, Wendy Chun's warning against "sourcery" (2011), or fetishizing source code as the ultimate underlying truth, is both a necessary caution and a reminder not to see code as a sole means or a definitive end. Nonetheless, to use and read code competently and consciously, one must understand its parameters, conventions, and effects. As a result, CCS involves some fluency in programming as well as working with those who have an intimate knowledge of language and programming paradigms. It is a moment in digital humanities that calls for collaboration, through which interpretation takes advantage of the same diversified skillsets that go into building software.

Until this point, my description of CCS has largely paralleled strains of media archaeology and science and technology studies. However, CCS also follows in the footsteps of critical race studies and critical legal studies in its calls for reflexive interpretation. That is, the "critical" dimension of CCS refers to not only a critique of conventional narratives (as mentioned earlier), but also the use of critical theory—a term applying loosely to philosophical hermeneutics (or "ways of interpreting") largely arising from Continental philosophy—as well as the critical approach of the examiner (or "theories of knowing"), including issues of ethics, social relations, ideology, or other aspects of epistemology and ontology. This approach presupposes that all is not apparent on the surface of code. Again, code means more than it shows as a symbol or signifier, and the conventions that frame how we interpret it are also constructed.

This challenge to conventional wisdom that code is what it does (i.e., its function) arises from a deconstructive approach. Associated with Jacques Derrida (1974), deconstruction is a practice of identifying fissures or gaps between the signifier and signified and then re-inscribing those gaps as resources fundamental to understanding the text at hand. While programmers must ask what any particular line of code does and how might it help them achieve a goal, deconstruction asks how the essence or source of code actually depends on its appearance or effects. Deconstruction does not take conventions or origins as gospel. It questions the underlying assumptions of those conventions and origins. Out of this deconstructive impulse comes Friedrich Kittler's claim that "there is no software" (1995), Wendy Chun's note that the source code is not exactly executable code (2011), and Tara McPherson's analysis of Unix and the Civil Rights movement (2012). Even if deconstruction has fallen out of favor, it is hard to imagine most contemporary forms of critical interpretation without its contributions to reading as a practice predicated on productive skepticism. The examples I have offered via Kittler, Chun, and McPherson show how critics of media and technology problematize simple interpretations by destabilizing systems of meaning, including the empirical "facts" or "natures" of computational systems.

While these gestures challenge the authority or essence of code, they do not detract from its ability to convey meaning. Ultimately, CCS must seek meaning in code. But where? In the comments? In the variable names? In how it executes processes? In the output or results? Obviously, there is no one answer. Meaning emerges from all of these aspects, yet CCS does not define code as a mere cipher, whose meaning need merely be revealed. Reading code, like reading any cultural text, is a creative and relational process, in which meaning arises from questions asked.

Case Studies in Reading Code

To illustrate some CCS methodologies, I will present a few examples drawn from my own work as well as from the CCS Working Groups, which are biennial online conferences that, since 2010, have gathered scholars from around the world to study culture through code. These working groups have helped grow CCS into a vibrant subfield such that code analysis is now a chief methodology of digital humanities. The case studies I have included here address code through examples that are relatively self-contained and easy to explain in a concise manner. As experimental works, they also perform a certain amount of commentary on code. Analyzing them thus offers a twofold critique, both the critique the works perform and the one emerging from my interpretations of them against various cultural contexts.

One week in the 2014 CCS Working Group focused on reading code through post-colonialism to critique and explore issues of power, subjugation, and identity formation after the period of large-scale colonial rule. The leaders of the discussion, Roopika Risam, Adaline Koh, and Amit Ray, examined the predominance of English in programming languages, by examining قلب or Alb ("heart"), a work presenting itself as an Arabic programming language (reposted 2014). Created by computer scientist and artist, Ramsey Nasser, in 2013, قلب is "a conceptual art piece exploring the difficulty of using any language other than English for practical software" (Nasser in McBride 2013). According to Nasser, the language is "LISP-based and similar to a variant called Scheme." Here is some sample code. Note the persistence of Roman characters and English words, such as "class," even in this snippet.

```
(قول "قلـب: لغة برمجة - مترجم ٠،١،٣")
(قول "رمـــزي نـــاصـــر ٢٠١٢")
(قول "")
(قول "<a class='execute' href='#أمثلة'>أمثلة</a> - <a class='execute'
href='#الـنجـدة'>النجدة</a> - <a class='execute' href='#ما هـذا؟'>ما-هذا؟</
a>")
(قول "")
```

```
(حدد أمثلة (لامدا () (
  (قول "سهل: <a class='load' href='#amthila/mrhba'>مرحبا يا عالم</a>")
  (قول "متوسط: <a class='load' href='#amthila/fybunatshi'>عدد فيبوناتشي</
a>")
  (قول "متقدم: <a class='load' href='#amthila/konway'>لعبة الحياة لكونواي</
a>")
  (عدم)
)))

(حدد النجدة (لامدا () (قول "هذا قلب!")))
(حدد ما-هذا؟ (لامدا ()
  (قول "قلب هي لغة برمجة هدفها إستكشاف")
  (قول "العلاقة بين الثقافة البشرية")
  (قول "والعلوم الحاسوبية، خصوصًا علاقة")
  (قول "الأبجدية اللاتينية بلغات البرمجة")
  (قول "المختلفة. للمزيد من المعلومات")
```

In many ways, Nasser's project already enacts a form of CCS by identifying the cultural dimension of programming, which is often considered purely logical or universal. However, the stakes are more apparent in an economic landscape, where many jobs in the technology sector depend on mastery of English-based programming languages (Vee 2013). Furthermore, قلب demonstrates programming's expressive potential, or how code is a creative medium for cultural intervention.

To discuss this code, the CCS hosts drew upon postcolonial theories of language, primarily Edgar Schneider's theorization of global Englishes in *Postcolonial English* (2007). In his analysis, Schneider maps the progress of English into a worldwide language through British colonization. Risam, Koh, and Ray make the argument that English has followed a similar course through programming languages, establishing its predominance specifically in American English. For instance, consider English words used in high-level programming languages (e.g., PRINT, if/then/else) as well as the left-to-right flow of code. However, programming languages do not operate through direct political colonization. Instead, their pervasive use in software makes them the lingua franca of the computational world. Risam, Koh, and Ray draw an argument from another trio, Bill Ashcroft, Gareth Griffiths, and Helen Tiffin, who, in *The Empire Writes Back* (1989), describe "a process through which writers disrupt the dominance of colonial English through forms of lexical resistance. Such writers, they suggest, take up the act of abrogation, refusing the dominant aesthetics and categories of imperial culture . . ." (Risam et al. 2013). By situating Nasser's code as an analogous act of abrogation, of disruption through code, these scholars gesture toward other potential acts of resistance to the colonizing force of English in programming languages.

When posing such questions of code and software, postcolonial criticism does something radical or perhaps unthinkable in work that adheres strictly to a particular discipline. In many ways, Nasser's code may be compared to the disruptive force of Rushdie's *Midnight's Children* (1981), Rhys's *Wide Sargasso Sea* (1966), or Achebe's *Things Fall Apart* (1958), as it resists popular colonial narratives. Nasser's project, together with its explication by Risam, Koh, and Ray, demonstrate how CCS extends discussions of programming by adding critical lenses that speak to other realms of communication.

If قلب and Risam, Koh, and Ray's interpretation disrupt programming by repositioning it in postcolonialism, then the next example resituates global positioning as part of geopolitical theater.

Transborder Immigrant Tool

In 2010, the Electronic Disturbance Theater (EDT) released the code for their provocative Transborder Immigrant Tool (TBT), a mobile phone application designed to help travelers who had crossed the Mexico-U.S. border survive their final mile's journey through the desert by offering them poetry and directions to water stations. Written mostly by Amy Sara Carroll, the poems take the form of prose modules, which offer guidance on how to survive in the desert, woven out of varied sources of knowledge, cultural allusions, and compelling imagery.

The code for the project, which was released before the project had been fully implemented—or, as I have argued elsewhere (Marino 2013), was released as a part of the piece's implementation—was written in Java, specifically to work on the J2ME platform of the Motorola i455 phone, chosen because it is inexpensive and relatively robust. In addition to the J2ME libraries, the code takes advantage of GPX, a platform Brett Stalbaum worked on to facilitate walking adventures. Importantly, this app was developed for a platform that predated and actually anticipated technologies we now take for granted. Stalbaum wrote much of the code, collaborating with Jason Najarro, an undergraduate at University of California, San Diego (UCSD) (Marino 2011a). Working on this code offered Najarro a chance to develop his skills for his résumé. However, that plan went astray when a *Vice* magazine piece about the TBT was picked up by conservative bloggers and then by conservative news outlets, specifically Glenn Beck and Fox News. The outrage did not end there as Todd Hunter and other U.S. politicians used the story to assail the public institution (UCSD) that funded the work (Hunter 2010). The controversy inevitably led to an audit of the TBT project and a fuller inquiry into the artistic activities of EDT member, Ricardo Dominguez (Su 2010).

This disruption was precisely the drama the EDT (consisting of micha cárdenas, Carroll, Dominguez, Elle Mehrmand, and Stalbaum) intended. In a personal interview (2011b), Dominguez explained to me that the TBT was developed as a Mayan technology in the tradition of the Zapatistas, conceived to confront and then confound authorities and other audiences. In that context, even the outrage of the politicians and pundits became part of the performance (Su 2010). However, the publicity also incited hate toward the artists, specifically physical threats directed toward the members and their families. Needless to say, the group had touched a nerve.

TBT's code offers conceptual frameworks that are not apparent in its audio or visual output. Most interesting are the metaphors used to name the functions related to finding water. Rather than using technical terms (e.g., "GPS" or "hotspot") or abstract names (e.g., "location" or "destination"), the team drew upon metaphors of "water witching." Water witching refers to finding water by means of a divining rod or dowsing compass in the form of a twig or stick. In contrast with technologies such as satellite positioning and cellular telephony, it uses parts of nature (e.g., broken branches) to find other parts of nature (e.g., the water which helped it grow). Consider the Java code activated when a water cache is found:

```
public void witchingEvent(TBCoordinates mc) {
    aheadCoords = mc;
    if (display.getCurrent().equals(tbDowsingCompass)) {
        waypointAheadAlert.setString(tbDowsingCompass.getInfo(mc));
```

```
waypointAheadAlert.setImage(aheadCoords.getIcon());
double distance = tbDowsingCompass.distanceTo(mc);
```

Although a full explanation of Java and object-oriented programming is beyond the scope of this chapter, "public" means this method can be called or accessed by any other class of objects. "Void" means this method does not return any values: it has no output to whatever code called it. This method takes two arguments: "TBCoordinates" and "mc." "TBCoordinates" represents where the traveler is; "mc" represents the destination of the traveler. A variable, "aheadCoords," is set to the target. Then, if the display is up to date, the waypoint is set and an alert is also set in the form of an icon. While the alerts are palpable (i.e., electronic notifications), the concept in the name of the function, "witchingEvent," is metaphysical.

More than just an arbitrary string, the method offers a new defining metaphor or conceptual framework (i.e., water witching) for how the app works. When a user arrives at the navigation point, this J2ME code is executed for an alert:

```
public void arrivedAtTarget(int distance) {
navigating = false;
// stop the compass from navigating
tbDowsingCompass.stopNavigation();
display.setCurrent(arrivedAlert);
display.vibrate(1000);
playAudioFile("arriving.wav", false);
}
```

Like the divining rod, the app makes the phone respond viscerally to proximity to water. It vibrates and plays an alert ("arriving.wav"), the physical signal necessary because the user may be undergoing heat exhaustion or heat stroke.

By turning a mobile phone into a dividing rod, the code also turns circuitry into a stick. But the stick does not just find water. For the person reading the code, it rearranges her relationship to the political drama of the Mexico-U.S. border—changing the tale from one of transgressions to one of survival. It rewrites the geopolitical narrative into a story that facilitates human sympathy and empathy. In fact, the code presents various scenarios, including one in which the traveler successfully reaches water:

```
waypointAheadAlert = new Alert (translation.translate("Site Ahead!")
arrivedAlert= new Alert(translation.translate("Arrived at Site")
```

A very different scenario is depicted in the code when the traveler stops moving:

```
If (isMoving) {// updated to moving
nearbyWPList =
tbDowsingCompass.getNearbyWaypoints (SEARCH_DISTANCE);//so update
nearby point
}else { //updated nt moving
display.vibrate(200).
If (moveWarningEnervator % 5 == 0) {//only play this file ~ every 5th time
playAudioFile("move.wav", false);//the "move for compass message can be too
frequent
```

In the first scenario, the alerts are sounded, the phone vibrates, and messages are sent, indicating that the waypoint has been found. In the second case, "movWarningEnervator" is triggered to keep the traveler going—to survive. It is hard to miss the pathos in this moment of code, demonstrating the emotional impact of its framing of a desperate moment in the life of its user.

Let us look at one more example to show how CCS can be used in conjunction with a variety of other approaches.

Tachistoscope

For 6 years, I have collaborated with Jessica Pressman and Jeremy Douglass to examine William Poundstone's work of electronic literature, *Project for Tachistoscope {Bottomless Pit}* (2005), which was composed in Adobe Flash. During the process of analyzing Poundstone's work, each of us took to our preferred methods of approaching a digital object, sharing our findings with the others to build collaborative readings. Douglass used various computational analysis methods, particularly visual analytics. Pressman used textual analysis and media archaeology, hunting through patents and other scholarship on the tachistoscope. To these, I added my analysis of the code. What we found in the code seriously affected the way we interpreted *Project*.

Project presents the story of a mysterious bottomless pit by displaying one word at a time in rapid succession on a screen. It is a busy work that challenges the reader to pay attention. In this way, it is similar to Young Hae Chang Heavy Industry's works, such as *Dakota* (2002; also see Pressman 2014). While flashing these words, *Project*'s interface also overlays a set of visual effects. At times, one can even perceive, though not consciously read, a set of words flashing in between the story words. The various introductory texts, accessible before the reader presses the "START" button, situate these as subliminal words, designed to prime the reader. Pressman pointed us toward the paratexts, or entry screens, that referred to this method of priming. Douglass's visual analysis of screenshots identified these subliminal words that seemed randomly drawn from a set. He asked me what I could find in the code about these subliminal words.

As it turns out, the code expresses a very different metaphor: spam. As in several of the previous cases, the metaphor resides in the most arbitrary aspect of the code: the variable and function names. In the ActionScript code of Poundstone's Flash file, the story's text is loaded from a TXT file into two variables. The story text is loaded in "storyvar," and the subliminal words are loaded into "spamvar" (not, as one might expect, "subliminalvar"). These rapidly interspersed words are not mere add-ons or incidental distractions but are instead central to the code's function: the call to display the spam initiates the story. In fact, the very first word displayed is not a story word but a spam word: "elongate."

When I revealed these findings to my collaborators, we found that it changed the way we interpreted the story, especially when processing the subliminal words. If subliminal messages claim to manipulate our subconscious desires, then spam are messages we consciously wish to block. If subliminal messages attempt to slip past our conscious blocks, then spam attempt to slip past our email filters. This new classification further helped us understand why the words have so little to do with the story or even each other, for that matter. Douglass noted that the spamvar words resemble the lists of words used at the end of spam emails to jam software that filters out spam. In a presentation in 2015, Poundstone confirmed these words were drawn from such an email. In light of the new conceptual framework of spam, the words changed their status in our reading—from hidden, barely perceived suggestions to egregious unwanted junk mail; from priming words to unsolicited messages. I should also mention that the hunt for the code and source files yielded an easy-to-read list of the subliminal and story words, a discovery which freed us from *Project*'s one-word-at-a-time animation.

Examining the code did not just affect the way we regarded the text. It also changed how we considered the interface effects that play throughout *Project for Tachistoscope*. While reading the code, I thought the distraction effects—or the flashing spam words—pulled the reader away from the primary text, or the story words. By extension, Poundstone's piece seemed to perform the war on attention that is so prevalent in digital environs (Hayles 2007; Davidson 2011). For example, one set of effects flashes the spam words in white. A set of white crosses, known in the code as "fixationCrosses," prime the reader to be attentive to these white words. (The term, "fixation crosses," references the small plus signs used as focal points in instruments that measure vision.) In *Project*, we initially thought the spam words *only* appear when they flash in white. However, we later realized they are in fact continuously flashing. Here is the ActionScript that renders the results:

```
if (index>.50) {
level = 3;
_level0.centerPoint.level2Effect_mc.unloadMovie();
var hue = Math.floor(Math.random()*(noOfColors+1));
myColor.setRGB(palette[hue]);
mySubliminalColor.setRGB(0xFFFFFF);
fixation_mc.attachMovie("fixationCrosses", "myFixationCrosses", 300);
}
```

Consequently, even the term "fixationCrosses" is a bit deceptive. It obscures how this piece directs and misdirects attention. It causes the eye to fixate on the white (FFFFFF) and notice the white words that follow. Yet, at the same time, it obscures the black words. Once again, Poundstone's piece is not only directing attention but also distracting the reader from noticing the subliminal words flashing by.

"fixationCrosses" helped us understand how Poundstone is playing with the language and conventions of tachistoscopes to challenge our relationships with the "flickering signifiers" of digital culture (Hayles 2008). By repurposing the tools of focus—the fixation crosses—Poundstone's version of a tachistoscope demonstrates how signifiers relayed for swift viewing entice a rich and methodical slow reading: the way those icons pull our eyes may be priming us to recognize one set of signs while obfuscating another. Only by looking at *Project*'s source files and code could we see how he confounded our perception. And yet, identifying this trick of the eye prompted us to examine this work more closely, using additional reading methods and machines to read the source code.

Note how this reading engages not just the natural language used to name objects and variables but also the realizations that can only be reached by examining code. Guided by the questions and observations of the other methodologies (i.e., visual analytics, textual analysis, and media archaeology), the examination of code yielded an insight into the design strategies of the piece. The code proves *Project* to be a distraction machine, but also a meditation on the nature of focus in a digital space. Similar to the analysis of the TBT, the code offers the conceptual metaphors used by designers, adding a layer of meaning to our interpretation of the piece. In this way, the study of code does not merely resume or promote the hunt for artistic intention. However, inasmuch as code is a material and mechanized manifestation of thought, it offers conceptual frameworks, organizational hierarchies, and ways of rendering that do more than merely complement the output of software—they define it. To study the code is to engage with these ideas as they express themselves through particular social and material conditions.

* * *

These examples demonstrate how CCS can be used in tandem with other approaches to develop multifaceted interpretations of texts and culture, where code is treated as a cultural text. They are not offered to delimit CCS—to draw a border around it—but instead to open it up and incite further exploration as well as further collaboration between those who build and those who interpret—*between the methods of making and partaking*—in the hope that we can realize how our technologies and our techniques for understanding them are mutually implicated and inextricably entwined.

Further Reading

Berry, D. M. (2011) *The Philosophy of Software: Code and Mediation in the Digital Age*, New York, NY: Palgrave Macmillan.

Brown, Jr., J. J. (2015) *Ethical Programs: Hospitality and the Rhetorics of Software*, Ann Arbor, MI: University of Michigan Press.

Chun, W. H. K. (2011) *Programmed Visions: Software and Memory*, Cambridge, MA: MIT Press.

Coleman, E. G. (2012) *Coding Freedom: The Ethics and Aesthetics of Hacking*, Princeton, NJ: Princeton University Press.

Cox, G. and A. McLean (2013) *Speaking Code: Coding as Aesthetic and Political Expression*, Cambridge, MA: MIT Press.

Jerz, D. G. (2007) "Somewhere Nearby Is Colossal Cave: Examining Will Crowther's Original Adventure in Code and in Kentucky," *Digital Humanities Quarterly* 1(2), retrieved from www.digitalhumanities.org/dhq/vol/1/2/000009/000009.html.

Vee, A. (2017) *Coding Literacy: How Computer Programming Is Changing Writing*, Cambridge, MA: The MIT Press.

References

Achebe, C. (1958) *Things Fall Apart*, London, UK: Heinemann.

Bigelow, S. (2011) "Code Is Poetry, CSS Is Art," *WordPress.com New*, retrieved from en.blog.wordpress.com/2011/11/24/code-is-poetry-css-is-art.

Chun, W. H. K. (2011) *Programmed Visions: Software and Memory*, Cambridge, MA: MIT Press.

Cox, G. and A. McLean. (2013) *Speaking Code: Coding as Aesthetic and Political Expression*, Cambridge, MA: MIT Press.

Davidson, C. N. (2011) *Now You See It: How Technology and Brain Science Will Transform Schools and Business for the 21st Century*, reprint edn, New York, NY: Penguin Books.

Derrida, J. (1974) *Of Grammatology*, G. C. Spivak (trans.), Baltimore, MD: Johns Hopkins University Press.

Du Gay, P., H. McKay, K. Negus, L. Janes, and S. Hall (2013) *Doing Cultural Studies: The Story of the Sony Walkman*, 2nd edn, London: Sage Publications.

Galloway, A. R. (2004) *Protocol: How Control Exists after Decentralization*, Cambridge, MA: MIT Press.

Hayles, N. K. (2007) "Hyper and Deep Attention: The Generational Divide in Cognitive Modes," *Profession* 13, 187–99.

Hayles, N. K. (2008) *How We Became Posthuman: Virtual Bodies in Cybernetics, Literature, and Informatics*, Chicago, IL: University of Chicago Press.

Hunter, D. (2010) "Taxpayers Should Be Outraged at this Use of Funds," *San Diego Union-Tribune*, retrieved from www.sandiegouniontribune.com/news/2010/mar/07/taxpayers-should-be-outraged-use-funds.

Kirschenbaum, M. (2008) *Mechanisms: New Media and the Forensic Imagination*, Cambridge, MA: MIT Press.

Kirschenbaum, M. (2011) "<!—opening thoughts—>;," Critical Code Studies, *HASTAC*, retrieved from www.hastac.org/comment/3711#comment-3711.

Kittler, F. (1995) "There Is No Software," *CTheory*, retrieved from www.ctheory.net/articles.aspx?id=74.

Knuth, D. E. (1992) "Literate Programming," *CSLI Lecture Notes, No. 27*, Stanford, CA: Center for the Study of Language and Information.

Marino, M. C. (2006) "Critical Code Studies," *electronic book review*, electropoetics, retrieved from www.electronicbookreview.com/thread/electropoetics/codology.

Marino, M. C. (2011a) Interview with Brett Stalbaum.

Marino, M. C. (2011b) Interview with Ricardo Dominguez.

Marino, M. C. (2013) "Code as Ritualized Poetry: The Tactics of the Transborder Immigrant Tool," *Digital Humanities Quarterly* 7(1), retrieved from www.digitalhumanities.org/dhq/vol/7/1/000157/000157.html.

McBride, S. (2013) "Arabic Code Language Won't Make Waves: Creator" ITP.net, retrieved from itp.net/592111-arabic-code-language-wont-make-waves-creator.

McPherson, T. (2012) "U.S. Operating Systems at Mid-Century: The Intertwining of Race and UNIX," in L. Nakamura and P. A. Chow-White (eds.) *Race after the Internet*, New York, NY: Routledge, 21–37.

Montfort, N., P. Baudoin, J. Bell, I. Bogost, J. Douglass, M. C. Marino, M. Mateas, C. Reas, M. Sample, and N. Vawter (2013) *10 PRINT CHR$(205.5+RND(1));_: GOTO 10*, Cambridge, MA: MIT Press.

Nasser, R. (2013) قلب, retrieved from nas.sr/%D9%82%D9%84%D8%A8/.

Obama, B. (2016) "Remarks of President Barack Obama—State of the Union Address As Delivered," Whitehouse.gov.

Poundstone, W. (2005) *Project for Tachistoscope {Bottomless Pit}*, www.williampoundstone.net.

Pressman, J. (2014) *Digital Modernism: Making It New in New Media*, New York, NY: Oxford University Press.

Pressman, J., M. C. Marino, and J. Douglass (2015) *Reading Project: A Collaborative Analysis of William Poundstone's Project for Tachistoscope {Bottomless Pit}*, Iowa City, IA: University of Iowa Press.

Risam, R., A. Koh, and A. Ray (2013) "PoCo Critcode: Coding in Global Englishes," Critical Code Studies Working Group, retrieved from roopikarisam.com/uncategorized/coding-in-global-englishes.

Rhys, J. (1966) *Wide Sargasso Sea*, London, UK: André Deutsch.

Rushdie, S. (1981) *Midnight's Children*, New York, NY: Random House.

Schneider, E. W. (2007) *Postcolonial English: Varieties around the World* Cambridge, UK: Cambridge University Press.

Spiegel-Rösing, I. and D. J. de Solla Price (1977) *Science, Technology, and Society: A Cross-Disciplinary Approach*, International Council for Science Policy Studies, London, UK: SAGE Publications.

Su, E. Y. (2010) "'Activist' UCSD Professor Facing Unusual Scrutiny," *San Diego Union Tribune*, retrieved from www.sandiegouniontribune.com/news/2010/apr/06/activist-ucsd-professor-facing-unusual-scrutiny.

Vee, A. (2013) "Understanding Computer Programming as a Literacy," *Literacy in Composition Studies* 1(2), 42–64.

Young-Hae Chang Heavy Industries (2005) *Dakota*, www.yhchang.com.

49

CRITICAL UNMAKING

Toward a Queer Computation

Jacob Gaboury

If there is an ethos that drives our contemporary digital culture, it is the belief that technology improves over time and that improvements in technology bring improvements to our lives. It is this desire for the new that supports our faith in the potential good of technology in bringing about a better future (Kurzweil 1990). Simply put: technology drives progress. This belief is by no means new—indeed, this progressivist faith in technology is a defining feature of the postindustrial west—but it has been accelerated by computational technologies whose exponential growth has become the self-fulfilling prophecy of our digital age (Moore 1965). With the release of each new software update, each new generation of smartphone or game console, and each new operating system, we update and upgrade. We want what is faster and newer, or perhaps what we have no longer functions as it should or once did. We are compelled to engage in this drive toward the new—this push toward a technological future that is always on the horizon, always deferred.

Left out of these narratives of progress are the many ways in which technology fails us and the ways we fail with and through technology. Not all digital technologies work as they should. Many fail to make money or disrupt, transform, and revolutionize the world as they so often claim. Often, technologies fail to be adopted by users, or simply fail to work altogether. Yet our belief in technological progress asks us to ignore the bugs, glitches, and obsolescence built into technical systems (Slade 2006; Krapp 2011; Parikka 2011). Moreover, it asks us to limit our use of these objects to their most productive forms, and to deny any use outside these sanctioned boundaries, disavowing them as somehow failed. Under these terms, failure becomes much more than an unfortunate or unforeseen error; it becomes a refusal of this impulse toward compulsory production, a disruptive withholding of one's identity, activity, and process time. Indeed, we might argue that the production of failure within technological systems in this way constitutes a radical queer practice.

Radical, perhaps, but why queer? To be sure, queerness is not the only means through which we might understand technological failure, and indeed many forms of failure or misuse might explicitly work against queer forms of life. One need only look to the disruptive and often violent use of technology to harass and threaten women, queer and trans people, and people of color online to see the limits of non-normative technological use as a radical practice (Massanari 2015). Likewise, failure is often reframed and recuperated as a useful step along the road to innovation and success (Farson & Keyes 2003; Harford 2011; Firestein 2015). Nonetheless, there is great value in thinking about queerness and computation together, as digital media technologies continue to have a transformative effect on the ways we construct identity and build community. As such, it seems crucial that we find new ways to make queer theory speak to technology on its own terms. To this end, this chapter looks to "compute queerness" by both making it subject to the logic of computation and asking it to act computationally; that is, to become executable (Galloway 2004: 165). In doing so, it proposes a practice of critical unmaking, foregrounding queer techniques of refusal, misuse, and disruption that must nonetheless work with and through contemporary digital technologies.

Fail

Queerness and queer theory offer us an ideal lens through which to understand and critique the progressivist teleology that drives the production of contemporary technology. Just as failure offers us a way to think outside the compulsion toward progress through technological production (Nunes 2011; Menkman 2011), queer theory has for decades worked to critique the demands of biological reproduction under compulsory heterosexuality and the drive toward a future that is inaccessible to queer forms of life.

This connection between queerness and failure is embodied in a wide range of theoretical practices and intellectual histories reaching back to the start of the twentieth century. As literary theorist, Heather Love, notes in her work on loss and the politics of queer history, "same-sex desire is marked by a long history of association with failure, impossibility and loss," such that "homosexuality and homosexuals serve as scapegoats for the failures and impossibilities of desire itself" (2009: 21). Queerness here is marked by failure in that it not only exists outside a given norm, but cannot be made legible or useful to a given society. For early queer theorist, Guy Hocquenghem, it is capitalism that marks the homosexual as failed, where failure is understood as an incapacity for proper reproductive love. Without a clear connection between sociality, relationality, family, sex, desire, and consumption as afforded to heterosexual reproduction, homosexuality cannot be made productive to capital and is re-territorialized as a failed state of being (Hocquenghem 1993 [1972]: 93–112). For literary scholars such as Lee Edelman, the queer subject has always been epistemologically bound to negativity, occupying the space of the social order's death drive, an irrecuperable excess whose ethical value lies in "accepting its figural status as resistance to the viability of the social while insisting on the inextricability of such resistance from every social structure" (2004: 3). Queerness here is marked by its own illegibility to the social order, a social order that Edelman identifies as reproductive futurism. Indeed, this illegibility is its very value. For Edelman, we must resist the legibility of a secure political identity lest we lose the radical difference that queerness offers. Refusing this move away from the political, Jack Halberstam (2011) has taken up the radical potential of queer failure to suggest that living within failure and refusing the terms of success pushed onto us by capitalism, patriarchy, heteronormativity, neoliberalism, and other compulsory norms might allow for new ways of being in the world that need not disavow the possibility of a political imaginary, that may indeed form the basis for a politics of refusal. Failure here becomes a radical practice, one that is not without a future but instead reimagines how that future might come into being.

Simply put, queer theory has, for decades, engaged in the difficult and at times contradictory task of marking a political identity bound by a refusal to be made useful or productive. Deploying queer theory in this way asks us to think through failure as not only a disruptive technical practice but also a radical lived experience that might allow for an embodied critique of technological futurism. To compute queerly, then, is to acknowledge, embrace, and enact a practice of radical technological failure. It is to engage in critical unmaking: to make central those externalities—exploits, bugs, breakdown, abuse, and misuse—of our digital culture that, while pervasive, we nonetheless disavow. To compute in this way is to work against the neoliberal drive toward the capture and exploitation of the self by technology; to work against the demands of pervasive visibility by means of always-on devices, against the quantification of affect, leisure, and solitude for the purpose of value extraction; and to disrupt the fantasy that technology—through the aggregation and quantification of data—allows us access to some unmediated truth (boyd & Crawford 2012; Crary 2013). In acknowledging, accepting, and even producing failure, queer computation seeks to make clear the values and assumptions that drive our culture of technological development and to offer alternate modes for living with and through technology. But what might a queer computing look like?

Glitch

There are several objects to which we might turn to identify a queer computational form, but perhaps the most immediately recognizable would be small but playful forms of disruption such as the error or glitch. A glitch is a temporary malfunction within a technical, usually computational, system. Glitches are unexpected, but importantly they do not shut down a system entirely. They temporarily transform a technical object by producing an unintended result or error, and in the process lay bare its material function. A glitch is an outlier, an aberration. As such, it should be no surprise that it has been for decades an extremely productive site for artistic and critical investigation into the aesthetics and politics of digital media. Early net art artists such as the European art collective, Jodi, have, since the 1990s, used markup languages and videogame modification as platforms for disruptive play (Jodi 2001; Adang 2013). This interest in shattering the illusion of a medium by laying bare the processes and materials that produce its technical form is a longstanding tradition in modernist art and the avant-garde. Nonetheless, the glitch offers a unique engagement not simply with the specificity of its medium, but in its negotiation with failure as a temporally delimited and unexpected transformation in the function of computational devices.

In recent years, the aesthetics of glitch have grown in both visibility and popularity, with a number of artists adopting techniques for producing glitch in a variety of visual works to both critical and aesthetic ends. The artist, Rosa Menkman, deals explicitly with the disruptive potential of glitch as both an unexpected and engineered form. In her 2010 work, "A Vernacular of File Formats," Menkman offers a didactic visual text that points at ways to exploit and deconstruct the organizations of file formats into new designs. Repeatedly glitching an image of herself in a variety of file formats (e.g., JPEG, BMP, TIFF, and RAW), Menkman attempts to demonstrate the particularity of each, making visible its method of compression, its bitmap structure, and its analog to digital conversion. In one example, Menkman databends a GIF file, producing a horizontal blur that resembles a VCR tracking error. The resulting image appears warped and smeared across the frame in jagged interlaced repetitions. Alongside the image, Menkman notes:

> The GIF format uses a four pass dimensional interlacing strategy. This basically means that the image, consisting of different rows of pixels, decodes some rows of pixels before other rows. The example image shows the displacement of the different rows

> during weaving (the putting together of the two layers), resulting in "combining artifacts" with "jagged edges."
>
> (Menkman 2011: 21)

Bending each format multiple times, Menkman produces a surprisingly diverse range of visual glitches. In breaking the technology in this way, Menkman shows that the verisimilitude of each image is highly dependent on the formal specificity of the image file. What we are left with after the glitch is not the image itself but the file format revealed (Sterne 2012).

Here, the glitch offers both a compelling and frustrating example of queer computation. To be sure, the work of Menkman and others demonstrates the disruptive and didactic potential of technological failure, but it is also readily recuperable as a visual aesthetic divorced from critique. The proliferation of glitch as an aesthetic practice in this way diminishes its radical potential, a transformation that Menkman openly acknowledges. Differentiating glitch from failure itself, Menkman notes, "while failure is a phenomenon to overcome, the glitch is a phenomenon that will be incorporated into new processes and conditions of technological design or cultural meaning" (2011: 27). Glitch is, like noise, a relative and subjective phenomenon. All channels are noisy channels. All systems contain glitch. These phenomena have no essential quality; they are simply that which we disavow as irregular, unwanted, or queer (Chang 2013; Halberstam 2013).

This contradiction, whereby the radical potential of glitch is transformed into a productive aesthetic practice, echoes the concerns of Edelman and others with regards to queerness. In marking failure as an explicit and repeatable practice, it is abstracted from its critical potential and recuperated by technological futurism. Here, we find ourselves in a double bind. While we may desire to identify or prescribe a queer computational form that we might use to disrupt or transform our digital landscape, we must acknowledge that any such prescription opens queerness to a radical visibility such that it may be repurposed to serve a normative ideology. How can we break free of this bind? What queer forms cannot be recuperated in this way?

Taken to an extreme, we might logically argue that the only truly queer computational form is one that fully embodies the radical potential of failure. If any investment in productivity or futurity is normatively recuperable, then the only queer computer is broken, nonfunctional, or destroyed. Surely, complete annihilation is the most radical, most extreme form of failure possible. Yet, while it may be compelling to smash our computers in an act of queer rebellion, the radical potential of such a gesture ends there. A broken machine cannot compute, queerly or otherwise. It is a brick, a doorstop; it has no radical potential for computation as it has no computational function. Likewise, it may be compelling to simply opt out of digital technologies altogether, supposing that digital media are irreconcilable with a radical queer politics. While Luddism is certainly a form of critique, it is deeply limited in its efficacy here. We cannot simply ignore the pervasive influence of digital technologies on all forms of contemporary life, queer and otherwise, and we must find ways to negotiate queer technological practices while working against the recuperative drive toward productivity and futurity.

Norm

It would appear that queer computation cannot simply offer an antinormative critique of digital media. Instead, it must offer a reframing of the goals, drives, and interests of these media as technologies in which queerness is necessarily situated. This presents a challenge, given how closely queer theory and indeed queer life hews to a politics of antinormativity. Indeed, antinormativity is in many ways the ground on which queer theory was formed. As Robyn Wiegman and Elizabeth Wilson have argued, "nearly every queer theoretical itinerary of analysis that now matters is informed by the prevailing supposition that a critique of normativity marks the spot where queer and theory meet" (2015: 1). And yet computation is built on and requires norms in order to function at all.

The computer is a precisely engineered machine, and computer science is a discipline made possible through the arrangement of incredibly complex systems that must function with consistency and accuracy if they are to function at all. This belief in the exceptional perfection of computation is a founding principle of the field. Writing in 1948, John von Neumann—a key conceptual inventor of the stored program digital computer—notes that:

> A computing machine is one of the exceptional artifacts. They not only have to perform a billion or more steps in a short time, but in a considerable part of the procedure (and this is a part that is rigorously specified in advance) they are permitted not a single error. In fact, in order to be sure that the whole machine is operative, and that no potentially degenerative malfunctions have set in, the present practice usually requires that no error should occur anywhere in the entire procedure.
>
> (von Neumann 1961: 292)

Computers require near perfect conditions to operate. A single error might produce an incorrect calculation or, worse still, cause a machine to fail altogether. Yet this ideal of a perfectly functioning technology is precisely that: an ideal. Far more common than the successful execution of a given calculation—particularly in von Neumann's own time—were bugs, errors, and failure. This was due in no small part to the high degree of human labor involved in the operation of a mechanical computer at that time. Programming, data input, and the interpretation of output were all dependent on mathematical calculation and interpretation by individuals known as either "human computers" or "computers," many of whom were women (Light 1999; Grier 2007; Ensmenger 2010). Likewise, the machines themselves were highly unstable, reliant on unreliable vacuum tubes and experimental hardware long since phased out of our modern machines. Yet our belief in the scientific precision of computation persists, due in part to the increasing malleability of computational systems, which have automated many of these processes in an attempt to account for human error, unexplained glitches, and other forms of inconsistency at those sites where the analog world interfaces with the logic of the digital. Put another way, in spite of this ideal of scientific precision, modern technical systems are, to a degree, incredibly tolerant of failure and misuse.

What, then, might we understand as the "normal" conditions under which a modern computer functions? If this ideal of a perfectly running machine is little more than a fantasy, perhaps a more accurate description might be that computation requires certain base conditions to be met, a set of rules or procedures known as protocols. These protocols constitute the control structure of a given computational form. Unless they are satisfied, a machine will not boot, run, or compute. Yet, problematically, these protocols are often designed and described as being without an explicit politics, that is, as postideological. On the topic of distributed network protocols, Alexander Galloway notes:

> [I]deology is a problem to be forgotten or subsumed: networks are specifically conceived and designed as those things that both are nonideological in their conception

> (we just want to "get things done"), but also post-ideological in their architecture (in that they acknowledge and co-opt the very terms of previous ideological debates, things like heterogeneity, difference, agency, and subject formation).
>
> (Galloway 2014)

Protocols are, by design, expansive and inclusive, but this disavowal of their own political agency also makes them insidious, even dangerous. While technical protocols are intended to facilitate communication and interaction rather than restrict use, they nonetheless shape what is permissible to a given technology. As such, while a technology may allow for queer uses, it will nonetheless demand strict adherence to certain base assumptions. In this way, protocols set the conditions for discourse itself.

This normalization of the terms of engagement can have wide-reaching effects, particularly on minority populations whose needs, desires, and bodies are often excluded from the norms that structure protocological assumptions. Scholars such as Dean Spade (2011), Simone Browne (2015), and Shoshana Magnet (2011) have shown the many ways that the norms we program into our technologies have a disproportionate effect on non-normative bodies and identities, enacting a double violence in which subjects are made hyper-visible in their difference and also violently excluded from those sites at which normalizing technologies are used: airport security, police surveillance, and state and national identification documentation, for instance.

In the face of these protocological norms that set the very terms of engagement in our digital society, antinormativity offers us very little. How, then, can we queer, if not as a resistance to the norms that govern a particular system?

Code

I would suggest that our queer imperative must be to identify the ideological assumptions that produce protocologial norms and then subvert them—to make visible through a queer critical practice the values that structure our technology. If it is not possible to work outside the conditions for engagement produced by a given technology, then we must work with technical practices to critique and disrupt the values and assumptions that structure that technology. We must acknowledge the value in *making* as a productive practice that creates the conditions for political intervention, as well as the need for a critical *unmaking* as both a means to resist recuperation and a mode of being that exists outside of protocological norms—that is, as a form of life that cannot be made productive to technology. In other words, we must begin by asking ourselves a question: What does our protocol value?

To begin to think through this challenge, I put forward here an exemplary practice: a playful, half-serious, yet deeply political form of computational subversion known as the esoteric programming language or *esolang*. Esolangs are a group of weird, largely unused technical languages built for the purpose of testing the limits of programming language design. They seem well suited to the kind of queer computation described here as they play at the limits of computational logic but generally strive to be computationally complete. Esolangs can theoretically be used to program anything that a more standard programming language could be used for. However, they are largely avoided due to their bizarre or intentionally frustrating form. Esolangs take on many forms, from playful parodies of existing languages to maddeningly complex languages that test the very limits of what we understand as code (Mateas & Montfort 2005).

The first known esolang is INTERCAL, and it was developed in 1972 by Don Woods and James Lyon (Raymond 2015). INTERCAL began largely as a send-up of programing languages from the 1960s, such as COBOL, FORTRAN, and APL. Borrowing and transforming the vocabulary and structure of these languages, INTERCAL "reads" as a series of clever puns and reversals designed for a technical audience. It confounds where it should clarify, plays language games, and makes bad jokes; it frustrates utility, but it also opens new avenues for playful expression not available to more rigid or purposeful linguistic forms. The name INTERCAL, for example, stands for "Compiler Language with No Pronounceable Acronym." The compiler itself, called simply "ick," is designed to skip over any text it does not understand and cannot compile, rather than return a compiling error as with all standard compilers. This makes debugging a particular challenge, but it also allows programmers to comment and converse in-program through the addition of noncompilable text.

This commentary form of esolang is also the most common for artists and scholars looking to critique the normative structure of technical language design through the lens of gender and sexuality. For example, the artist, Zach Blas, produced the transCoder programming language as part of his Queer Technologies (2007–12) suite. Drawing on queer linguistic traditions of coded and obfuscated language, such as the Polari cant slang used by queer men in Britain during the nineteenth and twentieth centuries (Baker 2002), transCoder seeks to produce new computational forms not normally accessible to technical languages. The language relies heavily on statements meant to play on the function of existing languages, such as C, replacing commands like INCLUDE and FOR with tongue-in-cheek formations such as finger(), which stimulates data, and qTime(), which permits the executions of a program to run outside of conventional computational narratives. In this sense, transCoder plays on a major feature of esolangs, a kind of structured play that allows for "double coding," where meaning may be expressed as computationally complete and compilable code, but also, on another level, as legible human language that either supplements or subverts that code.

Still other esolangs work in precisely opposite ways, obscuring code such that it loses all human-readable reference. One of the most famous esolangs to exhibit this feature is the Brainfuck language, which allows for an extremely limited set of only seven commands, each of which is represented by a single nonalphanumeric character. All commands in Brainfuck are produced through the assembly of these seven characters, but this lack of alphanumeric text alienates the language from anyone attempting to read it as text. This extreme minimalism and refusal of human-readable language are what make Brainfuck notorious, but the language is in fact Turing complete, which is to say it can be used for most any functional programming task. While we need not be too literal in our interpretation, Brainfuck's name seems apropos, given how it plays on our expectation of what a programming language is and can do, fucking with our desire for a language that prioritizes clarity and functionality. Read another way, the language fucks with our desire for simplicity, offering up an offensively simple set of characters that render the language all but useless. Here, we see the ways in which queer technologies might acknowledge and redeploy the assumptions that structure a technical object or practice, and in so doing draw attention to the ideological function of its protocols, that is, those ideologies that its producers and users disavow.

Brainfuck has also inspired a number of derivative languages, but most notable here is the bodyfuck language developed by artist and programmer, Nik Hanselmann, in which each of the seven Brainfuck commands is assigned a body movement or gesture. To "write" in bodyfuck, the programmer/performer must use their body in discrete and specific ways:

> Jumping increases the memory register, ducking decreases the memory register, moving left or right either swaps the memory register or sets a point in the "magnetic strip" by which the head will return upon the zeroing of the preceding register (a loop).
>
> (Hanselmann 2009–10)

In adding an additional layer of difficulty onto an already tedious process, and invoking the body as a physical and material apparatus that makes possible the coding of technical systems, bodyfuck renders explicit the ways in which embodiment is both inscribed and erased into digital technologies. As Hanselmann notes:

> bodyfuck as well as the performances that it engendered places conventional computability in tension with movements of the body. While bodyfuck maintains its ability as to automatically compute, the process of transcribing the code into the computer becomes an arduous task. The embedding of physical difficulty into the creation of a computer program reifies the gaps between machine performance and physical performance. The computer didn't get sore. I did.
>
> (Hanselmann 2009–10)

bodyfuck does not break the function or concept of the programming language, but instead opens it up to new forms of failure and play by asking its programmers to consider their body and its performance as part of a technical practice. While it is unlikely bodyfuck will ever be used outside its initial artistic context, it points to the great potential of queer interventions that take up and subvert the very technologies they employ.

End

To compute queerness, we must begin by acknowledging what queerness offers to a critique of computation. In doing so, we are left with few clear answers and are instead asked to imagine new ways to work against the normalizing influence of our technical culture while maintaining the general functionality of the systems we inhabit. While we need not give up on the radical potential of queerness as a means of imagining a future that is not yet here (Muñoz 2009), we must nonetheless acknowledge how futurity has been colonized by the cultural logic of contemporary technology, and as such cannot serve as the primary vector for queer computational critique. Thus, rather than mobilize queerness as a useful technological apparatus, we might deploy it as part of a critical practice of unmaking.

Further Reading

Blas, Z. and W. Schirmacher (eds.) (2011) *The Transreal: Political Aesthetics of Crossing Realities*, New York, NY: Atropos Press.

Gaboury, J. (2013) "On Uncomputable Numbers: The Origins of a Queer Computing," *Media-N: Journal of the New Media Caucus*, retrieved from median.newmediacaucus.org/caa-conference-edition-2013/on-uncomputable-numbers-the-origins-of-a-queer-computing.

Keeling, K. (2014) "Queer OS," *Cinema Journal* 53(2), 152–57.

Magnet, S. (2011) *When Biometrics Fail: Gender, Race, and the Technology of Identity*, Durham, NC: Duke University Press.

Mateas, M. and N. Montfort (2005) "A Box, Darkly: Obfuscation, Weird Languages, and Code Aesthetics," in *Proceedings of the 6th Digital Arts and Culture Conference*, IT University of Copenhagen, pp. 144–53.

References

Adang, L. (2013) "Untitled Project: A Cross-Disciplinary Investigation of Jodi's Untitled Game," New York: Rhizome, retrieved from media.rhizome.org/artbase/documents/Untitled-Project:-A-Cross-Disciplinary-Investigation-of-JODI%E2%80%99s-Untitled-Game.pdf.

Baker, P. (2002) *Polari—The Lost Language of Gay Men*, London and New York, NY: Routledge.

Blas, Z. (n.d.) TransCoder, retrieved from www.zachblas.info/projects/queer-technologies.

boyd, d. and K. Crawford (2012) "Critical Questions for Big Data: Provocations for a Cultural, Technological, and Scholarly Phenomenon," *Information, Communication & Society* 15(5), 662–79.

Browne, S. (2015) *Dark Matters: On the Surveillance of Blackness*, Durham, NC: Duke University Press.

Chang, E. (2014) "Queer Glitches, or, the Recuperation of Vanellope von Schweetz," *Society for Literature, Science, and the Arts Annual Conference*, Notre Dame, IN: University of Notre Dame.

Crary, J. (2014) *24/7: Late Capitalism and the Ends of Sleep*, London: Verso Books.

Edelman L. (2004) *No Future: Queer Theory and the Death Drive*, Durham, NC: Duke University Press.

Ensmenger, N. L. (2010) *The Computer Boys Take Over: Computers, Programmers, and the Politics of Technical Expertise*, Cambridge, MA: MIT Press.

Farson, R. and R. Keyes (2003) *The Innovation Paradox: The Success of Failure, the Failure of Success*, New York, NY: Simon and Schuster.

Firestein, S. (2015) *Failure: Why Science Is So Successful*, New York, NY: Oxford University Press.

Galloway, A. R. (2004) *Protocol: How Control Exists after Decentralization*, Cambridge, MA: MIT Press.

Galloway, A. R. (2014) "Network Pessimism," 11 November, retrieved from cultureandcommunication.org/galloway/network-pessimism.

Grier, D. A. (2005) *When Computers Were Human*, Princeton, NJ: Princeton University Press.

Halberstam, J. (2011) *The Queer Art of Failure*, Durham, NC: Duke University Press.

Halberstam, J. (2013) "Queer Gaming: Gaming, Hacking, and Going Gaga," *Queer Games Conference*, UC Berkeley, retrieved from www.twitch.tv/qgcon/c/3156423.

Hanselmann, N. (2009–10) "There Is No Hardware," M.F.A. Thesis, UC Santa Cruz, retrieved from nik.works/bodyfuck.

Harford, T. (2011) *Adapt: Why Success Always Starts with Failure*, New York, NY: Farrar, Straus and Giroux.

Hocquenghem, G. (1993 [1972]) "Capitalism, the Family and the Anus" in *Homosexual Desire*, Durham, NC: Duke University Press, pp. 93–112.

Jodi (2001) www.jodi.org/, retrieved from jodi.org.

Krapp, P. (2011) *Noise Channels: Glitch and Error in Digital Culture*, Minneapolis, MN: University of Minnesota Press.

Kurzweil, R. (1990) *The Age of Intelligent Machines*, Cambridge, MA: MIT Press.

Light, J. S. (1999) "When Computers Were Women," *Technology and Culture* 40(3), 455–83.

Love, H. (2009) *Feeling Backward*, Cambridge, MA: Harvard University Press.

Magnet, S. (2011) *When Biometrics Fail: Gender, Race, and the Technology of Identity*, Durham, NC: Duke University Press.

Massanari, A. (2015) "#Gamergate and The Fappening: How Reddit's Algorithm, Governance, and Culture Support Toxic Technocultures," *New Media & Society*, 9 October, retrieved from nms.sagepub.com/content/early/2015/10/07/1461444815608807.

Mateas, M. and N. Montfort (2005) "A Box, Darkly: Obfuscation, Weird Languages, and Code Aesthetics" in *Proceedings of the 6th Digital Arts and Culture Conference*, IT University of Copenhagen, pp. 144–53.

Menkman, R. (2010) "A Vernacular of File Formats," *Sunshine in My Throat*, retrieved from rosa-menkman.blogspot.ca/2010/08/vernacular-of-the-file-formats-2-workshop.html.

Menkman, R. (2011) *The Glitch Moment(um)*, Amsterdam: Institute of Network Cultures.

Moore, G. (1965) "Cramming More Components onto Integrated Circuits," *Electronics* 38(8), 114–17.

Muñoz, J. E. (2009) *Cruising Utopia: The Then and There of Queer Futurity*, New York and London: NYU Press.

Nunes, M. (ed.) (2011) *Error: Glitch, Noise, and Jam in New Media Cultures*, New York, NY: Continuum Books.

Parikka, J. (2011) "Mapping Noise: Techniques and Tactics of Irregularities, Interception, and Disturbance," in E. Huhtamo and J. Parikka (eds.) *Media Archaeology: Approaches, Applications, and Implications*, Berkley, CA: University of California Press, pp. 256–77.

Raymond. E. S. (2015) The INTERCAL Resources Page, retrieved from catb.org/esr/intercal.

Slade, G. (2006) *Made to Break: Technology and Obsolescence in America*, Cambridge, MA: Harvard University Press.

Spade, D. (2011) *Normal Life: Administrative Violence, Critical Trans Politics, and the Limits of Law*, Brooklyn, NY: South End Press.

Sterne, J. (2012) *MP3: The Meaning of a Format*, Durham, NC: Duke University Press.

von Neumann, J. (1961) "The General and Logical Theory of Automata," in A. H. Taub (ed.) *Collected Works: Vol. 5, Design of Computers, Theory of Automata, and Numerical Analysis*, Oxford: Pergamon Press, pp. 288–326.

Wiegman, R. and E. A. Wilson (2015) "Introduction: Antinormativity's Queer Conventions," *differences* 26(1), 1–25.

50

MAKING THINGS TO MAKE SENSE OF THINGS

DIY as Research and Practice

Kat Jungnickel

Figure 50.1 A time-lapse camera attached to the office ceiling added another perspective to the ethnography of making.

This image (see Figure 50.1) comes from a time-lapse camera fixed to the ceiling of my office. The camera took photos every 10 seconds, every day, for the last few weeks of a research project about cycling, gender, and citizenship. This frame captures a particular event. After many attempts, I had successfully sewn a buttonhole in a tricky position near the waistband of a Victorian convertible cycling skirt. But it was not just a buttonhole. In fact, there was no button involved. Instead, it was a critical component in an intricately designed technological system concealed in the framework of the costume. The mechanism comprised a hidden pulley system, stitched channels, long waxed cords, and weights that enabled the wearer to not only gather the front and back of the skirt up to a desired length (out of the danger of the bicycle wheels) but also quickly reverse this action when required. The purpose was to enable the wearer to adapt her costume at will depending on her mobility requirements, in particular regard to her cycling practices. I was following the step-by-step instructions of the inventor who had patented the complexly engineered costume in 1895. This buttonhole was the last component to be completed prior to installing the cords and testing it out.

Why was I doing this? Why was I making such a mess in my sociology office? Why was I sewing my research? I was working on a project called, "Freedom of Movement: The Bike, Bloomer and Female Cyclist in Late C19th Britain" (otherwise known as Bikes & Bloomers) about Victorian cycle wear. I had been researching contemporary cycling cultures and noted how often respondents, unprovoked, talked about what they wore to cycle and how certain clothing choices elicited welcome and sometimes less welcome responses from others. I quickly learned that cycle wear mattered. Brief archival research indicated this concern was not new, so I started to look for more in-depth answers to why cycle wear *still* matters.

In the process, I became fascinated by patents lodged by inventive women for new forms of cycle wear to address ideological and practical issues faced by early adopters of cycling, a new mobility technology of the period. For many enthusiastic women cyclists, their clothing, along with society's ideas of how, where, and in what ways women could move in public space, inhibited their freedom of movement. (See Jungnickel 2015 for more discussion on the social, cultural, and political context in which middle and upper class women were learning to cycle and how they shaped and were in turn shaped by Victorian society.) Some responded to these constraints by designing convertible garments. While there is evidence that some patented designs were commercialized and distributed across the UK, I have yet to find any existing artifacts of this nature in UK museums or galleries, and little has been written about this inventive cultural practice (with the exception of Khan 2000; Helvenston Gray & Peteu 2005; Peteu & Helvenston Gray 2009). In addition to exploring links between the advent of cycling at the turn of the last century and the politics of cycle wear today, I set out to answer the following question: What might making these costumes by hand reveal that reading and analyzing media in the from of a patent might not?

To do this I collaborated with a pattern cutter, weaver, and artist to make a collection of convertible Victorian women's costumes inspired by UK patents lodged from 1895 to 1899. Together we transformed these inventive women's ideas into 3-D artifacts and conducted an ethnography of making along the way. In total, 28 garments assembling five costumes were handmade by the research team (myself and one research assistant, with another joining us for the last month) in my sociology office over a 9-month period.

This chapter is about making as research or, more specifically, making things to make sense of things. From a practice-based research perspective, I examine the idea of media as something the researcher not only studies but also makes in the process of doing research. This chapter is also about DIY (do-it-yourself) as research *and* practice. I bring to this discussion how learnings from DIY and also DIT (do-it-together) technocultures can inform critical research methods, specifically the desire to engage materially with media, learn from doing, and, in the process, render public the visible and tangible mess, mistakes, and tangential happenings.

The argument that follows outlines the theoretical and methodological context in which making as a research practice is positioned. I specifically look to mobilities research and science and technology studies (STS), where there is a burgeoning interest in experimental sensory and material approaches. Throughout I discuss how making things to make sense of things presents opportunities for getting inside mobile, messy, and multiple social worlds.

The Politics of (Media) Making

Social science researchers make things in the process of making knowledge—notes, interviews, photos, drawings, arguments, charts, graphs, and presentations, among others. Yet, for a discipline engaged with a spectrum of inventive methods on many fascinating topics, the nature of knowledge objects and outputs predominantly takes the form of text and talk, which are surprisingly curtailed in terms of creativity, materiality, and form. While the senses are often central to an understanding of social processes, rarely do they feature in how we talk about society. As Guggenheim has argued, this marks out sociology in comparison to life and other natural sciences:

> When we compare this situation with other disciplines, such as biology, astronomy or chemistry, where all kinds of technologies are used to represent the world, from drawing, to computer models, from complex machines visualizing things very big and very small; to transform smells or heat into visual traces, it becomes apparent how unusual this situation is.
>
> (Guggenheim 2015: 346)

"Situations" are formed of disciplinary frameworks where specific kinds of knowledge practices are shaped, expected, and legitimized. They become normalized practices, mundane in their ubiquity and as a result hard to see. Yet situations are never fixed. They can change, and we can change, especially when we see our cultural norms in the context of others.

While the dominance of text in the social sciences remains an issue, this chapter is set against a growing interest in attending to less fixed and easily representable and more ambiguous and sensory socio-mobile constructions of everyday life (Büscher et al. 2011; Spinney 2011; Jungnickel & Aldred 2013). In the past, scholarship in the field of mobilities in particular has been criticized for a tendency to tidy up and stabilize mobile subjects in order to study them. This criticism has in part spurred the growth of "mobile methods," which Büscher et al. explain are an attempt "to move with, and to be moved by, the fleeting, distributed, multiple, noncausal, sensory, emotional and kinaesthetic" (2011: 2). Video is increasingly at the forefront of a desire for researchers to "be there" even when they are not (Spinney 2011). On its most basic level, this desire is an attempt to stay mobile in a mobile field site. For Spinney, the use of video is also "a tool to extend sensory vocabularies" (163). Aldred and I (2013) have looked at cyclists' "sensory strategies" and how assemblies of clothing and associated technologies such as headphones can be used to inhibit or amplify elements of the environment. This literature opens up new terrain for thinking about the intersection of mobilities, technologies, and bodies.

While mobilities scholars have been at the forefront of these methods, given the dynamism of their subject of study, similar moves are evident more broadly in the social sciences and especially in STS (Law 2004; Hine 2007; Back 2012; Back & Puwar 2012; Lury & Wakeford 2012; Orton-Johnson & Prior 2013; Guggenheim 2015). For many scholars, these methods entail bringing the researcher into a closer, more intimate and responsive entanglement with research subjects. They also evoke and provoke the social. Back, for instance, asks how we might "account for the social world without assassinating the life contained within it" (2012: 21). This is the premise of Back and Puwar's (2012) "live sociology," capable of responding in creative and spontaneous ways to rich, complex, multisensory, and multi-dimensional worlds. Critically, for this chapter I am struck by how Back emphasizes that live sociology is not just about interpreting things into words, given sometimes "what remains unspoken can be of even greater significance" (2012: 28). Instead, it involves developing "attentiveness to the multiple registers of life" and considering other ways in which the social can be explored, articulated, and known (29).

Another valuable contribution in this field is Lury and Wakeford's work on inventive methods. In an edited collection of seventeen chapters on different "devices," they explain how inventive methods "introduce answerability into a problem" and how they do not "leave that problem untouched" (Lury & Wakeford 2012: 3). Critically, for this chapter, the kinds of inventiveness enabled through these methods "can never be known in advance" (7). Or, as Fuller and Goriunova explain, "they are something that happens that make something happen" (2012: 168). Mess has also been a theme of much methodological discussion in the social sciences (Law 2004; Hine 2007). Law explores the idea of moving closer to the messy nature of social worlds when he argues that conventional sociological methods can serve to create realities that are "independent, prior, singular, definite and passive," all of which suggest realities are separate from researchers (2004: 147). Although these restrictions have their place, he says we should embrace and draw from mess to realize other modes of description and unlock the potential for expressing different versions of the world.

This chapter continues the move toward recognizing less conventional knowledge practices and the production of alternative research objects. However, it also shifts attention from mess and methods to making. In doing so, concern lies with the entire process. Making is a means of *doing* research. In the next two sections, I provide examples of some of the challenges and opportunities of this approach in my practice.

DIY as Subject, Method, and Practice

My interest in open source technology communities provoked my initial forays into hacking, tinkering, and critical making practice. During my PhD, I studied ethnographically the largest volunteer WiFi network group in Australia. In this group, individuals were collectively building a customized wireless network across the largely suburban city of Adelaide, capital of South Australia, by linking handmade antennas, many of which were located in backyards and on sheds. Rather than simply adding content *to* the internet, members were constructing the very architecture of the internet from the ground up, or in this case from the backyard out. They were making what they called "ournet not the internet." Their practices were imbued by a DIY ethic, but they were not doing it alone—they were doing it together.

For the purposes of the study, I defined DIY as a hands-on, physical engagement with a diverse set of materials and improvised methods for the purpose of creating or repairing something usually for not-for-profit use outside the times and spaces of traditional technology innovation. I defined DIT as an approach that marries collaborative social engagement with a willingness to tinker, predicated on an understanding of technology as open, malleable, and participatory (Jungnickel 2014).

While I was doing WiFi research, I stumbled into another grassroots technology culture, in the form of a freakbike club, which exposed me to yet another way of engaging with open source practices. Like WiFi makers, freakbikers customize and adapt discarded, freely available or cheaply purchased materials, re-inscribing them with new meanings and re-imagined possibilities of use. Freakbikers hand-build bicycles from rubbish and discarded materials that push the boundaries of conventional cycling and the nature of the bike (Jungnickel 2013). My engagement with freakbikers identified me as a maker of technology, interested in getting inside the "black box," which afforded me entry into a particular way of expressing engagement with materials and practices. Both groups rendered their making practice visible, invited people into a technology culture, and encouraged them to imagine how things might be "otherwise" (Bijker & Law 1992). Here, my mundane bicycle was as much an ethnographic tool as a vehicle of transportation.

Although very different, I was struck by similar elements of practice, which informed how I made sociological arguments about technology makers (Jungnickel 2010). Respondents appeared unfazed by uncertainty and mistakes, and tangents from experimental activities were not considered accidents to be tidied up or erased. Instead, they were built *into* systems. Mistakes were considered critical to practice and socio-technical storytelling. Making was a vehicle for expected and unexpected happenings. It resisted being contained neatly as topic, method, or process. Members made resourceful technologies capable of adapting to changing conditions as a result of, not in spite of, ambiguities. I drew inspiration from this practice of engaging with uncertainty and sharing haphazard improvised activities. I have since attempted to "remain faithful to experiences of mess" (Hine 2007: 12) by exposing vulnerable ideas and seeking responses and public engagement with multiple iterations of research in many forms.

Similarly, Bikes & Bloomers is fundamentally a project about DIY and DIT socio-technical cultures. At one level, the women who patented their new cycling costumes did so because what they considered to be appropriate cycle wear did not exist (see Figure 50.2). They had to do it themselves. Yet, they, too, did not do it alone. Although legal mechanisms attribute knowledge to a single author, the reality was more likely to resemble a messy collective of shared technologies and skills, circulating ideas, and social support. Making was at the core of their actions. They were engaged in the making of costumes for safer, more comfortable cycling and also making new forms of mobile gendered citizenship. Their actions were complicit in carving out new political and ideological ways in which newly mobile women could move in and through public space. Therefore, it is a story as much about the changing nature of mobile citizenship as it is about clothing inventions (Jungnickel 2015). Much like my point earlier about the bicycle as a dual tool, patents are simultaneously rich archival data, ethnographic tools, and political devices.

Patents as Media in the Making

Patents are classic "immutable mobiles" in that they are easily and infinitely reproducible and can also travel, recruit people, and enact power (Latour & Woolgar 1979). In addition to being valuable receptacles of archival data, they are also fascinating design objects. Inventors describe in detail the problem they attempt to solve, illustrating the process in text and annotated line drawings, and in doing so provide a glimpse into the socio-cultural context of the time. Yet, patents also conceal as much as they reveal. In their flattened form, they give the appearance of an incontrovertible list of claims. Their formulaic nature is deliberately designed to make complex knowledge appear ordered, neat, and, as a result, persuasive. In classic STS

Figure 50.2 Victorian patents are valuable historic records of invention.

language, patents are "black-boxed." STS scholars are particularly sensitive to artifacts and systems that look convincingly smooth, so much so that from the outside they become easy to overlook, under-examine, and accept without question. Many argue that, once paths of innovation and use become established, it is harder to see or change systems than when they are fresh and new; it is not long before they appear as if they have always been there (Callon 1986; Latour 1999; Graham & Thrift 2007). Graham and Thrift write about how systems can seem "characterized by perfect order, completeness, immanence and internal homogeneity rather than leaky, partial and heterogeneous entities" (2007: 10).

Making, then, can be viewed as an interruptive practice that shifts these conventional registers. From a making perspective, historical patents are transformed from a smooth, closed, and legally framed text into an invitation for "embodied entanglement" (Barad 2007) and 3-D argument. They are direct incitements to make and bring to light broader, messier, and complex (inter)connections. Making provides a means to explore the intentions of the original designer, revealing new entry points into research and eliciting feedback and interaction with diverse audiences. As a maker, I do not claim to replicate the exact patented design, but rather a version. I make public my work in progress and use it as a tool for my own meaning-making as well as engagement with others.

To make from a patent involves interpreting the inventors' instructions and paying close attention to the labor involved, including time to accomplish small tasks such as making buttonholes that enabled larger systems to operate. It invites a close consideration of materials, technologies, skills, and bodies in the making of knowledge, such as mine as the maker but also the communities of women in the 1890s who shared skills, devices (such as sewing machines), fabrics, patterns, patent agent recommendations, and ideas. This reflexive ethnographic approach draws on Star's techno-feminist work in *The Cultures of Computing*, where she considers the computer in relation to a richer, more complex and present politic of the body:

> Right now, typing this my neck aches and I am curled in an uncomfortable position. I try to think about my fingertips and the chips inside this Macintosh as a seamless "web of computing" to use Kling and Scacchi's classic phrase (1982). But chips make me think of the eyesight of women in Singapore and Korea, going blind during the process of crafting the fiddly little wires; of "clean rooms" I have visited in Silicon Valley and the Netherlands, where people dressed like astronauts etch bits of silicon and fabricate complex sandwiches of information and logic. I think of the silence of my European ancestors who wore Chinese embroidery, marveling at its intricate complexity, the near-impossible stitches woven over a lifetime with the eyesight of another generation of Asian women. I think, I want my body to include these experiences.
>
> (Star 1995: 2–3)

Star's powerful writing provokes us to look into, to think further or differently about, something that appears deceitfully smooth on the surface. Her work invites us, in the process of making, to claim our own positionalities and others in relation to the black box, to get beneath the surface to see how it is made, who is and is not involved, and how it came about. She reminds us about the fascinating aspects of the mundane and "boring" (Star 1999). The ethnography of making, captured in time-lapse photos, reveals through the mundane practice of sewing a buttonhole an emotional and physical entanglement in and with the research. In the outstretched body, the relieved face in respite from concentration, the raised arms, the labor of making is rendered visible and visceral. These close encounters with research bring the often ignored or hidden into a rich, embodied, affectual present.

Imagining Different Futures through Victorian Women's Convertible Cycle Wear

The cycling costume with the hidden pulley system was patented by Alice Louisa Bygrave on December 6, 1895. Her aim was to improve conventional skirts, to allow women to occupy dual identities—reputable lady *and* cyclist—at a time when the latter was socially difficult for some women. To make these garments, we collaborated with a team of talented people, and these interactions all helped to add texture and nuance to the project. For instance, the pattern cutter worked from patents and design briefs we provided from archival research. Together, we embarked upon a process of multidimensional dynamic translations: from drawings, photos, and text into mock-up toiles and pattern pieces. So often the act of research involves opening up and taking something apart—gaining entry into a smooth, closed black-boxed system. Here, we were engaged in the act of piecing things together. Equipped with patterns, we constructed various iterations, sewing scaled practice garments that slowly led to full-sized pieces. We tried on each one at various stages, using our bodies to make sense of them and make them work, making mistakes, mending, adjusting, and experimenting. This process revealed many challenges and surprises, such as the demanding presence of small, seemingly inconsequential buttonholes that were not only critical to the successful workings of the system but also important socio-cultural storytellers.

Stories about the future are often told in the authoritative fields of science and engineering by those Law has called "heroes, big men, important organisations or major projects"

(1991: 12). Feminist STS scholars have long drawn attention to the lesser-known roles, particularly of women, behind the scenes of technological systems (Cowan 1983; Star 1999; Khan 2000; Wajcman 2004). As Wajcman writes, "their absence is as telling as the presence of some other actors, and even a condition of that presence" (2004: 41). This scholarship foregrounds marginalized voices and perspectives and in the process raises questions about men's monopoly over the history of technology. In the past, few women's voices have been heard because their contributions have either been rendered invisible or not recognized as important, with many technological inventions appearing to come from a single (male) author, reinforcing the ideal of an independent inventor. In reality, groups of people were more likely to have worked on similar inventions at the same time.

As Cowan points out, we hear little about not just some inventors but also certain kinds of technologies, such as the baby bottle, which she argues, "transformed a fundamental human experience for vast numbers of infants and mothers" and "yet it finds no place in our histories of technology" (1983: 52). In a similar vein, Khan argues that studies in the history of technology exhibit many biases, but the two most significant are the tendency to mythologize supposed "heroes of invention," "macroinventions," and large discrete inventions and the failure to pay systematic attention to the relationship between women and technology (2000: 191). Reflecting on this argument, it is possible to consider how a wider range of inventors would tell different stories about modernity, mobility, and the body.

Overall, this form of making and entangling through design histories seeks out new and different ways of exploring mobilities, gender relations, and inventive practice. It is an attempt to (re)place women's stories in rich, messy, and dynamic socio-technical timelines. The Bikes & Bloomers project also builds on work by design and material culture scholars on the history of domestic dressmaking, which has long been undervalued and overlooked. As Burman writes, "[t]he ordinariness and domesticity of home dressmaking would seem to have contributed to its invisibility and the lack of analytical purchase on the part of historians in related fields" (1999: 3). Convertible cycle wear can be considered an extreme version of

Figure 50.3 The researcher's body was a critical tool for making sense of the convertible cycle wear designs.

this ordinariness in that it was deliberately designed to resist detection. With a focus on inventive women's clothing designs (see Figure 50.3), the research aims to give voice to less triumphal heroic narratives in cycling history, which has more often been dominated by stories of "young men of means and nerve" who would showcase their masculine verve in public (Bijker 1997: 41). Fundamentally, the project is a means of bringing to the surface different ways of understanding mobility and the design of mobile citizens.

Getting Inside Mobile, Messy, and Multiple Social Worlds

So, what does sewing bring to research practice? I have responded to this question through a discussion of Bikes & Bloomers: a multifaceted research project that interweaves new and unusual making perspectives, bringing them to bear on qualitative studies of mobility, gender, and citizenship. I also drew on learnings from DIY and DIT technology cultures in which WiFi and freakbike makers appeared to delight in instability, rendering their mistakes and tangents public rather than hiding or tidying them up. These are cultural practices through which individuals are encouraged to collectively experiment—to craft skills through trial and error and share results—and in the process build resilient and creative systems and artifacts that adapt to changing conditions. Throughout I have argued that a critical practice involving making provides the means for researchers to get closer to, and in this case *into*, a subject of study. Here, we have to make choices, make mess, learn from mistakes, clean up, do and re-do things, develop skills, and think not only about our subject area but also our own positionalities as we physically engage in the labor of knowledge making.

It is important to re-iterate that I am not arguing for the primacy of making over conventional research practices. Instead, what I have attempted to convey is that making provides an opportunity to broaden existing methods and research skills. For instance, one of the advantages of this approach lies in being able to move in and out of research, zoom up close, and then step back and walk around it. Shifts like this are discussed at length in many classic methods texts. In sociology, C. Wright Mills's *The Sociological Imagination* (1959) reminds us that micro-personal issues are always valuable as they can be linked to larger historical and social contexts. The history of Victorian women's convertible cycle wear is a fascinating and largely unexplored example of this value. On one hand, these are intimate personal stories of adaptation to restrictions posed on women who desired to cycle, yet they also speak of much larger socio-cultural, political, and ideological issues. Some of the inventions patented by women cyclists afford small incremental changes, while others promise radical transformations. And yet they share a common theme—all are deliberately hidden from view. The fact that cyclists could wear these garments undetected is a symbol of their success but also means that little is known of this inventive culture in British cycling histories.

Returning to the buttonhole image that opened this chapter, it is clear that I was wrestling with the costume. The image captures the moment of success, but in doing so it also renders visible, through absence, the hours of trial and error that led to that point. I had been hunched over the machine, ignoring all kinds of appropriate computer postures, sewing my way through a problem—and it was not a problem on the page; it only emerged in practice. I had not thought much about buttonholes prior to the project (I certainly did not anticipate writing a chapter on them). And if I had, it was in a functional context: buttonholes (with buttons) fasten things. Interestingly, the term also means to "attract the attention of and detain (someone) in conversation, typically against their will" (according to the *Oxford English Dictionary*). Both definitions are concerned with closure. Yet, within the context of making patented convertible cycling skirts, buttonholes were transformed into technologies for opening up new landscapes of possibility for the women who wore the cycling costumes, and for me as a researcher in understanding this cultural practice and deepening my own practice.

The buttonholing image is part triumph, part relief. I had finally worked it out. I could move on. But, in the process, I gained deeper insight into the research and the women inventors. The value of these small examples lies in how they render visible larger systems and practices, such as the politics of the body, socio-technical cultures, hidden infrastructures, and the skills, technologies, and labor involved. It is a valuable reminder that what might appear simple and boring, such as a buttonhole on a patent, might in fact be boring *and* something else entirely.

Social science's continued impact and relevance relies on not only what it says but also how it tells stories. This chapter contributes to a growing interest in alternative practices, objects of study, and sites and tools for making and engaging social worlds. This is an exciting time for our disciplines. While there is a lot of discussion about new methods, actually *doing* this kind of research occupies the fringes of the sociological imagination because making anything other than talk and text is not yet central to practice. Researchers are pressured to resist tidying up mess and flattening dynamic mobile social worlds, and yet many conventional academic mechanisms directly reflect and shape particular practices. How do we slowly change these mechanisms? Maybe through one small buttonhole at a time.

Acknowledgments

Bikes & Bloomers is part of the "Transmissions and Entanglements: Making, Curating and Representing Knowledge" project supported by an Economic and Social Research Council Knowledge Exchange grant with support from Intel Corporation (ES/K008048/1).

Further Reading

Back, L. and N. Puwar (eds.) (2012) *Live Methods*, Oxford: Wiley-Blackwell.

Lury, C. and N. Wakeford (eds.) (2012) *Inventive Methods: Happenings of the Social*, London: Routledge.

Michael, M. (2006) *Technoscience and Everyday Life: The Complex Simplicities of the Mundane*, London: Open University Press.

Orton-Johnson, K. and N. Prior (eds.) (2013) *Digital Sociology: Critical Perspectives*, New York, NY: Palgrave.

Wolf, M. (1992) *A Thrice Told Tale: Feminism, Postmodernism and Ethnographic Responsibility*, Stanford, CA: Stanford University Press.

References

Back, L. (2012) "Live Sociology: Social Research and Its Futures," in L. Back and N. Puwar (eds.) *Live Methods*, Oxford: Blackwell Publishing, pp. 18–39

Back, L. and N. Puwar (eds.) (2012) *Live Methods*, Oxford: Wiley-Blackwell.

Barad, K. (2007) *Meeting the University Halfway: Quantum Physics and the Entanglement of Matter and Meaning*, Raleigh, NC: Duke University Press.

Bijker, W. E. (1997) *Of Bicycles, Bakelites, and Bulbs: Toward a Theory of Sociotechnical Change*, Cambridge, MA: MIT Press.

Bijker, W. E. and J. Law (1992) *Shaping Technology Building Society: Studies in Sociotechnical Change*, Cambridge MA: MIT Press.

Burman, B. (ed.) (1999) *The Culture of Sewing: Gender, Consumption and Home Dressmaking*, London: Berg Publishing.

Büscher, M., J. Urry, and K. Witchger (eds.) (2011) *Mobile Methods*, London: Routledge.

"buttonhole, v.1" (2015) Oxford English Dictionary, Oxford: Oxford University Press.

Callon, M. (1986) "The Sociology of an Actor-Network: The Case of the Electric Vehicle," in M. Callon, J. Law, and A. Rip (eds.) *Mapping the Dynamics of Science and Technology: Sociology of Science in the Real World*, Basingstoke, UK: Macmillan, pp. 19–34.

Cowan, R. S. (1983) *More Work for Mother: The Ironies of Household Technology from the Open Hearth to the Microwave*, New York, NY: Basic Books.

Fuller, M. and O. Goriunova (2012) "Phrase," in C. Lury and N. Wakeford (eds.) *Inventive Methods: Happenings of the Social*, London: Routledge, pp. 163–71.

Graham, S. and N. Thrift (2007) "Out of Order: Understanding Repair and Maintenance," *Theory, Culture & Society* 24(1), 1–25.

Guggenheim, M. (2015) "The Media of Sociology: Tight or Loose Translations?" *British Journal of Sociology* 66(2), 345–72.

Helvenston Gray, S. and M. C. Peteu (2005) "Invention, 'The Angel of the Nineteenth Century': Patents for Women's Cycling Attire in the Nineteenth Century," *Dress* 32, 27–42.

Hine, C. (2007) "Multi-sited Ethnography as a Middle Range Methodology for Contemporary STS," *Science, Technology & Human Values* 32(6), 652–71.

Jungnickel, K. (2010) "Exhibiting Ethnographic Knowledge: Making Sociology about Makers of Technology," *Street Signs, Centre for Urban and Community Research*, London: Goldsmiths, pp. 28–31.

Jungnickel, K. (2013) "Getting There . . . and Back: How Ethnographic Commuting (by Bicycle) Shaped a Study of Australian Backyard Technologists," *Qualitative Research* 14(6), 640–55.

Jungnickel, K. (2014) *DiY WiFi: Re-imagining Connectivity*, London and New York, NY: Palgrave Pivot.

Jungnickel, K. (2015) "'One Needs to Be Very Brave to Stand All That': Cycling, Rational Dress and the Struggle for Citizenship in Late Nineteenth Century Britain," *Geoforum* 64, 362–71.

Jungnickel, K. (n.d.) Bikes & Bloomers Research website, retrieved from www.bikesandbloomers.com.

Jungnickel, K. and R. Aldred (2013) "Cycling's Sensory Strategies: How Cyclists Mediate Their Exposure to the Urban Environment," *Mobilities* 9(2), 238–55.

Khan, B. Z. (2000) "'Not for Ornament': Patenting Activity by Nineteenth-Century Women Inventors," *Journal of Interdisciplinary History* 31(2), 159–95.

Latour, B. (1999) *Pandora's Hope: Essays on the Reality of Science Studies*, Cambridge, MA: Harvard University Press.

Latour, B. and S. Woolgar (1979) *Laboratory Life: The Social Construction of Scientific Facts*, London: Sage.

Law, J. (2004) *After Method: Mess in Social Science Research*, London: Routledge.

Law, J. (1991) "Introduction: Monsters, Machines and Sociotechnical Relations," in (ed) *A Sociology of Monsters: Essays on Power, Technology and Domination*, London and New York, NY: Routledge, pp. 1–25

Lury, C. and N. Wakeford (eds.) (2012) *Inventive Methods: Happenings of the Social*, London: Routledge.

Mills, C. W. (1959) *The Sociological Imagination*, New York, NY: Oxford University Press.

Orton-Johnson, K. and N. Prior (eds.) (2013) *Digital Sociology: Critical Perspectives*, New York, NY: Palgrave.

Peteu, M. C. and S. Helvenston Gray (2009) "Clothing Invention: Improving the Functionality of Women's Skirts, 1846–1920," *Clothing and Textiles Research Journal* 27(1), 46–61.

Spinney, J. (2011) "A Chance to Catch a Breath: Using Mobile Video Ethnography in Cycling Research," *Mobilities* 6(2): 161–82.

Star, S. L. (ed.) (1995) *The Cultures of Computing*, Oxford: Blackwell Publishing.

Star, S. L. (1999) "The Ethnography of Infrastructure," in P. Lyman and N. Wakeford (eds.) *Analysing Virtual Societies: New Directions in Methodology, American Behavioral Scientist* 43(3), 377–91.

Wajcman, J. (2004) *TechnoFeminism*, Oxford: Polity Press.

51

ENVIRONMENTAL SENSING AND "MEDIA" AS PRACTICE IN THE MAKING

Jennifer Gabrys

Figure 51.1 Participant setting up Speck monitoring device, with logbook of monitoring practices.

Source: Citizen Sense 2014.

JENNIFER GABRYS

Introduction: Citizen Sensing

From ubiquitous computing to the Internet of Things, sensors that monitor and automate environmental processes are now proliferating. Along with the increasing prevalence of these devices, a diverse range of practices has arisen. Termed "citizen sensing," users equipped with low-cost sensing devices and sensor-enabled smart phones are able to monitor environments and collect real-time data. From recording air pollution levels to tracking the migrations of animals, sensing technologies allow citizens to observe environmental processes in increasing detail and communicate environmental observations to fellow citizens and policymakers. As an emerging set of practices and devices, however, citizen sensing also raises multiple questions about how environmental "citizenship" becomes articulated and even delimited as a technological and evidence-based mode of participation. This chapter outlines the key literature, practices, and technologies that have contributed to citizen sensing, and then discusses through the Citizen Sense research project how a practice-based and participatory study has sought to understand and contribute to this emerging area of citizen sensing and the development of digital media technologies.

On one level, citizen sensing inevitably resonates with a longer history of citizen science practices, where amateur natural historians conduct surveys and gather samples of environmental organisms and events, or alternatively might collect data on environmental pollution to advance social justice issues (Irwin 1995; Corburn 2005). Building on these areas, citizen sensing is also distinct in its use of digital monitoring technologies, such as sensors that enable new orders of data collection and real-time observations of environments. In its earlier uses, citizen sensing as a term often referred to "volunteered geographic information," where users provided data and developed applications for Open Street Map and Google Earth, among other platforms (Goodchild 2007). While sensors were notionally discussed as part of this early research on citizen sensing, which often focused on the validity of citizen-gathered datasets, a more thoroughgoing engagement has largely occurred through the development of low-cost sensing devices, such as the Air Quality Egg, Citizen Sensor, Air Casting, and Smart Citizen, which are projects located within maker communities. With citizen sensing, the focus has also shifted to include not just citizens providing geographic data across mapping platforms, but also the development of open hardware and low-cost physical computing that can generate data on phenomena such as urban air quality.

As an area of practice and study, citizen sensing crosses multiple fields, including geography and computer science, human-computer interaction, and media and communication studies, as well as art, design, and architecture. It also contributes to and is advanced by work in digital humanities, since many of the core issues that citizen sensing raises—in relation to participation, sensing, and citizenship—are longstanding discussions core to the humanities. At the same time, related and more extensive discussions within media theory have attended to questions about the nature and quality of participation within social media (Foth et al. 2011), as well as shifts from consumer to user, crowdsourcer, maker, and hacker modes of media engagement (Ratto & Boler 2014). The 2.0 designation of the internet and beyond captures this user-focused approach, which has proliferated from the internet to ubiquitous computing and multiple other forms of environmentally distributed digital devices (Galloway 2004; Dourish & Bell 2011). Citizen sensing activates digitally informed and practice-based engagements that put these concepts to the test within specific situations and in relation to distinct environmental problems.

The critical issues that define citizen sensing include questions related to which practices of citizenship and modes of participation digital sensing technologies might enable or delimit.

How do sensors and the environmental processes they trace influence relations and responsibilities toward environments? In what ways do the political, material, and affective orientations of sensing devices fulfill their performative potential? And to what extent do the diverse practices of citizens' everyday sensing practices reorient the intended programs of these devices? By enabling practices of environmental monitoring, data collection, and even technological tinkering, citizen sensing arguably prompts distinct types of participation that, on the one hand, activate particular forms of environmentalism and environmental responsibility that are largely data-focused. On the other hand, citizen sensing might be located within a broader context of environmental computing, where digital technologies and their modes of participation are moving from primarily screen- and platform-based engagements to more distributed and environmental sensory encounters. Citizen sensing thus has consequences for how the sites of digital media and digital media engagement might be located.

One way to research these developments might be to undertake an ethnographic study of an existing citizen sensing project. But as many technologies, communities, and practices related to citizen sensing are not yet stabilized as clear "objects" of research, undertaking a citizen sensing project is another way to research these emerging technologies and practices. The remainder of this chapter discusses once such effort: citizens sensing pollution stemming from unconventional natural gas extraction, or fracking, through the use of low-cost environmental sensors.

Pollution Sensing and the Citizen Sense Project

The Citizen Sense research project takes up the topic of citizen sensing as both a theoretical and practical area of inquiry and intervention. Structured in relation to three research areas, namely pollution sensing, urban sensing, and wild sensing, it focuses on environmental areas of citizen engagement to test, query, and potentially advance citizen sensing practices. The first project area, "pollution sensing," concentrates on the increasing use of sensors to detect environmental disturbance, including air and water pollution. The second project area, "urban sensing," focuses on urban sustainability or "smart city" projects that implement sensor technologies to attempt to realize more environmentally sound urban processes. The third project area investigates "wild sensing" and focuses on the use of sensors to map and track flora and fauna activity and habitats. The project areas set out to contextualize, question, and expand upon the understandings and possibilities of democratized environmental action through citizen sensing practices.

Within the first project area, "pollution sensing," the Citizen Sense research team first identified through desk-based research and fieldwork a range of existing citizen sensing projects and technologies. It became clear that a number of citizen sensing practices were already underway, monitoring air and water quality at sites, particularly in northeastern Pennsylvania, near fracking infrastructure and operations. Citizens engaged in monitoring activities might not have referred to their practices as "citizen sensing," and instead might have situated themselves within a wider context of monitoring practices aimed at environmental and social justice concerns, from fenceline monitoring at industrial sites to documenting health effects and keeping diaries of exposures. At what point, then, does citizen sensing become identifiable as a particular set of practices? Do maker-based digital technologies need to be introduced into settings to initiate citizen sensing engagements, or do existing practices provide another way of thinking about and practicing citizen sensing as something more than technology-focused?

In many ways, even from the early stages of identifying citizen sensing practices, the very use of this term prompted questions about how distinct digital practices stabilize and become recognizable. As part of the participatory aspect of the Citizen Sense research project, residents of northeastern Pennsylvania were consulted about which pollutants and environmental disturbances they were already in the process of monitoring, how they described and undertook their practices, what wider networks were important for communicating findings, and how it might be possible to work together to develop a "citizen sensing kit" that would be of use for monitoring air pollution in relation to the fracking industry.

As part of a back-and-forth dialogue, the Citizen Sense team developed a "logbook of monitoring practices" for residents to not only identify existing individual and institutional monitoring practices as well as issues related to their environments, but also make proposals for how to monitor or otherwise act on pollution concerns. Based on these logbook entries, along with images and video submitted by residents documenting their environments, a number of possible monitoring technologies and practices were identified that could assemble into a citizen sensing kit for use and testing. After several discussions with residents, and also through research into which technologies might be most adaptable, affordable, and accessible over a long period of use, the Citizen Sense Kit came together as a range of devices: Speck devices (borrowed from Create Lab at Carnegie Mellon University; see Figure 51.1) to monitor particulate matter ($PM_{2.5}$); analogue badges to monitor benzene, toluene, ethylbenzene, and xylene (BTEX) compounds commonly associated with petrochemical industries; a "Frackbox" (developed by the Citizen Sense team) to monitor nitrogen oxides (NO_x), ozone (O_3), and volatile organic compounds (VOCs) and also track wind direction, temperature, and humidity; and an online platform to locate and log environmental monitoring data.

As part of the process for distributing kits, the Citizen Sense team hosted a series of events in northeastern Pennsylvania, including a community workshop where the Citizen Sense Kit was introduced, a walk along fracking infrastructure where various monitoring equipment was tested, and a roundtable to discuss broader issues related to fracking and community organizing. Participants at these events included residents, technologists, environmental health practitioners, local ecologists, and community organizers. During the community workshop, components of the Citizen Sense Kit were then distributed to about 30 residents, who in turn used the environmental sensors for up to 7 months. Participants logged the approximate location of their monitoring on the Citizen Sense platform, primarily through the use of the Speck $PM_{2.5}$ monitor but also by logging their observations of industry and other activity that might generate high $PM_{2.5}$ levels. Data was then available to view both in real-time on actual Speck devices and on the platform once uploaded. Observations and readings could be compared across different monitoring locations, and in some cases discussion arose about the different readings, techniques, and events that might be causing elevated levels of pollutants in particular areas. Participants asked whether elevated readings could be attributed to nearby natural gas infrastructure, or if high pollen counts or other industries nearby were causing spikes they observed in their data.

In this brief account of the Citizen Sense Kit, it becomes clear that the kits developed into much more than digital gadgets or makery "stuff." By working in a context with identifiable environmental problems of concern, citizen sensing practices and technologies quickly become bound up with environments, communities, institutions, and wider politics. The accuracy of monitoring devices, the monitoring protocols used, the legitimacy of the data, and the agendas of users all come into play as factors influencing the techniques of environmental monitoring and the data gathered (see Bowker 2000).

In this respect, participation involves much more than merely using a sensor to gather a reading about a particular pollutant. Sensor use might be a more immediate, if limited, way of understanding what characterizes citizen sensing practices. Yet, in the context of monitoring, citizen sensing clearly moves beyond the often celebratory formula of gathering data for political action and change to open into particular worlds of inquiry and political contestation. New relations and communities might be put into play and activated through monitoring practices, or existing communities might re-encounter old problems with the difficulties of finding ways to hold environmental regulators and industry to account. Moreover, the data that is generated and gathered by monitoring devices is not obviously or immediately available in forms that are easily communicated or circulated to relevant agencies. Instead, data is potentially generated in excess, difficult to collate and present, and subject to disputes about its legitimacy.

Participation, Sensing, and Citizenship: "Media" as Practice in the Making

Returning to the questions posed at the beginning of this chapter, sensors can organize very particular ways of accounting for environmental problems such as pollution. Citizen sensing initiatives involve monitoring, reporting, managing, and even self-managing to establish environmental engagement. Data is collected as a form of "evidence" that might enable claims to be made to mitigate the effects of environmental harm. The hope is that, by undertaking a commitment to monitor environmental problems such as pollution over time, and to collect and systematically present evidence, environmental matters of concern will be taken more seriously by citizens, industry, and others. Yet, as has also become clear, citizen sensing gives rise to other difficulties related to the perceived accuracy of monitoring devices, the practices used for collecting data, and the perceived legitimacy of datasets, particularly when communicated to regulators and industry. In many ways, then, citizen sensing practices necessarily open up and reorient beyond the initial programs of monitoring devices, since the trajectory from sensing environments to collecting data and realizing political change does not play out in an uncomplicated manner.

Indeed, citizen sensing raises distinct points about the politics and practices of sense that emerge at the intersection of sensor technologies, citizen participation, and environmental change. Sensors do not simply detect external phenomena for reporting; they become entangled with particular values and means of informing citizen (and collective) action. Ways of articulating environmentalism and environmental problems, as well as attempts to realize environmental justice, become bound up with the distinct capacities of environmental sensing technology. For instance, air pollution as a problem is foregrounded by the capacity of air monitoring devices to not only make available distributed and widespread tracking of particular pollutants but also query state-led, corporate, and institutional approaches to monitoring and mitigating air pollution.

The issues that emerge through a practice-based study of citizen sensing then point back to the core topics mentioned at the beginning of this chapter—participation, sensing, and citizenship—and become newly encountered and constituted. As a challenge and provocation to media studies and digital humanities, practice-based research reworks the usual designations of these topics and concepts to indicate how a rather different set of issues emerge. Participation is not just, or even primarily, a matter of how individuals interact with digital technologies to achieve desired ends or partake of particular (often online) communities

Instead, participation through citizen sensing unfolds as a set of activities that require multiple other forms of community organizing that may not be recognized as "digital." At the same time, participation with sensor technologies can give rise to a hesitating and decidedly non-linear set of engagements, where learning about new technologies, establishing modes of consistent monitoring, and communicating findings are practices that come together through repeated attempts to use monitoring devices in effective and potentially unconventional ways.

Similarly, sensing as a concept and term is not a simple matter of sensing a pollutant. Instead, the very pollutants to be identified, the means and skills to conduct studies of pollutants over time, and the development or sourcing of technologies that will suitably and accurately "sense" pollutants materialize as particular practices for strategically monitoring environments. Sensing is thus less about a phenomenological encounter between a human body and external set of stimuli, and much more about particular technologies, concerns, and environmental problems, as well as bodies and politics, concretizing into specific occasions that can galvanize citizen sensing in certain ways (Gabrys 2007, 2016b). For instance, someone using an environmental sensor might have health effects only vaguely connected to air quality data, thereby requiring them to also rely on public health research, environmental policy, and community organizing to put together a case for addressing potentially high levels of pollutants. A practice-based encounter with citizen sensing explodes the assumed modes of detection to point toward a complex set of processes whereby environmental harm might be "sensed" and acted upon.

Regarding the "citizen" in citizen sensing, new insights emerge in practice by testing the very articulations of citizenship that technologies may facilitate. The notion that a device might embody and enable particular forms of environmental citizenship can be tested, challenged, and re-routed. By taking up citizen sensing technologies in practice, and through repeated use and asking how they actually do—or do not—allow for environmental citizenship, participants might challenge the claims made about devices, while also developing and inventing alternative capacities for citizen sensing technologies. In this respect, if we understand environmental citizenship to entail responsibilities for creating common inhabitations, then the practices of citizenship might emerge less as a scripted technological program and more as an open-ended and inventive set of collective engagements.

Conclusion: Re-orienting Practices toward Open Technology

Within the wider realm of digital technology, there is a proliferation of newly emerging digital practices, from social media activity to algorithms that match data flow with indicative behaviors, as well as electronic meters that modulate energy use, apps that track sleep and fitness, wearables that monitor heart rate, and devices that document how much pollution might be in any patch of air. These are specific practices enacted through digital technologies, which organize, manage, inform, and otherwise mediate everyday activities and give rise to distinct issues (such as surveillance, which is an important topic demanding further research). Citizen sensing is one such newly emerging practice that is concretizing at the intersection of environmental participation, digital sensors, data collection, and environmental citizenship. The diagram of citizen sensing as a practice is largely assumed in advance as drawing together citizens, entities to be monitored, environments, data, and politics in particular ways. Yet, what might begin as a relatively delineated practice starts to unfold in unexpected ways, overlapping with multiple other practices that blur the boundaries of what counts as citizen sensing.

By undertaking a practice-based study, the complexities as well as possibilities of citizen sensing become more fully apparent. The initial diagram of citizen sensing opens up and points to ways in which programs and their devices are reoriented and challenged by putting citizen sensing to work as both a concept and mode of participation. Citizen sensing might then be considered a *technique* in the sense raised by philosopher of science and technology, Georges Canguilhem (2008 [1965]). If technique presents a mode of engagement—here with machines—where the "facts" of environmental monitoring are not known in advance, but rather where capacities, skills, and potential new objects emerge through actual encounters, then citizen sensing is one such technique that requires an ongoing practice to not only understand the contours of digital engagements but also arrive at new and potentially inventive encounters with sensing technologies. A further point, then, is that citizen sensing as a practice has not yet solidified, and its very quality of being in-process may characterize it as a distinctly digital ontology (Gabrys 2016a).

Within newly emerging and established areas of digital research, a number of terms are solidifying to describe particular practice-based engagements, from making and critical making to hacking and tinkering to critical technical practice and participatory design (Agre 1997; Suchman 2009; DiSalvo et al. 2012). Within media studies, practice-based research might largely be seen to engage with the generation of creative form and content. And within science and technology studies, there is a long history of ethnographic observation and description of practices. There is also a much broader literature that investigates practice as both a topic of ethnographic concern and a methodology for undertaking research across the arts, social sciences, and humanities. Digital humanities research has similarly made a point of moving beyond text-based approaches to focus on experimental engagements, and to take up questions of materiality and making, embodiment, and action (Gold 2012; see also Chapters 9, 19 and 25, this volume). However, this distinction is arguably now less pressing given the proliferation of practice-based approaches that no longer depend upon classification apart from discursive or theoretical modes of research. Instead, practice-based research raises questions about how open-ended and inventive encounters with digital technologies might be one way of more fully researching and addressing the *qualities of technique* that are central to our technological engagements.

This chapter not only suggests that citizen sensing might be addressed as an emerging set of literatures, practices, and technologies; it also points to inventive modes for undertaking practice-based research to articulate the open-ended techniques that emerge through digital technologies. Such an approach allows for an understanding of how emerging practices settle—or not—into recognizable forms, as well as how the open, indeterminate, experimental, and speculative aspects of technologies might be an area for understanding how they unfold as provocations. Gilbert Simondon (2012), a philosopher of technology and student of Canguilhem, suggested that technologies articulate cultural values, and that these articulations might also serve as sites of cultural experimentation. According to Simondon, the openness of technology might then be pursued less as a question of open hardware or software and more as an investigation of how open technological engagements might be re-routed to be more democratic, inventive, and explicitly cultural. For Simondon, these lines of inquiry require an attention to and engagement with machines as they are taken up, used, and reworked through practice.

With these points in mind, citizen sensing research and practice might expand from their usual framing as sensing technologies enabling the collection of monitoring data toward political action to encompass a more inventive and open set of engagements. Moreover, digital media might be encountered as technologies that are always in the making, changing through practice, and which might be disrupted through programs of use that become sites of active cultural and political engagement.

Acknowledgments

The research leading to these results has received funding from the European Research Council under the European Union's Seventh Framework Programme (FP/2007–2013) / ERC Grant Agreement no. 313347, "Citizen Sensing and Environmental Practice: Assessing Participatory Engagements with Environments through Sensor Technologies." Thanks are due to participating residents in Pennsylvania; current and previous Citizen Sense researchers, including Helen Pritchard, Nerea Calvillo, Tom Keene, and Nick Shapiro; and consultants, including Kelly Finan, Benjamin Barratt, Lau Thiam Kok, and Raphael Faeh. Thanks are also due to the Create Lab at Carnegie Mellon University for loaning Speck devices for use in this study.

References

Agre, P. E. (1997) *Computation and Human Experience*, Cambridge, UK: Cambridge University Press.

Air Casting (n.d.) "Home," retrieved from aircasting.org.

Air Quality Egg (n.d.) retrieved from airqualityegg.com.

Bowker, G. C. (2000) "Biodiversity Datadiversity," *Social Studies of Science* 30(5), 643–83.

Canguilhem, G. (2008 [1965]) *Knowledge of Life*, trans. S. Geroulanos and D. Ginsburg, New York, NY: Fordham University Press.

Citizen Sense (n.d.) retrieved from www.citizensense.net.

Corburn, J. (2005) *Street Science: Community Knowledge and Environmental Health Justice*, Cambridge, MA: MIT Press.

DiSalvo, C., M. Louw, D. Holstius, I. Nourbakhsh, and A. Akin (2012) "Towards a Public Rhetoric through Participatory Design: Critical Engagements and Creative Expression in the Neighborhood Networks Project," *Design Issues* 28(3), 48–61.

Dourish, P. and G. Bell (2011) *Divining a Digital Future: Mess and Mythology in Ubiquitous Computing*, Cambridge, MA: MIT Press.

Foth, M., L. Forlano, C. Satchell, and M. Gibbs (eds.) (2011) *From Social Butterfly to Engaged Citizen: Urban Informatics, Social Media, Ubiquitous Computing, and Mobile Technology to Support Citizen Engagement*, Cambridge, MA: MIT Press.

Gabrys, J. (2007) "Automatic Sensation: Environmental Sensors in the Digital City," *The Senses and Society* 2(2), 189–200.

Gabrys, J. (2016a) "Citizen Sensing: Recasting Ontologies through Proliferating Digital Practices," *Cultural Anthropology (Theorizing the Contemporary)*, retrieved from culanth.org/fieldsights/823-citizen-sensing-recasting-digital-ontologies-through-proliferating-practices.

Gabrys, J. (2016b) *Program Earth: Environmental Sensing Technology and the Making of a Computational Planet*, Minneapolis, MN: University of Minnesota Press.

Galloway, A. (2004) "Intimations of Everyday Life: Ubiquitous Computing and the City," *Cultural Studies* 18(2–3), 384–408.

Gold, M. (ed.) (2012) *Debates in the Digital Humanities*, Minneapolis, MN: University of Minnesota Press.

Goodchild, M. F. (2007) "Citizens as Sensors: The World of Volunteered Geography," *GeoJournal* 69(4), 211–21.

Irwin, A. (1995) *Citizen Science: A Study of People, Expertise and Sustainable Development*, London: Routledge.

Ratto, M. and M. Boler (eds.) (2014) *DIY Citizenship: Critical Making and Social Media*, Cambridge, MA: MIT Press.

Saavedra, J. (n.d.) Citizen Sensor: DIY Pollution Monitoring, retrieved from www.citizensensor.cc.

Simondon, G. (2012) "Technical Mentality," in A. De Boever (trans.), A. De Boever, A. Murray, J. Roffe, and A. Woodward (eds.) *Gilbert Simondon: Being and Technology*, Edinburgh: Edinburgh University Press.

Smart Citizen (n.d.) retrieved from smartcitizen.me.

Speck (n.d.) "Meet Speck," retrieved from www.specksensor.com.

Suchman, L. (2009) "Agencies in Technology Design: Feminist Reconfigurations," in *Proceedings of the 5th European Symposium on Gender & ICT*, University of Bremen, retrieved from www.informatik.uni-bremen.de/soteg/gict2009/proceedings/GICT2009_Suchman.pdf.

52

APPROACHING DESIGN AS INQUIRY

Magic, Myth, and Metaphor in Digital Fabrication

Daniela K. Rosner

Over the last decade, a new project of reproduction has entered public life. Cultures of making have given rise to systems for digital fabrication that create tactile media out of metal, plastic, wood, and clay. At one end, advocates like Chris Anderson (2012) contend that such systems have created nothing short of a "revolution"—enabling new forms of small-scale manufacturing and technological empowerment (Hatch 2014; Lang and Demarest 2013). Laser cutters produce modular furniture in garages and workshops. Shoebox-sized 3-D printers create jewelry through additive manufacturing. And computer numerical control (CNC) looms weave textiles patterns with shared digital files. At the other end, analysts view digital fabrication as commodity fetishism: extending capitalist modes of production to accommodate small-scale, "means-end" production, often reinforcing privileged technical authority along the way (Ames et al. 2014; Bean and Rosner 2014; Reed 2016). For instance, maker enthusiast Leah Buechley (2016) emphasizes the tendency of "maker" publications and events to speak to college-educated, upper- and middle-class white men. Others break open the category of technology to detail forms of care work (Toombs 2015; Reed 2016) and craft (Rosner & Fox 2016).

This chapter departs from these productivist and critical framings to consider an integrative approach to *design-as-inquiry*: folding together practical tools of technical development (in this case, digital fabrication) with theoretical tools of social inquiry (in this case, the mimetic faculty). To examine emerging sites of digital and material production, I turn to metaphors of extraction and capture underpinning the mimetic discourse of Walter Benjamin and Michael Taussig. I draw on Taussig's "theory of magic" to critically examine what it means to build a mimetic machine via digital fabrication systems and forms (1993: 59). A mimetic machine not only imitates phenomena but also takes a certain "sheen" from the thing it seeks to represent (231). In this examination, I show how tactile media throw into question the bounds and competencies of production: how algorithms shape measurement and interpretation to become a source of magical power.

To begin this inquiry, I turn to the spectacle of fabrication in three projects: two programs of engineering from researchers at MIT (Follmer & Ishii 2012; Zoran & Paradiso 2013), and our research team's own development of an engraving tool, called "Arc," for ceramics. The first project, KidCAD, relinquishes object histories by physically copying an existing object on a scanning bed. The second project, FreeD, respecifies the machine's relationship to the hand by providing invisible haptic feedback. In the third project, Arc, our research team variously connects these questions of provenance, collision, and mimicry by moving an engraving instrument in response to surrounding gestures and sounds.

While the first two projects stem from productivist agendas that seek new processes for design, the final project develops out of our research team's collaboration with ceramicists through an approach to design-as-inquiry that comprises an integrative program of ethnographic interviews, conceptual development, and technology building. Treating design-as-inquiry here involves interventionist and collaborative methods of investigation that ask how an engagement with design may expand and shift what we know. Conversely, it prompts us to consider how social inquiry may help us, as analysts of the sociotechnical, get hold of design—to theorize and imagine design differently.

This approach draws on design-led approaches of critical, adversarial, and speculative design/making that consider the limits of digital production (Ratto 2011; DiSalvo 2012; Dunne & Raby 2013). For media studies scholars, processes of design present possibilities for empirical study of studio practice and downstream networks of maintenance and repair (Jackson & Kang 2014; Cheatle & Jackson 2015; Rosner & Turner 2015). For example, Elizabeth Goodman's (2013) ethnographic study of interaction design teams sheds light on the performative practices that organize work and enliven otherwise static deliverables. For digital humanists, processes of design offer unusual moments for conceptual interrogation. Approaches of this sort include Galey and Ruecker's (2010) assessment that digital prototypes may work as forms of argument and Matt Ratto's (2011) critical making workshops, which similarly rely on hardware programming to examine the limits of social theory, such as Marcel Mauss's theory of the gift economy. In other work, Hancock and colleagues (2013) suggest bibliotextual scholarship may productively work as a design-oriented practice, taking practices of "reflective design"—the promotion of critical, exploratory inquiry—to the study of the book. From printable prosthetics to portable water pumps, design projects shape the connections people make, the spaces they move through, and the sociopolitical infrastructures they inhabit (Bennett et al. 2016; de Laet & Mol 2000; Jungnickel 2015; Suchman 2011). The tools generated by each of these projects I have come to call "mimetic machines" (after Taussig 1993: 58–59, 219–20): systems that create sensuous (and not just functional) copies of existing forms, actions, and sounds. Beyond a study of mimesis, these cases serve to illustrate a program of design inquiry that proffers tactility as central to research practice.

Case Studies: Designing for Cultures of Making

This examination of digital fabrication as social and cultural inquiry begins with digital machinery for mimesis. From building circuitry to knitting sweaters, making practices have gained visibility within digital humanities due to the alternative framings of design and use they present. Although seemingly pervasive, making remains varied in its scale and purpose. Advocates claim makers "are reshaping how people consume and interpret the handmade" (Levine & Heimerl 2008: xi). While we often think of craft as domesticated by homemakers (often women) in living rooms and manufacturing as organized by professionals (often men) in factories, in these settings we see craft and manufacturing collide through material experimentation. Through examining how people make things and share them with others, scholars question how digital tools enable, enhance, circumvent, or detract from people's engagement and connection with the world (McCullough 1998; Gauntlett 2011; Roedl et al. 2015). Next I turn to three projects on digital fabrication that attempt to extend and clarify the work of makers through mimetic production. Each invites questions of development around systems that selectively limit the forms of agency bestowed upon humans and machines.

KidCAD: Mimicking Objects

Drawing on the metaphor of clay stamping, MIT Media Lab researchers Follmer and Ishii (2012) designed KidCAD to enable children to copy and reproduce toys. The machine uses existing physical objects as the "original" forms from which 3-D fabrication follows. To create the scanning bed, the designers used a substance that models objects as they deform its malleable surface. Like SketchChair's (2011) developers, who provide an interface for designing and building chairs with laser-cut and CNC-routed parts, makers can use KidCAD to modify and extend the objects without engaging a graphical user interface (GUI) or 3-D printing software. The machine also enables customization through varied textures and materials. Customization concerns the capacity for people (consumers) to change printed features in an ad-hoc manner rather than fall back on decisions made by a commercial product manufacturer (producers), an interaction Follmer and Ishii connect with "remix culture" (2012: 2402). In a "user evaluation" with thirteen children visiting their lab with parents in tow, they asked the children to create two animals and compose a story with the system. Looking for themes across the group, they found the system worked as a pictorial canvas, enabling children to create scenery as if drawing with objects (2409).

For digital humanists, this project may recall Elliott, MacDougall, and Turkel's (2012) discussion of "New Old Things" for historical research. The machine invites makers to appropriate already meaningful artifacts as a "new medium" for narration (Elliott et al. 2012: 122). The appropriation of the old allows for an exploration of how tacit knowledge and performance can produce (and limit) meaning. KidCAD users may develop a tactile version of "traditional copy and paste" (Follmer & Ishii 2012: 2402). In this process of copying, Follmer and Ishii "hope to expand children's view of what objects are and what they can be" (2401). Along the way, the apparatus may also enable children to shape the world in their own image. In circumventing prevailing market relations (consumer-producer), Follmer and Ishii not only develop tools for expression, but also rethink an "original" object through the technological imagination of the individual.

FreeD: Milling Against

In a second project of digital production, Zoran and Paradiso, also hailing from the MIT Media Lab, developed FreeD to "merge" qualities of digital fabrication and traditional craft, enabling "authentic engagement" with material through computational tools (Zoran & Paradiso 2013: 2613). FreeD is an interactive milling tool that pushes back at the hand that holds it. As a freehand apparatus, the device corresponds to a common hand tool, such as a chisel, which makers can use with skill and dexterity. Yet FreeD also keeps track of its location in space to reconnect the maker's motions with those of the machine. To accomplish this tracking, the system integrates a prespecified digital model with limited features of the maker's gestures, all with the goal of "re-introduc[ing] some of the craft values into digital fabrication"

(2614). The system reacts to the maker's actions when the actions "put the model at risk" (2614). For example, the designers developed an algorithm to minimize the chance that a bit will enter the volume of the model. The machine pulls the carving tool back when it senses this issue. As the bit moves farther from the surface, the software pushes the shaft to a pre-specified position. In subsequent tests, Zoran and Paradiso later assessed the accuracy of FreeD, producing artifacts within 2.5mm of the original form (2615).

Beyond guiding the development of form, the FreeD project positions the software's algorithm as a central yet hidden feature of production, prompting new questions of the handmade. What do Zoran and Paradiso mean when they assert the importance of handwork in digital production? Where do they locate the hand as evidence of intent? How do they account for the agency and responsibility of the maker when they take digital mimesis as a starting point for handwork? For FreeD users, the body and machine become part of the same machinery: collaboratively reproducing a digital model but with different degrees and arenas of control. The body follows an algorithmic pattern as well as the underlying digital specifications the algorithm interprets. Speed of the milling and movements of the shaft become a form of communication, showing the maker not only where the machine detects the location of the bit (in relation to the surface of the digital model), but also the very nature of digital specification, a technique paralleling the control mechanisms built into new autonomous vehicles (Markoff 2010). In that sense, Zoran and Paradiso do more than develop instrumental tools. They take up a procedure of minimizing risk to prompt new concerns for "authenticity" and what evidences the intention of the maker.

Arc: Milling Together

Our third project, Arc (see Figure 52.1), came about through a collaboration with University of Washington students, Hidekazu Saegusa and Thomas Tran, and Seattle-based ceramic artisans, John Ellefson and Adrien Miller (Saegusa et al. 2016). Saegusa is a design technologist with a master's degree in engineering, a bachelor's degree in media arts, and formal training in sound and image analysis. Tran is a photographer with a bachelor's degree in environmental science. Miller is a sculptor with a background in painting and photography. Much of his work takes the form of portraiture that he creates based on photos of individuals. By contrast, Ellefson calls himself a potter because of its less "pretentious" connotations, he explained to me. His ceramic objects focus on the urn and its narrative potential.

Together we created Arc, a machine that variously reproduces the actions and intensions of makers based on the computational analysis of surrounding gestures and sound. The machine consists of three parts: first, a mechanism that analyzes sound and gesture data captured by simple sensors; second, a custom engraving instrument that sculpts material on the potter's wheel in response to this analysis; and third, an interface for changing the sensitivity of the machine and software algorithms. For example, a maker can shift the association between pitch, volume, and gesture by repositioning a lever on a mobile phone interface. That interface then wirelessly communicates this analysis to the engraving mechanism. In early versions of the machine, the software focused on gesture alone. In response, Miller and Ellefson noted the machine's impoverished ability to mimic the hand. But once it involved mimicry of sound, the artisans read new possibilities. "You can record conversations on there," Miller told me as he created a pot with our design team (see Figure 52.2). Ellefson found the final version of Arc compelling for its variety of soft, vivid layers that contrasted with its initial version, which, he explained to me, "felt kind of like a ticker tape machine."

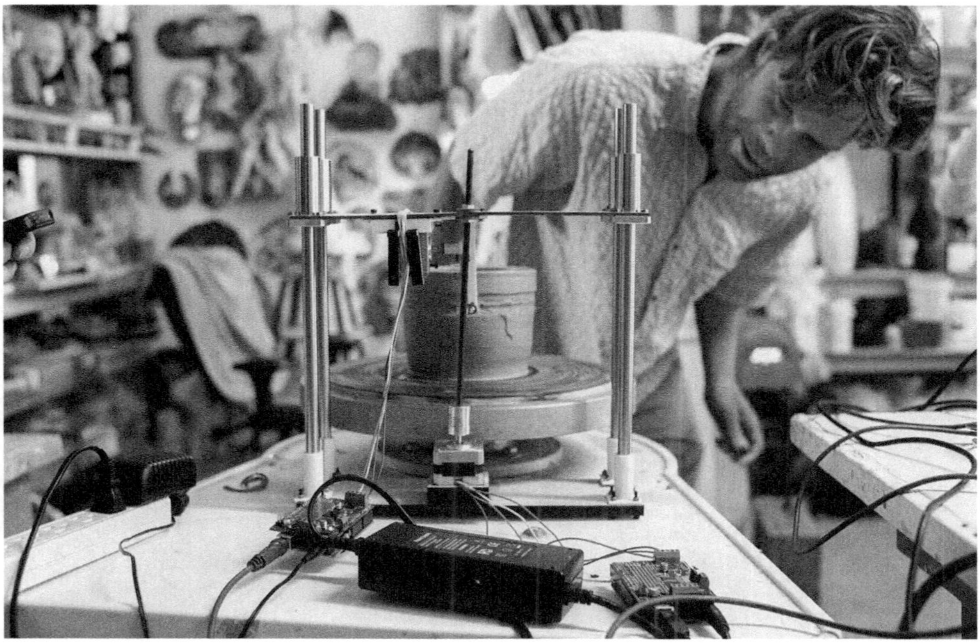

Figure 52.1 Ceramic artist Adrien Miller watches the Arc engraving tool, placed on top of his own pottery wheel, move across the clay as he gestures around it.

Source: Thomas Tran.

Figure 52.2 Ceramic artist Adrien Miller inspects the ceramic vessel he made with Arc.

Source: Thomas Tran.

Figure 52.3 Design and ethnography team (John Ellefson, Daniela Rosner, and Hidekazu Saegusa) discuss early experiments around the Arc machinery.

Source: Thomas Tran.

We developed Arc to explore responses to emerging practices around ceramic tooling (Saegusa et al. 2016; see Figure 52.3). As a medium that integrates manual, mechanical, and digital production, ceramics offers some interesting features for digital fabrication. Artist Geoffrey Mann's *Crossfire*, for example, uses 3-D printers to create ceramic vessels that visualize the sound of an argument passing through them. From encoding audio tracks in ceramic bowls (Rosner et al. 2015) to playing audio-recorded stories from ceramic vessels (Green Eyl 2009), clay blurs a contested boundary between craftsmanship and digital production. Here, Arc displays multiple roles in the workshop: as copier, translator, and connector. As copier, Arc reproduces the actions that came before, making precision and scope core concerns. As translator, Arc listens selectively to the digital descriptions of 3-D form, suggesting fabrication relies on ambiguity, neglect, and resistance. And as connector, Arc enlivens ideas of what fabricators could become—possibly an assistive tool for those living with limb loss, for example. By occupying the intellectual borderlands of technics and handwork, our project considers fabrication as a mode of inquiry, offering a window into the sociotechnical imagination of craft.

Situating Digital Production in Histories of the Mimetic Machine

Like the systems that came before them, emerging forms of digital production reproduce the workings of older technological ensembles. Film cameras create analogies with the phenomena depicted by moving imagery, and sound recorders apprehend the same from audio traces. In the projects above, KidCAD assumed a role similar to the photocopier, creating momentary links with an existing object. FreeD followed a standardized format much like Jonathan Sterne's (2012) descriptions of early audio recordings, selectively listening to (or ignoring) the gestures of the hand. Arc operated through negotiation and surprise, providing moments for reproduction, translation, and connection, and moments for overriding them. This machinery comprised a range of apparatuses, from engraving and etching to sonography and sound compression.

Across these projects, digital production took its power from the copy, a mystical sensuousness that Walter Benjamin calls "aura" in the context of cherished artworks (1978: 222–26). Michael Taussig sees the copy's capture and extraction of magic from the original as an explanation for how it produces a "fetishlike power" (1993: 59)—the growing urge, in Benjamin's words, "to get hold of an object at very close range by the way of its likeness" (1978: 223). Mimesis, Taussig argues (through Benjamin), long played a central role in ritual ceremonies within ancient societies. So, too, he asserts, has it impacted the ritual of modern machinery. What emerges from this two-part mimicry is a simultaneously historical and modernist ideal: the compulsion to act as someone or something else. Magic exists only to be subsequently extracted by technical means.

This argument recalls a rich literature on the magic of technological production emerging in histories of engineering and scientific infrastructure. Tracing the establishment of the American electrical industry in the late 1880s, historian Carolyn Marvin points to the audience emerging around electrical engineers (1990: 56). In a cry for public sympathy, this "scientific priesthood," in Marvin's terms, grew aware of their audience's affection for magic and myth. From this, Marvin surmises that, "[a]lthough an express mission of science was to kill magic and myth, electrical experts were deeply implicated in the production of both" (56). A yearning for spectacle remained strong. In a parallel analysis, David Nye traces this technological appeal to early American engineering achievements. Nearly a century after Marvin's sympathetic scientific priesthood, crowds gathering to celebrate the San Francisco Golden Gate Bridge led the bridge to sway and buckle, Nye explains (1994: xi). Unprepared for the unprecedented public turnout, officials perilously overlooked concerns for what Nye calls the "technological sublime," which concerns the representation of engineering developments as emblems of divinity. Water wheels display the same characteristics as the Grand Canyon as well as less engineered natural attractions such as Yellowstone National Park and Niagara (23). Vincent Mosco brings these themes into a sociology of cyberspace in his characterization of the "digital sublime," the magnetic power of the internet, which both enables and contributes to the enactment of myth (2005: 32). Building on Mosco's ideas, Morgan Ames (2014; 2015) introduces the term "charismatic technology" to describe the "uncanny holding power that some technologies seem to have" (2015: 1). She points to the Massachusetts Institute of Technology's One Laptop Per Child (OLPC) project's XO laptop as an artifact with this "charismatic authority" (after Weber 1947), highlighting the drawbacks of relying on the desires of MIT engineers to make the world in their own image (Ames 2014; 2015). Across these concepts—from scientific priesthood to charismatic technology—digital production is steeped in spectacle.

Yet, do the metaphors of "capture" and "extraction" comprise a persuasive paradigm for media studies? Do they help us make sense of this magic and spectacle? Borrowing from Taussig, the copy suggests "something ineffable is being 'brought out' by this interaction of miming bodies and mimetic machinery" (1993: 244): a magical correspondence with the original via engagement with digital tools. However, is something also *inscribed* in materials and then read back or "de-scribed" from them (Akrich 1992)? Is something *revealed* against Heideggerian (1977) background practices (those dominant ways of acting and speaking)? Is something *performed* in line with Butler's (1990) concern for the materialization of sexed bodies? Is something brought into being through—recalling Barad's (2007) attention to the mutual constitution of meaning and matter—its *entanglement* of tools and bodies?

Or what if we instead followed the logic of versions? Mary Ann Doane, for instance, provides an instructive example in her analysis of cinematic archives—collections that maintain "the aura of the original" film but rely on print and digital copies, or "copies without an original" (2002: 222). Further troubling concerns for originality and durability, Wendy Chun points to software as always open to iteration and alteration, just as its source code purportedly translates instructions in "dead repetition" (2011: 25). For historians of media, the "original" and "copy" flow from task-based interactions that tend to rationalize progress by giving the modern a historical referent.

Locating Fabrication in Theaters of Design Inquiry

Put in historical relief, the above projects suggest a *performative* mode to design. Rather than considering it a part of task-based production, design works as a theater of (re)production. This perspective helps scholars of media understand digital outputs as more than mere copies of an original toy or model. Digital prints (here, a KidCAD print, a FreeD sketch, or an Arc bowl) also evidence the moment of contact made with a phenomenon. This form of contagion—or what anthropologist James George Frazer (2004 [1890]) calls the "Law of Contact"—represents a crucial aspect of integration. The instrumental "user tests" of KidCAD and FreeD resemble Jonathan Sterne's description of early audio encoding listening tests, aiming to transcend their context to build a "universally communicable" format (2012: 153). The Arc project, by contrast, aims to examine its contexts of production, inviting interrogation of its specificity and communicable form (as copier, translator, and connector).

In locating fabrication in a performance of collaborative inquiry, this chapter asks scholars of media and technology to mutually engage their sites of study. This way of getting hold of the digital medium demands tactile intervention. It requires scholars to acknowledge an indefinable tactility of vision that often develops from habit and tacit appropriation (Benjamin 1978: 240). By talking about knowing something, we put ourselves (the knowers) in relation to that thing. In doing so, we create a kind of "relating to" that displaces the concept of "knowing" (Taussig 1993: 26), complicating the logics of "extraction" and "capture" that knowing inhabits. Examining exactly how "relating to" involves tactility calls for different approaches to studying algorithmic cultures. This interventionist, integrative approach to design-as-inquiry begins to address this plea: taking tactility more seriously—as an experience just as central as, and no less mediated than, vision or hearing—in the interrogation of our social world. Confronting the mimetic faculty of fabrication allows media scholars to pull back from the productivist framings of KidCAD and FreeD to use digital fabrication as a tool for comparing craft subjectivities—exposing their resistances, margins, and edges.

My objective here has been to create an account of digital fabrication that helps enrich a budding field of interventionist work across digital humanities and media studies. Toward this end, I have tried to impart some conceptual background and design exemplars and also outline their relation. Although the three projects presented above have different aims, they share a similar potential: suggesting new conceptual pathways emerge when we frame a design project as a mode of inquiry. We learn how machines not only draw readily and repeatedly on the spectacle, but also frame techne as a common ideal. Intersecting histories of technological magic with digital intervention, they serve as a backdrop for "mimetic machinery," exposing the limits of "capture" and "extraction" for explaining the shifting agency of the maker and machine.

Acknowledgments

I would like to thank Adrien Miller, John Ellefson, Hidekazu Saegusa, Thomas Tran, and the grants supported provided under NSF #1453329, NSF #1423074, and NSF #1523579.

Further Reading

Agre, P. (1997) *Computation and Human Experience*, New York, NY: Cambridge University Press.
DiSalvo, C. (2012) *Adversarial Design*, Cambridge, MA: MIT Press.
Lury, C. and N. Wakeford (eds.) (2012) *Inventive Methods: The Happening of the Social*, New York, NY: Routledge.

References

Akrich, M. (1992) "The De-Scription of Technical Objects," in W. E. Bijker and J. Law (eds.) *Shaping Technology/Building Society*, Cambridge, MA: MIT Press, pp. 205–24.
Ames, M. G., J. Bardzell, S. Bardzell, S. Lindtner, D. A. Mellis, and D. K. Rosner (2014) "Making Cultures: Empowerment, Participation, and Democracy—or Not?" in *CHI'14 Extended Abstracts on Human Factors in Computing Systems*, pp. 1087–92.
Ames, M. (2014) "10 Translating Magic: The Charisma of One Laptop per Child's XO Laptop in Paraguay," *Beyond Imported Magic: Essays on Science, Technology, and Society in Latin America*, Cambridge, MA: MIT Press, p. 207.
Ames, M. (2015) "Charismatic Technology," *Aarhus '15*, Critical Alternatives, retrieved from webfiles.uci.edu/mgames/research/Ames-charisma-aarhus.pdf.
Anderson, C. (2012) *Makers: The New Industrial Revolution*, New York, NY: Crown Business.
Barad, K. (2007) *Meeting the Universe Halfway: Quantum Physics and the Entanglement of Matter and Meaning*, Durham and London: Duke University Press.
Bean, J. and D. K. Rosner (2014) "Making: Movement or Brand?" *interactions* 21(1), pp. 26–27.
Benjamin, W. (1978) "On the Mimetic Faculty," in P. Demetz (ed.) and E. Jephcott (trans.) *Reflections*, New York, NY: Schocken Books, p. 334.
Benjamin, W. (2007 [1968]) *Illuminations*, H. Arendt (ed.) and H. Zohn (trans), New York, NY: Schocken Books.
Bennett, C. L., K. Cen, K. M. Steele, and D. K. Rosner (2016). "An Intimate Laboratory?: Prostheses as a Tool for Experimenting with Identity and Normalcy," in *Proceedings of the 2016 CHI Conference on Human Factors in Computing Systems*, pp. 1745–56.
Buechley, L. (2016) "A Critical Look at Making," *FabLearn* Conference, Stanford, CA: Stanford University.
Butler, J. (1990) *Gender Trouble: Feminism and the Subversion of Identity*, New York, NY: Routledge.
Cheatle, A. and S. J. Jackson (2015) "Digital Entanglements: Craft, Computation and Collaboration in Fine Art Furniture Production," in *Proceedings of the 18th ACM Conference on Computer Supported Cooperative Work & Social Computing*, New York, NY: ACM, pp. 958–68.
Chun, W. H. K. (2011) *Programmed Visions: Software and Memory*, Cambridge: MIT Press.
de Laet, M. and A. Mol. (2000) "The Zimbabwe Bush Pump: Mechanics of a Fluid Technology." *Social Studies of Science* 30(2), 225–63.
DiSalvo, C. (2012) *Adversarial Design*, Cambridge, MA: MIT Press.
Doane, M. A. (2002) *The Emergence of Cinematic Time: Modernity, Contingency, the Archive*, Cambridge, MA: Harvard University Press.
Dunne, A. and F. Raby (2013) *Speculative Everything: Design, Fiction, and Social Dreaming*, Cambridge, MA: MIT Press.
Ellefson, J. (2015) Interview with Daniela Rosner, 22 June/13 July.
Elliott, D., R. MacDougall, and W. J. Turkel (2012) "New Old Things: Fabrication, Physical Computing, and Experiment in Historical Practice," *Canadian Journal of Communication* 37(1), 121–28.
Follmer, S., and H. Ishii (2012) "KidCAD: Digitally Remixing Toys through Tangible Tools," in *Proceedings of the SIGCHI Conference on Human Factors in Computing Systems*, New York, NY: ACM, pp. 2401–10.
Frazer, J. G. (2004 [1890]) *The Golden Bough*, NuVision Publications, LLC.
Galey, A. and S. Ruecker (2010) "How a Prototype Argues," *Literary and Linguistic Computing* 25(4), 405–24.
Gauntlett, D. (2011) *Making Is Connecting*, Cambridge, UK: Polity.
Goodman, E. S. (2013) "Delivering Design: Performance and Materiality in Professional Interaction Design," dissertation, Berkeley, CA: University of California.
Green Eyl (2009) *Whispering Table*, retrieved from thegreeneyl.com/whispering-table.
Hancock, C., C. Hichar, C. Holl-Jensen, K. Kraus, C. Mozafari, and K. Skutlin (2013) "Bibliocircuitry and the Design of the Alien Everyday," *Textual Cultures: Texts, Contexts, Interpretation* 8(1), 72–100.

Hatch, M. (2014) *The Maker Movement Manifesto: Rules for Innovation in the New World of Crafters, Hackers, and Tinkerers*, New York, NY: McGraw-Hill Education.

Heidegger, M. (1977) *The Question Concerning Technology and Other Essays*, W. Lovitt (trans.), New York, NY: Garland Publishing

Jackson, S. J. and L. Kang (2014) "Breakdown, Obsolescence and Reuse: HCI and the Art of Repair," in *Proceedings of the 32nd Annual ACM Conference on Human Factors in Computing Systems*, New York, NY: AMC, pp. 449–58.

Jungnickel, K. (2015) "Sewing as a Design Method," *interactions* 22(6) (2015), pp. 72–75.

Lang, D. and R. Demarest (2013) *Zero to Maker: Learn (Just Enough) to Make (Just About) Anything*, Sebastopol, CA: Maker Media.

Levine, F. and C. Heimerl (2008) *Handmade Nation: The Rise of DIY, Art, Craft, and Design*, New York, NY: Princeton Architectural Press.

Markoff, J. (2010) "Google Cars Drive Themselves, in Traffic," *New York Times*, 9 October.

Marvin, C. (1990) *When Old Technologies Were New: Thinking about Electric Communication in the Late Nineteenth Century*, Oxford: Oxford University Press.

McCullough, M. (1998) *Abstracting Craft: The Practiced Digital Hand*, Cambridge, MA: MIT Press.

Miller, A. (2015) Fieldnotes from visit with Daniela Rosner, 13 July.

Mosco, V. (2005) *The Digital Sublime: Myth, Power, and Cyberspace*, Cambridge, MA: MIT Press.

Nye, D. E. (1994) *American Technological Sublime*, Cambridge, MA: MIT Press.

Ratto, M. (2011) "Critical Making: Conceptual and Material Studies in Technology and Social Life," *The Information Society* 27(4), 252–60.

Reed, A. (2016) "Craft and Care: The Maker Movement, Catherine Blake, and the Digital Humanities," *Essays in Romanticism* 23(1), pp. 23–38.

Roedl, D., S. Bardzell, and J. Bardzell (2015) "Sustainable Making? Balancing Optimism and Criticism in HCI Discourse," *ACM Transactions on Computer Human Interaction* 22(3), 15.

Rosner, D. K., M. Ikemiya, and T. Regan (2015) "Resisting Alignment: Code and Clay," in *Proceedings of the Ninth International Conference on Tangible, Embedded, and Embodied Interaction*, New York, NY: ACM, pp. 181–88.

Rosner, D. K., and S. E. Fox. (2016) "Legacies of Craft and the Centrality of Failure in a Mother-operated Hackerspace," *New Media & Society* 18(4), 558–80.

Rosner, D. K. and F. Turner (2015) "Theaters of Alternative Industry: Hobbyist Repair Collectives and the Legacy of the 1960s American Counterculture," in *Design Thinking Research*, New York: Springer International Publishing, pp. 59–69.

Saegusa, H., T. Tran, and D. K. Rosner (2016) "Mimetic Machines: Collaborative Interventions in Digital Fabrication with Arc," in *Proceedings of the 2016 CHI Conference on Human Factors in Computing Systems*, pp. 6008–13.

SketchChair (2011) retrieved from www.sketchchair.cc.

Sterne, J. (2012) *MP3: The Meaning of a Format*, Durham, NC: Duke University Press.

Suchman, L. (2011) "Anthropological Relocations and the Limits of Design." *Annual Review of Anthropology* 40(1), p. 1.

Tanenbaum, J. G., A. M. Williams, A. Desjardins, and K. Tanenbaum (2013) "Democratizing Technology: Pleasure, Utility and Expressiveness in DIY and Maker Practice," in *Proceedings of the SIGCHI Conference on Human Factors in Computing Systems*, New York, NY: ACM, pp. 2603–12.

Taussig, M. T. (1993) *Mimesis and Alterity: A Particular History of the Senses*, New York, NY: Psychology Press.

Toombs, A. (2015) "Enacting Care through Collaboration in Communities of Makers," in *Proceedings of the 18th ACM Conference Companion on Computer Supported Cooperative Work & Social Computing*, pp. 81–84.

Weber, M. (1947) "Charismatic Authority," in T. Parsons (ed.) *The Theory of Social and Economic Organization*, New York, NY: The Free Press, pp. 358–91.

Zoran, A. and J. A. Paradiso (2013) "FreeD: A Freehand Digital Sculpting Tool," in *Proceedings of the SIGCHI Conference on Human Factors in Computing Systems*, New York, NY: ACM, pp. 2613–16.

GLOSSARY OF ACRONYMS AND INITIALISMS

2-D	two-dimensional
3-D	three-dimensional
4-D	four-dimensional
AbTeC	Aboriginal Territories in Cyberspace
AI	artificial intelligence
AIDS	acquired immune deficiency syndrome
ANVC	Alliance for Networking Visual Culture
API	application programming interface
APL	programming language named after the book, *A Programming Language*
AR	augmented reality
ARG	alternate reality game
ARP Instruments	Alan Robert Pearlman Instruments, Inc.
ASL	average shot length
BASIC	Beginner's All-purpose Symbolic Instruction Code
BMP	bitmap image file
BTEX	benzene, toluene, ethylbenzene, and xylene
CAPTCHA	Completely Automated Public Turing test to tell Computers and Humans Apart
CCS	critical code studies
CD	compact disc
CD-ROM	compact disc read-only memory
CFC	Crunk Feminist Collective
CGI	computer-generated imagery
CNC	computer numerical control
COBOL	COmmon Business-Oriented Language
CPU	central processing unit
CRC	Canada research chair
C-SPAN	Cable-Satellite Public Affairs Network

CSS	Cascading Style Sheets
CSV	comma-separated values
CVR	cockpit voice recorder
CWILA	Canadian Women in the Literary Arts
DAW	digital audio workstation
DCT	discrete cosine transform
DH	digital humanities
DHSI	Digital Humanities Summer Institute
DIO	digital input/output
DIT	do it together
DIWO	doing it with others
DIY	do it yourself
DOCAM	Documentation and Conservation of the Media Arts Heritage
DOCC	distributed open collaborative course
DTD	document type definition
DVD	digital versatile disc or digital video disc
DVD-ROM	digital versatile disc or digital video disc read-only memory
DVR	digital video recorder
EDT	Electronic Disturbance Theater
ELL	Electronic Literature Laboratory
ELMCIP	Electronic Literature as a Model of Creativity and Innovation in Practice
ELO	Electronic Literature Organization
EPUB	e-book file format with the extension .epub
ETC	Experimental Television Center
FCC	Federal Communications Commission
FDR	flight data recorder
fMRI	functional magnetic resonance imaging
FOMO	fear of missing out
FORTRAN	FORmula TRANslation programming language
GCC	GNU compiler collection
GIF	graphics interchange format
GIS	geographic information system
GML	general markup language
GNU	A recursive acronym for "GNU's Not Unix!" (free software containing no Unix code)
GO::DH	Global Outlook::Digital Humanities
GPS	global positioning system
GSM	global system for mobile communications
GUI	graphical user interface
HASTAC	Humanities, Arts, Science and Technology Alliance and Collaboratory
HB recorder	an early attempt, by François Hussenot and Paul Beaudouin, to produce an FDR
HCI	human-computer interaction
HTML	HyperText Markup Language
HTTP	HyperText Transfer Protocol
HUD	heads-up display
HVAC	heating, ventilating/ventilation, and air conditioning

IBM	International Business Machines Corporation
I-CHASS	Institute for Computing in Humanities, Arts, and Social Sciences
ICT	information and communications technology
ICYMI	in case you missed it
IDE	integrated development environment
IML	integer matrix library
IMLS	Institute of Museum and Library Services
INKE	Implementing New Knowledge Environments
INTERCAL	compiler language with no pronounceable acronym
IoT	internet of things
IP	Internet Protocol
IQ	intelligence quotient
IRL	in real life
ISEA	International Symposium on Electronic Art
IT	information technology
JPEG	Joint Photographic Experts Group (a format for image files)
LED	light emitting diode
LGBTGNC	lesbian, gay, bisexual, transgender gender nonconforming
LIDAR	light detection and ranging or light imaging, detection, and ranging
LOC	lines of code
LOL	laugh out loud
M2M	machine-to-machine
Micro-CT	micro-computed tomography
MIT	Massachusetts Institute of Technology
MITH	Maryland Institute for Technology in the Humanities
MLA	Modern Language Association
MoMA	Museum of Modern Art
MOO	MUD object oriented
MOOC	massive open online course
MOU	memorandum of understanding
MP3	MPEG-1 or MPEG-2 Audio Layer III (a format for audio files)
MPEG	Moving Picture Experts Group (a format for various types of media)
MRI	magnetic resonance imaging
MUD	multi-user dungeon, multi-user dimension, and multi-user domain
MUFC	Mandela United Football Club
NEH	National Endowment for the Humanities
NER	named entity recognition
NFC	near-field communication
NO_x	nitrogen oxides
NPR	National Public Radio
O_3	ozone
OCR	optical character recognition
OED	Oxford English Dictionary
OLPC	One Laptop Per Child
PAR	participatory action research
PARC	Palo Alto Research Center Incorporated
PC	personal computer
PHP	recursive acronym for PHP: Hypertext Preprocessor

PICT	a graphics file format native to Macintosh computers
PLC	programmable logic controllers
PM	particulate matter
PM2.5	fine particulate matter
POC	people of color
POI	points of interest
PR	public relations
PSA	public service announcement
QGIS	quantum geographic information systems
QR	quick response code
QS	quantified self
RAF	Royal Air Force
RAM	random-access memory
RAW	rules as written
RFID	radio frequency identification
RGB-D	red, green, and blue, plus depth
RIAA	Recording Industry Association of America
RPG	role-playing game
RTI	reflectance transformation imaging
SES	scaled entity search
SGML	Standard Generalized Markup Language
SHGIS	Soweto Historical Geographic Information System
SIM	subscriber identity module
Soweto	South Western Townships
SOYCO	Soweto Youth Congress
SQL	structured query language
SRLP	Sylvia Rivera Law Project
SRR	Soul Rebel Radio
SSHRC	Social Sciences and Humanities Research Council of Canada
STEAM	science, technology, engineering, arts, and mathematics
STEM	science, technology, engineering, and mathematics
STS	science and technology studies
SXSW	South by Southwest
TBT	Transborder Immigrant Tool
TEACH Act	The Technology, Education and Copyright Harmonization Act
TED	Technology, Enterprise, Design
TEI	Text Encoding Initiative
TF-IDF	term frequency-inverse document frequency
THATCamp	The Humanities And Technology Camp
TIFF	Tagged Image File Format
TOS	terms of service
TRC	Truth and Reconciliation Commission
TV	television
TXT	a filename extension for text files
U.K.	United Kingdom of Great Britain and Northern Ireland
UMTS	universal mobile telephone system
URL	uniform (or universal) resource locator
U.S.	United States of America

V&A	Victoria and Albert Museum
VAT	Video Analysis Tableau
VCR	videocassette recorder
VIAF	Virtual International Authority File
VOC	volatile organic compound
VR	virtual reality
VRML	Virtual Reality Modeling Language or Virtual Reality Markup Language
WebGL	Web Graphics Library
WELL	Whole Earth 'Lectronic Link
WT	wearable technology
WWR	Women Who Rock
WWW	World Wide Web
WYSIWYG	what you see is what you get
XML	Extensible Markup Language
XSEDE	Extreme Science and Engineering Discovery Environment
ZKM	Center for Art and Media Technology, or Zentrum für Kunst und Medientechnologie Karlsruhe

GLOSSARY OF PROJECTS

#BlackLivesMatter: "[A]n online forum intended to build connections between Black people and our allies to fight anti-Black racism, to spark dialogue among Black people, and to facilitate the types of connections necessary to encourage social action and engagement." *See* blacklivesmatter.com and twitter.com/hashtag/blacklivesmatter.

#FeesMustFall: The Twitter hashtag associated with a protest movement that began in October 2015 in response to increasing fees at South African universities. *See* twitter.com/hashtag/feesmustfall.

#FemDH: The Twitter hashtag for an annual course at the University of Victoria's Digital Humanities Summer Institute titled, "Feminist Digital Humanities: Theoretical, Social, and Material Engagements." *See* twitter.com/hashtag/femdh.

#Ferguson: The Twitter hashtag associated with events in Ferguson, Missouri following the fatal shooting of Michael Brown by police officer, Darren Wilson, on August 9, 2014. *See* twitter.com/hashtag/ferguson.

#Gamergate: The Twitter hashtag associated with a harassment campaign concerning sexism in videogame culture. *See* twitter.com/hashtag/gamergate.

#RhodesMustFall: The Twitter hashtag associated with a protest movement directed against a statue that commemorates Cecil Rhodes at the University of Cape Town (UCT). *See* twitter.com/hashtag/rhodesmustfall.

#TransformDH: "[A]n academic guerrilla movement seeking to (re)define capital-letter Digital Humanities as a force for transformative scholarship by collecting, sharing, and highlighting projects that push at its boundaries and work for social justice, accessibility, and inclusion." *See* transformdh.org.

#TransHealthcareNOW: A social media campaign launched by Reina Gossett and other members of the Sylvia Rivera Law Project following their attendance at HX Refactored, a health care conference in New York City. *See* www.reinagossett.com/transhealthcarenow.

#YesWeCode: "[A] Dream Corps initiative that works with partners to help connect 100,000 underrepresented minorities to careers in technology." *See* www.yeswecode.org.

4'33": A mid-twentieth-century composition by experimental composer, John Cage. The score instructs performers to not play their instruments during the performance.

9/11 Memorial Museum: "The 9/11 Memorial Museum serves as the country's principal institution concerned with exploring the implications of the events of 9/11, documenting the impact of those events and exploring 9/11's continuing significance." *See* www.911 memorial.org/museum.

ActionScript: An object-oriented programming language originally designed to provide rich interactive abilities to the Adobe Flash Player platform, developed by Macromedia Inc.

Adobe Flash: "[T]he standard for delivering high-impact, rich Web content. Designs, animation, and application user interfaces are deployed immediately across all browsers and platforms, attracting and engaging users with a rich Web experience." *See* www. adobe.com/software/flash/about.

Adventure Game Studio: "[A] freeware tool that can be used to create both free and commercial graphical adventure games." *See* www.adventuregamestudio.co.uk.

afternoon, a story: An early piece of hypertext fiction by Michael Joyce (1987), published by Eastgate Systems in 1990. *See* www.wwnorton.com/college/english/pmaf/hypertext/ aft/index.html.

AIDS Quilt Touch: A mobile web app in development, and a collaboration between the University of Iowa Digital Studio for Public Humanities, The New School, and NAMES Project Foundation. *See* aidsquilttouch.org.

Air Casting: "[A]n open-source, end-to-end solution for collecting, displaying, and sharing health and environmental data using your smartphone. The platform consists of wearable sensors that detect changes in your environment and physiology, including a palm-sized air quality monitor." *See* aircasting.org.

Air Quality Egg: "A community-led air quality sensing network that gives people a way to participate in the conversation about air quality . . . The Air Quality Egg is a sensor system designed to allow anyone to collect very high resolution readings of NO2 and CO concentrations outside of their home." *See* airqualityegg.com.

Algorhythmic Sorting: "[A]n open source program and learning tool for people, who want to learn and analyze the diversity of sorting algorithms by hearing the different rhythmic and pattern generating behaviour of different sorting algorithms like bubble sort, merge sort, quick sort or heap sort and others." *See* sourceforge.net/projects/algorthythmics.

An Algorithm Audit: A collaborative proposal to audit online platforms. "These audits will ascertain whether algorithms result in harmful discrimination by class, race, gender, geography, or other important attributes." *See* www-personal.umich.edu/~csandvig/research/ An%20Algorithm%20Audit.pdf.

Alice Bag's website: "The official website of Alice Bag: musician, author, punk feminist, master troublemaker." *See* alicebag.com.

Alice in Dataland: "[A]n experiment in critical making created by Anastasia Salter . . . The project leverages material from the University of Florida *Afterlife of Alice & Her Adventures in Wonderland* collection as well as a range of Alice adaptations and remediations." *See* kairos.technorhetoric.net/20.1/inventio/salter/index.html.

Allied Media Conference: "Allied Media Projects cultivates media strategies for a more just, creative and collaborative world." *See* www.alliedmedia.org/amc.

Alvin Lucier Cover: Jonathan Sterne's cover of Alvin Lucier's "I Am Sitting in a Room" in which he repeatedly ran a recording through an MP3 encoder until it was over 50 minutes long. *See* sounds.sterneworks.org/projects/alvin-lucier-cover.

Amara: "Amara is home to an award winning subtitle editor that makes it easy to caption and translate video." *See* www.amara.org/en.

American Radio History: "[A] resource with thousands of publications about Broadcasting, Radio, TV, programming, electronics and ratings." *See* AmericanRadioHistory.com.

Amsterdam Smart Citizens Lab: "In the Smart Citizens Lab we explore tools and applications to map the world around us. Along with citizens, scientists, and designers, we deal with themes ranging from air quality to the conditions of bathing water to noise pollution." *See* waag.org/en/lab/amsterdam-smart-citizens-lab.

Analog Tara / Pink Noises: A collection of projects by Tara Rodgers (Analog Tara), "composer, historian and critic of electronic music, originally from upstate New York and now based in the Washington, DC area." *See* www.analogtara.net/wp/projects.

anarchive: "[A] series of interactive multi-media projects designed to explore an artist's overall oeuvre via diverse archival material." *See* www.anarchive.net/indexeng.htm.

Ancient Lives: "[A] project that asks volunteers to transcribe ancient Greek text on fragments from the Oxyrhynchus Papyri collection." *See* ancientlives.org.

Angels and Insects: An album by David Dunn (1992) containing *Tabula Angelorum Bonorum 49*, "a suite of seven pieces for computer-processed speaking voices based on the mystical work of Elizabethan alchemist John Dee" and *Chaos & the Emergent Mind of the Pond*, "made from field recordings of aquatic insect sounds." *See* www.nseq.org/releases/angels-insects.

A.nnotate: "[A]n online annotation, collaboration and indexing system for documents and images, supporting PDF, Word and other document formats." *See* a.nnotate.com.

Anthology of European Electronic Literature: From the ELMCIP researchers at the Blekinge Institute of Technology in Sweden, "the anthology is intended to provide educators, students and the general public with a free curricular resource of electronic literary works produced in Europe." *See* anthology.elmcip.net.

ANVIL: "[A] free video annotation tool, developed by Michael Kipp. It offers multi-layered annotation based on a user-defined coding scheme." *See* www.anvil-software.org.

APL: A Programming Language (APL) is a general-purpose programming language developed by Kenneth E. Iverson in the 1960s.

Arc: "A computer numerical controlled (CNC) engraving tool for ceramics. It offers a new window [into] traditional forms of craft . . . [by showing] that fabrication tools may integrate multiple, distinct roles." *See* faculty.washington.edu/dkrosner/craft.html.

ArcGIS: "Make and share beautiful maps, and do everything in between. It's possible only with ArcGIS Online, a scalable and secure software-as-a-service hosted by Esri." *See* www.arcgis.com/features/index.html.

Arduino: "[A]n open-source prototyping platform based on easy-to-use hardware and software." *See* www.arduino.cc.

ARIS: "[A] user-friendly, open-source platform for creating and playing mobile games, tours and interactive stories. Using GPS and QR Codes, ARIS players experience a hybrid world of virtual interactive characters, items, and media placed in physical space." *See* arisgames.org.

Around DH in 80 Days: "[A] multi-institutional, interdisciplinary Digital Humanities collaboration that seeks to introduce new and veteran audiences to the *global* field of DH scholarly practice by bringing together current DH projects from around the world." *See* www.arounddh.org.

artintact: "From 1994 to 1999, the Center for Art and Media in Karlsruhe presented pioneering works of interactive media art in the book-with-CD-ROM package entitled *artintact*." *See* on1.zkm.de/zkm/e/projekte/artintact_dvd.

Assassin's Creed: An action-adventure videogame series created by Ubisoft.

Augmented Reality Lab: "Situated in the Faculty of Fine Arts [at York University], the Augmented Reality Lab offers researchers the opportunity to explore new screen technologies, approaches and techniques through both production and theoretical study of this emerging medium." *See* ar.lab.yorku.ca.

Ausentes: "[An] interactive installation composed of printed digital images, neon lights, aluminum frames, six engines, two motion sensors, and PLC (Programmable Logic Controller)" by Isabel Restrepo (2007). *See* www.isabelrestrepo.com/index.php/8-portafolio/11-ausentes.

The Australian Institute for Aboriginal and Torres Strait Islander Studies: "[A] world-renowned research, collections and publishing organisation. We promote knowledge and understanding of Aboriginal and Torres Strait Islander cultures, traditions, languages and stories, past and present." *See* aiatsis.gov.au.

Authoring Software: "[A]n ongoing collection of statements about how writers and artists create electronic literature." *See* www.narrabase.net/judy_malloy.html.

Autonets: "*Local Autonomy Networks (Autonets)* is an artivist project focused on creating networks of communication to increase community autonomy and reduce violence against women, LGBTQI people, people of color and other groups who continue to survive violence on a daily basis." *See* faculty.washington.edu/michamc/autonets.

BASIC: Beginner's All-purpose Symbolic Instruction Code (BASIC) is a simple, high-level programming language designed by John G. Kemeny and Thomas E. Kurtz in the 1960s.

Becoming a Rap Genius: A list of resources related to "Becoming a Rap Genius," a course by Howard Rambsy II. *See* www.culturalfront.org/2013/12/becoming-rap-genius-resources.html.

Berlin Wall 3-D: A Mobile Augmented Reality experience that "puts history into its location context and encourages the interaction with that specific historic site." *See* www.hoppala-agency.com/article/berlin-wall-3d.

Bikes and Bloomers: An interdisciplinary research project led by Kat Jungnickel "about the bike, bloomer and female cyclist in late nineteenth century Britain." *See* bikesand bloomers.com.

BioShock: A first-person shooter videogame series designed by Ken Levine and developed by Irrational Games." *See* www.2kgames.com/bioshock.

Black Girls Code: A nonprofit organization; "By reaching out to the community through workshops and after school programs, Black Girls CODE introduces computer coding lessons to young girls from underrepresented communities in programming languages such as Scratch or Ruby on Rails." *See* www.blackgirlscode.com.

Blackfoot Digital Library: "[A] venue for sharing [Blackfoot family and community] stories, past and present. Most certainly it is intended to be an educational resource for all those now living in kitawahsinnoon." *See* www.blackfootdigitallibrary.com.

Bodyfuck: An adaptation of the Brainfuck programming language by Nik Hanselmann "that uses a camera as input." *See* nik.works/project/bodyfuck.

Book of Shadows: "A CD-ROM and book (64 pages b&w) titled 'Book of Shadows' released March 1996." *See* littlepig.org.uk/bos/index.htm.

Bookshare.org: "Bookshare opens up the world of reading for people with print disabilities . . . [and] offers the world's largest collection of accessible titles." *See* www.bookshare.org.

Brainfuck: An esoteric programming language created by Urban Müller in 1993, notable for its extreme minimalism.

Bronze: "A fractured fairy tale" piece of interactive fiction by Emily Short. *See* inform7.com/learn/eg/bronze/index.html.

Buffalo: The Name Dropping Game: "A card game of quick wits and zany combinations, *buffalo: the name dropping game* asks you to name-drop faster than your friends, collect the most cards, and win!" *See* www.tiltfactor.org/game/buffalo.

Build a Better Panel: Women in DH: A crowdsourced list of women who "you might invite for a keynote or other [DH related] conference event." *See* jwernimont.com/2015/09/19/build-a-better-panel-women-in-dh.

Burning the Interface: "[An] exhibition at the Museum of Contemporary Art, Sydney, curated by Mike Leggett and Linda Michael" (March–July 1996). *See* www.mikeleggett.com.au/projects/burning-interfaceinternational-artists-CD-ROM.

C: A high-level, procedural computer programming language originally developed for the UNIX operating system.

Canadian Women in the Literary Arts (CWILA): "[A]n inclusive national literary organization for people who share feminist values and see the importance of gender equity in Canadian literary culture." *See* cwila.com.

Center for Solutions to Online Violence: "[A] virtual hub for a distributed community working to address the myriad forms of violence drive designed to women offline." *See* sites.google.com/a/asu.edu/center-for-solutions-to-online-violence.

Chaos Cinema: A video essay by Matthias Stork that chronicles "[t]he decline and fall of action filmmaking." *See* video-cdn.indiewire.com/previews/0wKZtpxn-PbCxl3wn.

Charleston Syllabus: "[A] a list of readings that educators can use to broach conversations in the classroom about the horrendous events that unfolded in Charleston, South Carolina on the evening of June 17, 2015." *See* www.aaihs.org/resources/charleston syllabus.

Chicana por mi Raza: Uncovering the Hidden History of Chicana Feminism (1965–1985): "[A] public humanities project centered on the collection and digital preservation of archival materials, ephemera, and oral histories that document the development of Chicana feminist thought during the civil rights era." *See* chicanapor miraza.org.

Chicas Rockeras of Southest Los Angeles: "[A] day camp where girls ages 8–17 explore the joys and challenges of collaborative music-making while guided by inspirational female mentors." *See* www.chicasrockerassela.org.

Chronicles: "*Chronicles*, an extension of the *Pathfinders* project, focuses on *Chrono Trigger*, a video game, and applies best practices and methodologies from *Pathfinders* in order to capture and preserve these playing experiences, as well as document the articulation of culture in video games for generations to come." *See* scalar.usc.edu/works/chronicles/index.

Chrono Trigger: A role-playing videogame developed in 1995 for Super Nintendo and published by Square.

Cinemetrics: "Cinemetrics tools not only let one record data to analyze movies . . . but also publishes the gathered data on this web site for everyone to access. This is a collaborative project." *See* www.cinemetrics.lv.

Citizen Sense: A project led by Jennifer Gabrys that "investigates the relationship between technologies and practices of environmental sensing and citizen engagement." *See* www.citizensense.net.

Citizen Sense Kit: "The Citizen Sense kit developed in the course of the practice-based research on 'Pollution Sensing' is a response to the concerns of community members, who provided information via Citizen Sense 'logbooks' that asked for input on key environmental and health concerns related to natural gas infrastructure." *See* www.citizensense.net/kits/citizensense-kits.

Citizen Sensor: "[A] DIY and open-source hardware and software initiative to encourage personal and community pollution monitoring." *See* citizensensor.cc.

The Closed Captioning Project: "[A] 501c3 nonprofit dedicated to the improvement and increased accessibility of closed captioned media." *See* www.theclosedcaptioningproject.com.

COBOL: Common Business Oriented Language (COBOL) is a widely used computer programming language designed for business use.

Codecademy: "[A]n education company . . . committed to building the best learning experience inside and out, making Codecademy the best place for our team to learn, teach, and create the online learning experience of the future." *See* www.codecademy.com.

Code.org: "[A] nonprofit dedicated to expanding access to computer science, and increasing participation by women and underrepresented students of color. Our vision is that every student in every school should have the opportunity to learn computer science." *See* code.org.

Code Year: "Code Year takes you on a tour of important web technologies. Learn programming basics with Javascript, then add HTML and CSS to build interactive websites." *See* www.codecademy.com/en/tracks/code-year.

Colossal Cave Adventure: A text adventure game, developed by Will Crowther in 1976.

CommentPress: "[A]n open source theme and plugin for the *WordPress* blogging engine that allows readers to comment paragraph-by-paragraph, line-by-line or block-by-block in the margins of a text." *See* futureofthebook.org/commentpress.

Computational Culture: "[A]n online open-access peer-reviewed journal of inter-disciplinary enquiry into the nature of cultural computational objects, practices, processes and structures." *See* computationalculture.net.

Concret PH: A musique concrète piece by Iannis Xenakis, created and originally played in the Philips Pavilion at Expo 58.

Conditionally Accepted: "[A] career advice column for Inside Higher Ed . . . [that provides] news, information, personal stories, and resources for scholars who are, at best, conditionally accepted in academe." *See* www.insidehighered.com/users/conditionally-accepted.

Contact Zones: The Art of CD-ROM: A travelling exhibition curated by Timothy Murray (1999–2001). *See* contactzones.cit.cornell.edu/index.html.

Crash Override Network: "[A] crisis helpline, advocacy group and resource center for people who are experiencing online abuse." *See* www.crashoverridenetwork.com.

Critical Art Ensemble: "(CAE) is a collective of five tactical media practitioners of various specializations including computer graphics and web design, film/video, photography, text art, book art, and performance." *See* www.critical-art.net.

Critical Code Studies Working Groups: "Based at the University of Southern California, the HaCCS Lab [promotes] the development of critical vocabulary, case studies, and cross-disciplinary dialogue, specifically between the humanities and computer science." *See* haccslab.com/?cat=4.

Critical Making Lab: "The critical making laboratory is a shared space for opening up the practice of experimentation with embedded and material digital technology to students and faculty in the Faculty of Information [at the University of Toronto]." *See* criticalmaking.com.

Crunk Feminist Collective: "[A] space of support and camaraderie for hip hop generation feminists of color, queer and straight, in the academy and without." *See* www.crunkfeministcollective.com.

CSS: Cascading Style Sheets (CSS) is a style sheet language used to describe the layout of webpages written in a markup language.

CTheory Multimedia: "[A]n active collaboration of artists, programmers, and theorists who navigate the codes and anti-codes of digital organs in virtual space." *See* ctheory multimedia.cornell.edu.

CUNY Academic Commons: "[D]esigned to support faculty initiatives and build community through the use(s) of technology in teaching and learning." *See* commons.gc.cuny.edu.

Cyberflesh Girlmonster: An interactive animated "macabre comedy of monstrous femininity, of revenge, desire and violence." *See* www.lindadement.com/cyberflesh-girlmonster.htm.

Dames Making Games: "DMG is a not-for-profit feminist organization dedicated to supporting dames interested in making, playing, and changing games." *See* dmg.to.

Day of DH 2015: "[A]n open community publication project that will bring together scholars interested in the digital humanities from around the world to document what they do on one day" with the goal of creating "a web site that weaves together a picture of the participant's activities on the day which answers the question, 'Just what do digital humanists really do?'" *See* dayofdh2015.uned.es.

Deep Listening Institute: "Deep Listening Institute (DLI) promotes the music and Deep Listening practice of pioneer composer Pauline Oliveros, providing a unique approach to music, literature, art, meditation, technology and healing." *See* deeplistening.org/site.

Defense Distributed: A Texas corporation organized to "defend the human and civil right to keep and bear arms as guaranteed by the United States Constitution and affirmed by the United States Supreme Court; to collaboratively produce, publish, and distribute to the public information and knowledge related to the digital manufacture of arms." *See* defdist.org.

Desilusiones Ópticas: "Optical Delusions" is an interactive installation that recalls Argentina's celebrations during the 1978 World Cup. *See* www.leonunez.com.ar/desilusionesO.html.

Dickinson Electronic Archives: "A creative and critical collaboratory for reading Dickinson's material bodies and for featuring new critical and theoretical work about Emily Dickinson's writings, biography, reception, and influence." *See* www.emily dickinson.org.

Digital Africana Studies: A course offered by Bryan Carter, "exploring the intersections between African studies, technology, and digital humanities." *See* ibryancarter.com/dr-cs-classes.

Digital Archive of Japan's 2011 Disasters: "[A]n evolving, collaborative space for citizens, researchers, students, and policy makers, and a site of shared memory for those most directly affected by these events." *See* www.jdarchive.org/en/home.

Digital Dirt: "Digital Dirt is the first in a series of multimedia events curated by Arthur & Marilouise Kroker, editors of the electronic journal *CTheory*. Digital Dirt brings together electronic artists, new media designers, hyperdance performers, digital musicians, video makers, robotic visionaries and fleshmatic theorists." *See* ctheorymultimedia.cornell.edu/issue1/digidirt.htm.

Digital Durham: "The Digital Durham archive brings together numerous documents, maps, images, census data, and other primary source materials in a digital form accessible and searchable from the web." *See* web.duke.edu/digitaldurham and www.dukewired.org/projects/digital-durham-2.

Dorkbot: "[A] group of affiliated organizations worldwide that sponsor *grassroots* meetings of artists, engineers, designers, scientists, inventors, and anyone else working under the very broad umbrella of *electronic art*." *See* dorkbot.org.

Dwarf Fortress: "Dwarf Fortress is a part construction and management simulation, part rogue-like, indie video game created by Tarn and Zach Adams." *See* www.bay12games.com/dwarves.

Dynabook: A conceptual portable educational device, like a laptop computer, with eternal battery life, envisioned by Alan Kay.

the ear goes to sound: A film portrait of electronic sound artist Laetitia Sonami. *See* earsoundfilm.com.

eBlack Studies Workshop: "The first national workshop to launch eBlack Studies was organized and chaired by Abdul Alkalimat and held at the University of Illinois at Urbana-Champaign on July 24–27, 2008." *See* eblackstudies.org/workshop.

Edinburgh Film Festival: "Established in 1947, the Edinburgh International Film Festival is world renowned for discovering and promoting the very best in international cinema—and for heralding and debating changes in global filmmaking." *See* www.edfilmfest.org.uk.

Edmonton Pipelines Project: "[A] collection of digital maps and literary provocations . . . The main objective of the project is to construct a prototype for an interactive digital framework that makes meaning of the open data that the city of Edmonton makes freely available." *See* edmontonpipelines.org.

ELAN: "[A] professional tool for the creation of complex annotations on video and audio resources." *See* tla.mpi.nl/tools/tla-tools/elan.

Electric Dress: "[A] powerful conflation of the tradition of the Japanese komono with modern industrial technology," by Atsuko Tanaka (1957). *See* www.medienkunstnetz.de/works/electric-dress.

Electronic Beowulf: "The long-term goal of the project is to assemble an open-ended electronic archive of materials founded on, but by no means limited to, the only surviving manuscript of *Beowulf* and ancillary texts." *See* people.ucalgary.ca/~scriptor/kiernan/calgary.html.

Electronic Disturbance Theater: "[A] small group of cyber activists and artists engaged in developing the theory and practice of Electronic Civil Disobedience (ECD)." *See* www.thing.net/~rdom/ecd/EDTECD.html.

Electronic Literature Collection, Volume 1: The first volume of collected works released by the Electronic Literature Organization (ELO) in 2006. Editors: N. Katherine Hayles, Nick Montfort, Scott Rettberg, and Stephanie Strickland. *See* collection.eliterature.org/1.

Electronic Literature Collection, Volume 2: The second volume of collected works released by the Electronic Literature Organization (ELO) in 2011. Editors: Laura Borràs, Talan Memmott, Rita Raley, and Brian Stefans . *See* collection.eliterature.org/2.

Electronic Literature Collection, Volume 3: The third volume of collected works released by the Electronic Literature Organization (ELO) in 2016. Editors: Stephanie Boluk, Leonardo Flores, Jacob Garbe, and Anastasia Salter. *See* collection.eliterature.org/3.

Electronic Literature Lab: "Directed by Dr. Dene Grigar, ELL contains 47 vintage Macintosh computers, dating back from 1977 and a library of electronic literary works. It is used for the advanced inquiry into curating, preserving, and the production of born digital literary works." *See* dtc-wsuv.org/wp/ell.

ELIZA: A natural language processing program designed to mimic human interactions, originally developed in the 1960s by Joseph Weizenbaum.

-empyre-soft-skinned space: "[A] global community of new media artists, curators, theorists, producers, and others who participate in monthly thematic discussions via an e-mail listserv." *See* empyre.library.cornell.edu.

Esolang: "This wiki is dedicated to the fostering and documentation of programming languages designed to be unique, difficult to program in, or just plain weird." *See* esolangs.org/wiki/Main_Page.

Ev-ent-anglement: "[A]n experiment in digital embodied collective feminist media praxis . . . We use performance and technology to further entangle events and communities outside the logics of buying and selling." *See* ev-ent-anglement.com.

Evoke: A free, 10-week, social network game designed "to help empower people all over the world to come up with creative solutions to our most urgent social problems." *See* www.urgentevoke.com.

Facebook: A for-profit corporation and online social networking service. *See* www.facebook.com.

Facebook Demetricator: "A web browser extension that hides all the metrics on Facebook." *See* bengrosser.com/projects/facebook-demetricator.

Fashioning Circuits: "The goal of the project is twofold: to explore the ways in which fashion and emerging media intersect and to work with community partners to introduce beginners to making and coding through wearable media." *See* fashioningcircuits.com.

Fembot Collective: "[A] collaboration among faculty, graduate students, media producers, artists, and librarians promoting research on gender, new media and technology." *See* fembotcollective.org.

Feminist Online Spaces: "[A] project aimed at researching, teaching, talking about and otherwise building-towards online spaces that are defined by feminist and other progressive principles of community, visibility, discourse, and politics." *See* www.feministonlinespaces.com.

FemTechNet: "[A]n activated network of hundreds of scholars, students, and artists who work on, with, and at the borders of technology, science, and feminism in a variety of fields including Science and Technology Studies (STS), Media and Visual Studies, Art, Women's, Queer, and Ethnic Studies." *See* femtechnet.org.

FemTechNet Critical Race and Ethnic Studies Pedagogy Workbook: Launched by the Ethnic Studies Committee of FemTechNet and written in Scalar, the "workbook is an ongoing project to build resources for faculty members who are often overburdened at their home institutions, but are willing to take on the difficult task of teaching about gender and racial inequity in our information culture." *See* scalar.usc.edu/works/ftn-ethnic-studies-pedagogy-workbook-/index.

Ferguson Syllabus: A Google Doc intended "to gather resources for learning about the recent events in Ferguson, Missouri." *See* bit.ly/FergusonSyllabus.

Fibreculture Journal: "*The Fibreculture Journal* is a peer reviewed international journal, first published in 2003 to explore issues and ideas within the Fibreculture network." *See* fibreculturejournal.org.

Find the Future: The Game: An interactive experience that "combines real-world missions with virtual clues and online collaboration—all inspired by 100 works from the amazing collections of The New York Public Library." *See* exhibitions.nypl.org/100/digital_fun/play_the_game.

The First Mouse: "Doug Engelbart invented the computer mouse in the early 1960s in his research lab at Stanford Research Institute (now SRI International). The first prototype was built in 1964, the patent application for this 'X-Y position indicator for a display system' was filed in 1967, and US Patent 3,541,541 was awarded in 1970." *See* www.dougengelbart.org/firsts/mouse.html.

Flow.tv: "Flow is an online journal of television and media studies launched in October 2004, and since then, we have published 1400+ columns by over 700 authors from around the U.S. and the world." *See* www.flowjournal.org.

Forging the Future: "Building on the work of the Variable Media Network, Forging the Future refines and distributes free and open-source products that boost access and aid in preservation, including the Variable Media Questionnaire." *See* forging-the-future.net.

Fortran: A simple programming language well suited to number crunching and scientific procedures, originally developed in the 1950s by IBM.

Frankenstein: "Dave Morris' Frankenstein is an interactive novel that places you right inside the story, acting as Frankenstein's confidant, guide and conscience." *See* www.inklestudios.com/frankenstein.

FreeD: "[A] handheld augmented device that allows you to carve and sculpt manually with your hands without knowledge or skill in this process." *See* video.mit.edu/watch/the-freed-mit-smart-tools-meld-personal-technique-with-computerized-controls-26502.

Fun with Software: "In the latest exhibition 'Fun with Software' at Bristol's Arnolfini, curator Olga Goriunova seeks to document and explore how humorous approaches to software lead to innovation." *See* rhizome.org/editorial/2010/nov/3/interview-with-olga-goriunova-curator-of-fun-with-.

Future Everything: "[A]n award-winning innovation lab for digital culture and annual festival, established in Manchester in 1995." *See* futureeverything.org.

Game Changer Chicago Design Lab: "GCC develops serious games, interactive learning experiences, and digital media art with youth and for youth." *See* ci3.uchicago.edu/labs/game-changer-chicago.

Gamer Theory: "Together with the Institute for the Future of the Book, [McKenzie Wark] produced this website as a way to think about games." *See* www.futureofthebook.org/gamertheory2.0.

Games for Change: "Founded in 2004, Games for Change facilitates the creation and distribution of social impact games that serve as critical tools in humanitarian and educational efforts." *See* www.gamesforchange.org.

Geelriandre/Arthesis: Album by Eliane Radigue. *See* senufoeditions.bandcamp.com/album/geelriandre-arthesis.

Genius: "Genius breaks down text with line-by-line annotations, added and edited by anyone in the world." *See* genius.com.

GeoNames: "The GeoNames geographical database covers all countries and contains over eleven million placenames that are available for download free of charge." *See* www.geonames.org.

Girls Who Code: "[A] national nonprofit organization dedicated to closing the gender gap in technology . . . [by] building the largest pipeline of future female engineers in the United States" *See* girlswhocode.com.

GitHub: "Millions of developers use GitHub to build personal projects, support their businesses, and work together on open source technologies . . . GitHub fosters a fast, flexible, and collaborative development process that lets you work on your own or with others." *See* github.com.

Glass: "Glass is a hands-free device, for hands-on workers." *See* x.company/glass.

Global Outlook::Digital Humanities (GO::DH): "The purpose of GO::DH is to help break down barriers that hinder communication and collaboration among researchers and students of the Digital Arts, Humanities, and Cultural Heritage sectors in high, mid, and low income economies." *See* www.globaloutlookdh.org.

Gone Home: An interactive exploration simulator that enables the user to discover things about a family by rummaging through the objects in their home. *See* gonehome.game.

Google: "Search the world's information, including webpages, images, videos and more." *See* www.google.com.

Google Maps: "Find local businesses, view maps and get driving directions in Google Maps." *See* www.google.com/maps.

Great Wall of China: "The Great Wall of China is conceived for simultaneous realisation across media, including a Website (1995–1996), a CD-ROM with portfolio of prints (1997–1999) and an interactive installation (1999)." *See* littlepig.org.uk/wall/greatwall.htm.

GynePunk: A collective from Catalonia working to develop an emergency gynecological medicine tool kit. *See* gynepunk.hotglue.me.

Half the Sky: An innovative multiplatform initiative inspired by journalists Nicholas Kristof and Sheryl WuDunn's 2009 best-selling book, *Half the Sky: Turning Oppression into Opportunity for Women Worldwide*. *See* www.halftheskymovement.org

Handmade Cinema: "This web project visualizes the relationships detailed in [Gregory Zinman's] dissertation, 'Handmade: The Moving Image in the Artisanal Mode' . . . [which] seeks to enlighten our awareness of the intersection of art and media in the 20th century." *See* www.handmadecinema.com.

HASTAC: "HASTAC (Humanities, Arts, Science, and Technology Alliance and Collaboratory) is an interdisciplinary community of humanists, artists, social scientists, scientists, and technologists that are changing the way we teach and learn." *See* www.hastac.org.

HathiTrust: "[A] partnership of academic & research institutions, offering a collection of millions of titles digitized from libraries around the world." *See* www.hathitrust.org.

Hexacago: "Hexacago Health Academy (HHA) is a game-based science and health program [by the Game Changer Chicago Design Lab]." *See* hha.uchicago.edu.

Hidden Florence: "This website accompanies a free smartphone app that takes you on a unique tour of the Renaissance city through the eyes of a 'contemporary' guide, a 1490s wool worker called Giovanni." *See* hiddenflorence.org.

Honour Water: "*Honour Water* is a singing game for healing water available for free on iPads that passes on songs in Anishinaabemowin, the Anishinaabe language." *See* www.honourwater.com.

Hook and Eye: "[A]n intervention and an invitation: we write about the realities of being women working in the Canadian university system." *See* www.hookandeye.ca.

How Not to Be Seen: A video by Hito Steyerl (2013). *See* player.vimeo.com/video/125475136.

How to Truly Listen: "In this soaring demonstration, deaf percussionist Evelyn Glennie illustrates how listening to music involves much more than simply letting sound waves hit your eardrums." *See* www.ted.com/talks/evelyn_glennie_shows_how_to_listen?language=en.

HTML: HyperText Markup Language is the standard markup language for creating web pages.

Humument: An altered Victorian novel (*A Human Document* by W.H. Mallock, 1892) project by artist Tom Phillips, started in 1966. *See* www.tomphillips.co.uk/humument.

HyperCard: An application that enables Macintosh users to author hypertext pages without any programming knowledge, developed in the 1980s.

HyperCities: The online component to *HyperCities: Thick Mapping in the Digital Humanities* by Todd Presner, David Shepard, and Yoh Kawano (2014). *See* www.hypercities.com.

Hyper-Stacks: "Hyper-Stacks used the [Victoria and Albert Museum's] digital archives to analyse more than 1.14 million object records, and build a classification and connection engine." *See* hyper-stacks.com.

Hypothesis: An online "free, open, non-profit, neutral and lasting" annotation tool. *See* hypothes.is.

I Am Sitting in a Room: A sound artwork by Alvin Lucier (1969). *See* www.ubu.com/sound/lucier.html.

I Love Bees: A "groundbreaking alternate reality game" that served as a viral marketing campaign for the launch of Halo 2 in 2006. *See* www.42entertainment.com/work/ilovebees.

I Saw You on the Radio: Video by Angelica Macklin. *See* vimeo.com/24484214.

iBooks Author: "Available free on the Mac App Store, iBooks Author is an amazing app that allows anyone to create beautiful iBooks Textbooks—and just about any other kind of book—for iPad and Mac." *See* www.apple.com/ca/ibooks-author.

Ideas Box: "[A] portable multi-media toolkit . . . born from this challenge to access to information, culture and education for refugee populations." *See* www.ideas-box.org/index.php/en/the-ideas-box/discover-the-ideas-box.

ImageJ: "[A]n open source image processing program designed for scientific multidimensional images." *See* imagej.nih.gov/ij.

ImagePlot: "[A] free software tool that visualizes collections of images and video of any size. It is implemented as a macro which works with the open source image processing program ImageJ." *See* lab.softwarestudies.com/p/imageplot.html.

imagineNATIVE Film + Media Arts Festival: "imagineNATIVE is the world's largest presenter of Indigenous screen content. We are a registered charity committed to inspiring and connecting communities through original, Indigenous film and media arts." *See* www.imaginenative.org.

Implementing New Knowledge Environments (INKE): "an interdisciplinary initiative spawned in the methodological commons of the digital humanities that seeks to understand the future of reading and the book through a historical perspective." *See* inke.ca.

Index Thomisticus: "The Corpus Thomisticum project aims to provide scholars with a set of instruments of research on Thomas Aquinas, freely available via Internet." *See* www.corpusthomisticum.org/it/index.age.

Indigenous Routes Collective: "[A]n ad hoc group formed in August 2011 by Amanda Strong, Archer Pechawis and Ben Donoghue to carry out a community collaborative project producing an interactive documentary with six native youth." *See* www.indigenousroutes.ca.

Inform 7: "Inform is a design system for interactive fiction based on natural language." *See* inform7.com.

INFOS 2000: "Timothy Murray and Teo Spiller launched this experimental venture of featuring international net.art at the INFOS2000 Festival, in Ljubljana, Slovenia, in an 'off-line' format" and later released a CD-Rom format of the exhibition. *See* goldsen.library.cornell.edu/internet/infos.php.

Ingress: A location-based, story-based, augmented-reality massively multiplayer online game, originally developed by Google. *See* www.ingress.com.

Initiative for Indigenous Futures (IIF): "[A] partnership of universities and community organizations dedicated to developing multiple visions of Indigenous peoples tomorrow in order to better understand where we need to go today." *See* abtec.org/iif.

InscriptiFact: "The InscriptiFact Digital Image Library is designed to allow access via the Internet to high-resolution images of ancient inscriptions and artifacts, primarily from the Near Eastern and Mediterranean Worlds." *See* www.inscriptifact.com.

Institute for Multimedia Literacy (IML): "The IML is dedicated to sustaining and developing models of teaching and scholarship based on the use and development of new digital media technologies and applications." *See* cinema.usc.edu/iml.

Interaction Design Institute Ivrea: "[A]n independent non-profit organisation, founded by Telecom Italia and Olivetti, and now part of the Progetto Italia initiative of Telecom Italia." *See* interactionivrea.org/en/index.asp.

INTERCAL: INTERCAL (Compiler Language With No Pronounceable Acronym) is an esoteric programming language that was designed in the 1970s and is "now the center of an international community of technomasochists." *See* catb.org/esr/intercal.

Invaders: "Inspired by the art of Steven Paul Judd with design and programming by Elizabeth LaPensée and music by Trevino Brings Plenty, *Invaders* (2015) for web and mobile is a play on the classic arcade game, *Space Invaders*." *See* survivance.org/invaders and www.elizabethlapensee.com/#/games.

Iter: "*Iter*, meaning a journey or a path in Latin, is a not-for-profit partnership dedicated to the advancement of learning in the study and teaching of the Middle Ages and Renaissance (400–1700) through the development and distribution of online resources." *See* www.itergateway.org

Java: A general-purpose computer programming language designed to produce programs that will run on any computer system.

JavaScript: A popular, lightweight, interpreted programming language.

Jodi: An art collective and also a website created by Joan Heemskerk and Dirk Paesmans (1995). *See* wwwwww.jodi.org.

Kairos: A Journal of Rhetoric, Technology, and Pedagogy: "[A] refereed open-access online journal exploring the intersections of rhetoric, technology, and pedagogy." *See* kairos.technorhetoric.net.

KeyWorx: "[A]n application framework developed at Waag Society, originally suited for 'live' multi-user audio/visual performances. This code base, later called the classic application, was followed in 2006 by a successor named KeyWorx/Live, developed as an open source project." *See* www.keyworx.org.

KidCAD: "[A] digital clay interface for children to remix toys. KidCAD allows children to imprint 2.5D shapes from physical objects into their digital models by deforming a malleable gel input device, deForm." *See* tmg-trackr.media.mit.edu/publishedmedia/Papers/500-KidCAD%20digitally%20remixing%20toys/Published/PDF.

A Kiss: a kiss (for Jennifer) by Dan Waber (2008) is a novel-length hypertext. *See* www.logolalia.com/hypertexts/a-kiss.html#.

LambdaMOO: "LambdaMOO is both the name of a MUD and the name of MUD server software." *See* www.moo.mud.org.

Lantern: "[T]he search platform for the collections of the Media History Digital Library, an open access initiative led by David Pierce and Eric Hoyt. The Media History Digital

Library (MHDL) digitizes collections of classic media periodicals that belong in the public domain for full public access." *See* lantern.mediahist.org

Layar: "Founded in the summer of 2009, Layar quickly gained international attention as one of the first mobile augmented reality browsers to hit the market." *See* www.layar.com.

Learning from YouTube: "[A] unique video-book composed of approximately 250 texteos . . . YouTube is the subject, form, method, problem and solution of this video-book," by Alexandra Juhasz. *See* vectors.usc.edu/projects/learningfromyoutube.

Libraries Without Borders: "Founded in 2007 in France at the initiative of Patrick Weil, Libraries Without Borders is today one of the leading NGOs working in knowledge and culture-based development in the world and supporting libraries in developing countries." *See* www.librarieswithoutborders.org.

Lightbox Gallery: "This inaugural Lightbox Navigation program features a visual map of every object currently on display [at the Harvard Art Museum], and is a project by metaLAB (at) Harvard, a design and research group exploring the boundaries of digital culture." *See* www.harvardartmuseums.org/visit/calendar/lightbox-navigations-metalab-at-harvard.

Lightbox JS: By Lokesh Dhakar, "Lightbox is small javascript library used to overlay images on top of the current page." *See* lokeshdhakar.com/projects/lightbox2.

Lines and Nodes Symposium: A free event on September 19, 2014, hosted by the NYU Department of Media, Culture and Communication and Anthology Film Archives that brought "together artists and scholars to examine the mediated and aesthetic dimensions of extraction and infrastructure." *See* www.ecoarttech.net/lines-and-nodes.

Lisp: A high-level computer programming language, designed in 1958.

Logo: An educational programming language, designed in 1967 by Daniel G. Bobrow, Wally Feurzeig, Seymour Papert, and Cynthia Solomon, known mainly for its use of turtle graphics.

Long Table: An experimental open public forum that "combines theatricality and models for public engagement. It is at once a stylised appropriation and an open-ended, non-hierarchical format for participation." *See* publicaddresssystems.org/projects/long-table.

Lynda: An online education company "that helps anyone learn business, software, technology and creative skills to achieve personal and professional goals" through video tutorials. *See* www.lynda.com.

Made with Code: An initiative launched by Google to increase the representation of women in technology. *See* www.madewithcode.com.

Magic Clock: Open source code, hardware, and tutorials that enable people to create a clock that reveals their contacts' locations. *See* magicclock.de.

Maker Lab in the Humanities (MLab): Based at the University of Victoria, under the direction of Jentery Sayers, "with research priority areas in physical computing, digital fabrication, and multisite exhibits, the MLab intersects cultural criticism with experimental prototyping and electronics." *See* maker.uvic.ca.

Manifest.AR: "Manifest.AR is an international artists' collective working with emergent forms of augmented reality as interventionist public art." *See* manifestarblog.wordpress.com.

Marky: "[A] Web-based multi-purpose annotation tool. With this annotation tool you can annotate from simple documents (without any formatting) to HTML documents." *See* sing.ei.uvigo.es/marky.

Marvel Unlimited: Marvel Unlimited is an online service by Marvel Comics that grants members "instant access to over 17,000 Marvel Comics." *See* marvel.com/comics/unlimited.

Maryland Institute for Technology in the Humanities (MITH): Jointly supported by the University of Maryland College of Arts and Humanities and the University of Maryland Libraries, (MITH) "is a leading digital humanities center that pursues disciplinary innovation and institutional transformation through applied research, public programming, and educational opportunities." *See* mith.umd.edu.

Material Beliefs: Based at the Interaction Research Studio in the Department of Design at Goldsmiths, University of London, "Material Beliefs takes emerging biomedical and cybernetic technology out of labs and into public spaces." *See* materialbeliefs.co.uk/people.

Mauve Desert: "[A] CD-ROM Translation of Nicole Brossard's experimental novel Le désert mauve." *See* www.adrienejenik.net/mauvedesert.html.

The Media Ecology Project: "[P]rovides online access to primary moving image research materials, and engages dynamic new forms of scholarly production and online publishing." *See* sites.dartmouth.edu/mediaecology.

Media History Digital Library: "[A] non-profit initiative dedicated to digitizing collections of classic media periodicals that belong in the public domain for full public access." *See* mediahistoryproject.org.

metaLAB: "With partners at the Berkman Klein Center, across [Harvard University], and in the world at large, metaLAB explores the digital arts and humanities through research, experimentation, tool building, teaching, through publications in print and online, and via exhibition, performance, and social practice." *See* metalab.harvard.edu.

Metaverse Roadmap: "T]he Acceleration Studies Foundation (ASF) and its supporting foresight partners have explored the virtual and 3-D future of the World Wide Web in a first-of-its-kind cross-industry public foresight project, the Metaverse Roadmap (MVR)." *See* metaverseroadmap.org/index.html.

micro_research: "[A] mobile research platform exploring psychogeophysics and asking the question of where precisely the plague known as software executes." *See* 1010.co.uk/org.

Misogynoir: A term coined by Moya Bailey that combines "misogyny" with the French term for black, "noir," to describe the racialized sexism that black women face.

MIT Media Lab: Tangible Media Group: "The Tangible Media Group, led by Professor Hiroshi Ishii, explores the Tangible Bits & Radical Atoms visions to seamlessly couple the dual world of bits and atoms by giving dynamic physical form to digital information and computation." *See* tangible.media.mit.edu/vision.

Moments de Jean-Jacques Rousseau: "Moments of Jean-Jacques Rousseau is a project initiated by Jean-Louis Boissier and Liliane Terrier (Paris) (1994) that led to a particular edition of a CD-ROM." *See* circonstances.net/moments.

Mothership Hackermoms: "We give mothers of every gender the time and space to explore DIY craft and design, hacker/maker culture, community workshops, entrepreneurship and all manner of creative expression—with on-site childcare." *See* mothership.hackermoms.org.

Mukurtu Content Management System: "Mukurtu (MOOK-oo-too) is a grassroots project aiming to empower communities to manage, share, preserve, and exchange their digital heritage in culturally relevant and ethically-minded ways." *See* mukurtu.org.

Museum Without Walls: "[A] digital National Gallery of art and architecture in the public realm" formed through a collaboration between CultureNOW and "over 75 public art collections across America." *See* www.culturenow.org/mission.

Music, Language and Environment: An album by David Dunn (1996). *See* www.daviddunn.com/~david/HOME.htm.

Musqueam Place Names Web Mapping Portal: "Here you find information on Musqueam Place Names, hear audio of our hən̓q̓əmin̓əm̓ language from Musqueam elders past and present, view historical photographs and see where they are located." *See* www.musqueam.bc.ca/musqueam-our-history-web-map.

Mutant Giant Spider Dog: A viral YouTube video posted by Slywester Wardega (2014). *See* www.youtube.com/watch?v=YoB8t0B4jx4.

my body—a Wunderkammer: A piece of electronic literature by Shelley Jackson that "uses the HTML hypertext form to revitalize the memoir genre." *See* collection.eliterature.org/1/works/jackson__my_body_a_wunderkammer.html.

The NAMES Project Foundation: "Established in 1987, The NAMES Project Foundation, Inc. is the international, non-governmental, 501(c)(3) organization that is the custodian of The AIDS Memorial Quilt and its associated document and media archive." *See* www.aidsquilt.org/about/the-names-project-foundation.

Never Alone/Kisima Ingitchuna: "We paired world class game makers with Alaska Native storytellers and elders to create a game which delves deeply into the traditional lore of the Iñupiat people to present an experience like no other." *See* neveralonegame.com.

The New Aesthetic: A research project by James Bridle in which he collects material that "points towards new ways of seeing the world, an echo of the society, technology, politics and people that co-produce them." *See* new-aesthetic.tumblr.com.

Nivel de Confianza: "'Level of Confidence' is an art project to commemorate the mass kidnapping of 43 students from the Ayotzinapa normalista school in Iguala, Guerrero, Mexico" that uses a face-recognition camera. *See* www.lozano-hemmer.com/level_of_confidence.php.

Northwest Musuem of Arts and Culture: "The Museum's purpose is to inspire and foster understanding of the history, cultures, communities, commerce, and art of the Inland Northwest." *See* www.northwestmuseum.org.

Object Making/Exchange: A course "[d]eveloped by Anca Birzescu and Radhika Gajjala for Spring 2014 Graduate and Undergraduate classes taught by Radhika Gajjala at BGSU." *See* femtechnet.org/docc/object-makingexchange.

Occupy Wall Street: A protest movement "fighting back against the corrosive power of major banks and multinational corporations over the democratic process, and the role of Wall Street in creating an economic collapse that has caused the greatest recession in generations." *See* occupywallst.org.

Oculus Rift: A virtual reality headset that "radically redefines digital entertainment." *See* www.oculus.com.

One Laptop Per Child XO laptop: "The XO is a potent learning tool designed and built especially for children in developing countries, living in some of the most remote environments . . . It has built-in wireless and a unique screen that is readable under direct sunlight for children who go to school outdoors." *See* laptop.org/en/laptop.

Open Calais: "[T]he easiest and most accurate way to tag the people, places, companies, facts, and events in your content to increase its value, accessibility and interoperability." *See* www.opencalais.com.

Open Simulator: "[A]n open source multi-platform, multi-user 3D application server. It can be used to create a virtual environment (or world) which can be accessed through a variety of clients, on multiple protocols." *See* opensimulator.org/wiki/Main_Page.

Open Street Map (OSM): "[A] map of the world, created by people like you and free to use under an open license . . . Contributors use aerial imagery, GPS devices, and low-tech field maps to verify that OSM is accurate and up to date." *See* www.openstreetmap.org.

The Oregon Trail: A computer game developed in the 1970s to expose children to the realities of nineteenth-century pioneer life on the Oregon Trail.

Otsi:! Rise of the Kanien'kehá:ka Legends: An AbTeC PC videogame (2008–09). *See* abtec.org/iif/index.php/outputs/output-1.

Oxford English Dictionary of National Biography: "[T]he national record of men and women who have shaped British history and culture, worldwide, from the Romans to the 21st century. The Dictionary offers concise, up-to-date biographies written by named, specialist authors." *See* www.oxforddnb.com.

Papers, Please: A videogame about totalitarian government by Lucas Pope, developed and published under his pseudonym 3909. *See* papersplea.se.

Participatory Culture Foundation: "A 501c3 non-profit organization, working to build a more open, collaborative world" by "creating open and decentralized video tools and services." *See* pculture.org.

Patchwork Girl: A work of electronic literature by American author Shelley Jackson written in Storyspace and published by Eastgate Systems in 1995. *See* www.eastgate.com/catalog/PatchworkGirl.html.

Pathfinders: "'Pathfinders: Documenting the Experience of Early Digital Literature,' led by Dene Grigar (Washington State University Vancouver) and Stuart Moulthrop (University of Wisconsin-Milwaukee), is a digital preservation project that captures an important moment in literary history: the development of early digital literature." *See* dtc-wsuv.org/wp/pathfinders.

Pathfinders Book: A multimedia, open-source book published in June 2015 that "begins the necessary process of documenting early digital literature, specifically pre-web hypertext fiction and poetry, from 1986–1995." *See* scalar.usc.edu/works/pathfinders/index.

PeaceMaker: A game "inspired by real events in the Israeli-Palestinian conflict." *See* www.peacemakergame.com.

Perl: "Perl 5 is a highly capable, feature-rich programming language with over 29 years of development." *See* www.perl.org.

PHP: Hypertext Preprocessor (PHP) is an open-source, general-purpose programming language designed for web development by Rasmus Lerdorf in 1994.

The Plateau Peoples' Web Portal: "[A] gateway to Plateau peoples' cultural materials held in multiple repositories including WSU's Manuscripts, Archives and Special Collections, the Northwest Museum of Art and Culture, the National Anthropological Archives and the National Museum of the American Indian at the Smithsonian Institution." *See* plateauportal.libraries.wsu.edu.

Play the Past: "[A] student-directed field trip experience supported by technology. Students use iPods to explore the *Then Now Wow* exhibit." *See* education.mnhs.org/playthepast.

Play Your Place: An online game designed by Ruth Catlow and Mary Flanagan. "The free software, that enables anyone to draw, make and play their own platform game levels, developed with Soda was first published to Github [in] October 2013." *See* localplay.org.uk.

Political TV Ad Archive: "This site provides a searchable, viewable, and shareable online archive of 2016 political TV ads, married with fact-checking and reporting citizens can trust." *See* politicaladarchive.org.

The Probable Trust Registry: An installation and participatory group performance by Adrian Piper (2013). *See* www.adrianpiper.com/art/docs/TPTRGeneralizedPerformanceInstructionsWebsite.pdf.

Processing: "[A] flexible software sketchbook and a language for learning how to code within the context of the visual arts." *See* processing.org.

Project Arclight: "Arclight is a data mining and visualization tool for film and media history that allow users to analyze millions of pages of digitally scanned magazines and newspapers for trends related to a chosen subject." *See* search.projectarclight.org.

Project for Tachistoscope {Bottomless Pit}: A piece of hypertext by William Poundstone that contains a "bottomless (and looping) narrative of a geological anomaly though rapid serial visualization." *See* collection.eliterature.org/1/works/poundstone__project_for_tachistoscope_bottomless_pit.html.

Project Gutenberg: "Project Gutenberg was the first provider of free electronic books, or eBooks." *See* www.gutenberg.org.

Project Tango: A technology platform developed by Google that enables mobile devices to detect their locations without the use of GPS or other outside signals. *See* www.google.com/atap/project-tango.

Prom Week: "Prom Week is a social simulation game being developed at the University of California at Santa Cruz . . . [that combines] the dynamic simulation of games like the Sims with the detailed characters and dialog of story driven games." *See* promweek.soe.ucsc.edu.

Protocols for Native American Archival Materials: A list of "best professional practices for culturally responsive care and use of American Indian archival material held by non-tribal organizations." *See* www2.nau.edu/libnap-p.

Psy-Geo-Conflux: "[A]n annual event produced by Glowlab dedicated to current artistic and social investigations in psychogeography (the study of the effects of the geographic environment on the emotions and behavior of individuals)." *See* glowlab.blogs.com/psygeocon.

Puppet Motel: An interactive CD-ROM by Laurie Anderson and Hsin-Chien Huang (1995). *See* www.olats.org/reperes/offline/aout2003/puppetMotel.shtml.

Python: An open programming language developed by Guido van Rossum. *See* www.python.org.

(Qalb): "[A] programming language exploring the role of human culture in coding. Code is written entirely in Arabic, highlighting cultural biases of computer science and challenging the assumptions we make about programming. It is implemented as a tree-walking language interpreter in JavaScript." *See* nas.sr/%D9%82%D9%84%D8%A8.

QGIS: "[T]he best GIS tool in the free and open-source software (FOSS) community. QGIS is a user friendly Open Source Geographic Information System (GIS) licensed under the GNU General Public License." *See* www.qgis.org/en/site.

Quantified Self: Self Knowledge through Numbers: "Quantified Self Labs is a California-based company founded by Gary Wolf and Kevin Kelly that serves the Quantified Self user community worldwide by producing international meetings, conferences and expositions, community forums, web content and services, and a guide to self-tracking tools." *See* quantifiedself.com.

Queer Technologies: "[A]n organization that produces critical applications, tools, and situations for queer technological agency, interventions, and sociality." *See* www.zachblas.info/works/queer-technologies.

Queers in Love at the End of the World: A piece of hypertext fiction by Anna Anthropy (2013), built with the interactive fiction tool, Twine. *See* auntiepixelante.com/endoftheworld.

Raspberry Pi: "The Raspberry Pi is a credit card-sized computer that plugs into your TV and a keyboard. It is a capable little computer which can be used in electronics projects, and for many of the things that your desktop PC does, like spreadsheets, word processing, browsing the internet, and playing games." *See* www.raspberrypi.org.

Reacting to the Past: A series of "games, set in the past, in which students are assigned roles informed by classic texts in the history of ideas." *See* reacting.barnard.edu/about.

Reading Project: A Collaborative Analysis of William Poundstone's Project for Tachistoscope {Bottomless Pit}: "[A] collaboration between three scholars combining different interpretive methods of digital literature and poetics in order to think through how critical reading is changing—and, indeed, must change—to keep up with the emergence of digital poetics and practices." *See* scalar.usc.edu/aclsworkbench/reading-project/index.

Real Computer Music: "Some sort of computer music without any proper composer. Computer music as a side effect of computation." *See* sourceforge.net/projects/algorthythmics.

Reddit: "Reddit bridges communities and individuals with ideas, the latest digital trends, and breaking news (. . . okay, and maybe cats). Our mission is to help people discover places where they can be their true selves, and empower our community to flourish." *See* www.reddit.com.

Redshift & Portalmetal: A game by micha cárdenas with sound by Bobby Bray that "uses space travel as a lens through which to understand the experience of migration and settlement for a trans woman of color." *See* faculty.washington.edu/michamc/redshift-and-portalmetal.

Rose Goldsen Archive of New Media Art: "Named after the pioneering critic of the commercialization of mass media, the late Professor Rose Goldsen of Cornell University, the Archive was founded in 2002 by Timothy Murray to house international art work produced on CD-Rom, DVD-Rom, video, digital interfaces, and the internet." *See* goldsen.library.cornell.edu/index.php.

Ruby: "A dynamic, open source programming language with a focus on simplicity and productivity." *See* www.ruby-lang.org/en.

Rumah Hacker: A video by Stefanie Wuschitz that "compares women-centered tribe houses in West Sumatra with men-centered hackerspaces." *See* vimeo.com/79198342.

Scalar: "Scalar is a free, open source authoring and publishing platform that's designed to make it easy for authors to write long-form, born-digital scholarship online." *See* scalar.usc.edu/scalar.

Seattle Fandango Project: "The Seattle Fandango Project is dedicated to forging relationships through participatory music and dance." *See* www.seattlefandangoproject.org.

Second Life: "Second Life is a 3D world where everyone you see is a real person and every place you visit is built by people just like you." *See* secondlife.com.

Selfiecity: "Selfiecity investigates *selfies* using a mix of theoretic, artistic and quantitative methods." *See* www.selfiecity.net

Settlers of Catan: A multiplayer board game in which players "build roads and new settlements that eventually become cities." *See* www.catan.com.

Sexist Onesies and Feminist Viral Media: A storify account on "[w]hat happens when you tweet a juxtaposed pair of gender-stereotyped superheroes baby clothes . . . the Internet goes bananas, and the mass media follow suit." *See* storify.com/digiwonk/sexist-onesies-and-feminist-viral-media.

Shock in the Ear: "Shock in the Ear is an intense and poetic work, composed (and recomposed by the user) through interactive screens, stories, performances, music, and sound." *See* www.agencetopo.qc.ca/vitrine_blog/cd_shock/cd_shock_fr.html.

Sim City: A computer and console multiplayer videogame in which the player designs and develops a city from the ground up. *See* www.simcity.com.

Simple Astrolabe: "The 'tertiant' is a simple astrolabe similar to the quadrant or sextant. It is useful for measuring unreachable altitudes, discovering local latitude, and finding the average of inclines." *See* www.shapeways.com/product/FBS8F8973/simple-astrolabe.

Singuistics: An IOS app that teaches "traditional and original songs by Inuit musicians in a fun, three-step program." *See* pinnguaq.com/singuistics.

Skahiòn:hati: Legend of the Stone Giant: An AbTeC PC videogame (2011). *See* abtec.org/iif/index.php/outputs/output-2.

Skahiòn:hati: Rise of the Kanien'kehá:ka Legends: An AbTeC PC videogame (2012). *See* abtec.org/iif/index.php/outputs/output-3.

SketchChair: "[A] free, open-source software tool that allows anyone to easily design and build their own digitally fabricated furniture." *See* www.sketchchair.cc.

Skins Video Game Workshops: "Skins is a series of digital-media workshops for Aboriginal youth offered by an Aboriginally determined team of game designers, artists and educators known as Aboriginal Territories in Cyberspace." *See* skins.abtec.org.

Slashdot: "[A] website based on and running the Slashdot-Like Automated Story-Telling Homepage software." *See* slashdot.org.

Slow Reading: A manifesto by Antonio Tombolini on the practice of slow reading, which, he argues, faces extinction with the advent of digital media. *See* www.slowreading.org.

Small Dance: A film featuring Steve Paxton, shot and directed by Olive Bieringa (2010). *See* vimeo.com/19001115.

Smart Citizen: "Connecting data, people and knowledge, the objective of the platform is to serve as a node for building productive and open indicators, and distributed tools, and thereafter the collective construction of the city for its own inhabitants." *See* smartcitizen.me.

Smoke Dress: "A collaboration between fashiontech designer Anouk Wipprecht [NL] and technologist Aduen Darriba [NL]. The dress is a wireless and wearable tangible couture 'smoke screen' imbued with the ability to suddenly visually obliterate itself through the excretion of a cloud of smoke." *See* www.youtube.com/watch?v=G-0lTP90hVc#.

Smoke Stacks: A board game for youth from the Game Changer Chicago Design Lab that exposes the dangers of smoking. *See* ci3.uchicago.edu/labs/game-changer-chicago.

Social Edition of the Devonshire Manuscript: "The social edition is a work that brings communities together to engage in conversation around a text formed and reformed through an ongoing, iterative, public editorial process." *See* en.wikibooks.org/wiki/The_Devonshire_Manuscript and dms.itercommunity.org.

Social Justice History Platform: "[A] software platform designed to represent geographic and spatial data within an enhanced interface designed to contextualize locations and objects alongside the primary source documents that provide their historical narrative, and a range of related multimedia objects (including video, audio, images, and text)." *See* www.dhinitiative.org/node/274.

Socrates in the Labyrinth: David A. Kolb's "*Socrates in the Labyrinth* is one of the first works of hypertext non-fiction to examine and exploit the techniques of hypertext rhetoric discovered in the development of serious hypertext fiction." *See* www.eastgate.com/catalog/Socrates.html.

Software Studies Initiative: "[A] research lab and a design studio working on analysis of big cultural datasets. Our work combines methods and technologies from data science, data visualization, media design and humanities." *See* lab.softwarestudies.com.

Solr: An open source search platform that "is highly reliable, scalable and fault tolerant, providing distributed indexing, replication and load-balanced querying, automated failover and recovery, centralized configuration and more." *See* lucene.apache.org/solr.

Soul Rebel Radio: "[A] cutting edge youth based radio program hitting on topics as well as current events through comedy, youth voices, and interviews." *See* kpfk.org.

Sound Characters: An album by electronic musician Marianne Amacher (1999). *See* www.tzadik.com/volume.php?VolumeID=42.

A Sound Map of the Hudson River: A sound installation by Annea Lockwood (1982) commissioned by the Hudson River Museum. *See* www.annealockwood.com/compositions.htm.

Soundwalk: "[A] critically-acclaimed new media company based in NY . . . Our services range from multi-track sound installations to customized audio branding and tailor-made mixes." *See* www.soundwalk.com.

SourceForge: "[A]n Open Source community resource dedicated to helping open source projects be as successful as possible. We thrive on community collaboration to help us create a premiere resource for open source software development and distribution." *See* sourceforge.net.

The Soweto Historical Geographic Information System: "The primary objective of the Soweto Historical GIS Project (SHGIS) is to build a multi-layered historical geographic information system that explores the social, economic and political dimensions of urban development under South African apartheid regimes (1904/1948–1994) in Johannesburg's all-black township of Soweto." *See* www.dhinitiative.org/projects/shgis.

Spacebuster: A mobile inflatable structure created by Andrea Hofmann, Axel Timm, Benjamin Foerster-Baldenius, Christof Mayer, Markus Bader, and Matthias Rick (2009), "developed and designed to explore the qualities and possibilities of public space in New York City." *See* raumlabor.net/spacebuster.

Speck: "[A] low-cost, indoor fine particulate (PM2.5) monitor developed as a tool for citizen science and personal exposure tracking." *See* www.cmucreatelab.org/projects/Speck.

Spore: A game developed by Maxis in which players create their own species, guide them through evolution, and share with other players. *See* www.spore.com.

Steel: "[A] simple game about mining and smelting metals. A number of virtual mines (copper, iron and carbon) are located all around downtown Madison, and players collect the metals for profit." *See* arisgames.org/featured/steel.

Stone, Brick, Glass, Wood, Wire (Graphic Scores 1986–1996): A double live album comprised of graphic scores by English instrumentalist, composer, and improviser Fred Frith.

Storyspace: "Storyspace is a hypertext writing environment, especially well suited to creating large, complex, and challenging hypertexts." *See* www.eastgate.com/storyspace.

Streetmuseum: "Hundreds of images from the Museum of London's extensive collections showcase both everyday and momentous occasions in London's history, from the Great Fire of 1666 to the swinging sixties." *See* www.museumoflondon.org.uk/Resources/app/you-are-here-app/home.html.

Sylvia Rivera Law Project (SRLP): "SRLP is a collective organization founded on the understanding that gender self-determination is inextricably intertwined with racial, social and economic justice. Therefore, we seek to increase the political voice and visibility of low-income people and people of color who are transgender, intersex, or gender non-conforming." *See* srlp.org.

Tale-Spin: A piece of digital literature by James Meehan (1976). No known copy of the text's code exists today. *See* grandtextauto.soe.ucsc.edu/2006/09/13/the-story-of-meehans-tale-spin.

Tapp und Tastkino (Tap and Touch Cinema): A video by VALIE EXPORT (1968). *See* www.moma.org/collection/works/109931?locale=en.

Taroko Gorge: A piece of electronic poetry by Nick Montfort (2009). *See* nickm.com/taroko_gorge.

Teaching with Things: An award granted by the Harvard Initiative for Teaching and Learning "to expand an existing curatorial program at metaLAB and the museums to support object-based teaching in the humanities." *See* hilt.harvard.edu/pages/teaching-things-curation-hybrid-multimedia-and-object-oriented-pedagogy.

THATCamp (The Humanities And Technology Camp): "[A]n unconference: an open, inexpensive meeting where humanists and technologists of all skill levels learn and build together in sessions proposed on the spot." *See* thatcamp.org.

There.com: "[A] 3D social world that first launched in 2003 . . . today, nearly two million people have become members, making *There* the destination of choice for anyone who wants to experience the power of chat combined with the fun of online games." *See* www.there.com.

These Streets: A Rock 'n' Roll Story: "'These Streets' is [a play] inspired by over 40 interviews conducted with and about the many women rockers who were integral to the Seattle music scene during this legendary era." *See* thesestreets.org.

Tile: "[A] tiny Bluetooth tracker and easy-to-use app that finds everyday items in seconds . . . Tile's global community spans 200 countries and territories and helps people locate more than half a million items every day." *See* www.thetileapp.com.

Tiltfactor: "The interdisciplinary innovation studio dedicated to designing & studying games for social impact, was founded and is led by Dr. Mary Flanagan." *See* www.tiltfactor.org.

Timescape: An exhibition at the 9/11 Memorial Museum that won a silver MUSE award in the Applications and APIs category. *See* www.911memorial.org/blog/museum-exhibitions-honored-national-museum-association.

TOMS One Day Without Shoes: "Each year, we spend one day #withoutshoes to raise awareness for children's health and education." *See* www.toms.ca/one-day-without-shoes.

Transborder Immigrant Tool: A Mexico/U.S Border Disturbance Art Project by the Electronic Disturbance Theater/b.a.n.g. lab. "The Transborder Immigrant Tool (TBT) repurposes inexpensive used mobile phones that have GPS antennae." *See* faculty.washington.edu/michamc/wordpress-bang.

Transcriptions Center: "Transcriptions, begun in 1998, focuses on work in digital humanities and new media. Transcriptions is both a digital humanities lab and an interdisciplinary center . . . [that] work[s] to transcribe, translate and transform humanist engagement into digital inquiry and vice versa." *See* transcriptions.english.ucsb.edu.

Transformers: The Premake: A film by Kevin B. Lee that "turns 355 YouTube videos into a critical investigation of the global big budget film industry, amateur video making, and the political economy of images." *See* vimeo.com/94101046.

Turbulence: "Known as one of the 'premiere web sites for net art,' Turbulence.org (1996–2016) commissioned over 220 original Net | Web | Hybrid Art works and hosted over 20 real-time, multi-location performances." *See* turbulence.org.

TUTOR: A programming language initially developed for use in computer-assisted instruction (CAI) and computer-managed instruction (CMI) in the 1960s.

twarc: "[A] command line tool and Python library for archiving Twitter JSON data. Each tweet is represented as a JSON object that is exactly what was returned from the Twitter API." *See* github.com/edsu/twarc.

Twine: Originally created by Chris Klimas in 2009, "Twine is an open-source tool for telling interactive, nonlinear stories." *See* twinery.org.

Twitter: An online social networking service where users post and read 140-character entries called "tweets." *See* www.twitter.com.

Uncle Buddy's Phantom Funhouse: A hypermedia novel by John G. McDaid (1992) consisting of floppy disks and audio cassettes. *See* www.eastgate.com/catalog/Funhouse.html.

Uncle Roger: "Intertwining elements of magic realism with Silicon Valley culture, semiconductor industry lore, and early word processing, *Uncle Roger* is a pioneering work of hypertext narrative poetry [by Judy Malloy] that was first published beginning in 1986 on Art Com Electronic Network on the WELL." *See* www.well.com/user/jmalloy/uncleroger/partytop.html.

Unfit Bits: "At Unfit Bits, we are investigating DIY fitness spoofing techniques to allow you to create walking datasets without actually having to share your personal data. These techniques help produce personal data to qualify you for insurance rewards even if you can't afford a high exercise lifestyle." *See* www.unfitbits.com.

Unity: A game engine used to "create any 2D or 3D game. You can make it with ease, you can make it highly-optimized and beautiful, and you can deploy it with a click to more platforms than you have fingers and toes." *See* unity3d.com.

Unix: A multiuser, multi-tasking operating system initially developed in the 1960s at AT&T's Bell Labs, and continually developed since.

Unveiling Visions: The Alchemy of the Black Imagination: "Curated by artist John Jennings and Reynaldo Anderson, this exhibition includes artifacts from the Schomburg collections that are connected to Afrofuturism, black speculative imagination and Diasporan cultural production." *See* www.nypl.org/events/exhibitions/unveiling-visions.

Urban Armor: "[A]n artwork started by Kathleen McDermott, consisting of a series of playful electronic wearables which investigate the relationship between technology, the body, and personal and public space." *See* urbanarmor.org.

Usenet: A non-centralized, worldwide computer network through which individuals share discussions and files.

Values & Value: A project "interested in what happens when economic value is accumulated from spheres previously considered non-economic, and the distortions and alterations in both economic and non-economic values this process creates." *See* values.doc.gold.ac.uk.

Values at Play: "Values at Play investigates how designers can be more intentional about the ways in which they integrate human values into their game-based systems." *See* valuesatplay.org.

Variable Media Questionnaire: "[A]n instrument for determining how artists would like their work to be re-created in the future—if at all . . . The results of the questionnaire, the variable media kernel, enter a multi-institutional database that enables collecting institutions to share and compare data across artworks and genres." *See* www.variablemedia.net/pdf/Ippolito.pdf.

Vectors: Journal of Culture and Technology in a Dynamic Vernacular: "*Vectors* maps the multiple contours of daily life in an unevenly digital era, crystallizing around themes that highlight the social, political, and cultural stakes of our increasingly technologically-mediated existence." *See* vectorsjournal.org.

Victory Garden: "Stuart Moulthrop's Victory Garden is an enduring hypertext classic." *See* www.eastgate.com/catalog/VictoryGarden.html.

Video Analysis Tableau: "The Video Analysis Tableau (VAT) is an online toolkit created for automated video comparison, annotation and visualization." *See* thevatproject.org.

Virtual Harlem: "[A] virtual representation of Harlem, NY as it existed during the 1920s Jazz Age." *See* ibryancarter.com/research.

Virtual International Authority File: "A joint project with the Library of Congress, the Deutsche Nationalbibliothek, and the Bibliothèque nationale de France, in cooperation with an expanding number of other national libraries and other agencies, VIAF explores virtually combining the name authority files of participating institutions into a single name authority service." *See* www.oclc.org/research/activities/viaf.html.

Virtual Montmartre: "[C]ontent related to artistic, historic, geographical, musical and literary activities occurring in Montmartre during the early part of the 20th century." *See* www.montmartre-virt.paris-sorbonne.fr.

Virtual World Web: "A software platform for building virtual reality experiences." *See* virtualworldweb.com.

virus.circus: A video by micha cárdenas and Elle Mehrmand. *See* vimeo.com/12219412.

Visual Thesaurus: "[A]n interactive dictionary and thesaurus which creates word maps that blossom with meanings and branch to related words. Its innovative display encourages exploration and learning." *See* www.visualthesaurus.com.

Visualizing Venice: "[A] Digital Humanities initiative that consists of students, scholars and architects at all levels of their careers who are actively involved in research projects to generate digital models and maps of the city of Venice, its territories, and its lagoon." *See* www.visualizingvenice.org/visu.

Vive: A virtual reality headset developed by HTC and Valve Corporation. *See* www.htcvive.com/ca.

VNS Matrix: An artist collective founded in 1991 by Francesca da Rimini, Virginia Barrett, Julieanne Pierce, and Josie Starrs that "tried to redefine the role and image of women in art and technology." *See* www.medienkunstnetz.de/artist/vns-matrix/biography.

Wanisinowin: A videogame by Meagan Byrne (2015). *See* meaganbyrne.carbonmade.com/projects/5702517.

We Sing for Healing: "[A] musical text adventure game made from a place where Google Maps can't zoom in and Skype doesn't load, using Dreamweaver and Photoshop with SoundCloud tracks by Exquisite Ghost." *See* survivance.org/wesing.

Weasley-o-Meter: A tutorial to make a Weasley-o-Meter, featuring a Spark Core and Internet Button, "inspired by the clock in the Weasley house that is seen in the second Harry Potter." *See* www.instructables.com/id/Weasley-o-Meter/?ALLSTEPS.

Web Accessibility in Mind (WebAIM): A non-profit organization based at the Center for Persons with Disabilities at Utah State University, "WebAIM (Web Accessibility In Mind) has provided comprehensive web accessibility solutions since 1999." *See* webaim.org.

The WELL: "The WELL, launched back in 1985 as the *Whole Earth 'Lectronic Link*, continues to provide a cherished watering hole for articulate and playful thinkers from all walks of life." *See* www.well.com.

Wikibooks: A Wikimedia project for collaboratively writing open-content textbooks that anyone can edit.

William Bunge's Maps of Detroit: "Detroit Cartography/Geography = DETROIT-ography—we are all about maps and geography of Detroit. We like to write about maps that other people make about the City as well as create our own maps of Detroit." *See* detroitography.com/tag/william-bunge and architizer.com/blog/radical-cartography.

With Those We Love Alive: A piece of interactive fiction by Porpentine Charity Heartscape built using Twine. *See* aliendovecote.com/uploads/twine/empress/empress.html.

Women Who Rock: A community that "brings together scholars, musicians, media-makers, performers, artists, and activists to explore the role of women and popular music in the creation of cultural scenes and social justice movements in the Americas and beyond." *See* womenwhorockcommunity.org.

Women Who Rock Oral History Archive: "The Women Who Rock Digital Oral History Archive fosters the development of participant-driven scholarship, on-line exhibits, curriculum, and media production." *See* content.lib.washington.edu/wwrweb.

WordPress: "[W]eb software you can use to create a beautiful website, blog, or app . . . The core software is built by hundreds of community volunteers, and when you're ready for more there are thousands of plugins and themes available to transform your site into almost anything you can imagine." *See* wordpress.org.

World Wide Web / Million Man March: An interactive CD-ROM by Reginald Woolery that "suggests the fluidity of 'race and place' at play, yet denied, in contemporary dialogues centering on technology and emergent social bodies." *See* www.vdb.org/titles/world-wide-webmillion-man-march.

xxn: Jonathan Kemp. *See* xxn.org.uk.

YoHa: A partnership between Graham Harwood and Matsuko Yokokoji (est. 1994) who co-founded the artists group Mongrel (1996–2007) and established the Mediashed, a free-media lab in Southend-on-sea (2005–08). *See* yoha.co.uk.

Young-Hae Chang Heavy Industries: A Seoul-based web art group. *See* www.yhchang.com.

YouTube: "Enjoy the videos and music you love, upload original content, and share it all with friends, family, and the world on YouTube." *See* youtube.com

Zooniverse: "[T]he world's largest and most popular platform for people-powered research. This research is made possible by volunteers—hundreds of thousands of people around the world who come together to assist professional researchers." *See* zooniverse.org.

INDEX

#BlackLivesMatter 270, 400
#FemDH 57, 98, 100, 526
#Ferguson 38, 270; syllabus 37, 57
#ILookLikeAProfessor 57
#TransformDH 10, 39, 78, 125
#TransHealthcareNOW 36, 38

3-D environment 393–4, 400; models 429–30
4-D expression 384–5
9/11 433, 434–5, 440
9/11 Memorial Museum 433, 435

Aarseth, Espen 120, 354, 463, 464–5
Abelson, Robert 456–7
ableism 35, 38, 109
Aboriginal Territories in Cyberspace (AbTeC) 130
Abreu, Amelia 101, 103
accessibility 108, 110–1; and digital media 108, 114
ActionScript (programming language) 479–80
activism 4, 12–6, 18–31, 33–41, 56–65, 67–76, 78–85, 97–106, 111–4, 117–26, 128–37, 141–50, 183–93, 195–202, 204–12, 214–20, 227–8, 362–6, 377–8, 389, 391–401, 403–11, 424, 503–9
Adam, Alison 109
Adams, Vivian 409–10
Adler, Jerry 314
aesthetics of the network 276–7; aesthesia of networks 276, 278–9
affect 23–5, 48, 103–4, 277–8, 281; and games 177, 179–81; and online video 298
affective labor 57, 98, 280–1; materiality of 280
African American literary studies 345, 349–50; and digital humanities 345–6
AfroFuturism 345, 375, 385; *see also* Nelson, Alondra
afternoon, a story 364; *see also* Joyce, Michael
Agre, Philip 186, 454, 455, 509; *Computation and Human Experience* 454; *see also* critical technical practice
Ahmed, Sara 121; affect 25; feminist killjoy 119
AIDS Quilt Touch 145–9
Aldred, Rachel 494
Alexander, Bryan 463
algocracy 451; *see also* Aneesh, A.
algorhythmics 243–8
algorithms 243–4, 246–8, 251, 258, 296, 438–40, 451; audit 255; algorithmic literacy 305; algorithmic viewing 297
Ali, Syed Mustafa 80–1; *see also* decolonial computing
Alper, Meryl 110
alternate reality games (ARGs) 379, 467
Amacher, Maryanne 237–8; third ear music 238
Amara (software) 113–4
Amazon Kindle 170–1, 336, 339
Americans with Disabilities Act 113
Ames, Morgan 517
An Annotated Archive from the Cold War (virtual museum) 363; *see also* Legrady, George
Anarchive Project 365–6; *see also* Duguet, Anne-Marie
Anderson, Benedict 286
Anderson, Chris 511
Anderson, Laurie 363; *Puppet Motel* (CD-ROM) 363
Aneesh, A. 80, 451; *see also* algocracy
annotation 303, 345–6, 374–6, 378; collaborative 345, 347–50; documentary 374; interpretive 374–5
Anthropy, Anna 119, 467; *Queers in Love at the End of the World* (game) 467
ANVIL (software) 304
Anzaldúa, Gloria 70, 74
Anzelmo, Erin 224
Aoki, Tsuru 414, 418–20
Apache Solr (software) 416
Appadurai, Arjun 276–7; global sociality 276–7
Apple iBooks 339; iBooks Author 469; iPhone 224–5
apprehension 373–8; and comprehension 373–4
Aquinas, Thomas 337
Arc (project) 512, 514–6
archives 19, 23–4, 34–5, 68–76, 78, 81, 83, 145–7, 158, 268–70, 286, 287, 301, 304, 310–1, 316, 323, 333, 352, 358, 362–70, 392, 393–6, 403–4, 405, 414, 424, 518; Indigenous materials 403–4; colonialism 403
archivista praxis 68–9, 71–2
Arclight 414, 416–21
The Arden Shakespeare (digital edition) 338; *see also* Smith, Martha Nell

Arduino 102–3, 261, 264
ARIS 468
Around Digital Humanities in 80 days (project) 84; *see also* Gil, Alex
Arthur, Brian 162–3
artificial intelligence (AI) 454, 458
artintact (journal) 365
assemblage 149–50
AT&T crash (1990) 247
audification 246
audio technologies and gender 239
augmented reality (AR) 372–81, 388–90; annotation 374–5, 378; digital heritage 373; maps 378; space 376–7
Ausentes (project) 91–4
Austin, John L. 102
Australian Institute for Aboriginal and Torres Strait Islander Studies 404
Authoring Software (project) 351–2; *see also* Malloy, Judy
automation 222–4, 226, 302–3
Autonets (project) 104, 258–9; *see also* cárdenas, micha
avatar 89–90, 399–400; and race 52

Babbage, Charles 162
Back, Les 495
Badiou, Alain 20–1
Badu, Erykah 33
Bailey, Moya 33, 39, 40, 124
Balsamo, Anne 9, 15, 19, 74, 112, 141, 206–9, 303, 352; *Designing Culture: The Technological Imagination at Work* 15, 141; praxis 112; techno–body 206–9; *Technologies of the Gendered Body* 206
Banaji, Mahzarin 187
Barad, Karen 2, 21, 23, 24, 25, 244, 497, 518; agentive matter 24; diffraction 244; entanglement 23, 518; intra-action 25
Bardzell, Jeffrey 186
Bardzell, Shaowen 186
Barnett, Fiona 5
Baron, Jaimie 297–8
Barrett, Mark 465
Barrett, Paul 82
Barthes, Roland 89, 339–40, 343; "Death of the Author" 339–40; methodological fields 89
Barton, Jake 435, 438
BASIC (programming language) 445, 446–7, 472
Battles, Matthew 429
Baudelaire, Charles 284, 285, 378; "The Painter of Modern Life" 284, 285
Baudoin, Patsy 254, 448; *10 PRINT CHR$(205.5+RND(1)); : GOTO 10* 254, 448
Baudrillard, Jean 227, 260
Baym, Nancy 45
Bayonetta (videogame character) 122
Bell, John 254, 304, 448; *10 PRINT CHR$(205.5+RND(1)); : GOTO 10* 254, 448
Beller, Jonathan 260, 294
Belojevic, Nina 263; *Ghost Tree* (experimental media) 264–5; *Connect the Wires* (experimental media) 263; *Touch That Spot* (experimental media) 263–4
Benjamin, Walter 364, 378, 511, 517; *The Arcades Project* 378
Benmayor, Rina 68
Bennett, Jane 14–5
Berens, Kathi Inman 315–6
Berners-Lee, Tim 448
Bernstein, Daniel (the *Bernstein* case) 450
Berressem, Hanjo 331
Bhabha, Homi 81
Bialetti Moka Express 427–9
bibliowear 171–2
Bierylo, Michael 240
Big Data 226, 228, 252, 301, 423, 424, 435, 439–40
Bijker, Wiebe 496, 500
Bikes & Bloomers (project) 493, 496, 498–500
Biojewellery 209
biopolitics 207–9
biopower 47–8, 321
BioShock (videogame) 467
Birkerts, Sven 336
bit rot 368
Bivens, Rena 23
black boxes 259, 260, 263, 312–6, 416, 496–8
Black feminism 34, 40, 394–5; praxis 394–5
Black Girls Code 446, 449
Blackfoot Digital Library 407
Blake, William 162, 425
Blas, Zach 489; transCoder 489
Blast, Synthia China 34, 37–8
Blood Quantum (videogame) 134; *see also* Nejo, Renee
Bly, Bill 355; *We Descend* 355
Boal, Augusto 88
body 196–8, 490, 498, 499; in relation to machine 204, 514; materiality of 205; non-normative 488; and sound 235–7; and technology 259–60; and wearables 102–3
bodyfuck (programming language) 489–90
BodyPlay (project) 263–5
Bogost, Ian 174–6, 254, 465–6, 448; *10 PRINT CHR$(205.5+RND(1)); : GOTO 10* 254, 448; *see also* procedural rhetoric
Boissier, Jean-Louis 364
Boler, Megan 53
Bologna, Sergio 253
Bolter, Jay David 5, 336; *Remediation* 5
book history 340
Borges, Jorge Luis 170, 373, 380; "Funes the Memorious" 170; "On Exactitude in Science" 373; "The Garden of Forking Paths" 380
born-digital texts 351–3, 463
bots 297, 302
Bowker, Geoffrey 319, 322
boyd, danah 46, 296

bpNichol 352
Braidotti, Rosi 14
Brain, Tega 201–2
Brainfuck (programming language) 489
Bratton, Benjamin 253
Braxton, Anthony 239
Brice, Mattie 119, 122
Bridle, James 277, 428, 430; *see also Hyper-Stacks*
Brings Plenty, Trevino 128, 134
Brodbeck, Frederic 305
Brothman, Brien 170
Buechley, Leach 263, 511
Buffalo: The Name Dropping Game 187, 190
built environment 391, 393
Bunge, William 218; *see also* Where Commuters Run Over Black Children
Burgess, Jean 295
Burman, Barbara 499
Büscher, Monika 494
Butler, Judith 48, 518
Butler, Octavia 329
Bygrave, Alice Louisa 498
Byrne, Megan 134–5; *Wanisinowin* (game) 134–5
Byrne, Ruth 162–3

Cage, John 238
Caillois, Roger 129
Caldwell, John Thornton 287; televisuality 287
Callimachus 426
Canguilhem, Georges 509
capitalism 34, 48, 79, 118–9, 105, 118, 144, 149, 178–9, 259–60, 276, 279, 280, 362, 365, 395, 484
cárdenas, micha 83, 102, 103–4, 258–9; Transborder Immigrant Tool (project) 83, 102, 477; *Redshift & Portalmetal* (game) 83; *virus.circus* (video) 103
Carey, James 284
Cartwright, Lisa 131
Casetti, Francisco 295
Catlow, Ruth 188, 189
CD-ROM art 363–70
Cecire, Natalia 9–10
Chen, Jian 35–6; hidden labour 36
Chicana feminism 70–1, 83
Chicana por mi Raza (project) 83
Chinen, Michael T. 244
Christen, Kimberly 15, 83, 404, 405
Christian, Barbara 101
Chun, Wendy H. K. 2, 123, 262, 297, 331, 379, 474, 475, 518; empowerment of operators 262; *Programmed Visions* 379
cinema 9, 13, 120, 167, 205, 279, 280, 293, 297, 298, 300, 305, 306–7, 376, 418, 419, 464, 518
Cinemetrics 305
citizen science 269, 504
Citizen Sense (project) 504, 505–7; citizen sensing 504–10
Clarke, Gill 196
cockpit voice recorder (CVR) 313–4
code 1, 2, 4, 5, 10, 97, 99, 100, 101, 104, 111, 204, 243, 244, 254, 259, 260, 263, 265, 272, 296, 305, 337, 338, 353, 358, 364, 369, 445–51, 453, 457, 460, 472–81, 488–90, 518; as cultural text 472, 473
Code.org 446, 449
coding for everyone 446, 448–9
collaboration 3, 12, 19, 24, 27, 30, 33, 45, 68–76, 83, 89, 90, 92, 101, 104, 114, 121, 124, 132, 133, 134, 135, 141, 147, 153, 155, 156, 158, 175, 185, 192, 220, 240, 244, 269, 270, 273, 302, 318, 324, 340, 341, 342, 345–50, 363, 364, 366, 367, 368, 387, 389, 395, 397, 400, 407, 408–11, 427, 463, 467, 473, 474, 479, 481, 493, 495, 498, 512, 514, 518
colonialism 79, 98, 393, 403, 475, 476; and mapping 215; outpost 98–9; *see also* settler colonialism
Coman, Mihai 131–2
CommentPress 341–2
Completely Automated Public Turing test to tell Computers and Humans Apart (CAPTCHA) 269, 302
compulsory heterosexuality 484
computational culture 243–6, 250–2, 531
computational media 455–60; and ideology 457
computer literacy 445, 447–8
computer vision 259, 297–8, 302–3
Condit, Cecelia 12
conjectural criticism 162–4, 168–9
conjunction 278–80
Connect the Wires (experimental media) 263; *see also* Belojevic, Nina
Contact Zones: The Art of CD-ROM (exhibition) 366
convivencia 67–76
Cooley, Heidi Rae 141
copyright 297, 387, 417, 450; law 450
corporate funding 11–2
Coté, Mark 47–8
Cotera, Maria 83
counter-mapping 218–9, 378
counterpublics 209–10
Coverley, M.D. 352, 353; *Califia* 353
Coverley, Merlin 378; *Psychogeography* 378
Cowan, Ruth 499
Cowan, T. L. 23, 47
Cox, Geoff 473
Cox, Laverne 37
Crawford, Chris 464
Crenshaw, Kimberlé Williams 125
Critical Art Ensemble 186, 263
critical code studies 111–2, 472–81; and postcolonialism 475–6
critical making 12, 30, 97, 100, 102, 210, 212, 495, 512; Critical Making Lab 152, 155; *see also* Ratto, Matt
Critical Play 183–92
critical race studies 62, 474
critical technical practice 186, 455, 509; *see also* Agre, Philip

critical unmaking 485, 488, 490
Crockett, I'Nasah 63
crowdsourcing 269–70, 303–4
Crowther, Will 467; *Colossal Cave Adventure* 467
Crunk Feminist Collective 34, 40
cryptography 450
CTHEORY Multimedia 366–7
cyberethnography 44–53
cyberspace 267–8, 270, 387
cybertext 463
cyborg 204, 207–9

dance 195–7
data 225–6, 228, 267–8, 272–3, 424–5; and capta 273; and citizen sensing 504, 506–7, 508; collaborative production of 270; flight 310; forensics 310, 359, 370; materiality of 311; of the senses 425; and self 209; storage 310, 311; *see also* search; metadata
data halo 271, 272, 273, 425; *see also* Schnapp, Jeffrey
data-image 435–7
data journalism 439
data mining 405
data visualization 431, 433–40
Davidson, Cathy 5, 302; *Now You See It* 302; attention blindness 302
Davis, Christine 49–50
de Certeau, Michel 217, 378
De Filippi, Primavera 324
de Lima, Cecília 196–7
Dean, Jeremy 347
Dear, Michael 156
Debord, Guy 378; spectacle 227
decolonial computing 80
decolonial humanities 69, 71
decolonization 68–9, 71, 78–84
Deep Listening 235
deep mapping 214, 217, 218–21
Delagrange, Susan H. 468
Deleuze, Gilles 177
Depocas, Alain 368
Derrida, Jacques 474
design 3, 4, 5, 13, 18, 48, 50, 52, 68, 71, 80, 83, 84, 90–1, 97, 98, 101, 104, 105, 109, 110–3, 118, 119, 122, 132–6, 141–50, 152–9, 162–72, 174–81, 183–92, 195–202, 205, 209–10, 223–4, 226–9, 239–40, 258, 261–3, 272, 294, 313–4, 318, 320, 322–5, 330, 354, 359, 367, 372–81, 387, 393, 407, 408–10, 424–8, 434–5, 439–41, 454–60, 463–8, 480, 488–9, 493, 496–500, 509, 511–8
design-as-inquiry 511–8; theaters of 518
design fiction 271–2
Desilusiones Ópticas (project) 93; *see also* Nuñez, Leo
Dickinson Electronic Archives (digital edition) 338; *see also* Smith, Martha Nell
diegetic prototype 167–8
Dietrich, Craig 83
digital activism 35–7, 400; *see also* activism
Digital Africana Studies 384–90; and digital humanities 385; virtual reality 385–7, 389; augmented reality 388–9
digital art 363–70
digital curation 405–6
digital divide 121, 142, 345, 365, 369, 399
digital ethnography 44–53, 90–1, 392, 396
digital fabrication 511–8
digital heritage 372–3, 375–7, 380–1, 400, 403–11; and place 374–5
digital Humanities 1–5, 9–15, 33, 39, 41, 56, 68–76, 78–84, 101, 108, 111, 112, 114, 125, 141, 144–5, 149, 152–9 183, 191–2, 246, 267–73, 292, 301, 304, 311, 337, 338, 340, 345–6, 352, 384, 386, 391–400, 410, 440, 453, 462, 468, 474, 475, 504, 507, 509, 512; accessibility 33, 39, 41; critique of 108, 345–6; cultural studies 144; decolonization of 78–84; emergence of 267–8; feminism 100–1; intersectionality 78; neglect of African American subject matter 345–6; social justice 39, 41, 101, 125–6; and textual studies 338
Digital Humanities Manifesto 2.0 70
digital inequality 99
digital infrastructure 34, 318–9
digital labor 53, 260, 280, 293, 294, 348; women's work 49; *see also* immaterial labor
digital media accessibility 108, 109, 114
digital media studies 10; and digital humanities 14–5, 156
digital natives 46
digital ontology 46–8
digital patina 170–1
digital preservation 351, 353, 358–9, 362–70; emulation 353, 369–70; migration 353, 368
digital production and spectacle 517
digital reconstruction 391
Digital Townships (historical GIS project) 392–4
digitization 269, 407
Dijkstra, Edsger 101
disability 39, 78, 108–14, 121; accommodation 113–4; and glitch 108–9, 111–2, 114
disability studies 109–11, 121; digital accessibility 109; digital media 110
DiSalvo, Carl 209
Disch, Lisa 75
discursive interface analysis 111–2
disjunction 278–80
dispositif 48, 278, 285, 288
distant reading 301, 417
Distributed Open Collaborative Course (DOCC) 19; *see also* Massive Open Online Course (MOOC)
divinatory practices 168
do-it-together (DIT) 53, 493–5, 495–6; *see also* do-it-with-others
do-it-with-others (DIWO) 72, 211; *see also* do-it-together

do-it-yourself (DIY) 51–2, 72, 97, 100, 105, 258–9, 493–4, 495–6
Doane, Mary Ann 518
Doctorow, Cory 227
Dolmage, Jay 110
Dominguez, Ricardo 477
Doruff, Sher 276
Doty, Mark 425–6, 428
Douglass, Jeremy 254, 448, 479; *10 PRINT CHR$(205.5+RND(1)); : GOTO 10* 254, 448
Dourish, Paul 80, 154, 198, 200, 504
dress acts 101–3, 205, 207
dress-body-technology assemblage 207–8, 209–10
dressmaking 499
Driver, Susan 237
Drucker, Johanna 273, 340, 438–9
Duguet, Anne-Marie 365; *see also* Anarchive Project
Duguid, Paul 336, 338
Dunn, David 237
Dunne, Anthony 186, 209
Dyer-Witheford, Nick 260

e-readers 339
E2 Textiles Project 104
Earhart, Amy 100
Easterling, Keller 253
eBlack Studies 385
Eckmann, Sabine 206; *Window | Interface* 206
Edelman, Lee 484
Edinburgh Film Festival 13, 15
Edmonton Pipelines Project 219–20
Edwards, Paul 320, 454
Eisenstein, Sergei 307
ELAN (software) 304
Electronic Beowulf (digital edition) 338; *see also* Kiernan, Kevin
electronic book 336–7, 341, 462; materiality of 336, 338–41
Electronic Disturbance Theater (EDT) 102, 477; *see also* Transborder Immigrant Tool
electronic literature 351–9, 364, 462; preservation of 351–2; 358–9
Electronic Literature Laboratory 351, 352, 358
Eliza (AI) 458; effect 458, 460
Ellefson, John 514–6
Elliot, Devon 513
Ellis, Katie 110; *Disability and New Media* 110
Ellison, Nicole 296
embodied *poiesis* 102–5
embodied thinking 195–202
embodiment 3, 49, 101, 195, 210, 489–90; and making 497–8; and physical computing 262–5; and sound 235–7
Emerson, Lori 351, 353
-empyre- a soft-skinned space (listserv) 366, 367
emulation 353, 355, 369–70
Engels, Friedrich 44
entanglement 2, 3, 495, 518; with research subjects 497–8
Entwistle, Joanne 206
environmental storytelling 466–7
ephemerality 286, 310–6
Ernst, Wolfgang 247
Eskelinen, Markku 120, 353
esolangs (esoteric programming languages) 488–9
ethics 21, 26, 68, 117, 123, 124, 210, 297, 323–5, 403–11, 459–60, 474
Ev-ent-anglement (project) 19–29, 105
eversion 267–8, 270–3, 329
experience design 174–81, 375, 377, 378–9
experiential learning theory 373
Experimental Television Center (ETC) 362
EXPORT, VALIE 204, 206
expressive processing 445–6, 457–8, 460

Facebook 24, 26, 28, 29, 47, 331
failure 483–5, 486
Fanon, Frantz 78–9, 81; decolonization 78–9
Faraday pockets 227
Fashioning Circuits 210, 211
fear of missing out (FOMO) 292
Fembot Collective 125
feminism 15, 120, 210–2; backlash to 60–1; Chicana feminism 70–1, 83; digital humanities and 70–2; engagement with technology 97; and geography 216; makerspace 97–9, 209; praxis 99–100, 395; race 394–5; wearables 97; white 125, 395; women of color 68–70, 74
feminist film studies 12–4
feminist making 12, 15, 97–106, 210–2
FemTechNet 15, 19, 53, 74, 97
Ferguson, Kevin 305
Ferguson, Roderick 120, 121, 125
fiber-crafting 51–2
Fibreculture Journal 275
film 12–4, 279–81, 293–4, 297–8, 300; history 413, 418, 420
filmic media 300–1; affect 307; computational approaches 304, 307; metadata 302, 303; mixed methods 300–7
Fisher, Caitlin 338
Fitts, Mako 68, 75–6
Fitzpatrick, Kathleen 342
Flanagan, Mary 180, 323; *see also* Values at Play
flight recorder 310–6; materiality 313–4; ephemerality 313; wireless 314–5
Follmer, Sean 513
Fontana, Bill 237
Foucault, Michel 177, 217, 278, 395; *dispositif* 278; "Of Other Spaces and Heterotopias" 217
Fox, Christina 124
fracking 505, 506
Fraistat, Neil 270
Frankenstein (Morris) 353, 462, 466, 469
Frasca, Gonzalo 120, 465
Fraser, Nancy 209
FreeD (project) 512, 513–4
Freire, Paulo 88; *Pedagogy of the Oppressed* 88

Friedman, Batya 185
Frith, Fred 239
Fry, Ben 260–1
Fuchs, Christian 294
Fuller, Matthew 260
Future Everything 227–8

Gabrys, Jennifer 263
Galey, Alan 337, 339, 512
Gallardo, Heather 49–50
Galloway, Alexander 175, 178, 206, 474, 487–8; allegorithm 178
Game Changer Chicago Design Lab 174, 180
game mechanics 122, 176–7, 178, 180; and affect 174, 177, 179, 180–1
game studies 120, 464–6; and fun 118–9, 177, 187; and interactive stories 462; play-centric approach 174–6, 178; proceduralist approach 174–6, 178; procedural author 464; social justice 117, 124, 126, 183
GamerGate (#Gamergate) 64, 117, 124, 269
games 51, 117–8, 129, 464–6; indigenous representation in 131–2; and ludology 464–5; and narratology 120, 464–5, 467; and the classroom 462–3; *see also* videogames
Garcia, Linda 83
Gathering Native Foods (mini-games) 135
Gee, James Paul 180
Geertz, Clifford 50
Gehl, Robert W. 254–5
gender 14, 22, 25, 33–41, 45, 57, 58, 62, 63, 69, 71, 78, 79, 97, 102–5, 117, 120, 122, 153, 158, 183, 205–11, 234, 239, 287, 298, 303, 365, 397, 399, 400, 419, 489, 493–501, 517–8
Geographic Information System (GIS) 215–8, 219, 221, 267, 271, 377, 388, 393; ArcGIS 156; feminist 394, 396; historical 393, 396
geospatial Web 271
geoweb 215, 217, 219
Ghost Tree (project) 263–5; *see also* Belojevic, Nina
Gibson, J. J. 197
Gibson, William 267, 268, 329, 331, 384, 387; *Neuromancer* 267, 384; *Spook Country* 268
Gil, Alex 84
Gitelman, Lisa 333, 336, 339, 340
Glennie, Evelyn 235
Glitch 108–9, 485–6
Global Outlook::Digital Humanities 57, 81
Goffman, Erving 49
Goggin, Gerard 109; *Digital Disability* 109
Goldfarb, Charles 337
Goldsen Archive (Rose Goldsen Archive of New Media Art) 367, 369–70, 544
Goldwater Machine 456–7
Gone Home (videogame) 466, 467, 469
Gonzalez, Martha 67, 71, 75
Goodman, Elizabeth 512
Google 199–200, 388, 218, 270–1; Glass 199–200, 388; Maps 218, 270–1
Goriunova, Olga 255, 495; *Fun and Software* 255
Gotkin, Kevin 109; glitch 109
Grafton, Anthony 438
Graham, Stephen 319, 320, 497
graphical user interface (GUI) 250, 262
Greenwald, Alice 435, 438
Gregg, Melissa 23
Gregory, Karen 101
Greie, Antye 238
Griesemer, James 253
Grosser, Ben 254
Grosz, Elizabeth 207–8
Grundy, Saida 62–3
Grusin, Richard 5, 292; *Remediation* 5
Guggenheim, Michael 494
GynePunk 97

hackerspaces 97–8; exclusion in 97–8; feminist 97–8
hacking 10, 38, 222, 226–7
Halberstam, J. Jack 118–9, 484; queer failure 118–9, 484
Half the Sky 51–2; *Half the Sky Movement* (game) 51–2
Hall, Gary 11
Hall, Stuart 143
Hamilton, Trudy 34, 39, 40–1
Hanselmann, Nik 489–90
harassment 60–3, 99, 104, 117, 119, 123–5, 207–8, 397; doxing 38, 124–5
Haraway, Donna 3, 81, 101, 143–4, 207, 208–9, 234, 244, 263; cyborg 207; diffraction 244; play 101; reproductive technologies 143; situated knowledge 81, 263, 265
Harding, Sandra 80; postcolonial science and technology studies 80
Harlem Renaissance 385, 389
Harley, Gretta 73
Harley, J. B. 378
Harvard Art Museum 430–1
HASTAC v, 5, 125, 155
HathiTrust 271
Hayakawa, Sessue 414, 418–20
Hayles, N. Katherine 268, 338, 364, 340; mixed reality 268; "Translating Media: Why We Should Rethink Textuality" 338
Heidegger, Martin 142, 517
Helmond, Anne 254
Hemmings, Clare 120
Hernández, Pilar 87–8, 90
Hertz, Garnet 263
Hildebrand, Grant 379
Hocquenghem, Guy 484
Hofstadter, Douglas 163
Honour Water (videogame) 135
Hook & Eye (project) 57
hopeful monsters 163
How Not to Be Seen: A Fucking Didactic Educational .MOV File 322; *see also* Steyerl, Hito
Howse, Martin 253

HTML 111–2, 254, 337, 353, 448, 449
Huhtamo, Erkki 365
human agency 321
human-computer interaction (HCI) 186, 195–202, 258–63
human subjects 123–4
Hussenograph 313, 316
hybrid reality 372–3, 375, 379, 381; and gamespace 379–80
Hyper-Stacks (project) 428, 430; *see also* Bridle, James
HyperCard 354, 355, 357
HyperCities (platform) 156, 219, 221
Hypothes.is (project) 347, 350

I Am Sitting in a Room (music) 233–4, 238; *see also* Lucier, Alvin
I Love Bees (game) 467
Ideas Box (project) 324
ideology 10, 11, 12, 48, 49, 100, 108, 109, 117, 119, 125, 130, 131, 144, 149, 150, 174, 206, 207, 259, 269, 287, 303, 312, 320, 322, 323, 330, 334, 449, 456–7, 474, 486–90, 493, 496, 500
Igoe, Tom 258, 261, 262, 263; *Physical Computing* 258, 262
imagineNATIVE Film + Media Arts Festival 132
immaterial labor 46, 47–8, 51–3; *see also* digital labor
immutable mobiles 496
in case you missed it (ICYMI) 292
inclusion 110–1, 121–3
Indigenous archives 406–8
Indigenous games 128–30, 132–6; and language 136
Indigenous knowledge 135–6, 403–11
Inform 7 468, 469, 537
infrastructure 2, 12, 23, 34, 36, 46, 57, 80, 100, 143, 147, 152–9, 244, 253–4, 277–8, 285–6, 315, 316, 318–25, 366, 505–6, 517; and labor 321–5; *see also* digital infrastructure; media infrastructure
InnerSpace Adventure (project) 379–80
inscription 207, 208, 211, 310, 311, 316, 333–4
Instagram 24, 29
institutional space 153–8
intellectual middleware 153–4, 156–9
interactive art 365, 369
interactive narratives 87–95; trauma and 90–5
interactive stories 462–9
INTERCAL (programming language) 489
interface as process 205–6
Internet of Things 101, 222–9, 271, 504
Invaders (videogame) 128, 134
Ippolito, Jon 368
Irani, Lily 80
Ishii, Hiroshi 513
Ito, Mizuko 180
ivory tower 33–4, 39, 61–3, 114

Jackson, Shelley 352, 355, 357, 466; *Patchwork Girl* (e-lit) 355, 357; *my body– a Wunderkammer* (e-lit) 466
Jackson, Steven 163
James, William 278–9
Jansen, Fieke 46–7
Jenik, Adriene 364
Jenkins, Henry 16, 130, 294, 466–7
Jeremijenko, Natalie 186, 263
Jockers, Matthew 415
Jodi (collective) 276, 485
Johnston, Claire 13–5
Jones, Christopher 376
Jones, Steven E. 178, 179
Jorgensen, Danny 50
Joyce, Michael 89, 352, 354, 364; *afternoon, a story* (e-lit) 364; audience participation 89; traversal 354
Judd, Steven Paul 128, 134
Juhasz, Alexandra 15, 53, 105, 294; *Learning from YouTube* (video-book) 18, 19, 294

Kafer, Alison 109
Kairos: A Journal of Rhetoric, Technology, and Pedagogy 10
Kane, Shanley 61
Katamari Damacy (videogame) 178–9
Kavi, Krishna 314–5
Kay, Alan 447
Keen, Andrew 274
Kember, Sarah 15, 21, 98
Kemeny, John 445, 446–7, 448
Kemp, Jonathan 253
Kendall, Mikki 60
Kent, Mike 110; *Disability and New Media* 110
Ketchum, Karyl 123
KeyWorx (software) 276
Khan, B. Zorina 499
KidCAD (project) 513
Kiernan, Kevin 338; *Electronic Beowulf* (digital edition) 338
Kim, Dorothy 64
Kim, Eunsong 38–9, 64; "The Politics of Trending" 38–9
Kinetoscope 296
Kirby, David 167–8
Kirschenbaum, Matthew 164, 311, 334, 454, 473, 474; code 474; *Mechanisms: New Media and the Forensic Imagination* 164, 454; media forensics 334
Kitchin, Rob 253
Kittler, Friedrich 254, 475
Klein, Lauren F. 39
Knight, Kim 263
Knowles, Kelley 218
Knuth, Donald 445, 455, 472
Koepnick, Lutz 206; *Window | Interface* 206
Koh, Adeline 10, 475, 476
Kolb, David 359, 373; *Socrates in the Labyrinth* 359
Kopas, Merritt 119
Kozel, Susan 197–8
Krapp, Peter 108–9
Kraus, Kari 263, 272, 512; bibliocircuitry 512
Kreps, David 109

Kristeva, Julia 26
Kroker, Arthur 366
Kroker, Marilouise 366
Kuang, Cliff 435
Kuhn, Virginia 298, 413
Kurtz, Thomas 445, 446–7, 448

LaBelle, Brandon 235
laboratories 2, 3, 11, 12, 19, 75, 97, 101, 152, 153, 155, 158, 159, 167, 168, 172, 174, 180, 186, 187, 205, 226, 228, 260, 268, 272, 351, 376, 387, 388, 424, 430, 506, 513; *see also* makerspaces
Lachlan, Kenneth 49–50
LambdaMOO 275
Landow, George 90, 336
Lankoski, Petri 379
Larsen, Deena 352
Lash, Scott 250
Latour, Bruno 10, 191, 313, 333, 496, 497
Laurel, Brenda 91
Law, John 496, 498–9
Layar (software) 388–9
Lazzarato, Maurizio 47, 53, 260
Learning from YouTube (video-book) 18, 19, 294; *see also* Juhasz, Alexandra
Lebow, Alisa 23
Lee, Kevin 280–1; *see also Transformers: The Premake (a desktop documentary)*
Lefebvre, Henri 217, 376–7
Legrady, George 363; *see also An Annotated Archive from the Cold War*
Leggett, Mike 366
Leonard, David J. 63
Let's Play 298
Levy, Pierre 211, 364
Lewis, Jason Edward 130
Libraries Without Borders 324
The Lightbox Gallery 429–31
liminality 52, 450
Lippard, Lucy 219
Lisp (programming language) 475
literacy 445–6, 447, 451; infrastructural 322; and programming 445–51, 472; procedural 454, 457
Little Bear, Leroy 130
Liu, Alan 12, 108, 142, 304, 338; critique of digital humanities 108
live crisis archiving 424
live sociology 495
liveness 285, 287–8
Lockwood, Annea 240
Logo (programming language) 445, 447, 448
Lorde, Audre 81, 125; master's tools 81
Lothian, Alexis 71–2
Lotz, Amanda 289; post-network 289
Loukissas, Yanni 429
Love, Heather 484
Lozano-Hemmer, Rafael 94–5
Lucier, Alvin 233–4, 238; *see also I Am Sitting in a Room*
ludology 120, 464–7; *see also* game studies
Luddism 486
Lury, Celia 495; inventive methods 495
Lynch, Kevin 216, 377, 379; *The Image of the City* 216, 377, 379

MacDougall, Robert 513
machine-to-machine (M2M) communication 223–4
machinima 298
Mackenzie, Adrian 254, 321
macrohistory 392
McCartney, Andra 239
McConchie, Alan 218
McCoy, Josh 458
McDaid, John 352, 353, 354, 357–8; *Uncle Buddy's Phantom Funhouse* (e-lit) 353, 354, 357–8
McDermott, Kathleen 207–8
McGann, Jerome 338, 340
McGonigal, Jane 129, 376, 464
McKenzie, D. F. 338, 340, 342–3
McKenzie, Mia 64
McKitterick, David 336
McLean, Alex 473
McLeod, Dayna 47
McLuhan, Marshall 185
McMillan Cottom, Tressie 59, 61, 62, 63, 64
McPherson, Tara 2, 74, 76, 112–3, 123, 141, 158, 296, 435, 475; media studies 158; "Media Studies and the Digital Humanities" 2; volitional mobility 296
Madikizela-Mandela, Winnie 396–8
magic circle 379
maker culture 52–3, 98, 101–2, 159, 209, 259, 493–501, 504, 505, 506, 511–2, 514
Maker Lab in the Humanities 272
makerspaces 101, 105; exclusion in 97–8; *see also* laboratories
Maketivism 53
making 51–2, 272, 340, 488, 493–500, 509, 511–8; ethnography of 493, 498; feminist making 12, 15, 52–3, 97–106; as research 493–501
Malloy, Judy 351–2, 353, 354, 357, 358; *Authoring Software* (project) 351–2; *Uncle Roger* (e-lit) 353, 354, 357, 358
Mandela, Nelson 396, 398
Mann, Steve 204, 205
Manovich, Lev 2, 252, 297, 301, 305, 453, 454; *The Language of New Media* 2, 454
maps/mapping 214–6, 218–21; data 271; embedded technology 214; empiricism 215–6; as production 215
Marcuse, Herbert 144, 332
Marino, Mark 111, 254, 448; *10 PRINT CHR$(205.5+RND(1)); : GOTO 10* 254, 448
Markham, Annette 45
markup languages 206, 337, 338, 341, 448, 485
Marvin, Carolyn 517

Marvin, Simon 319, 320
Marx, Karl 44, 149
Maryland Institute for Technology in the Humanities (MITH) 270, 351, 355, 392
Massey, Doreen 216–7
Massey, Sharon Davis 88
Massive Open Online Course (MOOC) 15, 155, 449; *see also* Distributed Open Collaborative Course (DOCC)
Massumi, Brian 278
Mateas, Michael 254, 448, 465; *10 PRINT CHR$(205.5+RND(1)); : GOTO 10* 254, 448
materiality 3, 101, 103, 250–1; of computational processes 259–260; of digital text 334; of sound 234–5; of the cloud 314–5; and technocultural critique 262–3
Mattern, Shannon 155, 316
Mattu, Surya 201–2
Maxwell, John 337
Mäyrä, Frans 379
Mbembe, Achille 119
Meadows, Mark 467
media archaeology 165, 247, 311–2, 315, 395, 473, 474, 479
media history 311–2, 319–20, 413, 420; computational approaches 413–21
media History Digital Library (MHDL) 286, 413, 414, 416
media infrastructure 319–20
media praxis 18, 30
media studies 1–5, 9, 10, 12, 14, 15, 18, 23, 56, 74, 100, 108, 109, 111, 113, 118, 126, 131–2, 142, 146, 152, 153–9, 176, 180, 183, 186, 191–2, 210, 247, 263, 264, 269, 283, 284, 306, 311, 316, 372, 395, 434, 465, 507, 509, 517, 518; and data visualization 434; and digital heritage 372; and practice-based research 507, 509
Mehrmand, Elle 103, 477; *virus.circus* (video) 103
Mellencamp, Patricia 12
Memmi, Albert 81
memory 144–9, 286, 287, 289, 311–2, 314, 363, 397, 398–400
Menkman, Rosa 485–6
Merleau-Ponty, Maurice 197–8
Meronek, Toshio 34
mesh networks 104, 324
mess 3, 53, 100, 101, 105, 149, 396, 494–501
metadata 302, 303–4, 405–6, 409, 415, 426
metaLAB 272, 424, 429
micro-celebrity 56, 59
micro-computed tomography (Micro-CT) 428–9
micro-history 392, 395; spatial micro-history 396, 398
microhistorical reconstruction 392
microsound 238
Mifflin, Jeffrey 403, 404, 408
Miller, Adrien 514–6
Miller, Charlie 222
Miller, Laura 462
Mills, C. Wright 500; *The Sociological Imagination* 500
mimetic machines 511, 512, 516–8; *see also* Taussig, Michael
misogynoir 34, 39–41
misogyny 40, 60, 121–2; anti-black 40
MIT Media Lab 101, 167, 168, 172, 513
Mitchell, W.J.T. 2
Mitchem, Carl 142
mixed reality 268, 271–3; space and 271
Miyao, Daisuke 418–20
Miyazaki, Shintaro 254
mobilities research 494
Mohanty, Chandra Talpade 76
Monmonier, Mark 378
Montfort, Nick 122–3, 254, 260, 448, 466; *10 PRINT CHR$(205.5+RND(1)); : GOTO 10* 254, 448; "Taroko Gorge" (procedural poem) 466
Moon, Christina 323
Morse, Margaret 149; poetics of interactivity 149
Morse, Samuel 152–3
Mosco, Vincent 517
Moser, Ingunn 109
Mosley, Nicholas 163
Mothership HackerMoms (makerspace) 209
Moulthrop, Stuart 354; *Victory Garden* 354
moving images 1, 199, 279–81, 283, 292–8, 300–7
Mukurtu 82–3; *see also* Christen, Kimberly
Mulvey, Laura 12–3
Muntadas, Antoni 365, 368
Murray, Janet 89, 120, 174, 464
Museum Without Walls 374, 375
music 68–76, 233–40; and embodiment 235, 236; experimental music history 233; feminist narratives 69
Musqueam Place Names Web Mapping Portal 406
Mutant Giant Spider Dog (video) 293–4

Nakamura, Lisa 45, 112
Named Entity Recognition 440–1
narratology 120, 464–5, 467
Nasser, Ramsey 475–6
natural language processing system 455, 456
Neatline (software) 156
Necropolitics 119
Nejo, Renee 132, 134; *Blood Quantum* (videogame) 134
Nelson, Alondra 345
Nelson, Ted 447, 454; *Computer Lib / Dream Machines* 447, 454
neo-colonialism 79–80, 84
neogeography 217–8, 394
neoliberalism 11, 30, 45, 59, 60, 63, 142, 209, 210, 211, 226, 259, 278, 323, 332, 395, 449, 485
net art 250, 275, 276, 352, 362, 366, 367, 369, 485; and social media 366
network culture 274–6

network experience 275–7; affect and 276
Neumark, Norie 363, 369
neuroscience 306–7
Never Alone (videogame) 133
Nevitt, Barrington 185
New Aesthetic 277
new materialism 14, 23, 28
new media 1–5, 312, 365, 454
new media art 275, 362, 365–8; archives 367–8; exhibition 365, 366; ephemerality 367–8; obsolescence 367–8; preservation of 362–70
new media narratives 89
new media studies 56; and digital humanities 142, 157; and games 174; and practice 176, 180; and public scholarship 56–64; *see also* media studies
Newell, Christopher 109; *Digital Disability* 109
Nissenbaum, Helen 180, 185, 323
Nivel de Confianza (project) 94–5; *see also* Lozano-Hemmer, Rafael
Northwest Museum of Arts and Culture 407
Nowviskie, Bethany 10, 81
Nuñez, Leo 94
Nye, David 517

O'Brien, Jean 75
O'Sullivan, Dan 258, 262; *Physical Computing* 258, 262
obsolescence 316, 329–34, 352, 353, 368, 483; and innovation 329–34
Oliveras, Lissette 35–6
Oliveros, Pauline 235
online video 280–1, 292–5; and capital 295; genres of 297–8; and labor 293
ontogenetic perspective 170
optical character recognition (OCR) 269, 415, 417, 420
oral histories 71–3, 83
The Oregon Trail 379
Orth, Margaret 101–2
Ortiz, Simon J. 129
Otsì:!! Rise of the Kanien'kehá:ka Legends 132, 133

Packard, Vance 330
Paik, Nam June 362, 365
Panofsky, Erwin 300, 303, 307
Papers, Please (videogame) 189–90
Papert, Seymour 447–8
Paradiso, Joe 513–4
Parikka, Jussi 311–2
Parisi, Luciana 255
Park, Suey 63
Parks, Lisa 322
parthood 169–71
Patchwork Girl (e-lit) 352, 353, 355, 357; *see also* Jackson, Shelley
patents 3, 450, 479, 493, 496–8, 500
Pathfinders (project) 351, 353, 357–9
Pavlik, John 388
Paxton, Steve 197; small dance 197
PeaceMaker (videogame) 174–5
Pearce, Celia 105, 465
pedagogy 18–9, 68, 74–6; collaborative teaching 74, mentorship 73–5
Pedersen, Isabel 205; *Ready to Wear* 205
Pérez, Emma 71; *The Decolonial Imaginary* 71
Perlis, Alan 445, 446–7
Perry, Imani 236–7
Personal Space Dress (wearable) 207–8
pervasive mediation 224, 229
Peters, John Durham 330
Phan, Michelle 298
philanthropy 45, 50–2
Philip, Kavita 80
Phillips, Amanda 71–2
Phillips, Tom 353
philosophy of technology 142–4
photography 15, 21, 93, 219, 239, 285, 313, 316, 375, 393, 403, 409, 427, 428, 514
physical computing 100–1, 105, 258–65, 272
Pickles, John 378
Pinterest 24, 26, 28
Piper, Adrien 322–3; *see also Probable Trust Registry*
The Plateau Peoples' Web Portal (online archive) 408–11
platform studies 120, 122, 123, 468–9
Plato 243–4
Play Your Place (game) 186, 188, 189, 190
Playfair, William 433
Poe, Edgar Allan 378
Popular music studies 69, 74
Porpentine 467, 468
Posner, Miriam 10, 13, 99
postcolonial computing 80, 475–6
postcolonial studies 78, 81–2, 475–6
postcolonial theory 80; critique of 81–2
Poundstone, William 479–80; *see also Project for Tachistoscope*
Pratt, Mary Louise 157; contact zone 157
praxis 4, 14, 18, 21, 30, 68–76, 81, 84, 99, 110, 111, 112–4, 191, 192, 221, 394–5, 397, 398; *see also* archivista praxis; Balsamo, Anne; Black feminism; feminism; media praxis
Prensky, Marc 46, 449
Prescott, Andrew 158
Presner, Todd 219
Pressman, Jessica 479
Price, Margaret 110
Prince 274
Probable Trust Registry (installation) 322–3; *see also* Piper, Adrien
procedural rhetoric 174–8; *see also* Bogost, Ian
Processing (software) 260–1
programming 4, 5, 93, 101, 102, 104, 119, 224, 247, 228, 247, 252, 258, 259, 261, 267, 268, 445–51, 454, 455, 468, 472–81, 488–90; and embodiment 489–90; and language 476; and literacy 445–51, 455; and writing 445, 449–51

Project for Tachistoscope (e-lit) 479–80; *see also* Poundstone, William
Project Tango (Google) 259
Prom Week (videogame) 457–60
prosumerism 45, 49, 52–3, 218
Protocols for Native American Archival Materials 404
psychogeography 378–9
public memory 286, 287, 289, 373, 398–9, 407
public scholarship 56–7, 59, 61–4
Puppet Motel (CD-ROM) 363; *see also* Anderson, Laurie
Puwar, Nirmal 495
Pybus, Jennifer 47–8
Python (programming language) 270, 448

QR Codes 271, 374, 376
qualitative research 49–50
Quantified Self (QS) 103, 201, 205, 209
quantitative humanities 424, 453
queer computation 483–90
queer studies 33–41, 47, 100, 118–9, 121, 122, 237, 396, 398, 399, 400, 483–90; history 396, 398, 400, 484; theory 121, 122, 399, 484–5; and trans studies 33–9; zines 100
Queerness and Games Conference 125
Queneau, Raymond 463
Queers in Love at the End of the World (videogame) 467; *see also* Anthropy, Anna

Raby, Fiona 186, 209
race 14, 33–41, 45, 46, 57, 61, 62, 63, 69, 70, 78, 79, 105, 117, 120, 121, 125, 144, 153, 159, 187, 207, 208, 210, 218, 234, 236, 298, 345–6, 366, 391–400, 403, 418, 460
Radigue, Eliane 238
Radio Frequency Identification (RFID) 223, 258, 267–8
Radzikowska, Milena 379
Ramsay, Stephen 10
Rancière, Jacques 252
Rap Genius (project) 345–50
Raskin, Jef 262
Raspberry Pi 261, 272
Ratto, Matt 53, 210, 263, 512; *see also* critical making
Rault, Jasmine 47
Ray, Amit 475, 476
real time 223–4, 288
Reas, Casey 254, 260, 261, 448; *10 PRINT CHR$(205.5+RND(1)); : GOTO 10* 254, 448
reciprocal curation 407–8
recreation (of objects) 168
Redshift & Portalmetal (game) 83; *see also* cárdenas, micha
Reed, Alison 123
Reflectance Transformation Imaging (RTI) 428–9
remote sensing technologies 89–91
representation 121
respectability 37–8; framework of 37
Rettberg, Jill Walker 103, 205; *Seeing Ourselves Through Technology* 205
reverse-engineering 439–40
Rhizome (listserv) 366
Riot grrrl 100
Risam, Roopika 15, 475, 476
Rivera, Sylvia 35; Sylvia Rivera Law Project (SRLP) 37–8
Robinson, Zandria 62
Rock in Fist (game) 130
Rose, David 168; enchanted objects 168
Rosenberg, Daniel 438
Ross, Sara 418–20
Rothenbuhler, Eric 131–2
Ruberg, Bonnie 118–9
Rudy, Kathryn 171
Ruecker, Stan 340, 379, 512
Russ, Joanna 61
Ryan, Marie-Laure 89, 91, 464
Ryan, Susan Elizabeth 101–2, 205–7; *Garments of Paradise: Wearable Discourse in the Digital Age* 101, 205

Saegusa, Hidekazu 514–6
Sagar, Sharad Vivek 192
Said, Edward 81
Salt, Barry 305
Salter, Elizabeth 338; *The Wife of Bath's Tale* (digital edition) 338
Sample, Mark 252, 448; *10 PRINT CHR$(205.5+RND(1)); : GOTO 10* 254, 448
Sayers, Jentery 168, 263, 272, 359
Scalar (platform) 11, 83, 141, 357
Scaled Entity Search (SES) 414, 415, 416–7, 421
Schiphorst, Thecla 195, 198
Schnapp, Jeffrey T. 272–3
Schneider, Edgar 476; global Englishes 476
Schreiber, Loren 92
science and technology studies 78, 100, 110, 473, 495, 496–7, 509; feminist 499; postcolonial approaches 80
search 253, 414–21; affordances of 415; algorithms 416
Seaver, Nick 439
Second Life 48–9, 387
Seigworth, Gregory 23
self-determination 63, 129, 132, 136, 209
Semmelhack, Peter 226
Sengers, Phoebe 186
sensors 504–5, 507–8
sentient cities 318, 324
settler colonialism 82–3; *see also* colonialism
sewing 49, 102, 104, 210, 211, 258, 259, 493, 497, 498, 500
sexism 57–60, 269, 275
sexuality 14, 33–41, 45, 78, 97, 103, 117, 122, 125, 153, 210, 365, 366, 394, 400, 484, 489
Shah, Nishant 46–7, 101

Shatford Layne, Sara 303
Shaw, Adrienne 122, 400; *Gaming at the Edge: Sexuality and Gender at the Margins of Gamer Culture* 400
Shereen Sakr, Laila (VJ Um Amel) 15, 20, 23, 28–9
Shiga, Jason 466; *Meanwhile* 466
Short, Emily 468; *Bronze* 468
Sicart, Miguel 175–6
Siegel, Greg 313
SimCity 458; effect 458, 460
Simondon, Gilbert 509
Simone, AbdouMaliq 321
simulation 128, 158, 165, 170, 175, 259, 364, 372, 387, 455, 458, 460, 465, 466, 467; versus narrative 465
Sinclair, Stéfan 379
Singuistics (game) 135
Skawennati 130
Skins Video Game Workshops 130, 132, 133
Slack, Jennifer 149–50
Slade, Giles 329, 330; *Made to Break* 329, 330
small data 423, 424
smart cities 226, 228, 505; citizen 227–8; subject 223, 227–8
Smith, Linda 128–9
Smith, Martha Nell 12, 14, 338; *Dickinson Electronic Archives* (digital edition) 338*; The Arden Shakespeare* (digital edition) 338
Smoke Stacks (game) 179–81
Smoodin, Eric 413
Snapchat 28, 331
Snowden, Edward 229
Social Edition of the Devonshire Manuscript (project) 340–2
Social Justice 3–4, 19, 41, 63, 113, 117–26, 128, 400; and decolonization 79; games 51–2; music 71, 76; warrior 117
The Social Justice History Platform 393
social media 19, 28–30, 269–70, 277, 405; ecology of 292; and net.art 366; as text 123; and video 296
software art 250, 255
software studies 122, 250–5, 305, 453–5
Soja, Edward 156
Sonami, Laetitia 236
Sonification 244
sound 233–40, 246–7, 429, 430, 514–6; and interspecies communication 237
Soweto 392–3, 396–8, 399, 400; *Soweto '76: A Living Digital Archive* 392–3; *The Soweto Historical Geographic Information System* (SHGIS) 393
space 152–9, 214–21, 372–81, 391–400, 428–9, 430–1, 433–42; and apartheid 395; augmented reality 376–7; and place 215; and race 392; social 217; and visualization 430–1, 433–42
spam 479–80
spatial humanities 156, 217–8, 219, 394, 396; spatial turn 155, 156, 268, 394
speculative design 165, 168, 169, 172, 191, 318, 512; wear 168, 170–1
spimes 271–2
Spinney, Justin 494
Spinoza, Baruch 177
Squire, Kurt 130, 175
Stacey, Judith 120
Stanfill, Mel 112
Stanley, Eric A. 34
Star, Susan Leigh 253, 319, 322, 498; *The Cultures of Computing* 498
steampunk 163, 168–9
Stephenson, Neal 387
Sterling, Bruce 227, 271–2
Sterne, Jonathan 237, 239, 517, 518
stewardship 405–7, 410–1; collaborative 410–1; digital heritage 405–7
Steyerl, Hito 322; *How Not to Be Seen: A Fucking Didactic Education .MOV File* 322
Stoll, Clifford 274
stone soup 70
Stork, Matthias 298
Storyspace 354–5
strategic disloyalty 120–1; *see also* Stacey, Judith
Sturken, Marita 131
subjunctive knowledge 163; practices 164, 165, 168, 171
Suchman, Lucy 454; *Plans and Situated Actions* 454
Summers, Ed 270
Surkan, KJ 21–2
surveillance 47, 128, 204, 226–7, 229, 234, 322, 324, 403, 508
survivance 128, 129, 132, 136

Tale-Spin 458; effect 458
Tapp und Tastkino (Tap and Touch Cinema) 204–6
"Taroko Gorge" (procedural poem) 466; *see also* Montfort, Nick
Tate, Jamie 238
Taussig, Michael 511, 517; theory of magic 511, 517; *see also* mimetic machines
Taylor, T.L. 101
Teaching with Things (project) 429–30
techno-aesthetics 247–8
techno-body 102, 206, 207–9
technological embodiment 209
technological failure and queerness 483
technological progress 352, 483
Tekinbaş Katie S. 176–7
telegraph 162–3, 284–5
television 184, 283–90, 338, 362, 413; as bad object 283–4; critique of 283–4; early era 286–7; social networks and 288–9; and VCRs 287–8, 485
television Studies 283–90
Term Frequency-Inverse Document Frequency (TF-IDF) 440–1
Terranova, Tiziana 260
Text Encoding Initiative (TEI) 338
textual studies 337–8

THATCamps 9–10, 158–9
Thiel, Tamiko 375
Thobani, Sunera 63
Thrift, Nigel 246, 497
Tikka, Pia 307
Tile (project) 225–6
Tillequets, Jolena 409
Tiltfactor (studio) 187, 191
Timescape (exhibition) 433–40
Titchkosky, Tanya 110–1
Todd, Loretta 130
Toffler, Alvin 218
TOMS 50–1
Touch that Spot (experimental media) 263–4; *see also* Belojevic, Nina
Tran, Thomas 514–6
trans studies 33–9, 83, 103
Transborder Immigrant Tool (project) 83, 102, 477–9; *see also* cárdenas, micha; Electronic Disturbance Theater (EDT)
Transcriptions Center (UCSB) 155
transduction 237, 260, 263, 264, 265
Transformers: The Premake (a desktop documentary) 280–1
transphobia 34, 35, 37–8
Traversal (of e-lit) 351, 354–9
Tsivian, Yuri 304, 305
Tuan, Yi-Fu 376–7
Tuck, Eve 79; decolonization 79
Tufekci, Zeynep 270
Turing, Alan 254, 450
Turkel, William J. 81, 263, 513
Turkle, Sherry 192, 399
Twine 119, 468, 469
Twitter 24, 29, 30, 35, 38, 57–8, 60, 123–4, 155, 270

ubiquitous computing 224, 226–7, 229, 271, 504
unboxing 298
Uncle Buddy's Phantom Funhouse (e-lit) 353, 354, 355, 357–8; *see also* McDaid, John
Uncle Roger (e-lit) 353, 354, 357, 358, 359; *see also* Malloy, Judy
Underberg, Natalie M. 90
Underwood, Ted 415–6
Unity (software) 386–8, 469
universal design 110–2; for learning 110–1; in digital humanities 112
urban interfaces 324

Valasek, Chris 222
Values at Play (project) 185, 186, 191, 323; *see also* Flanagan, Mary; Nissenbaum, Helen
van Rossum, Guido 448
Variable Media Questionnaire 368–9, 370
Vasseleu, Cathryn 205
Vawter, Noah 254, 448; *10 PRINT CHR$(205.5+RND(1)); : GOTO 10* 254, 448
Vectors (journal) 11
Vee, Annette 101, 254
Vianello, Robert 286
Video Analysis Tableau (VAT) 305–6
videogames 52, 62, 128–30, 132, 174, 175, 176, 183; and social justice 117, 119–24, 126; and history 379; *see also* games
viral 56, 57, 59, 60, 61–3, 281
Virilio, Paul 311
The Virtual Harlem Project 385–9
virtual reality (VR) 268, 373, 385–7, 389, 393, 399; in the classroom 386, 387
virus.circus (video); *see also* cárdenas, micha; Mehrmand, Elle
Viseu, Ana 201
Visualizing Venice (project) 377
Vizenor, Gerald 128, 129, 131–2
VNS Matrix (collective) 275
von Helmholtz, Hermann 240
von Neumann, John 487
vulnerability 38, 62, 124, 222, 234, 313, 314, 315, 316, 496

wa Thiong'o, Ngũgĩ 79, 82
Waber, Dan 467; *A Kiss* 467
Wajcman, Judy 48, 499
Wakeford, Nina 495; inventive methods 495
Wanisinowin (game) 134–5; *see also* Byrne, Megan
Warde, Beatrice 339
Wardrip-Fruin, Noah 454–5, 456, 458; *Expressive Processing* 454–5, 456, 458
Wark, McKenzie 178–9, 260; *Gamer Theory* 178–9
Warren, David 313–4, 315
Warwick, Claire 10
Watson, Thomas 337
wearable technology 100–5, 195, 199, 200, 204–12; cultural and ethical dimensions 205; feminism 205; gender 102; technologies of care 104
Weaver, Lois 101
Web 2.0 19, 27, 47, 49, 52, 268, 504
Weiser, Mark 224
West, Lindy 61
wetware 321
What You See Is What You Get (WYSIWYG) 448
Where Commuters Run Over Black Children (map) 218; *see also* Bunge, William
Whereabouts Clock (*Harry Potter*) 165–8, 172
white supremacy 37, 62, 80, 118
Whole Earth 'Lectronic Link (WELL) 275, 357
Wiegman, Robyn 117, 120, 487
The Wife of Bath's Tale (digital edition) 338; *see also* Salter, Elizabeth
WiFi 495–6, 500
Wikipedia 40–1, 48–9, 75, 302; Wikibooks 341
Wilkens, Matthew 271
Willeford, Thomas 163
Williams, George 112
Williams, Mark 304
Williams, Raymond 143, 338

Williamson, Bess 111
Wilson, Elizabeth 487
Wipprecht, Anouk 103–4
women of color feminism 68–70, 74, 75
Women Who Rock (project) 67–76
Wood, Denis 215, 378
Wuschitz, Stefanie 97
Wyeth, Peter 307

X-reality 223
Xenakis, Iannis 238

Yakama Nation 408, 409–11
Yang, K. Wayne 79; decolonization 79
YouTube 18, 19, 24, 28–9, 280–1, 292–8

Zimmerman, Eric 129, 176–7
Žižek, Slavoj 20
Zoran, Amit 513–4
Zorn, Elayne 90
Zuckerman, Bruce 141; *InscriptiFact* 141
Zwicker, Heather 220
Zylinska, Joanna 15, 21, 23, 98

For Product Safety Concerns and Information please contact our EU representative GPSR@taylorandfrancis.com Taylor & Francis Verlag GmbH, Kaufingerstraße 24, 80331 München, Germany

Batch number: 10726294

Printed by Printforce, the Netherlands